The Theory and Practice of Investment Management

Second Edition

The Frank J. Fabozzi Series

Fixed Income Securities, Second Edition by Frank J. Fabozzi
Focus on Value: A Corporate and Investor Guide to Wealth Creation by James L. Grant and James A. Abate
Handbook of Global Fixed Income Calculations by Dragomir Krgin
Managing a Corporate Bond Portfolio by Leland E. Crabbe and Frank J. Fabozzi
Real Options and Option-Embedded Securities by William T. Moore
Capital Budgeting: Theory and Practice by Pamela P. Peterson and Frank J. Fabozzi
The Exchange-Traded Funds Manual by Gary L. Gastineau
Professional Perspectives on Fixed Income Portfolio Management, Volume 3 edited by Frank J. Fabozzi
Investing in Emerging Fixed Income Markets edited by Frank J. Fabozzi and Efstathia Pilarinu
Handbook of Alternative Assets by Mark J. P. Anson
The Global Money Markets by Frank J. Fabozzi, Steven V. Mann, and Moorad Choudhry
The Handbook of Financial Instruments edited by Frank J. Fabozzi
Collateralized Debt Obligations: Structures and Analysis by Laurie S. Goodman and Frank J. Fabozzi
Interest Rate, Term Structure, and Valuation Modeling edited by Frank J. Fabozzi
Investment Performance Measurement by Bruce J. Feibel
The Handbook of Equity Style Management edited by T. Daniel Coggin and Frank J. Fabozzi
Foundations of Economic Value Added, Second Edition by James L. Grant
Financial Management and Analysis, Second Edition by Frank J. Fabozzi and Pamela P. Peterson
Measuring and Controlling Interest Rate and Credit Risk, Second Edition by Frank J. Fabozzi,
    Steven V. Mann, and Moorad Choudhry
Professional Perspectives on Fixed Income Portfolio Management, Volume 4 edited by Frank J. Fabozzi
The Handbook of European Fixed Income Securities edited by Frank J. Fabozzi and Moorad Choudhry
The Handbook of European Structured Financial Products edited by Frank J. Fabozzi and Moorad Choudhry
The Mathematics of Financial Modeling and Investment Management by Sergio M. Focardi and
    Frank J. Fabozzi
Short Selling: Strategies, Risks, and Rewards edited by Frank J. Fabozzi
The Real Estate Investment Handbook by G. Timothy Haight and Daniel Singer
Market Neutral Strategies edited by Bruce I. Jacobs and Kenneth N. Levy
Securities Finance: Securities Lending and Repurchase Agreements edited by Frank J. Fabozzi and Steven V. Mann
Fat-Tailed and Skewed Asset Return Distributions by Svetlozar T. Rachev, Christian Menn, and
    Frank J. Fabozzi
Financial Modeling of the Equity Market: From CAPM to Cointegration by Frank J. Fabozzi, Sergio M.
    Focardi, and Petter N. Kolm
Advanced Bond Portfolio Management: Best Practices in Modeling and Strategies edited by
    Frank J. Fabozzi, Lionel Martellini, and Philippe Priaulet
Analysis of Financial Statements, Second Edition by Pamela P. Peterson and Frank J. Fabozzi
Collateralized Debt Obligations: Structures and Analysis, Second Edition by Douglas J. Lucas, Laurie S.
    Goodman, and Frank J. Fabozzi
Handbook of Alternative Assets, Second Edition by Mark J. P. Anson
Introduction to Structured Finance by Frank J. Fabozzi, Henry A. Davis, and Moorad Choudhry
Financial Econometrics by Svetlozar T. Rachev, Stefan Mittnik, Frank J. Fabozzi, Sergio M. Focardi, and
    Teo Jasic
Developments in Collateralized Debt Obligations: New Products and Insights by Douglas J. Lucas,
    Laurie S. Goodman, Frank J. Fabozzi, and Rebecca J. Manning
Robust Portfolio Optimization and Management by Frank J. Fabozzi, Petter N. Kolm,
    Dessislava A. Pachamanova, and Sergio M. Focardi
Advanced Stochastic Models, Risk Assessment, and Portfolio Optimizations by Svetlozar T. Rachev,
    Stogan V. Stoyanov, and Frank J. Fabozzi
How to Select Investment Managers and Evaluate Performance by G. Timothy Haight,
    Stephen O. Morrell, and Glenn E. Ross
Bayesian Methods in Finance by Svetlozar T. Rachev, John S. J. Hsu, Biliana S. Bagasheva, and
    Frank J. Fabozzi
Structured Products and Related Credit Derivatives by Brian P. Lancaster, Glenn M. Schultz, and Frank J. Fabozzi
Quantitative Equity Investing: Techniques and Strategies by Frank J. Fabozzi, Sergio M. Focardi, and
    Petter N. Kolm
Introduction to Fixed Income Analytics, Second Edition by Frank J. Fabozzi and Steven V. Mann
The Handbook of Traditional and Alternative Investment Vehicles by Mark J. P. Anson, Frank J. Fabozzi,
    and Frank J. Jones

The Theory and Practice of Investment Management

Second Edition

Asset Allocation, Valuation,
Portfolio Construction,
and Strategies

FRANK J. FABOZZI
HARRY M. MARKOWITZ

EDITORS

WILEY

John Wiley & Sons, Inc.

Library of Congress Cataloging-in-Publication Data

The theory and practice of investment management / Frank J. Fabozzi, Harry M. Markowitz,
editors.—2nd ed.
   p. cm.—(Frank J. Fabozzi series)
   Includes index.
   ISBN 978-0-470-92990-2 (hardback); 978-1-118-06741-3 (ebk); 978-1-118-06751-2
(ebk); 978-1-118-06756-7 (ebk)
   1. Investments. 2. Business enterprises—Finance. I. Fabozzi, Frank J. II. Markowitz,
H. (Harry), 1927-
HG4521.T455 2011
332.6—dc22
                                    2010054035

10 9 8 7 6 5 4 3 2 1

Contents

About the Editors

Frank J. Fabozzi is Professor in the Practice of Finance in the Yale School of Management. Prior to joining the Yale faculty, he was a Visiting Professor of Finance in the Sloan School at MIT. He is a Fellow of the International Center for Finance at Yale University and on the Advisory Council for the Department of Operations Research and Financial Engineering at Princeton University. Professor Fabozzi is the editor of the *Journal of Portfolio Management* and an associate editor of the *Journal of Fixed Income, Journal of Asset Management, Review of Futures Markets*, and *Quantitative Finance*. He is a trustee for the BlackRock family of closed-end funds. In 2002, he was inducted into the Fixed Income Analysts Society's Hall of Fame and is the 2007 recipient of the C. Stewart Sheppard Award given by the CFA Institute. He has authored numerous books in investment management. Professor Fabozzi earned a doctorate in economics from the City University of New York in 1972 and earned the designation of Chartered Financial Analyst and Certified Public Accountant.

Harry M. Markowitz has applied computer and mathematical techniques to various practical decision making areas. In finance, in an article in 1952 and a book in 1959, he presented what is now referred to as MPT, "modern portfolio theory." This has become a standard topic in college courses and texts on investments and is widely used by institutional investors for tactical asset allocation, risk control, and attribution analysis. In other areas, Dr. Markowitz developed "sparse matrix" techniques for solving very large mathematical optimization problems. These techniques are now standard in production software for optimization programs. He also designed and supervised the development of the SIMSCRIPT programming language. SIMSCRIPT has been widely used for programming computer simulations of systems like factories, transportation systems, and communication networks. In 1989, Dr. Markowitz received the John von Neumann Award from the Operations Research Society of America for his work in portfolio theory, sparse matrix techniques, and SIMSCRIPT. In 1990, he shared the Nobel Prize in Economics for his work on portfolio theory.

Contributing Authors

Andrew Alford	Goldman Sachs Asset Management
Noël Amenc	EDHEC-Risk Institute
Mark J. P. Anson	Oak Hill Investments
Stephen J. Antczak	Societe Generale
António Baldaque da Silva	Barclays Capital
Bülent Baygün	BNP Paribas
Bruce M. Collins	Western Connecticut State University
Chris P. Dialynas	Pacific Investment Management Company
Pamela P. Drake	James Madison University
Frank J. Fabozzi	Yale School of Management
Radu Găbudean	Barclays Capital
Felix Goltz	EDHEC-Risk Institute
James L. Grant	University of Massachusetts–Boston and JLG Research
Francis Gupta	Dow Jones Indexes
Bruce I. Jacobs	Jacobs Levy Equity Management
Robert R. Johnson	CFA Institute
Frank J. Jones	San Jose State University
Robert Jones	Goldman Sachs Asset Management
Petter N. Kolm	Courant Institute of Mathematical Sciences, New York University
Glen A. Larsen, Jr.	Indiana University Kelley School of Business–Indianapolis
Anthony Lazanas	Barclays Capital
Kenneth N. Levy	Jacobs Levy Equity Management
Terence Lim	Goldman Sachs Asset Management
Douglas J. Lucas	Moody's Investors Service
Steven V. Mann	The Moore School of Business, University of South Carolina

Harry M. Markowitz	Consultant
Lionel Martellini	EDHEC Business School, EDHEC-Risk Institute
Vincent Milhau	EDHEC-Risk Institute
Dessislava A. Pachamanova	Babson College
Ellen J. Rachlin	Mariner Investment Group, LLC
Arne D. Staal	Barclays Capital
Robert Tzucker	Credit Suisse
Raman Vardharaj	OppenheimerFunds
Raman Vardharaj	Oppenheimer Main Street Small Cap Fund
Guofu Zhou	Olin Business School, Washington University

Foreword

Then and Now in Investing, and Why Now Is So Much Better

Peter L. Bernstein

> This Foreword originally appeared in the first edition of *The Theory and Practice of Investment Management*. Peter Bernstein passed away in June 2009. References to the updated chapters mentioned in the Foreword are provided by the editors.

As I read this book for the first time, I was constantly reminded of the contrast between the investment world of today and what professional investing was like at the beginning of my career 50 years ago. The revolution in investing over the past half century has been far more remarkable than most people with a shorter memory bank can realize.

While sophisticated investors back then understood a few of the basic ideas and principles that drive today's investment practices, their methods were crude, undisciplined, purely intuitive, and wildly inaccurate in terms of achieving what they hoped to accomplish. Entire areas and techniques of investment management had yet to be discovered, many destined to appear only 20 or 30 years later. The momentous Nobel-prize-winning theoretical innovations that did develop during the 1950s—Markowitz's principles of portfolio selection, Modigliani-Miller's contribution to corporate finance and the uses of arbitrage, and Tobin's insights into the risk–reward trade-off—trickled at a snail's pace even into the academic world and were unknown to nearly all practitioners until many years later.

We did understand the importance of diversification, in both individual positions and in asset allocation. The diversification we provided, however, was determined by seat-of-the-pants deliberations, with no systematic evaluation beyond hunch. Although risk was an ever-present consideration, in our shop at least, the idea of attaching a number to investment risk was inconceivable. Performance measurement was a simple comparison to the Dow Jones Industrials. Institutional and tax-free investors were few and far between. Many of the individual clients who comprised our constituency kept their securities in safe deposit boxes instead of with brokers (risky) or custodian banks (costly), which was a major obstacle to making changes in portfolios, especially with bearer bonds.

We bought and sold stocks on the basis of their being "cheap" or "expensive," but we worked without any explicit methodology for quantifying what those words meant. The notion of growth as an investment consideration simply did not exist in the early 1950s, when stocks still yielded more than bonds. Although I attracted some attention with an article on the subject in the *Harvard Business Review* in 1956, growth as a central element of equity investing did not gain any traction until well into the 1960s.

We expected bond yields to rise and fall with business activity and stocks to do the opposite, which meant any suggestion of the two asset classes moving in tandem was unthinkable. Credit risk and interest rate risk were the only kinds of fixed income risk we thought about; inflation played no part in decisions concerning asset allocation, market timing, or managing the bond portions of our portfolios. Everybody knew long bonds were riskier than short-term obligations, but precisely how much riskier and the structure of risk and return in the bond market were never part of our deliberations. The uses of the complex and fascinating mathematics of fixed income securities were still largely undeveloped.

In any case, the fixed income universe available to us consisted only of Treasuries, corporates, and municipals; many of the corporates traded on the Big Board instead of in the dealer markets that are so familiar today. But that did not matter much because we acquired most of our clients' bonds on a buy-and-hold basis, as was the custom with all fixed income securities purchased by sober investors like insurance companies, college endowments, trustees for widows and orphans, and the small number of fee-only investment counsel firms like ours.

With the invention of the money market fund still some 20 years in the future, and Treasuries difficult to trade in small or odd amounts, cash management consisted of advising clients to deposit or withdraw money from savings accounts. Once in the savings account, the money became "their" money rather than "our" money. And that meant we had to call even clients with discretionary accounts and engage in a debate whenever we wanted to make a purchase without an offsetting sale.

The volume of information of interest to investors was infinitesimal from today's vantage point. At 10 minutes past every hour, a friendly broker would call on the phone to give us the latest hourly price of the Dow Jones

- Industrials and a rundown on the stocks we followed most closely. That was all we knew during the day about what was happening in the market. The Standard & Poor's averages were published only monthly because calculating values for market-weighted indexes took too long for the result to be timely; searching the ticker tape for the 30 Dow stocks, jotting down their prices, adding them up, and then dividing by the divisor was a dreary task, but it could be accomplished in just a few minutes.

- Research consisted primarily of the Value Line, which was way ahead of its time in working off a disciplined valuation procedure (although the saying went that if the stock's price did not move toward the Line after a while, the Line would manage to move toward the price). Wall Street research was spotty and superficial. As we and other leading investment advisors insisted

- that our clients choose their own brokers in order to avoid any odor of conflicts of interest, soft dollar research in such a world was nonexistent.

I need not elaborate on the difference the computer has made in preparing timely and elaborate client valuations, in organizing data for research

- purposes, and in speedy communication. But that was only the beginning: The computer has been the messenger of the investment revolution. If the world's stock of office equipment still consisted only of the slide-rules and hand-turned or electric (not electronic) desk-top calculators we used in the

- 1950s, the theories comprising the subject matter of this book, and that support today's investment practices, would never have moved beyond their pages in scholarly journals into the real world of investing.

• • •

To give you a flavor of the profound nature of the changes that have occurred, I suggest you peek ahead to a few chapters in this book. For example, skim through Chapter 3 on applying Markowitz's mean-variance analysis, Chapters 5 and 6 on asset pricing models, Chapter 19 on fixed income portfolio strategies, and Chapter 7 on asset allocation. Even a superficial view will reveal the radical difference between the way we managed portfolios in the 1950s and common practice today.

Markowitz won the Nobel Prize for his emphasis on two ancient homilies—nothing ventured, nothing gained, but do not put all your eggs into one basket. Markowitz's memorable achievement was to transform these two basic investment guidelines into a rigorous analytical procedure for composing investment portfolios. His primary innovation, in fact, was to distinguish between risk in a portfolio setting and the risk an investor faces in selecting individual security positions.

Markowitz uses his quantitative definition of risk to provide a means of calculating—in hard numbers—the price of risk, or the amount of additional risk an investor must face in order to increase the portfolio's expected return by a given amount. Investors can now employ diversification (distributing the eggs in many baskets) to minimize the amount of "venture," or risk, relative to a given amount of expected "gain," or return. Or, with the same process, the investor can choose to maximize the gain to be expected from a given amount of venture. Markowitz characterizes such portfolios as "efficient," because they optimize the combination of input (risk) per unit of output (return). This pioneering analysis was only a starting point, but it is still the inspiration for an extensive set of novel approaches for arriving at the most critical decisions in the portfolio-building process.

Despite his contribution to the measurement and understanding of investment risk, Markowitz skipped over a full-dress definition of the other side of the equation—expected return. Chapters 5 and 6 on asset pricing models detail striking advances in both defining and quantifying expected return. Nevertheless, the methodology in these chapters is still a variation on Markowitz's theme, for risk continues to play a central role in the prices investors set on individual assets as they go about building their portfolios.

This approach is a quantum leap from the way I used to guess whether a security was "cheap" or "expensive." We limited ourselves to trying to figure out what P/E or dividend yield was appropriate for each stock we considered, a judgment that ignored the correlations between that security and all the other securities in the portfolio or between that security and the market as a whole. But Markowitz made it clear that the selection of issues for a portfolio is not the same thing as valuing individual securities. Those choices must be set in terms of the interaction between each individual security and the rest of the portfolio; later variations by William Sharpe and others, also described in Chapters 4 and 5, emphasized the importance of the interaction between individual securities and the market as a whole. Consequently, the models in Chapters 4 and 5 have an entirely different goal from the traditional valuation parameters covered in Chapter 10.

This entire structure of portfolio formation is by no means limited to selecting stocks: It is equally important in the management of fixed-income portfolios. Here, as you will see in Chapter 19, the many aspects of fixed-income strategies are even further removed from traditional investment practices than the modern approach to equity selections. The proliferation of new forms of fixed income instruments has joined with the conversion of buy-and-hold into a broad set of active bond management strategies, creating a world of fixed-income investing unrecognizable to a Rip Van Winkle who went to sleep in the early 1950s and awoke in the early 2000s. Indeed, today's debt instruments are explicitly designed for agile and dynamic trading; the sanctified practice of holding bonds to maturity that I once knew would be dangerously inappropriate in today's world. Fixed income instruments may still be less risky than equities, but they nevertheless offer an immense and widening span of risk and return trade-offs. The result is a significant increase in total portfolio expected returns relative to the risks incurred. Here, too, portfolio efficiency can be enhanced.

• • •

Despite my enthusiasm for the whole long story within the covers of this book, I warn the reader against expecting magic potions showering instant riches on anyone who masters these lessons. The future faced by investors is just as unpredictable as it ever was. Do not believe any boasts to the contrary. Risk is an inescapable companion in the investment process.

But that is just the point. By making risk an integral part of the decisionmaking process, and by incorporating the rigor and discipline of quantification, modern theories and applications clarify as never before the multifarious paths linking the risk of loss to opportunities for gain. One of the most exciting features to me is how a few dominant principles can spawn an apparently unlimited supply of variations on the basic themes, opening investment possibilities we never dreamed of 50 years ago. While this book does a great job of describing the cat, it also provides a broad menu of effective methods to skin the cat.

The transformation in investing over the past 50 years is comparable to stepping from Charles Lindbergh's *Spirit of St. Louis* into a modern commercial aircraft. Lindbergh's flight from New York to Paris made him a hero before the whole world. A flight from New York to Paris now takes place without notice every hour of the day and into the night. But it is not only distance and time that modern technology has conquered. A glance into the cockpit of a contemporary aircraft reveals a fantastic array of controls and instruments whose entire purpose is to prevent the kinds of crashes that were as routine in Lindbergh's day as they are headline news in our own time—and to do so without any loss of speed. The secret of success is in control of an airliner at altitudes and velocity Lindbergh never dreamed of.

The metaphor is apt. As this book makes abundantly clear, the striking difference between today's investment world and the world to which I was introduced is in control over the consequences of decision making, under conditions of uncertainty, without any loss of opportunity. Indeed, the opportunity set has been greatly expanded. We will never know enough of what lies ahead to make greater wealth a certainty, but we can learn how to increase the odds and—equally important, I assure you—we can avoid losing our shirts because of foolish decisions.

The ideas in this book comprise a rich treasure. How I wish I had had it in my hands when I first entered the challenging world of investing back in 1951!

Instruments, Asset Allocation, Portfolio Selection, and Asset Pricing

Overview of Investment Management

Frank J. Fabozzi, Ph.D., CFA, CPA
Professor in the Practice of Finance
Yale School of Management

Harry M. Markowitz, Ph.D.
Consultant

T he purpose of this book is to describe the activities and investment vehicles associated with *investment management*. Investment management—also referred to as *portfolio management* and *money management*—requires an understanding of:

- How investment objectives are determined.
- The investment vehicles in which an investor can allocate funds.
- The way investment products are valued so that an investor can assess whether or not a particular investment is fairly priced, underpriced, or overpriced.
- The investment strategies that can be employed by an investor to realize a specified investment objective.
- The best way to construct a portfolio, given an investment strategy.
- The techniques for evaluating performance.

In this book, the contributors explain each of these activities. In this introductory chapter, we set forth in general terms the *investment management process*. This process involves the following five tasks:

1. Setting investment objectives.
2. Establishing an investment policy.
3. Selecting an investment strategy.

4. Constructing the portfolio.
5. Measuring and evaluating investment performance.

SETTING INVESTMENT OBJECTIVES

Setting investment objectives, begins with a thorough analysis of the investment objectives of the entity whose funds are being managed. These entities can be classified as *individual investors* and *institutional investors*. Within each of these broad classifications is a wide range of investment objectives.

Institutional investors include:

- Pension funds.
- Depository institutions (commercial banks, savings and loan associations, and credit unions).
- Insurance companies (life companies, property and casualty companies, and health companies).
- Regulated investment companies (mutual funds and closed-end funds).
- Endowments and foundations.
- Treasury department of corporations, municipal governments, and government agencies.

In general, we can classify institutional investors into two broad categories: those that must meet contractually specified liabilities and those that do not. We can classify those in the first category as institutions with "liability-driven objectives" and those in the second category as institutions with "nonliability driven objectives." A *liability* is a cash outlay that must be made at a specific time to satisfy the contractual terms of an issued obligation. An institutional investor is concerned with both the *amount* and *timing* of liabilities because its assets must produce the cash flow to meet any payments it has promised to make in a timely way.

Some institutions have a wide range of investment products that they offer investors, some of which are liability driven and others that are nonliability driven. Once the investment objective is clearly defined, it will then be possible to (1) establish a "benchmark" by which to evaluate the performance of the investment manager and (2) evaluate alternative investment strategies to assess the potential for realizing the specified investment objective.

ESTABLISHING AN INVESTMENT POLICY

Establishing an investment policy starts with the asset allocation decision. That is, a decision must be made as to how the funds to be invested should be distributed among the major classes of assets.

Asset Classes

Throughout this book, we refer to certain categories of investment products as an "asset class." In the next chapter, we take a closer look at what is meant by an asset class. From the perspective of a U.S. investor, the convention is to refer to the following as *traditional asset classes*: U.S. common stocks, non-U.S. (or foreign) common stocks, U.S. bonds, non-U.S. (or foreign) bonds, cash equivalents, and real estate. Common stock and bonds are further divided into different asset classes. Cash equivalents are defined as short-term debt obligations that have little price volatility. In addition to the traditional asset classes, there are asset classes commonly referred to as *alternative assets* or *alternative investments*. Two of the more popular ones are hedge funds and private equity. In the next chapter, we review three popular alternative assets.

Constraints

There are some institutional investors that make the asset allocation decision based purely on their understanding of the risk-return characteristics of the various asset classes and expected returns. The asset allocation will take into consideration any investment constraints or restrictions. Asset allocation models are commercially available for assisting those individuals responsible for making this decision.

In the development of an investment policy, the following factors must be considered: client constraints, regulatory constraints, and tax and accounting issues.

Examples of client-imposed constraints would be restrictions that specify the types of securities in which a manager may invest and concentration limits on how much or little may be invested in a particular asset class or in a particular issuer. When a benchmark is established, there may be a restriction as to the degree to which the manager may deviate from some key characteristics of that benchmark.

There are many types of regulatory constraints. These involve constraints on the asset classes that are permissible and concentration limits on investments. Moreover, in making the asset allocation decision, consideration must be given to any risk-based capital requirements. For depository institutions and insurance companies, the amount of statutory capital required is related to the quality of the assets in which the institution has invested.

Tax considerations are important for several reasons. First, certain institutional investors such as pension funds, endowments, and foundations are exempt from federal income taxation. Consequently, the assets in which they invest will not be those that are tax-advantaged investments. Second, there are tax factors that must be incorporated into the investment policy. For example, although a pension fund might be tax-exempt, there may be certain assets or the use of some investment vehicles in which it invests whose earnings may be taxed.

Generally accepted accounting principles (GAAP) and regulatory accounting principles (RAP) are important considerations in developing investment policies.

SELECTING A PORTFOLIO STRATEGY

The next task in the investment management process is selecting a portfolio strategy that is consistent with the investment objectives and investment policy guidelines. The selection can be made from a wide range of portfolio strategies. In general, portfolio strategies can be classified as either active or passive.

An *active portfolio strategy* uses available information and forecasting techniques to seek a better performance than a portfolio that is simply diversified broadly. Essential to all active strategies are expectations about the factors that have been found to influence the performance of an asset class. A *passive portfolio strategy* involves minimal expectational input, and instead relies on diversification to match the performance of some market index. In effect, a passive strategy assumes that market prices impound all available information. Between these extremes of active and passive strategies, several strategies have sprung up that have elements of both.

Given the choice among active and passive strategies, which should be selected? The answer depends on (1) the client's or money manager's view of how "price-efficient" the market is; (2) the client's risk tolerance; and (3) the nature of the client's liabilities. By "marketplace price efficiency," we mean how difficult it would be to earn a greater return than passive management after adjusting for the risk associated with a strategy and the transaction costs associated with implementing that strategy.

CONSTRUCTING THE PORTFOLIO

Once a portfolio strategy is selected, the next task is to construct the portfolio (i.e., select the specific assets to be included in the portfolio). It is in this phase of the investment management process that the investor attempts to construct an *efficient portfolio*. An efficient portfolio is one that provides the greatest expected return for a given level of risk, or equivalently, the lowest risk for a given expected return.

To construct an efficient portfolio, the investor must be able to quantify risk and provide the necessary inputs. As explained in Chapter 3, there are three key inputs that are needed: future expected return (or simply expected return), variance of asset returns, and correlation (or covariance) of asset returns. All of the investment tools described in the chapters that follow in this book are intended to provide the investor with information with which to estimate these three inputs.

MEASURING AND EVALUATING PERFORMANCE

Finally, there is the task of measuring and evaluating investment performance. *Performance measurement* involves the calculation of the return realized by a portfolio manager over some time interval, which we refer to as the *evaluation period*. There are several important issues that must be addressed in developing a methodology for calculating a portfolio's return and we discuss them below.

Performance evaluation is concerned with three issues: (1) determining whether the portfolio manager added value by outperforming the established benchmark; (2) identifying how the portfolio manager achieved the calculated return; and (3) assessing whether the portfolio manager achieved superior performance (i.e., added value) by skill or by luck. There are two approaches that have been employed in evaluating the performance of portfolio managers: single-index performance measures and performance attribution models.

Despite their popularity, single-index performance measures do not specify how or why a portfolio manager may have outperformed or underperformed a benchmark. Two popular measures are the Sharpe ratio[1] and information ratio. These two ratios are return/risk ratios. At this junction, an explanation of the information ratio is not easy to understand but it will be described in Chapter 9. The Sharpe ratio is equal to

$$\text{Sharpe ratio} = \frac{\text{Portfolio return} - \text{Risk-free rate}}{\text{Standard deviation of the portfolio return}}$$

The numerator of the Sharpe ratio is a measure of return. It is not the raw return but the return in excess of what could have been earned by investing in a risk-free security. The denominator is a measure of the risk associated with generating the portfolio return. As explained in Chapter 3, the standard deviation is a commonly used measure of risk. Thus, the

---

[1]William F. Sharpe, "Mutual Fund Performance," *Journal of Business* 39, S1 (1966): 119–138.

Sharpe ratio is a measure of the excess return relative to the variability of the portfolio return.

Performance attribution models (also called *return attribution models*) decompose the portfolio return so that a client can determine how the portfolio manager earned the return. As we explain in later chapters, a portfolio manager seeking to outperform a designated benchmark can do so by constructing a portfolio so that it differs from the risks embedded in the benchmark. Consequently, understanding the risk embedded in a benchmark are essential to understanding not only how to construct a portfolio, but also for employing return attribution models.

Measuring Performance

The starting point for evaluating the performance of a portfolio manager is measuring return. This might seem quite simple, but several practical issues make the task complex because one must take into account any cash distributions made from a portfolio during the evaluation period.

The dollar return realized on a portfolio for any evaluation period (i.e., a year, month, or week) is equal to the sum of:

1. The difference between the market value of the portfolio at the end of the evaluation period and the market value at the beginning of the evaluation period.
2. Any distributions made from the portfolio.

It is important that any capital or income distributions from the portfolio to a client or beneficiary of the portfolio be taken into account.

The rate of return, or simply return, expresses the dollar return in terms of the amount of the market value at the beginning of the evaluation period. Thus, the return can be viewed as the amount (expressed as a fraction of the initial portfolio value) that can be withdrawn at the end of the evaluation period while maintaining the initial market value of the portfolio intact.

In equation form, the portfolio's *return* can be expressed as follows:

$$R_P = \frac{MV_1 - MV_0 + D}{MV_0}$$

where

R_P = the portfolio's return

MV_1 = the portfolio's market value at the end of the evaluation period

MV_0 = the portfolio's market value at the beginning of the evaluation period

D = the cash distributions from the portfolio to the client during the evaluation period

To illustrate the calculation of a return, assume the following information for the portfolio manager of a common stock portfolio: The portfolio's market value at the beginning and end of the evaluation period is $250 million and $280 million, respectively, and, during the evaluation period, $10 million is distributed to the client from investment income. Therefore,

$$MV_1 = \$280{,}000{,}000 \quad MV_0 = \$250{,}000{,}000 \quad D = \$10{,}000{,}000$$

Then

$$R_P = \frac{\$280{,}000{,}000 - \$250{,}000{,}000 + \$10{,}000{,}000}{\$250{,}000{,}000} = 0.16 = 16\%$$

There are three assumptions in measuring return. The first assumption is that cash inflows (i.e., dividends and interest) into the portfolio during the evaluation period but are not distributed are reinvested in the portfolio. For example, suppose that during the evaluation period, $20 million is received from dividends. This amount is reflected in the market value of the portfolio at the end of the period.

The second assumption is that if there are distributions from the portfolio, they either occur at the end of the evaluation period or are held in the form of cash until the end of the evaluation period. In our example, $10 million is distributed to the client. But when did that distribution actually occur? To understand why the timing of the distribution is important, consider two extreme cases: (1) the distribution is made at the end of the evaluation period, as is assumed in the return calculation; and (2) the distribution is made at the beginning of the evaluation period. In the first case, the portfolio manager had the use of the $10 million to invest for the entire evaluation period. By contrast, in the second case, the portfolio manager loses the opportunity to invest the funds until the end of the evaluation period. Consequently, the timing of the distribution will affect the return, but this is not considered in the return calculation above.

The third assumption is that there is no cash contributed to the portfolio by the client. For example, suppose that sometime during the evaluation period, the client contributes $15 million to the portfolio manager to invest. Consequently, the market value of the portfolio at the end of the evaluation period, $280 million in our example, would reflect the contribution of

$15 million. The return calculation does not reflect that the portfolio's ending market value is affected by the cash contributed by the client. Moreover, the timing of this contribution will affect the calculated return.

Thus, while the return calculation for a portfolio can be evaluated for any length of time—such as one day, one month, five years—from a practical point of view, the assumptions of this approach limit its application. The longer the evaluation period, the more likely the assumptions will be violated. For example, it is highly likely that there may be more than one distribution to the client and more than one contribution from the client if the evaluation period is five years. Therefore, a return calculation made over a long period of time, if longer than a few months, would not be very reliable because of the assumption underlying the calculations that all cash payments and inflows are made and received at the end of the period.

Not only does the violation of the assumptions make it difficult to compare the returns of two portfolio managers over some evaluation period, but it is also not useful for evaluating performance over different periods. For example, the return calculation above will not give reliable information to compare the performance of a 1-month evaluation period and a 3-year evaluation period. To make such a comparison, the return must be expressed per unit of time, for example, per year.

The way to handle these practical issues is to calculate the return for a short unit of time such as a month or a quarter. We call the return so calculated the *subperiod return*. To get the return for the evaluation period, the subperiod returns are then averaged. So, for example, if the evaluation period is one year, and 12 monthly returns are calculated, the monthly returns are the subperiod returns, and they are averaged to get the 1-year return. If a 3-year return is sought, and 12 quarterly returns can be calculated, quarterly returns are the subperiod returns, and they are averaged to get the 3-year return. The 3-year return can then be converted into an annual return by the straightforward procedure described later.

Three methodologies have been used in practice to calculate the average of the subperiod returns: arithmetic average rate of return, time-weighted rate of return (also called the *geometric rate of return*), and dollar-weighted return.

Arithmetic Average (Mean) Rate of Return

The *arithmetic average (mean) rate of return* is an unweighted average of the subperiod returns. The general formula is

$$R_A = \frac{R_{P1} + R_{P2} + \cdots + R_{PN}}{N}$$

where

R_A = the arithmetic average rate of return
R_{Pk} = the portfolio return for subperiod k, where $k =1, \ldots, N$
N = the number of subperiods in the evaluation period

For example, if the portfolio returns were −10%, 20%, and 5% in months July, August, and September, respectively, the arithmetic average monthly return is 5%, as shown:

$$R_A = \frac{-0.10 + 0.20 + 0.05}{3} = 0.05 = 5\%$$

There is a major problem with using the arithmetic average rate of return. To see this problem, suppose a portfolio's initial market value is $280 million, and the market values at the end of the next two months are $560 million and $280 million, respectively. Furthermore, assume that there are no client distributions or contributions for either month. Then the subperiod return for the first month (R_{P1}) is 100%, and the subperiod return for the second month (R_{P2}) is −50%. The arithmetic average rate of return is then 25%. Not a bad return! But think about this number. The portfolio's initial market value was $280 million. Its market value at the end of two months is $280 million. The return over this 2-month evaluation period is zero. Yet the arithmetic average rate of return says it is a whopping 25%.

Thus it is improper to interpret the arithmetic average rate of return as a measure of the average return over an evaluation period. The proper interpretation is as follows: It is the average value of the withdrawals (expressed as a fraction of the portfolio's initial market value) that can be made at the end of each subperiod while keeping the portfolio's initial market value intact. In our first example, in which the average monthly return is 5%, the investor must add 10% of the initial portfolio market value at the end of the first month, can withdraw 20% of the initial portfolio market value at the end of the second month, and can withdraw 5% of the initial portfolio market value at the end of the third month. In our second example, the average monthly return of 25% means that 100% of the portfolio's initial market value ($280 million) can be withdrawn at the end of the first month, and 50% must be added at the end of the second month.

Time-Weighted Rate of Return

The *time-weighted rate of return* measures the compounded rate of growth of the portfolio's initial market value during the evaluation period, assuming that all cash distributions are reinvested in the portfolio. This return is also commonly referred to as the *geometric mean return* because it is computed by taking the geometric average of the portfolio subperiod returns. The general formula is

$$R_T = [(1 + R_{P1})(1 + R_{P2}) \dots (1 + R_{PN})]^{1/N} - 1$$

where R_T is the time-weighted rate of return, and R_{Pk} and N are as defined earlier.

For example, let us assume the portfolio returns were –10%, 20%, and 5% in July, August, and September, as in the first example above. Then the time-weighted rate of return is

$$R_T = \{[1 + (-0.10)] \, (1 + 0.20) \, (1 + 0.05)\}^{1/3} - 1$$
$$= [(0.90) \, (1.20) \, (1.05)]^{1/3} - 1 \ = 0.043$$

Because the time-weighted rate of return is 4.3% per month, $1 invested in the portfolio at the beginning of July would have grown at a rate of 4.3% per month during the 3-month evaluation period.

The time-weighted rate of return in the second example is 0%, as expected, as shown here:

$$R_T = \{(1 + 1.00)[1 + (-0.50)]\}^{1/2} - 1 = [(2.00)(0.50)]^{1/2} - 1 \ = 0\%$$

In general, the arithmetic and time-weighted average returns will give different values for the portfolio return over some evaluation period. This is because, in computing the arithmetic average rate of return, the amount invested is assumed to be maintained (through additions or withdrawals) at the portfolio's initial market value. The time-weighted return, in contrast, is the return on a portfolio that varies in size because of the assumption that all proceeds are reinvested.

In general, the arithmetic average rate of return will exceed the time-weighted average rate of return. The exception is in the special situation where all the subperiod returns are the same, in which case the averages are identical. The magnitude of the difference between the two averages is smaller the less the variation in the subperiod returns over the evaluation period. For example, suppose that the evaluation period is four months, and that the four monthly returns are as follows: R_{P1} = 0.04, R_{P2} = 0.06, R_{P3} = 0.02, and R_{P4} = –0.02. The arithmetic average rate of return is 2.5%, and the time-weighted average rate of return is 2.46%. Not much of a difference. In our earlier example, in which we calculated an average rate of return of 25% but a time-weighted average rate of return of 0%, the large discrepancy is due to the substantial variation in the two monthly returns.

Dollar-Weighted Rate of Return

The *dollar-weighted rate of return* is computed by finding the interest rate that will make the present value of the cash flows from all the subperiods in the evaluation period plus the portfolio's terminal market value equal to the portfolio's initial market value. The cash flow for each subperiod reflects the difference between the cash inflows due to investment income (i.e., dividends and interest) and to contributions made by the client to the portfolio and the cash outflows reflecting distributions to the client. Notice that it is not necessary to know the portfolio's market value for each subperiod to determine the dollar-weighted rate of return.

The dollar-weighted rate of return is simply an internal rate of return calculation, and, hence, it is also called the *internal rate of return*. The general formula for the dollar-weighted return is

$$V_0 = \frac{C_1}{(1+R_D)} + \frac{C_2}{(1+R_D)^2} + \cdots + \frac{C_N + V_N}{(1+R_D)^n}$$

where

R_D = the dollar-weighted rate of return
V_0 = the portfolio's initial market value
V_N = the portfolio's terminal market value
C_k = the portfolio's cash flow (cash inflows minus cash outflows) for subperiod k, where k = 1, 2, ..., N

The dollar-weighted rate of return and the time-weighted rate of return will produce the same result if no withdrawals or contributions occur over the evaluation period and if all investment income is reinvested. The problem with the dollar-weighted rate of return is that it is affected by factors that are beyond the control of the money manager. Specifically, any contributions made by the client or withdrawals that the client requires will affect the calculated return. This may make it difficult to compare the performance of two portfolio managers. Despite this limitation, the dollar-weighted rate of return does provide information about the growth of the fund. This growth, however, may not be solely attributable to the performance of the portfolio manager when there are contributions and withdrawals.

Annualizing Returns

The evaluation period may be less than or greater than one year. Typically, return measures are reported as an average annual return. This requires the annualization of the subperiod returns. The subperiod returns are usually calculated for a period of less than one year for the reasons described earlier. The subperiod returns are then annualized using the following formula:

$$\text{Annual return} = (1 + \text{Average period return})^{\text{Number of periods in year}} - 1$$

For example, suppose the evaluation period is three years, and a monthly period return is calculated. Suppose further that the average monthly return is 2%. Then the annual return would be

$$\text{Annual return} = (1.02)^{12} - 1 = 26.8\%$$

KEY POINTS

- The investment management process involves setting investment objectives, establishing an investment policy, selecting an investment strategy, constructing the portfolio, and measuring and evaluating investment performance.
- Investment objectives can be either based on some benchmark or liabilities.
- Investment policy begins with the decision as to how to allocate funds across the major asset classes taking into consideration client-imposed and regulatory constraints.
- In selecting a portfolio strategy that is consistent with its investment objectives, a client can select an active strategy or a passive strategy. The selection of a strategy depends on the client's view of the pricing efficiency of the market, as well as the client's risk tolerance.
- The portfolio construction task involves assembling assets so as to create an efficient portfolio: a portfolio that provides the greatest expected return for the target level of risk.
- In evaluating performance, return attribution analysis should be used.
- This tool allows a client to understand why a portfolio manager may have underperformed or outperformed a benchmark.
- Performance measurement involves computing the return over some time period.
- The three methods for computing a return over some evaluation period based on averaging subperiod returns are the arithmetic average rate of return, time-weighted rate of return, and dollar-weighted return. The last two measures will produce the same result if no withdrawals or contributions occur over the evaluation period and if all investment income is reinvested.

CHAPTER 2

Asset Classes, Alternative Investments, Investment Companies, and Exchange-Traded Funds

Mark J. P. Anson, Ph.D., JD, CPA, CFA, CAIA
Chief Investment Officer and Managing Partner
Oak Hill Investments

Frank J. Fabozzi, Ph.D., CFA, CPA
Professor in the Practice of Finance
Yale School of Management

Frank J. Jones, Ph.D.
Professor, Accounting and Finance Department
San Jose State University

In this chapter, we provide an overview of asset classes and then describe the various financial products available to investment managers. Because the focus is on the two major asset classes, common stock and bonds, in this book, we do not discuss them in any in any detail here. Instead, we provide an overview of alternatives asset classes and two important financial products that can be used to obtain exposure to all asset classes, regulated investment companies and exchange-traded funds.

ASSET CLASSES

In most developed countries, the four major asset classes are (1) common stocks, (2) bonds, (3) cash equivalents, and (4) real estate. Why are they referred to as asset classes? That is, how do we define an *asset class*? There are several ways to do so. The first is in terms of the investment attributes that the members of an asset class have in common. These investment characteristics include:

- The major economic factors that influence the value of the asset class and, as a result, correlate highly with the returns of each member included in the asset class.
- Risk and return characteristics that are similar.
- A common legal or regulatory structure.

Based on this way of defining an asset class, the correlation between the returns of two different asset classes—the key statistical measure for successful diversification as will be explained in the next chapter—would be low.

Mark Kritzman offers a second way of defining an asset class based simply on a group of assets that is treated as an asset class by asset managers. He writes:

[S]ome investments take on the status of an asset class simply because the managers of these assets promote them as an asset class. They believe that investors will be more inclined to allocate funds to their products if they are viewed as an asset class rather than merely as an investment strategy.[1]

Kritzman then goes on to propose criteria for determining asset class status which includes the attributes that we mentioned above and that will be described in more detail in later chapters.

Based on these two ways of defining asset classes, the four major asset classes above can be extended to create other asset classes. From the perspective of a U.S. investor, for example, the four major asset classes listed earlier have been expanded as follows by separating foreign securities from U.S. securities: (1) U.S. common stocks, (2) non-U.S. (or foreign) common stocks, (3) U.S. bonds, (4) non-U.S. bonds, (5) cash equivalents, and (6) real estate.

Common stocks and bonds are commonly further partitioned into more asset classes. For U.S. common stocks (also referred to as *U.S. equities*), asset classes are based on market capitalization and style (growth versus value).

The *market capitalization* of a firm, commonly referred to as "market cap," is the total market value of its common stock outstanding. For

---

[1]Mark Kritzman, "Toward Defining an Asset Class," *Journal of Alternative Investments* 2, no. 1(1999): 79.

example, suppose that a corporation has 400 million shares of common stock outstanding and each share has a market value of $100. Then the market capitalization of this company is $40 billion (400 million shares times $100 per share). The categories of common stock based on market capitalization are *mega-cap* (greater than $200 billion), *large cap* ($10 billion to $200 billion), *mid-cap* ($1 billion to $10 billion), *small cap* ($300 million to $1 billion), *micro-cap* ($50 million to $300 million), and *nano-cap* (less than $50 million).

While the market cap of a company is easy to determine given the market price per share and the number of shares outstanding, how does one define "value" and "growth" stocks? How this is done is explained in Chapter 10.

For U.S. bonds, also referred to as *fixed income securities*, the following are classified as asset classes: (1) U.S. government bonds, (2) corporate bonds, (3) U.S. municipal bonds (i.e., state and local bonds), (4) residential mortgage-backed securities, (5) commercial mortgage-backed securities, and (6) asset-backed securities. In turn, several of these asset classes are further segmented by the credit rating of the issuer. For example, for corporate bonds, investment-grade (i.e., high credit quality) corporate bonds and noninvestment-grade corporate bonds (i.e., speculative quality) are treated as two asset classes.

For non-U.S. stocks and bonds, the following are classified as asset classes: (1) developed market foreign stocks, (2) developed market foreign bonds, (3) emerging market foreign stocks, and (4) emerging market foreign bonds. The characteristics that market participants use to describe emerging markets is that the countries in this group:

- Have economies that are in transition but have started implementing political, economic, and financial market reforms in order to participate in the global capital market.
- May expose investors to significant price volatility attributable to political risk and the unstable value of their currency.
- Have a short period over which their financial markets have operated.

Loucks, Penicook, and Schillhorn describe what is meant by an emerging market as follows:

Emerging market issuers rely on international investors for capital. Emerging markets cannot finance their fiscal deficits domestically because domestic capital markets are poorly developed and local investors are unable or unwilling to lend to the government. Although emerging market issuers differ greatly in terms of credit risk, dependence on foreign capital is the most basic characteristic of the asset class.[2]

The asset classes above are referred to as *traditional asset classes*. Other asset classes are referred to as *nontraditional asset classes* or *alternative asset classes*. They include hedge funds, private equity, and commodities and are discussed later.

Real Estate

Before we discuss alternative asset classes, we provide a brief digression to consider where real estate belongs in our classification scheme. Real estate is a distinct asset class, but is it an alternative asset class? There are three reasons why we do not consider real estate to be an alternative asset class.

First, real estate was an asset class long before stocks and bonds became the investment of choice. Stocks and bonds evolved to support the financing needs of new enterprises that manufactured material goods and services. In fact, stocks and bonds became the "alternatives" to real estate instead of vice versa. Second, given the long-term presence of real estate as an asset class, models have been developed based on expected cash flows for valuing real estate.

Finally, real estate is not an alternative to stocks and bonds—it is a fundamental asset class that should be included within every diversified portfolio. Alternative assets are meant to diversify the stock-and-bond holdings within a portfolio context.

What Is an Alternative Asset Class?

Part of the difficulty of working with alternative asset classes is defining them. Are they a separate asset class or a subset of an existing asset class? Do they hedge the investment opportunity set or expand it? That is, in terms of Markowitz diversification that we describe in the next chapter, do they improve the efficient portfolio for a given level of risk? This means that for a given level of risk, do they allow for a greater expected return than by just investing in traditional asset classes?

In most cases, alternative assets are a subset of an existing asset class. This may run contrary to the popular view that alternative assets are separate asset classes. However, we take the view that what many consider separate "classes" are really just different investment strategies within an

---

[2]Maria Mednikov Loucks, John A. Penicook, and Uwe Schillhorn, "Emerging Markets Debt," Chapter 31 in Frank J. Fabozzi (ed.), *Handbook of Finance: Vol. I, Financial Markets and Instruments* (Hoboken, NJ: John Wiley, 2008): 340.

existing asset class. In most cases, they expand the investment opportunity set, rather than hedge it. Finally, with the exception of one alternative asset type, commodity futures, alternative assets are generally purchased in the private markets, outside of any exchange.

Alternative assets, then, are just alternative investments within an existing asset class. Specifically, most alternative assets derive their value from either the debt or equity markets. For instance, most hedge fund strategies involve the purchase and sale of either equity or debt securities. Additionally, hedge fund managers may invest in derivative instruments whose value is derived from the equity or debt market.

Efficient versus Inefficient Asset Classes

Another way to distinguish alternative asset classes from traditional asset classes is based on the efficiency of the marketplace in which the assets trade. The U.S. public stock-and-bond markets are generally considered to be the most price efficient marketplaces in the world. Often, these markets are referred to as "semistrong efficient." As explained in Chapter 9, this means that all publicly available information regarding a publicly traded corporation, both past information and present, is fully digested into the price of that company's traded securities.

Yet inefficiencies exist in all markets, both public and private. If there were no informational inefficiencies in the public equity market, there would be no case for pursuing a strategy that seeks to outperform the market. Such strategies are referred to as *active management strategies*. Nonetheless, whatever inefficiencies do exist, they are small and fleeting. The reason is that information is easy to acquire and disseminate in the publicly traded securities markets. Top-quartile portfolio managers who pursue active strategies in the public equity market earn returns in excess of their benchmark of approximately 1% a year.

In contrast, with respect to alternative assets, information is very difficult to acquire. Most alternative assets (with the exception of commodities) are privately traded. This includes private equity and hedge funds. The difference between top-quartile and bottom-quartile performance in private equity can be as much as 25%.

Consider venture capital, one subset of the private equity market. Investments in start-up companies require intense research into the product niche the company intends to fulfill, the background of the management of the company, projections about future cash flows, exit strategies, potential competition, beta testing schedules, and so forth. This information is not readily available to the investing public. It is time consuming and expensive to accumulate. Furthermore, most investors do not have the time or the talent to acquire and filter through the rough data regarding a private company. One reason why alternative asset managers charge large management and incentive fees is to recoup the cost of information collection.

This leads to another distinguishing factor between alternative asset classes and traditional asset classes: the investment intermediary. Continuing with our venture capital example, most investments in venture capital are made through limited partnerships, limited liability companies, or special-purpose vehicles. It is estimated that 80% of all private equity investments in the United States are funneled through a financial intermediary.

Investments in alternative assets are less liquid than their public market counterparts. Investments are closely held and liquidity is minimal. Furthermore, without a publicly traded security, the value of private securities cannot be determined by market trading. The value of the private securities must be estimated by book value or appraisal, or determined by a cash flow model.

Beta and Alpha Drivers

Two terms bandied about in asset management are "beta drivers" and "alpha drivers." To understand these terms, we must understand what is meant by a *market risk premium*. A market (or systematic) risk premium for an asset class is the difference in the return on an asset class and the return offered on a risk-free asset such as a U.S. Treasury security. Investors seek to capture that risk. An *excess return* is the return earned on an asset class that exceeds the return on a risk-free asset.

In constructing a portfolio, an investor seeks the most efficient trade-off between risk and return given a mix of asset classes. In the context of Markowitz diversification discussed in the next chapter, an efficient portfolio is sought—the portfolio that maximizes the expected portfolio return for a given level of risk. In this sense, the basic asset allocation is all about capturing the market risk premiums that exist for investing in different asset classes. However, if additional asset classes can be added to the mix of potential investment opportunities in which an investor may invest, the efficient frontier can be improved so as to provide a greater range of risk and return opportunities for an investor. Recall that in our earlier description of an asset class, we explained that it had a low correlation of returns with other asset classes.

Beta drivers capture market risk premiums in an efficient manner. We have already discussed the notion or beta or systematic risk. In contrast, *alpha drivers* seek pockets of excess return often without regard to benchmarks.

It is useful to think of traditional and alternative assets within the context of beta and alpha drivers. Alternative assets represent an alternative source of beta that is different from the mixture of traditional assets—

stocks and bonds. Access to alternative assets can provide new systematic risk premiums that are distinctly different than that obtained from stocks and bonds. Commodities are a good example—they provide a different risk exposure than stocks or bonds. Consequently, the risk premium associated with commodities is less than perfectly correlated with the markets for traditional asset classes.[3]

Alternative assets fall squarely into the category of alpha drivers. Alpha drivers seek excess return or added value. They tend to seek sources of return less correlated with traditional asset classes, which reduces risk in the entire portfolio via the process as we explained earlier in this chapter when we discussed diversification.

OVERVIEW OF ALTERNATIVE ASSET PRODUCTS

In this section, we describe three types of the best known alternative assets: hedge funds, private equity, and commodities.

Hedge Funds

The U.S. securities law does not provide a definition of the pools of investment funds run by asset managers that are referred to as *hedge funds*. These entities as of this writing are not regulated. George Soros, chairman of Soros Fund Management, a firm that advises a privately owned group of hedge funds (the Quantum Group of Funds), defines a hedge fund as follows:

> Hedge funds engage in a variety of investment activities. They cater to sophisticated investors and are not subject to the regulations that apply to mutual funds geared toward the general public. Fund managers are compensated on the basis of performance rather than as a fixed percentage of assets. "Performance funds" would be a more accurate description.[4]

The first page of a report by the President's Working Group on Financial Markets, *Hedge Funds, Leverage, and the Lessons of Long-Term Capital Management* published in April 1999, provides the following definition:

> The term "hedge fund" is commonly used to describe a variety of different types of investment vehicles that share some common

---

[3]This is a form of what is popularly referred to as *alternative beta*.
[4]George Soros, *Open Society: Reforming Global Capitalism* (New York: Public Affairs Press, 2000), 32n.

characteristics. Although it is not statutorily defined, the term encompasses any pooled investment vehicle that is privately organized, administered by professional money managers, and not widely available to the public.

The following is a description of hedge funds offered by the United Kingdom's Financial Services Authority, the regulatory body of all providers of financial services in that country:

The term can also be defined by considering the characteristics most commonly associated wih hedge funds. Usually, hedge funds:

- Are organised as private investment partnerships or offshore investment corporations.
- Use a wide variety of trading strategies involving position-taking in a range of markets.
- Employ an assortment of trading techniques and instruments, often including short-selling, derivatives and leverage.
- Pay performance fees to their managers.
- Have an investor base comprising wealthy individuals and institutions and a relatively high minimum investment limit (set at US$100,000 or higher for most funds).[5]

The definitions reproduced above help us understand several attributes of hedge funds. First and foremost, the word "hedge" in hedge funds is misleading because it is not a characteristic of hedge funds today. Second, hedge funds use a wide range of trading strategies and techniques in an attempt to not just generate abnormal returns but rather attempt to generate stellar returns regardless of how the market moves. The strategies used by a hedge fund can include one or more of the following:

- Leverage, which is the use of borrowed funds.
- Short selling, which is the sale of a financial instrument not owned in anticipation of a decline in that financial instrument's price.
- Derivatives to create leverage and/or to control risk.
- Simultaneous buying and selling of related financial instruments to realize a profit from the temporary misalignment of their prices.

Third, in evaluating hedge funds, investors are interested in the absolute return generated by the asset manager, not the relative return. *Absolute*

---

[5]Financial Services Authority, *Hedge Funds and the FSA*, Discussion Paper 16, 2002, p. 8.

return is simply the return realized rather than *relative return* which is the difference between the realized return and the return on some benchmark or index, which is quite different from the criterion used when evaluating the performance of an asset manager.[6]

Fourth, the management fee structure for hedge funds is a combination of a fixed fee based on the market value of assets managed plus a share of the positive return. The latter is a performance-based compensation referred to as an *incentive fee*.

We define *hedge fund* as a privately organized investment vehicle that manages a concentrated portfolio of public and private securities and derivative instruments on those securities, that can invest both long and short and can apply leverage.

Categories of Hedge Funds

Everyone has their own classification scheme for hedge funds.[7] This merely reflects the fact that hedge funds are a bit difficult to "box in." Here we break down hedge funds into broad categories as depicted in Exhibit 2.1.

We classify hedge funds into four broad buckets: market directional, corporate restructuring, convergence trading, and opportunistic. *Market directional hedge funds* are those that retain some amount of systematic risk exposure. For example, *equity long/short*[8] (or, as it is sometime called, *equity hedge*) are hedge funds that typically contain some amount of net long market exposure. As another example, activist hedge fund managers take large long-only positions in public companies and then try to effect value enhancement by becoming the catalyst for positive change to the corporate governance of the public company. While their portfolios are very concentrated and, therefore, have much more idiosyncratic risk, they still retain some amount of systematic market exposure through their net long position in public equities.

---

[6]The term *absolute return* comes from the skill-based nature of the industry. Hedge fund managers generally claim that their investment returns are derived from their skill at security selection rather than that of broad asset classes. This is due to the fact that most hedge fund managers build concentrated portfolios of relatively few investment positions and do not attempt to track a stock or bond index. The work of Fung and Hsieh shows that hedge funds generate a return distribution that is very different from mutual funds. See William Fund and David A. Hsieh, "Empirical Characteristics of Dynamic Trading Strategies: The Case of Hedge Funds," *Review of Financial Studies* 10, no. 2 (1997): 275–302.
[7]See, for example, Francois-Serg Lhabitant, *Hedge Funds: Quantitative Insight* (Hoboken, NJ: John Wiley & Sons, 2004).
[8]The equity long/short strategy is explained in Chapter 12.

EXHIBIT 2.1   Hedge Fund Styles and Risk Exposures

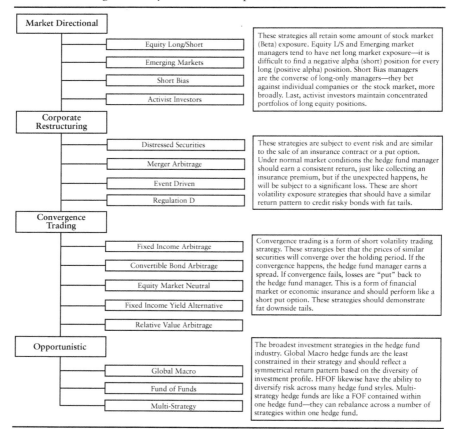

Corporate restructuring hedge funds take advantage of significant corporate transactions like a merger, acquisition, or bankruptcy. These funds earn their living by concentrating their portfolios in a handful of companies where it is more important to understand the likelihood that the corporate transaction will be completed than it is to determine whether the corporation is under or over valued. In fact, with respect to distressed securities hedge fund managers, there is some overlap with the private equity market. Both types of managers look for companies that are financially strapped for cash and can use either an infusion of new capital, or a restructuring of the company's outstanding debt. The skill set required is one that can navigate the bankruptcy process while being able to evaluate the fundamental price of an illiquid and distressed security—not an easy skill set to acquire.

Convergence trading hedge funds are the hedge funds that practice the art of arbitrage. In fact the specialized subcategories within this bucket typically contain the word *arbitrage* in their description such as statistical arbitrage, fixed income arbitrage, or convertible arbitrage. In general these hedge funds make bets that two similar securities but with dissimilar prices will converge to the same value over the investment holding period.

Last, we have the *opportunistic* category. We include in this category global macrohedge funds, hedge fund of funds, and multistrategy hedge funds. These funds are designed to take advantage of whatever opportunities present themselves—hence the word "opportunistic." For example, a multistrategy hedge fund might develop in house the expertise across several hedge fund strategies such as merger arbitrage, equity long/short, event driven, and convertible bond arbitrage. They then rebalance across these internal strategies in a form of tactical asset allocation depending upon what investment opportunities are available in the marketplace.

Private Equity

Private equity provides the long-term equity base of a company that is not listed on any exchange and therefore cannot raise capital via the public stock market. Private equity provides the working capital that is used to help private companies grow and succeed. It is a long-term investment process that requires patient due diligence and hands on monitoring.

Here we focus on the best known of the private equity categories: venture capital. Venture capital is the supply of equity financing to start-up companies that do not have a sufficient track record to attract investment capital from traditional sources (e.g., the public markets or lending institutions). Entrepreneurs that develop business plans require investment capital to implement those plans. However, these start-up ventures often lack tangible assets that can be used as collateral for a loan. In addition, start-up companies are unlikely to produce positive earnings for several years. Negative cash flows are another reason why banks and other lending institutions as well as the public stock market are unwilling to provide capital to support the business plan.

It is in this uncertain space where nascent companies are born that venture capitalists operate. Venture capitalists finance these high-risk, illiquid, and unproven ideas by purchasing senior equity stakes while the firms are still privately held. Venture capitalists are willing to underwrite new ventures with untested products and bear the risk of no liquidity only if they can expect a reasonable return for their efforts. Often venture capitalists set expected target rates of return of 33% or more to support the risks they bear. Venture capitalists have two roles within the industry. Raising money from investors is just the first part. The second is to invest that capital with start-up companies. Venture capitalists are not passive investors. Once they invest in a company, they take an active role either in an advisory capacity or as a director on the board of the company. They monitor the progress of the company, implement incentive plans for the entrepreneurs and management, and establish financial goals for the company. Besides providing management insight, venture capitalists usually have the right to hire and fire key managers, including the original entrepreneur. They also provide access to consultants, accountants, lawyers, investment bankers, and most importantly, other business that might purchase the start-up company's product.

Venture Capital Fees

Venture capitalists earn fees two ways: management fees and a percentage of the profits earned by the venture fund. Management fees can range anywhere from 1% to 3.5%, with most venture capital funds in the 2% to 2.5% range. Management fees are used to compensate the venture capitalist while looking for attractive investment opportunities for the venture fund.

A key point is that the management fee is assessed on the amount of committed capital, not invested capital. Investors pay the management fee on the amount of capital they have agreed to commit to the venture fund whether or not that capital has actually been invested.

The second part of the remuneration for a venture capitalist is the profit sharing or incentive fees. This is really where the venture capitalist makes money. Incentive fees provide the venture capitalist with a share of the profits generated by the venture fund. The typical incentive fee is 20% but the better known venture capital funds can charge up to 35%. That is, the best venture capitalists can claim one-third of the profits generated by the venture fund.

Fortunately, there is a check and balance on incentive fees in the venture capital world. Most, if not all, venture capital limited partnership agreements include some restrictive covenants on when incentive fees may be paid to the venture capitalist.

The Business Plan

The most important document upon which a venture capitalist will base his decision to invest in a start-up company is the business plan. The business plan must be comprehensive, coherent, and internally consistent. It must clearly state the business strategy, identify the niche that the new company will fill, and describe the resources needed to fill that niche.

The business plan also reflects the start-up management team's ability to develop and present an intelligent and strategic plan of action. The business plan not only describes the business opportunity but also gives the venture capitalist an insight into the viability of the management team.

Venture Capital Investment Vehicles

As the interest for venture capital investments has increased, venture capitalists have responded with new vehicles for venture financing. These include limited partnerships, limited liability companies, corporate venture funds, and venture capital fund of funds.

The predominant form of venture capital investing in the United States is the limited partnership. As a limited partnership, all income and capital gains flow through the partnership to the limited partner investors. The partnership itself is not taxed. An important element of limited partnership venture funds is that the general partner/venture capitalist has also committed investment capital to the fund. This assures the limited partners of an alignment of interests with the venture capitalist. Typically, limited partnership agreements specify a percentage or dollar amount of capital that the general partner must commit to the partnership.

Another financing vehicle in the venture capital industry is the *limited liability company* (LLC). Similar to a limited partnership, all items of net income or loss as well as capital gains are passed through to the shareholders in the LLC. LLCs and limited partnerships accomplish the same goal—the pooling of investor capital into a central fund from which to make venture capital investments.

A venture capital fund of funds is a venture pool of capital that, instead of investing directly in start-up companies, invests in other venture capital funds. The general partner of a fund of funds does not select start-up companies in which to invest. Instead, the general partner selects the best venture capitalists with the expectation that they will find appropriate start-up companies to fund.

The Life Cycle of a Venture Capital Fund

A venture capital fund is a long-term investment. Typically, investors' capital is locked up for a minimum of 10 years—the standard term of a venture capital limited partnership. During this long investment period, a venture capital fund will normally go through five stages of development.

The first stage is the fund raising stage where the venture capital firm raises capital from outside investors. Capital is committed—not collected. This is an important distinction noted above. Investors sign a legal agreement (typically a subscription) that legally binds them to make cash investments in the venture capital fund up to a certain amount. This is the committed, but not yet drawn, capital. The venture capital firm/general partner will also post a sizeable amount of committed capital. Fundraising normally takes six months to a year.

The second stage consists of sourcing investments, reading business plans, preparing intense due diligence on start-up companies and determining the unique selling point of each start-up company. This period begins the moment the fund is closed to investors and normally takes up the first five years of the venture fund's existence. During stage two, no profits are generated by the venture capital fund. In fact, quite the reverse, the venture capital fund generates losses because the venture capitalist continues to draw annual management fees (which can be up to 3.5% a year on the total committed capital). These fees generate a loss until the venture capitalist begins to extract value from the investments of the venture fund.

Stage three is the investment of capital. During this stage, the venture capitalist determines how much capital to commit to each start-up company, at what level of financing, and in what form of investment (convertible preferred shares, convertible debentures, etc.). At this stage the venture capitalist will also present capital calls to the investors in the venture fund to draw on the capital of the limited partners. Note that no cash flow is generated yet, the venture fund is still in a deficit.

Stage four begins after the funds have been invested and lasts almost to the end of the term of the venture capital fund. During this time the venture capitalist works with the portfolio companies in which the venture capital fund has invested. The venture capitalist may help to improve the management team, establish distribution channels for the new product, refine the prototype product to generate the greatest sales, and generally position the start-up company for an eventual public offering or sale to a strategic buyer. During this time period, the venture capitalist will begin to generate profits for the venture fund and its limited partner investors. These profits will initially offset the previously collected management fees until a positive net asset value is established for the venture fund.

The last stage of the venture capital fund is its windup and liquidation. At this point, all committed capital has been invested and now the venture capitalist is in the harvesting stage. Each portfolio company is either sold to a strategic buyer, brought to the public markets in an initial public offering, or liquidated through a Chapter 7 bankruptcy liquidation process. Profits are distributed to the limited partners and the general partner/venture capitalist now collects incentive and profit sharing fees.

These stages of a venture capital firm lead to what is known as the *J-curve effect*. Exhibit 2.2 demonstrates the J-curve. We can see that during

EXHIBIT 2.2   The Life Cycle of a Venture Capital Fund

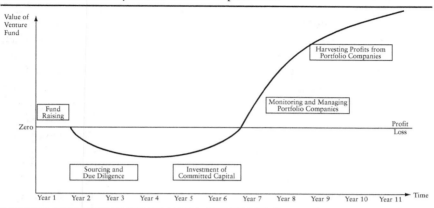

the early life of the venture capital fund, it generates negative revenues (losses) but eventually, profits are harvested from successful companies and these cash flows overcome the initial losses to generate a net profit for the fund. Clearly, given the initial losses that pile up during the first four to five years of a venture capital fund, this type of investing is only for patient, long-term investors.

Commodity Investments[9]

According to the academic literature, investments in commodity markets are considered an effective way for investors to diversify traditional portfolios. The diversification benefits of commodities come from their low (and sometimes even negative) correlation with equity and bond markets, as well as from their high positive correlation with inflation. Therefore, during times of price increases, commodities as real assets can function as effective inflation hedges. Moreover, the low correlation with stocks and bonds in general remains even in downward-trending markets (i.e., during phases when it is needed most). However, because commodities can be characterized as a heterogeneous asset class, commodity sector risk and return profiles can vary quite significantly, and may even move in opposite directions.

Commodity Sectors

Investments in global commodity markets differ greatly from other investments in several important ways. First, commodities are real assets—

---

[9]This section is coauthored with Roland Füss and Dieter G. Kaiser.

primarily consumption and not investment goods. They have an intrinsic value, and provide utility by use in industrial manufacturing or in consumption. Furthermore, supply is limited because in any given period, commodities have only a limited availability. For example, renewable commodities such as grains can be produced virtually without limitation. However, their yearly harvest is strictly limited. In addition, the supply of certain commodities shows a strong seasonal component. While metals can be mined almost all year, agricultural commodities like soybeans depend on the harvesting cycle.

Another important aspect of commodities as an asset class is its heterogeneity. The quality of commodities is not standardized; every commodity has its own specific properties. A common way to classify them is to distinguish between soft and hard commodities. *Hard commodities* are products from the energy, precious metals, and industrial metals sectors. *Soft commodities* are usually weather-dependent, perishable commodities from the agricultural sector serving consumptional purposes, such as grains, soybeans, or livestock such as cattle or hogs. Exhibit 2.3 shows the classification of commodity sectors.

Storability and availability (or renewability) are also important features of commodities. Since storability plays a decisive role in pricing, we distinguish between storable and nonstorable commodities. A commodity is said to have a high degree of storability if it is nonperishable and the costs of storage remain low with respect to its total value. Industrial metals such as aluminium or copper are prime examples: They fulfill both criteria to a high

EXHIBIT 2.3   Classification of Commodity Sectors

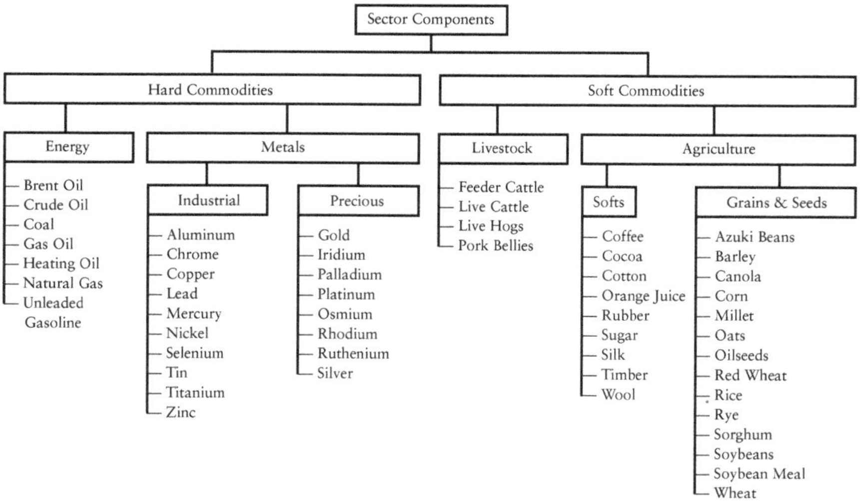

degree. In contrast, livestock is storable to only a limited degree, as it must be continuously fed and housed at current costs, and is only profitable in a specific phase of its lifecycle.

Commodities such as silver, gold, crude oil, and aluminium are non-renewable. The supply of nonrenewable commodities depends on the ability of producers to mine raw material in both sufficient quantity and quality.

The availability of commodity manufacturing capacities also influences supply. For some metals (excluding precious metals) and crude oil, the discovery and exploration of new reserves of raw materials is still an important issue. For a given supply, the price of nonrenewable resources depends strongly on current investor demand, while the price of renewable resources depends more on estimated future production costs.

The monetary benefit from holding a commodity physically instead of being long the respective futures is called the *convenience yield*. The convenience yield reflects market participants' expectations regarding a possible future scarcity of a short-term nonrenewable commodity. Another way to consider the convenience yield is that it is a call option on future price volatility of the underlying commodity. If the price of the commodity spikes due to some unfortunate news (frost, drought, war, embargo, mining strike, etc.), then the convenience yield is that value that is derived from holding onto the physical commodity at the time of the commodity shortage.

INVESTMENT COMPANIES

Investment companies (ICs) include open-end mutual funds, closed-end funds, and unit trusts. Shares in ICs are sold to the public and the proceeds invested in a diversified portfolio of securities. There is a wide range of ICs that invest in different asset classes and with different investment objectives. ICs can be actively managed or passively managed versus an index. Actively managed ICs offer investors to generate alpha returns as well as beta returns. Passively managed ICs offer only beta returns.

Types of Investment Companies

There are two primary types of ICs: open-end funds and closed-end funds.

Open-End Funds (Mutual Funds)

Open-end funds, commonly referred to simply as *mutual funds* (MFs), are portfolios of securities, mainly stocks, bonds, and money market instruments. There are several important aspects of MFs. First, investors in MFs own a pro rata share of the overall portfolio. Second, the investment manager of the MF manages the portfolio, that is, buys some securities and sells others.

Third, the value or price of each share of the portfolio, called the *net asset value* (NAV), equals the market value of the portfolio minus the liabilities of the MF divided by the number of shares owned by the MF investors. That is,

$$\text{NAV} = \frac{\text{Market value of portfolio} - \text{Liabilities}}{\text{Number of shares outstanding}}$$

For example, suppose that a MF with 20 million shares outstanding has a portfolio with a market value of $315 million and liabilities of $15 million. The NAV is

$$\text{NAV} = \frac{\$315,000,000 - \$15,000,000}{20,000,000} = \$15$$

Fourth, the NAV or price of the fund is determined only once each day, at the close of the day. For example, the NAV for a stock MF is determined from the closing stock prices for the day. Business publications provide the NAV each day in their MF tables. The published NAVs are the closing NAVs.

Fifth, and very importantly, all new investments into the fund or withdrawals from the fund during a day are priced at the closing NAV (investments after the end of the day or on a nonbusiness day are priced at the next day's closing NAV).

The total number of shares in the fund increases if there are more investments than withdrawals during the day, and vice versa. This is the reason such a fund is called an "open-end" fund. For example, assume that at the beginning of a day a MF portfolio has a value of $1 million, there are no liabilities, and there are 10,000 shares outstanding. Thus, the NAV of the fund is $100. Assume that during the day $5,000 is deposited into the fund, $1,000 is withdrawn, and the prices of all the securities in the portfolio remain constant. This means that 50 shares were issued for the $5,000 deposited (since each share is $100) and 10 shares redeemed for $1,000 (again, since each share is $100). The net number of new shares issued is then 40. Therefore, at the end of the day there will be 10,040 shares and the total value of the fund will be $1,004,000. The NAV will remain at $100. If, instead, the prices of the securities in the portfolio change, both the total size of the portfolio and, therefore, the NAV will change.

Overall, the NAV of a MF will increase or decrease due to an increase or decrease in the prices of the securities in the portfolio, respectively. The number of shares in the fund will increase or decrease due to the net deposits into or withdrawals from the fund, respectively. And the total value of the fund will increase or decrease for both reasons.

Closed-End Funds

The shares of a *closed-end fund* (CEF) are very similar to the shares of common stock of a corporation. The new shares of a CEF are initially issued by an underwriter for the fund. And after the new issue, the number of shares remains constant. This is the reason such a fund is called a "closed-end" fund. After the initial issue, there are no sales or purchases of fund shares by the fund company as there are for MFs. The shares are traded on a secondary market, either on an exchange or in the over-the-counter market.

The NAV of CEFs is calculated in the same way as for open-end funds. However, the price of a share in a CEF is determined by supply and demand, so the price can fall below or rise above the net asset value per share. Shares selling below NAV are said to be "trading at a discount," while shares trading above NAV are "trading at a premium." Newspapers list quotations of the prices of these shares under the heading "Closed-End Funds." Some sources also list the NAV and the discount or premium of the shares.

Consequently, there are two important differences between MFs and CEFs. First, the number of shares of a MF varies because the fund sponsor will sell new shares to investors and buy existing shares from shareholders. Second, by doing so, the share price is always the NAV of the fund. In contrast, CEFs have a constant number of shares outstanding because the fund sponsor does not redeem shares and sell new shares to investors (except at the time of a new underwriting). Thus, the price of the fund shares will be determined by supply and demand in the market and may be above or below NAV, as discussed above.

Under the Investment Company Act of 1940, CEFs are capitalized only once. They make an initial public offering (IPO) and then their shares are traded on the secondary market, just like any common stock. The number of shares is fixed at the IPO; CEFs cannot issue more shares. Since CEFs are traded like stocks, the cost to any investor of buying or selling a CEF is the same as that of a stock. The obvious charge is the stock broker's commission. The bid-offer spread of the market on which the stock is traded is also a cost.

Exhibit 2.4 summarizes the differences between MFs and CEFs.

Fund Sales Charges and Annual Operating Expenses

There are two types of costs borne by investors in ICs. The first is the *shareholder fee*, usually called the *sales charge* or *load*. ICs for which there is no shareholder fee are called no-load funds. For securities transactions, this

EXHIBIT 2.4   Mutual Funds (Open-End Funds) vs. Closed-End Funds

Characteristics	Mutual Fund	Closed-End Fund
1. Share Price (SP) vs. NAV	Always Equal (SP = NAV)	Can Differ: (SP > NAV: Premium) (SP < NAV: Discount)
2. Number of Shares Outstanding	Varies (Open-end)	Constant (Closed-end)
3. Determination of NAV	Once a day – at close of trading day	All during trading day – trade on exchange
4. Exchange of Shares	Buyers and sellers separately exchange via Mutual Fund Company	Between buyers and sellers via exchange
5. Issuance of Shares	Continuously (issuance and retirement) via Mutual Fund Company	Once, at initial public offering

charge is called a *commission*. This cost is a "one-time" charge debited to the investor for a specific transaction, such as a purchase, redemption or exchange. The type of charge is related to the way the fund is sold or distributed. The second cost is the annual fund operating expense, usually called the *expense ratio*, which covers the funds' expenses, the largest of which is for investment management. This charge is imposed annually.

The *operating expense*, also called the *expense ratio*, is debited annually from the investor's fund balance by the fund sponsor. The three main categories of annual operating expenses are the management fee, distribution fee, and other expenses. The *management fee*, also called the *investment advisory fee,* is the fee charged by the investment advisor for managing a fund's portfolio. If the investment advisor is part of a company separate from the fund sponsor, some or all of this investment advisory fee is passed on to the investment advisor by the fund sponsor. In this case, the fund manager is called a *subadvisor*. The management fee varies by the type of fund, specifically by the risk of the asset class of the fund.

Other expenses include primarily the costs of (1) custody (holding the cash and securities of the fund); (2) the transfer agent (transferring cash and securities among buyers and sellers of securities and the fund distributions, etc.); (3) independent public accountant fees; and (4) directors' fees.

The sum of the annual management fee, the annual distribution fee, and other annual expenses is called the expense ratio or annual operating expense. All the cost information on a fund, including selling charges and annual expenses, are included in the fund prospectus. In addition to the annual operating expenses, the fund prospectus provides the fees which are imposed only at the time of a fund transaction.

The operating expense is subtracted from the fund's NAV.

Advantages of Investing in Investment Companies

There are several advantages of the indirect ownership of securities by investing in ICs. The first is risk reduction through diversification. By investing in a fund, an investor can obtain broad-based ownership of a sufficient number of securities to reduce portfolio risk. While an individual investor may be able to acquire a broad-based portfolio of securities, the degree of diversification will be limited by the amount available to invest. By investing in an IC, however, the investor can effectively achieve the benefits of diversification at a lower cost even if the amount of money available to invest is not large.

The second advantage is the reduced cost of contracting and processing information because an investor purchases the services of a presumably skilled financial advisor at less cost than if the investor directly and individually negotiated with such an advisor. The advisory fee is lower because of the larger size of assets managed, as well as the reduced costs of searching for an investment manager and obtaining information about the securities. Also, the costs of transacting in the securities are reduced because a fund is better able to negotiate transactions costs; and custodial fees and recordkeeping costs are less for a fund than for an individual investor. For these reasons, there are said to be economies of scale in investment management.

Third, and related to the first two advantages, is the advantage of the professional management of the MF. Fourth is the advantage of liquidity. In the case of MFs, shares can be bought or liquidated any day at the closing NAV. Fifth is the advantage of the variety of funds available in terms of investment objective.

Taxation of Investment Companies

ICs must distribute at least 90% of their net investment income earned (bond coupons and stock dividends) exclusive of realized capital gains or losses to shareholders (along with meeting other criteria) to be considered a *regulated investment company* (RIC) and, thus, not be required to pay taxes at the fund level prior to distributions to shareholders. Consequently, funds always make these distributions. Taxes, if this criterion is met, are then paid on distributions, only at the investor level, not the fund level. Even though many IC investors choose to reinvest these distributions, the distributions are taxable to the investor, either as ordinary income or capital gains (long term or short term), whichever is relevant.

Capital gains distributions must occur annually, and typically occur late during the calendar year. The capital gains distributions may be either long-term or short-term capital gains, depending on whether the fund held the security for a year or more. IC investors have no control over the size of these distributions and, as a result, the timing and amount of the taxes paid on their fund holdings is largely out of their control. In particular, withdrawals by some investors may necessitate sales in the fund, which in turn cause realized capital gains and a tax liability to accrue to investors who maintain their holding.

New investors in the fund may assume a tax liability even though they have no gains. That is, all shareholders as of the date of record receive a full year's worth of dividends and capital gains distributions, even if they have owned shares for only one day. New investors may also receive a tax offset. This lack of control over capital gains taxes is regarded as a major limitation of ICs. In fact, this adverse tax consequence is one of the reasons suggested for a CEF's price selling below par value. Also, this adverse tax consequence is one of the reasons for the popularity of exchange traded funds to be discussed next.

Of course, the investor must also pay ordinary income taxes on distributions of income. Finally, when the fund investors sell the fund, they will have long-term or short-term capital gains, taxes, depending on whether they held the fund for a year or less.

EXCHANGE-TRADED FUNDS

Mutual funds (MFs) and closed-end funds (CEFs) are two types of managed portfolios valued relative to their net asset value (NAV) (the value of the assets in the portfolio less its liabilities). The structure of both of these investment vehicles has some practical defects.

MFs as an investment vehicle are often criticized for two major reasons. First, the shares of MFs are priced at and can be transacted (purchased and sold) only at the end of the trading day ("at the close"). That is, transactions cannot be made at intraday prices. The second criticism relates to taxes and investors' control over taxes. Withdrawals by some fund shareholders can cause taxable realized capital gains (or losses) for the other shareholders who have maintained their positions. CEFs, in contrast to MFs, trade throughout the trading day on stock exchanges. However, there is often a significant difference between the NAVs of the underlying portfolios and the price of a share of a CEF that is bought and sold.

Exchange-traded funds (ETFs) are a third type of managed funds, which overcome the practical defects of MFs and CEFs. Because most ETFs are based on indexes of some market, they offer pure beta returns.

Basics of Exchange-Traded Funds

Would it not be ideal if there were an investment vehicle that embodied a combination of the desirable aspects of both MFs and CEFs? The resolution to this dichotomy would require portfolios which could be traded throughout the day just like stocks but at a price equal to the continuously known NAV (i.e., the price is not at a premium or discount to the portfolio's NAV). Such a vehicle would be, in effect, a portfolio or fund which traded on an exchange, hence called an exchange-traded portfolio or as more commonly referred to as an *exchange-traded fund* (ETF).

At a very basic level, ETFs are easily understood. Most are based on indexes. ETFs are different, however, than conventional index mutual funds in the way they are bought and sold. An ETF is like a CEF and a stock in that it is traded throughout the day on an exchange. This means that investors can execute limit and stop-loss orders for ETFs,[10] just as with individual equities and CEFs. ETFs can also be sold short, and bought on margin (i.e., with borrowed money). Options are also available on many ETFs. Since ETFs trade on exchanges, they have a ticker symbol like stocks, as shown in Exhibit 2.5. Finally, ETFs are open-end funds like MFs since their number of shares outstanding can change. Just how the number of shares outstanding can change is explained later.

To maintain the equality, or near equality, of the NAV of the securities in the portfolio and the share price of an ETF requires some intervention by a third party. To assure that the price of the ETF on the exchange would be very close to the continuously known NAV, an agent is commissioned to arbitrage between the price of the ETF and the value of the underlying portfolio and keep their values equal. The agent is commissioned to conduct an arbitrage as follows. Suppose that the price of the ETF is less than the portfolio's NAV of the portfolio. The agent would purchase the cheap ETF and sell the expensive underlying portfolio at NAV. This would be a profitable arbitrage for the agent since it buys the cheap ETF and sells the expensive portfolios. If, instead, the price of the ETF exceeds the portfolio's NAV, the agent would sell the expensive ETF and buy the cheap underlying portfolio, thereby generating a profitable arbitrage.

These actions by an agent to capture the potential arbitrage would tend to cause the price of the ETF to trade very close (or equal) to that of the NAV. The agent who keeps the price of the ETF equal to (or close to)

---

[10]We describe these types of transactions for common stock in Chapter 8.

EXHIBIT 2.5 Largest U.S. Exchange-Traded Funds (June 30, 2010)

Name	Ticker	Broad Category Group	Morningstar Category	Net Assets-Share Class Base Currency	Annual Report Net Expense Ratio	Inception Date	Avg. Daily Volume (3 mo.)
SPDR S&P 500	SPY	Equity	ETF Large Blend	70,563,692,820.00	0.09	01/93	241,190,220
SPDR Gold Shares	GLD	—	ETF Commodities Precious Metals	50,041,100,299.00	0.40	11/04	17,154,253
iShares MSCI Emerging Markets Index	EEM	Equity	ETF Diversified Emerging Mkts	33,142,075,630.00	0.72	04/03	86,312,163
iShares MSCI EAFE Index	EFA	Equity	ETF Foreign Large Blend	31,443,064,971.00	0.35	08/01	25,764,754
Vanguard Emerging Markets Stock ETF	VWO	Equity	ETF Diversified Emerging Mkts	23,579,652,685.00	0.27	03/05	16,489,153
iShares S&P 500 Index	IVV	Equity	ETF Large Blend	21,655,254,747.00	0.09	05/00	4,469,955
iShares Barclays TIPS Bond	TIP	Fixed Income	ETF Inflation-Protected Bond	20,048,459,991.00	0.20	12/03	1,085,360
PowerShares QQQ	QQQQ	Equity	ETF Large Growth	18,060,393,603.00	0.20	03/99	98,281,596
Vanguard Total Stock Market ETF	VTI	Equity	ETF Large Blend	13,467,164,126.00	0.07	05/01	2,098,514
iShares Russell 2000 Index	IWM	Equity	ETF Small Blend	13,401,119,990.00	0.20	05/00	76,252,267
iShares iBoxx $ Invest Grade Corp Bond	LQD	Fixed Income	ETF Long-Term Bond	12,389,598,931.00	0.15	07/02	838,692
iShares Barclays Aggregate Bond	AGG	Fixed Income	ETF Intermediate-Term Bond	11,458,651,807.00	0.20	09/03	790,721
iShares Russell 1000 Growth Index	IWF	Equity	ETF Large Growth	10,660,837,235.00	0.20	05/00	3,338,780
iShares MSCI Brazil Index	EWZ	Equity	ETF Latin America Stock	9,319,509,854.00	0.65	07/00	23,410,402
iShares Russell 1000 Value Index	IWD	Equity	ETF Large Value	8,911,127,697.00	0.20	05/00	2,330,028
SPDR S&P MidCap 400	MDY	Equity	ETF Mid-Cap Blend	8,748,695,459.00	0.25	04/95	3,961,866
iShares Barclays 1-3 Year Treasury Bond	SHY	Fixed Income	ETF Short Government	8,451,453,093.00	0.15	07/02	1,180,547
SPDR Dow Jones Industrial Average	DIA	Equity	ETF Large Value	8,206,955,373.00	0.17	01/98	12,652,807
iShares FTSE/Xinhua China 25 Index	FXI	Equity	ETF Pacific/Asia ex-Japan Stk	7,484,084,047.00	0.73	10/04	32,066,995
Vanguard Total Bond Market ETF	BND	Fixed Income	ETF Intermediate-Term Bond	7,463,456,000.00	0.12	04/07	684,622
Market Vectors Gold Miners ETF	GDX	Equity	ETF Equity Precious Metals	7,307,259,935.00	0.54	05/06	13,218,787
iShares S&P MidCap 400 Index	IJH	Equity	ETF Mid-Cap Blend	7,209,729,851.00	0.20	05/00	1,130,362
Financial Select Sector SPDR	XLF	Equity	ETF Financial	6,718,417,437.00	0.22	12/98	122,503,457
iShares Barclays 1-3 Year Credit Bond	CSJ	Fixed Income	ETF Short-Term Bond	6,237,377,405.00	0.20	01/07	489,584
Energy Select Sector SPDR	XLE	Equity	ETF Equity Energy	6,132,852,187.00	0.22	12/98	23,473,691

Source: Morningstar Direct, June 30, 2010.

the portfolio's underlying NAV is, thus called, an *arbitrageur*. This agent is retained by the sponsor of the ETF, as discussed below.

The requirement for making this arbitrage process feasible is that the composition and the NAV of the underlying portfolio be known accurately and the securities in the portfolio be continuously traded throughout the trading day. An obvious example of such a portfolio would be the S&P 500 Index portfolio. The 500 stocks in the Index are very liquid and their prices and the value of the Index are quoted continuously throughout the trading day.

Thus, it is no coincidence that the first ETF was based on the S&P 500 Index. This ETF began trading on the American Stock Exchange on January 1, 1993. The ETF sponsor was State Street Global Advisers (SSgA) as its sponsor. Because its ticker symbol was SPY, it quickly became known as the "Spider." As shown in Exhibit 2.5, it remains the largest ETF. On the other hand, this process would not be feasible for the typical actively managed mutual fund because the composition of the portfolio and the prices of the securities comprising the portfolio are not known throughout the trading day. This is because mutual fund sponsors are required to make the composition of their funds public only four times a year and even then only 45 days after the date of portfolio report.

So ETFs are feasible for indexes on broad liquid security indexes but not on typical actively managed mutual funds. Like MFs, ETFs require a company to sponsor them. These companies are called *sponsors* or *providers* of ETFs. As of May 2010, the five major ETF sponsors according to *Morningstar ETF Investor* were as follows (assets in billions and market share shown in parentheses):

iShares BGI (BlackRock Global Investors) ($397; 47.2%)
State Street Global Advisors, SSgA ($200; 23.8%)
Vanguard ($109; 12.9%)
PowerShares ($50; 5.9%)
ProShares ($25; 3.0%)

MUTUAL FUNDS VS. ETFs: RELATIVE ADVANTAGES

As mentioned earlier, MFs are priced only once a day by being redeemed or offered by the mutual fund company at a price equal to the NAV. On the other hand, ETFs are traded on an exchange and so are priced continuously throughout the day. For MFs, the price of the fund is exactly the NAV of the underlying portfolio. For ETFs, there may be a discrepancy, although for actively traded funds, the discrepancy is very small. ETFs, since they are traded on an exchange, can also be shorted, leveraged and limit and stop orders can be used. This is not the case for MFs.

Both passive MFs and ETFs have low fees, but ETF fees tend to be somewhat lower. All ETFs trade on an exchange and, thus, incur a commission, ranging from a discount to a full-service commission depending on the broker used. MFs may be either no-load funds or load funds. For frequent, small investments—for example, monthly payroll deductions—MFs would most likely be better since no-load MFs cost nothing to trade and ETFs incur a commission cost. This is the reason that ETFs have not been widely used in employee retirement plans, such as 401(k) plans. For infrequent, large investments, ETFs may be better because of their somewhat lower expenses.

With respect to taxes, MFs, as discussed above, may lead to capital gains taxes for investors who do not even liquidate their fund. This is because the fund has to sell securities in their portfolio to fund the sales of shares of other investors. The sale of these shares may cause capital gains—and a capital gains tax liability—to the remaining shareholders, even though their holdings represent an unrealized loss. Thus, these shareholders incur a tax obligation even though they have not made a transaction. Because of the unique structure of ETFs discussed above, ETFs can fund redemptions by in-kind transfers without selling their holdings which have no tax consequences. ETFs are more tax efficient than MFs in this regard.

MFs may have some other advantages. Although ETFs have been exclusively passive or indexes, MF families offer many types of active funds as well as passive funds. In addition, no-load MFs, both active and passive, permit transactions with no loads or commissions.

Exhibit 2.6 provides a comparison of ETFs and MFs.

Uses of ETFs

ETFs can be used for:

- Long-term portfolio management or short-term trading.
- Long/short arbitrage strategies since ETFs can be shorted.
- Short-term asset reallocation by using long/short transactions.
- Many niche asset types.

All these strategies can be effectively conducted via ETFs because they are inexpensive and can be executed quickly. One disadvantage of ETFs is that at least at the time of mid 2010 they have been mostly passive. Therefore, they can be used for beta strategies only, not alpha-generating strategies. The reason they are inexpensive is that they are based on passive indexes. If, and when, active ETFs become successful, they will be more expensive than the existing passive ETFs and are likely to have higher tracking errors.

EXHIBIT 2.6   Mutual Funds versus Exchange-Traded Funds

	Mutual Funds	ETFs
Variety	Wide choice: Active and Passive	Mainly passive/indexes. Active ETFs are being developed
Taxation	Subject to taxation on dividend and realized capital gains. May have gains/losses when other investors redeem funds. May have gains/losses when stocks in index are changed.	Subject to taxation on dividend and realized capital gains. No gains/losses when other investors redeem funds. May have gains/losses when stocks in index are changed.
Valuation	NAV, based on actual price of underlying portfolio. Transactions via mutual fund company.	Creations and redemptions at NAV. Transactions via an exchange. Market price may be valued somewhat above or below NAV, but the deviation is typically small due to arbitrage.
Pricing	End-of-day.	Continuous.
Transaction Cost (initial)	None for no-load funds; Sales charge for load funds.	Commission or brokerage charge.
Management Fee (annual)	Depends on fund: Low for index funds. Higher for active funds.	Depends on ETF: Low and, in some cases, even lower than for index mutual funds. Higher for more active, less liquid underlying portfolios.

KEY POINTS

- The four major traditional asset classes are (1) common stocks, (2) bonds, (3) cash equivalents, and (4) real estate.
- One way of defining an asset class is in terms of the investment attributes that the members of an asset class have in common; a second way of defining an asset class is based simply on a group of assets that is treated as an asset class by asset managers.
- Nontraditional asset classes are referred to as alternative asset classes and include hedge funds, private equity, and commodities. Alternative assets typically are just different investment strategies within an existing asset class that derive their value from either the debt or equity markets
- Alternative asset classes can also be distinguished from traditional asset classes in terms of the efficiency of the marketplace in which the assets

trade. No case can be made for active management strategies in an asset class that is viewed to be characterized as informationally efficient such as one finds in most traditional asset classes; with most alternative assets, information is difficult to acquire and there are opportunities for active management.

- An asset classes' market (or systematic) risk premium is the difference in the return on an asset class and the return offered on a risk-free asset such as a U.S. Treasury security. Basic asset allocation seeks to capture the market risk premiums that exist for investing in different asset classes. Adding asset classes to the mix of potential investment opportunities in which an investor may invest can expand the efficient frontier so as to provide a greater range of risk and return opportunities.
- Beta drivers capture capture market risk premiums in an efficient manner, while alpha drivers seek pockets of excess return often without regard to benchmarks. Alternative assets represent an alternative source of beta that is different from the mixture of traditional assets, falling squarely into the category of alpha drivers
- A hedge fund is a privately organized investment vehicle that manages a concentrated portfolio of public and private securities and derivative instruments on those securities, that can invest both long and short, and that can apply leverage. There is no widely accepted definition of a hedge fund but they have certain attributes. The word "hedge" in hedge funds is misleading.
- Unlike the evaluation of asset managers of traditional asset classes where performance is evaluated relative to a benchmark, hedge fund managers are evaluated on an absolute return basis.
- Hedge funds can be classified into four broad categories: market directional, corporate restructuring, convergence trading, and opportunistic.
- Private equity provides the long-term equity base for a nonpublicly traded company. This investment vehicle requires a long-term investment horizon with constant monitoring of the company's activities.
- Venture capital, the best known of the private equity categories, is the supply of equity financing to start-up companies that do not have a sufficient track record to attract investment capital from traditional sources.
- Vehicles for venture financing investments include limited partnerships (the most common vehicle), limited liability companies, corporate venture funds, and venture capital fund of funds.
- A venture capital fund is a long-term investment (capital is locked up for a minimum of 10 years), during which time a venture capital fund will normally go through five stages of development: (1) raising capital, (2) sourcing investments, reading business plans, preparing intense

due diligence on start-up companies, and determining the unique selling point of each start-up company; (3) investing the capital; (4) working with the management of the companies in its portfolio to improve all phases of operations; and (5) winding up/liquidating by either a strategic sale of a company or bringing the company public via an initial public offering.

- It is argued that investments in commodity markets represent an effective manner for investors to diversify traditional portfolios because of their correlation with equity and bond markets, as well as from their high positive correlation with inflation.
- The quality of commodities is not standardized; every commodity has its own specific properties. Commodities are classified as hard commodities (products from the energy, precious metals, and industrial metals sectors) or soft commodities (usually weather-dependent, perishable commodities from the agricultural sector serving consumptional purposes, such as grains, soybeans, or livestock such as cattle or hogs.)
- The convenience yield is the monetary benefit from holding a commodity physically instead of being long a futures contract on that commodity.
- A share in an investment company represents a pro rata interest in the portfolio's net asset value. The net asset value is equal to the market value of the securities in the portfolio reduced by the liabilities divided by the total number of shares outstanding.
- The three types of investment companies are open-end (more popularly referred to as mutual funds), closed-end funds, and unit trusts. A wide range of funds with many different investment objectives is available.
- Mutual fund shares can only be transacted at the end of the trading day and at the NAV calculated at that time. Closed-end funds are traded on an exchange and therefore can be transacted at any time during the trading day at a price determined by supply and demand, just like any other stock. The price of a closed-end fund can be less than, equal to, or greater than the fund's NAV.
- There are drawbacks to mutual funds and closed-end funds from the perspective of investors. Exchange-traded funds overcome these problems.
- The advantages of ETFs over mutual funds is that they can be traded throughout the trading day on an exchange and thus have continuous pricing. This allows an investor to sell ETFs short, buy on margin, and place the types of orders that investors are accustomed to in trading stocks.
- Compared to a mutual fund, an ETF has tax advantages that include not being subject to capital gains tax when the investor does not liquidate a position and they typically have lower management fees.

- ETFs are based on portfolios which track an index; that is, they are passive vehicles. Authorized participants play a critical role in ETFs because it is their arbitrage activities that keep the ETF's price from deviating from the ETF's NAV.

QUESTIONS

1. In defining an asset class, why is the correlation between the returns of asset classes important?
2. Why are most alternative asset classes viewed as a subset of an existing asset class?
3. Why is it useful to think of alternative assets within the context of alpha drivers?
4. Decribe the four categories of hedge funds.
5. Why is an investor's horizon important in deciding on whether to invest in a venture capital fund?
6. What is the role of investments in commodities in an investor's portfolio?
7. How does the price of a mutual fund differ from that of a closed-end investment company?
8. What are the advantages of an exchange-traded fund relative to a:
   a. mutual fund?
   b. closed-end investment company?

CHAPTER 3

Portfolio Selection

Frank J. Fabozzi, Ph.D., CFA, CPA
Professor in the Practice of Finance
Yale School of Management

Harry M. Markowitz, Ph.D.
Consultant

Petter N. Kolm, Ph.D.
Director of the Mathematics in Finance M.S. Program
and Clinical Associate Professor
Courant Institute of Mathematical Sciences, New York University

Francis Gupta, Ph.D.
Director, Index Research & Design
Dow Jones Indexes

This chapter is an introduction to the theory of portfolio selection, which together with capital asset pricing theory provides the foundation and the building blocks for the management of portfolios. The goal of portfolio selection is the construction of portfolios that maximize expected returns consistent with individually acceptable levels of risk. Using both historical data and investor expectations of future returns, portfolio selection uses modeling techniques to quantify "expected portfolio returns" and "acceptable levels of portfolio risk" and provides methods to select an optimal portfolio.

The theory of portfolio selection presented in this chapter, often referred to as *mean-variance portfolio analysis* or simply *mean-variance analysis*, is a normative theory. A normative theory is one that describes a standard or norm of behavior that investors should pursue in constructing a portfolio rather than a prediction concerning actual behavior.

Asset pricing theory goes on to formalize the relationship that should exist between asset returns and risk if investors behave in a hypothesized manner. In contrast to a normative theory, asset pricing theory is a positive theory—a theory that hypothesizes how investors behave rather than how investors should behave. Based on that hypothesized behavior of investors, a model that provides the expected return (a key input for constructing portfolios based on mean-variance analysis) is derived and is called an *asset pricing model*.

Together, portfolio selection theory and asset pricing theory provide a framework to specify and measure investment risk and to develop relationships between expected asset return and risk (and hence between risk and required return on an investment). However, it is critically important to understand that portfolio selection is a theory that is independent of any theories about asset pricing. The validity of portfolio selection theory does not rest on the validity of asset pricing theory.

It would not be an overstatement to say that modern portfolio theory has revolutionized the world of investment management. Allowing managers to quantify the investment risk and expected return of a portfolio has provided the scientific and objective complement to the subjective art of investment management. More importantly, whereas at one time the focus of portfolio management used to be the risk of individual assets, the theory of portfolio selection has shifted the focus to the risk of the entire portfolio. This theory shows that it is possible to combine risky assets and produce a portfolio whose expected return reflects its components, but with considerably lower risk. In other words, it is possible to construct a portfolio whose risk is smaller than the sum of all its individual parts!

Though practitioners realized that the risks of individual assets were related, before modern portfolio theory, they were unable to formalize how combining these assets into a portfolio impacted the risk at the entire portfolio level, or how the addition of a new asset would change the return–risk characteristics of the portfolio. This is because practitioners were unable to quantify the returns and risks of their investments. Furthermore, in the context of the entire portfolio, they were also unable to formalize the interaction of the returns and risks across asset classes and individual assets. The failure to quantify these important measures and formalize these important relationships made the goal of constructing an optimal portfolio highly subjective and provided no insight into the return investors could expect and the risk they were undertaking. The other drawback before the advent of the theory of portfolio selection and asset pricing theory was that there was no measurement tool available to investors for judging the performance of their investment managers.

SOME BASIC CONCEPTS

Portfolio theory draws on concepts from two fields: financial economic theory and probability and statistical theory. This section presents the concepts from financial economic theory used in portfolio theory. While many of the concepts presented here have a more technical or rigorous definition, the purpose is to keep the explanations simple and intuitive so that the reader can appreciate the importance and contribution of these concepts to the development of modern portfolio theory.

Utility Function and Indifference Curves

There are many situations where entities (i.e., individuals and firms) face two or more choices. The economic "theory of choice" uses the concept of a utility function to describe the way entities make decisions when faced with a set of choices. A *utility function* assigns a (numeric) value to all possible choices faced by the entity. The higher the value of a particular choice, the greater the utility derived from that choice. The choice that is selected is the one that results in the maximum utility given a set of constraints faced by the entity.

In portfolio theory too, entities are faced with a set of choices. Different portfolios have different levels of expected return and risk. Typically, the higher the level of expected return, the larger the risk. Entities are faced with the decision of choosing a portfolio from the set of all possible risk–return combinations, where when they like return, they dislike risk. Therefore, entities obtain different levels of utility from different risk–return combinations. The utility obtained from any possible risk–return combination is expressed by the utility function. Put simply, the utility function expresses the preferences of entities over perceived risk and expected return combinations.

A utility function can be expressed in graphical form by a set of indifference curves. Exhibit 3.1 shows indifference curves labeled u_1, u_2, and u_3. By convention, the horizontal axis measures risk and the vertical axis measures expected return. Each curve represents a set of portfolios with different combinations of risk and return. All the points on a given indifference curve indicate combinations of risk and expected return that will give the same level of utility to a given investor. For example, on utility curve u_1, there are two points u and u', with u having a higher expected return than u', but also having a higher risk. Because the two points lie on the same indifference curve, the investor has an equal preference for (or is indifferent to) the two points, or, for that matter, any point on the curve. The (positive) slope of an indifference curve reflects the fact that, to obtain the same level of utility, the investor requires a higher expected return in order to accept higher risk.

EXHIBIT 3.1   Indifference Curves

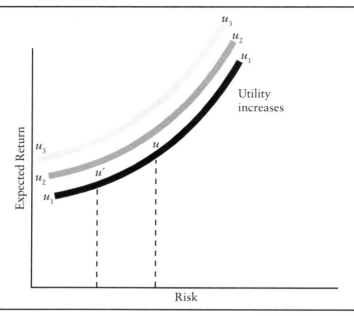

For the three indifference curves shown in Exhibit 3.1, the utility the investor receives is greater the further the indifference curve is from the horizontal axis because that curve represents a higher level of return at every level of risk. Thus, for the three indifference curves shown in the exhibit, u_3 has the highest utility and u_1 the lowest.

The Set of Efficient Portfolios and the Optimal Portfolio

Portfolios that provide the largest possible expected return for given levels of risk are called *efficient portfolios*. To construct an efficient portfolio, it is necessary to make some assumption about how investors behave when making investment decisions. One reasonable assumption is that investors are *risk averse*. A risk-averse investor is an investor who, when faced with choosing between two investments with the same expected return but two different risks, prefers the one with the lower risk.

In selecting portfolios, an investor seeks to maximize the expected portfolio return given his tolerance for risk.[1] Given a choice from the set of

---

[1]Alternatively stated, an investor seeks to minimize the risk that he is exposed to given some target expected return.

efficient portfolios, an *optimal portfolio* is the one that is most preferred by the investor.

Risky Assets vs. Risk-Free Assets

A risky asset is one for which the return that will be realized in the future is uncertain. For example, an investor who purchases the stock of Pfizer Corporation today with the intention of holding it for some finite time does not know what return will be realized at the end of the holding period. The return will depend on the price of Pfizer's stock at the time of sale and on the dividends that the company pays during the holding period. Thus, Pfizer stock, and indeed the stock of all companies, is a risky asset.

Securities issued by the U.S. government are also risky. For example, an investor who purchases a U.S. government bond that matures in 30 years does not know the return that will be realized if this bond is held for only one year. This is because changes in interest rates in that year will affect the price of the bond one year from now and that will impact the return on the bond over that year.

There are assets, however, for which the return that will be realized in the future is known with certainty today. Such assets are referred to as *risk-free* or *riskless assets*. The risk-free asset is commonly defined as a short-term obligation of the U.S. government. For example, if an investor buys a U.S. government security that matures in one year and plans to hold that security for one year, then there is no uncertainty about the return that will be realized. The investor knows that in one year, the maturity date of the security, the government will pay a specific amount to retire the debt. Notice how this situation differs for the U.S. government security that matures in 30 years. While the 1-year and the 30-year securities are obligations of the U.S. government, the former matures in one year so that there is no uncertainty about the return that will be realized. In contrast, while the investor knows what the government will pay at the end of 30 years for the 30-year bond, he does not know what the price of the bond will be one year from now.

MEASURING A PORTFOLIO'S EXPECTED RETURN

We are now ready to define the actual and expected return of a risky asset and a portfolio of risky assets.

Measuring Single-Period Portfolio Return

The actual return on a portfolio of assets over some specific time period is straightforward to calculate using the formula:

$$R_p = w_1 R_1 + w_2 R_2 + \ldots + w_G R_G \tag{3.1}$$

where

R_p = rate of return on the portfolio over the period
R_g = rate of return on asset g over the period
w_g = weight of asset g in the portfolio (i.e., market value of asset g as a proportion of the market value of the total portfolio) at the beginning of the period
G = number of assets in the portfolio

In shorthand notation, equation (3.1) can be expressed as follows:

$$R_p = \sum_{g=1}^{G} w_g R_g \tag{3.2}$$

Equation (3.2) states that the return on a portfolio (R_p) of G assets is equal to the sum over all individual assets' weights in the portfolio times their respective return. The portfolio return R_p is sometimes called the *holding period return* or the *ex post return*.

For example, consider the following portfolio consisting of three assets:

Asset	Market Value at the Beginning of Holding Period	Rate of Return over Holding Period
1	$6 million	12%
2	$8 million	10%
3	$11 million	5%

The portfolio's total market value at the beginning of the holding period is $25 million. Therefore,

w_1 = $6 million/$25 million = 0.24, or 24%   and R_1 = 12%
w_2 = $8 million/$25 million = 0.32, or 32%   and R_2 = 10%
w_3 = $11 million/$25 million = 0.44, or 44% and R_3 = 5%

Notice that the sum of the weights is equal to 1. Substituting into equation (3.1), we get the holding period portfolio return,

$$R_p = 0.24(12\%) + 0.32(10\%) + 0.44(5\%) = 8.28\%$$

The Expected Return of a Portfolio of Risky Assets

Equation (3.1) shows how to calculate the actual return of a portfolio over some specific time period. In portfolio management, the investor also wants to know the expected (or anticipated) return from a portfolio of risky assets. The expected portfolio return is the weighted average of the expected return of each asset in the portfolio. The weight assigned to the expected return of each asset is the percentage of the market value of the asset to the total market value of the portfolio. That is,

$$E(R_p) = w_1 E(R_1) + w_2 E(R_2) + \ldots + w_G E(R_G) \tag{3.3}$$

The $E(\ )$ signifies expectations, and $E(R_p)$ is sometimes called the *ex ante* return, or the expected portfolio return over some specific time period.

The expected return, $E(R_i)$, on a risky asset i is calculated as follows. First, a probability distribution for the possible rates of return that can be realized must be specified. A probability distribution is a function that assigns a probability of occurrence to all possible outcomes for a random variable. Given the probability distribution, the expected value of a random variable is simply the weighted average of the possible outcomes, where the weight is the probability associated with the possible outcome.

In our case, the random variable is the uncertain return of asset i. Having specified a probability distribution for the possible rates of return, the expected value of the rate of return for asset i is the weighted average of the possible outcomes. Finally, rather than use the term "expected value of the return of an asset," we simply use the term "expected return." Mathematically, the expected return of asset i is expressed as

$$E(R_i) = p_1 R_1 + p_2 R_2 + \ldots + p_N R_N \tag{3.4}$$

where,

R_n = the nth possible rate of return for asset i
p_n = the probability of attaining the rate of return R_n for asset i
N = the number of possible outcomes for the rate of return

How do we specify the probability distribution of returns for an asset? We shall see later on in this chapter that in most cases the probability distribution of returns is based on long-run historical returns. If there is no reason to believe that future long-run returns should differ significantly from historical long-run returns, then probabilities assigned to different return

EXHIBIT 3.2 Probability Distribution for the Rate of Return for Stock XYZ

n	Rate of Return	Probability of Occurrence
1	12%	0.18
2	10%	0.24
3	8%	0.29
4	4%	0.16
5	–4%	0.13
Total		1.00

outcomes based on the historical long-run performance of an uncertain investment could be a reasonable estimate for the probability distribution. However, for the purpose of illustration, assume that an investor is considering an investment, stock XYZ, which has a probability distribution for the rate of return for some time period as given in Exhibit 3.2. The stock has five possible rates of return and the probability distribution specifies the likelihood of occurrence (in a probabilistic sense) of each of the possible outcomes.

Substituting into equation (3.4) we get

$$E(R_{XYZ}) = 0.18(12\%) + 0.24(10\%) + 0.29(8\%) + 0.16(4\%) + 0.13(-4\%)$$
$$= 7\%$$

Thus, 7% is the expected return or mean of the probability distribution for the rate of return on stock XYZ.

MEASURING PORTFOLIO RISK

Investors have used a variety of definitions to describe risk. Harry Markowitz quantified the concept of risk using the well-known statistical measure: the *standard deviation* and the *variance*. The former is the intuitive concept. Most of any probability distribution is between its average plus or minus two standard deviations. Variance is standard deviation squared. Computations are simplest in terms of variance. Therefore, it is convenient to compute the variance of a portfolio and then takes its square root to obtain standard deviation.[2]

---

[2]See Harry Markowitz, "Portfolio Selection," *Journal of Finance* 7, no. 1 (1952): 77–91; Harry Markowitz, *Portfolio Selection: Efficient Diversification of Investments*, Cowles Foundation Monograph 16 (New York: John Wiley & Sons, 1959).

Variance and Standard Deviation as a Measure of Risk

The variance of a random variable is a measure of the dispersion or variability of the possible outcomes around the expected value (mean). In the case of an asset's return, the variance is a measure of the dispersion of the possible rate of return outcomes around the expected return.

The equation for the variance of the expected return for asset i, denoted $\text{var}(R_i)$, is

$$\text{var}(R_i) = p_1[r_1 - E(R_i)]^2 + p_2[r_2 - E(R_i)]^2 + \ldots + p_N[r_N - E(R_i)]^2$$

or

$$\text{var}(R_i) = \sum_{i=1}^{N} p_n[r_n - E(R_i)]^2 \tag{3.5}$$

Using the probability distribution of the return for stock XYZ, we can illustrate the calculation of the variance:

$$\text{var}(R_{XYZ}) = 0.18(12\% - 7\%)^2 + 0.24(10\% - 7\%)^2 + 0.29(8\% - 7\%)^2$$
$$+ 0.16(4\% - 7\%)^2 + 0.13(-4\% - 7\%)^2 = 24.1\%$$

The variance associated with a distribution of returns measures the tightness with which the distribution is clustered around the mean or expected return. Markowitz argued that this tightness or variance is equivalent to the uncertainty or riskiness of the investment. If an asset is riskless, it has an expected return dispersion of zero. In other words, the return (which is also the expected return in this case) is certain, or guaranteed.

Since the variance is squared units, as we know from earlier in this section, it is common to see the variance converted to the standard deviation by taking the positive square root:

$$SD(R_i) = \sqrt{\text{var}(R_i)}$$

For stock XYZ, then, the standard deviation is

$$SD(R_{XYZ}) = \sqrt{24.1\%} = 4.9\%$$

The variance and standard deviation are conceptually equivalent; that is, the larger the variance or standard deviation, the greater the investment risk. (A criticism of the variance or standard deviation as a measure is discussed later in this chapter.)

Measuring the Portfolio Risk of a Two-Asset Portfolio

Equation (3.5) gives the variance for an individual asset's return. The variance of a portfolio consisting of two assets is a little more difficult to calculate. It depends not only on the variance of the two assets, but also upon how closely the returns of one asset track those of the other asset. The formula is

$$\text{var}(R_p) = w_i^2 \, \text{var}(R_i) + w_j^2 \, \text{var}(R_j) + 2w_i w_j \, \text{cov}(R_i, R_j) \tag{3.6}$$

where

$\text{cov}(R_i, R_j)$ = covariance between the return for assets i and j

In words, equation (3.6) states that the variance of the portfolio return is the sum of the squared weighted variances of the two assets plus two times the weighted covariance between the two assets. We will see that this equation can be generalized to the case where there are more than two assets in the portfolio.

Covariance

The covariance has a precise mathematical translation. Its practical meaning is the degree to which the returns of two assets covary or change together. The covariance is not expressed in a particular unit, such as dollars or percent. A positive covariance means the returns on two assets tend to move or change in the same direction, while a negative covariance means the returns tend to move in opposite directions. The covariance between any two assets i and j is computed using the following formula:

$$\text{cov}(R_i, R_j) = p_1[r_{i1} - E(R_i)][r_{j1} - E(R_j)] + p_2[r_{i2} - E(R_i)][r_{j2} - E(R_j)]$$
$$+ \ldots + p_N[r_{iN} - E(R_i)][r_{jN} - E(R_j)] \tag{3.7}$$

where

r_{in} = the nth possible rate of return for asset i
r_{jn} = the nth possible rate of return for asset j
p_n = the probability of attaining the rate of return r_{in} and r_{jn} for assets i and j
N = the number of possible outcomes for the rate of return

To illustrate the calculation of the covariance between two assets, we use the two stocks in Exhibit 3.3. The first is stock XYZ from Exhibit 3.2 that we used earlier to illustrate the calculation of the expected return and

EXHIBIT 3.3 Probability Distribution for the Rate of Return for Asset XYZ and Asset ABC

n	Rate of Return for Asset XYZ	Rate of Return for Asset ABC	Probability of Occurrence
1	12%	21%	0.18
2	10%	14%	0.24
3	8%	9%	0.29
4	4%	4%	0.16
5	–4%	–3%	0.13
Total			1.00
Expected return	7.0%	10.0%	
Variance	24.1%	53.6%	
Standard deviation	4.9%	7.3%	

the standard deviation. The other hypothetical stock is stock ABC, whose data are shown in Exhibit 3.3. Substituting the data for the two stocks from Exhibit 3.3 in equation (3.7), the covariance between stocks XYZ and ABC is calculated as follows:

$$
\begin{aligned}
cov(R_{XYZ}, R_{ABC}) = {} & 0.18(12\% - 7\%)(21\% - 10\%) + 0.24(10\% - 7\%)(14\% - 10\%) \\
& + 0.29(8\% - 7\%)(9\% - 10\%) + 0.16(4\% - 7\%)(4\% - 10\%) \\
& + 0.13(-4\% - 7\%)(-3\% - 10\%) = 0.3396\%
\end{aligned}
$$

Relationship between Covariance and Correlation

The correlation is related to the covariance between the expected returns for two assets. Specifically, the correlation between the returns for assets i and j is defined as the covariance of the two assets divided by the product of their standard deviations:

$$cor(R_i, R_j) = cov(R_i, R_j)/[SD(R_i)SD(R_j)] \tag{3.8}$$

Dividing the covariance between the returns of two assets by the product of their standard deviations results in the correlation between the returns of the two assets. Because the correlation is a standardized number (i.e., it has been corrected for differences in the standard deviation of the returns), the correlation is comparable across different assets. The correlation between the returns for stock XYZ and stock ABC is

$$cor(R_{XYZ}, R_{ABC}) = 0.3396\%/(4.9\% \times 7.3\%) \approx 0.95$$

The correlation coefficient can have values ranging from +1.0, denoting perfect comovement in the same direction, to –1.0, denoting perfect comovement in the opposite direction. Also note that because the standard deviations are always positive, the correlation can only be negative if the covariance is a negative number. A correlation of zero implies that the returns are uncorrelated.

Measuring the Risk of a Portfolio Consisting of More than Two Assets

So far we have defined the risk of a portfolio consisting of two assets. The extension to three assets—i, j, and k—is as follows:

$$\operatorname{var}(R_p) = w_i^2 \operatorname{var}(R_i) + w_j^2 \operatorname{var}(R_j) + w_k^2 \operatorname{var}(R_k) + 2w_i w_j \operatorname{cov}(R_i, R_j)$$
$$+ 2w_i w_k \operatorname{cov}(R_i, R_k) + 2w_j w_k \operatorname{cov}(R_j, R_k) \qquad (3.9)$$

In words, equation (3.9) states that the variance of the portfolio return is the sum of the squared weighted variances of the individual assets plus two times the sum of the weighted pairwise covariances of the assets. In general, for a portfolio with G assets, the portfolio variance is given by,

$$\operatorname{var}(R_p) = \sum_{g=1}^{G} w_g^2 \operatorname{var}(R_g) + \sum_{g=1}^{G} \sum_{\substack{h=1 \\ \text{and } h \neq g}}^{G} w_g w_h \operatorname{cov}(R_g, R_h) \qquad (3.10)$$

PORTFOLIO DIVERSIFICATION

Often, one hears investors talking about diversifying their portfolio. By this an investor means constructing a portfolio in such a way as to reduce portfolio risk without sacrificing return. This is certainly a goal that investors should seek. However, the question is how to do this in practice.

Some investors would say that including assets across all asset classes could diversify a portfolio. For example, a investor might argue that a portfolio should be diversified by investing in stocks, bonds, and real estate. While that might be reasonable, two questions must be addressed in order to construct a diversified portfolio. First, how much should be invested in each asset class? Should 40% of the portfolio be in stocks, 50% in bonds, and 10% in real estate, or is some other allocation more appropriate? Second, given the allocation, which specific stocks, bonds, and real estate should the investor select?

Some investors who focus only on one asset class such as common stock argue that such portfolios should also be diversified. By this they mean that an investor should not place all funds in the stock of one corporation, but rather should include stocks of many corporations. Here, too, several questions must be answered in order to construct a diversified portfolio. First, which corporations should be represented in the portfolio? Second, how much of the portfolio should be allocated to the stocks of each corporation?

Prior to the development of portfolio theory, while investors often talked about diversification in these general terms, they did not possess the analytical tools by which to answer the questions posed above. For example, in 1945, D. H. Leavens wrote:

> An examination of some fifty books and articles on investment that have appeared during the last quarter of a century shows that most of them refer to the desirability of diversification. The majority, however, discuss it in general terms and do not clearly indicate why it is desirable.[3]

Leavens illustrated the benefits of diversification on the assumption that risks are independent. However, in the last paragraph of his article, he cautioned:

> The assumption, mentioned earlier, that each security is acted upon by independent causes, is important, although it cannot always be fully met in practice. Diversification among companies in one industry cannot protect against unfavorable factors that may affect the whole industry; additional diversification among industries is needed for that purpose. Nor can diversification among industries protect against cyclical factors that may depress all industries at the same time.[4]

A major contribution of the theory of portfolio selection is that using the concepts discussed above, a quantitative measure of the diversification of a portfolio is possible, and it is this measure that can be used to achieve the maximum diversification benefits.

The Markowitz diversification strategy is primarily concerned with the degree of covariance between asset returns in a portfolio. Indeed a key contribution of Markowitz diversification is the formulation of an asset's risk in terms of a portfolio of assets, rather than in isolation. Markowitz diversification seeks to combine assets in a portfolio with returns that are less than perfectly positively correlated, in an effort to lower portfolio risk (variance) without sacrificing return. It is the concern for maintaining return while

---

[3]D. H. Leavens, "Diversification of Investments," *Trusts and Estates* 80, no. 5 (1945): 469–473.
[4]Ibid, p. 473.

lowering risk through an analysis of the covariance between asset returns, that separates Markowitz diversification from a naive approach to diversification and makes it more effective.

Markowitz diversification and the importance of asset correlations can be illustrated with a simple two-asset portfolio example. To do this, we first show the general relationship between the risk of a two-asset portfolio and the correlation of returns of the component assets. Then we look at the effects on portfolio risk of combining assets with different correlations.

Portfolio Risk and Correlation

In our two-asset portfolio, assume that asset C and asset D are available with expected returns and standard deviations as shown:

Asset	$E(R)$	$SD(R)$
Asset C	12%	30%
Asset D	18%	40%

If an equal 50% weighting is assigned to both stocks C and D, the expected portfolio return can be calculated as shown:

$$E(R_p) = 0.50(12\%) + 0.50(18\%) = 15\%$$

The variance of the return on the two-stock portfolio from equation (3.6), using decimal form rather than percentage form for the standard deviation inputs, is

$$\mathrm{var}(R_p) = w_C^2 \, \mathrm{var}(R_C) + w_D^2 \, \mathrm{var}(R_D) + 2w_C w_D \, \mathrm{cov}(R_C, R_D)$$
$$= (0.5)^2(0.30)^2 + (0.5)^2(0.40)^2 + 2(0.5)(0.5)\,\mathrm{cov}(R_C, R_D)$$

From equation (3.8),

$$\mathrm{cor}(R_C, R_D) = \mathrm{cov}(R_C, R_D)/[SD(R_C)SD(R_D)]$$

so

$$\mathrm{cov}(R_C, R_D) = SD(R_C)SD(R_D)\mathrm{cor}(R_C, R_D)$$

Since $SD(R_C) = 0.30$ and $SD(R_D) = 0.40$, then

$$\mathrm{cov}(R_C, R_D) = (0.30)(0.40)\,\mathrm{cor}(R_C, R_D)$$

Substituting into the expression for $\text{var}(R_p)$, we get

$$\text{var}(R_p) = (0.5)^2(0.30)^2 + (0.5)^2(0.40)^2 + 2(0.5)(0.5)(0.30)(0.40)\text{cor}(R_C, R_D)$$

Taking the square root of the variance gives

$$
\begin{aligned}
SD(R_p) \\
&= \sqrt{(0.5)^2(0.30)^2 + (0.5)^2(0.40)^2 + 2(0.5)(0.5)(0.30)(0.40)\text{cor}(R_C, R_D)} \\
&= \sqrt{0.0625 + (0.06)\text{cor}(R_C, R_D)}
\end{aligned}
\tag{3.11}
$$

The Effect of the Correlation of Asset Returns on Portfolio Risk

How would the risk change for our two-asset portfolio with different correlations between the returns of the component stocks? Let's consider the following three cases for $\text{cor}(R_C, R_D)$: +1.0, 0, and –1.0. Substituting into equation (3.11) for these three cases of $\text{cor}(R_C, R_D)$, we get:

$\text{cor}(R_C, R_D)$	$E(R_p)$	$SD(R_p)$
+1.0	15%	35%
0.0	15%	25%
–1.0	15%	5%

As the correlation between the expected returns on stocks C and D decreases from +1.0 to 0.0 to –1.0, the standard deviation of the expected portfolio return also decreases from 35% to 5%. However, the expected portfolio return remains 15% for each case.

This example clearly illustrates the effect of Markowitz diversification. The principle of Markowitz diversification states that as the correlation (covariance) between the returns for assets that are combined in a portfolio decreases, so does the variance (hence the standard deviation) of the return for the portfolio.

The good news is that investors can maintain expected portfolio return and lower portfolio risk by combining assets with lower (and preferably negative) correlations. However, the bad news is that very few assets have small to negative correlations with other assets! The problem, then, becomes one of searching among large numbers of assets in an effort to discover the portfolio with the minimum risk at a given level of expected return or, equivalently, the highest expected return at a given level of risk.

The stage is now set for a discussion of efficient portfolios and their construction.

EXHIBIT 3.4   Portfolio Expected Returns and Standard Deviations for Five Mixes of Assets C and D

Asset C: $E(R_C) = 12\%$, $SD(R_C) = 30\%$
Asset D: $E(R_D) = 18\%$, and $SD(R_D) = 40\%$
Correlation between Asset C and D = $cor(R_C, R_D) = -0.5$

Portfolio	Proportion of Asset C	Proportion of Asset D	$E(R_p)$	$SD(R_p)$
1	100%	0%	12.0%	30.0%
2	75%	25%	13.5%	19.5%
3	50%	50%	15.0%	18.0%
4	25%	75%	16.5%	27.0%
5	0%	100%	18.0%	40.0%

CHOOSING A PORTFOLIO OF RISKY ASSETS

Diversification in the manner suggested by Markowitz leads to the construction of portfolios that have the highest expected return for a given level of risk. Such portfolios are called *efficient portfolios*.

Constructing Efficient Portfolios

The technique of constructing efficient portfolios from large groups of stocks requires a massive number of calculations. In a portfolio of G securities, there are $(G^2 - G)/2$ unique covariances to estimate. Hence, for a portfolio of just 50 securities, there are 1,224 covariances that must be calculated. For 100 securities, there are 4,950. Furthermore, in order to solve for the portfolio that minimizes risk for each level of return, a mathematical technique called *quadratic programming* must be used. A discussion of this technique is beyond the scope of this chapter. However, it is possible to illustrate the general idea of the construction of efficient portfolios by referring again to the simple two-asset portfolio consisting of assets C and D.

Recall that for two assets, C and D, $E(R_C) = 12\%$, $SD(R_C) = 30\%$, $E(R_D) = 18\%$, and $SD(R_D) = 40\%$. We now further assume that $cor(R_C, R_D) = -0.5$. Exhibit 3.4 presents the expected portfolio return and standard deviation for five different portfolios made up of varying proportions of C and D.[5]

Feasible and Efficient Portfolios

A *feasible portfolio* is any portfolio that an investor can construct given the assets available. The five portfolios presented in Exhibit 3.4 are all feasible

---

[5]These calculations are simple enough to verify using a calculator.

portfolios. The collection of all feasible portfolios is called the *feasible set of portfolios*. With only two assets, the feasible set of portfolios is graphed as a curve, which represents those combinations of risk and expected return that are attainable by constructing portfolios from all possible combinations of the two assets.

Exhibit 3.5 presents the feasible set of portfolios for all combinations of assets C and D. As mentioned earlier, the portfolio mixes listed in Exhibit 3.4 belong to this set and are shown by the points 1 through 5, respectively. Starting from 1 and proceeding to 5, asset C goes from 100% to 0%, while asset D goes from 0% to 100%—therefore, all possible combinations of C and D lie between portfolios 1 and 5, or on the curve labeled 1–5. In the case of two assets, any risk–return combination not lying on this curve is not attainable since there is no mix of assets C and D that will result in that risk–return combination. Consequently, the curve 1–5 can also be thought of as the feasible set.

In contrast to a feasible portfolio, an *efficient portfolio* is one that gives the highest expected return of all feasible portfolios with the same risk. An efficient portfolio is also said to be a *mean-variance efficient portfolio*. Thus, for each level of risk there is an efficient portfolio. The collection of all efficient portfolios is called the *efficient set*.

The efficient set for the feasible set presented in Exhibit 3.5 is differentiated by the bold curve section 3–5. Efficient portfolios are the combinations of assets C and D that result in the risk–return combinations on the bold section of the curve. These portfolios offer the highest expected return

EXHIBIT 3.5   Feasible and Efficient Portfolios for Assets C and D

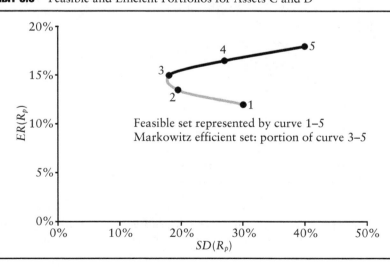

at a given level of risk. Notice that two of our five portfolio mixes—portfolio 1 with $E(R_p) = 12\%$ and $SD(R_p) = 20\%$ and portfolio 2 with $E(R_p) = 13.5\%$ and $SD(R_p) = 19.5\%$—are not included in the efficient set. This is because there is at least one portfolio in the efficient set (for example, portfolio 3) that has a higher expected return and lower risk than both of them. We can also see that portfolio 4 has a higher expected return and lower risk than portfolio 1. In fact, the whole curve section 1–3 is not efficient. For any given risk–return combination on this curve section, there is a combination (on the curve section 3–5) that has the same risk and a higher return, or the same return and a lower risk, or both. In other words, for any portfolio that results in the return/risk combination on the curve section 1–3 (excluding portfolio 3), there exists a portfolio that dominates it by having the same return and lower risk, or the same risk and a higher return, or a lower risk and a higher return. For example, portfolio 4 dominates portfolio 1, and portfolio 3 dominates both portfolios 1 and 2.

Exhibit 3.6 shows the feasible and efficient sets when there are more than two assets. In this case, the feasible set is not a line, but an area.

EXHIBIT 3.6   Feasible and Efficient Portfolios with More Than Two Assets[a]

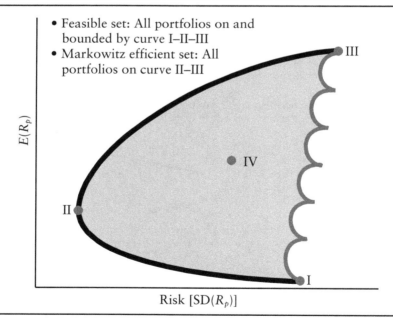

[a]The picture is for illustrative purposes only. The actual shape of the feasible region depends on the returns and risks of the assets chosen and the correlation among them.

This is because, unlike the two-asset case, it is possible to create asset portfolios that result in risk–return combinations that not only result in combinations that lie on the curve I–II–III, but all combinations that lie in the shaded area. However, the efficient set is given by the curve II–III. It is easily seen that all the portfolios on the efficient set dominate the portfolios in the shaded area.

The efficient set of portfolios is sometimes called the *efficient frontier* because graphically all the efficient portfolios lie on the boundary of the set of feasible portfolios that have the maximum return for a given level of risk. Any risk–return combination above the efficient frontier cannot be achieved, while risk–return combinations of the portfolios that make up the efficient frontier dominate those that lie below the efficient frontier.

Choosing the Optimal Portfolio in the Efficient Set

Now that we have constructed the efficient set of portfolios, the next step is to determine the optimal portfolio.

Since all portfolios on the efficient frontier provide the greatest possible return at their level of risk, an investor or entity will want to hold one of the portfolios on the efficient frontier. Notice that the portfolios on the efficient frontier represent trade-offs in terms of risk and return. Moving from left to right on the efficient frontier, the risk increases, but so does the expected return. The question is which one of those portfolios should an investor hold? The best portfolio to hold of all those on the efficient frontier is the *optimal portfolio.*

Intuitively, the optimal portfolio should depend on the investor's preference over different risk–return trade-offs. As explained earlier, this preference can be expressed in terms of a utility function.

In Exhibit 3.7, three indifference curves representing a utility function and the efficient frontier are drawn on the same diagram. An indifference curve indicates the combinations of risk and expected return that give the same level of utility. Moreover, the farther the indifference curve from the horizontal axis, the higher the utility.

From Exhibit 3.7, it is possible to determine the optimal portfolio for the investor with the indifference curves shown. Remember that the investor wants to get to the highest indifference curve achievable given the efficient frontier. Given that requirement, the optimal portfolio is represented by the point where an indifference curve is tangent to the efficient frontier. In Exhibit 3.7, that is the portfolio P^*_{MEF}. For example, suppose that P^*_{MEF} corresponds to portfolio 4 in Exhibit 3.5. We know from Exhibit 3.4 that this portfolio is made up of 25% of asset C and 75% of asset D, with an $E(R_p)$ = 16.5% and $SD(R_p)$ = 27.0%.

EXHIBIT 3.7 Selection of the Optimal Portfolio

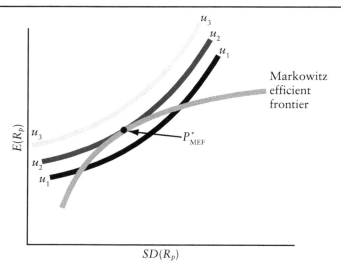

u_1, u_2, u_3 = indifference curves with $u_1 < u_2 < u_3$

P^*_{MEF} = optimal portfolio on Markowitz efficient frontier

Consequently, for the investor's preferences over risk and return as determined by the shape of the indifference curves represented in Exhibit 3.7, and expectations for asset C and D inputs (returns and variance-covariance) represented in Exhibit 3.4, portfolio 4 is the optimal portfolio because it maximizes the investor's utility. If this investor had a different preference for expected risk and return, there would have been a different optimal portfolio.

At this point in our discussion, a natural question is how to estimate an investor's utility function so that the indifference curves can be determined. Economists in the field of behavioral and experimental economics have conducted a vast amount of research in the area of utility functions. Though the assumption sounds reasonable that individuals should possess a function that maps the different preference choices they face, the research shows that it it not so straightforward to assign an individual with a specific utility function. This is because preferences may be dependent on circumstances, and those may change with time.

The inability to assign an investor with a specific utility function does not imply that the theory is irrelevant. Once the efficient frontier is constructed, it is possible for the investor to *subjectively* evaluate the trade-offs for the different return–risk outcomes and choose the efficient portfolio that is appropriate given his or her tolerance to risk.

Example Using the MSCI World Country Indexes

Now that we know how to calculate the optimal portfolios and the efficient frontier, let us take a look at a practical example. We start the example using only four assets and later show these results change as more assets are included. The four assets are the four country equity indexes in the MSCI World Index for Australia, Austria, Belgium, and Canada.[6]

Let us assume that we are given the annualized expected returns, standard deviations, and correlations between these countries as presented in Exhibit 3.8. The expected returns vary from 7.1% to 9%, whereas the standard deviations range from 16.5% to 19.5%. Furthermore, we observe that the four country indexes are not highly correlated with each other—the highest correlation, 0.47, is between Austria and Belgium. Therefore, we expect to see some benefits of portfolio diversification.

Exhibit 3.9 shows the efficient frontier for the four assets. We observe that the four assets, represented by the diamond-shaped marks, are all below the efficient frontier. This means that for a targeted expected portfolio return, the mean-variance portfolio has a lower standard deviation. A utility maximizing investor, measuring utility as the trade-off between expected return and standard deviation, will prefer a portfolio on the efficient frontier over any of the individual assets.

The portfolio at the leftmost end of the efficient frontier (marked with a solid circle in Exhibit 3.9) is the portfolio with the smallest obtainable standard deviation. It is called the *global minimum variance* (GMV) portfolio.

Increasing the Asset Universe

We know that by introducing more (low correlating) assets, for a targeted expected portfolio return, we should be able to decrease the standard deviation of the portfolio. In Exhibit 3.10, the assumed annualized expected

EXHIBIT 3.8 Annualized Expected Returns, Standard Deviations, and Correlations between the Four Country Equity Indexes: Australia, Austria, Belgium, and Canada

Expected Returns	Standard Deviation	Correlations		1	2	3	4
7.9%	19.5%	Australia	1	1			
7.9%	18.2%	Austria	2	0.24	1		
9.0%	18.3%	Belgium	3	0.25	0.47	1	
7.1%	16.5%	Canada	4	0.22	0.14	0.25	1

[6]This example draws from Frank J. Fabozzi, Sergio M. Focardi and Petter N. Kolm, *Financial Modeling of the Equity Market: From CAPM to Cointegration* (Hoboken, N.J.: John Wiley & Sons, 2006).

EXHIBIT 3.9 The Mean-Variance Efficient Frontier of Country Equity Indexes of Australia, Austria, Belgium, and Canada

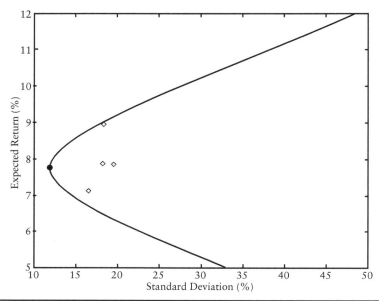

Note: Constructed using the data in Exhibit 3.8. The expected return and standard deviation combination of each country index is represented by a diamond-shaped mark. The global minimum variance portfolio (GMV) is represented by a solid circle. The portfolios on the curves above the GMV portfolio constitute the efficient frontier.

returns, standard deviations, and correlations of 18 countries in the MSCI World Index are presented.

Exhibit 3.11 illustrates how the efficient frontier moves outwards and upwards as we go from 4 to 12 assets and then to 18 assets. By increasing the number of investment opportunities, we increase the level of possible diversification thereby making it possible to generate a higher level of return at each level of risk.

Adding Short Selling Constraints

So far in this section, our theoretical derivations imposed no restrictions on the portfolio weights other than having them add up to one. In particular, we allowed the portfolio weights to take on both positive and negative values; that is, we did not restrict short selling. In practice, many portfolio

EXHIBIT 3.10 Annualized Expected Returns, Standard Deviations, and Correlations between 18 Countries in the MSCI World Index

Expected Returns	Standard Deviation	Correlations		1	2	3	4	5	6	7	8	9	10	11	12	13	14	15	16	17	18
7.9%	19.5%	Australia	1	1																	
7.9%	18.2%	Austria	2	0.24	1																
9.0%	18.3%	Belgium	3	0.25	0.47	1															
7.1%	16.5%	Canada	4	0.22	0.14	0.25	1														
12.0%	18.4%	Denmark	5	0.24	0.44	0.48	0.21	1													
10.3%	20.4%	France	6	0.22	0.41	0.56	0.35	0.45	1												
9.5%	21.8%	Germany	7	0.26	0.48	0.57	0.35	0.48	0.65	1											
12.0%	28.9%	Hong Kong	8	0.31	0.17	0.17	0.19	0.18	0.22	0.24	1										
11.6%	23.3%	Italy	9	0.20	0.36	0.42	0.22	0.38	0.47	0.47	0.16	1									
9.5%	22.1%	Japan	10	0.32	0.28	0.28	0.18	0.28	0.27	0.29	0.24	0.21	1								
10.9%	19.7%	Netherlands	11	0.26	0.38	0.57	0.39	0.45	0.67	0.67	0.24	0.44	0.28	1							
7.9%	22.7%	Norway	12	0.33	0.37	0.41	0.27	0.41	0.45	0.47	0.21	0.32	0.28	0.50	1						
7.6%	21.5%	Singapore	13	0.34	0.22	0.23	0.20	0.22	0.22	0.26	0.44	0.19	0.34	0.24	0.28	1					
9.9%	20.8%	Spain	14	0.26	0.42	0.50	0.27	0.43	0.57	0.54	0.20	0.48	0.25	0.51	0.39	0.25	1				
16.2%	23.5%	Sweden	15	0.27	0.34	0.42	0.31	0.42	0.53	0.53	0.23	0.41	0.27	0.51	0.43	0.27	0.49	1			
10.7%	17.9%	Switzerland	16	0.26	0.47	0.59	0.32	0.49	0.64	0.69	0.23	0.45	0.32	0.67	0.48	0.25	0.53	0.51	1		
9.8%	18.5%	United Kingdom	17	0.25	0.34	0.47	0.38	0.40	0.58	0.53	0.22	0.40	0.28	0.68	0.43	0.24	0.46	0.45	0.57	1	
10.5%	16.5%	United States	18	0.05	0.05	0.21	0.62	0.11	0.29	0.29	0.13	0.17	0.08	0.32	0.15	0.12	0.21	0.22	0.26	0.31	1

EXHIBIT 3.11   The Efficient Frontier Widens as the Number of Low Correlated Assets Increase

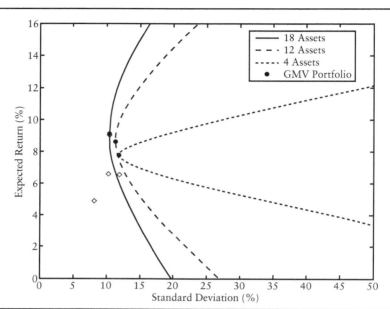

Note: The efficient frontiers have been constructed with 4, 12, and 18 countries (from the innermost to the outermost frontier) from the MSCI World Index. The portfolios on the curves above the GMV portfolio constitute the efficient frontiers for the three cases.

managers cannot sell assets short. This could be for investment policy or legal reasons, or sometimes just because particular asset classes are difficult to sell short such real estate. In Exhibit 3.12, we see the effect of not allowing for short selling. Since we are restricting the opportunity set by constraining all the weights to be positive, the resulting efficient frontier is inside the unconstrained efficient frontier.

ISSUES IN PORTFOLIO SELECTION

In this section, we look at some issues surrounding the theory of portfolio selection and the practical implementation of the model.

Index Model's Approximations to the Covariance Structure

The inputs to mean-variance analysis include expected returns, variance of returns, and either covariance or correlation of returns between each pair

EXHIBIT 3.12 The Effect of Restricting Short Selling: Constrained versus Unconstrained Efficient Frontiers Constructed from 18 Countries from the MSCI World Index

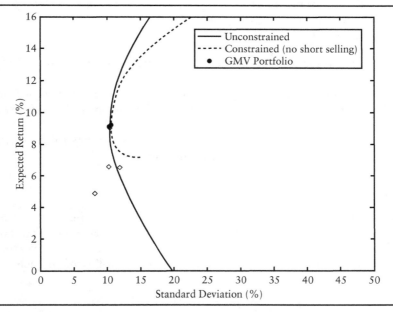

Note: The portfolios on the curves above the GMV portfolio constitute the efficient frontiers.

of securities. For example, an analysis that allows 200 securities as possible candidates for portfolio selection requires 200 expected returns, 200 variances of return, and 19,900 correlations or covariances. An investment team tracking 200 securities may reasonably be expected to summarize their analyses in terms of 200 means and variances; but it is clearly unreasonable for them to produce 19,900 carefully considered correlations or covariances.

It was clear to Markowitz that some kind of model of covariance structure was needed for the practical application of normative analysis to large portfolios. One model he proposed to explain the correlation structure among security returns assumed that the return on the security depends on an "underlying factor, the general prosperity of the market as expressed by some index." Mathematically, the relationship is expressed as follows:[7]

$$r_i = \alpha_i + \beta_i F + u_i \qquad (3.12)$$

---

[7]See Markowitz, *Portfolio Selection: Efficient Diversification of Investments*, pp. 96–101 and, in particular, footnote 1 on page 100.

where

r_i = the return on security i
F = value of some index[8]
u_i = error term

The expected value of u_i is zero and u_i is uncorrelated with F and all other u_j ($j \neq i$).

The parameters α_i and β_i are parameters to be estimated. When measured using regression analysis, β_i is the ratio of the covariance of asset i's return and F to the variance of F.

Markowitz further suggested that the relationship need not be linear and that there could be several underlying factors.

Single-Index Market Model

In 1963, William Sharpe tested equation (3.12) as an explanation of how security returns tend to go up and down together with general market index, F.[9] For the index in the market model he used a market index for F. Specifically, Sharpe estimated using regression analysis the following model:

$$r_{it} = \alpha_i + \beta_i\, r_{mt} + u_{it} \qquad (3.13)$$

where

r_{it} = return on asset i over the period t
r_{mt} = return on the market index over the period t
α_i = a term that represents the nonmarket component of the return on asset i
β_i = the ratio of the covariance of the return of asset i and the return of the market index to the variance of the return of the market index
u_{it} = a zero mean random error term

The model given by equation (3.13) is called the *single-index market model* or simply the *market model*. It is important to note that when Markowitz discussed the possibility of using equation (3.12) to estimate the covariance structure, the index he suggested was not required to be a market index.

Regression analysis is used to calculate the values for β_i and α_i.

---

[8]Markowitz used the notation I in proposing the model given by equation (3.12).
[9]William F. Sharpe, "A Simplified Model for Portfolio Analysis," *Management Science* 9, no. 2 (1963): 277–293.

For a portfolio of assets, the portfolio beta (β_p) is simply a weighted average of the computed betas of the individual assets in the portfolio, where the weight is the percentage of the market value of the individual asset relative to the total market value of the portfolio. That is,

$$\beta_p = \sum_{i=1}^{G} w_i \beta_i$$

where G is the number of assets.

Multi-Index Market Models

Sharpe concluded that the model represented by equation (3.12) is reasonable for the purposes of estimating variances and covariances among assets in a portfolio. This conclusion was supported by research of Kalman Cohen and Gerald Pogue.[10] Benjamin King found strong evidence for industry factors in addition to the marketwide factor.[11] Barr Rosenberg found other sources of risk beyond a marketwide factor and industry factor.[12] We discuss other factor models that can be used to construct an optimal portfolio in Chapter 13.

In Chapter 1, the range of approaches to portfolio construction was described. One approach to full mean-variance analysis is the use of these multi-index or factor models to obtain the covariance structure.

Limitations of the Variance as a Risk Measure

If the return distribution is normally distributed, then the variance is a useful measure of risk. The normal distribution is symmetric so outcomes above and below the expected value are equally likely. However, there are both empirical studies of real-world financial markets as well as theoretical arguments that would suggest that the normal distribution assumption should be rejected.

The original empirical evidence that refuted the assumption that return distributions are not normally distributed was first presented in the 1960s by Benoit Mandelbrot,[13] and further supported by Eugene Fama. Mandelbrot argued that return distributions follow a non-normal probability dis-

---

[10]Kalman J. Cohen and Gerald A. Pogue, "An Empirical Evaluation of Alternative Portfolio Selection Models," *Journal of Business* 40, no. 2 (1967): 166–193.
[11]Benjamin F. King, "Market and Industry Factors in Stock Price Behavior," *Journal of Business* 39, no. 1 (1966): 139–190.
[12]Barr Rosenberg, "Extra-Market Components of Covariance in Security Returns," *Journal of Financial and Quantitative Analysis* 9, no. 2 (1974): 263–274.
[13]Benoit Mandelbrot, "The Variation in Certain Speculative Prices," *Journal of Business* 36, no. 3 (1963): 394–419.

tribution called a *stable Paretian distribution*. Although a discussion of the stable Paretian distribution is beyond the scope of this chapter, the important point here is that it has only been in recent years that more attention has been paid to this distribution in asset management.[14]

The following three properties have been reported in numerous studies of asset returns. First, real-world return distributions have "fatter" or "heavier" tails than the normal distribution. The "tails" of the return distribution are where the extreme outcomes occur. If a probability distribution for the return of assets exhibits fat tails, extreme outcomes are more likely than would be predicted by the normal distribution. As a result, between periods when the market exhibits relatively modest changes in returns, there will be periods when there are changes that are much higher than the normal distribution predicts. Such extreme outcomes are referred to as crashes and bubbles. Second, a normal distribution assumes symmetry of asset returns. In many markets, return distributions have been found to be asymmetric. As a result, asset return distribution may exhibit greater downside risk than suggested by a normal distribution.

Alternative Risk Measures for Portfolio Selection

It would be wrong to think that Markowitz did not carefully consider the problems associated with using the variance of returns as a measure of investment risk. In fact, Markowitz recognized that an alternative to the variance is the semivariance. The *semivariance* is similar to the variance except that in the calculation no consideration is given to returns above the expected return. Portfolio selection could be recast in terms of mean-semivariance. However, if the return distribution is symmetric, Markowitz notes that "an analysis based on (expected return) and (standard deviation) would consider these . . . (assets) as equally desirable."[15] In discussing the semivariance, he noted that the variance "is superior with respect to cost, convenience, and familiarity" and when the asset return distribution is symmetric, either measure "will produce the same set of efficient portfolios."[16]

---

[14]There are many other types of probability distributions that can describe a nonnormal distribution. The technical reason supporting the stable Paretian distribution is that it is the only member of a large and flexible class of probability distributions that allows for the skewness and fat tails that explain what has been observed for real-world asset returns. For a further discussion, see Svetlozar T. Rachev, Christian Menn, and Frank J. Fabozzi, *Fat-Tailed and Skewed Asset Return Distributions: Implications for Risk Management, Portfolio Selection, and Option Pricing* (Hoboken, N.J.: John Wiley & Sons, 2005).

[15]Markowitz, *Portfolio Selection: Efficient Diversification of Investment*: 190.

[16]Ibid., pp.193–194.

There is an ongoing debate on risk measures used for valuing and optimizing the investor's portfolio. In this section and the next, we will describe the various portfolio risk measures proposed in the literature. However, we do not include the mathematical formulation here for each of these measures.

According to the literature on portfolio theory, two disjointed categories of risk measures can be defined: dispersion measures and safety-risk measures. We describe some of the most well-known dispersion measures and safety-first measures next.

Dispersion Measures

The variance or standard deviation is a dispersion measure. Several alternative portfolio mean dispersion approaches have been proposed in the last few decades. The most commonly used measure (and easiest to understand) is the mean-absolute deviation. The *mean-absolute deviation* (MAD) dispersion measure is based on the absolute value of the deviations from the mean rather than the squared deviations as in the case of the mean-standard deviation. The MAD is more robust with respect to outliers (i.e., observations in the tail of the return distribution).

Safety-First Risk Measures

Safety-first rules as a criterion for decision making under uncertainty were first proposed by Roy.[17] In these models, a subsistence, a benchmark, or a disaster level of returns is identified. The objective is the maximization of the probability that the returns are above the benchmark. Thus, most of the safety-first risk measures proposed in the literature are linked to the benchmark-based approach.

Some of the most well-known safety-first risk measures proposed in the literature are classical safety-first, Value at Risk, conditional Value at Risk/expected tail loss, and lower partial moment.

In the *classical safety-first* portfolio choice problem as formulated by Roy, the risk measure is the probability of loss or, more generally, the probability of portfolio return less than some specified value.

Probably the most well-known downside risk measure is *Value at Risk* (VaR). This measure is related to the percentiles of loss distributions, and measures the predicted maximum loss at a specified probability level (for example, 95%) over a certain time horizon (for example, 10 days). The main characteristic of VaR is that of synthesizing in a single value the possible losses which could occur with a given probability in a given temporal

---

[17]A. D. Roy, " Safety-First and the Holding of Assets," *Econometrica* 20, no. 3 (1952): 431–449.

horizon. This feature, together with the (very intuitive) concept of maximum probable loss, allows investors to figure out how risky a portfolio or trading position is. There are various ways to calculate the VaR of a security or a portfolio but a discussion of these methodologies are beyond the scope of this chapter.

Despite the advantages cited for VaR as a measure of risk, it does have several theoretical limitations—and VaR has been shown not to be a coherent risk measure. Specifically, there are properties that a risk measure should specify; and risk measures that satisfy these properties are referred to as "coherent risk" measures.[18] Moreover, VaR ignores returns beyond the VaR (i.e., it does not consider the concentration of returns in the tails beyond VaR). To overcome these limitations and problems, *conditional Value at Risk* (CVaR) is an alternative risk measure. CVaR, also called *expected shortfall* or *expected tail loss*, measures the expected value of portfolio returns, given that the VaR has been exceeded. CVaR is a coherent risk measure, and portfolio selection using this risk measure can be reduced to a linear optimization problem.

A natural extension of semivariance is the lower *partial moment* risk measure.[19] This measure, also called *downside risk* or *probability-weighted function of deviations below a specified target return*, depends on two parameters: (1) a power index that is a proxy for the investor's degree of risk aversion and (2) the target rate of return that is the minimum return that must be earned.

Robust Portfolio Optimization

Despite the great influence and theoretical impact of modern portfolio theory, today full risk–return optimization at the asset level is primarily done only at the more quantitatively oriented asset management firms. The availability of quantitative tools is not the issue—today's optimization technology is mature and much more user-friendly than it was at the time Markowitz first proposed the theory of portfolio selection—yet many asset managers avoid using the quantitative portfolio allocation framework altogether.

A major reason for the reluctance of portfolio managers to apply quantitative risk-return optimization is that they have observed that it may be unreliable in practice. Specifically, mean-variance optimization (or any

---

[18]Philippe Artzner, Freddy Delbaen, Jean-Marc Eber, and David Heath, "Coherent Measures of Risk," *Mathematical Finance* 9, no. 3 (1999): 203–228.
[19]See V. S. Bawa, "Admissible Portfolio for All Individuals," *Journal of Finance* 31, no. 4 (1976): 1169–1183; and Peter C. Fishburn, "Mean-Risk Analysis with Risk Associated with Below-Target Returns," *American Economic Review* 67, no. 2 (1977): 116–126.

measure of risk for that matter) is very sensitive to changes in the inputs (in the case of mean-variance optimization, such inputs include the expected return and variance of each asset and the asset covariance between each pair of assets). While it can be difficult to make accurate estimates of these inputs, estimation errors in the forecasts significantly impact the resulting portfolio weights. As a result, the optimal portfolios generated by the mean-variance analysis generally have extreme or counterintuitive weights for some assets.[20] Such examples, however, are not necessarily a sign that the theory of portfolio selection is flawed; rather, that when used in practice, the mean-variance analysis as presented by Markowitz has to be modified in order to achieve reliability, stability, and robustness with respect to model and estimation errors.

It goes without saying that advances in the mathematical and physical sciences have had a major impact upon finance. In particular, mathematical areas such as probability theory, statistics, econometrics, operations research, and mathematical analysis have provided the necessary tools and discipline for the development of modern financial economics. Substantial advances in the areas of robust estimation and robust optimization were made during the 1990s, and have proven to be of great importance for the practical applicability and reliability of portfolio management and optimization.

Any statistical estimate is subject to error—that is, estimation error. A *robust estimator* is a statistical estimation technique that is less sensitive to outliers in the data and is not driven by one particular set of observations of the data. For example, in practice, it is undesirable that one or a few extreme returns have a large impact on the estimation of the average return of a stock. Nowadays, statistical techniques such as Bayesian analysis and robust statistics are more commonplace in asset management. Taking it one step further, practitioners are starting to incorporate the uncertainty introduced by estimation errors directly into the optimization process. This is very different from traditional mean-variance analysis, where one solves the portfolio optimization problem as a problem with deterministic inputs (i.e., inputs that are assumed to be known with certainty), without taking the estimation errors into account. In particular, the statistical precision of individual estimates is explicitly incorporated

---

[20]See Michael J. Best and Robert R. Grauer, "On the Sensitivity of Mean-Variance Efficient Portfolios to Changes in Asset Means: Some Analytical and Computational Results," *Review of Financial Studies* 4, no. 2 (1991): 315–342; and Vijay K. Chopra and William T. Ziemba, "The Effect of Errors in Means, Variances, and Covariances on Optimal Portfolio Choice," *Journal of Portfolio Management* 19, no. 2 (1993): 6–11.

into the portfolio allocation process. Providing this benefit is the underlying goal of *robust portfolio optimization.*[21]

Modern robust optimization techniques allow a portfolio manager to solve the robust version of the portfolio optimization problem in about the same time as needed for the traditional mean-variance portfolio optimization problem. The robust approach explicitly uses the distribution from the estimation process to find a robust portfolio in a single optimization, thereby directly incorporating uncertainty about inputs in the optimization process. As a result, robust portfolios are less sensitive to estimation errors than other portfolios, and often perform better than optimal portfolios determined by traditional mean-variance portfolios. Moreover, the robust optimization framework offers greater flexibility and many new interesting applications. For instance, robust portfolio optimization can exploit the notion of statistically equivalent portfolios. This concept is important in large-scale portfolio management involving many complex constraints such as transaction costs, turnover, or market impact. Specifically, with robust optimization, a portfolio manager can find the best portfolio that (1) minimizes trading costs with respect to the current holdings and (2) has an expected portfolio return and variance that are statistically equivalent to those of the classical mean-variance portfolio.[22]

KEY POINTS

- Markowitz quantified the concept of diversification through the statistical notion of the covariances between individual securities that make up a portfolio and the overall standard deviation of the portfolio.

---

[21]There are two approaches that have been suggested for dealing with this problem. One is the application of estimation by using a statistical technique known as *Bayesian analysis*. See Svetlozar T. Rachev, John Hsu, Biliana Bagasheva, and Frank J. Fabozzi, *Bayesian Methods in Finance* (Hoboken, N.J.: John Wiley & Sons, 2008). The Black-Litterman model uses this approach. (See F. Black and R. Litterman, "Asset Allocation: Combining Investor Views With Market Equilibrium," Goldman, Sachs & Co., *Fixed Income Research*, September 1990.) The other is using a resampling methodology as suggested in Richard Michaud, *Efficient Asset Management: A Practical Guide to Stock Portfolio Optimization and Asset Allocation* (New York: Oxford University Press, 2001). One study found that the resampled approach is superior to that of a Bayesian approach. See Harry M. Markowitz and Nilufer Usmen, "Diffuse Priors vs. Resampled Frontiers: An Experiment," *Journal of Investment Management* 1 (2003): 9–25.
[22]For a discussion of these models, see Frank J. Fabozzi, Petter N. Kolm, Dessislava Pachamanova, and Sergio M. Focardi, *Robust Portfolio Optimization and Management* (Hoboken, N.J.: John Wiley & Sons, 2007).

- A basic assumption behind modern portfolio theory is that an investor's preferences over portfolios with different expected returns and variances can be represented by a function (utility function).
- The basic principle underlying modern portfolio theory is that for a given level of expected return an investor would choose the portfolio with the minimum variance from amongst the set of all possible portfolios.
- Minimum variance portfolios are called mean-variance efficient portfolios. The set of all mean-variance efficient portfolios is called the efficient frontier. The portfolio on the efficient frontier with the smallest variance is called the global minimum variance portfolio (GMVP).
- The efficient frontier moves outwards and upwards as the number of (not perfectly correlated) securities increases. The efficient frontier shrinks as constraints are imposed upon the portfolio.
- Index models are used as an alternative to estimating the full variance-covariance structure of a set of securities
- The stable Paretian distribution has been proposed as an alternative to the normal distribution for modelling asset returns. This is because it is more consistent with two empirically observed behavior of asset returns: fat tails and asymmetry.
- In addition to axiomatic properties that a risk measure should satisfy, desirable features of investment risk measures include relativity of risk, multidimensionalility of risk, and asymmetry of risk.
- The various measures of risk for valuing and optimizing an investor's portfolio are open to debate. The two categories of risk measures that have been suggested are classified those that measure dispersion measures and those that are based on the individual's level of safety-risk.
- The variance and mean-absolute deviation are the most commonly used measures of dispersion.
- Safety-first measures require the investor to specify a benchmark or a worst-case scenario level of return. The objective then is to maximize the liklihood that the selected portfolio's return is above the benchmark or the worst-case scenario level of return. The most well-known safety-first risk measures used are classical safety-first, Value at Risk, conditional Value at Risk/expected tail loss, and lower partial moments.
- An advancement in the theory of portfolio selection is the development of estimation techniques that generate more robust mean-variance estimates along with optimization techniques that result in optimized portfolios being more robust to the mean-variance estimates used.

QUESTIONS

1. **a.** What is "utility" in an economic sense?
   b. How do indifference curves express the utility function of a person?
   c. What does it mean that an investor is risk-averse?

2. **a.** How is the expected return of a portfolio calculated from the expected returns of the assets?
   b. What other information is needed for this calculation?

3. **a.** Why are covariances (or correlations) important in selecting a portfolio?
   b. How do they impact diversification and portfolio risk?

4. **a.** What is the feasible set of portfolios?
   b. What are the important subsets of a feasible set?
   c. How does one determine the optimal portfolio for an investor?

5. What method can be used as an approximation to the full covariance structure of a group of assets?

6. **a.** What approach is generally used to determine the critical inputs used in the Markowitz model?
   b. What are some problems with this approach?
   c. How can robust portfolio optimization be used in portfolio construction?

7. **a.** What are some reasons for constraining the allocation of certain assets in a portfolio?
   b. What is the cost of such constraints?

8. What do empirical studies suggest about the probability distribution of asset returns?

9. **a.** What is the Value-at-Risk measure?
   b. What are limitations of the Value-at-Risk measure?
   c. What is the conditional Value-at-Risk measure and why is it superior to the Value-at-Risk measure?

CHAPTER 4

Capital Asset Pricing Models

Frank J. Fabozzi, Ph.D., CFA, CPA
Professor in the Practice of Finance
Yale School of Management

Harry M. Markowitz, Ph.D.
Consultant

Risk-return analysis in finance is a "normative" theory: It does not purport to describe, rather it offers advice. Specifically, it offers advice to an investor regarding how to manage a portfolio of securities. The investor may be an institution, such as a pension fund or endowment; or it may be an institution with multiple portfolios to manage, such as a Fidelity or Vanguard, which manage various mutual funds as well as funds for institutional clients. The focus of risk-return analysis is on advice for each individual portfolio.

This contrasts with capital asset pricing models (CAPMs), the focus of this chapter, which are hypotheses concerning capital markets as a whole. They are "positive" models, that is, they are hypotheses about that which *is*—as opposed to "normative" models which advise on what should be or, more precisely, advise on what an investor should do.

Despite the importance of CAPMs in finance, there is considerable confusion regarding certain aspects of the theory. So, in addition to describing CAPMs in this chapter, we explain the sources of the confusion and their implications.

SHARPE-LINTNER CAPM

The first CAPM was that of Sharpe[1] and Lintner.[2] The *Sharpe-Lintner CAPM* (SL-CAPM) assumes the following:

[1] William F. Sharpe, "Capital Asset Prices: A Theory of Market Equilibrium under Conditions of Risk," *Journal of Finance* 19, no. 3 (1964): 425–442.
[2] John Lintner, "The Valuation of Risk Assets and the Selection of Risky Investments in Stock Portfolios and Capital Budgets," *Review of Economics and Statistics* 47, no. 1 (1965): 13–37.

- All investors have the same beliefs concerning security returns.
- All investors have mean-variance efficient portfolios.
- All investors can lend all it has or can borrow all it wants at the same risk-free interest rate that the U.S. federal government pays to borrow money.

By the *mean* it is meant the expected value of the return of a security or portfolio. Thus, throughout this chapter, we use the terms "mean return" and "expected return" interchangeably. By *variance*, we mean the variance of the returns of a security or portfolio. This is the square of the standard deviation, the most commonly used measure in statistics to quantify the dispersion of the possible outcomes of some random variable. Standard deviation is the more intuitively meaningful measure: Most of any probability distribution is between its mean minus two standard deviations and mean plus two distributions. It is not true that most of a distribution is between the mean and plus or minus two variances, or any other number of variances. While standard deviation is the more intuitive measure, formulas are more conveniently expressed in terms of variance. One can most easily compute the variance of a portfolio and then take its square root to obtain its standard deviation.

As explained in the previous chapter, by *mean-variance efficient portfolios*, we mean that of all the possible portfolios that can be created from all of the securities in the market, the ones that have highest mean for a given variance.

The two major conclusions of the SL-CAPM are:

CAPM Conclusion 1. The market portfolio is a mean-variance efficient portfolio.
CAPM Conclusion 2. The difference between the expected return and the risk-free interest rate, referred to as the *excess return*, of each security is proportional to its beta.

The "market portfolio" includes all securities in the market. The composition of the portfolio is such that the sum of the weights allocated to all the securities is equal to one. That is, denoting X_i^M as the percentage of security i in the market portfolio (denoted by M), then

$$\sum_{i=1}^{n} X_i^M = 1 \tag{4.1}$$

Each holding of a security is proportional to its part of the total market capitalization. That is,

$$X_i^M = \frac{\text{Market value of } i\text{-th security}}{\text{Total market value of all securities}} \quad (4.2)$$

CAPM Conclusion 1 is that this "market portfolio" is on the mean-variance efficient frontier.

Let r_i stand for the return on the *i-th* security during some period. The return on the market portfolio then is

$$r^M = \sum_{i=1}^{n} X_i^M r_i \quad (4.3)$$

The beta (β) referred to in CAPM Conclusion 2 can be estimated using regression analysis from historical data on observed returns for a security and observed returns for the market. In this regression analysis, security return is the "dependent variable" and market return is the "independent variable." However, the beta produced by this analysis should be interpreted as a measure of association rather than causation. That is, it is a measure of the extent that the two quantities move up and down together, not as the so-called "independent variable" causing the level of the "dependent variable." Below we examine why there is this association (not causation) in CAPM between security returns and market return.

The excess return, denoted by e_i, is the difference between the security's expected return, $E(r_i)$, and the risk-free interest rate, r_f, at which all investors are assumed to lend or borrow:

$$e_i = E(r_i) - r_f \quad (4.4)$$

CAPM Conclusion 2 is that the excess return for security i is proportional to its β. That is, letting k be a constant then

$$e_i = k\beta_i, \quad i = 1, ..., n \quad (4.5)$$

It can also be shown that equation (4.5) applies to portfolios as well as individual securities. Thus in an SL-CAPM world, each security and portfolio has an excess return that is proportional to the regression of the security or portfolio's return against the return of the market portfolio.

ROY CAPM

A second CAPM, which appeared shortly after that of the writings of Sharpe and Lintner, differs from the SL-CAPM only in its assumption concerning the investment constraint imposed by investors. More specifically, it assumes that each investor (I) can choose any portfolio that satisfies

$$\sum_{i=1}^{n} X_i^I = 1 \tag{4.6}$$

without regard to the sign of the variables. Positive X_i^I is interpreted as a long position in a security while a negative X_i^I is interpreted as a short position in a security.

However, a negative X_i^I is far from a realistic model of real-world constraints on shorting. For example, equation (4.6) would consider feasible a portfolio with

$$X_1 = -1,000$$
$$X_2 = 1,001$$
$$X_i = 0 \qquad i = 3, ..., n$$

since the above sums to one. This would correspond to an investor depositing $1,000 with a broker; shorting $1,000,000 of stock 1; then using the proceeds of the sale, plus the $1,000 deposited with the broker to buy $1,001,000 worth of stock 2. In fact, in this example, Treasury Regulation T (Reg T) would require that the sum of long positions, plus the value of the stocks sold short, not exceed $2,000.

Equation (4.6), as the only constraint on portfolio choice, was first proposed by Roy,[3] albeit not in a CAPM context. Since it is difficult to pin down who first used this constraint set in a CAPM (more than one did so almost simultaneously), we refer to this as the *Roy CAPM* as distinguished from the SL-CAPM.

CONFUSIONS REGARDING THE CAPM

Probably no other part of financial theory has been subject to more confusion, by professionals and amateurs alike, than the CAPM. Major areas of confusion include the following:

Confusion 1. Failure to distinguish between the following two statements:

The market is efficient in that each participant has correct beliefs and uses them to their advantage.

---

[3]Andrew D. Roy, "Safety First and the Holding of Assets," *Econometrica* 20, no. 3 (1952): 431–449.

and

The market portfolio is a mean-variance efficient portfolio.

Confusion 2. Belief that equation (4.5) shows that CAPM investors get paid for bearing "market risk." That this view—held almost universally until quite recently—is in error is easily demonstrated by examples in which securities have the same covariance structure but different excess returns.

Confusion 3. Failure to distinguish between the beta in Sharpe's one-factor model of covariance,[4] and that in Sharpe's CAPM.[5]

The following sections present the assumptions and conclusions of the SL-CAPM and the Roy CAPM, and discuss the nature of these three historic sources of confusion, and their practical implications.

TWO MEANINGS OF MARKET EFFICIENCY

CAPM is an elegant theory. With the aid of some simplifying assumptions, it reaches dramatic conclusions about practical matters. For example:

- How can an investor choose an efficient portfolio? The answer: Just buy the market.
- How can you forecast expected returns? The answer: Just forecast betas.
- How should you price a new security? The answer is once again: Forecast its beta.

CAPM's simplifying assumptions make it easier to deduce properties of market equilibria, which is like computing falling body trajectories while assuming there is no air. But, before betting the ranch that the feather and the brick will hit the ground at the same time, it is best to consider the implications of some of the omitted complexities. The present section mostly explores the implications of generalizing one of CAPMs simplifying assumptions.

Note the difference between the statement "The market is efficient," in the sense that market participants have accurate information and use it correctly to their benefit, and the statement "The market portfolio is a mean-

---

[4]William F. Sharpe, "A Simplified Model for Portfolio Analysis," *Management Science* 9, no. 2 (1963): 277–293

[5]Sharpe, "Capital Asset Prices: A Theory of Market Equilibrium under Conditions of Risk."

variance efficient portfolio." Under some assumptions the two statements are equivalent. Specifically, if we assume:

Assumption 1. Transaction costs and other illiquidities can be ignored.

Assumption 2. All investors hold mean-variance efficient portfolios.

Assumption 3. All investors hold the same (correct) beliefs about means, variances, and covariances of securities.

Assumption 4. Every investor can lend all she or he has or can borrow all she or he wants at the risk-free interest rate.

Then based on these four assumptions we get CAPM Conclusion 1: The market portfolio is a mean-variance efficient portfolio. This CAPM conclusion also follows if Assumption 4 is replaced by the following assumption:

Assumption 4'. Equation (4.6) is the only constraint on the investor's choice of portfolio.

As noted earlier, a negative X_i is interpreted as a short position; but this is clearly a quite unrealistic model of real-world short constraints. Equation (4.6) would permit any investor to deposit \$1,000 with a broker, sell short \$1,000,000 worth of one security, and buy long \$1,001,000 worth of another security.

In addition to CAPM Conclusion 1, Assumptions 1 through 4 imply CAPM Conclusion 2: In equilibrium, excess returns are proportional to betas, as in equation (4.5). This CAPM conclusion is the basis for the CAPM's prescriptions for risk adjustment and asset valuation.

Since a Roy CAPM world may or may not have a risk-free asset, Assumptions 1–3 plus Assumption 4' cannot imply CAPM Conclusion 2. These assumptions do, however, imply the following:

CAPM Conclusion 2'. Expected returns are a linear function of betas, i.e., there are constants, a and b, such that

$$E(r_i) = a + b\beta_i \quad i = 1, \ldots, n \tag{4.7}$$

Equation (4.5) of the SL-CAPM is the same as equation (4.7) of the Roy CAPM with $a = r_f$.

CAPM Conclusions 1 and 2 (or 2') do not follow from Assumptions 1, 2, and 3 if 4 (or Assumption 4') is replaced by a more realistic description of the investor's investment constraints. This is illustrated by an example

EXHIBIT 4.1 Expected Returns and Standard Deviations for Three Hypothetical Securities[a]

Security	Expected Return	Standard Deviation
1	0.15%	0.18%
2	0.10%	0.12%
3	0.20%	0.30%

[a] Security returns are uncorrelated.

with the expected returns and standard deviations given in Exhibit 4.1. In this example, it is assumed that the returns are uncorrelated (but similar results occur with correlated returns). The example assumes that investors cannot sell short or borrow. The same results hold if investors can borrow limited amounts or can sell short but are subject to Reg T or a similar constraint.

Assumptions 1 through 3 are assumed in this example. Rather than Assumption 4 or Assumption 4′, the example assumes that the investor can choose any portfolio that meets the following constraints:

$$X_1 + X_2 + X_3 = 1.0 \qquad (4.8a)$$

and

$$X_1 \geq 0, \ X_2 \geq 0, \ X_3 \geq 0 \qquad (4.8b)$$

This is the "standard" portfolio selection constraint set presented in Markowitz.[6] It differs from the Roy constraint set in the inclusion of nonnegativity constraints, the inequalities given by (4.8b).

In Exhibit 4.2, X_1—the fraction invested in Security 1—is plotted on the horizontal axis; X_2—the fraction invested in Security 2—is plotted on the vertical axis; and X_3—the fraction invested in the third security—is given implicitly by the relationship $X_3 = 1 - X_1 - X_2$. In the exhibit, the portfolio labeled "c" has smaller variance than any other portfolio that satisfies the equation (4.8a) constraint. In general, such a minimum-overall-variance portfolio may or may not satisfy the inequalities given by (4.8b) constraints. In other words, the minimum-overall-variance portfolio may or may not be feasible for the original Markowitz constraint set.[7] In the present example

---

[6] Harry M. Markowitz, "Portfolio Selection," *Journal of Finance* 7, no. 1 (1952): 77–91.
[7] Markowitz, "Portfolio Selection."

EXHIBIT4.2 Example Illustrating that When Short Sales are Not Allowed, the Market Portfolios is Typically Not Mean-Variance Efficient

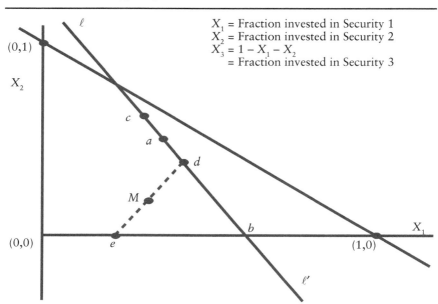

it is. Results similar to those we illustrate here also typically hold when c is not feasible for the standard model.[8]

The line $\ell\ell'$ connects all points (portfolios) which minimize variance, on the portfolio-as-a-whole, for various levels of portfolio expected return, subject to equation (4.8a), ignoring nonnegativity inequalities (4.8b). Using differential calculus, one can minimize a function such as

$$V = \sum_{i=1}^{3} X_i^2 V_i \qquad (4.9a)$$

[8]Markowitz presents examples of three-security standard analyses in which "c" is feasible in some cases and not feasible in others. It is possible in the latter case for the set of mean-variance efficient portfolios to be a single line segment or even a single point. But typically, when "c" is outside of the feasible triangle, as well as when it is within it, the set of efficient portfolios consists of two or more line segments (the "efficient segments"), which meet at "corner portfolios." Thus the construction in Exhibit 4.2 can typically be carried out in cases in which "c" is not feasible. (See Markowitz, "Portfolio Selection"and Chapter 7 in Harry M. Markowitz, *Portfolio Selection: Efficient Diversification of Investments*, 2nd ed. (New York: John Wiley & Sons, 1991).

subject to constraints

$$\sum_{i=1}^{3} X_i = 1 \qquad\qquad (4.9b)$$

$$E_0 = \sum_{i=1}^{3} X_i E(r_i) \qquad\qquad (4.9c)$$

One can do so with the expected returns and standard deviations from Exhibit 4.1, letting E_0 vary, and thereby obtain the line in Exhibit 4.2. Moving downward and to the right on $\ell\ell'$, the portfolio expected return increases. This downward direction for increasing expected return does not always hold: it depends on the choice of security expected returns.

In the Roy model, every point in the exhibit is feasible since they all satisfy equation (4.6) or, equivalently, equation (4.8a). It follows that, in the Roy CAPM, *all* points on $\ell\ell'$, from "*c*" downward in the direction of increasing *E*, are efficient. But in the standard model, including nonnegativity inequalities (4.8b), all points on $\ell\ell'$ below the point "*b*" are not feasible (since they have negative X_2) and therefore cannot be efficient. In this example, when portfolio choice is subject to the standard constraint set, the set of efficient portfolios is the same as that of the Roy constraint set from portfolio *c* to portfolio *b*. After that, the set of efficient portfolios moves horizontally along the X_1 axis, ending at point (0, 0). This represents the portfolio with everything invested in Security 3, which has maximum expected return in the example.

Suppose that some investors select the cautious portfolio *d*, while the remainder selects the more aggressive portfolio *e*. The market portfolio *M* lies on the straight line that connects *d* and *e* (e.g., halfway between if both groups have equal amounts invested).

But *M* is not an efficient portfolio, either for the standard constraint set or for the Roy constraint set. Thus, even though all investors hold mean-variance efficient portfolios, the market portfolio is not mean-variance efficient!

A Simple Market

Exhibit 4.2 demonstrates that if the expected returns and variances for our three hypothetical securities in Exhibit 4.1 reflect equilibrium beliefs, then the market portfolio would not be a mean-variance efficient portfolio. But can these be equilibrium beliefs? Consider the following simple market: Inhabitants of an island live on coconuts and produce them from their own gardens. The island has three enterprises, namely, three coconut farms. Once a year, a stock market convenes to trade the shares of the three farms.

Each year the resulting share prices turn out to be the same as those of preceding years. Thus the only source of uncertainty of return is the dividend each stock pays during the year, which is the stock's pro rata share of the farm's production. Markowitz[9] shows that means, variances, and covariances of coconut production exist that imply the efficient set in Exhibit 4.2, or in any of the other three-security efficient sets presented in Markowitz's initial works.[10]

With such probability distributions of returns, the market is rational in the sense that each participant knows the true probability distribution of returns, and each seeks and achieves mean-variance efficiency. Nevertheless, in contrast to the usual CAPM conclusion, the market portfolio is not an efficient portfolio. It also follows that there is no representative investor since no one wants to hold the market portfolio.

Arbitrage

Suppose that most investors are subject to the non-negativity requirement of inequalities (4.8b), but one investor can short in the CAPM sense. (Perhaps the CAPM investor has surreptitious access to a vault containing stock certificates that he or she can "borrow" temporarily without posting collateral.) Would this CAPM investor, with unlimited power to short and use the proceeds to buy long, arbitrage away the inefficiency in the market portfolio?

Exhibit 4.3 shows an investor would not do so. Suppose that portfolio P is the one most preferred by the Roy CAPM investor. If this investor shorts M and uses the proceeds to buy more P, then the resulting portfolio will be on the straight line connecting M and P—but this time on the far side of P (e.g., at Q) rather than between M and P. But Q is not efficient for the Roy CAPM investor since it does not lie on the $\ell\ell'$ line. The Roy CAPM investor is better off just holding P rather than shorting M to buy more P.

With market participants holding portfolios d, e, and P and with the weighted average of the d and e investors being at M, the new market portfolio will be on the straight line between M and P, such as at M^a, M^b, or M^c in Exhibit 4.4. M^c cannot be the market equilibrium since this would imply a negative market value for Security 2. Similarly, M^b implies a zero market value for Security 2, therefore a zero price.

Thus the only points (portfolios) between M and P that are consistent with positive prices for all securities lie strictly between M and M^b, such as

[9]Harry M. Markowitz, "Market Efficiency: A Theoretical Distinction and So What?" *Financial Analysts Journal* 61, no. 5 (2005): 17–30.
[10]Markowitz, "Portfolio Selection" and Chapter 7 in *Portfolio Selection: Efficient Diversification of Investments.*

EXHIBIT 4.3 Illustration that an Investor who can Sell Short and Use the Proceeds to Buy Long Should Not Short an Inefficient Market

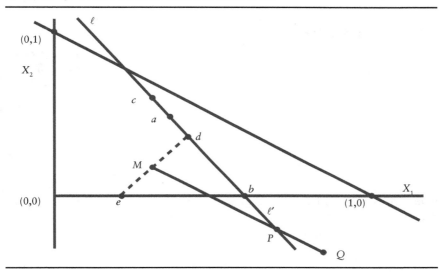

EXHIBIT 4.4 Illustration that the Presence of a CAPM Short Seller Does Not Make the Market Portfolio Efficient

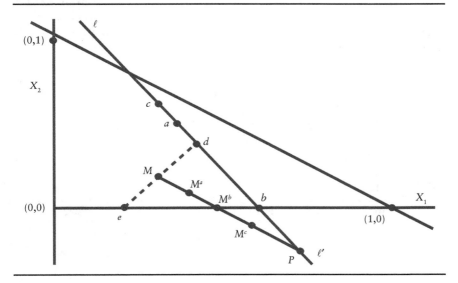

M^a; but M^a is not efficient for either the investors with a standard or a Roy constraint set.

Expected Returns and Betas

If Assumptions 1 through 4 (or Assumption 4′) are true, then CAPM Conclusion 2′ follows: Expected returns are linearly related to the betas of each security as in equation (4.7), that is,

$$E_1 = a + b\beta_1$$

$$E_2 = a + b\beta_2$$

$$E_3 = a + b\beta_3$$

where β_i is the coefficient of regression of the return on the ith security against the return on the market portfolio. In other words, all (E_i, β_i) combinations lie on the straight line

$$Y = a + bX$$

But equation (4.7) does not typically hold if Assumptions 1 through 3 are true but neither Assumption 4 nor Assumption 4′ is also true, as illustrated using the data in Exhibits 4.5 and 4.6, and the diagram in Exhibit 4.7. Exhibit 4.5 shows the β_i for portfolio P; Exhibit 4.6 shows them for portfolio M. These betas are computed using the fact that the regression coefficient $\beta_{s,r}$ of random variable s against a random variable r is

$$\beta_{s,r} = \frac{\text{Covariance}(r,s)}{\text{Variances}(s)} \tag{4.10}$$

Exhibit 4.7 shows the plot of these betas against the expected returns given in Exhibit 4.1 The relationship between beta and expected return is linear for regressions against P, as implied by equation (4.7), but not against

EXHIBIT 4.5   Betas versus Portfolio P

Security	Percent in P	$\text{cov}_{i,P} = P_i V_i$	$\text{beta}_{i,P}$
1	0.70%	0.0227	0.52
2	−0.25	−0.0036	−0.08
3	0.55	0.0495	1.12

Note: var(P) = 0.0440; Beta$_{i,P}$ = cov$_{i,P}$/var(P).

EXHIBIT 4.6   Betas versus Portfolio M

Security	Percent in M	$\text{cov}_{i,M} = M_i V_i$	$\text{beta}_{i,M}$
1	0.30	0.0097	0.36
2	0.19	0.0027	0.10
3	0.51	0.0459	1.71

Note: $\text{var}(M) = 0.0268$; $\text{beta}_{i,M} = \text{cov}_{i,M}/\text{var}(M)$.

EXHIBIT 4.7   Linear Relationship between Expected Returns and Betas if and only if the Regression is Against a Portfolio on the line $\ell\ell'$ in Exhibit 4.2

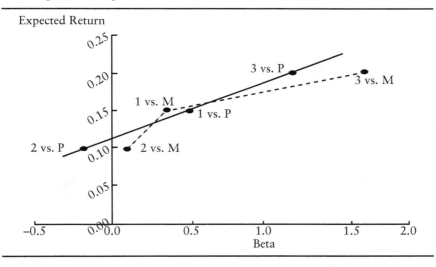

M. In general, expected returns are a linear function of betas if and only if the regressions are against a portfolio on the $\ell\ell'$ line.[11]

Limited Borrowing

Thus far we have seen that the market portfolio is not necessarily an efficient portfolio, and there is usually no linear relationship between expected returns and betas (regressions against the market portfolio) if the SL-CAPM or Roy CAPM is replaced by the standard, Markowitz constraint set, constraints given by (4.8). Exhibit 4.8 illustrates that the same conclusions hold if borrowing and lending at a risk-free interest rate are permitted, but borrowing is limited, e.g., to 100% of the equity in the portfolio. In Exhibit 4.8,

---

[11]See Chapter 12 in Harry M. Markowitz and Peter Todd, *Mean-Variance Analysis in Portfolio Choice and Capital Markets* (New York: John Wiley & Sons, 2000).

EXHIBIT 4.8   Illustration that if Borrowing is Permitted but Limited, the Market Portfolio is still Typically not an Efficient Portfolio

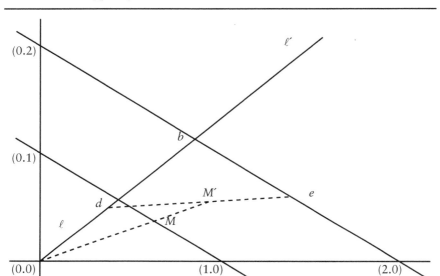

Security 3 is the risk-free asset. With 100% borrowing permitted, the set of feasible portfolios is no longer on and in the triangle with (0, 0), (1, 0), and (0, 1) as its vertices. Rather, the feasible region is on and in the triangle whose vertices are (0, 0), (2, 0), and (0, 2). For example, the (2, 0) point represents the portfolio with 200% invested in Security 1.

In the SL-CAPM, the efficient set starts at the portfolio (0, 0), which holds only the risk-free asset. From there, the efficient set moves along a straight line in the first quadrant of Exhibit 4.8.[12] In the SL-CAPM, this efficient line would continue in the same direction without limit. In the model with borrowing limited to at most 100% of equity, the ray extending from (0, 0) is no longer feasible (therefore no longer efficient) when it crosses the line connecting (0, 2) and (2, 0)—at b in the figure. The efficient set then moves towards the leveraged portfolio with highest expected return: (2, 0) in the present case. Thus in Exhibit 4.8 the set of efficient portfolios is the line segment connecting (0, 0) to b, followed by the segment connecting b to (2, 0). As in our analysis using the standard

---

[12]The SL-CAPM requires nonnegative investments. Thus if the parameters of an example were such that the straight line would move into, say, the fourth quadrant, X_2 would equal zero on the line and would, in effect, drop out of the market, and out of the analysis.

constraint set, if some investors hold portfolio d and the remainder hold portfolio e, then the "market portfolio" will be between them (e.g., at M') and will not be an efficient portfolio.

We put "market portfolio" in quotes above because M' is a leveraged portfolio. In order to meet the definition of market portfolio in equation (4.1), so that the holdings in the market portfolio sum to one, we must rescale M'. This gives us the market portfolio (no quotation marks) M, which is also not an efficient portfolio.

Finally, as in the analysis of the standard case since M is not on the $\ell\ell'$ line, there does not exist a linear relationship between expected returns and betas. Also, there is no "representative investor," since no investor wants to hold the market portfolio.

Further Generalizations

Suppose that there are n securities (for $n = 3$ or 30 or 3,000). Suppose that one security has the highest expected return, and that the n securities have a "nonsingular covariance matrix." This means that there is no riskless combination of risky securities. If the only constraint on the choice of portfolio is equation (4.6), then the portfolios that minimize portfolio variance V_p for various values of portfolio expected return E_p lie on a single straight line in n-dimensional portfolio space. This is not true for an investor also subject to nonnegativity constraints such as in the inequalities given by (4.8b).

The "critical line algorithm" (CLA) for tracing out all efficient portfolios begins with the portfolio that is 100% invested in the security with highest expected return.[13] It traces out the set of efficient portfolios in a series of iterations. Each iteration computes one piece (one linear segment) of the piecewise linear efficient set. Each successive segment has either one more or one less security than the preceding segment. If the universe consists of, say 10,000 securities, and if all securities are to be demanded by someone, then this universal efficient frontier must contain at least 10,000 segments. If investors have sufficiently diverse risk tolerances, they will choose portfolios on many different segments. The market portfolio is a weighted average of individual portfolios and typically will not be on any efficient segment.

This characterization of efficient sets remains true if limited borrowing is allowed, as we saw. It also remains true when short selling is permitted but is subject to a Reg T or a similar constraint.[14]

---

[13]See Markowitz and Todd, *Mean-Variance Analysis in Portfolio Choice and Capital Markets.*

[14]See Bruce I Jacobs, Kenneth N. Levy, and Harry M. Markowitz, "Portfolio Optimization with Factors, Scenarios, and Realistic Short Positions," *Operations Research* 53, no. 4 (2005): 586–599.

CAPM INVESTORS DO NOT GET PAID FOR BEARING RISK

Recall that if the SL-CAPM assumptions are made then a stock's beta (regression against the market portfolio) is proportional to its excess return, as shown in equation (4.5). Markowitz shows that this does *not* imply that CAPM investors are paid to bear risk.[15]

This is most easily seen if we assume that risks are uncorrelated. (CAPM should cover this case too.) In this case, we show that two securities can have the same variance but different expected returns, or the same expected returns and different variances. Therefore, it cannot be true that the investor is paid for bearing risk!

According to equation (4.10), the beta of r_i against r_M is

$$\beta_i = \frac{\text{Covariance } (r_i, r^M)}{\text{variance } (r^M)}$$

Therefore, equation (4.5) holds if and only if we also have

$$e_i = \tilde{b} \text{ covariance}(r_i, r^M) \tag{4.11}$$

where

$$\tilde{b} = b / Var(r^M)$$

In other words, excess return is proportional to β_i if and only if it is proportional to the covariance between r_i and r^M.

As a calculus exercise one can show that, in the uncorrelated case, the SL-CAPM investor minimizes portfolio variance for given portfolio mean if and only if the investor choose a portfolio such that

$$VX_i^I = k^I e_i \tag{4.12a}$$

where V_i is the variance of r_i and k^I depends on the investor's risk aversion.

Equation (4.12a) implies a similar relationship for the market portfolio:[16]

---

[15]Harry M. Markowitz, "CAPM Investors Do Not Get Paid for Bearing Risk," *Journal of Portfolio Management* 34, no. 2 (2008): 91–94.
[16]If we multiply both sides of equation (4.12a) by w^I, the I-th investor's equity as a fraction of total market equity, and sum we get

$$V_i \left(\sum_I w^I X_i^I \right) = \left(\sum w^I k^I \right) e_i$$

If we sum the above over all securities, the second factor on the left, namely

$$V_i X_i^M = k^M e_i \qquad (4.12\text{b})$$

Therefore,

$$X_i^M = k^M \left(\frac{e_i}{V_i} \right) \text{ for } i = 1, ..., n \qquad (4.12\text{c})$$

Thus if two securities have the same positive excess return but different variances, the market portfolio will contain a larger dollar value of the one with the lower variance. Conversely, if two securities have the same variance but different positive excess returns, the market portfolio will contain a larger dollar value of the one with higher excess return.

Now let us consider where the linear relationship in equation (4.5), or (4.11), comes from in this case of uncorrelated returns. It can be shown that in equation (4.12b), $V_i X_i^M$ is the covariance of the r_i with the market. Therefore, covariance with the market is proportional to excess return (and vice versa) because the security with the higher ratio of excess return to variance is a larger part of the market portfolio.

Thus, in the uncorrelated case, the relationship between beta and excess return in equation (4.5) results from the security with higher excess return (per unit variance) being a larger part of the market portfolio. The beta in equation (4.5) is the regression of r_i against the market portfolio and, in the uncorrelated case, the only security in the market portfolio with which it is correlated is itself.

When returns are correlated, the formula for the covariance between security return and market portfolio return is more complicated, but the basic principle is the same. For example, two securities have the same covariance structure, the one with the higher expected return will constitute a larger share of the market portfolio—despite the presence in the market portfolio of securities with which it is correlated—and hence have its own returns more correlated with returns on the market portfolio.

THE "TWO BETA" TRAP

Two distinct meanings of the word "beta" are used in modern financial theory. These meanings are sufficiently alike for people to converse—some

$$S = \sum_i \left(\sum_I w^I X_i^I \right)$$

will not necessarily sum to one since nothing in the SL-CAPM assumptions prevents market participants from being either net borrowers or net lenders. However, if we divide both sides of equation (4.12c) by S, we get equation (4.12b) for the market portfolio as defined in equations (4.1) and (4.2).

with one meaning in mind, some with the other—without realizing they are talking about two different things. The meanings are sufficiently different, however, that one can validly derive diametrically opposite conclusions depending on which one is used. The net result of all this can be like an Abbot and Costello vaudeville comedy routine with portfolio theory rather than baseball as its setting. This is what Markowitz calls the "two beta trap."[17] Below we first review the background of the two betas and then tabulate propositions that are true for one concept and false for the other.

Beta$_{1963}$

In Chapter 3, we discussed Sharpe's "single-index" (or one-factor) model of covariance introduced in 1963.[18] This model assumes that the returns of different securities are correlated with each other because each is dependent on some underlying systematic factor. This can be written as

$$r_i = \alpha_i + \beta_i F + u_i \qquad (4.13)$$

where the expected value of u_i is zero, and u_i is uncorrelated with F and every other u_j.

Originally F was denoted by I and described as an "underlying factor, the general prosperity of the market as expressed by some index." We have changed the notation from I to F to emphasize that r_i depends on the underlying factor rather than the index used to estimate the factor. The index never measures the factor exactly, no matter how many securities are used in the index, provided that each security has positive variance of u_i, since the index I equals:

$$
\begin{aligned}
I &= \sum w_i r_i \\
&= \sum \alpha_i w_i + F(w_i \beta_i) + \sum u_i w_i \\
&= A + BF + U,
\end{aligned}
\qquad (4.14)
$$

where w_i is the weight of return r_i in the index, and

$$
\begin{aligned}
A &= \sum \alpha_i w_i \\
B &= \sum w_i \beta_i, \\
U &= \sum u_i w_i.
\end{aligned}
$$

---

[17]Harry M. Markowitz, "The Two Beta Trap," *Journal of Portfolio Management* 11, no. 1 (1984): 12–20.
[18]Sharpe, "A Simplified Model for Portfolio Analysis."

U is the error in the observation of F. Under the conditions stated, the variance of U is

$$V_U = \sum_{i=1}^{N} w_i^2 V_{u_i} > 0 \tag{4.15}$$

Sharpe tested equation (4.13) as an explanation of how security returns tend to go up and down together.[19] He concluded that equation (4.13) was as complex a model of covariance as seemed to be needed. This conclusion was supported by research of Cohen and Pogue.[20] King found strong evidence for industry factors in addition to the market-wide factor.[21] Rosenberg found other sources of systematic risk beyond the market-wide factor and industry factors.[22]

We refer to the beta coefficient in equation (4.13) as "beta$_{1963}$" since it is the subject of Sharpe's 1963 article. We contrast the properties of this beta with that of the beta that arises from the Sharpe-Lintner CAPM. The latter we will refer to as "beta$_{1964}$" since it is the subject of Sharpe's 1964 article.

Beta$_{1964}$

We noted that the SL-CAPM makes various assumptions about the world, including that all investors are mean-variance efficient, have the same beliefs, and can lend or borrow all they want at the same "risk-free" interest rate. Note, however, one assumption that the SL-CAPM does *not* make is that the covariances among securities satisfy equation (4.13). On the contrary, the assumptions it makes concerning covariances are quite general.[23] They are consistent with equation (4.13) but do not require it. They are also consistent with the existence of industry factors as noted by King, or other sources of systematic risk such as those identified by Rosenberg.

As previously noted, the beta that appears in the CAPM relationship of equation (4.5) (which we now refer to as beta$_{1964}$) is the regression of the i-th security's return against the return on the market portfolio. This is defined

---

[19]Sharpe, "A Simplified Model for Portfolio Analysis."
[20]Kalman J. Cohen and Jerold A. Pogue, "An Empirical Evaluation of Alternative Portfolio-Selection Models," *Journal of Business*, 40, no. 2 (1967): 166–193.
[21]Benjamin F. King, "Market and Industry Factors in Stock Price Behavior," *Journal of Business* 39, no. 1 [part 2] (1966): 139–190.
[22]Barr Rosenberg, "Extra-Market Components of Covariance in Security Returns," *Journal of Financial and Quantitative Analysis* 9, no. 2 (1974): 263–273.
[23]Mossin provides a precise statement of the assumptions behind the Sharpe-Lintner CAPM. Specifically all that Mossin assumes about covariances is that the covariance matrix is nonsingular (i.e., that no portfolio of risky securities is riskless). See Jan Mossin, "Equilibrium in a Capital Asset Market," *Econometrica*, 34, no. 4 (1966): 768–783.

whether or not the covariance structure is generated by the single-factor model of equation (4.13). Equation (4.5) is an assertion about the expected return of a security and how it relates to the regression of the security's return against the market-portfolio return. Unlike equation (4.13), it is not an assertion about how security returns covary.

One source of confusion between beta$_{1963}$ and beta$_{1964}$ is that William Sharpe presented each of them. Sharpe, however, has never been confused on this point. In particular, when explaining beta$_{1964}$ he emphasizes that he derived it without assuming equation (4.13).

Propositions about Betas

Exhibit 4.9 lists various propositions about betas and indicates whether they are true or false for beta$_{1963}$ or beta$_{1964}$. The first column presents each proposition, the second indicates whether the proposition is true or false for beta$_{1963}$, and the third column indicates the same for beta$_{1964}$. Most of the propositions in Exhibit 4.9 are true for one of the betas and false for the other.

Proposition 1

Because of the definition of a regression beta in general, both beta$_{1963}$ and beta$_{1964}$ equal

EXHIBIT 4.9 Propostions about Beta

	β_{1963}	β_{1964}
1. The β_i of the ith security equals $\mathrm{cov}(r_i,R)/V(R)$ for some random variable R.	T	T
2. R is "observable;" specifically, it may be computed exactly from security returns (r_i) and market values (X_i).	F	T
3. R is a *value*-weighted average of the (r_i).	F	T
4. An index I that estimates R should ideally be weighted by a combination of $(1/V_{u_i})$ and (β_i/V_i). Unfortunately, the β_i and V_{u_i} needed to determine these weights are unobservable.	T	F
5. If ideal weights are not used, then equal weights are "not bad" in computing I; specifically, nonoptimum weights can be compensated for by increased sample size.	T	F
6. Essentially, all that is important in computing I is to have a large number of securities; it is not necessary to have a large fraction of all securities.	T	F
7. The ideally weighted index is an efficient portfolio.	F	T

$$\beta_i = \operatorname{cov}(r_i, R) / V(R)$$

for some random variable R. In the case of beta$_{1963}$, R is F for equation (4.13); in the case of beta$_{1964}$ R is the M in equations (4.1) and (4.2).

Proposition 2

Equation (4.15) implies that F cannot be observed exactly no matter how many securities are used to estimate it, provided that no security has a zero variance of u_i. In contrast, portfolio M in equation (4.2) is observable, at least in principle, if only we are diligent enough to measure each X_i^M in the market. Thus, the assertion that R is observable is true in principle for beta$_{1964}$ and false for beta$_{1963}$.

Propositions 3 and 4

One source of confusion about the two betas concerns whether an index estimating R should be "value weighted"; that is, should the w_i used in computing an estimate of R from the r_i equal the X_i^M? We have seen that in the case of beta$_{1964}$:

$$R = \sum X_i^M r_i$$

In this case $w_i = X_i^M$ = market-value weights.

The answer is different in the case of beta$_{1963}$. Ideally, we would like to eliminate the error term U from equation (4.14). Our index would be perfect if $V_U = 0$, provided of course $B \ne 0$. Nevertheless, as long as no security has $V_{u_i} = 0$, the perfect index cannot be achieved with a finite number of securities. Short of this, it might seem that the best to be wished is for V_U be a minimum. In this case, w_i would equal $1 / V_{u_i}$. The optimum choice of weights for estimating the underlying factor F is more complicated, depending also on β_i / V_i.[24] and more complicated still, since V_{u_i} and β_i are not known.

Proposition 5

The fifth proposition in Exhibit 4.9 asserts that if ideal weights cannot be obtained, equal weights are good enough. In particular, an increase in the number of securities can compensate for nonoptimum weights. We have already seen that this proposition is false for beta$_{1964}$. It is easily seen to be true for beta$_{1963}$ under mild restrictions on how fast the V_{u_i} increase as i increases.

---

[24]See Markowitz, "The Two Beta Trap."

Proposition 6

The next proposition asserts that all that is important in designing a good index is to have many securities, as opposed to having a large percentage of the population represented in the index. This proposition is true for I_{1963} and false for I_{1964}, as may be illustrated by two extreme examples.

First, suppose that there are only a few securities in the entire population, and all of them are used in computing a value-weighted index. Then I_{1964} would, in fact, be M and would be precisely correct. In the case of I_{1963}, on the other hand, equation (4.15) implies that if $n = 6$, for example, the error term V_U is the same regardless of whether the six securities are 100% or 1% of the universe.

At the other extreme, imagine that the sample is large but is a small percentage of the total population. For example, suppose $N = 1,000$ out of 100,000 securities. Then I_{1963} will give a good reading for F, and therefore beta$_{1963}$ but I_{1964} may lead to serious mis-estimates of beta$_{1964}$. First, the covariance with I_{1964} of an asset not in this index will tend to be too low. Second, if the index contains more of certain kinds of assets than is characteristic of the entire population, then assets of this sort will tend to have a higher correlation with the index than with the true M, and assets of other sorts will tend to have lower correlations. More precisely, the covariance between return r_i and the market is a weighted average of the covariances σ_{ij} (including $V_i = \sigma_{ii}$) weighted by market values. If the index chosen does not have approximately the same average σ_{ij} for a given i, the estimates of $\beta_{i,1964}$ will be in error.

Proposition 7

This proposition asserts that the ideal index is an efficient portfolio. This is true for I_{1964} and false for I_{1963} since one of the conclusions of the SL-CAPM assumptions is that the market portfolio is efficient. In fact, the market portfolio is the only combination of *risky* assets that is efficient in this CAPM. All other efficient portfolios consist of either investment in the market portfolio plus lending at the risk-free rate, or of investment in the market portfolio financed in part by borrowing at the risk-free rate. On the other hand, beta$_{1963}$ has nothing to do with expected returns or market efficiency.

KEY POINTS

- The two major conclusions of the Sharpe-Lintner CAPM are that (1) the market portfolio is a mean-variance efficient portfolio; and (2) the excess return of each security is proportional to its beta.

- The "market portfolio" includes all securities in the market.
- The beta (β) in CAPM is estimated using regression analysis using historical data on observed returns for a security (response variable) and observed returns for the market (explanatory variable).
- The Roy CAPM differs from the Sharpe-Lintner CAPM only in its assumption concerning the investment constraint imposed by investors. More specifically, it assumes that each investor can short securities.
- Confusion regarding the CAPM involves (1) the failure to distinguish between the following two statements: the market is efficient in that each participant has correct beliefs and uses them to their advantage on the one hand, and the market portfolio is a mean-variance efficient portfolio on the other hand; (2) belief that CAPM investors get paid for bearing nondiversifiable risk; and (3) failure to distinguish between the beta in Sharpe's one-factor model of covariance (1963 beta) and that in Sharpe's CAPM (1964 beta).

QUESTIONS

1. What are the assumptions of the Sharpe-Lintner Capital Asset Pricing Model?

2. What are the two main conclusions of the Sharpe-Lintner CAPM?

3. How does the Roy formulation of the CAPM differ from the Sharpe-Lintner CAPM?

4. What is meant by the "two beta trap"?

5. With respect to an index used in calculating the beta from the Sharpe-Lintner CAPM and the Sharpe single-index factor model, in which case is the following proposition true: "The ideal index is an efficient portfolio."

CHAPTER 5

Factor Models

Guofu Zhou, Ph.D.
Frederick Bierman and James E. Spears Professor of Finance
Olin Business School, Washington University

Frank J. Fabozzi, Ph.D., CFA, CPA
Professor in the Practice of Finance
Yale School of Management

Given a set of assets or asset classes, an important task in the practice of investment management is to understand and estimate their expected returns and the associated risks. Factor models are widely used by investors to link the risk exposures of the assets to a set of known or unknown factors. The known factors can be economic or political factors or industry factors or country factors, and the unknown factors are those that best describe the dynamics of the asset returns in the factor models. However, they are not directly observable or easily intrepreted by investors and have to be estimated from the data.

Applications of the mean-variance analysis and portfolio selection theories in general require the estimation of asset expected asset returns and their covariance matrix. Those market participants who can identify those true factors that drive asset returns should have much better estimates of the true expected asset returns and the covariance matrix to form a much better portfolio than otherwise possible. Hence, there is a lot of research and resources devoted to analyzing factor models in practice by the investment community. There is an intellectual "arms race" to find the best portfolio strategies to outperform competitors.

Factor model estimation depends crucially on whether the factors are identified (known) and unidentified (latent), and depend on the sample size and the number of assets. In addition, factor models can be used not only for explaining asset returns, but also for predicting future returns. In this chapter, we review the factor models in the case of known and latent factors in order to provide a big picture and then discuss the details of estimation.

ARBITRAGE PRICING THEORY

One of the fundamental problems in finance is to explain the cross-section differences in asset expected returns. Specifically, what factors can explain the observed differences. Those factors that systematically affect the differences in expected returns are therefore the risks that investors are compensated for. Hence, the term factors is interchangeabley with the term risk factors.

The Arbitrage Pricing Theory (APT), formulated by Stephen Ross,[1] posits that expected returns of assets are linearly related to K systematic factors and the exposure to these factors is measured by factor betas; that is,

$$E[\tilde{r}_i] = r_f + \gamma_1 \beta_{i1} + \cdots + \gamma_K \beta_{iK} \qquad (5.1)$$

where β_{ik} is the beta or risk exposure on the k-th factor, and γ_k is the factor risk premium, for $k = 1, 2, ..., K$.

Technically, the APT assumes a K-factor model for the return-generating process, that is, the asset returns are influenced by K factors in the economy via linear regression equations,

$$\tilde{r}_{it} - r_{ft} = \alpha_i + \beta_{i1}\tilde{f}_{1t} + \cdots + \beta_{iK}\tilde{f}_{Kt} + \tilde{\varepsilon}_{it} \qquad (5.2)$$

where $\tilde{f}_1, \tilde{f}_2, ..., \tilde{f}_K$ are the systematic factors that affect all the asset returns on the left-hand side, $i = 1, 2, ..., N$; and $\tilde{\varepsilon}_{it}$ is the asset specific risk. Note that we have placed a tilde sign ($\sim$) over the random asset returns, factors, and specific risks. By so doing, we distinguish between factors (random) and their realizations (data), which are important for understanding the estimation procedure below.

Theoretically, under the assumption of no arbitrage, the asset pricing relation of the APT as given by equation (5.1) must be true as demonstrated by Ross. There are two important points to note. First, the return-generating process as given by equation (5.2) is fundamentally different from the asset pricing relation. The return-generating process is a statistical model used to measure the risk exposures of the asset returns. It does not require drawing an economic conclusion, nor does it say anything about what the expected returns on the assets should be. In other words, the α_is in the

[1]Stephen A. Ross, "The Arbitrage Theory of Capital Asset Pricing," *Journal of Economic Theory* 13, no. 3 (1976): 341–360.

return-generating process can statistically be any numbers. Only when the no-arbitrage assumption is imposed, can one claim the APT, which says that the α_is should be linearly related to their risk exposures (betas).

Second, the APT does not provide any specific information about what the factors are. Nor does the theory make any claims on the number of factors. It simply assumes that if the returns are driven by the factors, and if smart investors know the betas (via learning or estimating), then an arbitrage portfolio, which requires no investment but yields a positive return, can be formed if the APT pricing relation is violated in the market. Hence, in equilibrium if there are no arbitrage opportunities, we should not observe deviations from the APT pricing relation.

TYPES OF FACTOR MODELS

In this section we describe the different types of factor models.

Known Factors

The simplest case of factor models is where the K factors are assumed known or observable, so that we have time-series data on them. In this case, the K-factor model for the return-generating process as given by equation (5.2) is a multiple regression for each asset, and is a multivariate regression if all of the individual regressions are pooled together. For example, if one believes that the gross domestic product (GDP) is the driving force for a group of stock returns, one would have a one-factor model,

$$\tilde{r}_{it} - r_{ft} = \alpha_i + \beta_{i1}\tilde{GDP}_t + \tilde{\varepsilon}_{it}$$

The above equation corresponds to equation (5.1) with $K = 1$ and $f_1 = \tilde{GDP}$. In practice, one can obtain time-series data on both the asset returns and GDP, and then one can estimate the regressions to obtain all the parameters, including in particular the expected returns.

Another popular one-factor model is the market model regression

$$\tilde{r}_{it} - r_{ft} = \alpha_i + \beta_{i1}(\tilde{r}_{mt} - r_{ft}) + \tilde{\varepsilon}_{it}$$

where $\tilde{r}_{mt}$ is the return on a stock market index.

To understand the covariance matrix estimation, it will be useful to write the K-factor model in matrix form,

$$\tilde{R}_t = \alpha + \beta\tilde{f}_t + \tilde{\varepsilon}_t$$

or

$$\begin{bmatrix} \tilde{R}_{1t} \\ \vdots \\ \tilde{R}_{Nt} \end{bmatrix} = \begin{bmatrix} \alpha_1 \\ \vdots \\ \alpha_N \end{bmatrix} + \begin{bmatrix} \beta_{11} & \cdots & \beta_{1K} \\ \vdots & \ddots & \vdots \\ \beta_{N1} & \cdots & \beta_{NK} \end{bmatrix} \begin{bmatrix} \tilde{f}_{1t} \\ \vdots \\ \tilde{f}_{Kt} \end{bmatrix} + \begin{bmatrix} \tilde{\varepsilon}_{1t} \\ \vdots \\ \tilde{\varepsilon}_{Nt} \end{bmatrix}$$

where

$\tilde{R}_t$ = an N-vector of asset excess returns
α = an N-vector of the alphas
β = an $N \times K$ of betas or factor loadings
$\tilde{f}_t$ = a K-vector of the factors
$\tilde{\varepsilon}$ = an N-vector of the model residuals

For example, we can write a model with $N = 3$ assets and $K = 2$ factors as

$$\begin{bmatrix} \tilde{R}_{1t} \\ \tilde{R}_{2t} \\ \tilde{R}_{3t} \end{bmatrix} = \begin{bmatrix} \alpha_1 \\ \alpha_2 \\ \alpha_3 \end{bmatrix} + \begin{bmatrix} \beta_{11} & \beta_{12} \\ \beta_{21} & \beta_{22} \\ \beta_{31} & \beta_{32} \end{bmatrix} \begin{bmatrix} \tilde{f}_{1t} \\ \tilde{f}_{2t} \end{bmatrix} + \begin{bmatrix} \tilde{\varepsilon}_{1t} \\ \tilde{\varepsilon}_{2t} \\ \tilde{\varepsilon}_{3t} \end{bmatrix}$$

Taking covariance on both sides of equation (5.2), we have the return covariance matrix

$$\Sigma = \beta' \Sigma_f \beta + \Sigma_\varepsilon \tag{5.3}$$

where Σ_f is the covariance matrix of the factors, and Σ_ε is the covariance matrix of the residuals. Σ_f can be estimated by using the sample covariance matrix from the historical returns. This works for Σ_ε too if N is small relative to T. However, when N is large relative to T, the sample covariance matrix of the residuals will be poorly behaved.

Usually an additional assumption that the residuals are uncorrelated is imposed, so that Σ_ε becomes a diagonal matrix, and can then be estimated by using the sample variances of the residuals. Plugging in the estimates of all the parameters into the right-hand side of equation (5.3), we obtain the covariance matrix needed for applying mean-variance portfolio analysis.

In the estimation of a multifactor model, it is often implicitly assumed that the number of time series observations T is far greater than K, the number of factors. Otherwise, the regressions will perform poorly. For the case in which K is close to T, some special treatments are needed. This will be addressed later in this chapter.

Examples of Multifactor Models with Known Factors

Before discussing latent factors, let's briefly describe four multifactor models where known factors are used: (1) Fama-French three-factor model,[2] (2) MSCI Barra fundamental factor model,[3] (3) Burmeister-Ibbotson-Roll-Ross (BIRR) macroeconomic factor model,[4] and (4) Barclay Group Inc. factor model.[5] The first three are equity factor models and the last is a bond factor model.

The widely used Fama-French three-factor model is a special case of equation (5.1) with $K = 3$,

$$\tilde{r}_{it} - r_{ft} = \alpha_i + \beta_{im}(\tilde{r}_{mt} - r_{ft}) + \beta_{is}\tilde{SMB}_t + \beta_{ib}\tilde{HML}_t + \tilde{\varepsilon}_{it}$$

where $\tilde{r}_{mt}$ as before, is the return on a stock market index, $\tilde{SMB}_t$ and $\tilde{HML}_t$ are two additional factors. SMB_t (small minus big) is defined as the difference between the returns on diversified portfolios of small and big stocks (where small and big are measured in terms of stock market capitalization) and HML_t (high minus low) is defined as the difference between the returns on diversified portfolios of high and low book value-to-market value (B/M) stocks. The introduction of these factors by Fama and French is to better capture the systematic variation in average return for typical portfolios than using a stock market index alone. These factors are supported by empirical studies, and are consistent with classifying stocks in terms of growth and value.[6]

Fundamental factor models use company and industry attributes and market data as "descriptors." Examples are price–earnings ratios, book–price ratios, estimated earnings growth, and trading activity. The estimation of a fundamental factor model begins with an analysis of historical stock returns and descriptors about a company. In the MSCI Barra model, for example, the process of identifying the factors begins with monthly returns for hundreds of stocks that the descriptors must explain. Descriptors are

---

[2]See Eugene F. Fama and Kenneth R. French, "Common Risk Factors in the Returns on Stocks and Bonds," *Journal of Financial Economics* 33, no. 1 (1993): 3–56. For an extension of the Fama–French Model to four factors by a momentum factor, see Mark M. Carhart, "On Persistence in Mutual Fund Performance," *Journal of Finance* 52, no. 1 (1997): 57–82.

[3]A description of this model is provided in Chapter 13.

[4]See Edwin Burmeister, Richard R. Roll, and Stephen A. Ross, A Practitioner's Guide to Arbitrage Pricing Theory," in *A Practitioner's Guide to Factor Model* (Charlottesville, VA: Institute of Chartered Financial Analysts, 1993)

[5]A description of this factor model is provided in Chapter 21.

[6]See Chapter 9 for an explanation of equity style management and the meaning of growth and value.

not the "*r* factors" but instead they are the candidates for risk factors. The descriptors are selected in terms of their ability to explain stock returns. That is, all of the descriptors are potential risk factors but only those that appear to be important in explaining stock returns are used in constructing risk factors. Once the descriptors that are statistically significant in explaining stock returns are identified, they are grouped into "risk indexes" to capture related company attributes. For example, descriptors such as market leverage, book leverage, debt-to-equity ratio, and company's debt rating are combined to obtain a risk index referred to as "leverage." Thus, a risk index is a combination of descriptors that captures a particular attribute of a company. For example, in the MSCI Barra fundamental multifactor model, there are 13 risk indexes and 55 industry groups. The 55 industry classifications are further classified into sectors.

In a *macroeconomic factor model*, the inputs to the model are historical stock returns and observable macroeconomic variables. In the BIRR macroeconomic multifactor model, the macroeconomic variables that have been pervasive in explaining excess returns and which are therefore included in the market are:

- *The business cycle:* Changes in real output that are measured by percentage changes in the index of industrial production.
- *Interest rates:* Changes in investors' expectations about future interest rates that are measured by changes in long-term government bond yields.
- *Investor confidence:* Expectations about future business conditions as measured by changes in the yield spread between high- and low-grade corporate bonds.
- *Short-term inflation:* Month-to-month jumps in commodity prices, such as gold or oil, as measured by changes in the consumer price index.
- *Inflationary expectations:* Changes in expectations of inflation as measured by changes in the short-term risk-free nominal interest rate.

Additional variables, such as the real GDP growth and unemployment rates, are also among the macroeconomic factors used by asset managers in other macroeconomic multifactor models. Moreover, some asset managers also have identified technical variables, such as trading volume and market liquidity, as factors.

The Barclay Group Inc. (BGI) bond factor model (previously the Lehman bond factor model) uses two categories of systematic risk factors: term structure factors and nonterm structure risk factors. The former include changes in the level of interest and changes in the shape of the yield curve. The nonterm structure factors are sector risk, credit risk, optionality risk, and a series of risks associated with investing in mortgage-backed securities.[7]

The search for factors is a never-ending task of asset managers. In practice, many popular investment softwares use dozens of factors. Some academic studies, such as Ludvigson and Ng, use hundreds of them.[8]

Latent Factors

While some applications use observed factors, some use entirely latent factors; that is, they view that the factors f_t in the K-factor model,

$$\tilde{R}_t = \alpha + \beta \tilde{f}_t + \tilde{\varepsilon}_t$$

are not directly observable. An argument for the use of latent factors is that the observed factors may be measured with errors or have been already anticipated by investors. Without imposing what f_t are from our likely incorrect belief, we can statistically estimate the factors based on the factor model and data.

It important to understand that in the field of statistics, there is statistical methodology known as "factor analysis" and the model generated is referred to as a "factor model." Factor models as used by statisticians are statistical models that try to explain complex phenomena through a small number of basic causes or factors with the factors being latent. Factor models as used by statisticians serve two main purposes: (1) They reduce the dimensionality of models to make estimation possible; and (2) they find the true causes that drive data. In the following discussion of multifactor models, we are using the statistical tool of factor analysis to try to determine the latent factors driving asset returns.

While the estimation procedures for determining the set of factors is discussed in the next section, it will be useful to know some of the properties of the factor model here. The first property is that the factors are not uniquely defined in the model, but all sets of factors are linear combinations of each other. This is because if $\tilde{f}_t$ is a set of factors, then, for any $K \times K$ invertible matrix A, we have

$$\tilde{R}_t = \alpha + \beta \tilde{f}_t + \tilde{\varepsilon}_t = \alpha + (\beta A^{-1})(A \tilde{f}_t) + \tilde{\varepsilon}_t \tag{5.4}$$

which says that if $\tilde{f}_t$ with regression coefficients β (known as *factor loadings* in the context of factor models) explains well asset returns, so does $\tilde{f}_t^* = A \tilde{f}_t$

---

[7]Bond risk factors are described in Chapter 21.
[8]Sydney C. Ludvigson and Serena Ng, "The Empirical Risk-Return Relation: A Factor Analysis Approach," *Journal of Financial Economics* 83, no. 1 (2007): 171–222.

with loadings βA^{-1}. The linear transformation of $\tilde{f}_t$, $\tilde{f}_t^*$, is also known as a *rotation* of f_t.

The second property is that we can assume all the factors have zero mean (i.e., $E[\tilde{f}_t] = 0$). This is because if $\mu_f = E[f_t]$, then the factor model can be rewritten as

$$\tilde{R}_t = \alpha + \beta \tilde{f}_t + \tilde{\varepsilon}_t = (\alpha + \beta \mu_f) + \beta(\tilde{f}_t - \mu_f) + \tilde{\varepsilon}_t \qquad (5.5)$$

If we rename $\alpha + \beta \mu_f$ as the new alphas, and $f_t - \mu_f$ as the new factors, then the new factors will have zero means, and the new factor model is statistically the same as the old one. Hence, without loss of generality, we assume that the mean of the factors are zeros in our estimation in the next section.

Note that the return covariance matrix formula, equation (5.3) or

$$\Sigma = \beta' \Sigma_f \beta + \Sigma_\varepsilon \qquad (5.6)$$

holds regardless of whether the factors are observable or latent. However, through factor rotation, we can make a new set of factors so as to have the identity covariance matrix. In this case with $\Sigma_f = I_K$, we say that the factor model is *standardized*, and the covariance equation then simply becomes

$$\Sigma = \beta' \beta + \Sigma_\varepsilon \qquad (5.7)$$

In general, Σ_ε can have nonzero off-diagonal elements, implying that the residuals are correlated. If we assume that the residuals are uncorrelated, then Σ_ε becomes a diagonal matrix, and the factor model is known as a *strict factor model*. If we assume further that Σ_ε has equal diagonal elements, that is, $\Sigma_\varepsilon = \sigma^2 I_N$ for some $\sigma > 0$ with I_N an N identity matrix, then the factor model is known as a *normal factor model*.

Both Types of Factors

Rather than taking the view of either only observable factors or only latent factors, we can consider a more general factor model with both types of factors,

$$\tilde{R}_t = \alpha + \beta \tilde{f}_t + \beta_g \tilde{g}_t + \tilde{\varepsilon}_t \qquad (5.8)$$

where $\tilde{f}_t$ is a K-vector of latent factors, $\tilde{g}_t$ is an L-vector of observable factors, and β_g are the betas associated with $\tilde{g}_t$. This model makes intuitive sense. If we believe a few fundamental and macroeconomic factors are the driving forces, they can be used to create the $\tilde{g}_t$ vector. Since we may not account for all the possible factors, we need to add K unknown factors which are to be estimated from the data.

The estimation of the above factor model given by equation (5.8) usually involves two steps. In the first step, a regression of the asset returns on the known factors is run in order to obtain $\hat{\beta}_g$, an estimate of β_g. This allows us to compute the residuals,

$$\hat{u}_t = R_t - \hat{\beta}_g g_t \qquad (5.9)$$

that is, the difference of the asset returns from their fitted values by using the observed factors for all the time periods. Then, in the second step, a factor estimation approach is used to estimate the latent factors for $\hat{u}_t$,

$$\tilde{u}_t = \alpha + \beta \tilde{f}_t + \tilde{v}_t \qquad (5.10)$$

where $\tilde{u}_t$ is the random residuals whose realized values are $\hat{u}_t$. The estimation method for this model is the same as estimating a latent factor model, and will be detailed in the next section. With the factor estimates, we can treat the latent factors as known, and then use equation (5.8) to determine the expected asset returns and covariance matrix.

Predictive Factor Models

An important feature of factor models is that they use time t factors to explain time t returns. This is to estimate the long-run risk exposures of the assets, which are useful for both risk control and portfolio construction. On the other hand, portfolio managers are also very concerned about time-varying expected returns. In this case, they often use a predictive factor model such as the following to forecast the returns,

$$\tilde{R}_{t+1} = \alpha + \beta \tilde{f}_t + \beta_g \tilde{g}_t + \tilde{\varepsilon}_t \qquad (5.11)$$

where as before $\tilde{f}_t$ and $\tilde{g}_t$ are the latent and observable factors, respectively. The single difference is that the earlier $\tilde{R}_t$ is now replaced by $\tilde{R}_{t+1}$. Equation (5.11) uses time t factors to forecast future return $\tilde{R}_{t+1}$.

Computationally, the estimation of the predictive factor model is the same as for estimating the standard factor models. However, it should be emphasized that the regression R^2, a measure of model fitting, is usually very good in the explanatory factor models. For example, in a regression of industry portfolio returns on the market, the R^2 is usually in the range of 65% to 92%, indicating a good fitting or strong explanatory power. In contrast, if a predictive factor model is used to forecast the expected returns of various assets, the R^2 rarely exceeds 2%. This simply reflects the fact that assets returns are extremely difficult to predict in the real world. For example, one study finds that that the R^2 are mostly less than 1% when forecasting industry returns using a variety of past economic variables and past industry returns.[9]

FACTOR MODEL ESTIMATION

In this section, we provide first a step-by-step procedure for estimating the factor model based on the popular and implementable approach, the *principal components analysis* (PCA), to which a detailed and intuitive introduction is provided in the appendix. PCA is a statistical tool that is used by statisticians to determine factors with statistical learning techniques when factors are not observable. That is, given a variance–covariance matrix, a statisician can determine factors using the technique of PCA. Then, after introducing the computational procedure, we provide an application to identify three factors for bond returns. Finally, we outline some alternative procedures for estimating the factor models and their extensions.

Computational Procedure

Based on our latent models, we need to consider only how to estimate the latent factors $\tilde{f}_t$ from the K-factor model,

$$\tilde{Y}_t = \beta \tilde{f}_t + \tilde{\varepsilon}_t \tag{5.12}$$

where

$$E(\tilde{f}_t) = 0, \quad E[\tilde{Y}_t] = 0$$

This version of the factor model is obtained in two steps. We de-mean first the factor f_t so that the alphas are the expected returns of the assets. Second, we de-mean again the asset returns. In other words, we let $\tilde{Y}_t = \tilde{R}_t - \alpha$.

In practice, suppose that we have return data on N risky assets over T time periods. Then the realizations of the random variable $\tilde{Y}_t$ can be summarized by a matrix,

---

[9]David E. Rapach, Jack K. Strauss, Jun Tu, and Guofu Zhou, "Industry Return Predictability: Is It There Out of Sample?" Working paper, Washington University in St. Louis, 2009.

$$Y = \begin{pmatrix} Y_{11} & Y_{21} & \cdots & Y_{N1} \\ \vdots & \vdots & \vdots & \vdots \\ Y_{1T} & Y_{2T} & \cdots & Y_{NT} \end{pmatrix} \tag{5.13}$$

where the rows are the N asset returns subtracting from their sample means at time t for $t = 1, 2, \ldots, T$. Our task is to estimate the realizations (unobserved) on the K factors, $\tilde{f}_t$, over the T periods,

$$F = \begin{pmatrix} F_{11} & F_{21} & \cdots & F_{K1} \\ \vdots & \vdots & \vdots & \vdots \\ F_{1T} & F_{2T} & \cdots & F_{KT} \end{pmatrix} \tag{5.14}$$

We will now apply PCA estimation methodology

There are two important cases, both of which calling for a different way of applying PCA. The first case is the one of traditional factor analysis in which N is treated as fixed, and T is allowed to grow. We refer to his case as the "fixed N" below. The second case is N is allowed to grow but T is either fixed or allowed to grow. We refer to this case simply as "large N."

Case 1: Fixed N

In the case of fixed N, we have a relatively smaller number of assets and relatively large sample size. Then the covariance matrix of the asset returns, which is the same as the covariance matrix of $\tilde{Y}_t$, can be estimated by the sample covariance matrix,

$$\Psi = \frac{Y'Y}{T} \tag{5.15}$$

which is an N by N matrix since Y is T by N. For example, if we think there are K (say $K = 5$) factors, we can use standard software to compute the first K eigenvectors of Ψ corresponding to the first K largest eigenvalues of Ψ, each of which is an N vector. Let $\hat{\beta}$ be the N by K matrix formed by these K eigenvectors. Then $\hat{\beta}$ will be an estimate of β. Based on this, the factors are estimated by

$$\hat{F}_t = Y_t\hat{\beta}, \quad t = 1, 2, \ldots, T \tag{5.16}$$

where Y_t is the t-th row of Y, and $\hat{F}_t$ is the estimate of F_t, the t-th row of F. The $\hat{F}_t$'s are the estimated realizations of the first K factors. Seber explains why the $\hat{F}_t$'s are good estimates of the true and unobserved factor realizations.[10] However, theoretically, they, though close, will not necessarily converge to the true values, unless the factor model is normal, as T increases. Nevertheless, despite this problem, this procedure is widely used in practice.

Case 2: Large N

In the case of large N, we have a large number of assets. We now form a new matrix based on the product of Y with Y',

$$\Omega = \frac{YY'}{T} \tag{5.17}$$

which is a T by T matrix since Y is T by N. Given K, we use standard software to compute the first K eigenvectors of Ω corresponding to the first K largest eigenvalues of Ω, each of which is a T vector. Letting $\hat{F}$ be the T by K matrix formed by these K eigenvectors, the PCA says that $\hat{F}$ is an estimate of the true and unknown factor realizations F of equation (5.14), up to a linear transformation. Connor and Korajczyk provided the first study in the finance literature to apply the PCA as described above.[11] The method is also termed *asymptotic PCA* since it allows the number of assets to increase without bound. In contrast, traditional PCA keeps N fixed, while allowing the number of time periods, T, to be large.

Theoretically, if the true factor model is the strict factor model or is not much too different from it (i.e., the residual correlations are not too strong), Bai shows that $\hat{F}$ converges to F up to a linear transformation when both T and N increase without limit.[12] The estimation errors are of order the larger of $1/T$ or $1/\sqrt{N}$, and converge to zero as both T and N grow to infinity. However, when T is fixed, we need a stronger assumption that the the true factor model is close to a normal model, then the estimation errors are of order of $1/\sqrt{N}$. Intuitively, at each time t, given that there are only a few factors to pricing so many assets, we should have enough information to back out the factors accurately.

Based on the estimated factors, the factor loadings are easily estimated from equation (5.12). For example, we can obtain the loadings for each asset by estimating the standard ordinary least squares (OLS) regression of the asset returns on the factors. Mathematically, this is equivalent to computing all the loadings from the formula

---

[10]George Seber, *Multivariate Observations* (New York: John Wiley & Sons, 1984).
[11]Gregory Conner and Robert Korajzcyk, "Performance Measurement with the Arbitrage Pricing Theory: A New Framework For Analysis," *Journal of Financial Economics* 15 (1986): 373–394.
[12]Jushan Bai, "Inferential Theory for Factor Models of Large Dimensions," *Econometrica* 71, no. 1 (2003): 135–172.

$$\hat{\beta}' = (\hat{F}'\hat{F})^{-1}\hat{F}'X \qquad (5.18)$$

Under the same conditions above, ⎯⎯⎯ also converges to β up to a linear transformation.

The remaining question is how to determine K. In practice, this may be determined by trial and error depending on how different K's perform in model fitting and in meeting the objectives where the model is applied. From an econometrics perspective, there is a simple solution. Bai and Ng provide a statistical criterion[13]

$$IC(K) = \log(V(K)) + K\left(\frac{N+T}{NT}\right)\log\left(\frac{NT}{N+T}\right) \qquad (5.19)$$

where

$$V(K) = \sum_{i=1}^{N}\sum_{t=1}^{T}(Y_{it} - \hat{\beta}_{i1}\hat{f}_{1t} - \hat{\beta}_{i2}\hat{f}_{2t} - \cdots - \hat{\beta}_{iK}\hat{f}_{Kt})^2 \qquad (5.20)$$

For a given $K, V(K)$ is the sum of the fitted squared residual errors of the factor model across both asset and time. This is a measure of model fitting. The smaller the $V(K)$, the better the K-factor model in explaining the asset returns. So we want to choose such a K that minimizes $V(K)$. However, the more the factors, the smaller the $V(K)$, but at a cost of estimating more factors with greater estimation errors. Hence, we want to penalize too many factors. This is the same as the case in linear regressions where we also want to penalize too many regressors. The second term in equation (5.19) plays this role. It is an increasing function of K. Therefore, the trade-off between model fitting and estimation errors requires us to minimize the $IC(K)$ function. Theoretically, assuming that the factor model is indeed true for some fixed K^*, Bai and Ng show that the K that minimizes $IC(K)$ will converge to K^* as either N or T or both increase to infinity.

Alternative Approaches and Extensions

The standard statistical approach for estimating the factor model is the maximum likelihood (ML) method. Consider factor model given by equation (5.12) where $E(\tilde{f}_t) = 0, E[\tilde{Y}_t] = 0$. The de-meaned returns and standardized factors are usually assumed to have normal distributions.

---

[13]Jushan Bai and Serena Ng, "Determining the Number of Factors in Approximate Factor Models," *Econometrica* 70, no. 1 (2002): 191–221.

In addition, the factors are usually standardized so that $\Sigma_f = I_K$, and the residuals are assumed uncorrelated so that Σ_ε is diagonal. Then the log likelihood function, as the log density function of the returns, is

$$\log L(\beta, \Sigma_\varepsilon) = -\frac{NT}{2}\log(2\pi) - \frac{T}{2}\log|\beta'\beta + \Sigma_\varepsilon| - \frac{1}{2}\sum_{t=1}^{T} Y_{t'}(\beta'\beta + \Sigma_\varepsilon)^{-1} Y_t \quad (5.21)$$

The ML estimator of the parameters β and Σ_ε are those values that maximize the log likelihood function. Since β enters into the function in a complex nonlinear way, an analytical solution to the maximization problem is very difficult to obtain. Numerically, it is still difficult if maximizing $\log L(\beta, \Sigma_\varepsilon)$ directly.

There is, however, a data-augmentation technique known as the *expectation maximization* (EM) algorithm that can be applied.[14] The EM algorithm can be effective in numerically solving the earlier maximization problem. The idea of the EM algorithm is simple. The key difficulty here is that the factors are unobserved. But conditional on the parameters and the factor model, we can learn them. Consider now given the factors $\tilde{f}_t$, the log likelihood function conditional on f_t is

$$\log L_c(\beta, \Sigma_\varepsilon) = -\frac{NT}{2}\log(2\pi) - \frac{T}{2}\log|\Sigma_\varepsilon| - \frac{1}{2}\sum_{t=1}^{T}(Y_t - \beta f_t)'\Sigma_\varepsilon^{-1}(Y_t - \beta f_t) \quad (5.22)$$

Because it is conditional on f_t, the factor model is the usual linear regression. In other words, integrating out f_t from equation (5.22) yields the unconditional $\log L(\beta, \Sigma_\varepsilon)$. The beta estimates conditional on f_t are straightforward. They are the usual OLS regression coefficients, and the estimates for Σ_ε are the residual variances.

On the other hand, conditional on the parameters, we can learn the factors by using their conditional expected values obtained easily from their joint distribution with the returns. Hence, we can have an iterative algorithm. Starting from an initial guess of the factors, we maximizie the conditional likelihood function to obtain the OLS β and Σ_ε estimates, which is the M-step of the EM algorithm Based on these estimates, we update a new estimate of f_t using their expected value. This is the EM algortihm's E-step. Using the new f_t, we learn new estimates of β and Σ_ε in the M-step. With the new estimates, we can again update the f_t. Iterating between the EM steps, the limits converge to the unconditional ML estimate and the factor estimates converge to the true ones.

---

[14]Lehmann and Modest were the first in finance to apply the EM algorithm to study factor models. See Bruce N. Lehmann and David M. Modest, "The Empirical Foundations of the Arbitrage Pricing Theory," *Journal of Financial Economics* 21, no. 2 (1998): 213–254.

As an alternative to the ML method, Geweke and Zhou[15] propose a Bayesian approach which treats all parameters as random variables.[16] It works in a way similar to the EM algorithm. Conditional on parameters, we learn the factors, and conditional on the factors, we learn the parameters. Iterating after a few thousand times, we learn the entire joint distribution of the factors and parameters, which are all we need in a factor model. The advantage of the Bayesian approach is that it can incorporate prior information and can provide exact inference. In contrast, the ML method cannot use any priors, nor can it obtain the exact standard errors of both parameters and functions of interest due to complexity of the factor model. Nardari and Scruggs[17] extend the Bayesian approach to allow a more general model in which the covariance matrix can vary over time and the APT restrictions can be imposed.

Finally, we provide two important extensions of the factor model which are useful in practice. Note that the factors we discussed thus far assume identifical and independently distributed returns and factors. These are known as *static factor models*. The first extension is *dynamic factor models* which allow the factors to evolve over time according to a vector autoregression,

$$\tilde{f}_t = A_1 \tilde{f}_{t-1} + A_2 \tilde{f}_{t-2} + \cdots + A_m \tilde{f}_{t-m} + \tilde{v}_t \qquad (5.23)$$

where the As are the regression coefficient matrices, m is the order of the autoregression that determines how far past factor realizations still affect today's realizations, and v_t is the residual. In practice, many economic variables are highly persistent, and hence it will be important to incorporate this as above.[18]

The second extension is to allow the case with a large number of factors. Consider our earlier factor model

$$\tilde{R}_t = \alpha + \beta \tilde{f}_t + \beta_g \tilde{g}_t + \tilde{\varepsilon}_t \qquad (5.24)$$

[15]John Geweke and Guofu Zhou, "Measuring the Pricing Error of the Arbitrage Pricing Theory," *Review of Financial Studies* 9, no. 2 (1996): 557–587.

[16]For a discussion of Bayesian methods and their applications to finance, see Svetlozar T. Rachev, John S.J. Hsu, Biliana Bagasheva, and Frank J. Fabozzi, *Bayesian Methods in Finance* (Hoboken, N.J.: John Wiley & Sons, 2008).

[17]Federico Nardari and John Scruggs, "Bayesian Analysis of Linear Factor Models With Latent Factors, Multivariate Stochastic Volatility, and APT Pricing Restrictions," *Journal of Financial and Quantitative Analysis* 42, no. 4 (2007): 857–892.

[18]Amengual and Watson discuss the estimation for dynamic factor models. See Dante Amengual and Mark Watson, "Consistent Estimation of the Number of Dynamic Factors in a Large N and T Panel," *Journal of Business and Economic Statistics* 25, no. 1 (2007): 91–96.

where $\tilde{f}_t$ is a K vector of latent factors, $\tilde{g}_t$ is an L vector of observable factors. The problem now is that L is large, about 100 or 200, for instance. This requires at least a few hundred or more time series observations for the regression of R_t on g_t to be well behaved, and this can cause a problem due to the lack of long-term time series data or due to concerns of stationarity. The idea is to break $\tilde{g}_t$ into two sets, $\tilde{g}_{1t}$ and $\tilde{g}_{2t}$, with the first having a few key variables and the second having the rest. We then consider the modified model

$$\tilde{R}_t = \alpha + \beta \tilde{f}_t + \beta_{g1} \tilde{g}_{1t} + \beta_h \tilde{h}_t + \tilde{\varepsilon}_t \qquad (5.25)$$

where $\tilde{h}(t)$ has a few variables too that represents a few major driving forces that summarize the potentially hundreds of variables of $\tilde{g}_{2t}$ via another factor model,

$$\tilde{g}_{2t} = B\tilde{h}_t + \tilde{u}_t \qquad (5.26)$$

where $\tilde{u}_t$ is the residual. This second factor model provides a large dimension reduction that transforms the hundreds of variables into a few, which can be estimated by the PCA. In the end, we have only a few factors in equation (5.25), making the analysis feasible based on the methods we discussed earlier. Ludvigson and Ng[19] appear to be the first to apply such a model in finance. They find that the model can effectively incorporate a few hundred variables so as to make a significant difference in understanding stock market predictability.

KEY POINTS

- The Arbitrage Pricing Theory is a general multifactor model for pricing assets. The theory does not provide any specific information about what the factors are. Moreover, the APT does not make any claims on the number of factors either.
- The APT asserts that only taking the systematic risks are rewarded.
- The APT simply assumes that if the returns are driven by the factors, and if investors know the betas for the factors, then an arbitrage portfolio, which requires no investment but yields a positive return, can be formed if the APT pricing relation is violated in the market. In equilibrium, therfore, if there are no arbitrage opportunities, deviations from the APT pricing relation should not be observed.

---

[19]Sydney C. Ludvigsona and Serena Ng, "The Empirical Risk–Return Relation: A Factor Analysis Approach," *Journal of Financial Economics* 83, no. 1 (2007): 171–222.

- In practice, factor models are widely used as a tool for estimating expected asset returns and their covariance matrix. The reason is that if investors can identify the factors that drive asset returns, they will have much better estimates of the true expected asset returns and the covariance matrix, and hence to form a much better portfolio than otherwise possible.
- Factor model estimation depends crucially on (1) whether the factors are identified (known) and unidentified (latent) and (2) the sample size and the number of assets. Furthermore, factor models can be used not only for explaining asset returns, but also for predicting future returns.
- The simplest case of factor models is where the factors are assumed to be known or observable, so that time-series data are those factors can be used to estimate the model.
- In practice there are three commonly used equity multifactor models where known factors are used: (1) Fama-French three-factor model, (2) MSCI Barra fundamental factor model, and (3) the Burmeister-Ibbotson-Roll-Ross model macroeconomic factor model. Fundamental factor models use company and industry attributes and market data as descriptors. In a macroeconomic factor model, the inputs to the model are historical stock returns and observable macroeconomic variables.
- An argument for the use of latent factors is that the observed factors may be measured with errors or have been already anticipated by investors. Without imposing what the factors are from likely incorrect belief, asset managers can statistically estimate the factors based on the factor model and data.
- Two important extensions of the static factor model used in practice are (1) dynamic factor models, which allow the factors to evolve over time according to a vector autoregression; and (2) allowance for a large number of factors. This second factor model provides a large dimension reduction that transforms the hundreds of variables into a few, which can be estimated by the principal components analysis.
- Principal component analysis is a simple statistical approach that can be applied to estimate a factor model easily and effectively.

APPENDIX: PRINCIPAL COMPONENT ANALYSIS IN FINANCE

Principal component analysis (PCA) is a widely used tool in finance. It is useful not only for estimating factor models as explained in this chapter, but also for extracting a few driving variables in general out of many for the covariance matrix of asset returns. Hence, it is important to understand the statistical intuition behind it. To this end, we provide a simple introduction to it in this appendix.

Perhaps the best way to understand the PCA is to go through an example in detail. Suppose there are two risky assets, whose returns are denoted by $\tilde{r}_1$ and $\tilde{r}_2$, with covariance matrix

$$\Sigma = \begin{bmatrix} \sigma_1^2 & \sigma_{12} \\ \sigma_{21} & \sigma_2^2 \end{bmatrix} = \begin{bmatrix} 2.05 & 1.95 \\ 1.95 & 2.05 \end{bmatrix}$$

That is, we assume that they have the same variances of 2.05 and covariance of 1.95. Our objective is to find a linear combination of the two assets so that it has a large component in the covariance matrix, which will be clear below. For notation brevity, we assume first that the expected returns are zeros; that is,

$$E[\tilde{r}_1] = 0, \quad E[\tilde{r}_1] = 0$$

and will relax this assumption later in this appendix.

Recall from linear algebra that we call any vector $(a_1, a_2)'$ satisfying

$$\Sigma \begin{pmatrix} a_1 \\ a_2 \end{pmatrix} = \lambda \begin{pmatrix} a_1 \\ a_2 \end{pmatrix}$$

an eigenvector of Σ, and the associated λ the eigenvalue. In our example here, it is easy to verify that

$$\begin{bmatrix} 2.05 & 1.95 \\ 1.95 & 2.05 \end{bmatrix} \cdot \begin{pmatrix} 1 \\ 1 \end{pmatrix} = 4 \times \begin{pmatrix} 1 \\ 1 \end{pmatrix}$$

and

$$\begin{bmatrix} 2.05 & 1.95 \\ 1.95 & 2.05 \end{bmatrix} \cdot \begin{pmatrix} 1 \\ -1 \end{pmatrix} = 0.1 \times \begin{pmatrix} 1 \\ -1 \end{pmatrix}$$

so 4 and 0.1 are the eigenvalues, and $(1,1)'$ and $(1,-1)'$ are the eigenvectors.

In practice, computer software is available to compute the eigenvalue and eigenvectors of any covariance matrix. The mathematical result is that for a covariance matrix of N assets, there are exactly N different eigenvectors and N associated positive eigenvalues (these eigenvalues can be equal in some cases). Moreover, the eigenvectors are orthogonal to each other; that is, their inner product or vector product is zero. In our example, it is clear that

$$(1,\ 1)' \cdot \begin{pmatrix} 1 \\ -1 \end{pmatrix} = 1 - 1 = 0$$

It should be noted that the eigenvalue associated with each eigenvector is unique, but any scale of the eigenvector remains an eigenvector. In our example, it is obvious that a double of the first eigenvector, $(2,2)'$, is also an eigenvector. However, the eigenvectors will be unique if we standardize them, making the sum of the elements be 1. In our example,

$$A_1 = \begin{bmatrix} 1/\sqrt{2} \\ 1/\sqrt{2} \end{bmatrix}, \quad A_2 = \begin{bmatrix} 1/\sqrt{2} \\ -1/\sqrt{2} \end{bmatrix}$$

are the standardized eigenvectors, which are obtained by scaling the earlier eigenvectors by $1/\sqrt{2}$. These are indeed standardized since

$$A_1'A_1 = (1/\sqrt{2})^2 + (1/\sqrt{2})^2 = 1$$
$$A_2'A_2 = (1/\sqrt{2})^2 + (-1/\sqrt{2})^2 = 1$$

Now let us consider two linear combinations (or portfolios without imposing the weights summing to 1) of the two assets whose returns are $\tilde{r}_1$ and $\tilde{r}_2$,

$$\tilde{P}_1 = \frac{1}{\sqrt{2}}\tilde{r}_1 + \frac{1}{\sqrt{2}}\tilde{r}_2 = A_1'\tilde{R}$$
$$\tilde{P}_2 = \frac{1}{\sqrt{2}}\tilde{r}_1 - \frac{1}{\sqrt{2}}\tilde{r}_2 = A_2'\tilde{R}$$

where $\tilde{R} = (\tilde{r}_1, \tilde{r}_2)'$. Both $\tilde{P}_1$ and $\tilde{P}_2$ are called the *principal components* (PCs). There are three important and interesting mathematical facts about the PCs.

- *Fact 1.* The variances of the PCs are exactly equal to the eigenvalues corresponding the eigenvectors used to form the PCs.

That is,

$$Var(\tilde{P}_1) = 4$$
$$Var(\tilde{P}_2) = 1$$

Note that the two PCs are random variables since they are the linear combination of random returns. So, their variances are well defined. The equalities to the eigenvalues can be verified directly.

- *Fact 2*. The returns can also be written as a linear combinations of the PCs.

The PCs are defined as linear combinations of the returns. Inverting them, the returns are linear functions of the PCs too. Mathematically, $\tilde{P} = A\tilde{R}$, and so $\tilde{R} = A^{-1}\tilde{P}$. Since A is orthogonal, $A^{-1} = A'$, thus $\tilde{R} = A'\tilde{P}$. That is, we have

$$\tilde{r}_1 = \frac{1}{\sqrt{2}}\tilde{P}_1 + \frac{1}{\sqrt{2}}\tilde{P}_2$$
$$\tilde{r}_2 = \frac{1}{\sqrt{2}}\tilde{P}_1 - \frac{1}{\sqrt{2}}\tilde{P}_2 \tag{5A.1}$$

- *Fact 3*. The asset return covariance matrix can be decomposed as the sum of the products of eigenvalues with the cross products of eigenvectors.

Mathematically, it is known that

$$\Sigma = [A_1, A_2]\begin{bmatrix} \lambda_1 & 0 \\ 0 & \lambda_2 \end{bmatrix}[A_1, A_2]'$$
$$= \lambda_1 A_1 A_1' + \lambda_2 A_2 A_2' = 4A_1 A_1' + 0.1A_2 A_2'$$

which is also easy to verify in our example. The economic interpretation is that the total risk profile of the two assets, as captured by their covariance matrix, is a sum of two components. The first component is determined by the first PC, and the second is determined by the second PC. In other words, in the return linear combinations, equation (5A.1), if we ignore P_2, we will get only $\lambda_1 A_1 A_1'$, the first component in the covariance matrix decomposition, and only the second if we ignore P_1. We obtain the entire Σ if we ignore neither.

The purpose of the PCA is finally clear. Since 4 is 40 times as big as 0.1, the second component in the Σ decomposition has little impact, and hence may be ignored. Then, ignoring $\tilde{P}_2$, we can write the returns simply as, based on equation (5A.1),

$$\tilde{r}_1 \approx (1/\sqrt{2})\tilde{P}_1$$
$$\tilde{r}_2 \approx (1/\sqrt{2})\tilde{P}_1$$

This says that we can reduce the analysis of $\tilde{r}_1$ and $\tilde{r}_2$ by analyzing simple functions of $\tilde{P}_1$. In this example, the result tells us that the two assets are almost the same. In practice, there may be hundreds of assets. By using PCA, we can reduce the dimensionality of the problem substantially to an analysis of perhaps a few, say five, PCs.

In general, when there are N assets with return $\tilde{R} = (\tilde{r}_1, \ldots, \tilde{r}_N)'$, computer software can be used to obtain the N eigenvalues and N standardized eigenvectors. Let $\lambda_1 \geq \lambda_2 \geq \ldots \geq \lambda_N \geq 0$ be the N eigenvalues in decreasing order, and $A_i = (a_{i1}, a_{i2}, \ldots, a_{iN})'$ be the standardized eigenvector associated with λ_i, and A be an $N \times N$ matrix formed by the all the eigenvectors. Then, the i-th PC is defined as $\tilde{P}_i = A_i'\tilde{R}$, all of which can be computed in matrix form,

$$
\tilde{P} = \begin{bmatrix} \tilde{P}_1 \\ \tilde{P}_2 \\ \vdots \\ \tilde{P}_N \end{bmatrix} = \begin{bmatrix} A_1'\tilde{R} \\ A_2'\tilde{R} \\ \vdots \\ A_N'\tilde{R} \end{bmatrix} = A'\tilde{R} \tag{5A.2}
$$

The decomposition for Σ is

$$
\Sigma = [A_1, \ldots, A_N] \begin{bmatrix} \lambda_1 & 0 & \cdots & 0 \\ 0 & \lambda_2 & \cdots & 0 \\ 0 & 0 & \cdots & \lambda_N \end{bmatrix} [A_1, \ldots, A_N]' \tag{5A.3}
$$

$$
= \lambda_1 A_1 A_1' + \lambda_2 A_2 A_2' + \cdots + \lambda_N A_N A_N'
$$

It is usually the case that, for some K, the first K eigenvalues are large, and the rest are too small, and can then be ignored. In such situations, based on the first K PCs, we can approximate the asset returns by

$$
\begin{aligned}
\tilde{r}_1 &\approx a_{11}\tilde{P}_1 + a_{12}\tilde{P}_2 + \cdots + a_{1K}\tilde{P}_K \\
\tilde{r}_2 &\approx a_{21}\tilde{P}_1 + a_{22}\tilde{P}_2 + \cdots + a_{2K}\tilde{P}_K \\
&\vdots \qquad \vdots \qquad \qquad \vdots \\
\tilde{r}_N &\approx a_{N1}\tilde{P}_1 + a_{N2}\tilde{P}_2 + \cdots + a_{NK}\tilde{P}_K
\end{aligned} \tag{5A.4}
$$

In most studies, the K PCs may be interpreted as K factors that (approximately) derive the movements of all the N returns. Our earlier example is a case with $K = 1$ and $N = 2$.

In the above PCA discussion, the expected returns of the asset are assumed to be zero. If they are nonzero and given by a vector $(\mu_1, \mu_2, \ldots, \mu_N)'$, Σ will remain the same, and so will the eigenvalues and eigenvectors. However, in this case we need to replace all the $\tilde{r}_i$'s in equation (5A.2) by

$\tilde{r}_i - \mu_i$'s, and add μ_i's on the right-hand side of equation (5A.4). The interpretation will be, of course, the same as before.

In Case 1 of the factor model estimation (i.e., known or observable factors) discussed in the chapter, the K PCs clearly provide a good approximation of the first K factors since they explain the asset variations the most given K. Moreover, in either Case 1 or Case 2 (latent factors), the PCA is equivalent to minimizing the model errors, as given by equation (5.20), by choosing both the loadings and factors, and hence the solution should be close to the true factors and loadings.

QUESTIONS

1. a. What does the arbitrage pricing theory as formulated by Stephen Ross say about factors and the number of factors?
   b. What is meant by a factor beta?

2. a. In the estimation of a multifactor model, what is the implicit assumption about the number of observations in a time series used to estimate the model and the number of factors?
   b. Why is this assumption important?

3. What is meant by a fundamental factor model?

4. a. What is meant by latent factors?
   b. How are latent factors estimated?
   c. Why do statisticians use factor models?

5. What are the steps involved in estimating a multifactor model that includes both known and latent factors?

CHAPTER 6

Modeling Asset Price Dynamics

Dessislava A. Pachamanova, Ph.D.
Associate Professor of Operations Research
Babson College

Frank J. Fabozzi, Ph.D., CFA, CPA
Professor in the Practice of Finance
Yale School of Management

Many classical asset pricing models, such as the Capital Asset Pricing Theory and the Arbitrage Pricing Theory, take a myopic view of investing: They consider events that happen one time period ahead, where the length of the time period is determined by the investor. In this chapter, we present apparatus that can handle asset dynamics and volatility over time. The dynamics of price processes in discrete time increments are typically described by two kinds of models: *trees* (such as *binomial trees*) and *random walks*. When the time increment used to model the asset price dynamics becomes infinitely small, we talk about *stochastic processes in continuous time*.

In this chapter, we introduce the fundamentals of binomial tree and random walk models, providing examples for how they can be used in practice. We briefly discuss the special notation and terminology associated with stochastic processes at the end of this chapter; however, our focus is on interpretation and simulation of processes in discrete time. The roots for the techniques we describe are in physics and the other natural sciences. They were first applied in finance at the beginning of the twentieth century, and have represented the foundations of asset pricing ever since.

FINANCIAL TIME SERIES

Let us first introduce some definitions and notation. A financial *time series* is a sequence of observations of the values of a financial variable, such as an

EXHIBIT 6.1   S&P 500 Index Level Between August 19, 2005, and August 19, 2009

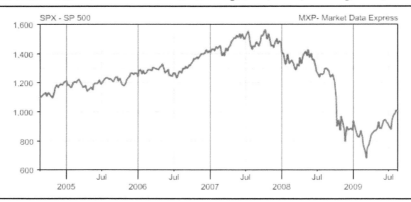

asset price (index level) or asset (index) returns, over time. Exhibit 6.1 shows an example of a time series, consisting of weekly observations of the S&P 500 price level over a period of five years (August 19, 2005, to August 19, 2009).

When we describe a time series, we talk about its drift and volatility. The term *drift* is used to indicate the direction of any observable trend in the time series. In the example shown in Exhibit 6.1, it appears that the S&P 500 time series has a positive drift up from August 2005 until about the middle of 2007, as the level of prices appears to have been generally increasing over that time period. From the middle of 2007 until the beginning of 2009, there is a negative drift. The volatility was smaller (the time series was less "squiggly") from August 2005 until about the middle of 2007, but increased dramatically between the middle of 2007 and the beginning of 2009.

We are usually interested also in whether the volatility increases when the price level increases, decreases when the price level increases, or remains constant independently of the current price level. In this example, the volatility was lower when the price level was increasing, and was higher when the price level was decreasing. Finally, we talk about the *continuity* of the time series—is the time series smooth, or are there jumps whose magnitude appears to be large relative to the price movements the rest of the time? From August 2005 until about the middle of 2007, the time series is quite smooth. However, some dramatic drops in price levels can be observed between the middle of 2007 and the beginning of 2009—notably in the fall of 2008.

For the remainder of this chapter, we will use the following notation:

- S_t is the value of underlying variable (price, interest rate, index level, etc.) at time t.
- S_{t+1} is the value of underlying variable (price, interest rate, etc.) at time $t + 1$.

- ω_t is the random error term observed at time t. (For the applications in this chapter, it will follow a normal distribution with mean equal to 0 and standard deviation equal to σ.)
- ε_t is the realization of a normal random variable with mean equal to 0 and standard deviation equal to 1 at time t.

BINOMIAL TREES

Binomial trees (also called *binomial lattices*) provide a natural way to model the dynamics of a random process over time. The initial value of the security S_0 (at time 0) is known. The length of a time period, Δt, is specified before the tree is built.[1] The binomial tree model assumes that at the next time period, only two values are possible for the price; that is, the price may go up with probability p or down with probability $(1 - p)$. Usually, these values are represented as multiples of the price at the beginning of the period. The factor u is used for an up movement, and d is used for a down movement. For example, the two prices at the end of the first time period are $u \cdot S_0$ and $d \cdot S_0$. If the tree is recombining, there will be three possible prices at the end of the second time period: $u^2 \cdot S_0$, $u \cdot d \cdot S_0$, and $d^2 \cdot S_0$. Proceeding in a similar manner, we can build the tree in Exhibit 6.2.

EXHIBIT 6.2   Example of a Binomial Tree

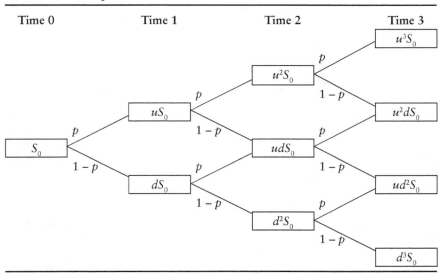

[1]The symbol Δ is often used to denote *difference*. The notation Δt therefore means time difference, that is, length of one time period.

The binomial tree model may appear simple because, given a current price, it only allows for two possibilities for the price at each time period. However, if the length of the time period is small, it is possible to represent a wide range of values for the price after only a few steps. To see this, notice that each step in the tree can be thought of as a Bernoulli trial[2]—it is a "success" with probability p, and a "failure" with probability $(1 - p)$. (The definition of success and failure here is arbitrary because an increase in price is not always desirable, but we define them in this way for the example's sake.) After n steps, each particular value for the price will be reached by realizing k successes and $(n - k)$ failures, where k is a number between 0 and n. The probability of reaching each value for the price after n steps will be

$$P(k \text{ successes}) = \frac{n!}{k!(n-k)!} p^k (1-p)^{n-k}$$

For large values of n, the shape of the binomial distribution becomes more and more symmetric, and the range of possible values looks like a continuum. (See Exhibit 6.3.) In fact, it approximates a normal distribution with specific mean and standard deviation related to the probability of success and the number of trials.[3] (See Exhibit 6.4 for a graph of the standard normal distribution, which has a mean of zero and a standard deviation of 1.) One can therefore represent a large range of values for the price as long as the number of time periods used in the binomial tree is large. Practitioners often use also trinomial trees, that is, trees with three branches emanating from each node, in order to obtain a better representation of the range of possible prices in the future.

ARITHMETIC RANDOM WALKS

Instead of assuming that at each step the asset price can only move up or down by a certain multiple with a given probability, we could assume that the price moves by an amount that follows a normal distribution with mean μ and standard deviation σ. In other words, the price for each period is determined from the price of the previous period by the equation

$$S_{t+1} = S_t + \mu + \tilde{\omega}_t$$

[2]One can think of the Bernoulli random variable as the numerical coding of the outcome of a coin toss, where one outcome is considered a "success" and one outcome is considered a "failure." The Bernoulli random variable takes the value 1 ("success") with probability p, and the value of 0 ("failure") with probability $1 - p$.
[3]The normal distribution is a continuous probability distribution. It is represented by a bell-shaped curve, and the shape of the curve is entirely described by the distribution mean and variance.

EXHIBIT 6.3   Binomial Distribution

A.

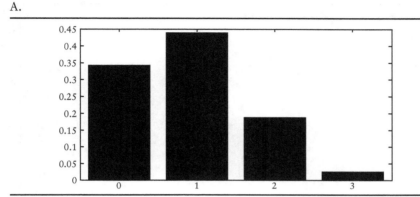

B.

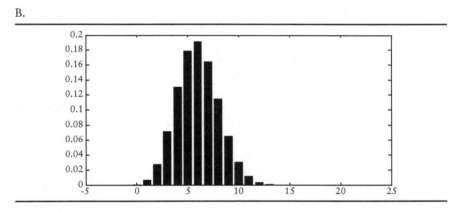

C.

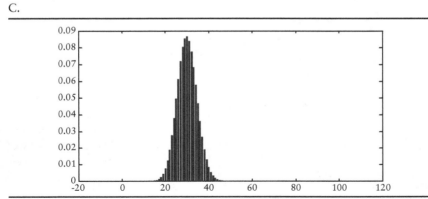

Note: Probability of success (p) assumed to be 0.3. Number of trials (A) $n = 3$; (B) $n = 20$; (C) $n = 100$.

EXHIBIT 6.4   Standard Normal Distribution

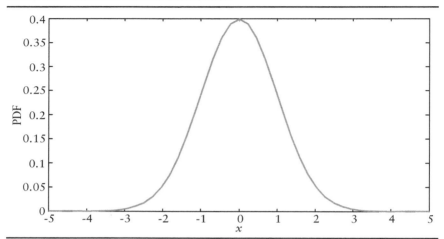

where $\tilde{\omega}_t$ is a normal random variable with mean 0 and standard deviation σ. We will also assume that the random variable $\tilde{\omega}_t$ describing the change in the price in one time period is independent of the random variables describing the change in the price in any other time period.[4] A sequence of independent and identically distributed (IID) random variables $\tilde{\omega}_0, \dots, \tilde{\omega}_t, \dots$ with zero mean and finite variance σ^2 is sometimes referred to as *white noise*.

The movement of the price expressed through the equation above is called an *arithmetic random walk with drift*. The drift term, μ, represents the average change in price over a single time period. Note that for every time period t, we can write the equation for the arithmetic random walk as

$$
\begin{aligned}
S_t &= S_{t-1} + \mu + \tilde{\omega}_{t-1} \\
&= (S_{t-2} + \mu + \tilde{\omega}_{t-2}) + \mu + \tilde{\omega}_{t-1} \\
&= (S_{t-3} + \mu + \tilde{\omega}_{t-3}) + 2 \cdot \mu + \tilde{\omega}_{t-1} + \tilde{\omega}_{t-2} \\
&= \cdots \\
&= S_0 + \mu \cdot t + \sum_{i=0}^{t-1} \tilde{\omega}_i
\end{aligned}
$$

Therefore, an arithmetic random walk can be thought of as a sum of two terms: A deterministic straight line $S_t = S_0 + \mu \cdot t$ and a sum of all past noise terms (see Exhibit 6.5).

---

[4]This is known as the *Markov property*. It implies that past prices are irrelevant for forecasting the future, and only the current value of the price is relevant for predicting the price in the next time period.

EXHIBIT 6.5   Five Paths of an Arithmetic Random Walk Assuming $\mu = -0.1697$ and $\sigma = 3.1166$

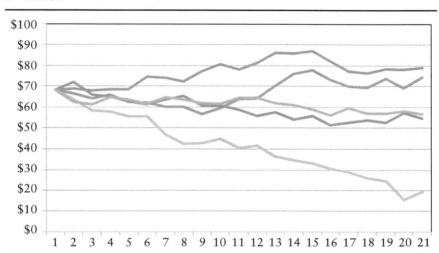

Simulation

The equation for the arithmetic random walk can be expressed also as

$$S_{t+1} = S_t + \mu + \sigma \cdot \tilde{\varepsilon}_t$$

where $\tilde{\varepsilon}_t$ is a standard normal random variable.[5] This equation makes it easy to generate paths for the arithmetic random walk by simulation. All we need is a way of generating the normal random variables $\tilde{\varepsilon}_t$.

We start with an initial price S_0, which is known. We also know the values of the drift μ and the volatility σ over one period. To generate the price at the next time period, S_1, we add μ to S_0, simulate a normal random

---

[5]To show this, we need to mention that every normal distribution can be expressed in terms of the standard normal distribution, which has mean of 0 and standard deviation of 1. Namely, if $\tilde{\varepsilon}$ is a standard normal variable with mean 0 and standard deviation 1, and $\tilde{x}$ is a normal random variable with mean μ and standard deviation σ, we have

$$\tilde{\varepsilon} = \frac{\tilde{x} - \mu}{\sigma} \quad \text{(equivalently, } \tilde{x} = \sigma \cdot \tilde{\varepsilon} + \mu)$$

This is a property unique to the normal distribution—no other family of probability distributions can be transformed in the same way. In the context of the equation for the arithmetic random walk, we have a normal random variable $\tilde{\omega}$ with mean 0 and standard deviation σ. It can be expressed through a standard normal variable $\tilde{\varepsilon}_t$ as $\sigma \cdot \tilde{\varepsilon} + 0$.

variable from a standard normal distribution, multiply it by σ, and add it to $S_0 + \mu$. At the next step (time period 2), we use the price at time period 1 we already generated, S_1, add to it μ, simulate a new random variable from a standard normal distribution, multiply it by σ, and add it to $S_1 + \mu$. We proceed in the same way until we generate the desired number of steps of the random walk.[6]

Parameter Estimation

In order to simulate paths of the arithmetic random walk, we need to have estimates of the parameters (μ and σ). We need to assume that these parameters remain constant over the time period of estimation. Note that the equation for the arithmetic random walk can be written as

$$S_{t+1} - S_t = \mu + \sigma \cdot \tilde{\varepsilon}_t$$

Given a historical series of T prices for an asset, we can therefore do the following to estimate μ and σ:

1. Compute the price changes $S_{t+1} - S_t$ for each time period t, $t = 0,..., T-1$.
2. Estimate the drift of the arithmetic random walk, μ, as the average of all the price changes.
3. Estimate the volatility of the arithmetic random walk, σ, as the standard deviation of all the price changes.

An important point to keep in mind is the units in which the parameters are estimated. If we are given time series in monthly increments, then the estimates of μ and σ we will obtain through steps 1 through 3 will be for monthly drift and monthly volatility. If we then need to simulate future paths for monthly observations, we can use the same μ and σ. However, if, for example, we need to simulate weekly observations, we will need to adjust μ and σ to account for the difference in the length of the time period. In general, the parameters should be stated as annual estimates. The annual estimates can then be adjusted for daily, weekly, monthly, etc. increments.

For example, suppose that we have estimated the weekly drift and the weekly volatility. To convert the weekly drift to an annual drift, we multiply the number we found for the weekly drift by 52, the number of weeks in a year. To convert the weekly volatility to annual volatility, we multiply the number we found for the weekly volatility by the square root of the number of weeks in a year, i.e., by $\sqrt{52}$. Conversely, if we are given annualized

---

[6]For example, given a current price S, in Microsoft Excel the price for the next time period can be generated with the formula $S + \mu + \sigma*NORMINV(RAND(),0,1)$.

values for the drift and the volatility, we can obtain weekly values by dividing the annual drift and the volatility by 52 and $\sqrt{52}$, respectively.

Arithmetic Random Walks: Some Additional Facts

In general, if we use the arithmetic random walk model, any price in the future, S_t, can be expressed through the initial (known) price S_0 as

$$S_t = S_0 + \mu \cdot t + \sigma \cdot \sum_{i=0}^{t-1} \tilde{\varepsilon}_i$$

The random variable corresponding to the sum of t independent normal random variables $\tilde{\varepsilon}_0, \ldots, \tilde{\varepsilon}_{t-1}$ is a normal random variable with mean equal to the sum of the means and standard deviation equal to the square root of the sum of variances. Since $\tilde{\varepsilon}_0, \ldots, \tilde{\varepsilon}_{t-1}$ are independent standard normal variables, their sum is a normal variable with mean 0 and standard deviation equal to

$$\underbrace{\sqrt{1 + \ldots + 1}}_{t \text{ times}} = \sqrt{t}$$

Therefore, we can have a closed-form expression for computing the asset price at time t given the asset price at time 0:

$$S_t = S_0 + \mu \cdot t + \sigma \cdot \sqrt{t} \cdot \tilde{\varepsilon}$$

where $\tilde{\varepsilon}$ is a standard normal random variable.

Based on the discussion so far in this section, we can state the following observations about the arithmetic random walk:

- The arithmetic random walk has a constant drift μ and volatility σ, that is, at every time period, the change in price is normally distributed, on average equal to μ, with a standard deviation of σ.
- The overall noise in a random walk never decays. The price change over t time periods is distributed as a normal distribution with mean equal to $\mu \cdot t$ and standard deviation equal to $\sigma\sqrt{t}$. That is why in industry one often encounters the phrase "The uncertainty grows with the square root of time."
- Prices that follow an arithmetic random walk meander around a straight line $S_t = S_0 + \mu \cdot t$. They may depart from the line, and then cross it again.
- Because the distribution of future prices is normal, we can theoretically find the probability that the future price at any time will be within a given range.

- Because the distribution of future prices is normal, future prices can theoretically take infinitely large or infinitely small values. Thus, they can be negative, which is an undesirable consequence of using the model.

Asset prices, of course, cannot be negative. In practice, the probability of the price becoming negative can be made quite small as long as the drift and the volatility parameters are selected carefully. However, the possibility of generating negative prices with the arithmetic random walk model is real.

Another problem with the assumptions underlying the arithmetic random walk is that the change in the asset price is drawn from the same random probability distribution, independent of the current level of the prices. A more natural model is to assume that the parameters of the random probability distribution for the change in the asset price vary depending on the current price level. For example, a $1 change in a stock price is more likely when the stock price is $100 than when it is $4. Empirical studies confirm that over time, asset prices tend to grow, and so do fluctuations. Only returns appear to remain stationary, that is, to follow the same probability distribution over time. A more realistic model for asset prices may therefore be that returns are an IID sequence. We describe such a model in the next section.

GEOMETRIC RANDOM WALKS

Consider the following model:

$$r_t = \mu + \sigma \cdot \tilde{\varepsilon}_t$$

where $\tilde{\varepsilon}_0, \ldots, \tilde{\varepsilon}_t$ is a sequence of independent normal variables, and r_t, the return, is computed as

$$r_t = \frac{S_{t+1} - S_t}{S_t}$$

Returns are therefore normally distributed, and the return over each interval of length 1 has mean μ and standard deviation σ. How can we express future prices if returns are determined by the equations above?

Suppose we know the price at time t, S_t. The price at time $t + 1$ can be written as

$$S_{t+1} = S_t \cdot \frac{S_{t+1}}{S_t}$$

$$= S_t \cdot \left(\frac{S_t}{S_t} + \frac{S_{t+1} - S_t}{S_t} \right)$$

$$= S_t \cdot \left(1 + \frac{S_{t+1} - S_t}{S_t}\right)$$

$$= S_t \cdot \left(1 + \tilde{r}_t\right)$$

$$= S_t + \mu \cdot S_t + \sigma \cdot S_t \cdot \tilde{\varepsilon}_t$$

This last equation is very similar to the equation for the arithmetic random walk, except that the price from the previous time period appears as a factor in all of the terms.

The equation for the geometric random walk makes it clear how paths for the geometric random walk can be generated. As in the case of the arithmetic random walk, all we need is a way of generating the normal random variables $\tilde{\varepsilon}_t$. We start with an initial price S_0, which is known. We also know the values of the drift μ and the volatility σ over one period. To generate the price at the next time period, S_1, we add $\mu \cdot S_0$ to S_0, simulate a normal random variable from a standard normal distribution, multiply it by σ and S_0, and add it to $S_0 + \mu \cdot S_0$. At the next step (time period 2), we use the price at time period 1 we already generated, S_1, add to it $\mu \cdot S_1$, simulate a new random variable from a standard normal distribution, multiply it by σ and S_1, and add it to $S_1 + \mu \cdot S_1$. We proceed in the same way until we generate the desired number of steps of the geometric random walk.[7]

Using similar logic to the derivation of the price equation earlier, we can express the price at any time t in terms of the known initial price S_0. Note that we can write the price at time t as

$$S_t = S_0 \cdot \frac{S_1}{S_0} \cdot \ldots \cdot \frac{S_{t-1}}{S_{t-2}} \cdot \frac{S_t}{S_{t-1}}$$

Therefore,

$$S_t = S_0 \cdot \left(1 + \tilde{r}_0\right) \cdot \ldots \cdot \left(1 + \tilde{r}_{t-1}\right)$$

In the case of the arithmetic random walk, we determined that the price at any time period follows a normal distribution. This was because if we know the starting price S_0, the price at any time period could be obtained by adding a sum of independent normal random variables to a constant term and S_0. The sum of independent normal random variables is a normal random variable itself. In the equation for the geometric random walk, each of the terms $\left(1 + \tilde{r}_0\right), \ldots, \left(1 + \tilde{r}_{t-1}\right)$ is a normal random variable as well. (It is the sum of a normal random variable and a constant.) However, they are

---

[7]For example, given a current price S, in Excel the price for the next time period can be generated with the formula $S + \mu*S + \sigma*S*\text{NORMINV(RAND(),0,1)}$.

multiplied together. The product of normal random variables is not a normal random variable, which means that we cannot have a nice closed-form expression for computing the price S_t based on S_0.

To avoid this problem, let us consider the natural logarithm of prices.[8] If we take logarithms of both sides of the equation for S_t, we get

$$\ln(S_t) = \ln\left(S_0 \cdot (1+\tilde{r}_0) \cdot \ldots \cdot (1+\tilde{r}_{t-1})\right)$$
$$= \ln(S_0) + \ln\left(1+\tilde{r}_0\right) + \ldots + \ln\left(1+\tilde{r}_{t-1}\right)$$

Log returns are in fact differences of log prices. To see this, note that

$$\ln(1+r_t) = \ln\left(1+\frac{S_{t+1}-S_t}{S_t}\right)$$
$$= \ln\left(\frac{S_{t+1}}{S_t}\right)$$
$$= \ln\left(S_{t+1}\right) - \ln\left(S_t\right)$$

Now assume that log returns (not returns) are independent, and follow a normal distribution with mean μ and standard deviation σ:

$$\ln(1+\tilde{r}_t) = \ln(S_{t+1}) - \ln(S_t) = \mu + \sigma \cdot \tilde{\varepsilon}_t$$

As a sum of independent normal variables, the expression

$$\ln(S_0) + \ln(1+\tilde{r}_0) + \ldots + \ln(1+\tilde{r}_{t-1})$$

is also normally distributed. This means that $\ln(S_t)$ (rather than S_t) is normally distributed, that is, S_t is a lognormal random variable.[9,10]

---

[8]In many references, as well as software packages such as Excel, the abbreviation used for the natural logarithm is ln. The natural logarithm is the function ln so that $e^{\ln(x)} = x$, where e is the number 2.7182.... Unless otherwise specified, we use "logarithm" to refer to the natural logarithm, that is, the logarithm of base e.
[9]If $\tilde{Y}$ is a normal random variable, then the random variable $\tilde{X} = e^{\tilde{Y}}$ is lognormal. In this case, $\ln(S_t)$ is a normal random variable. Therefore, $e^{\ln(S_t)}$, i.e., S_t, is lognormally distributed.
[10]As a general matter, if the logarithm of a random variable is normally distributed, then the random variable itself follows a lognormal distribution. The lognormal distribution has a very convenient property, which is that products of independent lognormal random variables are themselves lognormal random variables. This is another way to see that S_t is a lognormal random variable given S_0: it is a product of lognormal random variables, scaled by a constant (S_0):
$$S_t = (1+\tilde{r}_{t-1}) \cdot \ldots \cdot (1+\tilde{r}_0) \cdot S_0$$

In fact, similarly to the case of an arithmetic random walk, we can compute a closed-form expression for the price S_t given S_0:

$$\ln(S_t) = \ln(S_0) + (\mu - \frac{1}{2} \cdot \sigma^2) \cdot t + \sigma \cdot \sqrt{t} \cdot \tilde{\varepsilon}$$

or, equivalently,

$$S_t = S_0 \cdot e^{(\mu - \frac{1}{2}\sigma^2) \cdot t + \sigma \cdot \sqrt{t} \cdot \tilde{\varepsilon}}$$

where $\tilde{\varepsilon}$ is a standard normal variable.

Notice that the only inconsistency with the formula for the arithmetic random walk is the presence of the extra term

$$(-\frac{1}{2} \cdot \sigma^2) \cdot t$$

in the drift term

$$(\mu - \frac{1}{2} \cdot \sigma^2) \cdot t$$

Why is there an adjustment of one half of the variance in the expected drift? In general, if $\tilde{Y}$ is a normal random variable with mean μ and variance σ^2, then the random variable, which is an exponential of the normal random variable $\tilde{Y}, \tilde{X} = e^{\tilde{Y}}$, has mean

$$E[\tilde{X}] = e^{\mu + \frac{1}{2}\sigma^2}$$

At first, this seems unintuitive—why is the expected value of $\tilde{X}$ not

$$E[\tilde{X}] = e^{\mu} ?$$

The expected value of a linear function of a random variable is a linear function of the expected value of the random variable. For example, if a is a constant, then

$$E[a \cdot \tilde{Y}] = a \cdot E[\tilde{Y}]$$

However, determining the expected value of a nonlinear function of a random variable (in particular, the exponential function, which is the function we are using here) is not as trivial. For example, there is a well-known relationship, the *Jensen Inequality*, which states that the expected value of a convex function of a random variable is less than the value of the function at the expected value of the random variable.

In our example, $\tilde{X}$ is a lognormal random variable, so its probability distribution has the shape shown in Exhibit 6.6. The random variable $\tilde{X}$ cannot take values less than 0. Since its variance is related to the variance of the normal random variable $\tilde{Y}$, as the variance σ^2 of $\tilde{Y}$ increases, the distribution of $\tilde{X}$ will spread out in the upward direction. This means that the mean of the lognormal variable $\tilde{X}$ will increase not only as the mean of the normal variable $\tilde{Y}$, μ, increases, but also as $\tilde{Y}$'s variance, σ^2, increases. In the context of the geometric random walk, $\tilde{Y}$ represents the normally distributed log returns, and $\tilde{X}$ is in fact the factor by which the asset price from the previous period is multiplied in order to generate the asset price in the next time period. In order to make sure that the geometric random process grows exponentially at average rate μ, we need to subtract a term (that term turns out to be $\sigma^2/2$), which will correct the bias.

Specifically, suppose that we know the price at time t, S_t. We have

$$\ln\left(S_{t+1}\right) = \ln\left(S_t\right) + \ln(1 + \tilde{r}_t)$$

that is,

$$S_{t+1} = S_t \cdot e^{\ln(1+\tilde{r})}$$

EXHIBIT 6.6 Example of a Lognormal Distribution with Mean of 1 and Standard Deviation of 0.8

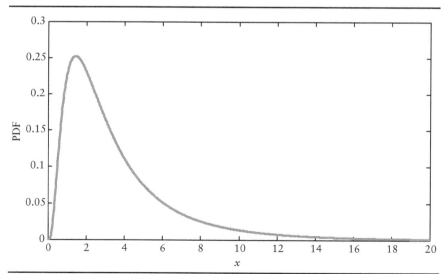

Note that we are explicitly assuming a *multiplicative model* for asset prices here—the price in the next time period is obtained by multiplying the price from the previous time period by a random factor. In the case of an arithmetic random walk, we had an *additive model*—a random shock was added to the asset price from the previous time period.

If the log-return $\ln(1 + \tilde{r}_t)$ is normally distributed with mean μ and standard deviation σ, then the expected value of

$$e^{\ln(1+\tilde{r}_t)}$$

is

$$e^{\mu + \frac{1}{2}\sigma^2}$$

and hence

$$E[S_{t+1}] = S_t \cdot e^{\mu + \frac{1}{2}\sigma^2}$$

In order to make sure that the geometric random walk process grows exponentially at an average rate μ (rather than $\mu + 0.5 \cdot \sigma^2$), we need to subtract the term $0.5 \cdot \sigma^2$ when we generate the future price from this process. This argument can be extended to determining prices for more than one time period ahead.

We will understand better why this formula holds when we review stochastic processes at the end of this chapter.

Simulation

It is easy to see how future prices can be generated based on the initial price S_0. First, we compute the term in the power of e: We simulate a value for a standard normal random variable, multiply it by the standard deviation and the square root of the number of time periods between the initial point and the point we are trying to compute, and subtract the product from the drift term adjusted for the volatility and the number of time periods. We then raise e to the exponent we just computed, and multiply the resulting value by the value of the initial price.[11]

One might wonder whether this approach for simulating realizations of an asset price following a geometric random walk is equivalent to the simulation approach mentioned earlier when we introduced geometric random walks, which is based on the discrete version of the equation for a random

---

[11]For example, given a current price S, in Excel we use the formula
$S * \exp((\mu - 0.5*\sigma^2) * t - \sigma * \sqrt{t} * \text{NORMINV}(\text{RAND}(),0,1))$.

walk. The two approaches are different (for example, the approach based on the discrete version of the equation for the geometric random walk does not produce the expected lognormal price distribution), but it can be shown that the differences in the two simulation approaches tend to cancel over many steps.

Parameter Estimation

In order to simulate paths of the geometric random walk, we need to have estimates of the parameters (μ and σ). The implicit assumption here, of course, is that these parameters remain constant over the time period of estimation. (We discuss how to incorporate considerations for changes in volatility later in this chapter.) Note that the equation for the geometric random walk can be written as

$$\ln\left(S_{t+1}\right) - \ln\left(S_t\right) = \ln(1 + \tilde{r}_t)$$

Equivalently,

$$\ln\left(\frac{S_{t+1}}{S_t}\right) = \mu + \sigma \cdot \tilde{\varepsilon}_t$$

Given a historical series of T prices of an asset, we can therefore do the following to estimate μ and σ:

1. Compute $\ln(S_{t+1}/S_t)$ for each time period t, $t = 0,\ldots, T-1$.
2. Estimate the volatility of the geometric random walk, σ, as the standard deviation of all $\ln(S_{t+1}/S_t)$.
3. Estimate for the drift of the arithmetic random walk, μ, as the average of all $\ln(S_{t+1}/S_t)$, plus one half of the standard deviation squared.

If we are given data on the returns r_t of an asset rather than the prices of the asset, we can compute $\ln(1 + r_t)$, and use it to replace $\ln(S_{t+1}/S_t)$ in steps 1 through 3 above. This is because

$$\log\left(\frac{S_{t+1}}{S_t}\right) = \log\left(1 + \frac{S_{t+1} - S_t}{S_t}\right) = \log(1 + \tilde{r}_t)$$

Geometric Random Walk: Some Additional Facts

To summarize, the geometric random walk has several important characteristics:

- It is a multiplicative model, that is, the price at the next time period is a multiple of a random term and the price from the previous time period.
- It has a constant drift μ and volatility σ. At every time period, the *percentage change* in price is normally distributed, on average equal to μ, with a standard deviation of σ.
- The overall noise in a geometric random walk never decays. The *percentage price change* over t time periods is distributed as a normal distribution with mean equal to $\mu \cdot t$ and standard deviation equal to $\sigma\sqrt{t}$.
- The exact distribution of the future price knowing the initial price can be found. The price at time t is lognormally distributed with specific probability distribution parameters.
- Prices that follow a geometric random walk in continuous time never become negative.

The geometric random walk model is not perfect. However, its computational simplicity makes the geometric random walk and its variations the most widely used processes for modeling asset prices. The geometric random walk defined with log returns never becomes negative because future prices are always a multiple of the initial stock price and a positive term (see Exhibit 6.7). In addition, observed historical stock prices can actually be quite close to lognormal.

EXHIBIT 6.7 Five Paths of a Geometric Random Walk with $\mu = -0.0014$ and $\sigma = 0.0411$

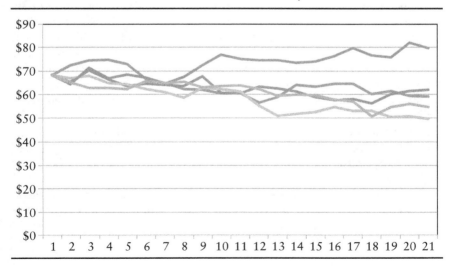

Note: Although the drift is slightly negative, it is still possible to generate paths that generally increase over time.

It is important to note that, actually, the assumption that log returns are normal is not required to justify the lognormal model for prices. If the distribution of log returns is non-normal, but the log returns are IID with finite variance, the sum of the log returns is asymptotically normal.[12] Stated differently, the log return process is approximately normal if we consider changes over sufficiently long intervals of time.

Price processes, however, are not always geometric random walks, even asymptotically. A very important assumption for the geometric random walk is that price increments are independently distributed; if the time series exhibits autocorrelation, the geometric random walk is not a good representation. We will see some models that incorporate considerations for autocorrelation and other factors later in this chapter.

MEAN REVERSION

The geometric random walk provides the foundation for modeling the dynamics for asset prices of many different securities, including stock prices. However, in some cases it is not justified to assume that asset prices evolve with a particular drift, or can deviate arbitrarily far from some kind of a representative value. Interest rates, exchange rates, and the prices of some commodities are examples for which the geometric random walk does not provide a good representation over the long term. For example, if the price of copper becomes high, copper mines would increase production in order to maximize profits. This would increase the supply of copper in the market, therefore decreasing the price of copper back to some equilibrium level. Consumer demand plays a role as well—if the price of copper becomes too high, consumers may look for substitutes, which would reduce the price of copper back to its equilibrium level.

Exhibit 6.8 illustrates the behavior of the 1-year Treasury bill yield from the beginning of January 1962 through the end of July 2009. It can be observed that, even though the variability of Treasury bill rates has changed over time, there is some kind of a long-term average level of interest rates to which they return after deviating up or down. This behavior is known as *mean reversion*.

The simplest mean reversion (MR) model is similar to an arithmetic random walk, but the means of the increments change depending on the current price level. The price dynamics are represented by the equation

$$S_{t+1} = S_t + \kappa \cdot (\mu - S_t) + \sigma \cdot \tilde{\varepsilon}_t$$

---

[12]This is based on a version of the Central Limit Theorem.

EXHIBIT 6.8 Weekly Data for One-Year Treasury Bill Rates: January 5, 1962–July 31, 2009

where $\tilde{\varepsilon}_t$ is a standard normal random variable. The parameter κ is a non-negative number that represents the *speed of adjustment* of the mean-reverting process—the larger its magnitude, the faster the process returns to its long-term mean. The parameter μ is the long-term mean of the process. When the current price S_t is lower than the long-term mean μ, the term $(\mu - S_t)$ is positive. Hence, on average there will be an upward adjustment to obtain the value of the price in the next time period, S_{t+1}. (We add a positive number, $\kappa \cdot (\mu - S_t)$, to the current price current price S_t.) By contrast, if the current price S_t is higher than the long-term mean μ, the term $(\mu - S_t)$ is negative. Hence, on average there will be a downward adjustment to obtain the value of the price in the next time period, S_{t+1}. (We add a negative number, $\kappa \cdot (\mu - S_t)$, to the current price current price S_t.) Thus, the mean-reverting process will behave in the way we desire—if the price becomes lower or higher than the long-term mean, it will be drawn back to the long-term mean.

In the case of the arithmetic and the geometric random walks, the cumulative volatility of the process increases over time. By contrast, in the case of mean reversion, as the number of steps increases, the variance peaks at

$$\frac{\sigma^2}{\kappa \cdot (2 - \kappa)}$$

In continuous time, this basic mean-reversion process is called the *Ornstein-Uhlenbeck process*. (See the last section of this chapter.) It is

EXHIBIT 6.9 Five Paths with 50 Steps Each of a Mean-Reverting Process with $\mu = 1.4404$, $\kappa = 0.0347$, and $\sigma = 0.0248$

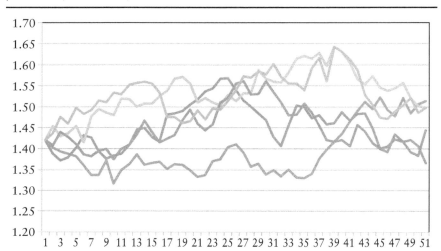

widely used when modeling interest rates and exchange rates in the context of computing bond prices and prices of more complex fixed-income securities. When used in the context of modeling interest rates, this simple mean-reversion process is also referred to as the *Vasicek model*.[13]

The mean-reversion process suffers from some of the disadvantages of the arithmetic random walk—for example, it can technically become negative. However, if the long-run mean is positive, and the speed of mean reversion is large relative to the volatility, the price will be pulled back to the mean quickly when it becomes negative. Exhibit 6.9 contains an example of five paths generated from a mean-reverting process.

Simulation

The formula for the mean-reverting process makes it clear how paths for the mean-reverting random walk can be generated. As in the case of the arithmetic and the geometric random walks, all we need is a way of simulating the normal random variables $\tilde{\varepsilon}_t$. We start with an initial price S_0, which is known. We know the values of the drift μ, the speed of adjustment κ, and the volatility σ over one period. To generate the price at the next time period, S_1, we add $\kappa \cdot (\mu - S_0)$ to S_0, simulate a normal random variable from a

[13]See Oldrich Vasicek, "An Equilibrium Characterization of the Term Structure," *Journal of Financial Economics* 5, no. 2 (1977): 177–188.

standard normal distribution, multiply it by σ, and add it to $S_0 + \kappa \cdot (\mu - S_0)$. At the next step (time period 2), we use the price at time period 1 we already generated, S_1, add to it $\kappa \cdot (\mu - S_1)$, simulate a new random variable from a standard normal distribution, multiply it by σ, and add it to $S_1 + \kappa \cdot (\mu - S_1)$. We proceed in the same way until we generate the desired number of steps of the random walk.[14]

Parameter Estimation

In order to simulate paths of the mean-reverting random walk, we need to have estimates of the parameters (κ, μ, and σ). Again, we assume that these parameters remain constant over the time period of estimation. The equation for the mean-reverting process can be written as

$$S_{t+1} - S_t = \kappa \cdot (\mu - S_t) + \sigma \cdot \tilde{\varepsilon}_t$$

or, equivalently,

$$S_{t+1} - S_t = \kappa \cdot \mu - \kappa \cdot S_t + \sigma \cdot \tilde{\varepsilon}_t$$

This equation has the characteristics of a linear regression model, with the absolute price change $(S_{t+1} - S_t)$ as the response variable, and S_t as the explanatory variable. Given a historical series of T prices for an asset, we can therefore do the following to estimate κ, μ, and σ:

1. Compute the price changes $(S_{t+1} - S_t)$ for each time period t, $t = 0,...,$ $T - 1$.
2. Run a linear regression with $(S_{t+1} - S_t)$ as the response variable and S_t as the explanatory variable.
3. Verify that the estimates from the linear regression model are valid:
   a. Plot the values of S_t versus $(S_{t+1} - S_t)$. The points in the scatter plot should approximately vary around a straight line with no visible cyclical or other patterns.
   b. The p-value[15] for the coefficient in front of the explanatory variable S_t should be small, preferably less than 0.05.
4. An estimate for the speed of adjustment of the mean-reversion process, κ, can be obtained as the negative of the coefficient in front of S_t. Since

---

[14]For example, given a current price S, in Excel the price for the next time period can be generated with the formula $S + \kappa*(\mu - S) + \sigma*\text{NORMINV(RAND(),0,1)}$.

[15]The p-values of the regression coefficients are part of standard regression output for most software packages. Most generally, they measure the degree of significance of the regression coefficient for explaining the response variable in the regression.

the speed of adjustment cannot be a negative number, if the coefficient in front of S_t is positive, the regression model cannot be used for estimating the parameters of the mean reverting process.

5. An estimate for the long-term mean of the mean-reverting process, μ, can be obtained as the ratio of the intercept term estimated from the regression and the slope coefficient in front of S_t (if that slope coefficient is valid, i.e., negative and with low p-value).

6. An estimate for the volatility of the mean-reverting process, σ, can be obtained as the standard error of the regression.[16]

Geometric Mean Reversion

A more advanced mean-reversion models that bears some similarity to the geometric random walk is the geometric mean reversion (GMR) model[17]

$$S_{t+1} = S_t + \kappa \cdot (\mu - S_t) \cdot S_t + \sigma \cdot S_t \cdot \tilde{\varepsilon}_t$$

The intuition behind this model is similar to the intuition behind the discrete version of the geometric random walk—the variability of the process changes with the current level of the price. However, the GMR model allows for incorporating mean reversion. Even though it is difficult to estimate the future price analytically from this model, it is easy to simulate.[18] Exhibit 6.10 contains an example of five paths generated from a geometric mean reversion model.

To estimate the parameters κ, μ, and σ to use in the simulation, we can use a series of T historical observations for the price of an asset. Assume that the parameters of the geometric mean reversion remain constant during the time period of estimation.

Note that the equation for the geometric mean-reverting random walk can be written as

$$\frac{S_{t+1} - S_t}{S_t} = \kappa \cdot (\mu - S_t) + \sigma \cdot \tilde{\varepsilon}_t$$

or, equivalently, as

---

[16]The standard error of the regression measures the standard deviation of the points around the regression line.

[17]This is a special case of the mean reversion model $S_{t+1} = S_t + \kappa \cdot (\mu - S_t) \cdot S_t + \sigma \cdot S_t^{\gamma} \cdot \tilde{\varepsilon}_t$, where γ is a parameter selected in advance. The most commonly used models have $\gamma = 1$ or $\gamma = 1/2$.

[18]For example, given a current price S, in Excel the price for the next time period can be generated with the formula $S + \kappa*(\mu - S)*S + \sigma*S*\text{NORMINV}(\text{RAND}(),0,1)$.

EXHIBIT 6.10 Five Paths with 50 Steps Each of a Geometric Mean Reversion Process with μ = 1.4464, κ = 0.0253, and σ = 0.0177

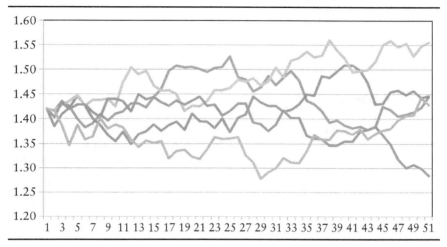

$$\frac{S_{t+1} - S_t}{S_t} = \kappa \cdot \mu - \kappa \cdot S_t + \sigma \cdot \tilde{\varepsilon}_t$$

Again, this equation bears characteristics of a linear regression model, with the percentage price change $(S_{t+1} - S_t)/S_t$ as the response variable, and S_t as the explanatory variable. Given a historical series of T prices of an asset, we can therefore do the following to estimate κ, μ, and σ:

1. Compute the percentage price changes $(S_{t+1} - S_t)/S_t$ for each time period t, $t = 0, ..., T - 1$.
2. Run a linear regression with $(S_{t+1} - S_t)/S_t$ as the response variable and S_t as the explanatory variable.
3. Verify that the estimates from the linear regression model are valid:
   a. Plot the values of S_t versus $(S_{t+1} - S_t)/S_t$. The points in the scatter plot should approximately vary around a straight line with no visible cyclical or other patterns.
   b. The p-value for the coefficient in front of the explanatory variable S_t should be small, preferably less than 0.05.
4. An estimate for the speed of adjustment of the geometric mean-reverting process, κ, can be obtained as the negative of the coefficient in front of S_t. Since the speed of adjustment cannot be a negative number, if the coefficient in front of S_t is positive, the regression model cannot be used for estimating the parameters of the geometric mean-reverting process.

5. An estimate for the long-term mean of the geometric mean-reverting process, μ, can be obtained as the ratio of the intercept term estimated from the regression and the slope coefficient in front of S_t (if that slope coefficient is valid, i.e., negative and with low p-value).

6. An estimate for the volatility of the geometric mean-reverting process, σ, can be obtained as the standard error of the regression.

ADVANCED RANDOM WALK MODELS

The models we described so far provide building blocks for representing the asset price dynamics. However, observed real-world asset price dynamics has features that cannot be incorporated in these basic models. For example, asset prices exhibit correlation—both with each other, and with themselves over time. Their volatility typically cannot be assumed constant. This section reviews several techniques for making asset price models more realistic depending on observed price behavior.

Correlated Random Walks

So far, we have discussed models for asset prices that assume that the dynamic processes for the prices of different assets evolve independently of each other. This is an unrealistic assumption—it is expected that market conditions and other factors will have an impact on the prices of groups of assets simultaneously. For example, it is likely that stock prices for companies in the oil industry will generally move together, as will stock prices for companies in the telecommunications industry.

The argument that asset prices are codependent has theoretical and empirical foundations as well. If asset prices were independent random walks, then large portfolios would be fully diversified, have no variability, and therefore be completely deterministic. Empirically, this is not the case. Even large aggregates of stock prices, such as the S&P 500, exhibit random behavior.

If we make the assumption that log returns are jointly normally distributed, then their dependencies can be represented through the covariance matrix (equivalently, through the correlation matrix).[19]

Let us give an example of how one can model two correlated stock prices assumed to follow geometric random walks. Suppose we are given

---

[19]In general, covariance and correlation are not equivalent with dependence of random variables. Covariance and correlation measure only the strength of linear dependence between two random variables. However, in the case of a multivariate normal distribution, covariance and correlation are sufficient to represent dependence.

two historical series of T observations each of observed asset prices for Stock 1 and Stock 2. We follow the steps described in the previous sections of this chapter to estimate the drifts and the volatilities of the two processes. To estimate the correlation structure, we find the correlation between

$$\ln\left(\frac{S_{t+1}^{(1)}}{S_t^{(1)}}\right) \text{ and } \ln\left(\frac{S_{t+1}^{(2)}}{S_t^{(2)}}\right)$$

where the indexes (1) and (2) correspond to Stock 1 and Stock 2, respectively.[20] This correlation can then be incorporated in the simulation.[21] Basically, at every step, we generate correlated normal random variables, $\varepsilon_t^{(1)}$ and $\varepsilon_t^{(2)}$, with means of zero, and with a given covariance structure. Those realizations of the correlated normal random variables are then used to compute the next period's Stock 1 price and the next period's Stock 2 price.

When we consider many different assets, the covariance matrix becomes very large, and cannot be estimated accurately. Factor models can be used to reduce the dimension of the covariance structure. Multivariate random walks are in fact *dynamic factor models* for asset prices. A multifactor model for the return of asset i can be written in the following general form:

$$r_t^{(i)} = \mu^{(i)} + \sum_{k=1}^{K} \beta^{(i,k)} \cdot f_t^{(k)} + \varepsilon_t^{(i)}$$

where the K factors $f^{(k)}$ follow random walks, $\beta^{(i,k)}$ are the factor loadings, and $\varepsilon_t^{(i)}$ are normal random variables with zero means.

It is important to note that the covariance matrix cannot capture correlations at lagged times (i.e., correlations of dynamic nature). Furthermore, the assumptions that log returns behave as multivariate normal variables is not always applicable—some assets exhibit dependency of nonlinear kind, which cannot be captured by the covariance or correlation matrix. Alternative tools for modeling covariability include *copula functions* and *transfer entropies*.[22]

---

[20]In Excel, the correlation between two data series stored in Array1 and Array2 can be computed with the function CORREL(Array1, Array2).

[21]Excel cannot generate correlated normal random variables. A number of Excel add-ins for simulation are available, however, and they have the capability to do so. Such add-ins include @RISK (sold by Palisade Corporation, http://www.palisade.com), Crystal Ball (sold by Oracle, http://www.oracle.com), and Risk Solver (from Frontline Systems, the developers of the original Excel Solver, http://www.solver.com).

[22]See, for example, Chapter 17 and Appendix B in Frank J. Fabozzi, Sergio Focardi, and Petter N. Kolm, *Financial Modeling of the Equity Markets: CAPM to Cointegration* (Hoboken, N.J.: John Wiley & Sons, 2006).

Incorporating Jumps

Many of the dynamic asset price processes used in industry assume continuous sample paths, as was the case with the arithmetic, geometric, and the different mean-reverting random walks we considered earlier in this chapter. However, there is empirical evidence that the prices of many securities incorporate jumps. The prices of some commodities, such as electricity and oil, are notorious for exhibiting "spikes." The logarithm of a price process with jumps is not normally distributed, but is instead characterized by a high peak and heavy tails, which are more typical of market data than the normal distribution. Thus, more advanced models are needed to incorporate realistic price behavior.

A classical way to include jumps in models for asset price dynamics is to add a Poisson process to the process (geometric random walk or mean reversion) used to model the asset price. A Poisson process is a discrete process in which arrivals occur at random discrete points in time, and the times between arrivals follow an exponential distribution with average time between arrivals equal to $1/\lambda$. This means that the number of arrivals in a specific time interval follows a Poisson distribution with mean rate of arrival λ. The "jump" Poisson process is assumed to be independent of the underlying "smooth" random walk.

The Poisson process is typically used to figure out the times at which the jumps occur. The magnitude of the jumps itself could come from any distribution, although the lognormal distribution is often used for tractability.

Let us explain in more detail how one would model and simulate a geometric random walk with jumps. At every point in time, the process moves as a geometric random walk, and updates the price S_t to S_{t+1}. If a jump happens, the size of the jump is added to S_t as well to obtain S_{t+1}. In order to avoid confusion about whether or not we have included the jump in the calculation, let us denote the price right before we find out whether or not a jump has occurred $S_{t+1}^{(-)}$, and keep the total price for the next time period as S_{t+1}. We therefore have

$$S_{t+1}^{(-)} = S_t + \mu \cdot S_t + \sigma \cdot S_t \cdot \tilde{\varepsilon}_t$$

that is, $S_{t+1}^{(-)}$ is computed according to the normal geometric random walk rule. Now suppose that a jump of magnitude $\tilde{J}_t$ occurs between time t and time $t + 1$. Let us express the jump magnitude as a percentage of the asset price, that is, let

$$S_{t+1} = S_{t+1}^{(-)} \cdot \tilde{J}_t$$

If we restrict the magnitude of the jumps $\tilde{J}_t$ to be non-negative, we will make sure that the asset price itself does not become negative.

Let us now express the changes in price in terms of the jump size. Based on the relationship between S_{t+1}, $S_{t+1}^{(-)}$, and $\tilde{J}_t$, we can write

$$S_{t+1} - S_{t+1}^{(-)} = S_{t+1}^{(-)} \cdot (\tilde{J}_t - 1)$$

and hence

$$S_{t+1}^{(-)} = S_{t+1} - S_{t+1}^{(-)} \cdot (\tilde{J}_t - 1)$$

Thus, we can substitute this expression for $S_{t+1}^{(-)}$, and write the geometric random walk with jumps model as

$$S_{t+1} = S_t + \mu \cdot S_t + \sigma \cdot S_t \cdot \tilde{\varepsilon}_t + S_{t+1}^{(-)} \cdot (\tilde{J}_t - 1)$$

How would we simulate a path for the jump-geometric random walk process? Note that given the relationship between S_{t+1}, $S_{t+1}^{(-)}$, and $\tilde{J}_t$, we can write

$$\ln(S_{t+1}) = \ln(S_{t+1}^{(-)}) + \ln(\tilde{J}_t)$$

Since $S_{t+1}^{(-)}$ is the price resulting only from the geometric random walk at time t, we already know what $\ln(S_{t+1}^{(-)})$ is. Recall based on our discussion of the geometric random walk that

$$\ln(S_{t+1}^{(-)}) = \ln(S_t) + (\mu - 0.5 \cdot \sigma^2) + \sigma \cdot \tilde{\varepsilon}_t$$

Therefore, the overall equation will be

$$\ln(S_{t+1}) = \ln(S_t) + (\mu - 0.5 \cdot \sigma^2) + \sigma \cdot \tilde{\varepsilon}_t + \sum_i \ln(J_t^{(i)})$$

where $J_t^{(i)}$ are all the jumps that occur during the time period between t and $t + 1$. This means that

$$S_{t+1} = S_t \cdot e^{\mu - 0.5 \cdot \sigma^2 + \sigma \cdot \tilde{\varepsilon}_t} \cdot \prod_i J_t^{(i)}$$

where the symbol Π denotes product. (If no jumps occurred between t and $t + 1$, we set the product to 1.)

Hence, to simulate the price at time $t + 1$, we need to simulate

- A standard normal random variable $\tilde{\varepsilon}_t$, as in the case of a geometric random walk.

- How many jumps occur between t and $t + 1$.
- The magnitude of each jump.[23]

As Merton pointed out, if we assume that the jumps follow a lognormal distribution, then $\ln(\tilde{J}_t)$ is normal, and the simulation is even easier.[24,25]

Stochastic Volatility

The models we considered so far all assumed that the volatility of the stochastic process remains constant over time. Empirical evidence suggests that the volatility changes over time, and more advanced models recognize that fact. Such models assume that the volatility parameter σ itself follows a random walk of some kind. Since there is some evidence that volatility tends to be mean-reverting, often different versions of mean-reversion models are used.[26]

STOCHASTIC PROCESSES

In this section, we provide an introduction to what is known as *stochastic calculus*. Our goal is not to achieve a working knowledge in the subject, but rather to provide context for some of the terminology and the formulas encountered in the literature on modeling asset prices with random walks.

So far, we discussed random walks for which every step is taken at a specific discrete point in time. When the time increments are very small, almost zero in length, the equation of a random walk describes a *stochastic process in continuous time*. In this context, the arithmetic random walk model is known as a *generalized Wiener process* or *Brownian motion* (BM). The geometric random walk is referred to as *geometric Brownian motion*

---

[23]For more details, see Chapter 12 in Dessislava A. Pachamanova and Frank J. Fabozzi, *Simulation and Optimization in Finance: Modeling with MATLAB, @RISK and VBA* (Hoboken, N.J.: John Wiley & Sons, 2010); and Paul Glasserman, *Monte Carlo Methods in Financial Engineering* (New York: Springer-Verlag, 2004).
[24]See Robert C. Merton, "Option Pricing When Underlying Stock Returns Are Discontinuous," *Journal of Financial Economics* 3, nos. 1 & 2 (1976): 125–144.
[25]See Paul Glasserman, *Monte Carlo Methods in Financial Engineering* (New York: Springer-Verlag, 2004) for more advanced examples.
[26]For more details on stochastic volatility models and their simulation see, for example, Paul Glasserman, *Monte Carlo Methods in Financial Engineering*, and John Hull, *Options, Futures and Other Derivatives*, 7th ed. (Upper Saddle River, N.J.: Prentice Hall, 2008).

(GBM), and the arithmetic mean-reverting walk is the Ornstein-Uhlenbeck process mentioned earlier.

Special notation is used to denote stochastic processes in continuous time. Increments are denoted by d or Δ. (For example, $(S_{t+1} - S_t)$ is denoted dS_t, meaning a change in S_t over an infinitely small interval.) The equations describing the process, however, have a very similar form to the equations we introduced earlier in this section:

$$dS_t = \mu\, dt + \sigma\, dW$$

Equations involving small changes ("differences") in variables are referred to as *differential equations*. In words, the equation above reads: "The change in the price S_t over a small time period dt equals the average drift μ multiplied by the small time change plus a random term equal to the volatility σ multiplied by dW, where dW is the increment of a Wiener process." The Wiener process, or Brownian motion, is the fundamental building block for many of the classical asset price processes.

A standard Wiener process $W(t)$ has the following properties:

1. For any time $s < t$, the difference $W(t) - W(s)$ is a normal random variable with mean zero and variance $(t - s)$. It can be expressed as $\sqrt{t - s} \cdot \tilde{\varepsilon}$, where $\tilde{\varepsilon}$ is a standard normal random variable.[27]
2. For any times $0 \le t_1 < t_2 \le t_3 < t_4$, the differences $(W(t_2) - W(t_1))$ and $(W(t_4) - W(t_3))$ (which are random variables) are independent.[28] Note that independent implies uncorrelated.
3. The value of the Wiener process at the beginning is zero, $W(t_0) = 0$.

Using the new notation, the first two properties can be restated as

---

[27]To show this, we need to mention that every normal distribution can be expressed in terms of the standard normal distribution. Namely, if $\tilde{\varepsilon}$ is a standard normal variable with mean 0 and standard deviation 1, and $\tilde{x}$ is a normal random variable with mean μ and standard deviation σ, we have

$$\tilde{\varepsilon} = \frac{\tilde{x} - \mu}{\sigma} \quad \text{(equivalently, } \tilde{x} = \sigma \cdot \tilde{\varepsilon} + \mu)$$

This is a property unique to the normal distribution—no other family of probability distributions can be transformed in the same way. In the context of Property 1 of the Wiener process, we have a normal random variable $(W(t) - W(s))$ with mean 0 and standard deviation $\sqrt{t - s}$. It can be expressed through a standard normal variable $\tilde{\varepsilon}$ as $\sqrt{t - s} \cdot \tilde{\varepsilon} + 0$.

[28]These differences are the actual increments of the process at different points in time.

Property 1. The change dW during a small period of time dt is normally distributed with mean 0 and variance dt, and can be expressed as $\sqrt{dt} \cdot \tilde{\varepsilon}$.

Property 2. The values of dW for any two nonoverlapping time intervals are independent.

The arithmetic random walk can be obtained as a *generalized Wiener process*, which has the form

$$dS_t = a\,dt + b\,dW$$

The appeal of the generalized Wiener process is that we can find a closed-form expression for the price at any time period. Namely,

$$S_t = S_0 + a \cdot t + b \cdot W(t)$$

The generalized Wiener process is a special case of the more general class of *Ito processes*, in which both the drift term and the coefficient in front of the random term are allowed to be nonconstant. The equation for an Ito process is

$$dS_t = a(S,t)\,dt + b(S,t)\,dW$$

GBM and the Ornstein-Uhlenbeck process are both special cases of Ito processes.

In contrast to the generalized Wiener process, the equation for the Ito process does not allow us to write a general expression for the price at time t in closed form. However, an expression can be found for some special cases, such as GBM. We now show how this can be derived.

The main relevant result from stochastic calculus is the so-called *Ito Lemma*, which states the following. Suppose that a variable x follows an Ito process

$$dx_t = a(x,t)\,dt + b(x,t)\,dW$$

and let y be a function of x, that is,

$$y_t = f(x,t)$$

Then, y evolves according to the following differential equation:

$$dy_t = \left(\frac{\partial f}{\partial x} \cdot a + \frac{\partial f}{\partial t} + \frac{1}{2} \cdot \frac{\partial^2 f}{\partial x^2} \cdot b^2 \right) dt + \frac{\partial f}{\partial x} \cdot b \cdot dW$$

where the symbol ∂ is standard notation for the partial derivative of the function f with respect to the variable in the denominator. For example, $\partial f/\partial t$ is the derivative of the function f with respect to t assuming that all terms in the expression for f that do not involve t are constant. Respectively, ∂^2 denotes the second derivative of the function f with respect to the variable in the denominator, that is, the derivative of the derivative.

This expression shows that a function of a variable that follows an Ito process also follows an Ito process.

A rigorous proof of Ito's Lemma is beyond the scope of this chapter, but let us provide some intuition. Let us see how we would go about computing the expression for y in Ito's Lemma.

In ordinary calculus, we could obtain an expression for a function of a variable in terms of that variable by writing the Taylor series extension:

$$dy = \frac{\partial f}{\partial x} \cdot dx + \frac{\partial f}{\partial t} \cdot dt + \frac{1}{2} \cdot \frac{\partial^2 f}{\partial x^2} \cdot dx^2 + \frac{1}{2} \cdot \frac{\partial^2 f}{\partial t^2} \cdot dt^2 + \frac{\partial^2 f}{\partial x \partial x} \cdot dx\, dt + \ldots$$

We get rid of all terms of order dt^2 or higher, deeming them "too small." We need to expand the terms that contain dx, however, because they contain terms of order dt. We have

$$dy = \frac{\partial f}{\partial x} \cdot (a(x,t)\, dt + b(x,t)\, dW) + \frac{\partial f}{\partial t} \cdot dt + \frac{1}{2} \cdot \frac{\partial^2 f}{\partial x^2} \cdot (a(x,t)\, dt + b(x,t)\, dW)^2$$

The last expression in parentheses, when expanded, becomes (dropping the arguments of a and b for notational convenience)

$$(a\, dt + b\, dW)^2 = a^2 (dt)^2 + b^2 (dW)^2 + 2ab \cdot dt \cdot dW$$
$$= b^2\, dt$$

To obtain this expression, we dropped the first and the last term in the expanded expression because they are of order higher than dt. The middle term, $b^2(dW)^2$, in fact equals $b^2 \cdot dt$ as dt goes to 0. The latter is not an obvious fact, but it follows from the properties of the standard Wiener process. The intuition behind it is that the variance of $(dW)^2$ is of order dt^2, so we can ignore it and treat the expression as deterministic and equal to its expected value. The expected value of $(dW)^2$ is in fact dt.[29]

---

[29]To see this, recall from the properties of the standard Wiener process that the difference between the values of the process between any two points in time is distributed as a normal random variable with mean 0 and variance equal to the time difference itself. Therefore, dW (the difference over a very small time interval dt) is distributed as a normal random variable with mean 0 and variance dt, that is,

$$dW = \varepsilon \cdot \sqrt{dt}$$

Substituting this expression back into the expression for dy, we obtain the expression in Ito's Lemma.

Using Ito's Lemma, let us derive the equation for the price at time t, S_t, that was the basis for the exact simulation method for the geometric random walk. Suppose that S_t follows the GBM

$$dS_t = (\mu \cdot S_t)\, dt + (\sigma \cdot S_t)\, dW$$

We use Ito's Lemma to compute the equation for the process followed by the logarithm of the stock price. In other words, in the notation we used in the definition of Ito's Lemma, we have

$$y_t = f(x,t) = \ln S_t$$

We also have

$$a = \mu \cdot S \text{ and } b = \sigma \cdot S$$

Finally, we have

$$\frac{\partial f}{\partial x} = \frac{\partial(\ln S)}{\partial S} = \frac{1}{S} \text{ and } \frac{\partial^2 f}{\partial x^2} = \frac{\partial(1/S)}{\partial S} = -\frac{1}{S^2}$$

Plugging into the equation for y in Ito's Lemma, we obtain

$$d \ln S = \left(\frac{1}{S} \cdot a + 0 + \frac{1}{2} \cdot \left(-\frac{1}{S^2} \right) \cdot b^2 \right) dt + \frac{1}{S} \cdot b \cdot dW$$

$$= \left(\mu - \frac{1}{2} \cdot \sigma^2 \right) dt + \sigma \cdot dW$$

which is the equation we presented earlier. This explains also the presence of the

$$-\frac{1}{2} \cdot \sigma^2$$

term in the expression for the drift of the GBM.

---

where ε is a standard normal random variable. Finding the distribution of the squared difference $(dW)^2 = \varepsilon^2 \cdot dt$ is not as easy (it is no longer normal). However, we can say something about the mean and the variance of that distribution. The variance of a standard normal variable ε equals 1, and can be expressed as $E[\varepsilon^2] - (E[\varepsilon])^2$. Since $E[\varepsilon] = 0$, we must have $E[\varepsilon^2] = 1$. Therefore, the expected value of $(dW)^2 = E[\varepsilon^2] \cdot dt = 1 \cdot dt = dt$.

KEY POINTS

- Models of asset dynamics include trees (such as binomial trees) and random walks (such as arithmetic, geometric, and mean-reverting random walks). Such models are called discrete when the changes in the asset price are assumed to happen at discrete time increments. When the length of the time increment is assumed infinitely small, we refer to them as stochastic processes in continuous time.
- The arithmetic random walk is an additive model for asset prices—at every time period, the new price is determined by the price at the previous time period plus a deterministic drift term and a random shock that is distributed as a normal random variable with mean equal to zero and a standard deviation proportional to the square root of the length of the time period. The probability distribution of future asset prices conditional on a known current price is normal.
- The arithmetic random walk model is analytically tractable and convenient; however, it has some undesirable features such as a nonzero probability that the asset price will become negative.
- The geometric random walk is a multiplicative model for asset prices—at every time period, the new price is determined by the price at the previous time period multiplied by a deterministic drift term and a random shock that is distributed as a lognormal random variable. The volatility of the process grows with the square root of the elapsed amount of time. The probability distribution of future asset prices conditional on a known current price is lognormal.
- The geometric random walk is not only analytically tractable, but is more realistic than the arithmetic random walk because the asset price cannot become negative. It is widely used in practice, particularly for modeling stock prices.
- Mean reversion models assume that the asset price will meander, but will tend to return to a long-term mean at a speed called the *speed of adjustment*. They are particularly useful for modeling prices of some commodities, interest rates, and exchange rates.
- The codependence structure between the price processes for different assets can be incorporated directly (by computing the correlation between the random terms in their random walks), by using dynamic multifactor models, or by more advanced means such as copula functions and transfer entropies.
- A variety of more advanced random walk models are used to incorporate different assumptions, such as time-varying volatility and "spikes," or jumps, in the asset price. They are not as tractable analytically as the classical random walk models, but can easily be simulated.

- The Wiener process, a stochastic process in continuous time, is a basic building block for many of the stochastic processes used to model asset prices. The increments of a Wiener process are independent, normally distributed random variables with variance proportional to the length of the time period.
- An Ito process is a generalized Wiener process with drift and volatility terms that can be functions of the asset price and time.
- An important result in stochastic calculus is Ito's Lemma, which states that a variable that is a function of a variable that follows an Ito process follows an Ito process itself with specific drift and volatility terms.

QUESTIONS

1. **a.** What are the main assumptions of arithmetic random walks?
   b. What are their main disadvantages when modeling asset prices?

2. **a.** What are the main assumptions of geometric random walks?
   b. What is the probability distribution of asset prices that follow geometric random walks?

3. **a.** What are the main assumptions of mean reversion?
   b. When would you model asset prices using mean-reverting walks instead of arithmetic or geometric random walks?

4. Explain in detail how you would simulate a geometric random walk when the volatility is assumed to follow a mean-reverting process.

5. Let us evaluate a simple trading strategy whose goal is to limit downside risk. Suppose you are holding one share of stock. You sell the stock as soon your loss (relative to the original price of stock) exceeds 10% of the original stock value; otherwise you keep the stock. Once you have sold the stock, you do not buy it back for three months. If you have not sold the stock, you sell it at the end of three months.

   Pick a stock, and determine its drift and volatility from historical data. Check also if a mean-reverting process appears to apply. Implement a simulation model in which the price of the stock is assumed to follow (1) an arithmetic random walk, (2) a geometric random walk, (3) mean reversion, and (4) geometric mean reversion with the parameters you estimated. Discuss the performance of the trading strategy depending on the process the price of the stock is assumed to follow.

CHAPTER 7

Asset Allocation and Portfolio Construction

Noël Amenc, Ph.D.
Professor of Finance, EDHEC Business School
Director, EDHEC-Risk Institute

Felix Goltz, Ph.D.
Head of Applied Research, EDHEC-Risk Institute

Lionel Martellini, Ph.D.
Professor of Finance, EDHEC Business School
Scientific Director, EDHEC-Risk Institute

Vincent Milhau, Ph.D.
Senior Research Engineer, EDHEC-Risk Institute

A sset management is justified as an industry by the capacity of adding value through the design of investment solutions that match investors' needs. For more than 50 years, the industry has in fact mostly focused on security selection decisions as a single source of added value. This sole focus has somewhat distracted the industry from another key source of added value, namely portfolio construction and asset allocation decisions. In the face of recent crises, and given the intrinsic difficulty in delivering added-value through security selection decisions only, the relevance of the old paradigm has been questioned with heightened intensity, and a new paradigm is starting to emerge.

In a nutshell, the new paradigm recognizes that the art and science of portfolio management consists of constructing dedicated portfolio *solutions*, as opposed to one-size-fits-all investment *products*, so as to reach the return objectives defined by the investor, while respecting the investor's constraints expressed in terms of (absolute or relative) risk budgets. In this broader context, asset allocation and portfolio construction decisions appear as the main source of added-value by the investment industry, with security selection being a third-order problem. As argued throughout this chapter, asset allocation and portfolio construction decisions are intimately related to risk management. In the end, the quintessence of investment management is essentially about finding optimal ways to spend risk budgets that investors are reluctantly willing to set, with a focus on allow for the highest possible access to performance potential while respecting such risk budgets. Risk diversification, risk hedging, and risk insurance are shown to be three useful approaches to optimal spending of investors' risk budgets.

Academic research has provided very useful guidance with respect to how asset allocation and portfolio construction decisions should be analyzed so as to best improve investors' welfare. In a nutshell, the "fund separation theorems" that lie at the core of modern portfolio theory advocate a separate management of performance and risk control objectives. In the context of asset allocation decisions with consumption/liability objectives, it can be shown that the suitable expression of the fund separation theorem provides rational support for *liability-driven investment* (LDI) techniques that have recently been promoted by a number of investment banks and asset management firms. These solutions involve on the one hand the design of a *customized liability-hedging portfolio* (LHP), the sole purpose of which is to hedge away as effectively as possible the impact of unexpected changes in risk factors affecting liability values (most notably interest rate and inflation risks), and on the other hand the design of a *performance-seeking portfolio* (PSP), which raison d'être is to provide investors with an optimal risk-return trade-off.[1]

One of the implications of this LDI paradigm is that one should distinguish two different levels of asset allocation decisions: allocation decisions involved in the design of the performance-seeking or the liability-hedging portfolio (design of better building blocks, or BBBs), and asset allocation decisions involved in the optimal split between the PSP and the LHP (designed of advanced asset allocation decisions, or AAAs). We address both questions (BBB and AAA) in this chapter. More specifically, we first focus here on how to construct efficient performance-seeking and liability-hedging portfolios, and then move on to provide information regarding how to optimally allocate to these two building blocks once they have been designed.

---

[1]More generally, other forms of hedging demand exist that allow investors to neutralize the impact of unexpected changes in risk factors affecting the opportunity set or the wealth process. This is discussed in more detail later in this chapter where we cover dedicated to life-cycle investment strategies.

The objective of this chapter is not to provide a thorough and rigorous treatment of all technical questions related to asset allocation and portfolio construction. It is to provide an overview of the key conceptual challenges involved.

In the next section, we present the challenges related to asset allocation and portfolio construction decisions within the PSP. We then discuss the challenges related to asset allocation and portfolio construction decisions within the LHP. The last section provides an introduction to how to optimally allocate to the PSP versus the LHP for a long-term investor facing short-term constraints, once these two key building blocks have been properly designed.

ASSET ALLOCATION AND PORTFOLIO CONSTRUCTION DECISIONS IN THE OPTIMAL DESIGN OF THE PERFORMANCE-SEEKING PORTFOLIO

Modern portfolio theory provides again some useful guidance with respect to the optimal design of a PSP that would best suit investors' needs. More precisely, the prescription is that the PSP should be obtained as the result of a portfolio optimization procedure aiming at generating the highest risk-reward ratio.

Portfolio optimization is a straightforward procedure, at least in principle. In a mean-variance setting for example, the prescription consists of generating a maximum Sharpe ratio (MSR) portfolio based on expected return, volatility and pairwise correlation parameters for all assets to be included in the portfolio, a procedure which can even be handled analytically in the absence of portfolio constraints.

More precisely, consider a simple mean-variance problem:

$$\max_{w} \mu_p - \frac{1}{2}\gamma\sigma_p^2$$

Here, the control variable is a vector w of optimal weight allocated to various risky assets, μ_p denotes the portfolio expected return, and σ_p denotes the portfolio volatility. We further assume that the investor is facing the following investment opportunity set: a riskless bond paying the risk-free rate r, and a set of N risky assets with expected return vector μ (of size N) and covariance matrix Σ, (of size $N \times N$), all assumed constant so far.

With these notations, the portfolio expected return and volatility are respectively given by:

$$\mu_p = w'(\mu - re) + r$$
$$\sigma_p^2 = w'\Sigma w$$

In this context, it is straightforward to show by standard arguments that the only efficient portfolio composed with risky assets is the maximum Sharpe ratio portfolio, also known as the tangency portfolio. This chapter's appendix provides more details.

Finally, the Sharpe ratio reads (where we further denote by e a vector of ones of size N):

$$SR = \frac{w'(\mu - re)}{(w'\Sigma w)^{\frac{1}{2}}}$$

And the optimal portfolio is given by

$$\max_w \left(\mu_p - \frac{1}{2}\gamma\sigma_p^2 \right) \Rightarrow w_0^* = \frac{1}{\gamma}\Sigma^{-1}(\mu - re) = \frac{e'\Sigma^{-1}(\mu - re)}{\gamma} \underbrace{\frac{\Sigma^{-1}(\mu - re)}{e'\Sigma^{-1}(\mu - re)}}_{PSP} \quad (7.1)$$

This is a two-fund separation theorem, which gives the allocation to the MSR performance-seeking portfolio (PSP), with the rest invested in cash, as well as the composition of the MSR performance-seeking portfolio.

In practice, investors end up holding more or less imperfect proxies for the truly optimal performance-seeking portfolio, if only because of the presence of parameter uncertainty which makes it impossible to obtain a perfect estimate for the maximum Sharpe ratio portfolio. Denoting by λ the Sharpe ratio of the (generally inefficient) PSP actually held by the investor, and by σ its volatility, we obtain the following optimal allocation strategy:

$$w_0^* = \frac{\lambda}{\gamma\sigma} PSP \quad (7.2)$$

Hence the allocation to the performance-seeking portfolio is a function of two objective parameters, the PSP volatility and the PSP Sharpe ratio, and one subjective parameter, the investor's risk aversion. The optimal allocation to the PSP is inversely proportional to the investor's risk aversion. If risk aversion goes to infinity, the investor only holds the risk-free asset only, as should be expected. For finite risk-aversion levels, the allocation to the PSP is inversely proportional to the PSP volatility, and it is proportional to the PSP Sharpe ratio. As a result, if the Sharpe ratio of the PSP is increased, one can invest more in risky assets. Hence, risk management is not only about risk reduction; it is also about performance enhancement through a better spending of investors' risk budgets. We revisit this point later in the chapter.

The expression (7.1) is useful because it provides in principle a straightforward expression for the optimal portfolio starting from a set of N risky assets. In the presence of a realistically large number N of securities, the curse of dimensionality, however, makes it practically impossible for investors to implement such direct one-step portfolio optimization decisions involving all individual components of the asset mix. The standard alternative approach widely adopted in investment practice consists instead in first grouping individual securities in various asset classes according to various dimensions, such as, country, sector and style within the equity universe, or country, maturity and credit rating within the bond universe, and subsequently generating the optimal portfolio through a two-stage process. On the one hand, investable proxies are generated for MSR portfolios within each asset class in the investment universe. We call this step, which is typically delegated to professional money managers, the *portfolio construction step*. On the other hand, when the MSR proxies are obtained for each asset class, an optimal allocation to the various asset classes is eventually generated so as to generate the maximum Sharpe ratio at the global portfolio level. This step is called the *asset allocation step*, and it is typically handled by a centralized decision maker (e.g., a pension fund CIO) with or without the help of specialized consultants, as opposed to be delegated to decentralized asset managers. We discuss both of these steps in what follows.

Portfolio Construction Step: Designing Efficient Benchmarks

In the absence of active views, the default option consists of using market-cap-weighted indexes as proxies for the asset class MSR portfolio. Academic research, however, has found that such market-cap-weighted indexes were likely to be severely inefficient portfolios (see for example Haugen and Baker,[2] Grinold,[3] or Amenc, Goltz and Le Sourd[4]). In a nutshell, market-cap-weighted indexes are not good choices as investment benchmarks because they are poorly diversified portfolios. In fact, cap weighting tends to lead to exceedingly high concentration in relatively few stocks. As a consequence of their lack of diversification, cap-weighted indexes have empirically be found

---

[2]Robert A. Haugen and Nardin L. Baker, "The Efficient Market Inefficiency of Capitalization-Weighted Stock Portfolios," *Journal of Portfolio Management* 17, no. 3 (1991): 35–40.

[3]Richard C. Grinold, "Are Benchmark Portfolios Efficient?" *Journal of Portfolio Management* 19, no. 1 (1992): 34–40.

[4]Noël Amenc, Felix Goltz and Véronique Le Sourd, "Assessing the Quality of Stock Market Indices," EDHEC-Risk Institute Publication (September 2006).

EXHIBIT 7.1 Inefficiency of Cap-Weighted Benchmarks, and the Quest for an Efficient Proxy for the True Tangency Portfolio

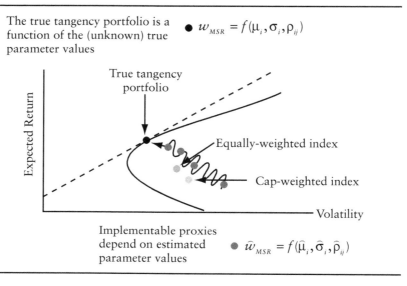

The true tangency portfolio is a function of the (unknown) true parameter values

$$\bullet\ w_{MSR} = f(\mu_i, \sigma_i, \rho_{ij})$$

Implementable proxies depend on estimated parameter values

$$\bullet\ \hat{w}_{MSR} = f(\hat{\mu}_i, \hat{\sigma}_i, \hat{\rho}_{ij})$$

to be severely inefficient portfolios, which do not provide investors with the fair reward given the risk taken. As a result of their poor diversification, they have been found to be dominated by equally weighted benchmarks,[5] which are naïvely diversified portfolios that are optimal if and only if all securities have identical expected return, volatilities, and of all pairs of correlation are identical.

In what follows, we analyze in some details a number of alternatives based on practical implementation of modern portfolio theory that have been suggested to generate more efficient proxies for the MSR portfolio in the equity or fixed income investment universes (see Exhibit 7.1).

Modern portfolio theory was born with the efficient frontier analysis of Markowitz in 1952.[6] Unfortunately, early applications of the technique, based on naïve estimates of the input parameters, have been found of little use because leading to unreasonable portfolio allocations.

Below we first explain how to help bridge the gap between portfolio theory and portfolio construction by showing how to generate enhanced parameter estimates so as to improve the quality of the portfolio optimization

---

[5]Victor DeMiguel, Lorenzo Garlappi, and Raman Uppal, "Optimal versus Naive Diversification: How Inefficient is the 1/N Portfolio Strategy?" *Review of Financial Studies* 22, no. 3 (2009): 1915–1953.
[6]Harry M. Markowitz, "Portfolio Selection," *Journal of Finance* 7, no. 1 (1952): 77–91.

outputs (optimal portfolio weights). We begin by focusing on enhanced covariance parameter estimates, and explain how to meet the main challenge of sample risk reduction.[7] Against this backdrop, we present the state-of-the art methodologies for reducing the problem dimensionality and estimating the covariance matrix with multi-factor models. We then turn to expected return estimation. We argue that statistical methodologies are not likely to generate any robust expected return estimates, which suggests that economic models such as the Capital Asset Pricing Model (CAPM) and the Arbitrage Pricing Theory (APT) should instead be used for expected return estimation. Finally, we also present evidence that proxies for expected return estimates should not only include systematic risk measures, but they should also incorporate idiosyncratic risk measures as well as downside risk measures.

Robust Estimators for Covariance Parameters

In practice, the success in the implementation of a theoretical model relies not only upon its conceptual grounds but also on the reliability of the inputs to the model. In the case of mean-variance (MV) optimization the results will highly depend of the quality of the parameter estimates: the covariance matrix and the expected returns of assets.

Several improved estimates for the covariance matrix have been proposed, including most notably the factor-based approach,[8] the constant correlation approach,[9] and the statistical shrinkage approach.[10] In addition, Jagannathan and Ma find that imposing (non-short selling) constraints on the weights in the optimization program improves the risk-adjusted out-of-sample performance in a manner that is similar to some of the aforementioned improved covariance matrix estimators.[11]

In these papers, the focus was on testing the out-of-sample performance of *global minimum variance* (GMV) portfolios, as opposed to the MSR

---

[7]Another key challenge is the presence of nonstationary risk parameters, which can be accounted for with conditional factor models capturing time-dependencies (e.g., GARCH-type models) and state-dependencies (e.g., Markov Regime Switching models) in risk parameter estimates.

[8]William F. Sharpe, "A Simplified Model for Portfolio Analysis," *Management Science* 9, no. 2 (1963): 277–293.

[9]Elton Elton and Martin Gruber, "Estimating the Dependence Structure of Share Prices: Implications for Portfolio Selection," *Journal of Finance* 28, no. 5 (1973): 1203–1232.

[10]Olivier Ledoit and Michael Wolf, "Honey, I Shrunk the Sample Covariance Matrix," *Journal of Portfolio Management* 30, no. 4 (2004): 110–119.

[11]Ravi Jagannathan and Tongshu Ma, "Risk Reduction in Large Portfolios: Why Imposing the Wrong Constraints Helps," *Journal of Finance* 58, no. 4 (2003): 1651–1684.

portfolios (also known as *tangency portfolios*), given that there is a consensus around the fact that purely statistical estimates of expected returns are not robust enough to be used, a point that we return to later in this chapter when we look at expected return estimation.

The key problem in covariance matrix estimation is the curse of dimensionality; when a large number of stocks are considered, the number of parameters to estimate grows exponentially, where the majority of them are pairwise correlations.

Therefore, at the estimation stage, the challenge is to reduce the number of factors that come into play. In general, a multifactor model decomposes the (excess) return (in excess in excess of the risk-free asset) of an asset into its expected rewards for exposure to the "true" risk factors as

$$r_{it} = \alpha_{it} + \sum_{j=1}^{K} \beta_{i,jt} \cdot F_{jt} + \varepsilon_{it}$$

or in matrix form for all N assets, that is

$$r_t = \alpha_t + \beta_t F_t + \varepsilon_t$$

where β_t is a $N \times K$ matrix containing the sensitivities of each asset i with respect to the corresponding j-*th* factor movements; r_t is the vector of the N assets' (excess) returns, F_t a vector containing the K risk factors' (excess) returns and ε_t the $N \times 1$ vector containing the zero mean uncorrelated residuals ε_{it}. The covariance matrix for the asset returns, implied by a factor model is given by

$$\Omega = \beta \cdot \Sigma_F \cdot \beta^T + \Sigma_\varepsilon$$

where Σ_F is the $K \times K$ covariance matrix of the risk factors and Σ_ε a $N \times N$ covariance matrix of the residuals corresponding to each asset.

While the factor-based estimator is expected to allow for a reasonable trade-off between sample risk and model risk, still remains, however, the problem of choosing the "right" factor model. One popular approach aims at relying as little as possible on strong theoretical assumptions by using *principal component analysis* (PCA) to determine the underlying risk factors from the data. The PCA method is based on a spectral decomposition of the sample covariance matrix and its goal is to explain covariance structures using only a few linear combinations of the original stochastic variables that will constitute the set of (unobservable) factors.

Bengtsson and Holst[12] and Fujiwara et al.,[13] motivate the use of PCA in a similar way, extracting principal components in order to estimate expected correlation within MV portfolio optimization. The latter find that the realized risk-return of portfolios based on the PCA method outperforms the one based on a single index and that the optimization gives a practically reasonable asset allocation. Overall, the main strength of the PCA approach at this stage is that it leads to "letting the data talk" and having them tell us what are the underlying risk factors that govern most of the variability of the assets at each point in time. This strongly contrasts with having to rely on the assumption that a particular factor model is the true pricing model and reduces the specification risk embedded in the factor-based approach while keeping the sample risk reduction.

The question of determining the appropriate number of factors to structure the correlation matrix is critical for the risk estimation when using PCA as a factor model. Several options have been proposed to answer this question, some of them with more theoretical grounds than others.

As a final note, we need to recognize that the discussion is so far cast in a mean-variance setting, which can in principle only be rationalized for normally distributed asset returns. In the presence of non-normally distributed asset returns, optimal portfolio selection techniques require estimates for variance-covariance parameters, along with estimates for higher-order moments and co-moments of the return distribution. This is a formidable challenge that severely exacerbates the dimensionality problem already present with mean-variance analysis. In a recent paper, Martellini and Ziemann[14] extend the existing literature, which has mostly focused on the covariance matrix, by introducing improved estimators for the coskewness and cokurtosis parameters. On the one hand, they find that the use of these enhanced estimates generates a significant improvement in investors' welfare. On the other hand, they find that also that when the number of constituents in the portfolios is large (e.g., more than 20), the increase in sample risk related to the need to estimate higher-order comoments by far outweighs the benefits related to considering a more general portfolio optimization procedure.

---

[12]Christoffer Bengtsson and Jan Holst, "On Portfolio Selection: Improved Covariance Matrix Estimation for Swedish Asset Returns," Working paper (Lund University and Lund Institute of Technology, 2002).

[13]Yoshi Fujiwara, Wataru Souma, Hideki Murasato, and Hiwon Yoon, "Application of PCA and Random Matrix Theory to Passive Fund Management," in *Practical Fruits of Econophysics*, ed. Hideki Takayasu (Tokyo: Springer, 2006), 226–230.

[14]Lionel Martellini and Volker Ziemann, "Improved Estimates of Higher-order Comoments and Implications for Portfolio Selection," *Review of Financial Studies* 23, no. 4 (2010): 1467–1502.

When portfolios with large numbers of assets are optimized, maximizing the Sharpe ratio leads to better out-of-sample results than does maximizing a return-to-VaR ratio. It does so even when portfolio performance is assessed with measures that rely on VaR rather than on volatility to adjust for risk. Similar arguments hold for other extreme risk measures such as CVaR. In the end, using extreme risk measures in portfolios with large numbers of assets leads to a formidable estimation problem, and empirical results suggest that it is sensible to stay with the mean-variance approach, in which reliable input estimates can be derived.

Robust Estimators for Expected Returns

While it appears that risk parameters can be estimated with a fair degree of accuracy, it has been shown that expected returns are difficult to obtain with a reasonable estimation error.[15] What makes the problem worse is that optimization techniques are very sensitive to differences in expected returns, so that portfolio optimizers typically allocate the largest fraction of capital to the asset class for which estimation error in the expected returns is the largest.[16]

In view of the difficulty of using sample-based expected return estimates in a portfolio optimization context, a reasonable alternative consists in using some risk estimate as a proxy for excess expected returns.[17] This approach is based on the most basic principle in finance, that is, the natural relationship between risk and reward. In fact, standard asset pricing theories such the APT imply that expected returns should be positively related to systematic volatility, such as measured through a factor model that summarizes individual stock return exposure with respect to a number of rewarded risk factors.

More recently, a series of papers have focused on the explanatory power of idiosyncratic, as opposed to systematic, risk for the cross section of expected returns. In particular, Malkiel and Xu,[18] extending an insight from

---

[15]Robert C. Merton, "On Estimating the Expected Return on the Market: an Exploratory Investigation," *Journal of Financial Economics* 8, no. 4 (1980): 323–361.

[16]See, example, Mark Britten-Jones, "The Sampling Error in Estimates of Mean-Variance Efficient Portfolio Weights," *Journal of Finance* 54, no. 2 (1999): 655–671; and Richard Michaud, *Efficient Asset Management: A Practical Guide to Stock Portfolio Optimization and Asset Allocation* (Cambridge, Mass.: Harvard Business School Press, 1998).

[17]This discussion focuses on estimating the fair neutral reward for holding risky assets. If one has access to active view on expected returns, one may use a disciplined approach (e.g., the Black-Litterman model) to combine the active views with the neutral estimates.

[18]Burton Malkiel and Yexiao Xu, "Idiosyncratic Risk and Security Returns," Working paper, University of Texas at Dallas, 2006.

Merton,[19] show that an inability to hold the market portfolio, whatever the cause, will force investors to care about total risk to some degree in addition to market risk so that firms with larger firm-specific variances require higher average returns to compensate investors for holding imperfectly diversified portfolios.[20] That stocks with high idiosyncratic risk earn higher returns has also been confirmed in a number of recent empirical studies.[21]

Taken together, these findings suggest that *total* risk, a model-free quantity given by the sum of systematic and specific risk, should be positively related to expected return. Most commonly, total risk is the volatility of a stock's returns. Martellini has investigated the portfolio implications of these findings, and has found that tangency portfolios constructed on the assumption that the cross-section of excess expected returns could be approximated by the cross-section of volatility posted better out-of-sample risk-adjusted performance than their market-cap-weighted counterparts.[22]

More generally, recent research suggests that the cross-section of expected returns might be best explained by risk indicators taking into account higher-order moments. Theoretical models have shown that, in exchange for higher skewness and lower kurtosis of returns, investors are willing to accept expected returns lower (and volatility higher) than those of the mean-variance benchmark.[23] More specifically, skewness and kurtosis in individual stock returns (as opposed to the skewness and kurtosis of aggregate portfolios) have been shown to matter in several papers. High skewness is associated with lower expected returns in several studies.[24] The

---

[19]Robert C. Merton, "A Simple Model of Capital Market Equilibrium with Incomplete Information," *Journal of Finance* 42 (1987): 483–510.

[20]For a similar conclusion from a behavioral perspective, see Nicholas C. Barberis and Ming Huang, "Mental Accounting, Loss Aversion and Individual Stock Returns," *Journal of Finance* 56, no. 4 (2001): 1247–1292.

[21]See, in particular, Seha Tinic and Richard West, "Risk, Return and Equilibrium: A Revisit," *Journal of Political Economy* 94, no. 1 (1986): 126–147; Burton Malkiel and Yexiao Xu, "Risk and Return Revisited," *Journal of Portfolio Management* 23, no. 3 (1997): 9–14; and Malkiel and Xu, "Idiosyncratic Risk and Security Returns."

[22]Lionel Martellini, "Towards the Design of Better Equity Benchmarks: Rehabilitating the Tangency Portfolio from Modern Portfolio Theory," *Journal of Portfolio Management* 35, no. 4 (Summer 2008): 34–41.

[23]Mark E. Rubinstein, "The Fundamental Theorem of Parameter-preference Security Valuation," *Journal of Financial and Quantitative Analysis* 8, no. 1 (1973): 61–69; and Alan Krauz and Robert H. Litzenberger, "Skewness Preference and the Valuation of Risk Assets," *Journal of Finance* 31, no. 4 (1976): 1085–1100.

[24]Nicholas C. Barberis and Ming Huang, "Stock as Lotteries: The Implication of Probability Weighting for Security Prices," Working paper, Stanford and Yale University, 2004; Markus K. Brunnermeier, Christian Gollier, and Jonathan A. Parker, "Optimal Beliefs, Asset Prices, and the Preference for Skewed Returns," *American*

intuition behind this result is that investors like to hold positively skewed portfolios. The highest skewness is achieved by concentrating portfolios in a small number of stocks that themselves have positively skewed returns. Thus investors tend to be underdiversified and drive up the price of stocks with high positive skewness, which in turn reduces their future expected returns. Stocks with negative skewness are relatively unattractive and thus have low prices and high returns. The preference for kurtosis is in the sense that investors like low kurtosis and thus expected returns should be positively related to kurtosis. Two studies provide empirical evidence that individual stocks' skewness and kurtosis are indeed related to future returns.[25] An alternative to direct consideration of the higher moments of returns is to use a risk measure that aggregates the different dimensions of risk. In this line, Bali and Cakici[26] show that future returns on stocks are positively related to their Value-at-Risk and Estrada[27] and Chen, Chen, and Chen[28] show that there is a relationship between downside risk and expected returns.

Implications for Benchmark Portfolio Construction

Once careful estimates for risk and return parameters have been obtained, one may then design efficient proxies for asset class benchmarks with an attractive risk-return profile. For example Amenc et al.[29] find that efficient equity benchmarks designed on the basis of robust estimates for risk and expected return parameters substantially outperform in terms of risk-adjusted performance market-cap-weighted indexes that are often used as default options for investment benchmarks in spite of their well-documented lack of efficiency.[30]

Economic Review 97 (2007): 159–165; and Todd Mitton and Keith Vorkink, "Equilibrium Underdiversification and the Preference for Skewness," *Review of Financial Studies* 20 (2007): 1255–1288.

[25]Brian Boyer, Todd Mitton, and Keith Vorkink, "Expected Idiosyncratic Skewness," *Review of Financial Studies* 23, no. 1 (2010): 169–202; and Jennifer Conrad, Robert F. Dittmar, and Eric Ghysels, "Ex ante Skewness and Expected Stock Returns," Working paper, University of North Carolina at Chapel Hill, 2008.

[26]Turan Bali and Nusret Cakici, "Value at Risk and Expected Stock Returns," *Financial Analysts Journal* 60, no. 2 (2004): 57–73.

[27]Javier Estrada, "The Cost of Equity in Emerging Markets: A Downside Risk Approach," *Emerging Markets Quarterly* 4, no. 3 (2000): 19–30.

[28]Dar-Hsin Chen, Chun-Da Chen, and Jianguo Chen, "Downside Risk Measures and Equity Returns in the NYSE," *Applied Economics* 41, no. 8 (2009): 1055–1070.

[29]Noël Amenc, Felix Goltz, Lionel Martellini, and Patrice Retkowsky, "Efficient Indexation: An Alternative to Cap-Weighted Indices," Working paper, EDHEC Risk Institute, 2010.

[30]See, for example, Haugen and Baker, "The Efficient Market Inefficiency of Capitalization-Weighted Stock Portfolios," and Grinold, "Are Benchmark Portfolios Efficient?"

Exhibit 7.2 shows summary performance statistics for an efficient index constructed according to the afore-mentioned principles. For the average return, volatility and the Sharpe ratio, we report differences with respect to cap-weighting and assess whether this difference is statistically significant.

Exhibit 7.2 shows that the efficient weighting of index constituents leads to higher average returns, lower volatility, and higher Sharpe ratio. All these differences are statistically significant at the 10% level, whereas the difference in Sharpe ratios is significant even at the 0.1% level. Given the data, it is highly unlikely that the unobservable true performance of efficient weighting was not different from that of capitalisation weighting. Economically, the performance difference is pronounced, as the Sharpe ratio increases by about 70%.

Asset Allocation Step: Putting the Efficient Benchmarks Together

After efficient benchmarks have been designed for various asset classes, these building blocks can be assembled in a second step, the asset allocation step, to build a well-designed multiclass performance-seeking portfolio. While the methods we have discussed so far can in principle be applied in both contexts, a number of key differences should be emphasized.

In the asset allocation context, the number of constituents is small, and using time- and state-dependent covariance matrix estimates is reasonable; nonetheless, these estimates do not necessarily improve the situation in portfolio construction contexts, in which the number of constituents is large. Similarly, while it is not feasible in general, as explained above, to perform portfolio optimization with higher-order moments in a portfolio construction context, in which the number of constituents is typically large, it is reasonable to go beyond mean-variance analysis in an asset allocation context, in which the number of constituents is limited.

Furthermore, in an asset allocation context, the universe is not homogeneous, which has implications for expected returns and covariance estimation. In terms of covariance matrix, it will not prove easy to obtain a universal factor model for the whole investment universe. In this context, it is is arguably better to use statistical shrinkage towards say the constant correlation model, than to take a factor model approach.[31]

---

[31]See Olivier Ledoit and Mark Wolf, "Improved Estimation of the Covariance Matrix of Stock Returns with an Application to Portfolio Selection," *Journal of Empirical Finance* 10, no. 5 (2003): 603–621; and Ledoit and Wolf, "Honey, I Shrunk the Sample Covariance Matrix."

EXHIBIT 7.2 Risk and Return Characteristics for the Efficient Index

Index	Annual Average Return (compounded)	Annual Standard Deviation	Sharpe Ratio (compounded)	Information Ratio	Tracking Error
Efficient index	11.63%	14.65%	0.41	0.52	4.65%
Cap weighted	9.23%	15.20%	0.24	0.00	0.00%
Difference (efficient minus cap weighted)	2.40%	-0.55%	0.17	—	—
p-value for difference	0.14%	6.04%	0.04%	—	—

Note: The table shows risk and return statistics portfolios constructed with the same set of constituents as the cap-weighted index. Rebalancing is quarterly subject to an optimal control of portfolio turnover (by setting the reoptimization threshold to 50%). Portfolios are constructed by maximising the Sharpe ratio given an expected return estimate and a covariance estimate. The expected return estimate is set to the median total risk of stocks in the same decile when sorting by total risk. The covariance matrix is estimated using an implicit factor model for stock returns. Weight constraints are set so that each stock's weight is between $1/2N$ and $2/N$, where N is the number of index constituents. P-values for differences are computed using the paired t-test for the average, the F-test for volatility, and a Jobson-Korkie test for the Sharpe ratio. The results are based on weekly return data from 1/1959 to 12/2008.

ASSET ALLOCATION AND PORTFOLIO CONSTRUCTION DECISIONS IN THE OPTIMAL DESIGN OF THE LIABILITY-HEDGING PORTFOLIO

Risk diversification is only one possible form of risk management, merely focusing at achieving the best risk-return trade-off regardless of investment objectives and constraints. On the other hand, one should recognize that diversification is simply not the appropriate tool when it comes to protecting long-term liability needs.

One key academic insight emanating from the pioneering work of Robert Merton in the 1970s is that the presence of state variables impacting the asset return and/or wealth process will lead to the introduction of dedicated *hedging demands*, in addition to cash and optimally diversified PSP (which is still needed).

In particular, it clearly appears that the risk factors impacting pension liability values should not be diversified away, but instead should be hedged away. Amongst those, two main risk factors stand out, namely interest rate risk and inflation risk. Although constructing interest rate and inflation hedging benchmarks might seem straightforward compared to constructing performance-seeking benchmarks, some challenges remain, which we discuss now.

Towards the Design of Improved Interest Rate Risk Benchmarks

A first approach to the design of the LHP, called *cash-flow matching*, involves ensuring a perfect *static* match between the cash flows from the portfolio of assets and the commitments in the liabilities. Let us assume for example that a pension fund has a commitment to pay out a monthly pension to a retired person. Leaving aside the complexity relating to the uncertain life expectancy of the retiree, the structure of the liabilities is defined simply as a series of cash outflows to be paid, the real value of which is known today, but for which the nominal value is typically matched with an inflation index. It is possible in theory to construct a portfolio of assets whose future cash flows will be identical to this structure of commitments. Doing so, assuming that securities of that kind exist on the market, would involve purchasing inflation-linked zero-coupon bonds with a maturity corresponding to the dates on which the monthly pension installments are paid out, with amounts that are proportional to the amount of real commitments.

While this technique provides the advantage of simplicity and allows, in theory, for perfect risk management, it presents a number of limitations and raises a series of implementation challenges. In particular, finding bond portfolios with the proper duration is hardly feasible, especially when looking at the corporate bond segment.

The conflict of interests between issuers and investors about the duration of corporate bonds is known as the duration problem. Each bond investor has a specific time horizon of his investment in mind, and there is no reason to expect that these needs correspond to the optimal financing plan of the issuers. In fact, the duration structure of outstanding bonds reflects the preferences of the issuers in their aim to minimize the cost of capital. This minimization is fundamentally opposed to the interest of the investors, who usually try to maximize their returns. Although as such a part of the suitability problem mentioned above, the duration mismatch in the corporate bond market is of primordial importance to investors. Pension funds have some fixed nominal liabilities originating from their defined benefit plans. Given this long-term perspective, long-term bonds are a much better hedge than short-term debt. Issuers of such bonds therefore have to pay only a small yield premium—even though they are more volatile. In contrast, for short-term investors with no fixed time horizon in mind such investments are far less attractive. The duration of the indexes is however a result of the sell-side of corporate bonds—so that no investor should hold just this benchmark duration. Hence, many corporate bonds indexes are not well suited to serving as benchmark for corporate bond investors.

More worrisome perhaps is the fact that the characteristics of corporate bond indexes can change over time, and can therefore hardly be optimized over. So, efforts are required towards the design of stable corporate bond indexes that are optimized not only in an attempt to maximize their risk-adjusted performance, but also so as to display a (quasi) constant duration and allocation by rating class over time.

Towards the Design of Improved Inflation Hedging Benchmarks

A recent surge in worldwide inflation has increased the need for investors to hedge against unexpected changes in price levels. Inflation hedging has in fact become a concern of critical importance for private investors, who consider inflation as a direct threat with respect to the protection of their purchasing power, but also for pension funds, which must make pension payments that are typically indexed with respect to consumer price or wage level indexes.

In this context, novel forms of institutional investment solutions have been promoted by asset managers and investment banks, focusing on the design of a customized liability-matching portfolios, the sole purpose of which is to hedge away as effectively as possible the impact of unexpected changes in risk factors, most notably inflation risk, affecting liability values. A variety of cash instruments (Treasury inflation protected securities, or

TIPS) as well as dedicated OTC derivatives (such as inflation swaps) are used in practice to achieve a customized exposure with respect to consumer price inflation. One outstanding problem, however, is that such solutions generate very modest performance given that real returns on inflation-protected securities, negatively impacted by the presence of a significant inflation risk premium, are typically very low. In this context, it has been argued that some other asset classes, such as stocks, real estate or commodities, could provide useful inflation protection, especially when long-term horizons are considered, at a lower cost compared to investing in TIPS.

Empirical evidence suggests that there is in fact a negative relationship between expected stock returns and expected inflation, which is consistent with the intuition that higher inflation leads to lower economic activity, and thus depresses stock returns. On the other hand, higher future inflation leads to higher dividends and thus higher returns on stocks, and thus equity investments should offer significant inflation protection over long-horizons. (As it happens, several recent empirical studies have confirmed that equities provide a good hedge against inflation over the long term, see, e.g., Boudoukh and Richardson[32] and Schotman and Schweizer.[33]) This property is particularly appealing for long-term investors such as pension fund, who need to match increases in price level at the horizon, but not on a monthly basis. Obviously, different kinds of stocks offer contrasted inflation-hedging benefits, and it is in fact possible to select stocks or sectors on the basis of their ability to hedge against inflation. For example, utilities and infrastructures companies typically have revenues that are highly correlated with inflation, and as a result they tend to provide better-than-average inflation protection. As a result, it seems possible to select stocks or sectors on the basis of their ability to hedge against inflation (hedging demand), as opposed to selecting them as a function of their outperformance potential (speculative demand). In this context, one can envision selecting stocks or sectors in an attempt to maximize the inflation-hedging property of equity-based inflation hedging solutions. The analysis typically involves two separate stages, the selection stage and the optimization stage. The goal of the selection stage is to select the set of stocks that are likely to exhibit the most attractive inflation hedging properties. In a second step, a portfolio of selected stocks will be formed so as to optimize the expected inflation-hedging benefits.

Going beyond the equity universe, similar inflation hedging properties are expected for bond returns. Indeed, bond yields may be decomposed into

---

[32]Jacob Boudoukh and Matthew Richardson, "Stock Returns and Inflation: A Long-Horizon Perspective," *American Economic Review* 83, no. 5 (1993): 1346–55.
[33]Peter Schotman and Mark Schweitzer, "Horizon Sensitivity of the Inflation Hedge of Stocks," *Journal of Empirical Finance* 7, nos. 3 & 4 (2000): 301–315.

a real yield and an expected inflation components. Since expected and realized inflation move together on the long-term, a positive long-term correlation between bond returns and changes in inflation is expected. In the short-term, however, expected inflation may deviate from the actual realized inflation, leading to low or negative correlations in the short-term. It has also been recently argued that alternative forms of investments offer attractive inflation-hedging benefits. Commodity prices, in particular, are argued to be leading indicators of inflation in that they are quick to respond to economy-wide shocks to demand. Commodity prices generally are set in highly competitive auction markets and consequently tend to be more flexible than prices overall. Beside, recent inflation is heavily driven by the increase in commodity prices, in particular in the domain of agriculture, minerals and energy. In the same vein, it has also been found that commercial and residential real estate provide at least a partial hedge against inflation and that portfolios that include real estate realize an increase in inflation hedgeability, especially over long-horizons.

Exhibit 7.3 (borrowed from Amenc, Martellini and Ziemann[34] to which we refer for further details on the calibration of the VAR and VECM models), which displays a set of estimated term structure of correlation coefficients between asset returns and inflation-linked liability returns, confirms that various asset classes have contrasted inflation-hedging properties over various horizons, with an inflation-hedging capacity that increases with the horizon for stocks, bonds and real estate.

As a consequence of the afore mentioned findings, it is tempting to investigate whether novel liability-hedging investment solutions can be designed so as to decrease the cost of inflation insurance from the investor's perspective. In particular, it is possible to construct different versions of the inflation-hedging portfolio so as to assess the impact of introducing investment classes such as equities, commodities and real estate in addition to inflation-linked bonds. Amenc, Martellini, and Ziemann have shown that the increased expected return potential generated by the introduction of asset classes with good long-term inflation-hedging property allows the sponsor company to maintain the level of contributions and lower exposure to downside risk.

Other advanced solutions may involve hedging a particular segment of inflation distribution, with an expected focus on hedging large, as opposed to moderate, inflation shocks, in an attempt to again reduce the costs of inflation hedging, and hence enhance the performance of the inflation-hedging portfolio.

---

[34]Noël Amenc, Lionel Martellini and Volker Ziemann, "Inflation-Hedging Properties of Real Assets and Implications for Asset–Liability Management Decisions," *Journal of Portfolio Management* 35, no. 4 (2009): 94–110.

EXHIBIT 7.3 Term Structure of Correlation Coefficients Between Different Asset Returns and Inflation-Linked Liability Returns for Various Horizons

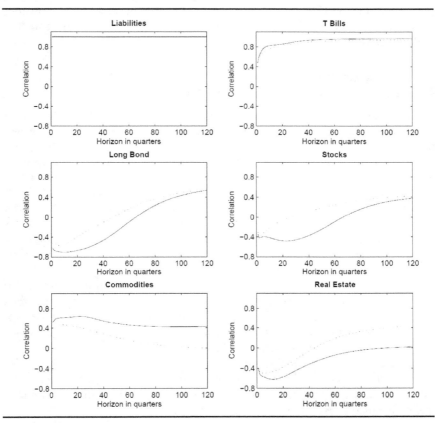

Dotted lines correspond to implied correlations estimated from a Vector Auto Regressive (VAR) model, while solid lines correspond to implied correlations estimated from a Vector Error Correction Model (VECM).

Source: Noël Amenc, Lionel Martellini, and Volker Ziemann, "Inflation-Hedging Properties of Real Assets and Implications for Asset–Liability Management Decisions," *Journal of Portfolio Management* 35, no. 4 (2009): 98.

This copyrighted material is reprinted with permission from Institutional Investor, Inc., *Journal of Portfolio Management*, 225 Park Avenue, New York, NY 10003.

As a final note, we analyze in the next section situations in which the strict separation between the performance-seeking and liability-hedging portfolios does not apply in a strict sense. More specifically, we consider situations in which multiple and equally attractive candidates exist for the PSP and LHP.

Performance-Seeking Portfolios with Attractive Liability/Inflation Hedging Properties

As previously mentioned, asset pricing theory is grounded on *separation theorems*, stating that risk and performance are two conflicting objectives that are best managed when managed separately. According to this paradigm, performance generation is first obtained through an optimal exposure to rewarded risk factors so as to alleviate the burden on contributions, while hedging against unexpected shocks that impact current value of (assets and) liabilities is accounted for by a separate dedicated portfolio.

This clear separation between performance and hedging portfolios is very useful, and has a number of important implications, not only in terms of portfolio construction and asset allocation techniques, but also in terms of the organizational structure at the institutional investors' level.

One might wonder, however, what would happen if an investor was to be given a choice between two (or more) performance-seeking portfolios with identical risk-reward ratios but distinct liability hedging properties. Obviously in this situation, an investor would tend to favor the performance portfolio with the most attractive liability-hedging property.

In fact this hypothetical question would not arise if the efficient frontier were strictly concave, which would ensure the existence and uniqueness of the maximum risk–reward ratio portfolio, as is the case in the standard mean-variance paradigm with perfect information.

It has been shown, however, that when using a general non strictly convex risk measure, the efficient frontier may not be strictly concave, and as a result the maximum reward–risk portfolio may not be unique.[35] A similar result would hold for a mean-variance objective in the absence of perfect information regarding the risk return parameters. See Exhibit 7.4 for an illustration.

As a result, in most realistic situations, if given a choice between seemingly attractive portfolio-seeking portfolios, it would be rational for an investor to aim at selecting the performance portfolio with the most attractive liability-hedging properties, and this would not conflict with the fund separation theorem. Conversely, if an investor had a choice of liability-hedging portfolios with equally attractive inflation-hedging benefits, the investor

---

[35]Stoyan V. Stoyanov, Svetlozar T. Rachev, and Frank J. Fabozzi, "Optimal Financial Portfolios," *Applied Mathematical Finance* 14, no. 5 (2007): 401–436.

EXHIBIT 7.4   Multiple True or Estimated Tangency Portfolios

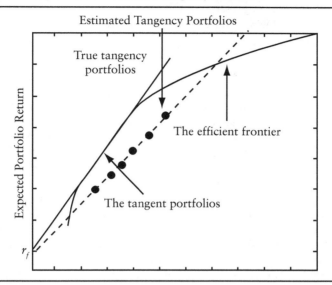

would tend to favour the hedging portfolio with the most attractive risk–reward ratio.

DYNAMIC ALLOCATION DECISIONS TO THE PERFORMANCE-SEEKING AND LIABILITY-HEDGING PORTFOLIOS

Assuming that reasonable proxies for performance-seeking and liability-hedging portfolios have been designed using some of the afore-mentioned methodologies, we must still determine the optimal allocation strategy to those two building blocks. A series of novel paradigms, which we describe next, are reshaping our approaches to long-term investment decisions for long-term investors facing liability commitments and short-term performance constraints.

Accounting for the Presence of Investors' Liability Commitments: The Liability-Driven Investment Paradigm

As explained earlier in this chapter, investors endowed with consumption/liability objectives need to invest in two distinct portfolios, in addition to cash: one performance-seeking portfolio and one liability-hedging portfolio, construction methods that have been discussed in previous sections.

Formally, under the assumption of a constant opportunity set,[36] we obtain the following expression of the fund separation theorem in the intertemporal context when trading is possible between current date and investment horizon:

$$w_t^* = \frac{\lambda}{\gamma\sigma} PSP + \left(1 - \frac{1}{\gamma}\right)\beta \ LHP$$

This expression is similar to that in equation (7.2), extended to the asset-liability management setting. As appears from this equation, the allocation to the "risky" building block is a decreasing function of the PSP Sharpe ratio λ and a decreasing function of the investor's risk aversion γ and PSP volatility σ, as was already the case in equation (7.2).[37] The allocation to the "safe" building block is an increasing function of the beta of liability portfolio with respect to the liability-hedging portfolio. If there exists an asset portfolio that perfectly matches the liability portfolio, then the beta is 1, and an infinitely risk-averse investor fully allocates to the LHP. This is consistent with the intuition that for an investor facing liability commitments, the LHP, as opposed to cash, is the true risk-free asset.

Equation (7.2) is the solution to a static optimization problem, and the corresponding strategy is (by construction) of the buy-and-hold kind. Equation (7.3) is the solution to a dynamic optimization problem, as shall be evidenced by the presence of an explicit time-dependency in the expression for the optimal allocation strategy. The corresponding strategy is a fixed-mix strategy, where in principle constant trading occurs so as to rebalance the portfolio allocation back to the constant target. The fund separation theorem is expressed here under the assumption of a constant opportunity set. In later sections, we shall relax this assumption and analyze how the allocation is impacted in particular by the introduction of time-variation in the PSP expected return and volatility.

In Exhibit 7.5, we present the distribution the distribution of the funding ratio, defined as asset value divided by liability value, at horizon. The initial funding ratio is assumed to be 100%, the horizon is 11.32 years (taken to be the duration of liabilities of a Dutch defined benefit pension fund).[38] On the left–hand side the Sharpe ratio of the PSP is assumed to be 0.24, while it assumed to be improved by 50% at 0.36 on the right-hand

---

[36]See this chapter's appendix for details.

[37]Risk-aversion is not observable, and not even well-defined for institutions, but it should be treated as an implicit parameter that can be backed out from a given risk-budget, often expressed in terms of expected shortfall with respect to liabilities.

[38]For more details, see Lionel Martellini and Vincent Milhau, "Measuring the Benefits of Dynamic Asset Allocation Strategies in the Presence of Liability Constraints," EDHEC-Risk Institute Publication, March 2009.

EXHIBIT 7.5   Distribution of Funding Ratio with Inefficient versus Efficient PSP

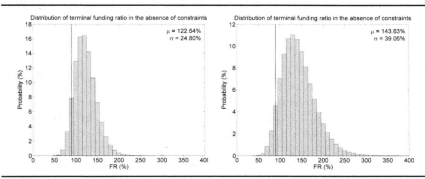

Note: The initial funding ratio is assumed to be 100%, the horizon is 11.32 years (taken to be the duration of liabilities of a Dutch defined benefit pension fund). On the left-hand side the Sharpe ratio of the PSP is assumed to be 0.24, while it assumed to be improved by 50% at 0.36 on the right-hand side.

side. The idea here is to capture possible improvements to the performance-seeking Sharpe ratio that would result from the use of efficient, as opposed to cap weighted, benchmarks, as discussed in previous sections.

The expected level of the funding ratio has been significantly increased. The volatility increases as well, but this is mostly due to higher dispersion on the upside. Regarding downside risk, the shortfall probability (formally defined as the probability that the funding ratio ends up below 100%) decreases from 19.23% down to 11.97% when the Sharpe ratio of the PSP portfolio is improved from 0.24 to 0.36. Overall, the substantial improvement in the distribution of funding ratio at horizon is the result of two effects. On the one hand, if the Sharpe ratio of the PSP is increased, the expected value of the funding ratio is improved, with associated benefits from an ALM perspective. On the other hand, the allocation to the PSP is also increased. Overall, we obtain that improving the risk-reward ratio is a key component in meeting investors' long-term objective.

Accounting for the Presence of Investors' Long-Term Objectives: The Life-Cycle Investment Paradigm

While assuming a constant opportunity set can be acceptable when investors have a short-term horizon, the presence of a long-horizon, typical to most investors' problems, makes it necessary to go beyond Markowitz static portfolio selection analysis. The next important step after Markowitz[39]

---

[39]Markowitz, "Portfolio Selection," 3.

is Merton[40] who extends portfolio construction techniques beyond the static setting, and shows how to solve dynamic portfolio optimization problems using dynamic programming approach. In terms of industry implications, the development of dynamic asset pricing theory has led to the emergence of improved investment solutions that take into account the changing nature of investment opportunities. These novel forms of investment solutions are broadly referred to as *life-cycle investing* strategies.

Current forms of implementation of the life-cycle investing concept are sometimes severely suboptimal. For example, a popular asset allocation strategy for managing equity risk on behalf of a private investor in the context of a defined contribution pension plan is known as deterministic life investing. In the early stages, when the retirement date is far away, the contributions are invested entirely in equities. Then, beginning on a predetermined date (e.g., 10 years) prior to retirement, the assets are switched gradually into bonds at some pre-defined rate (e.g., 10% per year). By the date of retirement, all the assets are held in bonds.[41] This is somewhat reminiscent of the rule of thumb put forward by Shiller,[42] advocating a percentage allocation to equity given by 100 minus investor's age in years.

While deterministic life investing is a simple strategy that is popular amongst investment managers and consultants, and it is widely used by defined-contribution pension providers, there is no evidence that it is an optimal strategy in a rational sense, and we will argue below that these strategies are very imperfect proxies for truly optimal stochastic life-cycle investing strategies. Overall, the presence of risk factors can impact the opportunity set (risk-and-return parameters) and it can have a direct impact on the wealth process for non-self-financed portfolios when inflows and outflows of cash are taking place.

Accounting for Risk Factors Impacting the Investment Opportunity Set

A vast amount of empirical research has documented that interest and inflation rates, but also expected return, volatility and correlation parameters

---

[40]Robert C. Merton, "Lifetime Portfolio Selection under Uncertainty: The Continuous Time Case," *Review of Economics and Statistics* 51, no. 3 (1969): 247–257 and Robert C. Merton, "Optimum Consumption and Portfolio Rules in a Continuous-time Model," *Journal of Economic Theory* 3, no. 4 (1971): 373–413.

[41]In fact the rationale behind the strategy is to reduce the impact on the pension of a catastrophic fall in the stock market just before the plan member retires and to hedge the interest-rate risk inherent in the pension-related liability value. As we will argue later, holding a zero exposure to equity is a very trivial way of managing equity risk, and one that does not allow to let investors benefit from equity upside potential.

[42]Robert Shiller, "The Lifecycle Personal Accounts Proposal for Social Security: A Review," Working paper WP No. 11300, National Bureau of Economic Research, 2005.

are stochastically time varying, as a function of key state variables that describe the state of the business cycle. Unexpected changes in these variables have an impact on portfolio risk and performance (through changes in interest rates and risk premium process parameters), which should be optimally managed.[43] In fact, one can show that the dynamic asset allocation problem involves an optimal hedging of the state variables impacting the risk-free rate and the risk-premium processes. Except for a myopic investor, the optimal dynamic solution does not consist in merely taking the static solution, and updating it with time-varying parameters; one should also introduce dedicated *hedging* portfolios.

For example, when interest rates are stochastic, cash is no longer a risk-free asset; the risk-free asset is instead a bond with maturity matching the investor's horizon. It is therefore somewhat unsurprising that the optimal allocation decision in the presence of interest rate risk involves an additional building block, the bond with a maturity matching the investor horizon, in addition to cash and the highest risk-reward performance-seeking portfolio (a three-fund, as opposed to two-fund separation theorem). As another illustration, let us assume that the expected return on most risky assets is for example negatively impacted by increases in oil prices. So as to compensate for the deterioration of the investment opportunity set in case of a sharp increase in oil prices, the investor will benefit from holding a long position in a dedicated portfolio optimized to exhibit the highest possible correlation with oil prices.

For example, Kim and Omberg[44] have analyzed a model including a stochastic equity risk premium with a mean-reverting component. In the context of this model, one can show that the optimal allocation involves not only a deterministic decrease of the allocation to equity as the investor gets closer to the time-horizon, which is consistent with standard target date fund practice. One can also show, on the other hand, that the optimal strategy displays a state-dependent component, suggesting that the allocation to equity should be increased (respectively, decreased) when equity has become cheap (respectively, expensive), as measured through a proxy like dividend yield or price-earning ratios.

We obtain the following expression for the optimal allocation strategy, assuming for simplicity that an equity benchmark is the only risky asset so that the PSP is 100% invested in that benchmark (see this chapter's appendix for details):

---

[43]See, for example, Jérôme Detemple and Marcel Rindisbacher, "Dynamic Asset Allocation: Portfolio Decomposition Formula and Applications," *Review of Financial Studies* 23, no. 1 (2010): 25–100, as well as references therein.

[44]Tong Suk Kim and Edward Omberg, "Dynamic Nonmyopic Portfolio Behavior," *Review of Financial Studies* 9, no. 1 (1996): 141–161.

$$w_t^* = \frac{\lambda_t^s}{\gamma \sigma_S} PSP + \underbrace{\left(1 - \frac{1}{\gamma}\right) \frac{\rho_{\lambda s} \sigma_\lambda}{\sigma_s} \left[A(T-t) + B(T-t) \lambda_t^s \right]}_{\text{Hedging demand } HD_{t,T}^\lambda}$$

Here we let $\rho_{\lambda S}$ be the correlation between the Sharpe ratio of the equity index, denoted by λ^S, and the equity index return; a negative correlation means that high realized return periods tend to be followed by low expected return periods, which is supported by empirical evidence. Beside, σ_λ is the volatility of the equity Sharpe ratio process and σ_s is the volatility on the stock index.

The hedging demand $HD_{t,T}^\lambda$ against unexpected changes in the PSP Sharpe ratio has the following properties (for $\rho_{\lambda S} < 0$ and $\gamma > 1$):

- The investor with $\gamma > 1$ holds more stocks when equity Sharpe ratio is mean-reverting than when it is constant ($\sigma_\lambda = 0$).
- The hedging demand disappears if there is no equity risk premium risk ($\sigma_\lambda = 0$), or if the risk exists but cannot be hedged away ($\rho_{\lambda s} = 0$).
- The investment in stock decreases when approaching horizon T; this is consistent with target date funds prescription.

We also confirm that there is one additional state-dependent factor: if/when equity prices are low (high), and therefore expected return is high (low), one should allocate more (less) to stocks, regardless of horizon.

Accounting for Risk Factors Impacting the Wealth Process

As noted earlier, the presence of risk factors can also have a direct impact on the wealth process, even in the case of a constant opportunity set. In fact, most portfolios are not self-financed portfolios because of the presence of outflows of cash (consumption, liability payments) or inflows of cash (endowment, contribution, income, and so on). For example, labor income risk will have an impact on optimal portfolio decisions, and will legitimate the introduction of a dedicated hedging demand. More generally, the present value of liability and endowment flows are impacted by state variables (interest rate risk, inflation risk, income risk, etc.), the impact of which needs to be hedged away.

For example, a pension fund should hold a long position in a liability-hedging portfolio to hedge away the implicit short position in liability flows. Conversely, a sovereign wealth fund from an oil-rich country should hold a short position in oil prices to hedge away implicit long position in endowment flows. The intuition is rather straightforward: The sovereign wealth fund is implicitly holding a long position in an asset whose value is given as the present value of future sovereign contributions. If the fund implements the standard asset allocation decision optimal in the absence of contribution, it will invest in the highest risk-reward portfolio and cash as a function of risk aversion. This will result in an overexposure to oil prices with respect to the optimal composition of the highest risk-reward portfolio. This position should be compensated away by holding a short position in securities positively correlated with oil prices or a long position in securities negatively correlated with oil prices.

Generally speaking, a sound investment solution involves a dynamic asset allocation strategy that takes into account (1) the stochastic features of the investor's lifetime income progression (where is the money coming from); (2) the stochastic features of the investor's expected pension value (what the money is going to be used for); and (3) the stochastic features of the assets held in his portfolio. These advances in dynamic asset allocation decisions have potential applications for the design of stochastic, state-dependent, asset allocation policies, which stand in contrast to the deterministically time-dependent allocation strategies embedded within existing life-cycle investment products.

If we focus on a retirement product, the optimal asset allocation strategy will involve a state-dependent allocation to three building-blocks: (1) a performance-seeking portfolio (heavily invested in equities, but also in bonds and real estate); (2) an income-hedging portfolio (heavily invested in cash but also invested in equities, which exhibit appealing wage inflation hedging properties, especially over long-horizons); and (3) a pension hedging portfolio (heavily invested in bonds for interest rate hedging motives, and also in real estate for inflation hedging motives). In the early stages of the plan, the income hedging fund is the dominant low-risk component of the investment strategy, but as the retirement date approaches, there is a gradual, albeit nondeterministic, switch from the income hedging building block into the pension hedging building block. This switching only superficially resembles deterministic life-cycle investing; instead of switching from high-risk assets to low-risk assets, as in the case of deterministic life-cycle investing, the optimal stochastic lifestyle strategy involves a switch between different types of hedging demands. Moreover, the relative weights of the hedging portfolios are no longer deterministic; they take into account the current level of all variables of interest.

In other words, stochastic life-cycle investing has at least two advantages over deterministic life-cycle investing: (1) consistent with the fund separation theorem, it focuses on fundamental building blocks, as opposed to asset classes; and (2) it involves a stochastic allocation to these three building blocks, which evolves as a function of the current values of state variables of interest (and most notably interest rate, inflation rate and income rate). Overall, the state-dependent asset allocation strategies can be shown to strongly dominate various static and deterministic strategies, and the utility costs associated to such inefficient strategies have been found substantial.[45] A similar result is obtained by Martellini and Milhau,[46] who confirm that the opportunity cost involved in purely deterministic life-cycle strategies such as those implemented by available target date funds is substantial for reasonable parameter values. Perhaps surprisingly, they also find that even very reasonably fine partitions of the set of investors and market conditions, perfectly consistent with implementation in a retail money management context and only marginally more complex than current partitions solely based on time-horizon, allow for substantial welfare gains compared to deterministic life-cycle strategies. These results have important potential implications for the design of improved forms of target date funds since they suggest that more financial innovation can be used to design improved forms of target date funds based on stochastic, as opposed to deterministic, life-cycle investing.

Accounting for the Presence of Investors' Short-Term Constraints: The Risk-Controlled Investment Paradigm

One key element that is missing in the analysis presented so far is the integration of short-term constraints into the design of the optimal allocation strategy. In fact, it can be argued that most if not all investors, even those (such as pension funds or sovereign wealth funds) with the longest possible horizons inevitably face a number of short-term performance constraints, imposed by accounting and/or regulatory pressure, political pressure, peer pressure, etc. In a private wealth management context, there is also strong evidence that investors typically face (mostly self-imposed) short-term constraints, e.g., maximum drawdown constraints.

These constraints are not managed through diversification strategies (which are dedicated to the design of the PSP) or hedging strategies, but through insurance strategies. From a technical standpoint, the introduction of short-term constraints can be formalized in a portfolio selection problem based on a key insight regarding the deep correspondence between pricing and portfolio problems. On the one hand, asset-pricing problems are equivalent

---

[45]Andrew J. G. Cairns, David Blake, and K. Dowd, "A Two-Factor Model for Stochastic Mortality with Parameter Uncertainty," *Journal of Risk and Insurance* 73, no. 4 (2006): 687–718.
[46]Lionel Martellini and Vincent Milhau, "From Deterministic to Stochastic Life-Cycle Investing—Implications for the Design of Improved Forms of Target-Date Funds," Working paper, EDHEC-Risk Institute, 2010.

to dynamic asset allocation problems: Merton's[47] interpretation of the Black and Scholes[48] option pricing formula. On the other hand, dynamic asset allocation problems[49] are equivalent to asset pricing problems: *martingale* or *convex duality* approach to dynamic asset allocation problems.[50]

The practical implication of the introduction of short-term constraints is that optimal investment in a performance-seeking satellite portfolio (PSP) is not only a function of risk aversion, but also of risk budgets (margin for error), as well as probability of the risk budget to be spent before horizon. In a nutshell, a precommitment to risk management allows one to adjust risk exposure in an optimal state-dependent manner, and therefore to generate the highest exposure to upside potential of PSP while respecting risk constraints.

Dynamic Liability-Driven Investing

The procedure of constant proportion portfolio insurance techniques, originally designed to ensure the respect of absolute performance, can be extended to a relative return context. Martellini and Milhau[51] show that an approach similar to standard constant proportion portfolio insurance (CPPI) can be taken to offer the investor a guarantee on the relative level of performance, with a cap on underperformance with respect to the liability-driven benchmark.[52] The techniques of traditional CPPI still apply, provided that the risky asset is reinterpreted as the performance-seeking portfolio, which contains relative risk with respect to the liability benchmark, and the risk-free asset is reinterpreted as the liability-hedging portfolio, which contains no relative risk with respect to the liability benchmark.

---

[47]Robert C. Merton, "Theory of Rational Option Pricing," *Bell Journal of Economics and Management Science* 4, no. 1 (1973): 141–183.

[48]Fischer Black and Myron Scholes, "Pricing of Options and Corporate Liabilities," *Journal of Political Economy* 81, no. 3 (1973): 637–654.

[49]Merton, "Theory of Rational Option Pricing," 13.

[50]See Ioannis Karatzas, John P. Lehoczky and Steve Shreve, "Optimal Portfolio and Consumption Decisions for a 'Small Investor' on a Finite Horizon," *SIAM Journal on Control and Optimization* 25 (1987): 1557–1586; and John C. Cox and Chi-fu Huang, "Optimal Consumption and Portfolio Policies when Asset Prices Follow a Diffusion Process," *Journal of Economic Theory* 49, no. 1 (1989): 33–83.

[51]Martellini and Milhau, "From Deterministic to Stochastic Life-Cycle Investing—Implications for the Design of Improved Forms of Target-Date Funds," 33.

[52]For an introduction to the basic CPPI technique see Fischer Black and Robert Jones, "Simplifying Portfolio Insurance," *Journal of Portfolio Management* 14, no. 1 (1987): 48–51; and Fischer Black and Andre Perold, "Theory of Constant Proportion Portfolio Insurance," *Journal of Economic Dynamics and Control* 16, nos. 3 & 4 (1992): 403–426.

Investors endowed with consumption and liability objectives must still invest in two distinct portfolios: the "risky" and the "safe" part; their allocation to the risky part must still be increasing in the PSP Sharpe ratio λ and decreasing in the investor's risk aversion γ and PSP volatility σ. The novelty is that the allocation to the PSP versus LHP is also a function of the risk-budget, a quantity that is defined as the difference between the asset value A_t and a (probability-weighted) floor $p_{t,T}F_t$. When implemented in continuous-time, this portfolio strategy allows truncating the final distribution of the funding ratio to the minimum funding ratio level denoted by F_t.

In what follows, we present the optimal allocation strategy:[53]

$$w_t^{*c} = \frac{1}{\gamma}\frac{\lambda}{\sigma}\left(1 - p_{t,T}\frac{F_t}{A_t}\right)PSP + \left(1 - \frac{1}{\gamma}\left(1 - p_{t,T}\frac{F_t}{A_t}\right)\right)\beta\,LHP \qquad (7.4)$$

A simplified version exists, which consists in the following expression:

$$w_t^{*c} = \frac{1}{\gamma}\frac{\lambda}{\sigma}\left(1 - \frac{F_t}{A_t}\right)PSP + \left(1 - \frac{1}{\gamma}\left(1 - \frac{F_t}{A_t}\right)\right)\beta\,LHP \qquad (7.5)$$

The allocation strategy presented in equation (7.5) has a constant proportion portfolio insurance (CPPI) flavor: the dollar allocation to the risky PSP is not only a function of risk aversion, as well as the PSP volatility and Sharpe ratio; it is also a function of the risk budget (or margin for error) defined as the distance between the asset value A_t and the short-term floor level F_t (typically known as the "cushion" in CPPI terminology):

$$A_t w_t^{*c} = \frac{1}{\gamma}\frac{\lambda}{\sigma}\left(A_t - F_t\right)PSP + \left(A_t - \frac{1}{\gamma}\left(A_t - F_t\right)\right)\beta\,LHP$$

When the margin for error disappears, that is, when the investor's short-term risk budget is spent, then the allocation to the PSP becomes 0, as it should.

Equation (7.4) defines a more general allocation strategy, with a more aggressive spending of the risk budget. The risk budget is here defined to be $A_t - p_{t,T}F_t$ as opposed to $A_t - F_t$, where the number $p_{t,T}$ is like a probability, hence between 0 and 1, and can be interpreted as the estimated probability that the risk budget will be violated by the corresponding unconstrained strategy (see Exhibit 7.6).

While the risk budget $A_t - p_{t,T}F_t > A_t - F_t$ looks higher than investor's wishes, we still have that $A_t \geq F_t$ for all t because $p_{t,T}$ adjusts itself in an optimal manner in the sense that $p_{t,T} \to 1$ when and if the satellite portfolio does

---

[53]See this chapter's appendix for details.

EXHIBIT 7.6   Violations of Risk Budgets with Unconstrained Strategies

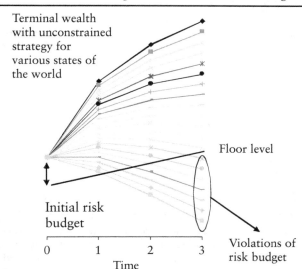

Terminal wealth with unconstrained strategy for various states of the world

Floor level

Initial risk budget

Violations of risk budget

0   1   2   3

Time

so poorly that the risk budget is almost entirely spent. Conversely, when the margin for error increases, we have that $p_{t,T} \to 0$, thus allowing for a fuller access to the upside potential of the satellite. Intuitively, it is straightforward to understand that a state-dependent spending of the risk budget is better than a deterministic (constant) spending scheme. Having a constant spending of the risk budget is in general suboptimal and has an opportunity cost for the investor with finite time horizon.

In fact, the equation (7.4) describes an asset allocation strategy that is somewhat reminiscent of (dynamic replication of) option-based portfolio insurance (OBPI) strategies, which it extends in a number of dimensions. First, the underlying asset is not a risky asset but the underlying optimal unconstrained strategy. Moreover, the risk-free asset is no longer cash, but the investor's liability benchmark. These modifications to the standard OBPI strategy allow one to transport its structure to relative risk management.

Formally, the terminal wealth A_T^{*c} generated by the optimal constrained strategy with minimum funding level is given by F_t:[54]

$$A_T^{*c} = F_T + \max\left(\xi A_T^{*u} - F_T, 0\right)$$

Here A_T^{*u} is the terminal wealth generated by the optimal unconstrained strategy, which is a fixed-mix strategy when the opportunity set is constant,

---

[54]See this chapter's appendix for details.

EXHIBIT 7.7   Distribution of Terminal Funding Ratio under a Risk-Controlled Strategy with an Inefficient PSP

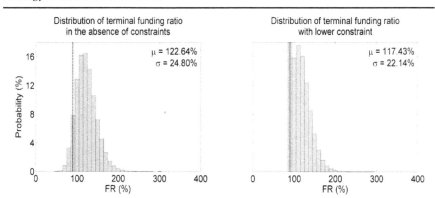

Note: The initial funding ratio is assumed to be 100%, the horizon is 11.32 years (taken to be the duration of liabilities of a Dutch defined benefit pension fund). The distribution in the right panel is the one generated by a risk-controlled strategy with a minimum funding ratio at 90%.
Source: Lionel Martellini and Vincent Milhau, "From Deterministic to Stochastic Life-Cycle Investing—Implications for the Design of Improved Forms of Target-Date Funds," Working paper, EDHEC-Risk Institute, 2010.

and in general has a life-cycle component in the presence of a stochastic opportunity set. Obviously, no such long-maturity options written on customized dynamic liability-driven investing (LDI)/life-cycle investing (LCI) strategies can be found, even as OTC contracts, and investors will have to implement some form of dynamic allocation strategy that will allow for the replication of the optimal payoff.

This approach, known as *risk-controlled investing*, allows an investor to truncate the relative return distribution so as to allocate the probability weights away from severe underperformance relative to the liabilities in favor of more potential for outperformance. In Exhibit 7.7, we present on the right panel the distribution of the funding ratio at horizon under the same assumption as in Exhibit 7.5, but under a risk-controlled strategy with a minimum funding ratio at 90% (for comparison, the left panel presents the base case unconstrained strategy analyzed in Exhibit 7.5). Here, the Sharpe ratio of the PSP is assumed to be taken at the base case value 0.24.

We find that the introduction of the risk-controlled strategy allows one to truncate the left-side of the distribution of the final funding ratio at the 90% level, as expected. Downside risk protection has a cost, however, as can be seen from the fact that the expected terminal funding ratio is lower

EXHIBIT 7.8   Distribution of Terminal Funding Ratio under a Risk-Controlled Strategy with an Improved PSP

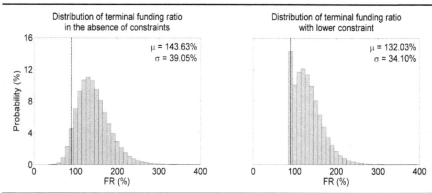

Note: The initial funding ratio is assumed to be 100%, the horizon is 11.32 years (taken to be the duration of liabilities of a Dutch defined benefit pension fund.
Source: Lionel Martellini and Vincent Milhau, "From Deterministic to Stochastic Life-Cycle Investing—Implications for the Design of Improved Forms of Target-Date Funds," Working paper, EDHEC-Risk Institute, 2010.

for the risk-controlled strategy (117.43% on the right panel) than for the unconstrained strategy (122.64% on the left panel).

In Exhibit 7.8, we present the distribution of the funding ratio at horizon under the same assumption as in Exhibit 7.7, but under the assumption of a Sharpe ratio of a PSP improved by 50% (taken to be 0.36 as opposed to 0.24).

We find that again that the introduction of the risk-controlled strategy allows one to truncate the left-side of the distribution of the final funding ratio at the 90% level, as expected. The implicit cost of downside risk protection can be seen from the fact that the expected terminal funding ratio is lower for the risk-controlled strategy (132.03% on the right panel) than for the unconstrained strategy (143.63% on the left panel). Interestingly, we find that the use of an improved PSP has a very substantial impact in terms of final distribution of the constrained funding ratio. In particular, the mean of the distribution of the funding ratio is higher with the risk-controlled strategy and the efficient PSP than it is with the base case strategy and the inefficient PSP, and this while allowing for downside protection below the 90% minimum level.

In practice, the starting point consists of generating stochastic scenarios for the return on risky asset classes, as well as the return on liabilities. These scenarios will be used to analyze the distribution of the final surplus, expected return, volatility, max drawdown, etc. generated by risk-controlled strategies. Most notably, they allow one to provide a formal analysis of the costs *and* benefits of (1) increasing/decreasing multiplier and protection levels and (2) introducing various floors and goals as discussed below. These scenarios can be generated using a standard Monte-Carlo analysis or some form of historical simulation (bootstrapping).

Beyond the calibration stage, there are a number of key improvements that can be used in implementation. The first of these improvements relates to the introduction of a time-varying multiplier, allowing one to benefit from the clustering effect in volatility dynamics, with increases in volatility typically associated with bear market environments. The second of these improvements relates to strategies based on a trading frequency that takes place at regular space, as opposed to time, intervals.

While the original approach was developed in a simple framework, it can be extended in a number of important directions, allowing for the introduction of more complex floors. A large variety of floors can in fact be introduced (simultaneously if necessary) so as to accommodate the needs of different kinds of investors. Among the possible floors, the following possibly stand out in terms of their relevance for various kinds of investors: capital guarantee floors allowing for the protection of a fraction of the initial capital, benchmark protection floors allowing for the protection of a fraction of the value of any given stochastic benchmark (with the liability portfolio being the most natural benchmark for investors facing liabilities), max drawdown floors allowing for the respect of limits on maximum consecutive losses, trailing performance floors allowing for the protection of a fraction of the prior value of the portfolio on a rolling basis, and the like.

In addition to accounting for the presence of floors, the dynamic risk-controlled strategies can also accommodate the presence of various forms of *goals* or *ceilings*. Goal-directed strategies recognize that the investor has no utility over a *ceiling* target level of wealth G_t, which represents the investor's goal (actually a cap), which can be a constant, deterministic or stochastic function of time. Goal-directed strategies involve an optimal switching at some suitably-defined threshold level, which defines the switching point between fear-dominated and hope-dominated behavior.[55] From a conceptual standpoint, it is not clear *a priori* why any investor should want to impose a strict limit on upside potential. The intuition is that by forgiving performance beyond a certain threshold, where they have relatively lower utility from higher wealth, investors benefit from a decrease in the cost of the downside protection (short position in a convex payoff in addition to

---

[55]See, for example, Jiah-Shing Chen and Benjamin Penyang Liao, "Piecewise Linear Goal-Directed CPPI Strategy," *Asian Journal of Information Technology* 5, no. 7 (2006): 720–724; and Sid Browne, "Risk-Constrained Dynamic Active Portfolio Management," *Management Science* 46, no. 9 (2000): 1188–1199.

EXHIBIT 7.9 Distribution of Terminal Funding Ratio under a Risk-Controlled Strategy with Upper and Lower Bound and the Funding Ratio (and an inefficient PSP)

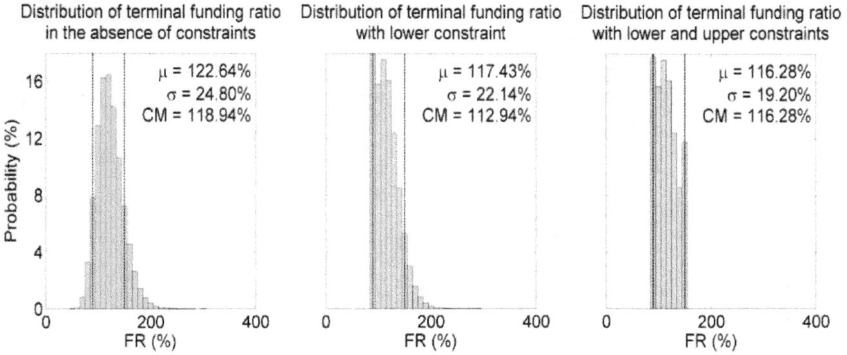

Note: The initial funding ratio is assumed to be 100%, the horizon is 11.32 years (taken to be the duration of liabilities of a Dutch defined benefit pension fund. The distribution in the middle panel is the one generated by a risk-controlled strategy with a minimum funding ratio at 90% and the distribution in the right panel is the one generated by a risk-controlled strategy with a minimum funding ratio at 90% and a maximum at 150%.

Source: Lionel Martellini and Vincent Milhau, "From Deterministic to Stochastic Life-Cycle Investing—Implications for the Design of Improved Forms of Target-Date Funds," Working paper, EDHEC-Risk Institute, 2010.

the long position—collar flavor). Putting it differently, without the performance cap, investors have a greater chance of failing an almost reached-goal when their wealth level is very high.

In Exhibit 7.9, we present on the right panel the distribution of the funding ratio at horizon under the same assumption as in Exhibit 7.5, but under a risk-controlled strategy with a minimum funding ratio at 90% and a maximum funding ratio of 150% (for comparison, the left panel presents the base case unconstrained strategy analyzed in Exhibit 7.5, and the panel in the middle presents the strategy with minimum funding ratio constraint analyzed in Exhibit 7.7). Here the Sharpe ratio of the PSP is assumed to be taken at the base case value 0.24.

By giving up part of the upside potential beyond levels where marginal utility of wealth (relative to liabilities) is low or almost zero, the investor can decrease the cost of downside protection, as can be seen from the fact that the conditional mean of the funding ratio CM for values between the minimum 90% and the maximum 150% is higher on the left panel (116.28%) compared to the panel in the middle (112.94%).

EXHIBIT 7.10 Distribution of Terminal Funding Ratio under a Risk-Controlled Strategy with Upper and Lower Bound on the Funding Ratio and an Improved PSP

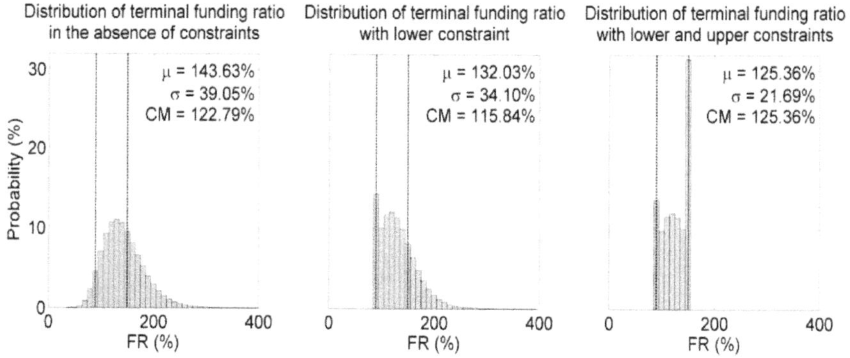

Note: The initial funding ratio is assumed to be 100%, the horizon is 11.32 years (taken to be the duration of liabilities of a Dutch defined benefit pension fund). *Source:* Lionel Martellini and Vincent Milhau, "From Deterministic to Stochastic Life-Cycle Investing—Implications for the Design of Improved Forms of Target-Date Funds," Working paper, EDHEC-Risk Institute, 2010.

Again, using an improved PSP would lead to substantially improved results, as can be seen from Exhibit 7.10.

Putting the Pieces Together: Stochastic Life-Cycle Investing with Risk Budgets

In closing, we briefly discuss the extension to a setting with a stochastic opportunity set, and we argue that the two motivations behind dynamic asset allocation decisions, namely the risk management and the revision of strategic asset allocation motivations, are often perceived as inconsistent and mutually exclusive.

In practice, dynamic risk-controlled strategies, which typically imply a reduction to equity allocation when a drop of equity prices has led to a substantial diminution of the risk budget, have often been blamed for their procyclical nature. Long-term investors are often reluctant to sell equity holdings after a fall in equity prices because they know that the phenomenon of mean reversion in equity risk premium makes equity markets particularly attractive after falls.

In other words, it is widely perceived that a tension exists between a focus on hedging long-term risk and a focus on insurance with respect to short-term constraints. In fact, recent research suggests that long-term objectives and short-term constraints need not be mutually exclusive, and can be integrated in a comprehensive asset allocation framework.[56]

In fact, an explicit analytical representation of the relationship between optimal strategies in the presence and in the absence of short-term constraints can be derived, which allows us to disentangle the impact of short-term constraints from the impact of return predictability on the optimal allocation decision.

For example, in the presence of a stochastic Sharpe ratio for the PSP, the optimal dollar allocation to the PSP can be defined as

$$A_t w_t^{*PSP} = \frac{1}{\gamma} \frac{\lambda_t}{\sigma} \left(A_t - p_{t,T} F_t \right) PSP$$

Depending on market conditions and parameter values the procyclical risk-controlled motivation $A_t - p_{t,T} F_t$ may outweigh the revision of strategic asset allocation motivation $\lambda_t / \gamma \sigma$, or vice versa, with risk management always prevailing ultimately. In other words, the risk-control methodology can be made entirely consistent with internal or external processes aiming at generating active asset allocation views. In fact, casting the active view generation process within the formal framework of a dynamic risk-control strategy appears to be the only way to successfully implement active asset allocation decisions while ensuring the respect of risk limits.

KEY POINTS

- Meeting the challenges of modern investment practice involves the design of novel forms of investment solutions, as opposed to investment products, customized to meet investors' expectations.
- These new forms of investment solutions rely on the use of improved, more efficient performance-seeking portfolio and liability-hedging portfolio building blocks, as well as on the use of improved dynamic allocation strategies.
- While each of these ingredients can be found in various current investment products, it is only by putting the pieces of the puzzle together, and by combining all these sources of expertise, that the asset management industry will satisfactorily address investors' needs.
- From the technical perspective, these advanced investment solutions also rely on a sophisticated exploitation of the benefits of the three competing approaches to risk management, namely risk diversification

---

[56]See Lionel Martellini and Vincent Milhau, "Hedging versus Insurance: Long-Term Investing with Short-Term Constraints," Working paper, EDHEC-Risk Institute, 2010.

(key ingredient in the design of better benchmarks for performance-seeking portfolios), risk hedging (key ingredient in the design of better benchmarks for hedging portfolios) and risk insurance (key ingredient in the design of better dynamic asset allocation benchmarks for long-term investors facing short-term constraints), each of which represents a so far largely unexplored potential source of added-value for the asset management industry.

- Risk management is often mistaken for risk measurement. This is a problem since the capacity of properly measuring risk is at best a necessary but not sufficient condition to ensure proper risk management.
- Another misconception is that risk management is about risk reduction. It is at least as much about return enhancement as it is about risk reduction. In fact, risk management is about maximizing the probability of achieving investors' long-term objectives while respecting the short-term constraints they face.
- Traditional static strategies (e.g., asset-liability management) without dynamic risk-controlled ingredient inevitably lead to underspending of investors' risk budget in normal market conditions (with a strong associated opportunity cost), and overspending of investors' risk budget in extreme market conditions.

APPENDIX

Static Asset Allocation Problem

First find the MSR portfolio:

$$SR_w = 0 \Leftrightarrow \left(w'\Sigma w\right)e'\Sigma^{-1}\left(\mu - re\right) = w'\left(\mu - re\right)e'w$$
$$\Leftrightarrow w'\left(\mu - re\right) = \left(w'\Sigma w\right)e'\Sigma^{-1}\left(\mu - re\right)$$
$$\Leftrightarrow \left(\mu - re\right) = \Sigma w e'\Sigma^{-1}\left(\mu - re\right)$$
$$\Leftrightarrow \Sigma^{-1}\left(\mu - re\right) = w e'\Sigma^{-1}\left(\mu - re\right)$$

We multiply by e' on the left-hand side to obtain

$$SR_w = \left(\mu - re\right)\left(w'\Sigma w\right)^{-\frac{1}{2}} - w'\left(\mu - re\right)\left(w'\Sigma w\right)^{-\frac{3}{2}}\Sigma w$$
$$SR_w = 0 \Leftrightarrow \left(\mu - re\right) = w'\left(\mu - re\right)\left(w'\Sigma w\right)^{-1}\Sigma w$$
$$SR_w = 0 \Leftrightarrow \left(w'\Sigma w\right)\Sigma^{-1}\left(\mu - re\right) = w'\left(\mu - re\right)w$$

Finally (note that weights sum up to 1),

$$w_{MSR}^* = \frac{\Sigma^{-1}(\mu - re)}{e'\Sigma^{-1}(\mu - re)}$$

The next step consists of finding the right allocation as a function of the investor's risk aversion:

$$\underset{w}{Max}\ \mu_p - \frac{\gamma}{2}\sigma_p^2 = \underset{w}{Max}\ w'(\mu - re) - \frac{\gamma}{2}w'\Sigma w$$

We obtain the solution by writing the first-order condition (L is the Lagrangian for the problem and L_w is its first derivative with respect to portfolio weights):

$$L_w = (\mu - re) - \gamma \Sigma w = 0 \Rightarrow w_0^* = \frac{1}{\gamma}\Sigma^{-1}(\mu - re) = \frac{e'\Sigma^{-1}(\mu - re)}{\gamma}\frac{\Sigma^{-1}(\mu - re)}{e'\Sigma^{-1}(\mu - re)}$$

Dynamic Asset-Liability Allocation Problem with Constant Opportunity Set

We now consider a dynamic asset allocation problem, with an investor allowed to rebalance portfolio between dates 0 and T. In this intertemporal context, information about asset return distribution over the horizon is not sufficient, and one needs to know the distribution of asset return at all points in time.

In what follows, we assume that the investor has access to N locally risky assets and one risk-free asset paying the constant interest rate, with the following dynamics (where W is a standard N-dimensional Brownian motion process):

$$\begin{cases} dS_t = diag(S_t)\left[(re + \sigma_S'\lambda_S)dt + \sigma_S'dW_t\right] \\ \dfrac{dB_t}{B_t} = rdt \Leftrightarrow B_t = B_0 e^{rt} \end{cases}$$

Here λ_s is the price of risk vector for the N assets, assumed to be constant, and σ_s is the volatility matrix, which is not necessarily constant. The investor needs to finance the payment of a liability portfolio which value is modeled here as an exogenous geometric Brownian motion process:[57]

---

[57]For some investors, e.g. defined-benefit pension funds, the liability process L can be endogenously identified as the present value of future liability payments. See for example, Martellini and Milhau, "Measuring the Benefits of Dynamic Asset Allocation Strategies in the Presence of Liability Constraints," 20.

$$dL_t = L_t \left[\mu_L dt + \sigma_L' dW_t \right]$$

The asset value process for a given (self-financed) portfolio strategy is given by

$$dA_t = A_t \left[w_t' \left(\text{diag } S_t \right)^{-1} dS_t + \left(1 - w_t' e \right) \frac{dB_t}{B_t} \right]$$

$$= A_t \left[\left(r_t + w_t' \sigma_S' \lambda_t \right) dt + w_t' \sigma_S' dW_t \right]$$

The optimal dynamic asset allocation decisions with constant opportunity set, with CRRA preferences $u(x) = x^{1-\gamma}/1 - \gamma$, is given by equation (7.2), that is

$$\max_{(w_t)} E \left[u \left(\frac{A_T}{L_T} \right) \right] \Rightarrow w_t^* = \frac{\lambda}{\gamma \sigma} PSP + \left(1 - \frac{1}{\gamma} \right) \beta \ LHP$$

Here the *PSP* is again the portfolio that achieves the highest Sharpe ratio, and we denote by λ its Sharpe ratio, and σ its volatility. *LHP* is the portfolio that achieves the highest correlation with the liability process; β is the beta of changes in the liability portfolio value with respect to changes in the LHP value.

The expressions for the PSP, the LHP and the weights are as follows:

$$PSP = \frac{\sigma_S^{-1} \lambda_S}{e' \sigma_S^{-1} \lambda_S}, \ LHP = \frac{\sigma_S^{-1} \sigma_L}{e' \sigma_S^{-1} \sigma_L} \ , \ \frac{\lambda}{\sigma} = e' \sigma_S^{-1} \lambda_S, \ \beta = e' \sigma_S^{-1} \sigma_L$$

The expression for the PSP in this dynamic model is actually the same as the expression for the MSR PSP in the static case. Formally, the relationship can be established as follows. Consider the vector of log-returns over the period $[0,T]$, $\ln S_T - \ln S_0$. Under the assumption of constant parameters, its first two moments are given by

$$E \left[\ln S_T - \ln S_0 \right] = \left[re + \sigma_S' \lambda_S - \frac{1}{2} \text{diag}(\sigma_S' \sigma_S) \right] T, \ V \left[\ln S_T - \ln S_0 \right] = \sigma_S' \sigma_S T$$

Then define μ and Σ as

$$\mu = E \left[\ln S_T - \ln S_0 \right] + \frac{1}{2} \text{diag} \left(V \left[\ln S_T - \ln S_0 \right] \right), \ \Sigma = V \left[\ln S_T - \ln S_0 \right]$$

where we observe that diag($V[\ln S_T - \ln S_0]$) is the vector of variances.
Then we have

$$PSP = \frac{\Sigma^{-1}(\mu - re)}{e'\Sigma^{-1}(\mu - re)}$$

which is the same expression as in the static case. The quantities μ and Σ can be obtained using a proper econometric model for asset returns.[58]

The proof of the result in equation (7.2) can be obtained by applying the martingale approach of Cox and Huang.[59] First the dynamic portfolio problem is mapped into a static problem where the control variable is the terminal wealth:

$$\max_{A_T} E\left[\left(\frac{A_T}{L_T}\right)\right], \quad \text{s.t. } E[M_T A_T] = A_0$$

where M_T is the pricing kernel:

$$M_T = \exp\left[-\left(r + \frac{\|\lambda_s\|^2}{2}\right)T - \lambda_s' W_T\right]$$

The optimal terminal wealth reads

$$A_T^* = \frac{A_0}{E\left[(M_T L_T)^{1-\frac{1}{\gamma}}\right]} M_T^{-\frac{1}{\gamma}} L_T^{1-\frac{1}{\gamma}}$$

and the optimal wealth process is

$$A_t^* = \frac{A_0}{E\left[(M_T L_T)^{1-\frac{1}{\gamma}}\right]} E_t\left[\left(\frac{M_T L_T}{M_t L_t}\right)^{1-\frac{1}{\gamma}}\right] M_t^{-\frac{1}{\gamma}} L_t^{1-\frac{1}{\gamma}}$$

---

[58]See for example Amenc, Martellini, Milhau, and Ziemann, "Inflation-Hedging Properties of Real Assets and Implications for Asset–Liability Management Decisions" and the references therein.

[59]Cox and Huang, "Optimal Consumption and Portfolio Policies when Asset Prices Follow a Diffusion Process." For notational simplicity, we present the proof in the case where the market is dynamically complete, that is, the volatility matrix σ_s is square and invertible. The result is not impacted by this assumption; the proof in the general case of a possibly incomplete market would proceed exactly as in the complete case, up to some notational modifications.

Applying Ito's Lemma to both sides of this equality and matching the diffusion terms, one obtains the optimal portfolio.

Dynamic Asset Allocation Problem with Time-Varying Opportunity Set (Focus on Time-Varying Sharpe Ratio)

We now assume that the equity risk-premium is time-varying with the business cycle, with a mean-reverting component. We let $\rho_{\lambda S}$ be the correlation between λ^S and S; a negative correlation means that high realized return periods tend to be followed by low expected return periods, which is supported by empirical evidence:

$$d\lambda_t^s = a_\lambda \left(b_\lambda - \lambda_t^s \right) dt + \sigma_\lambda dW_t^\lambda$$

$$dS_t = S_t \left[r + \sigma_S \lambda_t^s \right] dt + S_t \sigma_S dW_t^S$$

The interest rate r is assumed to be constant for simplicity, and the stock index is assumed to be the only risky asset; this is an incomplete market setting except for a perfect negative correlation $\rho_{\lambda S} = -1$.

Because of market incompleteness, we use the dynamic programming approach, with a value function defined, assuming again CRRA preferences, as follows

$$J\left(t,\lambda_t^s, A_t\right) = \sup_{(\omega_s)_{s \geq t}} E_t \left[\frac{A_T^{1-\gamma}}{1-\gamma} \right]$$

The Hamilton-Jacobi-Bellman (HJB) equation for J reads

$$0 = J_t + \sup_{w_S} \left[\frac{1}{2} w_S^2 \sigma_S^2 A_t^2 J_{AA} + w_S \left(\mu_S - r \right) A_t J_A + w_S \rho_{\lambda S} \sigma_\lambda \sigma_S A_t J_{A\lambda^s} \right]$$

$$+ rA_t J_A + \frac{1}{2} \sigma_\lambda^2 J_{\lambda^s \lambda^s} + a_\lambda \left(b_\lambda - \lambda_t^s \right) J_{\lambda^s}$$

and the optimal portfolio strategy is

$$w_t^S = -\frac{J_A}{A_t J_{AA}} \frac{\mu_S - r}{\sigma_S} - \frac{J_{A\lambda^s}}{A_t J_{AA}} \frac{\rho_{\lambda S} \sigma_\lambda}{\sigma_S} = -\frac{J_A}{A_t J_{AA}} \frac{\lambda_t^s}{\sigma_S} - \frac{J_{A\lambda^s}}{A_t J_{AA}} \frac{\rho_{\lambda S} \sigma_\lambda}{\sigma_S}$$

Plugging back the optimal portfolio strategy into the HJB equation, we finally obtain the following partial differential equation (PDE):

$$0 = J_t + rA_t J_A + \frac{1}{2}\sigma_\lambda^2 J_{\lambda^S \lambda^S} + a_\lambda \left(b_\lambda - \lambda_t^S \right) J_{\lambda^S}$$

$$- \frac{J_A^2}{2J_{AA}}(\lambda_t^S)^2 - \frac{J_{A\lambda^S}^2}{2J_{AA}}\rho_{\lambda S}^2 \sigma_\lambda^2 - \frac{J_A J_{A\lambda^S}}{J_{AA}}\sigma_\lambda \rho_{\lambda S}\lambda_t^S$$

Given the affine structure of the model, we guess a solution to HJB equation of the form

$$J(t, A_t, \lambda_t^S) = \frac{A_t^{1-\gamma}}{1-\gamma}\exp\left[\frac{1-\gamma}{\gamma}\left[A(T-t)\lambda_t^S + \frac{1}{2}B(T-t)(\lambda_t^S)^2 + C(T-t)\right]\right]$$

Plugging the relevant derivatives of J back into HJB equation, we obtain a system of 3 coupled ordinary differential equations (ODEs) for A, B and C, which can be solved to yield

$$A(s) = -\frac{1}{\gamma}\frac{a_\lambda b_\lambda \left(1 - e^{-\sqrt{q}s}\right)^2}{\sqrt{q}\left[2\sqrt{q} - \left(\sqrt{q} - \bar{b}_\lambda\right)\left(1 - e^{-2\sqrt{q}s}\right)\right]}$$

$$B(s) = -\frac{1}{\gamma}\frac{1 - e^{-2\sqrt{q}s}}{2\sqrt{q} - \left(\sqrt{q} - \bar{b}_\lambda\right)\left(1 - e^{-2\sqrt{q}s}\right)}$$

$$\bar{b}_\lambda = b_\lambda - \frac{1-\gamma}{\gamma}\rho_{\lambda S}\sigma_\lambda; \quad q = \bar{b}_\lambda^2 - \sigma_\lambda^2(\rho_{\lambda S}^2 + \gamma(1-\rho_{\lambda S}^2))\frac{1-\gamma}{\gamma^2}$$

The optimal portfolio strategy is then obtained by taking the derivatives of the J function in

$$w_t^* = -\frac{J_A}{A_t J_{AA}}\frac{\lambda_t^S}{\sigma_S} - \frac{J_{A\lambda^S}}{A_t J_{AA}}\frac{\rho_{\lambda S}\sigma_\lambda}{\sigma_S}$$

Dynamic Asset-Liability Allocation Problem with Short-Term Performance Constraints

We consider the case of an investor maximizing expected utility from terminal funding ratio, subject to a short-term performance constraint, here a minimum funding ratio constraint formally defined as $A_t \geq F_t = kL_t$ for all $t \leq T$:

$$\max_{(w_t)} E\left[\left(\frac{A_T}{L_T}\right)\right], \quad \text{s.t. } A_t \geq kL_t \text{ for all } t \leq T$$

In order to avoid technical issues, we assume that the liability L is fully replicable by the LHP. In this context, the static form of the dynamic portfolio problem is a program where the series of short-term constraints can be replaced with a single long-term performance constraint:

$$\max_{A_T} E\left[\left(\frac{A_T}{L_T}\right)\right], \quad \text{s.t. } A_T \geq kL_T \quad \text{and} \quad E[M_T A_T] = A_0$$

The optimal payoff is then given by

$$A_T^* = kL_T + \left(\xi A_T^{*u} - kL_T\right)^+$$

where A_T^{*u} is the terminal wealth that would be optimal in the absence of performance constraints and ξ is some constant whose value is adjusted so as to make the budget constraint $E[M_T A_T^*] = A_0$ hold. Under the assumption of a constant opportunity set, the exchange option between the unconstrained payoff and the floor can be valued using Margrabe's formula:[60]

$$A_t^* = kL_t + \xi A_t^{*u} N\left(d_{1,t}\right) - kL_t N\left(d_{2,t}\right)$$

$$d_{1,t} = \frac{1}{\Sigma_{t,T}}\left[\ln\frac{\xi A_t^{*u}}{kL_t} + \frac{1}{2}\Sigma_{t,T}^2\right], \quad d_{2,t} = d_{1,t} - \Sigma_{t,T}$$

where $\Sigma_{t,T}$ is the cumulated volatility of the unconstrained funding ratio A^{*u}/L over the time span $[t,T]$. Applying Ito's Lemma and identifying diffusion terms, we obtain the optimal strategy:

$$w_t^{*c} = \frac{\lambda}{\gamma\sigma}\left(1 - \frac{kN\left(-d_{2,t}\right)L_t}{A_t^*}\right)PSP + \left[1 - \frac{1}{\gamma}\left(1 - \frac{kN\left(-d_{2,t}\right)L_t}{A_t^*}\right)\right]\beta \, LHP$$

where $N(-d_{2,t})$ can be interpreted as the risk-neutral probability that the exchange option ends out-of-the-money.[61]

QUESTIONS

1. What is wrong with cap-weighted indexes?

---

[60]William Margrabe, "The Value of an Option To Exchange One Asset For Another," *Journal of Finance* 33, no. 1 (1978): 177–186.
[61]Under the assumption of a perfect liability matching portfolio, the parameter β would be equal to 1.

2. How can one obtain risk parameter estimates needed for portfolio construction decisions?

3. How can one obtain expected return parameter estimates needed for portfolio construction decisions?

4. What are the main limitations of existing bond indexes?

5. What are the main challenges involved in deciding how much to allocate to the performance-seeking portfolio versus the liability-hedging portfolio?

Equity Analysis and Portfolio Management

Fundamentals of Common Stock

Frank J. Fabozzi, Ph.D., CFA, CPA
Professor in the Practice of Finance
Yale School of Management

Frank J. Jones, Ph.D.
Professor, Accounting and Finance Department
San Jose State University

Robert R. Johnson, Ph.D., CFA
Senior Managing Director
CFA Institute

Pamela P. Drake, Ph.D., CFA
J. Gray Ferguson Professor Finance
College of Business
James Madison University

Common stocks are also called *equity securities*. Equity securities represent an ownership interest in a corporation. Holders of equity securities are entitled to the earnings of the corporation when those earnings are distributed in the form of *dividends*; they are also entitled to a pro rata share of the remaining equity in case of liquidation.

Common stock is only one type of equity security. Another type is preferred stock. The key distinction between the two forms of equity securities is the degree to which their holders may participate in any distribution of earnings and capital and the priority given to each class in the distribution of earnings. Typically, preferred stockholders are entitled to a fixed dividend, which they receive before common stockholders may receive any dividends. Therefore, we refer to preferred stock as a senior corporate security, in the sense that preferred stock interests are senior to the interests of common stockholders.

In this chapter, we explain the fundamental factors of earnings and dividends and we look at common stock as an investment, their relations with share price as expressed in such commonly-used ratios as the price-earnings ratio and the dividend yield, where stocks are traded, the mechanics of stock trading, and trading costs.

EARNINGS

A commonly used measure of a company's performance over a period of time is its *earnings*, which is often stated in terms of a return—that is, earnings scaled by the amount of the investment. But earnings can really mean many different things depending on the context. If a common stock analyst is evaluating the performance of a company's operations, the focus is on the operating earnings of the company—its *earnings before interest and taxes*, EBIT. If the analyst is evaluating the performance of a company overall, the focus is upon net income, which is essentially EBIT less interest and taxes. If the analyst is evaluating the performance of the company from a common shareholder's perspective, the earnings are the earnings available to common shareholders—EBIT less interest, taxes, and preferred stock dividends. Finally, if the analyst is forecasting future earnings and cash flows, the focus is on earnings from continuing operations. Therefore, it is useful to be very specific about the meaning of "earnings."

There is a possibility that reported financial information may be managed by the judicious choice of accounting methods and timing employed by management. In particular, earnings can be managed using a number of accounting devices. There are many pressures that a company may face that affect the likelihood of earnings management. These pressures include executive compensation based on earnings targets, reporting ever-increasing earnings (especially when the business is subject to variations in the business cycle), and meeting or beating analyst forecasts.

Earnings targets comes in various forms, but typically schemes on earnings targets provide for a bonus if earnings meet or exceed a specified target such as a return on equity. One-sided incentives such as this—rewards for beating the target return, but no penalty for not making the target—can create problematic situations. Combine this with the tendency of stock prices to be affected by whether or not analysts' forecasts are met or beat, and there is significant potential for problems. If, for example, management knows that the earnings target cannot be met in a period, there may be an incentive to either (1) manage earnings, through such mechanics as accruals, changes in estimates, or changes in accounting method; or (2) take large write-offs in that period, increasing chances of making earnings targets in future periods—referred to as taking a "big bath."

Meeting analysts' forecasts presents still another pressure for the management of earnings. We know from the wealth of empirical evidence that stock prices react to earnings surprises, where surprises are defined as the difference between expected and actual earnings. Because there is a market reaction to surprises—negative for earnings less than expected and positive for earnings better than expected—companies have an incentive to manage earnings to meet or exceed forecasted earnings. The pressure to report constant or constantly increasing earnings may also result in earnings management, manipulation, or, in extreme cases, even fraud.

Evidence suggests that there is a strong incentive to meet analysts' forecasts. More companies meet or beat earnings forecasts than miss these forecasts.[1] Stock prices are sensitive to whether earnings meet analysts' forecasts.[2] Finally, management is more likely to sell their shares of the company's stock after meeting or beating forecasts, than if the company fails to meet forecasts.[3] As a result of these incentives, investors should not only look for unusual patterns in earnings, but also earnings that are perhaps *too* predictable.

Is there a relation between earnings and stock value? The research into the relation between earnings and value concludes the following. First, stock prices change in response to an announcement of unexpected earnings. Second, accounting earnings are correlated with stock returns, especially returns measured over a long horizon following the release of earnings.[4] The strong relation between earnings and stock prices may be due to reported earnings being strongly correlated with true earnings (that is, earnings in the absence of earnings management). Or the earnings–stock price relation may be due to the valuation of stocks being dependent on reported earnings.

Earnings Per Share

Earnings per share (EPS) is earnings available for common shareholders, divided by the number of common shares outstanding:

[1]See Carla Hayn, "The Information Content of Losses," *Journal of Accounting and Economics*, 20, no. 2 (1995): 125–153; and Sarah McVay, Venky Nagar, and Vivki Tang, "Trading Incentives to Meet Earnings Thresholds," Working paper, University of Michigan, January 2005.
[2]See E.D. Bartov, D. Givoly, and Carla Hayn, "The Rewards to Meeting or Beating Earnings Expectations," *Journal of Accounting and Economics* 33, no. 2 (2002): 173–204.
[3]McVay, Nagar, and Tang, "Trading Incentives to Meet Earnings Thresholds."
[4]See, for example, Peter D. Easton, Trevor S. Harris, and James A. Ohlson, "Aggregate Accounting Earnings Can Explain Most of Security Returns," *Journal of Accounting and Economics* 15, nos. 2 & 3 (1992): 119–142.

Earnings per share

$$= \frac{\text{Earnings available to common stockholders}}{\text{Weighted average number of common shares outstanding}}$$

This ratio indicates each share's portion of how much is earned by the company in a given accounting period.

The EPS doesn't tell us anything about the preferred shareholders. And that's acceptable because preferred shareholders, in most cases, receive a fixed dividend amount. Because the common shareholders are the residual owners of the firm—they are the last ones in line after creditors and preferred shareholders—we are interested in seeing just what is left over for them.

When we see an amount given for EPS, we have to be sure we know what it really means. But what is there to interpret? Net income available to common shares is pretty clear-cut (with some exceptions). What about the number of common shares outstanding? Can that change during the period of time under consideration? It can, affecting the calculated value of earnings per share. The number of common shares outstanding can change for two reasons. First, net income is earned over a specific period of time, yet the number of shares outstanding may change over this period. This is the reason why the weighted average number of shares over the time period is used in the denominator of the EPS calculation. Second, the company may have securities outstanding that can be converted into common stock or employee stock options and warrants that may be exercisable, so the number of shares of common that potentially may share in this net income is greater than the number reported as outstanding. These securities are referred to as *dilutive securities*.

For a company with securities that are dilutive—meaning they could share in net income—there are two earnings per share amounts that are reported in financial statements. *Basic earnings per share* are earnings (minus preferred dividends), divided by the average number of shares outstanding. *Diluted earnings per share* is earnings (minus preferred dividends) divided by the number of shares outstanding considering all dilutive securities. Accounting principles require that the diluted earnings per share may never be reported as greater than basic earnings per share.

DIVIDENDS

A *dividend* is the cash, stock, or any type of property a corporation distributes to its shareholders. The board of directors may declare a dividend at any time, but dividends are not a legal obligation of the corporation—it is the choice of the board of directors. Unlike interest on debt securities, if a corporation does not pay a dividend, there is no violation of a contract, nor any legal recourse for shareholders.

When the board of directors declares a distribution, it specifies the amount of the distribution, the date on which the distribution is paid, and the *date of record*, which determines who has the right to the distributions. Because shares are traded frequently and it takes time to process transactions, the exchanges have devised a way of determining which investors receive the dividend: the exchanges take the record date, as specified by the board of directors, and identify the *ex dividend date*, which is two business days prior to the record date. The ex dividend date is often referred to simply as the *ex date*.

The cash dividends that a corporation pays is described in terms of *dividend per share*, calculated as follows:

$$\text{Dividend per share} = \frac{\text{Cash dividends paid to common stockholders}}{\text{Number of common shares outstanding}}$$

Another way of describing cash dividends is in terms of the percentage of earnings paid out in dividends, which we refer to as the *dividend payout ratio*. We can express the dividend in terms of the proportion of earnings over a fiscal period:

$$\text{Dividend payout ratio} = \frac{\text{Cash dividends paid to common stockholders}}{\text{Earnings available to common shareholders}}$$

Alternatively, the dividend payout ratio can be calculated as follows:

$$\text{Dividend payout ratio} = \frac{\text{Dividend per share}}{\text{Earnings per share}}$$

The dividend payout ratio is the complement of the *retention ratio*, also referred to as the *plowback ratio*:

Retention ratio

$$= \frac{\text{Earnings available to common shareholders} - \text{Cash dividends}}{\text{Earnings available to common shareholders}}$$

$$= 1 - \text{Dividend payout ratio}$$

The retention ratio is the proportion of earnings that the company retains, that is, the proportion of earnings reinvested back into the company.

Corporations have different dividend policies. A dividend policy is a corporation's decision about the payment of cash dividends to shareholders. There are several basic ways of describing a corporation's *dividend policy*:

(1) no dividends, (2) constant growth in dividends per share, (3) constant payout ratio, and (4) low regular dividends with periodic extra dividend.

The corporations that typically do not pay dividends are those that are generally viewed as younger, faster growing companies. For example, Microsoft Corporation was founded in 1975 and went public in 1986, but it did not pay a cash dividend until January 2003.

A common pattern of cash dividends tends to be the constant growth of dividends per share. Another pattern is the constant payout ratio. Many companies in the food processing industry, such as Kellogg and Tootsie Roll Industries, pay dividends that are a relatively constant percentage of earnings. Some companies display both a constant dividend payout and a constant growth in dividends. This type of dividend pattern is characteristic of large, mature companies that have predictable earnings growth—the dividends growth tends to mimic the earnings growth, resulting in a constant payout.

U.S. corporations that pay dividends tend to pay either constant or increasing dividends per share. Dividends tend to be lower in industries that have many profitable opportunities in which to invest their earnings. But as a company matures and finds fewer and fewer profitable investment opportunities, it generally pays out a greater portion of its earnings in dividends.

Many corporations are reluctant to cut dividends because the corporation's share price usually falls when a dividend reduction is announced. For example, the U.S. auto manufacturers cut dividends during the recession in the early 1990s. As earnings per share declined, the automakers did not cut dividends until earnings per share were negative—and in the case of General Motors, not until it had experienced two consecutive loss years. But as earnings recovered in the mid-1990s, dividends were increased. (General Motors increased dividends until cutting them once again in 2006 as it incurred substantial losses.)

Because investors tend to penalize companies that cut dividends, corporations tend to only raise their regular quarterly dividend when they are sure they can keep it up in the future. By giving a special or extra dividend, the corporation is able to provide more cash to the shareholders without committing itself to paying an increased dividend each period into the future.

Dividends and Stock Prices

By buying common stock, an investor obtains a financial position that represents an ownership interest in the corporation. Shares of common stock are a perpetual security—there is no maturity. The investor who owns shares of common stock has the right to receive a certain portion of any dividends—but dividends are not a sure thing. Whether a firm will pay dividends is up to its board of directors—the representatives of the common shareholders.

Typically we see some pattern in the dividends companies pay: Dividends per share are either constant or grow at a constant rate. But there is no guarantee that dividends will be paid in the future.

It is reasonable to assume that what an investor pays for a share of stock should reflect what in the aggregate investors expect to receive from it—the stock's return on investment. What an investor receives are cash dividends in the future. How can we relate that return to what a share of common stock is worth? Well, the value of a share of stock should be equal to the present value of all the future cash flows investors expect to receive from that share. Because common stock never matures, today's value is the present value of an infinite stream of cash flows. And also, common stock dividends are not fixed. Not knowing the amount of the dividends—or even if there will be future dividends—makes it difficult to determine the value of common stock.

So what are investors to do? They can grapple with the valuation of common stock by looking at its current dividend and making assumptions about any future dividends the company may pay. This is the basic idea behind the financial models used to value common stock. Because these models involve the discounting of future dividends, they are called *dividend discount models*. A discussion of these models is provided in Chapter 10.

THE U.S. EQUITY MARKETS

The U.S. equity markets have undergone considerable change in recent years. Traditionally, the U.S. markets have been driven by two exchanges, the New York Stock Exchange (also called "the Big Board") and Nasdaq (the acronym for the National Association of Securities Dealers Automated Quotation System).

An *exchange* is typically defined as a market where intermediaries meet to deliver and execute customer orders. There are, however, some off-exchange markets which perform this function. In the United States, exchanges must be registered with the Securities and Exchange Commission (SEC). The U.S. markets have been based on two different market models. The first model is "order-driven," in which public participants who are owners of securities meet and provide buy and sell orders ("orders") and via an auction system which establishes market prices at which other public participants can trade. This mechanism is an *auction-based, order-driven market*. The second model involves intermediaries, referred to as *market makers* or *dealers*, who provide quotes (bid quotes to buy and offer quotes to sell) at which market participants can trade. This mechanism is a *dealer-based, quote-driven market*.

The NYSE has been mainly an order-driven, auction market. The NYSE has not, however, been purely an order-driven market because it provides "specialists" for each stock who function as dealers for their allocated stocks and buy or sell these stocks for their own account to maintain "orderly markets." The NYSE is often called a *specialist system*. Nasdaq has always (since it was founded in 1971) been a pure quote-driven, dealer market. The American Stock Exchange (Amex) has been a third, much smaller, national exchange which functions like the NYSE. There have also been regional stock exchanges in Chicago, Philadelphia, Boston, San Francisco, and other cities which have functioned similarly to the NYSE.

Off-exchange markets (also called *alternative electronic markets*) have also evolved. There are two major types. The first and most important is *electronic communication networks* (ECNs) which are direct descendents of Nasdaq. Archipelago ("Arca") and Instinet are early and important examples of ECNs. The second type is, in general, *alternative trading systems* (ATS) which involve the direct trading of stock between two customers without an intermediary, either a broker or an exchange. An ATS is essentially for-profit broker's brokers that match investor orders. There are two types of ATS. The first type is a *crossing network* which is an electronic venue that does not display quotes but simply anonymously matches (or crosses) large institutional customer orders. The second type is a *dark pool*. A dark pool is a neutral gathering place which provides private crossing networks where participants submit orders to cross trades at externally specified prices. No quotes are involved, only orders at externally determined prices. Dark pools, thus, provide anonymous sources of liquidity (hence the name "dark").

In addition to the development of off-exchange markets, the two major exchanges, particularly the NYSE, have transformed themselves since 2000. During December 2005, the NYSE acquired Archipelago, a leading ECN and a public company. This permitted the NYSE to both become a public company and also become a hybrid of an order-driven auction (specialist) market and a quote-driven (dealer) market (called electronic trading) (initially named the NYSE Hybrid Market). Since then, however, the new electronic trading component of NYSE has dominated the traditional specialist trading component. In fact, during early 2006, the NYSE closed one of its traditional trading rooms. During April 2007, the NYSE acquired Euronext, the trans-European fully electronic stock exchange, making NYSE the first transatlantic stock exchange. The current name of the exchange is NYSE Euronext, Inc. During October 2008, the NYSE acquired the Amex.

Nasdaq has also been very acquisitive and transformative. During July 2002, Nasdaq bought a controlling interest in OMX, a Nordic-based exchange which operated eight stock exchanges in Europe. At the same time, on July 2, 2002, Nasdaq publicly listed its own stock. Its name is the NASDAQ OMX Group, Inc. In April 2005 (two days after NYSE acquired Archipelago), Nasdaq acquired Instinet, the largest and oldest ECN. During

2007, Nasdaq also acquired the Philadelphia Stock Exchange and the Boston Stock Exchange.

As of mid-2010, there were changes in the composition of stock exchanges. In addition to the disappearance of the regional exchanges due to their acquisitions by the NYSE and Nasdaq, these major exchanges have become public companies, international exchanges, and multiproduct exchanges (including options and exchange-traded funds). The second trend was the formation of new independent exchanges from previous ECNs. The major new exchanges formed in this way were BATS (an acronym for Better Alternative Trading System) and Direct Edge. BATS was founded in June 2005 as an ECN and by early 2009 was the third largest stock exchange in the world, after the NYSE and Nasdaq. Direct Edge, an ECN which had previously operated as a stock exchange using the International Securities Exchange (ISE) stock platform, was approved by the SEC as a stock exchange in March 2010. Direct Edge is the fourth largest U.S. stock exchange.

TRADING MECHANICS

The equity markets have been characterized by major innovations in trading by investors. Specifically, *algorithmic trading* (also called *algo trading* and *black box trading*) involves using computer-based algorithms to determine the timing, pricing, and quantities of trades. Algorithmic trading is often used by institutions to divide single large orders into many small orders to reduce market impact and disguise their trades. One type of algorithmic trading is *high-frequency trading* (HFT), in which computers use information received electronically to generate orders without human input. There are many uses for this type of trading, including market-making, arbitrage and simply filling orders. HFT is estimated to account for over 70% of stock trading in the United States in 2010. A subset of HFT is *flash trading* in which traders are permitted, for a fee, to view incoming buy or sell orders for a brief amount of time (often 30 milliseconds) before they are exposed to the entire market.

There have been two dramatic effects of algorithmic trading. First, fast computers and advanced algorithms have significantly reduced the average trade sizes on exchanges. Specifically, the average trade size of a NYSE-listed stock declined from 724 shares in 2005 to 268 shares in 2009. Second, the time it takes to complete a trade, called *latency*, has declined significantly. Trading times are measured in milliseconds and even microseconds (one-thousandth and one-millionth of a second, respectively). Trading in single digit microseconds is a realistic goal of market participants. With latency becoming so small and important for market participants, colocation (using space in exchange-owned facilities) has become essential.

Another type of investor change is *Direct Market Access* (DMA), which refers to the ability of investors (the "buy side") to interact directly with the exchanges or markets rather than go through a broker-dealer. HFT has encouraged the use of DMA, which often occurs with the buy-side traders using sell-side systems. Latency of less than 500 milliseconds can be achieved in this way.

Undoubtedly, with multiple active exchanges, ECNs, dark pools, and DMA, stock trading has become more fragmented, that is less centralized. The common ongoing debate about these trading strategies is whether they improve the liquidity of the markets (as proponents of these techniques assert) or whether they provide an unfair advantage to some traders (as critics of these techniques assert).

Next we describe the key features involved in trading stocks. Later in the chapter, we discuss trading arrangements (block trades and program trades) that developed specifically for coping with the needs of institutional investors.

Types of Orders and Trading Priority Rules

When an investor wants to buy or sell a share of common stock, the price and conditions under which the order is to be executed must be communicated to a broker. The simplest type of order is the *market order*, an order to be executed at the best price available in the market. If the stock is listed and traded on an organized exchange, the best price is assured by the exchange rule that when more than one order on the same side of the buy/sell transaction reaches the market at the same time, the order with the best price is given priority. Thus, buyers offering a higher price are given priority over those offering a lower price; sellers asking a lower price are given priority over those asking a higher price.

Another priority rule of exchange trading is needed to handle receipt of more than one order at the same price. Most often, the priority in executing such orders is based on the time of arrival of the order—first orders in are the first orders executed—although there may be a rule that gives higher priority to certain types of market participants over other types of market participants seeking to transact at the same price. For example, on exchanges, orders can be classified as either *public orders* or orders of those member firms dealing for their own account (both nonspecialists and specialists). Exchange rules require that public orders be given priority over orders of member firms dealing for their own account.

The danger of a market order is that an adverse move may take place between the time the investor places the order and the time the order is executed. To avoid this danger, the investor can place a *limit order* that designates a price threshold for the execution of the trade. A *buy limit order* indicates that the stock may be purchased only at the designated price or lower. A *sell limit order* indicates that the stock may be sold only at the designated price or higher. The key disadvantage of a limit order is that there is no guarantee that it will be executed at all; the designated price may simply not be obtainable. A limit order that is not executable at the time it reaches the market is recorded in the limit order book.

The limit order is a *conditional order*: It is executed only if the limit price or a better price can be obtained. Another type of conditional order is the *stop order*, which specifies that the order is not to be executed until the market moves to a designated price, at which time it becomes a market order. A *buy stop order* specifies that the order is not to be executed until the market rises to a designated price, that is, until it trades at or above, or is bid at or above, the designated price. A *sell stop order* specifies that the order is not to be executed until the market price falls below a designated price— that is, until it trades at or below, or is offered at or below, the designated price. A stop order is useful when an investor cannot constantly monitor the market. Profits can be preserved or losses minimized on a stock position by allowing market movements to trigger a trade. In a sell (buy) stop order, the designated price is lower (higher) than the current market price of the stock. In a sell (buy) limit order, the designated price is higher (lower) than the current market price of the stock.

There are two dangers associated with stop orders. Stock prices sometimes exhibit abrupt price changes, so the direction of a change in a stock price may be quite temporary, resulting in the premature trading of a stock. Also, once the designated price is reached, the stop order becomes a market order and is subject to the uncertainty of the execution price noted earlier for market orders.

A *stop-limit order*, a hybrid of a stop order and a limit order, is a stop order that designates a price limit. In contrast to the stop order, which becomes a market order if the stop is reached, the stop-limit order becomes a limit order if the stop is reached. The stop-limit order can be used to cushion the market impact of a stop order. The investor may limit the possible execution price after the activation of the stop. As with a limit order, the limit price may never be reached after the order is activated, which therefore defeats one purpose of the stop order—to protect a profit or limit a loss.

An investor may also enter a *market if touched order*. This order becomes a market order if a designated price is reached. A market if touched order to buy becomes a market order if the market falls to a given price, while a stop order to buy becomes a market order if the market rises to a given price. Similarly, a market if touched order to sell becomes a market order if the market rises to a specified price, while the stop order to sell becomes a market order if the market falls to a given price. We can think of the stop order as an order designed to get out of an existing position at an acceptable price (without specifying the exact price), and the market if touched order as an order designed to get into a position at an acceptable price (also without specifying the exact price).

Orders may be placed to buy or sell at the open or the close of trading for the day. An opening order indicates a trade to be executed only in the opening range for the day, and a closing order indicates a trade is to be executed only within the closing range for the day.

An investor may enter orders that contain order cancellation provisions. A *fill-or-kill order* must be executed as soon as it reaches the market or it is immediately canceled. Orders may designate the time period for which the order is effective—a day, week, month, or perhaps by a given time within the day. An *open order*, or good till canceled order, is good until the investor specifically terminates the order.

Orders are also classified by their size. One round lot is typically 100 shares of a stock. An *odd lot* is defined as less than a round lot. A *block trade* is defined on the NYSE as an order of 10,000 shares of a given stock or a total market value of $200,000 or more.

Short Selling

Short selling involves the sale of a security not owned by the investor at the time of sale. The investor can arrange to have a broker borrow the stock from someone else, and the borrowed stock is delivered to implement the sale. To cover the short position, the investor must subsequently purchase the stock and return it to the party that lent the stock. The short position benefits if the price declines and realizes a loss if the price appreciates.

Two costs will reduce the return from selling short. First, a fee will be charged by the lender of the stock and we will discuss this shortly. Second, if there are any dividends paid while the stock is borrowed, the short seller must compensate the lender of the stock for the dividends that the lender would have been entitled to.

Margin Transactions

Investors can borrow cash to buy securities and use the securities themselves as collateral. The funds borrowed to buy the additional stock will be provided by the broker, and the broker gets the money from a bank. By doing so, the investor is creating leverage. The interest rate that banks charge brokers for these funds is the *call money rate* (also referred to as the *broker loan rate*). The broker charges the borrowing investor the call money rate plus a service charge.

Margin Requirements

The brokerage firm is not free to lend as much as it wishes to the investor to buy securities. The Securities Exchange Act of 1934 prohibits brokers from lending more than a specified percentage of the market value of the securities. The *initial margin requirement* is the proportion of the total market value of the securities that the investor must pay as an equity share, and the remainder is borrowed from the broker. The 1934 act gives the Board of Governors of the Federal Reserve (the Fed) the responsibility to set initial margin requirements. The initial margin requirement has been below 40%, and is 50% as of this writing.

The Fed also establishes a *maintenance margin requirement*. This is the minimum proportion of the equity in the investor's margin account to the total market value. If the investor's margin account falls below the minimum maintenance margin (which would happen if the share price fell), the investor is required to put up additional cash. The investor receives a margin call from the broker specifying the additional cash to be put into the investor's margin account. If the investor fails to put up the additional cash, the broker has the authority to sell the securities in the investor's account. There are also margin requirements for short selling.

Stock Lending

An investor who shorts a stock must be able to borrow that stock in order to deliver it to the buyer of the stock. A short seller can use a mechanism called *stock lending* to borrow the stock. The two parties in a stock lending transaction are the owner of a stock who agrees to lend that stock to the party that sold the stock short. In a stock lending transaction, the former party is referred to as the *stock lender* or the *beneficial owner*. The second party is the entity that agrees to borrow the stock, called the *stock borrower*. Hence, a stock lending transaction is one in which the stock lender loans the requested stock to the stock borrower at the outset and the stock borrower agrees to return the same stock to the stock lender at some time in the future. The loan may be terminated by the stock lender upon notice to the stock borrower.

To protect against credit (counterparty) risk, the stock lender will require that the stock borrower provide collateral. Typically the collateral is cash that is equal to at least the value of the stock lent. The stock lender must pay the stock borrower a fee and this fee is called a *rebate*. Effectively, the stock borrower has provided a loan to the stock lender, charging the stock lender the rebate. The cash received by the stock lender is then invested. The stock lender faces all the risks associated with investing the cash received from the stock borrower. The stock lender only earns a profit if the amount earned on investing the cash collateral exceeds the rebate. In fact, if the amount earned is less than the rebate, the stock lender incurs this cost.

Institutional investors with a stock portfolio to lend can either (1) lend directly to counterparties that need stocks, (2) use the services of an intermediary, or (3) employ a combination of (1) and (2). If a party decides to lend directly, it must have the in-house capability of assessing counterparty risk. When an intermediary is engaged, the intermediary receives a fee for its services and can guarantee against counterparty risk. Moreover, when cash is reinvested, a stock lender must decide whether it will reinvest the cash or use the services of an external money manager to invest the funds. As noted earlier, stock lenders may realize a return on the cash collateral that is less than the rebate. Reinvesting cash collateral requires an understanding of the risks associated with investing.

TRADING COSTS

A critical element in investment management is controlling the trading costs necessary to implement a strategy. While important, the measurement of trading costs is very difficult.

We begin by defining trading costs. Trading costs can be decomposed into two major components: *explicit costs* and *implicit costs*. Explicit costs are the direct costs of trading, such as broker commissions, fees, and taxes. Implicit costs represent such indirect costs as the price impact of the trade and the opportunity costs of failing to execute in a timely manner or at all. Whereas explicit costs are associated with identifiable charges, no such reporting of implicit costs occurs.

Explicit Costs

The main explicit cost is the commission paid to the broker for execution. Commission costs are fully negotiable and vary systematically by broker type and market mechanism. The commission may depend on both the price per share and the number of shares in the transaction. In addition to commissions, there may be other explicit costs. These explicit costs include custodial fees (the fees charged by an institution holding securities in safekeeping for an investor) and transfer fees (the fees associated with transferring an asset from one owner to another).

Implicit Costs

Implicit trading costs include impact costs, timing costs, and opportunity costs.

Impact Costs

The impact cost of a transaction is the change in market price due to supply/demand imbalances as a result of the trade. Bid-ask spread estimates, although informative, fail to capture the fact that large trades—those that exceed the number of shares the market maker is willing to trade at the quoted bid and ask prices—may move prices in the direction of the trade. That is, large trades may increase the price for buy orders and decrease the price for sell orders. The resulting market impact or price impact of the transaction can be thought of as the deviation of the transaction price from the "unperturbed price" that would have prevailed had the trade not occurred. As discussed above, crossing networks are designed to minimize impact costs.

Timing Cost

The *timing cost* is measured as the price change between the time the parties to the implementation process assume responsibility for the trade and the time they complete the responsibility. Timing costs occur when orders are on the trading desk of a buy-side firm (e.g., an investment management firm), but have not been released to the broker because the trader fears that the trade may swamp the market.

Opportunity Costs

The opportunity cost is the "cost" of securities not traded. This cost results from missed or only partially completed trades. These costs are the natural consequence of the release delays. For example, if the price moves too much before the trade can be completed, the manager will not make the trade. In practice, this cost is measured on shares not traded based on the difference between the market price at the time of decision and the closing price 30 days later.

While commissions and impact costs are actual and visible out-of-pocket costs, opportunity costs and timing costs are the costs of foregone opportunities and are invisible. Opportunity costs can arise for two reasons. First, some orders are executed with a delay, during which the price may move against the investor. Second, some orders incur an opportunity cost because they are only partially filled or are not executed at all.

Institutional Trading

With the increase in trading by institutional investors, trading arrangements more suitable for these investors were developed. Institutional needs include trading in large size and trading groups of stocks, both at a low commission and with low market impact. This has resulted in the evolution of special arrangements for the execution of certain types of orders commonly sought by institutional investors: (1) orders requiring the execution of a trade of a large number of shares of a given stock and (2) orders requiring the execution of trades in a large number of different stocks at as near the same time as possible. The former types of trades are called *block trades*; the latter are called *program trades*.

Block trades for stocks are trades that are negotiated off an exchange's trading facility (called the "upstairs market") because the order is equal to or in excess of a minimum threshold an exchange establishes for the quantity of shares. For example, the NYSE, block trades are defined as either trades of at least 10,000 shares of a given stock, or trades of shares with a market value of at least $200,000, whichever is less.

Program trades involve the buying and selling of a large number of names simultaneously. Such trades are also called *basket trades* because effectively a "basket" of stocks is being traded. The NYSE defines a program trade as any trade involving the purchase or sale of a basket of at least 15 stocks with a total value of $1 million or more. (It is estimated that program trades account for about a quarter of all stock market trading.) The rationale for treating a portfolio or basket of stocks as a single asset is that it diversifies the risk of trading and thus reduces costs. Brokers can offer a much lower commission rate if the portfolio is submitted as a single asset rather than submitting each individual name. In addition, the trades are typically motivated by an investor's desire for broad market exposure and are therefore "informationless," which should not result in large price concessions.

There are several commission arrangements available to an institution for a program trade, and each arrangement has numerous variants. Considerations in selecting one (in addition to commission costs) are the risk of failing to realize the best execution price and the risk that the brokerage firms to be solicited about executing the program trade will use their knowledge of the program trade to benefit from the anticipated price movement that might result—in other words, that they will frontrun the transaction (for example, buying a stock for their own account before filling the customer buy order).

STOCK MARKET INDICATORS

Stock market indicators have come to perform a variety of functions, from serving as benchmarks for evaluating the performance of professional money managers to answering the question "How did the market do today?" In general, market indexes rise and fall in fairly similar patterns. Although the correlations among indexes are high, the indexes do not move in concert at all times. The differences in movement reflect the different manner in which the indexes are constructed. Three factors enter into that construction: the universe of stocks represented by the sample underlying the index, the relative weights assigned to the stocks included in the index, and the method of averaging across all the stocks.

The stocks included in a stock market index must be combined in certain proportions (i.e., each stock must be given a weight). The three main approaches to weighting are: (1) weighting by the market capitalization, which is the number of shares times price per share; (2) weighting by the price of the stock; and (3) equal weighting for each stock, regardless of its price or its firm's market value. With the exception of the Dow Jones industrial averages (such as the DJIA) and the Value Line Composite Index, nearly all of the most widely used indexes are market-value weighted. The DJIA is a price-weighted average, and the Value Line Composite Index is an equal-weighted index.

Stock market indicators can be classified into three groups: (1) Those produced by stock exchanges based on all stocks traded on the exchanges; (2) those produced by organizations that subjectively select the stocks to be included in indexes; and (3) those where stock selection is based on an objective measure, such as the market capitalization of the company.

The New York Stock Exchange Composite Index and, although it is not an exchange, the Nasdaq Composite Index, fall into the first group. The two most popular stock market indicators in the second group are the DJIA and the Standard & Poor's 500 (S&P 500). The DJIA is constructed from 30 of the largest and most widely held U.S. companies. The companies included in the average are those selected by Dow Jones & Company, publisher of the *Wall Street Journal*. The S&P 500 represents stocks chosen from the New York Stock Exchange and the Nasdaq. The stocks in the index at any given time are determined by a committee of the Standard & Poor's Corporation, which may occasionally add or delete individual stocks or the stocks of entire industry groups. The aim of the committee is to capture present overall stock market conditions as reflected in a broad range of economic indicators. The Value Line Composite Index, produced by Value Line Inc., covers a broad range of widely held and actively traded NYSE, Nasdaq, and Toronto Stock Exchange issues selected by Value Line.

Some indexes represent a broad segment of the stock market while others represent a particular sector such as technology, oil and gas, and financial. In addition, because the notion of an equity investment style (discussed in Chapter 9) is widely accepted in the investment community, early acceptance of equity style investing (in the form of growth versus value and small market capitalization versus large capitalization) led to the creation and proliferation of published *style indexes*.

In the third group, we have the Wilshire indexes produced by Wilshire Associates (Santa Monica, California) and the Russell indexes produced by the Frank Russell Company (Tacoma, Washington), a firm that consults with pension funds and other institutional investors. The criterion for inclusion in each of these indexes is solely a firm's market capitalization. The most comprehensive index is the Wilshire 5000, which actually includes more than 6,700 stocks now, up from 5,000 at its inception. The Wilshire 4500 includes all stocks in the Wilshire 5000 except for those in the S&P 500. Thus, the shares in the Wilshire 4500 have smaller capitalization than those in the Wilshire 5000. The Russell 3000 encompasses the 3,000 largest companies in terms of their market capitalization. The Russell 1000 is limited to the largest 1,000 of those, and the Russell 2000 has the remaining smaller firms.

The MSCI (Morgan Stanley Capital International) indexes are U.S. capitalization-weighted stock indexes which have received increased acceptance.

KEY POINTS

- Common stock is an equity security representing an ownership interest in a corporation. As an equity owner, common stockholders are entitled to the earnings of the corporation when those earnings are distributed in the form of dividends.
- The most commonly used measure of the performance of a corporation is its earnings. Earnings per share—the ratio of earnings available for common shareholders divided by the number of common shares outstanding—indicates each share's portion of how much is earned by the company in a given accounting period. Because of potential dilution of earnings due to the presence of dilutive securities, earnings per share is reported in two ways in the financial statement: basic earnings per share and dilutive earnings per share.
- A dividend is the cash, stock, or any type of property a corporation distributes to its shareholders. The cash dividends that a corporation pays are described in terms of dividend per share or dividend payout ratio. The dividend payout ratio is the complement of the retention ratio. A corporation's dividend policy is usually one of the following: (1) no dividends, (2) constant growth in dividends per share, (3) constant payout ratio, or (4) low regular dividends with periodic extra dividends.
- Because common stock never matures, today's value is the present value of an infinite stream of cash flows. For the valuation of common stock,

investors look at the current dividend and make assumptions about any future dividends the company may pay, and then discounting those future earnings. This basic idea for valuing common stock is referred to as a dividend discount model.

- The U.S. stock markets have been based on two different market models: (1) auction-based, order-driven and (2) dealer-based, quote-driven. In an auction-based, order-driven market, public participants who are owners of securities meet and provide buy and sell orders via an auction system to establish market prices at which other public participants can trade. In a dealer-based, quote-driven market, market makers/dealers provide quotes at which market participants can trade.

- An exchange is typically defined as a market where intermediaries meet to deliver and execute customer orders. There are two types of off-exchange markets (alternative electronic markets): electronic communication networks and alternative trading systems. The latter include crossing networks and dark pools.

- There are various types of orders that investors can submit for execution that have different objectives. These include market orders, limit orders, conditional orders, stop orders, stop-limit orders, market-if-touched orders, kill-or-fill orders, and open orders.

- Short selling involves the sale of a stock not owned by the investor at the time of sale. A mechanism for borrowing the stock sold short is available. The costs of selling short include a fee charged by the lender of the stock and any dividends paid while the stock is borrowed.

- Buying a stock on margin involves an investor borrowing funds using the stock purchased as collateral for the loan. The investor is charged the call money interest rate for borrowing the funds plus a service fee. There are restrictions imposed by the Federal Reserve as to how much can be borrowed at the time of purchase (i.e., initial margin requirement) and how much must be maintained if the price of the stock declines (i.e., maintenance margin requirement).

- Algorithmic trading is often used by institutions to divide single large orders into many small orders to reduce market impact and disguise their trades. High-frequency trading involves computers utlizing information received electronically to generate orders without human input. Flash trading is particular type of high-frequency trading.

- Trading costs are made up of two components: explicit and implicit costs. Explicit costs are the direct cost of trading such as broker commissions, fees, and taxes. Implicit costs represent the price impact of the trade and the opportunity costs of failing to execute a trade in a timely manner or at all.

- Special trading arrangements have evolved that are more suitable for institutional investors who must place orders requiring the execution of a trade of a large number of (1) shares of a given stock and (2) trades in a large number of different stocks at as near the same time as possible. Blocks trades are used for the former and program trades are used for the latter.
- There are three types of stock market indicators: (1) those produced by stock exchanges based on all stocks traded on the exchanges (e.g., New York Stock Exchange Composite Index and Nasdaq Composite Index); (2) those produced by organizations that subjectively select the stocks to be included in indexes (e.g., Dow Jones Industrial Index and the Standard & Poor's 500); and, (3) those where stock selection is based on an objective measure, such as the market capitalization of the company (e.g., Wilshire and Russell indexes).

QUESTIONS

1. Following is information from General Mills' fiscal 2011 first quarter results:

Earnings per share—basic	$0.73
Earnings per share—diluted	$0.70
Dividends per share	$0.28

   a. What is the difference between the two earnings per share for General Mills for the period reported?
   b. What is meant by the dividends per share?
   c. Based on dilutive earnings per share, what is the dividend payout ratio?

2. What is the basic idea behind a dividend discount model?

3. a. What is meant by a market order?
   b. What risk is an investor exposed to when placing a market order?
   c. When is a limit order executed?

4. The following appeared as the opening paragraph in an article appearing in the *Wall Street Journal* (March 31, 2010):

   SHANGHAI—China will launch its long-awaited trial program for margin trading and short selling Wednesday, removing the last bit of uncertainty over its latest effort to introduce risky alternative-investment tools to its huge but still immature stock market.

   a. What is meant by "margin trading" and why is it viewed as a risky strategy?

   b. What is "short selling" and why is it viewed as a risk strategy?

5. What are the costs associated with short selling?

6. The following is the opening paragraph of a *Bloomberg Business-week* story published on March 25, 2010 (http://www.businessweek.com/news/2010-03-25/fsa-probe-is-said-to-focus-on-front-running-of-block-trades.html):

   March 26 (Bloomberg)—Britain's financial regulator is examining whether some of the seven people arrested in an insider-trading probe engaged in the front-running of block trades, a person with direct knowledge of the case said.

   a. What is meant by a block trade?

   b. What is meant by "front-running of block trades"?

7. The following is a quote from a May 6, 2010 article published by Fox-Business ("Dow Plunge: Program Trading's Role"):

   Program trading has been the subject of massive controversy in recent years as many traders and analysts feel it creates dangerous volatility in the market. Such trading began in the 1970s as trades were manually walked around to specialists' posts. But sophisticated computer systems now allow traders to place trades directly into the exchange computer, increasing the speed of trading exponentially.

   a. What is meant by "program trading"?

   b. Why do traders use this form of trading?

CHAPTER 9

Common Stock Portfolio Management Strategies

Frank J. Fabozzi, Ph.D., CFA, CPA
Professor in the Practice of Finance
Yale School of Management

James L. Grant, Ph.D.
Assistant Professor of Accounting and Finance
University of Massachusetts Boston
and
President
JLG Research

Raman Vardharaj, CFA
Vice President and Portfolio Manager
OppenheimerFunds

In this chapter, we review equity portfolio strategies, taking a close look at active and passive management, the decision as to whether or not to pursue an active or passive management, style investing, and the different types of active strategies that can be employed. We begin the chapter with a discussion of the equity portfolio management process.

INTEGRATING THE EQUITY PORTFOLIO MANAGEMENT PROCESS

In Chapter 1, the investment management process was described as a series of five distinct tasks. In practice, portfolio management requires an integrated approach. There must be recognition that superior investment performance results when valuable ideas are implemented in a cost-efficient

EXHIBIT 9.1 The Investing Process

Information Value	less	Implementation Cost	equals	Captured Value

Source: See Wayne H. Wagner and Mark Edwards, "Implementing Investment Strategies: The Art and Science of Investing," Chapter 11 in *Active Equity Portfolio Management*, ed. Frank J. Fabozzi (Hoboken, N.J.: John Wiley & Sons, 1998).

manner. The process of investing—as opposed to the process of investment—includes innovative stock selection and portfolio strategies as well as efficient cost structures for the implementation of any portfolio strategy.[1] Exhibit 9.1 highlights the importance of an integrated approach to managing equity portfolios. It recognizes that the value added by the manager is the result of information value less the implementation cost of trading. This difference in value is referred to as *captured value*, a term coined by Wayne Wagner and Mark Edwards.[2]

This view that an investing process requires an integrated approach to portfolio management is reinforced by MSCI BARRA, a vendor of analytical systems used by portfolio managers. This service provider emphasizes that superior investment performance is the product of careful attention paid by equity managers to the following four elements:

- Forming reasonable return expectations.
- Controlling portfolio risk to demonstrate investment prudence.
- Controlling trading costs.
- Monitoring total investment performance.

Accordingly, the investing process that includes these four elements are all equally important in realizing superior investment performance. As for the second element, we will discuss the process of controlling risk in Chapter 13. Trading costs are explained in Chapter 8.

CAPITAL MARKET PRICE EFFICIENCY

Later in this chapter, we explain the two major types of portfolio strategies: active versus passive. The decision as to which of the two approaches to pursue depends on the price efficiency of the market. A price efficient market

---

[1]Wayne H. Wagner and Mark Edwards, "Implementing Investment Strategies: The Art and Science of Investing," Chapter 11 in *Active Equity Portfolio Management*, ed. Frank J. Fabozzi (Hoboken, N.J.: John Wiley & Sons, 1998).
[2]Ibid.

is one where security prices at all times fully reflect all available information that is relevant to their valuation. When a market is price efficient, investment strategies pursued to outperform a broad-based stock market index will not consistently produce superior returns after adjusting for risk and transaction costs.

Numerous studies have examined the pricing efficiency of the stock market. While it is not our intent in this chapter to provide a comprehensive review of these studies, we can summarize the basic findings and implications for common stock portfolio management strategies.

Forms of Efficiency

There are three different forms of pricing efficiency: (1) weak form, (2) semistrong form, and (3) strong form. The distinctions among these forms rests in the relevant information that is believed to be taken into consideration in the price of the security at all times. Weak-form efficiency means that the price of the security reflects the past price and trading history of the security. Semistrong-form efficiency means that the price of the security fully reflects all public information (which, of course, includes but is not limited to, historical price and trading patterns). Strong-form efficiency exists in a market where the price of a security reflects all information, whether it is publicly available or known only to insiders such as the firm's managers or directors.

The preponderance of empirical evidence supports the claim that the U.S. common stock market is efficient in the weak form. The evidence emerges from numerous sophisticated tests that explore whether or not historical price movements can be used to project future prices in such a way as to produce returns above what one would expect from market movements and the risk class of the security. Such returns are known as *positive abnormal returns*. The implications are that investors who follow a strategy of selecting common stocks solely on the basis of price patterns or trading volume—such investors are referred to as *technical analysts* or *chartists*—should not expect to do better than the market. In fact, they may fare worse because of higher transactions costs associated with frequent buying and selling of stocks.

Evidence on price efficiency in the semistrong form is mixed. Some studies support the proposition of efficiency when they suggest that investors who select stocks on the basis of fundamental security analysis—which consists of analyzing financial statements, the quality of management, and the economic environment of a company—will not outperform the market. This result is certainly reasonable. There are so many analysts using the same approach, with the same publicly available data, that the price of the stock remains in line with all the relevant factors that determine value. On the other hand, a sizable number of studies have produced evidence indicating that there have been instances and patterns of pricing inefficiency in the stock market over long periods of time. Economists and financial analysts often label these examples of inefficient pricing as "anomalies" in the market, that is, phenomena that cannot be easily explained by accepted theory.

Empirical tests of strong form pricing efficiency fall into two groups: (1) studies of the performance of professional money managers and (2) studies of the activities of insiders (individuals who are either company directors, major officers, or major stockholders). Studying the performance of professional money managers to test the strong form of pricing efficiency has been based on the belief that professional managers have access to better information than the general public. Whether or not this is true is moot because the empirical evidence suggests professional managers have been unable to outperform the market consistently. In contrast, evidence based on the activities of insiders has generally revealed that this group often achieves higher risk-adjusted returns than the stock market. Of course, insiders could not consistently earn those high abnormal returns if the stock prices fully reflected all relevant information about the values of the firms. Thus, the empirical evidence on insiders fails to support the notion that the market is efficient in the strong-form sense.

Implications for Investing in Common Stock

Common stock investment strategies can be classified into two broad categories: active strategies and passive strategies. Active strategies are those that attempt to outperform the market by one or more of the following: (1) timing market transactions, such as in the case of technical analysis, (2) identifying undervalued or overvalued stocks using fundamental security analysis, or (3) selecting stocks according to one of the market anomalies. Obviously, the decision to pursue an active strategy must be based on the belief that there is some type of gain from such costly efforts, but gains are possible only if pricing inefficiencies exist. The particular strategy chosen depends on why the investor believes this is the case.

Investors who believe that the market prices stocks efficiently should accept the implication that attempts to outperform the market cannot be systematically successful, except by luck. This implication does not mean that investors should shun the stock market, but rather that they should pursue a passive strategy, one that does not attempt to outperform the market. Is there an optimal investment strategy for someone who holds this belief in the pricing efficiency of the stock market? Indeed there is. The theoretical basis rests on modern portfolio theory and capital market theory. According to modern portfolio theory, the market portfolio offers the highest level of return per unit of risk in a market that is price efficient. A portfolio of financial assets with characteristics similar to those of a portfolio consisting of the entire market—the market portfolio—will capture the pricing efficiency of the market.

But how can such a passive strategy be implemented? More specifically, what is meant by a market portfolio, and how should that portfolio be constructed? In theory, the market portfolio consists of all financial assets, not just common stock. The reason is that investors compare all investment opportunities, not just stock, when committing their capital. Thus, our principles of investing must be based on capital market theory, not just stock market theory. When the theory is applied to the stock market, the market portfolio has been interpreted as consisting of a large universe of common stocks. But how much of each common stock should be purchased when constructing the market portfolio? Theory states that the chosen portfolio should be an appropriate fraction of the market portfolio; hence, the weighting of each stock in the market portfolio should be based on its relative market capitalization. Thus, if the aggregate market capitalization of all stocks included in the market portfolio is $T and the market capitalization (i.e., number of shares times the share price) of one of these stocks is $A, then the fraction of this stock that should be held in the market portfolio is $A/$T.

The passive strategy that we have just described is called *indexing*. As pension fund sponsors in the 1990s increasingly came to believe that managers were unable to outperform the stock market, the amount of funds managed using an indexing strategy has grown substantially. That being said, the passive indexing approach to investing has been called into question by some plan sponsors due to the flat-to-negative average performance of the stock market in the decade following 2000.

TRACKING ERROR AND RELATED MEASURES

Tracking error is a key concept in understanding the potential performance of a common stock portfolio relative to a benchmark index, as well as the actual performance of a common stock portfolio relative to a benchmark index. Tracking error can be used to measure the degree of active management by a portfolio manager.

Definition of Tracking Error

As explained in Chapter 3, a portfolio's risk can be measured by the standard deviation of portfolio returns. This statistical measure provides a range around the portfolio's average return within which the actual return over a period is likely to fall with some specific probability. The mean return and standard deviation (or volatility) of a portfolio can be calculated over a period of time.

The standard deviation or volatility of a portfolio or a market index is an absolute number. A portfolio manager or client can also ask what the variation of the portfolio's return is relative to a specified benchmark. Such variation is called the portfolio's *tracking error*.

Specifically, tracking error measures the dispersion of a portfolio's returns relative to the benchmark's returns. That is, tracking error is the standard deviation of the portfolio's *active return* where active return is defined as

Active return = Portfolio's actual return − Benchmark's actual return

A portfolio created to match the benchmark (i.e., an index fund) that regularly has zero active returns (that is, always matches its benchmark's actual return) would have a tracking error of zero. But a portfolio that is actively managed that takes positions substantially different from the benchmark would likely have large active returns, both positive and negative, and thus would have an annual tracking error of, say, 5% to 10%.

To find the tracking error of a portfolio, it is first necessary to specify the benchmark. The tracking error of a portfolio, as indicated, is its standard deviation relative to the benchmark, *not* its total standard deviation. For example, an index fund that exactly matches the S&P 500 would have a tracking error of 0% but is likely to have an overall standard deviation that is different from zero, which is the standard deviation of its benchmark. Exhibit 9.2 presents the information used to calculate the tracking error for a hypothetical portfolio and benchmark using 30 weekly observations. The fourth column in the exhibit shows the active return for the week. It is from the data in this column that the tracking error is computed. As reported in the exhibit, the standard deviation of the weekly active returns is 0.54%. This value is then annualized by multiplying by the square root of 52—52 representing the number of weeks in a year.[3] This gives a value of 3.89%.

Given the tracking error, a range for the possible portfolio active return and corresponding range for the portfolio can be estimated assuming that the active returns are normally distributed. For example, assume the following:

Benchmark = S&P 500
Expected return on S&P 500 = 20%
Tracking error relative to S&P 500 = 2%

then:[4]

---

[3] If the observations were monthly rather than weekly, the monthly tracking error would be annualized by multiplying by the square root of 12.
[4] The probabilities are based on a normal probability distribution.

EXHIBIT 9.2 Data and Calculation for Active Return, Alpha, and Information Ratio

	Weekly Returns (%)		
Week	Portfolio	Benchmark	Active
1	3.69%	3.72%	–0.03%
2	–0.56	–1.09	0.53
3	–1.41	–1.35	–0.06
4	0.96	0.34	0.62
5	–4.07	–4.00	–0.07
6	1.27	0.91	0.36
7	–0.39	–0.08	–0.31
8	–3.31	–2.76	–0.55
9	2.19	2.11	0.08
10	–0.02	–0.40	0.38
11	–0.46	–0.42	–0.04
12	0.09	0.71	–0.62
13	–1.93	–1.99	0.06
14	–1.91	–2.37	0.46
15	1.89	1.98	–0.09
16	–3.75	–4.33	0.58
17	–3.38	–4.22	0.84
18	0.60	0.62	–0.02
19	–10.81	–11.60	0.79
20	6.63	7.78	–1.15
21	3.52	2.92	0.60
22	1.24	1.89	–0.66
23	–0.63	–1.66	1.03
24	3.04	2.90	0.14
25	–1.73	–1.58	–0.15
26	2.81	3.05	–0.24
27	0.40	1.64	–1.24
28	1.03	1.03	0.00
29	–0.94	–0.95	0.01
30	1.45	1.66	–0.21

Notes:

Average of active returns = 0.035%
Standard deviation of active returns = 0.54%

Annualizing
Annual average = Weekly average × 52
Annual std dev = Weekly std dev × $(52^{0.5})$

Hence, on an annual basis,
Alpha = 1.82% (= 0.035% × 52 = Annualized average of weekly active returns)
Tracking error = 3.89% (= 0.54% × $[52^{0.5}]$ = Annualized std dev of weekly active returns)
Information ratio = Alpha/Tracking error = 1.82%/3.89%= 0.47

Number of Standard Deviations	Range for Portfolio Active Return	Corresponding Range for Portfolio Return	Probability
1	±2%	18%–22%	67%
2	±4%	16%–24%	95%
3	±6%	14%–26%	99%

A manager can pursue a blend of an active and passive (i.e., indexing) strategy. That is, a manager can construct a portfolio such that a certain percentage of the portfolio is indexed to some benchmark and the balance actively managed. Assume that the passively managed portion (i.e., the indexed portion) has a zero tracking error relative to the benchmark. For such a strategy, we can show (after some algebraic manipulation) that the tracking error for the overall portfolio would be as follows:

Portfolio tracking error relative to index
= (Percent of portfolio actively managed)
× (Tracking error of the actively managed portion relative to index)

An *enhanced index fund* differs from an index fund in that it deviates from the index holdings in small amounts and hopes to slightly outperform the index through those small deviations. In terms of an active/passive strategy, the manager allocates a small percentage of the portfolio to be actively managed. The reason is that in case the bets prove detrimental, then the underperformance would be small. Thus, realized returns would always deviate from index returns only by small amounts. There are many enhancing strategies. Suppose that a manager whose benchmark is the S&P 500 pursues an enhanced indexing strategy allocating only 5% of the portfolio to be actively managed and 95% indexed. Assume further that the tracking error of the actively managed portion is 15% with respect to the S&P 500. The portfolio would then have a tracking error calculated as follows:

Percent of portfolio actively managed relative to S&P 500 = 5%
Tracking error relative to S&P 500 = 15%
Portfolio's tracking error relative to S&P 500 = 5% × 15% = 0.75%

Forward-Looking vs. Backward-Looking Tracking Error

In Exhibit 9.1 the tracking error of the hypothetical portfolio is shown based on the active returns reported. However, the performance shown is the result of the portfolio manager's decisions during those 30 weeks with respect to portfolio positioning issues such as beta, sector allocations, style tilt (i.e., value versus growth), stock selections, and the like. Hence, we can call the tracking error calculated from these trailing active returns a *back-ward-looking tracking error*. It is also called an *ex post tracking error*.

One problem with a backward-looking tracking error is that it does not reflect the effect of current decisions by the portfolio manager on the future active returns and hence the future tracking error that may be realized. If, for example, the manager significantly changes the portfolio beta or sector allocations today, then the backward-looking tracking error that is calculated using data from prior periods would not accurately reflect the current portfolio risks going forward. That is, the backward-looking tracking error will have little predictive value and can be misleading regarding portfolio risks going forward.

The portfolio manager needs a forward-looking estimate of tracking error to accurately reflect the portfolio's risk going forward. The way this is done in practice is by using the services of a commercial vendor that has a model, called a multifactor risk model, that has defined the risks associated with a benchmark. Such a model is described in Chapter 13. Statistical analysis of the historical return data of the stocks in the benchmark are used to obtain the factors and quantify their risks. (This involves the use of variances and correlations.) Using the manager's current portfolio holdings, the portfolio's current exposure to the various factors can be calculated and compared to the benchmark's exposures to the same factors. Using the differential factor exposures and the risks of the factors, a portfolio's *forward-looking tracking error* can be computed. This tracking error is also referred to as the *predicted tracking error* or *ex ante tracking error*.

There is no guarantee that the forward-looking tracking error at the start of, say, a year would exactly match the backward-looking tracking error calculated at the end of the same year. There are two reasons for this. The first is that as the year progresses and changes are made to the portfolio, the forward-looking tracking error estimate would change to reflect the new exposures. The second is that the accuracy of the forward-looking tracking error depends on the extent of the stability in the variances and correlations that were used in the analysis. These problems notwithstanding, the average of forward-looking tracking error estimates obtained at different times during the year will be reasonably close to the backward-looking tracking error estimate obtained at the end of the year.

Each of these estimates has its use. The forward-looking tracking error is useful in risk control and portfolio construction. The manager can immediately see the likely effect on tracking error of any planned change in the portfolio. Thus, a portfolio manager can do a what-if analysis of various portfolio strategies and eliminate those that would result in a tracking error that exceeds a specified risk tolerance. The backward-looking tracking error can be useful for assessing actual performance analysis, such as the information ratio discussed next.

Information Ratio

Alpha is the average active return over a time period. Since backward-looking tracking error measures the standard deviation of a portfolio's active return, it is different from alpha. A portfolio does not have backward-looking tracking error simply because of outperformance or underperformance. For instance, consider a portfolio that outperforms (or underperforms) its benchmark by exactly 10 basis points every month. This portfolio would have a backward-looking tracking error of zero and a positive (negative) alpha of 10 basis points. In contrast, consider a portfolio that outperforms its benchmark by 10 basis points during half the months and underperforms by 10 bp during the other months. This portfolio would have a backward-looking tracking error that is positive but an alpha equal to zero.[5]

The *information ratio* combines alpha and tracking error as follows:

$$\text{Information ratio} = \frac{\text{Alpha}}{\text{Backward-looking tracking error}}$$

The information ratio is essentially a reward-to-risk ratio. The reward is the *average* of the active return, that is, alpha. The risk is the standard deviation of the active return, the tracking error, and, more specifically, backward-looking tracking error. The higher the information ratio, the better the manager performed relative to the risk assumed.

To illustrate the calculation of the information ratio, consider the active returns for the hypothetical portfolio shown in Exhibit 9.2. The weekly average active return is 0.035%. Annualizing the weekly average active return by multiplying by 52 gives an alpha of 1.82%. Since the backward tracking error is 3.89%, the information ratio is 0.47 (1.83%/3.89%)

Marginal Contribution to Tracking Error

Since tracking error arises from various bets (some intentional and some unintentional) placed by the manager through overweights and underweights relative to the benchmark, it would be useful to understand how sensitive the tracking error is to small changes in each of these bets.

---

[5]Note that in some texts, alpha and tracking error are calculated respectively as the average and the standard deviation of the beta-adjusted active return, instead of the total active return.

Suppose, for example, a portfolio initially has an overweight of 3% in the semiconductor industry relative to its benchmark, and that the tracking error is 6%. Suppose that the tracking error subsequently increases to 6.1% due to the semiconductor industry weight in the portfolio increasing by 1% (and hence the overweight increases to 4%). Then, it can be said that this industry adds 0.1% to tracking error for every 1% increase in its weight. That is, its *marginal contribution to tracking error* is 0.1%. This would hold only at the margin, that is, for a small change, and not for large changes.

Marginal contributions can be also calculated for individual stocks. If the risk analysis employs a multifactor risk model, then similar marginal contribution estimates can be obtained for the risk factors also.

Generally, marginal contributions would be positive for overweighted industries (or stocks) and negative for underweighted ones. The reason is as follows. If a portfolio already holds an excess weight in an industry, then increasing this weight would cause the portfolio to diverge further from the benchmark. This increased divergence adds to tracking error, leading to a positive marginal contribution for this industry. Suppose, however, the portfolio has an underweight in an industry. Then, increasing the portfolio weight in this industry would make the portfolio converge towards the benchmark, thus reducing tracking error. This leads to a negative marginal contribution for this industry.

An analysis of the marginal contributions can be useful for a manager who seeks to alter the portfolio's tracking error. Suppose a manager wishes to reduce the tracking error, then portfolio overweights in industries (or stocks) with the highest positive marginal contributions should be reduced. Alternatively, a manager can reduce the underweights (i.e., increase the overall weights) in industries (or stocks) with the most negative marginal contributions. Such changes would be most effective in reducing the tracking error while minimizing the necessary turnover and the associated expenses.

ACTIVE VS. PASSIVE PORTFOLIO MANAGEMENT

While earlier in this chapter we distinguished between the extremes of equity portfolio management—passive versus active—in practice there are investors who pursue different degrees of active management and different degrees of passive management. It would be helpful to have some way of quantifying the degree of active or passive management. Fortunately, there is a way to do that.

EXHIBIT 9.3 Measures of Management Categories

	Indexing	Active Management	Enhanced Indexing
Expected alpha	0%	2.0% or higher	0.5% to 2.0%
Tracking error	0% to 0.2%	4% or higher	0.5% to 2.0%

Source: Exhibit 2 in John S. Loftus, "Enhanced Equity Indexing," Chapter 4 in *Perspectives on Equity Indexing*, ed. Frank J. Fabozzi (Hoboken, N.J.: John Wiley & Sons, 2000), 84.

John Loftus has suggested that one way of classifying the various types of equity strategies is in terms of alpha and tracking error.[6] Based on these measures, Loftus proposes the classification scheme shown in Exhibit 9.3. While there may be disagreements as to the values proposed by Loftus, the exhibit does provide some guidance. In an indexing strategy, the portfolio manager seeks to construct a portfolio that matches the risk profile of the benchmark, the expected alpha is zero and, except for transaction costs and other technical issues discussed later when we cover the topic of indexing, the tracking error should be, in theory, zero. Due to these other issues, tracking error will be a small positive value. At the other extreme, a manager who pursues an active strategy by constructing a portfolio that significantly differs from the risk profile of the benchmark has an expected alpha of more than 2% and a large tracking error—a tracking error of 4% or higher.

Using tracking error as our guide and the fact that a manager can construct a portfolio whose risk profile can differ to any degree from the risk profile of the benchmark, we have a conceptual framework for understanding common stock portfolio management strategies. For example, there are managers that will construct a portfolio with a risk profile close to that of the benchmark but intentionally not identical to it. Such a strategy as we mentioned earlier is enhanced indexing. This strategy will result in the construction of a portfolio that has greater tracking error relative to an indexing strategy. In the classification scheme proposed by Loftus, for an enhanced indexer the expected alpha does not exceed 2% and the tracking error is 0.5% to 2%.

EQUITY STYLE MANAGEMENT

Before we discuss the various types of active and passive strategies, let's discuss an important topic regarding what has come to be known as *equity investment styles*. Several academic studies found that there were

---

[6]John S. Loftus, "Enhanced Equity Indexing," Chapter 4 in *Perspectives on Equity Indexing*, ed. Frank J. Fabozzi (Hoboken, N.J.: John Wiley & Sons, 2000).

categories of stocks that had similar characteristics and performance patterns. Moreover, the returns of these stock categories performed differently than other categories of stocks. That is, the returns of stocks within a category were highly correlated and the returns between categories of stocks were relatively uncorrelated. As a result of these studies, practitioners began to view these categories of stocks with similar performance as a "style" of investing. Using size as a basis for categorizing style, some managers became "large cap" investors while others "small cap" investors. ("Cap" means market capitalization.) Moreover, there was a commonly held belief that a manager could shift "styles" to enhance performance return. Today, the notion of an equity investment style is widely accepted in the investment community. There are three major services that provide popular style indexes.

Types of Equity Styles

Stocks can be classified by style in many ways. The most common is in terms of one or more measures of "growth" and "value." Within a growth and value style there is often a substyle based on some measure of size. The motivation for the value/growth style categories can be explained in terms of the most common measure for classifying stocks as growth or value—the price-to-book value per share (P/B) ratio.[7] Earnings growth will increase the book value per share. Assuming no change in the P/B ratio, a stock's price will increase if earnings grow—as higher book value times a constant P/B ratio leads to higher stock price. A manager who is growth oriented is concerned with earnings growth and seeks those stocks from a universe of stocks that have higher relative earnings growth. The growth manager's risks are that growth in earnings will not materialize and/or that the P/B ratio will decline.

For a value manager, concern is with the price component rather than with the future earnings growth. Stocks would be classified as value stocks within a universe of stocks if they are viewed as cheap in terms of their P/B ratio. By cheap it is meant that the P/B ratio is low relative to the universe of stocks. The expectation of the manager who follows a value style is that the P/B ratio will return to some normal level and thus even with book value per share constant, the price will rise. The risk is that the P/B ratio will not increase.

Within the value and growth categories there are substyles. In the value category, there are three substyles: low price-to-earnings (P/E) ratio,

[7]Support for the use of this measure is provided in Eugene F. Fama and Kenneth R. French, "Common Risk Factors on Stocks and Bonds," *Journal of Financial Economics* 33, no. 1 (1993): 3–56.

contrarian, and yield.[8] The *low-P/E manager* concentrates on companies trading at low prices relative to their P/E ratio.[9] (The P/E ratio can be defined as the current P/E, a normalized P/E, or a discounted future earnings.) The *contrarian manager* looks at the book value of a company and focuses on those companies that are selling at low valuation relative to book value. The companies that fall into this category are typically depressed cyclical stocks or companies that have little or no current earnings or dividend yields. The expectation is that the stock is on a cyclical rebound or that the company's earnings will turn around. Both these occurrences are expected to lead to substantial price appreciation. The most conservative value managers are those that look at companies with above average dividend yields that are expected to be capable of increasing, or at least maintaining, those yields. This style is followed by a manager who is referred to as a *yield manager*.

Growth managers seek companies with above average growth prospects. In the growth manager style category, there tends to be two major substyles.[10] The first is a growth manager who focuses on high-quality companies with consistent growth. A manager who follows this substyle is referred to as a *consistent growth manager*. The second growth substyle is followed by an *earnings momentum growth manager*. In contrast to a consistent growth manager, an earnings momentum growth manager prefers companies with more volatile, above-average growth. Such a manager seeks to buy companies in expectation of an acceleration of earnings.

There are some managers who follow both a growth and value investing style but have a bias (or tilt) in favor of one of the styles. The bias is not sufficiently identifiable to categorize the manager as either a growth or value manager. Most managers who fall into this hybrid style are described as *growth at a price managers* or *growth at a reasonable price managers*. These managers look for companies that are forecasted to have above-average growth potential selling at a reasonable value.

Range of Equity Style Opportunities

There are different equity styles used by managers of mutual funds. There are organizations that classify managers based on several broad style

---

[8]Jon A. Christopherson and C. Nola Williams, "Equity Style: What It Is and Why It Matters," Chapter 1 in *The Handbook of Equity Style Management*, 2nd ed., ed. T. Daniel Coggin, Frank J. Fabozzi, and Robert D. Arnott (Hoboken, N.J.: John Wiley & Sons, 1997).

[9]For a discussion of an approach based on low price-earnings, see Gary G. Schlarbaum, "Value-Based Equity Strategies," Chapter 7 in *The Handbook of Equity Style Management*.

[10]Christopherson and Williams, "Equity Style: What It Is and Why It Matters."

classifications. One of these organizations is Morningstar which introduced the Morningstar Style Box™ in 1992. Morningstar classifies equity mutual funds on the basis of size—in terms of market capitalization of the stocks held—and style—value versus growth. Based on size and style, Morningstar classifies mutual funds according to the following 3 × 3 (or nine-box) matrix range of equity styles:

	Value	Blend	Growth
Large cap	Lge V	Lge B	Lge G
Mid-cap	Mid V	Mid B	Mid G
Small cap	Sm V	Sm B	Sm G

Morningstar believes that combining these two variables offers investors a broad view of a mutual fund's holdings and risk. The actual size measure used by Morningstar for an equity fund is based on the geometric mean of the market capitalizations of the stocks in the fund. For example, if a mutual fund held equal proportions in three large-cap stocks with market capitalizations of $15 billion, $20 billion, and $25 billion, respectively, then the Morningstar size measure for the equity fund would be:

$$\text{Size} = \$15^{1/3} \times \$20^{1/3} \times \$25^{1/3} = \$19.57 \text{ billion}$$

For reporting, the size value of the mutual fund would be shown by Morningstar as the average market capitalization of the stocks in the fund. In turn, Morningstar uses composite scores based on five value and five growth variables to distinguish the value and growth orientation of the stocks in the fund. The Morningstar growth score for a stock is based on an evaluation of both long-term projected earnings growth, at 50% weight, and historical growth measures, with a 12.5% weighting on sales growth, earnings growth, cash flow growth and book growth, respectively. Growth stocks score high on these growth rate measures. While we indicated earlier that the value style of a fund is often related to the P/B ratio, the Morningstar value orientation of a stock in a fund is based on an assessment of the forward-looking P/E, at 50% weight, and historical price multiples, with a 12.5% weighting on P/B, P/S, P/CF, and dividend yield, respectively. Based on these price relatives, value stocks generally have low price multiples and high dividend yields (to the extent that a stock pays dividends). Stocks that do not exhibit either a value or growth orientation would fall into the Morningstar core or blend style.

The Morningstar value and growth orientation for equity mutual funds are consistent across U.S. and non-U.S. markets, as the style of each fund is determined relative to the appropriate regional (or country) index. The regions of the world covered by Morningstar in their mutual fund reporting include the United States, Canada, Europe, Japan, Asia ex-Japan, Australia and New Zealand, and Latin America. In the case of U.S. domestic stocks, size is a measure of the average market cap of a mutual fund's holdings as it compares to the average market cap of stocks in the Morningstar equity database of the 5,000 largest domestic stocks.

Depending on size (market capitalization), Morningstar places a mutual fund into a large cap, mid-cap, or small cap grouping. As noted, the style orientation of a stock in a fund is based on a composite of fundamentals including price multiples for value stocks and growth rates for growth stocks. An average of these scores is computed for each of the size categories. The average style score of a mutual fund's holdings is then compared to the average for its size category. Mutual funds whose average style scores are well above the average are categorized as "growth," and those with scores that are well below the average are categorized as "value." This style classification system is supported (although not necessarily) by the observation that growth stocks (i.e., stocks with higher than average earnings growth rates) have high P/E and P/B ratios, while value stocks have low P/E and P/B ratios.

In terms of size definitions, conventional wisdom holds that large-cap stocks have an average market capitalization of more than $5 billion. Mid-cap stocks often range from $1 to $5 billion on the size scale, while small caps have an equity capitalization of less than $1 billion. The following 5 × 3 (or 15-box) matrix range includes giant-cap funds and expands the range of opportunities for classifying equity mutual funds by size and style:

	Value	Blend	Growth
Giant cap	*Giant V*	*Giant B*	*Giant G*
Large cap	Lge V	Lge B	Lge G
Mid-cap	Mid V	Mid B	Mid G
Small cap	Sm V	Sm B	Sm G
Micro-cap	*Mic V*	*Mic B*	*Mic G*

In the 5 × 3 equity style matrix, giant cap value- and giant cap growth funds have been added to the traditional 3 × 3 style matrix to recognize that another equity size classification is needed—namely giant-cap or maxi-cap stocks—as many U.S. large capitalization firms have market values well in excess of $100 billion. Moreover, in terms of the possible creation of style active or passive (indexing) opportunities, it is noteworthy that at the lowest end of the equity size spectrum, *micro*-cap stocks have an equity cap of about $250 million, or less.

For consistency across U.S. and non-U.S. markets, Morningstar uses the following size convention for classifying giant-cap, large-cap, mid-cap, small-cap, and micro-cap funds. Again, fund size is reported by Morningstar as the average market capitalization of component stocks in a mutual fund.

Giant cap = highest 40% of total market capitalization
Large cap = next 30% of total market capitalization
Mid-cap = next 20% of total market capitalization
Small cap = next 7% of total market capitalization
Micro-cap = remaining 3% of total market capitalization

Moreover, the determination of the value and growth styles for mutual funds comprising the 5 × 3 equity style matrix is the same as that outlined before. In addition to the 3 × 3 style box for equity mutual funds, Morningstar conducts investment style analysis on fixed income funds, balanced funds, exchange-traded funds, and hedge funds, among other investment fund vehicles. In recent years, Morningstar has developed the dual concepts of the fund centroid and the Ownership Zone[SM]. In simple terms, the fund centroid reflects the asset-weighted average of the funds' holdings, while the Ownership Zone reflects the possible range of styles across the equity style box that includes 75% of a fund's holdings. While caveats apply, particularly for active equity managers, the concepts of the fund centroid and the Ownership Zone can be used by investors to assess the location and consistency of a particular style, whether value, growth, or blend orientation within the equity style box.

PASSIVE STRATEGIES

There are two types of passive strategies: a buy-and-hold strategy and an indexing strategy. In a *buy-and-hold strategy*, a portfolio of stocks based on some criterion is purchased and held to the end of some investment horizon. There is no active buying and selling of stocks once the portfolio is created. While referred to as a passive strategy, there are elements of active management. Specifically, the investor who pursues this strategy must determine which stock issues to buy.

An indexing strategy is the more commonly followed passive strategy. With this strategy, the manager does not attempt to identify undervalued or overvalued stock issues based on fundamental security analysis. Nor does the manager attempt to forecast general movements in the stock market and then structure the portfolio so as to take advantage of those movements. Instead, an indexing strategy involves designing a portfolio to track the total return performance of a benchmark index. Next we explain how that is done.

Constructing an Indexed Portfolio

In constructing a portfolio to replicate the performance of the benchmark index, sometimes referred to as the *indexed portfolio* or the *tracking portfolio*, there are several approaches that can be used. One approach is to purchase all stock issues included in the benchmark index in proportion to their weightings. A second approach, referred to as the *capitalization approach*, is one in which the manager purchases a number of the largest capitalized names in the benchmark index and equally distributes the residual stock weighting across the other issues in the benchmark index. For example, if the top 150 highest-capitalization stock issues are selected for the replicating portfolio and these issues account for 70% of the total capitalization of the benchmark index, the remaining 30% is evenly proportioned among the other stock issues.

Another approach is to construct an indexed portfolio with fewer stock issues than the benchmark index. Two methods used to implement this approach are the cellular (or stratified sampling) method and the multifactor risk model method.

In the *cellular method*, the manager begins by defining risk factors by which the stocks that make up a benchmark index can be categorized. A typical risk factor is the industry in which a company operates. Other factors might include risk characteristics such as beta or capitalization. The use of two characteristics would add a second dimension to the stratification. In the case of the industry categorization, each company in the benchmark index is assigned to an industry. This means that the companies in the benchmark have been stratified by industry. The objective of this method is then to reduce residual risk by diversifying across all industries in the same proportion as the benchmark index. Stock issues within each cell or stratum, or in this case industry, can then be selected randomly or by some other criterion such as capitalization ranking.

The second method is using a multifactor risk model to construct a portfolio that matches the risk profile of the benchmark index as explained in Chapter 13. By doing so, a predicted tracking error close to zero can be obtained. In the case of smaller portfolios, this approach is ideal since the manager can assess the trade-off of including more stock issues versus the higher transaction costs for constructing the indexed portfolio. This can be measured in terms of the effect on predicted tracking error.

ACTIVE INVESTING

In contrast with passive investing, active investing makes sense when a moderate to low degree of capital market efficiency is present in the financial markets (or areas thereof). This happens when the active investor has (1) better information than most other investors (namely, the "consensus" investors), and/or (2) the investor has a more productive way of looking at a given information set to generate active rewards.

In general, active strategies can be classified as following either a top-down approach or a bottom-up approach. We discuss each approach in this section.

Top-Down Approaches to Active Investing

Before delving into the "top-down" approach to investing, it should be noted that those who actually use portfolio analysis to select portfolios do so in one of two major ways: top-down approach and all-at-once approach.

In the top-down approach, a "top-down" portfolio analysis is performed at the asset class level. Then, the asset class allocation is implemented either passively or actively. If implemented actively, this can be done quantitatively or informally. If done quantitatively, then the asset class index becomes the benchmark for the manager with this mandate. In this approach to portfolio analysis, expected returns for asset classes can be based on macroeconomic models or other considerations. This was demonstrated in Chapter 3 where we discussed Markowitz portfolio selection. In the "all-at-once" approach to portfolio analysis, means, variances, and covariances are supplied at the individual stock level and an efficient frontier is computed at the security level rather than at the asset class level.

With this background, we can now distinguish between two types of top-down active investing. Namely (1) top-down active investing that involves the utilization and forecasts of key variables that impact the macroeconomic outlook (such as consumer confidence, commodity prices, interest rates, inflation, and economic productivity), and (2) top-down active investing by equity management styles such as value or growth. We'll look at the macroeconomic outlook approach to top-down active investing with recognition that active investing (or tilting) by equity styles such as value or growth is to some degree a by-product of the former approach to top-down active investing.

Macroeconomic Approach to Top-Down Investing

With the macroeconomic variables approach to top-down active investing, an equity manager[11] begins by assessing the macroeconomic environment and forecasting its near-term outlook. Based on this assessment and forecast, an equity manager decides on how much of the portfolio's funds to allocate among the different sectors of the equity market and how much to cash equivalents (i.e., short-term money market instruments).

Given the amount of the portfolio's funds to be allocated to the equity market, the manager must then decide how much to allocate among the sectors and industries of the equity market. The sectors of the equity market can be classified as follows: basic materials, communications, consumer staples, financials, technology, utilities, capital goods, consumer cyclical, energy, health care, and transportation.[12] Industry classifications give a finer breakdown and include, for example, aluminum, paper, international oil, beverages, electric utilities, telephone and telegraph, and so forth.

In making the active asset allocation decision, a manager who follows a macroeconomic approach to top-down investing often relies on an analysis of the equity market to identify those sectors and industries that will benefit the most on a relative basis from the anticipated economic forecast. Once the amount to be allocated to each sector and industry is made, the manager then looks for the individual stocks to include in the portfolio. The top-down approach looks at changes in several macroeconomic factors to assess the expected active return on securities and portfolios. As noted before, prominent economic variables include changes in commodity prices, interest rates, inflation, and economic productivity.

Additionally, the macroeconomic outlook approach to top-down investing can be both quantitative and qualitative in nature. From the former perspective, equity managers employ factor models in their top-down attempt at generating abnormal returns (that is, positive alpha).

The power of top-down factor models is that given the macroeconomic risk measures and factor sensitivities, a portfolio's risk exposure profile can be quantified and controlled. In this way, it is possible to see why a portfolio is likely to generate abnormally high or low returns in the marketplace. However, one of the practical limitations of these quantitatively based approaches to equity management is that there can be considerable disagreement about the right number of macro-risk pricing factors.

---

[11]In the discussion that follows, we take an institutional perspective where the active portion of the client's portfolio (pension fund, endowment, etc.) is managed by a professional money manager.

[12]These are the categories used by Standard & Poor's Corporation. There is another sector labeled "miscellaneous" that includes stocks that do not fall into any of the other sectors.

Style Active Approach to Top-Down Investing

Tilting or rotating by equity style—such as value or growth—is another form of top-down active investing. In this context, the enhanced equity style matrix presented earlier in this chapter has several active management implications. For example, if abnormal return opportunities exist in the giant-cap or maxi-cap universe—due perhaps to leftover corporate restructurings and or acquisitions—then investors could tilt their portfolios in the relevant "giant-cap" value or growth direction. Also, if untapped opportunities exist way down in "micro-cap land," then active equity allocations can be tilted toward micro-cap stocks having a value or growth orientation.

From a style-active perspective, it is interesting to note that several studies document the risk-adjusted return superiority of a value style of investing over a growth style. While the empirical evidence seems compelling regarding the performance superiority of a value style of investing, the findings are problematic in several respects. First, the empirical findings contradict the long-established view in finance that investors should be compensated for bearing market or systematic risk. Second, according to one study,[13] there is ample reason to believe that equity styles per se—such as value, growth, and small cap—reflect both macroeconomic and monetary influences. Third, the findings on value versus growth investing imply that active value managers may be penalized over active growth managers for their low-risk investment successes because their equity style benchmarks—due to unexplained empirical regularities—have comparatively high expected returns.[14]

Bottom-Up Approaches to Active Investing

The "bottom-up" approach to active investing makes sense when numerous pricing inefficiencies exist in the capital markets (or components thereof). An investor who follows a bottom-up approach to investing focuses either

---

[13]See, Gerald R. Jensen, Robert R. Johnson, and Jeffrey M. Mercer, "The Inconsistency of Small-Firm and Value Stock Premiums," *Journal of Portfolio Management* 24, no. 2 (1998): 27–36.

[14]One study supports the view that it may be easier for growth managers to outperform their equity-style benchmarks, while value managers have an added measure of return responsibility. See T. Daniel Coggin and Charles Trzcinka, "Analyzing the Performance of Equity Managers: A Note on Value versus Growth," in *The Handbook of Equity Style Management*, pp. 167–170. Coggin, Fabozzi, and Rahman find that institutional equity managers not only outperformed the stock market in general, but that their active performance measures (alpha) for benchmarked-growth portfolios were higher than the corresponding security-selection measures for value-focused managers. See, T. Daniel Coggin, Frank J. Fabozzi, and Shafiqur Rahman, "The Investment Performance of U.S. Equity Pension Fund Managers: An Empirical Investigation," *Journal of Finance* 48, no. 3 (1993): 1039–1055.

on (1) technical aspects of the market or (2) the economic and financial analysis of individual companies, giving relatively less weight to the significance of economic and market cycles.

The investor who pursues a bottom-up strategy based on certain technical aspects of the market is said to be basing stock selection on technical analysis. The primary research tool used for investing based on economic and financial analysis of companies is called *security analysis*. We describe security analysis next and technical analysis later.

The following three types of security analysis can now be distinguished in practice:

- Traditional fundamental analysis
- Quantitative fundamental analysis
- Value-based metric analysis

Traditional Fundamental Analysis

Traditional fundamental analysis often begins with the financial statements of a company in order to investigate its revenue, earnings, and cash flow prospects, as well as its overall corporate debt burden. Growth in revenue, earnings, and cash flow on the income statement side (current and proforma) and the relative magnitude of corporate leverage (namely, debt-to-capital ratio among others) from current and anticipated balance sheets are frequently used by fundamental equity analysts in forming an opinion of the investment merits of a particular company's stock.

In this type of security analysis, the investor also looks at the firm's product lines, the economic outlook for the products (including existing and potential competitors), and the industries in which the company operates. Based on the growth prospects of earnings, the fundamental analyst attempts to determine the fair market value (or the "intrinsic value") of the stock, using, for example, a price-to-earnings or price-to-book value multiplier. The estimated "fair value" of the firm is then compared to the actual market price to see if the stock is correctly priced in the capital market. "Cheap stocks," or potential buy opportunities, have a current market price below the estimated intrinsic value, while "expensive" or overvalued stocks have a market price that exceeds the calculated present worth of the stock. Benjamin Graham and David Dodd developed the classical approach to equity securities analysis.[15] Notable investors who have successfully employed the traditional approach to equity security analysis include Warren Buffett of Berkshire Hathaway, Inc. and Peter Lynch of Fidelity Management & Research Co.

---

[15]See, Benjamin Graham and David Dodd, *Security Analysis, 6th ed.* (1934; reprint, New York: McGraw-Hill, 2008).

Quantitative Fundamental Analysis

Quantitative fundamental analysis seeks to assess the value of securities using a statistical model derived from historical information about security returns. The most commonly used model is the *fundamental multifactor risk model* or simply fundamental factor model. One fundamental factor model is the MSCI BARRA model which is described in Chapter 13. Without getting into the statistical details here, this model is both jointly quantitative and fundamental in nature because it has several systematic *non*market or "common factors" measures that are used in traditional fundamental analysis such as equity size, book-to-price, dividend yield, earnings growth rate, among others, as well as many industry classifications that can be used to identify active rewards on individual securities and portfolios.

Value-Based Metrics Analysis

A rapidly emerging form of security analysis is called the *economic profit* or value-based metrics (VBM) approach to securities analysis. The VBM approach is based on metrics such as EVA® (for Economic Value Added), CFROI® (for Cash Flow Return on Investment), residual income, abnormal earnings, among other names for economic profit measures.[16] While the VBM analysis has been used by corporate managers for many years to measure financial success, Grant and Abate developed the economic profit approach to securities analysis and common stock portfolio management during the mid-1990s to early 2000s.[17] In practice, economic profit measures such as EVA and CFROI fall into the realm of securities analysis

---

[16]There are several value based metrics used in practice including EVA®, CFROI®, residual income, and abnormal earnings. Economic Value Added (EVA®) is a registered trademark of Stern Stewart & Co. For explanation and application of EVA, see G. Bennett Stewart III, *The Quest for Value* (New York: Harper Collins, 1991) and James L. Grant, *Foundations of Economic Value Added* (Hoboken, N.J.: John Wiley & Sons, 2003). For explanation of Cash Flow Return on Investment (CFROI®), see Bartley J. Madden, *CFROI® Valuation: A Total Systems Approach to Valuing the Firm* (Woburn, Mass.: Butterworth-Heinemann, 1999). The analogous VBM concepts of residual income and abnormal earnings are explained respectively in John D. Stowe, Thomas R. Robinson, Jerald E. Pinto, and Dennis W. McLeavey, *Equity Asset Valuation*, CFA Institute Investment Series (Hoboken, N.J.: John Wiley & Sons, 2007) and Paul M. Healy and Krishna G. Palepu, *Business Analysis and Valuation: Using Financial Statements* (Mason, Ohio: Southwestern Thomson, 2007).

[17]The foundation on the value-based metrics approach to securities analysis and common stock portfolio management is developed in James L. Grant, "Foundations of EVA for Investment Managers," *Journal of Portfolio Management* 23, no. 1 (1996): 41–48; and James A. Abate and Grant, *Focus on Value: A Corporate and Investor Guide to Wealth Creation* (Hoboken, N.J.: John Wiley & Sons, 2001).

because they are related to the firm's underlying net present value (NPV).[18] In this way, the VBM approach is different from traditional accounting measures of profit such as net income and operating earnings (EBITDA or EBIT) because this approach looks at the firm's profitability net of the overall dollar-cost of debt and equity capital. In this context, economic profit is a second bottom line which fully reflects the firm's revenue and operating costs, debt financing cost (interest expense), taxes, and, uniquely, the opportunity cost of equity financing (via the required rate of return on equity measured in dollar terms). In the EVA framework, for example, companies with discounted positive EVA—or equivalently, positive NPV—are viewed as "wealth creators," while firms with discounted negative EVA are viewed as wealth wasters due to the negative NPV outcomes.

In the VBM or EVA approach to securities analysis and common stock portfolio management, wealth creators (i.e., good companies) have the fundamental ability to rationalize capital, while wealth wasters (i.e., the bad- or risky-troubled companies) cannot earn their weighted average cost of capital (WACC) on a consistent basis. In terms of stock selection, Grant and Abate develop an EVA style (or quadrants) approach to show that companies with positive EVA momentum (i.e., the wealth-creating growth and positive restructuring companies) are potential buy opportunities, while the stocks of companies with negative EVA momentum (i.e., the wealth-destroying growth and stagnant companies) are possible sell or short-sell candidates, assuming that market implied expectations of economic profit growth are not fully impounded in share price. This VBM approach to securities analysis and common stock portfolio management—with its central focus on the ability of companies to rationalize capital (return on capital higher or lower than WACC) joined with their capital spending growth rates (positive or negative)—is now known as an "EVA style of investing."

Fundamental Law of Active Management

The information ratio is the ratio of alpha to the tracking error. It is a reward (as measured by alpha) to risk (as measured by tracking error) ratio. The higher the information ratio, the better the performance of the manager. Two portfolio managers, Richard Grinold and Ronald Kahn, have developed a framework—which they refer to as the "fundamental law of active

---

[18]Indeed, the NPV of any company is equal to the present value of its expected economic profit. This implies that wealth creators have positive average EVA while wealth destroyers have negative average EVA. Given market inefficiencies, Abate and Grant explain that active investors could reap abnormal profits by buying the stocks of companies having positive economic profit momentum and selling or shorting the stocks of companies with discounted negative economic profit happenings.

management"—for explaining how the information ratio changes as a function of:[19]

1. The *depth* of an active manager's skill
2. The *breadth* or number of independent insights or investment opportunities.

In formal terms, the information ratio can be expressed as

$$IR = IC \times BR^{0.5}$$

IR = the information ratio
IC = the information coefficient
BR = the number of independent insights or opportunities available to the active manager

In the above expression, the information ratio (IR) is the reward-to-risk ratio for an active portfolio manager. (This measure is explained earlier in this chapter.) In turn, the information coefficient (IC) is a measure of the depth of an active manager's skill. On a more formal basis, IC measures the "correlation" between actual returns and those predicted by the portfolio manager. According to the fundamental law of active management, the information ratio also depends on breadth (BR), which reflects the number of creative insights or active investment opportunities available to the investment manager.

There are several interesting implications of the fundamental law of active management. First, we see that the information ratio goes up when manager skill level rises for a given number of independent insights or active opportunities. This fact should be obvious, as a more skillful manager should produce higher risk-adjusted returns, compared with a less skilled manager whose performance is evaluated over the *same* set of investment opportunities (possibly securities). Second, a prolific manager with a large number of independent insights for a given skill level can, in principle, produce a higher information ratio than a manager with the same skill but a limited number of investment opportunities.

Equally important, the fundamental law of active management suggests that a manager with a high skill level but a limited set of opportunities may end up producing the *same* information ratio as a manager having a relatively lower level of skill but more active opportunities. According

---

[19]Richard Grinold and Ronald Kahn, *Active Portfolio Management* (New York: McGraw-Hill, 1999).

to Ronald Kahn,[20] a market timer with an uncanny ability to predict the market may end up earning the same information ratio on the average as a somewhat less skillful stock picker. This might happen because the stock picker has numerous potentially mispriced securities to evaluate, while the otherwise successful market timer may be constrained by the number of realistic market forecasts per year (due, perhaps, to quarterly forecasting or macroeconomic data limitations). Thus, the ability to profitably evaluate an investment opportunity (skill) and the number of independent insights (breadth) is key to successful active management.

With an understanding of the fundamental law of active management, we can now look at the risk of failing to produce a given level of active portfolio return. In this context, Bruce Jacobs and Kenneth Levy suggest that even traditional equity managers face a portfolio management dilemma involving a trade-off between the depth, or "goodness," of their equity management insights and the breadth or scope of their equity management ideas.[21] According to Jacobs and Levy, the breadth of active research conducted by equity managers is constrained in practical terms by the number of investment ideas (or securities) that can be implemented (researched) in a timely and cost efficient manner. This trade-off is shown in Exhibit 9.4.

The exhibit displays the relationship between the depth of equity manager insights (vertical axis) and the breadth of those insights (horizontal axis). The depth of equity manager insights is measured in formal terms by the information coefficient (IC, on the vertical axis), while the breadth (BR) of manager insights can be measured by the potential number of investment ideas or the number of securities in the manager's acceptable universe. When the breadth of equity manager insights is low—as in the case of traditional equity management, according to Jacobs and Levy—then the depth, or "goodness" of each insight needs to be high in order to produce a constant level of active reward-to-active risk (information ratio, IR). Exhibit 9.4 shows that this low breadth/high depth combination produces the same level of active reward that would be associated with a pair-wise high number of investable ideas (or securities) and a relatively low level of equity manager "goodness" or depth per insight.

In a risk management context, one can say that the probability of failure to achieve a given level of active reward is quite high when the breadth of investment ideas or securities to be analyzed is very low. If the market is price efficient, that scenario is likely in the traditional fundamental analysis approach to active equity management discussed earlier. On the other

---

[20]See Ronald N. Kahn, "The Fundamental Law of Active Management," *BARRA Newsletter* (Winter 1997).
[21]Jacobs and Levy, "Investment Management: An Architecture for the Equity Market."

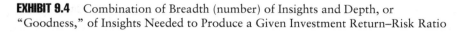

EXHIBIT 9.4 Combination of Breadth (number) of Insights and Depth, or "Goodness," of Insights Needed to Produce a Given Investment Return–Risk Ratio

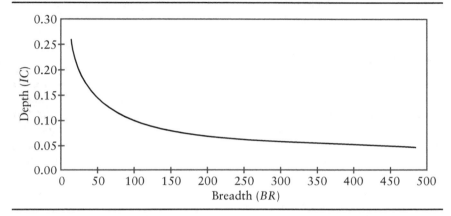

Source: See Bruce I. Jacobs and Kenneth N. Levy, "Investment Management: An Architecture for the Equity Market," Chapter 1 in *Active Equity Portfolio Management*, ed. Frank J. Fabozzi (Hoboken, N.J.: John Wiley & Sons, 1998).

hand, the risk of not achieving a given level of active reward is low when the breadth of implementable manager ideas is high. This can happen in a world where active managers employ an engineered approach to active portfolio management. However, if the capital market is largely price efficient, then the probability of failing to produce any level of active reward is high (near one). With market efficiency, investable ideas are transparent, and their active implications are already fully impounded in security prices.

Strategies Based on Technical Analysis

Given the preceding developments, we would be remiss for not shedding some insight on active strategies based on technical analysis. In this context, various common stock strategies that involve only historical price movement, trading volume, and other technical indicators have been suggested since the beginning of stock trading. Many of these strategies involve investigating patterns based on historical trading data (past price data and trading volume) to forecast the future movement of individual stocks or the market as a whole. Based on observed patterns, mechanical trading rules indicating when a stock should be bought, sold, or sold short are developed. Thus, no consideration is given to any factor other than the specified technical indicators. This approach to active management is called *technical analysis*. Because some of these strategies involve the analysis of charts that plot price and volume movements, investors who follow a technical analysis approach are sometimes called *chartists*. The overlying principle of these strategies is to detect changes in the supply of and demand for a stock and capitalize on the expected changes.

Dow Theory

The grandfather of the technical analysis school is Charles Dow. During his tenure as editor of the *Wall Street Journal*, his editorials theorized about the future direction of the stock market. This body of writing is now referred to as the "Dow Theory." This theory rests on two basic assumptions. First, according to Charles Dow, "The averages in their day-to-day fluctuations discount everything known, everything foreseeable, and every condition which can affect the supply of or the demand for corporate securities." This assumption sounds very much like the efficient market theory. But there's more. The second basic assumption is that the stock market moves in trends—up and down—over periods of time. According to Charles Dow, it is possible to identify these stock price trends and predict their future movement.

According to the Dow Theory, there are three types of trends or market cycles. The "primary trend" is the long-term movement in the market. Primary trends are basically four-year trends in the market. From the primary trend a trend line showing where the market is heading can be derived. The secondary trend represents short-run departures of stock prices from the trend line. The third trend is day-to-day fluctuations in stock prices. Charles Dow believed that upward movements in the stock market were tempered by fallbacks that lost a portion of the previous gain. A market turn occurred when the upward movement was not greater than the last gain. In assessing whether or not a gain did in fact occur, he suggested examining the comovements in different stock market indexes such as the Dow Jones Industrial Average and the Dow Jones Transportation Average. One of the averages is selected as the primary index and the other as the "confirming index." If the primary index reaches a high above its previous high, the increase is expected to continue if it is confirmed by the other index also reaching a high above its previous high.

Simple Filter Rules

The simplest type of technical strategy is to buy and sell on the basis of a predetermined movement in the price of a stock; the rule is basically if the stock increases by a certain percentage, the stock is purchased and held until the price declines by a certain percentage, at which time the stock is sold.

The percentage by which the price must change is called the "filter." Each investor pursuing this technical strategy decides his or her own filter.

Moving Averages

Some technical analysts make decisions to buy or sell a stock based on the movement of a stock over an extended period of time (for example, 200 days). An average of the price over the time period is computed, and a rule is specified that if the price is greater than some percentage of the average, the stock should be purchased; if the price is less than some percentage of the average, the stock should be sold. The simplest way to calculate the average is to calculate a simple moving average. Assuming that the time period selected by the technical analyst is 200 days, then the average price over the 200 days is determined. A more complex moving average can be calculated by giving greater weight to more recent prices.

Advance/Decline Line

On each trading day, some stocks will increase in price or "advance" from the closing price on the previous trading day, while other stocks will decrease in price or decline from the closing price on the previous trading day. It has been suggested by some market observers that the cumulative number of advances over a certain number of days minus the cumulative number of declines over the same number of days can be used as an indicator of short-term movements in the stock market.

Relative Strength

The *relative strength* of a stock is measured by the ratio of the stock price to some price index. The ratio indicates the relative movement of the stock to the index. The price index can be the index of the price of stocks in a given industry or a broad-based index of all stocks. If the ratio rises, it is presumed that the stock is in an uptrend relative to the index; if the ratio falls, it is presumed that the stock is in a downtrend relative to the index. Similarly, a relative strength measure can be calculated for an industry group relative to a broad-based index. Relative strength is also referred to as *price momentum* or *price persistence*.

Short Interest Ratio

Some technical analysts believe that the ratio of the number of shares sold short relative to the average daily trading volume is a technical signal that is valuable in forecasting the market. This ratio is called the *short interest ratio.* However, the economic link between this ratio and stock price movements can be interpreted in two ways. On one hand, some market observers believe that if this ratio is high, this is a signal that the market will advance. The argument is that short sellers will have to eventually cover their short position by buying the stocks they have shorted and, as a result, market prices will increase. On the other hand, there are some market observers who believe this a bearish signal being sent by market participants who have shorted stocks in anticipation of a declining market.

Market Overreaction

To benefit from favorable news or to reduce the adverse effect of unfavorable news, investors must react quickly to new information.[22] According to cognitive psychologists, people tend to overreact to extreme events. People tend to react more strongly to recent information and they tend to heavily discount older information.

The question is, do investors follow the same pattern? That is, do investors overreact to extreme events? The *overreaction hypothesis* suggests that when investors react to unanticipated news that will benefit a company's stock, the price rise will be greater than it should be given that information, resulting in a subsequent decline in the price of the stock. In contrast, the overreaction to unanticipated news that is expected to adversely affect the economic well-being of a company will force the price down too much, followed by a subsequent correction that will increase the price.

If, in fact, the market does overreact, investors may be able to exploit this to realize positive abnormal returns if they can (1) identify an extreme event, and (2) determine when the effect of the overreaction has been impounded in the market price and is ready to reverse. Investors who are capable of doing this will pursue the following strategies. When positive news is identified, investors will buy the stock and sell it before the correction to the overreaction. In the case of negative news, investors will short the stock and then buy it back to cover the short position before the correction to the overreaction.

Nonlinear Dynamic Models: Chaos Theory

Some market observers—like Edgar Peters[23]—believe that the pattern of stock price behavior is so complex that linear (simple, or otherwise) mathematical

---

[22]Werner DeBondt and Richard Thaler, "Does the Market Overreact?" *Journal of Finance* 40 (1985): 793–805.
[23]See Edgar E. Peters, *Chaos and Order in the Capital Markets: A New View of Cycles, Prices, and Market Volatility* (New York: John Wiley & Sons, 1991).

models are insufficient for detecting historical price patterns and developing models for forecasting future return volatility. While stock prices may appear to change randomly, there could be an undiscovered *nonlinear* pattern that is missed when using simple mathematical tools. Scientists have developed complex mathematical models for detecting patterns from observations of some phenomenon that appear to be random. Generically, these models are called *nonlinear dynamic models* because the mathematics used to detect any structure or pattern is based on a system of nonlinear equations.

Nonlinear dynamic models have been suggested for analyzing stock price patterns. In recent years, there have been several studies that suggest that stock prices exhibit the characteristics of a nonlinear dynamic model.[24] The particular form of nonlinear dynamic models that has been suggested is chaos theory. At this stage, the major insight provided by *chaos theory* is that stock price movements that appear to be random may in fact have a structure that can be used to generate abnormal returns. However, some market observers caution that the actual application of nonlinear return models falls short of the mark.

Strategies Based on Fundamental Analysis

As explained earlier, fundamental analysis involves an economic analysis of a firm with respect to earnings growth prospects, ability to meet debt obligations, competitive environment, and the like.

Proponents of semistrong market efficiency argue that strategies based on fundamental analysis will not produce abnormal returns in the long run. Semistrong-form efficiency means that the price of the security fully reflects all public information (which, of course, includes but is not limited to, historical price and trading patterns).[25] The reason is simply that there are many independent analysts undertaking basically the same sort of analysis, with the same publicly available data, so that the price of the stock reflects all the relevant factors that determine value.

A fundamental tenet of finance theory is that there is a relationship between risk and return. Risk itself cannot be eliminated. If there were no risk, finance theory would be reduced to accounting. Abnormal returns always have to be compared to the inherent risk. One cannot simply say that a given level of return is abnormal unless the relative amount of risk is given.

---

[24]See José Scheinkman and Blake LeBaron, "Nonlinear Dynamics and Stock Returns," *Journal of Business* 62 (1989): 311–337; and Peters, *Chaos and Order in the Capital Markets.*

[25]Eugene F. Fama, "Efficient Capital Markets: A Review of Theory and Empirical Work," *Journal of Finance* 24, no. 2 (1970): 383–417.

Stated differently, even in an efficient market we can still make forecasts, but we have to consider the risk associated with our forecasts.

Earnings Surprises

Studies have found that it is not merely the absolute change in earnings that is important. The reason is that analysts have a consensus forecast of a company's expected earnings. What might be expected to generate abnormal returns is the extent to which the market's forecast of future earnings differs from actual earnings that are subsequently announced. The divergence between the actual earnings announced and the forecasted earnings by the consensus of analysts is called an *earnings surprise*. When the actual earnings exceed the market's forecast, then this is a positive earnings surprise; a negative earnings surprise arises when the actual earnings are less than the market's forecast.

There have been numerous studies of earnings surprises. These studies seem to suggest that identifying stocks that may have positive earnings surprises and purchasing them may generate abnormal returns. Of course, the difficulty is identifying such stocks.

Low Price-Earnings Ratio

The legendary Benjamin Graham proposed a classic investment model in 1949 for the "defensive investor"—one without the time, expertise, or temperament for aggressive investment. The model was updated in each subsequent edition of his book, *The Intelligent Investor*, first published in 1949. Some of the basic investment criteria outlined in the 1973 edition are representative of the approach:

1. A company must have paid a dividend in each of the past 20 years.
2. Minimum size of a company is $100 million in annual sales for an industrial company and $50 million for a public utility.
3. Positive earnings must have been achieved in each of the past 10 years.
4. Current price should not be more than 1.5 times the latest book value.
5. Market price should not exceed 15 times the average earnings for the past three years.

Graham considered the P/E ratio as a measure of the price paid for value received. He viewed high P/Es with skepticism and as representing a large premium for difficult-to-forecast future earnings growth. Hence, lower-P/E companies were viewed favorably as having less potential for earnings disappointments and the resulting downward revision in price.

While originally intended for the defensive investor, numerous variations of Graham's low-P/E approach are currently followed by a number of professional investment advisors.

Market-Neutral Long-Short Stratregy

An active strategy that seeks to capitalize on the ability of an investor to select stocks is a market-neutral long-short strategy. The basic idea of this strategy is as follows. First, a quantitative model is used to analyze the expected return of individual stocks within a universe of stocks. Based on this analysis, the stocks analyzed are classified as either "high-expected return stocks" or "low-expected return stocks." Based on this classification of each stock, one of the following strategies is pursued: (1) purchase only high-expected return stocks, (2) short low-expected return stocks, or (3) simultaneously purchase high-expected return stocks and short low-expected return stocks.[26]

The problem with the first two strategies is that general movements in the market can have an adverse affect. For example, suppose an investor selects high-expected return stocks and the market declines. Because of the positive correlation between the return on all stocks and the market, the drop in the market will produce a negative return even though the investor may have indeed been able to identify high-expected return stocks. Similarly, if an investor shorts low-expected return stocks and the market rallies, the portfolio will realize a negative return. This is because a rise in the market means that the investor must likely cover the short position of each stock at a higher price than which a stock was sold.

Let's look at the third alternative—simultaneously purchasing stocks with high-expected returns and shorting those stocks with low-expected returns. Consider what happens to the long and the short positions when the market in general moves. A drop in the market will hurt the long position but benefit the short position. A market rally will hurt the short position but benefit the long position. Consequently, the long and short positions provide a hedge against each other.

While the long-short position provides a hedge against general market movements, the degree to which one position moves relative to the other is not controlled by simply going long the high-expected return stocks and going short the low-expected return stocks. That is, the two positions do not neutralize the risk against general market movements. However, the long and short positions can be created with a market exposure that neutralizes any market movement. Specifically, long and short positions can be constructed

---

[26]Bruce L. Jacobs and Kenneth N. Levy, "The Long and Short on Long-Short," *Journal of Investing* 6, no. 1 (1997): 78–88.

to have the same beta and, as a result, the beta of the collective long-short position is zero. For this reason, this strategy is called a *market-neutral long-short strategy*. If, indeed, an investor is capable of identifying high- and low-expected return stocks, then neutralizing the portfolio against market movements will produce a positive return whether the market rises or falls.

Market Anomaly Strategies

While there are investors who are skeptical about technical analysis and others who are skeptical about fundamental analysis, some investors believe that there are pockets of pricing inefficiency in the stock market. That is, there are some investment strategies that have historically produced statistically significant positive abnormal returns. Some examples of these anomalies are the small-firm effect, the low-price-earnings ratio effect, the neglected-firm effect, and various calendar effects. There are also strategies based on following the trading transactions of the insiders of a company.

Some of these anomalies are a challenge to the semistrong form of market efficiency. This includes the small-firm effect and the low price-earnings effect. The calendar effects are a challenge to the weak form of pricing efficiency. Following insider activities with regard to buying and selling the stock of their company is a challenge to both the weak and strong forms of pricing efficiency. (Recall that weak-form efficiency means that the price of the security reflects the past price and trading history of the security; strong-form efficiency exists in a market where the price of a security reflects all information, whether it is publicly available or known only to insiders such as the firm's managers or directors.) The challenge to the weak form is that, as will be explained shortly, information on *insider activity* is publicly available and, in fact, has been suggested as a technical indicator. Thus, the question is whether "outsiders" can use information about trading activity by insiders to generate abnormal returns. The challenge to the strong form of pricing efficiency is that insiders are viewed as having special (insider) information and therefore based on this information they may be able to generate abnormal returns from their special relationship with the firm.

Small-Firm Effect The *small-firm effect* emerges from several studies that have shown that portfolios of small firms (in terms of total market capitalization) have outperformed large firms. Because of these findings, there has been increased interest in stock market indicators that monitor small-capitalization firms.

Low P/E Effect   Earlier we discussed Benjamin Graham's strategy for defensive investors based on low P/Es. The *low P/E effect* is supported by several studies showing that portfolios consisting of stocks with a low P/E have outperformed portfolios consisting of stocks with a high P/E. However, other studies found that after adjusting for the transaction costs necessary to rebalance a portfolio, as prices and earnings change over time, the superior performance of portfolios of low P/E stocks no longer holds. An explanation for the presumably superior performance is that stocks trade at low P/Es because they are temporarily out of favor with market participants. As fads change, companies not currently in vogue will rebound at some time in the future.

Neglected-Firm Effect   Not all firms receive the same degree of attention from security analysts. One school of thought is that firms that are essentially neglected by security analysts will outperform firms that are the subject of considerable attention. This market anomaly is referred to as the *neglected-firm effect*.

Calendar Effects   While some empirical work focuses on selected firms according to some criterion such as market capitalization, P/E, or degree of analysts' attention, the calendar effect looks at the best time to implement strategies. Examples of *calendar anomalies*, as these strategies are referred to, are the January effect, month-of-the-year effect, day-of-the-week effect, intra-day effect, and holiday effect. It seems from the empirical evidence that there are times when the implementation of a strategy will, on average, provide a superior performance relative to other calendar time periods.

Following Insider Activity   While the U.S. Securities and Exchange Commission (SEC) has a more comprehensive definition of an insider, we can think of insiders of a corporation as the corporate officers, directors, and holders of large amounts of a company's common stock. The SEC requires that all trading activity by insiders be reported within a specified number of days of the month following the trade. The SEC then releases this information in a report called the *SEC Insider Transaction Report*. Thus, after a time lag, the information is made publicly available. Studies have found that insiders have been able to generate abnormal returns using their privileged position. However, when outsiders use this information, one study found that after controlling for the other anomalies discussed above and transaction costs, outsiders cannot benefit from this information. In other words, insider activity information published by the SEC is not a useful technical indicator for generating abnormal returns.

One of the difficulties with assessing all of the strategies described here is that the factors that are believed to generate market anomalies are interrelated. For example, small firms may be those that are not given much attention by security analysts and that therefore trade at a low P/E. Even a study of insider activity must carefully separate abnormal returns that may be the result of a market anomaly having nothing to do with insider activity. For example, one study that found no abnormal returns from following insiders also found that if there are any abnormal returns they are due to the size and low P/E effects. There have been many attempts to disentangle these effects.

Momentum and Reversal Strategies

Families of strategies that have gained popularity are *momentum strategies* and *reversal strategies*. Momentum and reversal strategies are based on the empirical fact that large ensembles of stock prices exhibit a pattern of persistence and reversals of returns. Persistence of returns means that those stocks that had the highest returns in a given period will likely continue to exhibit high returns in the future. Conversely, those stocks that had the lowest returns in a given period will likely continue to exhibit low returns in the future.

Reversals mean that those stocks that had the highest returns in given time windows will exhibit low returns in the future, while those stocks that had the lowest returns in given time windows will exhibit high returns in the future.

The important, and somewhat surprising, fact is that there seems to be stable patterns of both momentum and reversals in the stock market. Indeed, stock prices exhibit reversals over short time windows, from a few days to one month, momentum in medium time periods from 6 to 12 months, and reversals over long periods, from two to five years. It has been empirically found that these patterns have remained stable for several decades in the United States and Europe. Some studies, however, seem to conclude that as of the early 2000s, it has become more difficult in some markets to profit from patterns of momentum and reversals.

PERFORMANCE EVALUATION

Performance evaluation is concerned with three questions: (1) determining whether the portfolio manager added value by outperforming the established benchmark; (2) identifying how the portfolio manager achieved the calculated return; and, (3) assessing whether the portfolio manager achieved superior performance (i.e., added value) by skill or by luck. As explained in

Chapter 1, single-index performance measures such as the Sharpe ratio does not help us address these three questions. Performance attribution models, which decompose the portfolio return so that a client can determine how the portfolio manager earned the return, are commonly used for this reason.

In broad terms, the return performance of a portfolio can be explained by three actions followed by a portfolio manager. The first is actively managing a portfolio to capitalize on factors that are expected to perform better than other factors. The second is actively managing a portfolio to take advantage of anticipated movements in the market. For example, the manager of a common stock portfolio can increase the portfolio's beta when the market is expected to increase, and decrease it when the market is expected to decline. The third is actively managing the portfolio by buying securities that are believed to be undervalued, and selling (or shorting) securities that are believed to be overvalued.

The methodology for answering these questions is called *performance attribution analysis*. There are commercially available models that can be used to do this analysis. We do not describe these models here. These models employ the factor model approach described in Chapter 13. Instead, we provide an illustration of how these models are used.

Rennie and Cowhey[27] report the performance of three external money managers for Bell Atlantic (now Verizon Communications).[28] Exhibit 9.5 shows the results for the three money managers since they began managing funds for Bell Atlantic. The values shown in parentheses in the exhibit are statistical measures that indicate the probability that the estimated value is statistically different from zero. The value in parentheses is referred to as a confidence level. The higher the confidence level, the more likely the estimated value is different from zero and, therefore, performance can be attributed to skill rather than luck.

The active management return represents the difference between the actual portfolio return and the benchmark return. Manager A's active management return is 420 basis points and, therefore, seems to have outperformed the benchmark. But was this by investment skill or luck? The confidence level of 99% suggests that it was through investment skill. The lower panel of the table shows how this was achieved. Of the four components of return, two are statistically significant—sector emphasis and security selection. The other two components—market timing and industry exposure—are not statistically significant. This means that either manager A's

---

[27]Edward P. Rennie and Thomas J. Cowhey, "The Successful Use of Benchmark Portfolios," in *Improving Portfolio Performance with Quantitative Models*, ed. Darwin M. Bayston and H. Russell Fogler (Charlottesville, Va.: Institute of Chartered Financial Analysts, 1989): 32–44.

[28]Bell Atlantic merged with GTE to form Verizon Communications, Inc.

EXHIBIT 9.5 Performance Attribution Analysis for Three Money Managers

	Manager A		Manager B		Manager C	
Actual return	19.1%		17.0%		12.6%	
Benchmark portfolio	14.9		15.2		12.6	
Active management return	4.2%	(99)	1.8%	(53)	0.0%	(3)
Components of return:						
Market timing	−0.2%	(40)	−0.6%	(64)	−0.5%	(73)
Industry exposure	0.2	(20)	−2.0	(89)	0.3	(34)
Sector emphasis	2.2	(99)	3.9	(99)	0.3	(51)
Security selection	1.9	(84)	0.6	(43)	0.1	(7)
Unreconciled return[a]	0.1		−0.1		−0.2	

Note: Numbers set in parentheses denote confidence level.
[a]Difference between actual management return and sum of components of return.

Source: Adapted from Edward P. Rennie and Thomas J. Cowhey, "The Successful Use of Benchmark Portfolios," in *Improving Portfolio Performance with Quantitative Models*, ed. Darwin M. Bayston and H. Russell Fogler (Charlottesville, Va.: Institute of Chartered Financial Analysts, 1989), 37.

skills in these two areas did not significantly impact the portfolio's return, or the manager did not emphasize these skills. In fact, this manager's stated investment style is to add value through sector emphasis and security selection and neutralize market timing and industry exposure. The results of the performance attribution analysis are consistent with this investment style.

An analysis of the results of manager B indicates that the manager outperformed the benchmark by 180 basis points. The confidence level, however, is 53%. In most statistical tests, this confidence level would suggest that the 180 basis points is not statistically different from zero. That is, the 180-basis-point active management return can be attributed to luck rather than skill. However, Rennie and Cowhey state that this is an acceptable level of confidence for Bell Atlantic, but that it does provide a warning to the company to carefully monitor this manager's performance for improvement or deterioration. The stated investment style of this manager is to identify undervalued securities. The component return of 60 basis points from security selection with a confidence level of only 43% suggests that this manager is not adding value in this way. This is another warning sign that this manager must be more carefully monitored.

Manager C has to be carefully monitored because this manager did not outperform the benchmark, and none of the component returns are statistically significant. This manager is a candidate for termination. What is the minimum active management return that Bell Atlantic expects from its active equity managers? According to Rennie and Cowhey, it is 1% per year over a 2.5-year investment horizon with a confidence level of at least 70%. Moreover, the component analysis should corroborate what the manager states is the manager's investment style.

KEY POINTS

- The decision as to whether to pursue an active or passive strategy depends on the view of the price efficiency of the market. A price efficient market is one where security prices at all times fully reflect all available information that is relevant to their valuation. The distinction between the three forms of pricing efficiency—weak form, semi-strong form, and strong form—rests in the relevant information that is believed to be embodied in the price of the security at all times.
- Active strategies are those that seek to outperform the market based on the belief that there are abnormal returns due to the existence of some pricing inefficiencies. Investors who believe that the market prices stocks efficiently and that active management will not generate abnormal returns will pursue a passive strategy, the most popular passive strategy being indexing.
- Tracking error measures the dispersion of a portfolio's returns relative to the benchmark's returns. That is, tracking error is the standard deviation of the portfolio's active return where active return is the difference between the portfolio return and the benchmark return. Backward-tracking error is calculated from historical active returns; forward-tracking error is computed using the portfolio's current holdings based on a statistical model developed using historical tracking error.
- The information ratio is a reward-to-risk ratio where the numerator is the average active return (alpha) and denominator is the backward-looking tracking error. The higher the information ratio, the better the manager performed relative to the risk assumed.
- Managers can be classified based on investment style. A manager's style depends on the characteristics of the stocks purchased. Stocks can be classified by style in many ways. The most common is in terms of one or more measures of growth and value. Moreover, within a growth and value style there is often a substyle based on size (i.e., market capitalization).
- In constructing an indexed portfolio, a manager can purchase all the stocks in the index or only purchase the largest market capitalization stocks (capitalization approach). Two alternative methodologies for

constructing an indexed portfolio where less than all the stocks are purchased are the cellular method and the multifactor risk model method.

- Active strategies can be classified as following either a top-down approach or a bottom-up approach. In a bottom-up approach to active management, there are three types of security analysis styles that are employed in practice: traditional fundamental analysis, quantitative fundamental analysis, and value-based metric analysis.
- The fundamental law of active management is used to explain how the information ratio changes as a function of time. According to the fundamental law, the information ratio depends on the manager's skill (as measured by the information coefficient) and the breadth or number of independent insights or investment opportunities available to the manager.
- Technical analysis involves investigating patterns based on historical trading data (past price data and trading volume) to forecast the future movement of individual stocks or the market as a whole. Based on observed patterns, mechanical trading rules indicating when a stock should be bought, sold, or sold short are developed without any consideration given to any factor other than the specified technical indicators.
- Fundamental analysis involves an economic analysis of a firm with respect to earnings growth prospects, ability to meet debt obligations, competitive environment, and the like.
- Performance evaluation is concerned with three questions: (1) determining whether the portfolio manager added value by outperforming the benchmark; (2) identifying how the portfolio manager achieved the calculated return; and (3) assessing whether the portfolio manager achieved superior performance by skill or by luck. Performance attribution models can answer these three questions by decomposing the portfolio return into the factors that affect performance and then assess the statistical significance of the decisions made by the manager.

QUESTIONS

1. In constructing an equity portfolio, which type of tracking error—backward-looking or forward-looking should be used?

2. Calculate the annualized alpha, tracking error, and information ratio based on the 12 monthly returns that follows:

Month	Active Return %
1	0.37
2	−0.31
3	−0.55
4	0.09
5	0.37
6	−0.05
7	−0.62
8	0.06
9	0.46
10	−0.09
11	0.58
12	0.84

3. Assuming active returns are normally distributed, calculate the expected returns about the benchmark at the 67%, 95%, and 99% confidence levels assuming the following data:

Expected active return %	0.02
Tracking error %	0.03
Benchmark expected return %	0.08

4. Explain the philosophy of a:
   a. contrarian manager
   b. yield manager

5. Determine the size and style orientation of the following equity mutual fund:

	$ Market Cap (MC)		Portfolio	
	(in billions)	MC$^{(1/n)}$	Cap Weight	PB Ratio
Stock A	18	2.620488909	0.2000	0.8
Stock B	30	3.106880249	0.3333	1.0
Stock C	42	3.475593597	0.4667	1.4

6. Construct a graph showing combinations of breadth and depth to produce constant information ratio (IR) with an alpha of 3% and a tracking error of 4%.

7. Use portfolio attribution analysis to assess the active strategies of two managers with the same alpha:

	Manager X	Manager Y
Active management return (alpha) %	3.5	3.5
Components of active return:		
Market timing	−0.2	−0.1
Sector emphasis	0.5	2
Industry exposure	1.5	1.4
Security selection	2	0.5
Unreconciled return	−0.3	−0.3

CHAPTER 10

Approaches to Common Stock Valuation

Pamela P. Drake, Ph.D., CFA
J. Gray Ferguson Professor Finance
College of Business
James Madison University

Frank J. Fabozzi, Ph.D., CFA, CPA
Professor in the Practice of Finance
Yale School of Management

Glen A. Larsen Jr., Ph.D., CFA
Professor of Finance
Indiana University Kelley School of Business–Indianapolis

In this chapter, we discuss practical methods of valuing common stock using two methods: discounted cash flow models and relative valuation models. Both methods require strong assumptions and expectations about the future. No one single valuation model or method is perfect. All valuation estimates are subject to model error and estimation error. Nevertheless, common stock analysts use these models to help form their expectations about a fair market price. In later chapters, other valuation models and approaches are discussed.

DISCOUNTED CASH FLOW MODELS

If an investor buys a common stock, he or she has bought shares that represent an ownership interest in the corporation. Shares of common stock are a perpetual security—that is, there is no maturity. The investor who owns shares of common stock has the right to receive a certain portion of any cash dividends—but dividends are not a sure thing. Whether or not a corporation pays dividends is up to its board of directors—the representatives of the common shareholders. Typically, we see some pattern in the dividends companies pay: Dividends are either constant or grow at a constant rate.

But there is no guarantee that dividends will be paid in the future. It is reasonable to figure that what an investor pays for a share of stock should reflect what he or she expects to receive from it—a return on the investor's investment. What an investor receives are cash dividends in the future. How can we relate that return to what a share of common stock is worth? Well, the value of a share of stock should be equal to the present value of all the future cash flows an investor expects to receive from that share.

To value stock, therefore, common stock analysts must project future cash flows, which, in turn, means projecting future dividends. This approach to the valuation of common stock is referred to the *discounted cash flow approach*. There are various discounted cash flow (DCF) models that we can use to value common stock. We do not describe all of the models. Rather our primary focus is on models that are referred to as dividend discount models.

Dividend Discount Models

Most *dividend discount models* (DDM) use current dividends, some measure of historical or projected dividend growth, and an estimate of the required rate of return. Popular models include the basic dividend discount model, which assumes a constant dividend growth, and the multiple-phase models. Here we discuss these dividend discount models and their limitations, beginning with a review of the various ways to measure dividends. Then we look at how dividends and stock prices are related.

Dividend Measures

Dividends are measured using three different metrics: dividends per share, dividend yield, and dividend payout ratio. The value of a share of stock today is the market's assessment of today's worth of future cash flows for each share. Because future cash flows to shareholders are dividends, we need a measure of dividends for each share of stock to estimate future cash flows per share.

The *dividends per share* is the dollar amount of dividends paid out during the period per share of common stock:

$$\text{Dividends per share} = \frac{\text{Dividends paid to common shareholders}}{\text{Number of shares of common stock outstanding}}$$

Another measure of dividends is the *dividend yield*, which is the ratio of dividends to the common stock's current price:

$$\text{Dividend yield} = \frac{\text{Annual cash dividend per common share}}{\text{Market price per common share}}$$

The dividend yield is also called the *dividend-price ratio*.[1]

Still another way of describing dividends paid out during a period is to state the dividends as a portion of earnings for the period. This is the *dividend payout ratio*:

$$\text{Dividend payout ratio} = \frac{\text{Dividends paid to common shareholders}}{\text{Earnings available to common shareholders}}$$

The complement to the dividend payout ratio is the *plowback ratio*, which is the percentage of earnings retained by the company during the period.

The proportion of earnings paid out in dividends varies by company and industry. If the board of directors of companies focuses on maintaining a constant dividends per share or a constant growth in dividends per share in establishing their dividend policy, the dividend payout ratio will fluctuate along with earnings. Typically corporate boards set the dividend policy such that dividends per share grow at a relatively constant rate, resulting in dividend payouts that fluctuate from year to year.

Basic Dividend Discount Models

As discussed, the basis for the dividend discount model is simply the application of present value analysis, which asserts that the fair price of an asset is the present value of the expected cash flows.[2] The cash flows are the expected dividends per share.

We can express the basic DDM mathematically as

$$P_0 = \frac{D_1}{(1+r_1)^1} + \frac{D_2}{(1+r_2)^2} + \frac{D_3}{(1+r_3)^3} + \cdots$$

or

---

[1]Historically, the dividend yield for U.S. stocks has been a little less than 5% according to a study by John Y. Campbell and Robert J. Shiller, "Valuation Ratios and the Long-Run Stock Market Outlook," *Journal of Portfolio Management* 24 (1998): 11–26.

[2]This model was first suggested by John Burr Williams, *The Theory of Investment Value* (Boston, Mass.: Harvard University Press, 1938).

$$P_0 = \sum_{t=1}^{\infty} \frac{D_t}{(1+r_t)^t} \qquad (10.1)$$

where

P_0 = the current price of the stock
D_t = the dividend per share in period t
r_t = the discount rate appropriate for the cash flow in period t

In this model, the company is expected to pay dividends in the future. If the company is never expected to pay a dividend, this model implies that the stock would have no value. To reconcile the fact that stocks not paying a current dividend do, in fact, have a positive market value with this model, analysts assume that the company will pay cash someday, at some time N, even if only a liquidating dividend.

The Finite-Life General Dividend Discount Model

We can modify the DDM given by equation (10.1) by assuming a finite life for the expected cash flows. In this case, the expected cash flows are the expected dividends per share and the expected sale price of the stock at some future date. We refer to this expected price in the future as the terminal price, and it captures the future value of all subsequent dividends. This model is the *finite-life general DDM* and which we can express mathematically as

$$P_0 = \frac{D_1}{(1+r_1)^1} + \frac{D_2}{(1+r_2)^2} + \cdots + \frac{P_N}{(1+r_N)^N}$$

or

$$P_0 = \left[\sum_{t=1}^{N} \frac{D_t}{(1+r_t)^t} \right] + \frac{P_N}{(1+r_N)^N}$$

where P_N is the expected value of the stock at the end of period N.

Assuming a Constant Discount Rate   A special case of the finite-life general DDM that is more commonly used in practice assumes that the discount rate is constant. That is, we assume each r_t is the same for all t. Denoting this constant discount rate by r, the value of a share of stock today becomes

$$P_0 = \frac{D_1}{(1+r)^1} + \frac{D_2}{(1+r)^2} + \cdots + \frac{P_N}{(1+r)^N}$$

or

$$P_0 = \left[\sum_{t=1}^{N} \frac{D_t}{(1+r)^t} \right] + \frac{P_N}{(1+r)^N} \tag{10.2}$$

Equation (10.2) is the constant discount rate version of the finite-life general DDM, and is the more general form of the model.

Required Inputs   The finite-life general DDM requires three sets of forecasts as inputs to calculate the fair value of a stock:

- Expected terminal price, P_N.
- Dividends up to the assumed horizon, D_1 to D_N.
- Discount rates, r_1 to r_N, or r in the case of the constant discount rate version.

Thus, the relevant issue is how accurately these inputs can be forecasted.

The terminal price is the most difficult of the three forecasts. According to theory, P_N is the present value of all future dividends after N; that is, $D_{N+1}, D_{N+2}, \ldots, D_\infty$. Also, we must estimate the discount rate, r. In practice, analysts make forecasts of either dividends (D_N) or earnings (E_N) first, and then the price P_N based on an "appropriate" requirement for yield, price-earnings ratio, or capitalization rate. Note that the present value of the expected terminal price $P_N \div (1 + r)^N$ becomes very small if N is very large.

The forecasting of dividends is somewhat easier. Usually, information on past dividends is readily available and we can estimate cash flows for a given scenario. The discount rate, r, is the required rate of return, and forecasting this rate is more complex. In practice for a given company, analysts assume that r is constant for all periods, and typically estimate this rate from the capital asset pricing model (CAPM). The CAPM can be used to estimate the expected return for a company based on the expected risk-free rate, the expected market risk premium, and the stock's systematic risk, its beta.[3]

Assessing Relative Value   Once analysts have an estimate of a stock's value from using the DDM, they then compare their estimate of the stock's value with the observed price of the stock, if this price is readily available. If the market price is below the fair price derived from the model, the stock is undervalued or cheap. The opposite holds for a stock whose market price is greater than the model-derived price. In this case, the stock is said to be overvalued or expensive. A stock trading equal to or close to its fair price is fairly valued.

---

[3]Using the CAPM, the expected return is the sum of the risk-free rate of interest and a premium for bearing risk. The premium for bearing risk of a specific asset is the product of the asset's beta and the market's risk premium.

The use of the DDM tells the analyst the relative value but does not indicate when the price of the stock should be expected to move to its fair price. That is, the model says that based on the inputs generated by the analyst, the stock may be cheap, expensive, or fair. However, it does not tell the analyst, if the stock is mispriced, how long it will take before the market recognizes the mispricing and corrects it. As a result, an investor may hold onto a stock perceived to be cheap for an extended period of time and may underperform during that period.

While a stock may be mispriced, an analyst must also consider how mispriced it is in order to take the appropriate action (that is, buy a cheap stock and expect to sell it when the price rises, or sell short an expensive stock expecting its price to decline). This will depend on (1) how much the stock is trading from its fair value, and (2) transactions costs. An analyst should also consider that a stock may look as if it is mispriced (based on the estimates and the model), but this may be the result of estimates that may introduce error in the valuation.

Constant Growth Dividend Discount Model If we assume that future dividends grow at a constant rate, g, and we use a single discount rate, r, the finite-life general DDM assuming a constant growth rate given by equation (10.2) becomes

$$P_0 = \frac{D_0(1+g)^1}{(1+r)^1} + \frac{D_0(1+g)^2}{(1+r)^2} + \cdots + \frac{D_0(1+g)^N}{(1+r)^N} + \frac{P_N}{(1+r)^N}$$

It can be shown that if N is assumed to approach infinity, this equation is equal to

$$P_0 = \frac{D_0(1+g)}{r-g} \tag{10.3}$$

Equation (10.3) is the *constant growth dividend discount model*.[4] Therefore, the greater the expected growth rate of dividends, the greater the estimated value of a share of stock.

In estimating g, if the analyst believes that dividends will grow in the future at a similar rate as they grew in the past, the dividend growth rate can be estimated by using the compounded rate of growth of historical dividends. The compound growth rate, g, is found using the following formula:[5]

---

[4]Myron Gordon and Eli Shapiro, "Capital Equipment Analysis: The Required Rate of Profit," *Management Science* 3 (1956): 102–110.
[5]This formula is equivalent to calculating the geometric mean of 1 plus the percentage change over the number of years.

$$g = \left(\sqrt[\text{Number of years}]{\frac{\text{Last year's dividend}}{\text{First year's dividend}}} \right) - 1 \qquad (10.4)$$

What if an analyst estimates a stock's value, and the estimated value is considerably off the mark when compared to the stock's actual price? The reasons for this discrepancy may include:

- The market's expectations of the company's dividend growth pattern may not be for constant growth.
- The growth rate of dividends in the past may not be representative of what investors expect in the future.

Another problem that arises in using the constant growth rate model is that the estimated growth rate of dividends may exceed the discount rate, r. Therefore, there are some cases in which it is inappropriate to use the constant rate DDM.

Multiphase Dividend Discount Models The assumption of constant growth may be unrealistic and can even be misleading. Instead, most practitioners modify the constant growth DDM by assuming that companies will go through different growth phases, but within a given phase, it is assumed that dividends grow at a constant rate.[6]

The most popular multiphase model employed by practitioners appears to be the *three-stage DDM*. This model assumes that all companies go through three phases, analogous to the concept of the product life cycle. In the growth phase, a company experiences rapid earnings growth as it produces new products and expands market share. In the transition phase, the company's earnings begin to mature and decelerate to the rate of growth of the economy as a whole. At this point, the company is in the maturity phase in which earnings continue to grow at the rate of the general economy.

A three-phase model can be designed to fit different growth patterns. For example, an emerging growth company would have a longer growth phase than a more mature company. Some companies are considered to have higher initial growth rates and hence longer growth and transition phases. Other companies may be considered to have lower current growth rates and hence shorter growth and transition phases.

---

[6]For a pioneering work that modified the DDM to accommodate different growth rates, see Nicholas Molodovsky, CatherineMay, and Sherman Chattiner, "Common-Stock Valuation—Principles, Tables, and Applications," *Financial Analysts Journal* 21 (1965): 104–123.

Expected Returns and Dividend Discount Models

Thus far we have seen how to calculate the fair price of a stock given the estimates of dividends, discount rates, terminal prices, and growth rates.[7] An analyst then compares the model-derived price to the actual price and the appropriate action is taken.

We can recast the model in terms of expected return. This is found by calculating the interest rate that will make the present value of the expected cash flows equal to the market price. Mathematically, we can express this as

$$r = \frac{D_0(1+g)}{P_0} + g = \frac{D_1}{P_0} + g \qquad (10.5)$$

In other words, the expected return is the discount rate that equates the present value of the expected future cash flows with the present value of the stock. The higher the expected return—for a given set of future cash flows—the lower the current value.

This rearrangement of the dividend discount model provides a perspective on the expected return: the expected return is the sum of the dividend yield (that is, D_1/P_0) and the expected rate of growth of dividends. The latter represents the appreciation (or depreciation, if negative) anticipated for the stock. Therefore, this is the expected capital gain or loss (or, simply, capital yield) on the stock.

Given the expected return and the required return (that is, the value for r), any mispricing can be identified. If the expected return exceeds the required return, then the stock is undervalued; if it is less than the required return then the stock is overvalued. A stock is fairly valued if the expected return is equal to the required return.

With the same set of inputs, the identification of a stock being mispriced or fairly valued will be the same regardless of whether the fair value is determined and compared to the market price or the expected return is calculated and compared to the required return.

RELATIVE VALUATION METHODS

Although stock and company valuation is very strongly tilted toward the use of DCF methods, it is impossible to ignore the fact that many analysts use other methods to value equity and entire companies. The primary alternative valuation method is the use of multiples (that is, ratios) that have

---

[7]The formula for this model can be found in Eric Sorensen and Williamson, "Some Evidence of the Value of Dividend Discount Models," *Financial Analysts Journal* 41 (1985): 60–69.

price or value as the numerator and some form of earnings or cash flow generating performance measure for the denominator and that are observable for other similar or like-kind companies.

These multiples are sometimes called "price/X ratios," where the denominator "X" is the appropriate cash flow generating performance measure and the numerator is either a market value per share or a total market value. For example, the price/earnings (P/E) ratio is a popular multiple used for relative valuation, where an earnings estimate is the cash flow generating performance measure. Keep in mind that the terms relative valuation and valuation by multiples are used interchangeably here as are the terms price and value.

The essence of valuation by multiples assumes that similar or comparable companies are fairly valued in the market. As a result, the scaled price or value (the present value of expected future cash flows) of similar companies should be much the same. That is, comparable companies should have similar price/X ratios. The key for the analyst is to find the comparable companies that can be used for valuing a target company using valuation by multiples.

Valuation by multiples, or simply relative valuation, is quick and convenient. The simplicity and convenience of valuation by multiples, however, constitute both the appeal of this valuation method and the problems associated with its use. Simplicity, however, means that too many facts are swept under the carpet and too many questions remain unasked. Multiples should never be an analyst's only valuation method and preferably not even the primary focus because no two companies, or even groups of companies, are exactly the same. The term "similar" entails just as much uncertainty as the concept of "expected future cash flows" in DCF valuation methods. Actually, when an analyst has more than five minutes to value a company, the DCF method, which forces an analyst to consider the many aspects of an ongoing concern, is the preferred valuation method and the use of multiples should be secondary.

Having said this, valuation by multiples can provide a valuable "sanity check." If an analyst has completed a thorough valuation, he can compare his predicted multiples, such as the P/E ratio or market value to book value (MV/BV) ratio, to representative multiples of similar companies. In the MV/BV ratio, the book value of assets is the cash flow generating performance measure. That is, each dollar of book value of assets is assumed to generate cash flow for the company. If an analyst's predicted multiples are comparable, he can, perhaps, feel more assured of the validity of his analysis. On the other hand, if an analyst's predicted multiples are out of line with the representative multiples of the market, the analyst should reexamine the assumptions, the appropriateness of the comparables, and the appropriateness of the multiple to the situation at hand.

When using relative valuation, an analyst does not attempt to explain observed prices of companies. Instead, an analyst uses the appropriately scaled average price of similar companies to estimate values without specifying why prices are what they are. That is, the average price of similar companies is scaled by the appropriate "price/X" ratio. In addition, there is nothing to say that multiple price/X ratios can be used or is appropriate for the situation and that each one will generally provide a different estimate of value. Hence, the trick in valuing with multiples is selecting truly comparable companies and choosing the appropriate scaling bases—the appropriate "X" measure.

The Basic Principles of Relative Valuation

To use the word "multiples" is a fancy name for market prices divided (or "scaled") by some measure of performance, a Price/X ratio where X is the measure of performance that is highly correlated with cash flow. In a typical valuation with multiples, the average multiple—the average price scaled (that is, divided) by some measure of performance—is applied to a performance measure of the target company that an analyst is attempting to value.

For example, suppose an analyst chooses earnings as the scaling measure; that is, the analyst chooses earnings to be the performance measure by which prices of similar companies will be scaled. To scale the observed prices of companies by their earnings, the analyst computes for each company the ratio of its price to its earnings—its P/E ratio or its earnings multiple. He then averages the individual P/E ratios to estimate a "representative" P/E ratio, or a representative earnings multiple. To value a company, an analyst multiplies the projected profits of the company being valued by the representative earnings multiple, the average P/E.

When valuing with multiples, the analyst is agnostic regarding what determines prices. This means that there is no theory to guide the analyst on how best to scale observed market prices by one of the following: net earnings, earnings before interest and taxes (EBIT), sales, or book value of assets. In practice, this means that valuation with multiples requires the use of several scaling factors or, in other words, several multiples.

Often the best multiples for one industry may not be the preferred multiples in another industry. This implies, for example, that the practice of comparing P/E ratios of companies in different industries is problematic (and in many cases inappropriate altogether). This further implies that when the analyst performs a multiple-based valuation, it is important first to find what the industry considers as the best measure of relative values.

Although valuation by multiples differs from valuation by discounting cash flows, its application entails a similar procedure—first projecting

EXHIBIT 10.1   The Process of Relative Valuation

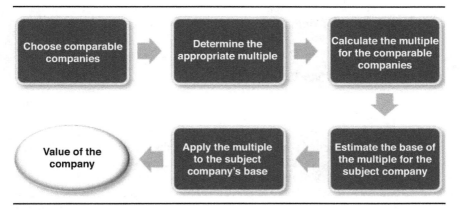

performance, and then converting projected performance to values using market prices, as we detail in Exhibit 10.1. Specifically, if an analyst believes, based on a study of comparable companies, that an appropriate forward-looking P/E (or any price/X ratio) for a subject company is 17 and expects earnings to be $3.00 per share in the next period, an estimate of a fair market price based on relative valuation assumptions is

Appropriate P/E ratio × Expected earnings = 17 × $3 = $51 per share

Choose Comparable Companies

The whole idea is to estimate a value of the subject company using the multiple implicit in the pricing of the comparable companies. Therefore, we want to select comparable companies that are as similar as possible to the company being valued. The flip-side of this argument, however, is that by specifying too stringent criteria for similarity, the analyst ends up with too few companies to compare. With a small sample of comparable companies, the idiosyncrasies of individual companies affect the average multiples too much so that the average multiple is no longer a representative multiple. In selecting the sample of comparable companies, an analyst has to balance these two conflicting considerations. The idea is to obtain as large a sample as possible so that the idiosyncrasies of a single company do not affect the valuation by much, yet not to choose so large a sample that the "comparable companies" are not comparable to the one being valued.

Financial theory states that assets that are of equivalent risk should be priced the same, all else equal. The key idea here is that we assume that comparable companies are of equivalent risk. Thus, the concept of being able to find comparable companies is the foundation for valuation by multiples. If there are no comparable companies, then valuation by multiples is not an option.

Determine an Appropriate Multiple

To convert market prices of comparable companies to a value for the company being analyzed, an analyst has to scale the valued company relative to the comparable companies. This is typically done by using several bases of comparison. Some generic measures of relative size often used in valuation by multiples are sales, gross profits, earnings, and book values.

Often, however, industry-specific multiples are more suitable than generic multiples. Examples of industry-specific multiples are price per restaurant for fast-food chains, paid miles flown for airlines, and price per square foot of floor space for retailers. In general, the higher-up that the scaling basis is in the income statement, the less it is subject to the vagaries of accounting principles. Thus, scaling basis of sales is much less dependent on accounting methods than earnings per share (EPS). For example, depreciation or treatment of convertible securities critically affect EPS calculations, but hardly affect sales. On the other hand, the higher-up that the scaling basis is in the income statement, the less it reflects differences in operating efficiency across companies—differences that critically affect the values of the comparable companies as well as the value of the company being analyzed.

Calculate the Multiple for the Comparable Companies

Once an analyst has a sample of companies that he is considering similar to the company being valued, an average of the multiples provides a measure of what the market is willing to pay for comparable companies in order to estimate a "fair" price for the subject company. For example, after dividing each comparable company's share price by its EPS to get individual P/E ratios, the analyst can average the P/E ratios of all comparable companies to estimate the earnings multiple that analysts think is fair for companies with these characteristics. The same thing can be done for all the scaling bases chosen, calculating a "fair price" per dollar of sales, per restaurant, per square foot of retail space, per dollar of book value of equity, and so on.

Note that we put "fair price" in quotation marks because there is no market for either EPS or sales or any other scaling measure. The computation of average multiples is merely a scaling exercise and not an exercise in finding "how much the market is willing to pay for a dollar of earnings."

Investors do not want to buy earnings; they only want cash flows (in the form of either dividends or capital gains). Earnings (or sales) are paid for only to the extent that they generate cash. In computing average ratios for various bases, an analyst implicitly assumes that the ability of companies to convert each basis (e.g., sales, book value, and earnings) to cash is the same. Keep in mind that this assumption is more tenable in some cases than in others and for some scaling factors than for others.

Realize that we use the word "average" to mean the appropriate value that is determined by the average company in the comparable group. It may not be the strict average. It may be a mean, median, or mode. The analyst is also free to throw out outliers that do not seem to conform to the majority of companies in the group. Outliers are most likely so because the market has determined that they are different for any number of reasons.

Estimate to Base of the Multiple for the Subject Company

Once we have the multiple for the comparable, we apply it to the projected performance of the company that we are valuing. Therefore, an analyst needs to project the same measures of the relative size used in scaling the prices of the comparable companies for the company being valued.

Consider an example in which we want to value Company X, using the comparables A, B, and C. And suppose we estimate the average P/E of companies A, B, and C to be 15. If we project earnings per share of Company X as $2, then applying the comparables' multiple of 15 gives us an estimate of the value per share for Company X of $30.

The simplest application of valuation with multiples is by projecting the scaling bases one year forward and applying the average multiple of comparable companies to these projections. For example, the comparable companies' average P/E ratio to the projected next year's earnings of the company being valued is applied. Clearly, by applying the average multiple to the next year's projections, an analyst overemphasizes the immediate prospects of the company and gives no weight to more distant prospects.

To overcome this weakness of the one-step-ahead projections, an analyst can use a more sophisticated approach, applying the average multiples representative projections—projections that better represent the long-term prospects of the company. For example, instead of applying the average P/E ratio to next year's earnings, we can apply the comparable P/E ratio to the projected average EPS over the next five years. In this way, the representative earnings' projections can also capture some of the long-term prospects of the company, while next year's figures (with their idiosyncrasies) do not dominate valuations.

Apply the Multiple to the Subject Company's Base

In the final step, an analyst combines the average multiples of comparable companies to the projected parameters of the subject company (i.e., the company to be valued) to obtain an estimated value. On the face of it, this is merely a simple technical step. Yet often it is not. The values that we obtain from various multiples (i.e., by using several scaling bases) are typically not the same; in fact, frequently they are quite different. This means that this step requires some analysis of its own—explaining why valuation by the average P/E ratio yields a lower value than the valuation by the sales multiple (e.g., the valued company has higher than normal selling, general, and administrative expenses) or why the MV/BV ratio yields a relatively low value. The combination of several values into a final estimate of value, therefore, requires an economic analysis of both "appropriate" multiples and how multiple-based values should be adjusted to yield values that are economically reasonable.

KEY POINTS

- The basis for the dividend discount model is simply the application of present value analysis, which asserts that the fair price of an asset is the present value of its expected cash flows.
- Most dividend discount models use current dividends, some measure of historical or projected dividend growth, and an estimate of the required rate of return. The three most common dividend measures are dividends per share, dividend yield, and dividend payout.
- Variations of the dividend discount models allow an analyst to vary assumptions regarding dividend growth to accommodate different patterns of dividends. Popular models include the finite-life general dividend discount model, the constant growth dividend discount model, and multiphase dividend discount model.
- A dividend discount model can be recast in terms of expected return. The expected return is found by calculating the interest rate that will make the present value of the expected cash flows equal to the market price.
- An alternative valuation method to the dividend discount model is the use of multiples that have price or value as the numerator and some form of earnings or cash flow generating performance measure for the denominator and that are observable for other similar or like-kind companies. These multiples are sometimes called "price/X ratios," where the denominator X is the appropriate cash flow generating performance measure.
- The essence of valuation by multiples assumes that similar or comparable companies are valued fairly in the market. When using relative

valuation, no attempt is made by an analyst to explain observed prices of companies. Rather, an analyst employs suitably scaled average price of similar companies to estimate values without specifying why prices are what they are.
- Despite the fact that valuation by multiples differs from valuation by discounting cash flows, the application entails a similar procedure, which involves first forecasting performance, and then converting projected performance to values using market prices.

QUESTIONS

1. Consider three companies, A, B, and C. Suppose that a common stock analyst estimates that the market risk premium is 5% and the risk-free rate is 4.63%. The analyst estimated the beta for each company to be as follows: Company A, 0.9; Company B, 1.0, and; Company C, 1.2. The analyst uses to CAPM to estimate the discount rate. The CAPM says that the expected return is equal to the risk-free rate plus the product of the market risk premium and the company's beta. What is the estimated discount rate for each company?

2. Estimate the value of a share of stock for each of the following companies using the constant growth model and estimating the average annual growth rate of dividends from 20X1 through 20X6 as given below as the basis for estimated growth beyond 20X6:

	Dividends per Share		
Company	20X1	20X6	Discount Rate
1	$1.00	$1.20	8%
2	$2.00	$1.80	9%
3	$0.50	$0.60	7%
4	$0.25	$0.30	12%

3. Estimate the expected return for each of the following companies:

Company	Current Dividends per Share	Expected Growth Rate of Dividends	Value of the Stock
T	$1.00	2%	$25
U	$0.50	3%	$20
V	$1.25	1%	$10
W	$0.25	2%	$15

4. Consider Company RV that has projected earnings per share of $2.5 and a projected book value per share of $20. Determine the estimated value of this Company RV, based on a relative value using the price-earnings ratio and the market value to book value ratio. Use the average of the respective multiples of the following three comparables companies:

Comparable	Value per Share	Earnings per Share	Book Value per Share
X	$15	$1	$10
Y	$32	$2	$8
Z	$60	$5	$40

5. Why would an analyst use a multiphase dividend discount model?

6. Why might an analyst prefer to use a measure of cash flow generating ability such as earnings instead of sales in relative valuation?

7. To what extent is the procedure for valuation based on discounting cash flows and valuation by multiples similar?

8. In seeking to establish comparable companies in relative valuation analysis, what is the problem with specifying too stringent criteria for companies to be included in the comparable group?

CHAPTER 11

Quantitative Equity Portfolio Management

Andrew Alford, Ph.D.
Managing Director
Quantitative Investment Strategies Group
Goldman Sachs Asset Management

Robert Jones, CFA
Managing Director
Quantitative Investment Strategies Group
Goldman Sachs Asset Management

Terence Lim, Ph.D., CFA
Managing Director
Quantitative Investment Strategies Group
Goldman Sachs Asset Management

Equity portfolio management has evolved considerably since Benjamin Graham and David Dodd published the original edition of their classic text on security analysis in 1934.[1] For one, the types of stocks available for investment have shifted dramatically, from companies with mostly physical assets (such as railroads and utilities) to companies with mostly intangible assets (such as technology stocks and pharmaceuticals). Moreover, theories such as Modern Portfolio Theory and the Capital Asset Pricing Model, in conjunction with new data sources and powerful computers, have revolutionized the way investors select stocks, create portfolios, and execute trades. Consequently, what was once mostly an art is increasingly becoming a dynamically evolving science: Loose rules of thumb are being replaced by rigorous research and complex implementation.

---

[1]Benjamin Graham and David Dodd, *Security Analysis* (New York: McGraw-Hill, 1934).

Of course, these new advances, while greatly expanding the frontiers of finance, have not necessarily made it any easier for portfolio managers to beat the market. In fact, the increasing sophistication of the typical investor has probably made it more difficult to find—and exploit—pricing errors. Several studies show that the majority of professional money managers have been unable to beat the market.[2] There are no sure bets, and mispricings, when they occur, are rarely both large and long lasting. Successful managers must therefore constantly work to improve their existing strategies and to develop new ones. Understanding fully the equity management process is essential to accomplishing this challenging task.

These new advances, unfortunately, have also allowed some market participants to stray from a sound investment approach. It is now easier than ever for portfolio managers to use biased, noisy, or unfamiliar data in a flawed strategy, one developed from untested conjecture or haphazard trial and error. Investors, too, must be careful not to let the abundance of data and high-tech techniques distract them when allocating assets and selecting managers. In particular, investors should not allow popular but narrow rankings of short-term performance obscure important differences in portfolio managers' style exposure or investment process. To avoid these pitfalls, it helps to have a solid grasp of the constantly advancing science of equity investing.

This chapter provides an overview of quantitative equity portfolio management aimed at current and potential investors, analysts, investment consultants, and portfolio managers. We begin with a discussion of the two major approaches to equity portfolio management: the traditional, or qualitative, approach and the quantitative approach. The remaining sections of the chapter are organized around four major steps in the investment process: (1) forecasting the unknown quantities needed to manage equity portfolios—returns, risks, and transaction costs; (2) constructing portfolios that maximize expected risk-adjusted return net of transaction costs; (3) trading stocks efficiently; and (4) evaluating results and updating the process.

These four steps should be closely integrated: The return, risk, and transaction cost forecasts, the approach used to construct portfolios, the way stocks are traded, and performance evaluation should all be consistent with one another. A process that produces highly variable, fast-moving return forecasts, for example, should be matched with short-term risk forecasts, relatively high expected transaction costs, frequent rebalancing, aggressive trading, and short-horizon performance evaluation. In contrast,

---

[2]See, for example, Burton G. Malkiel, "Returns from Investing in Equity Mutual Funds, 1971 to 1991," *Journal of Finance* 50, no. 2 (1995): 549–572; and Eugene F. Fama and Kenneth R. French, "Luck versus Skill in the Cross Section of Mutual Fund Returns," *Journal of Finance* 65, no. 5 (2010): 1915–1947.

stable, slower-moving return forecasts can be combined with longer term risk forecasts, lower expected transaction costs, less frequent rebalancing, more patient trading, and longer-term evaluation. Mixing and matching incompatible approaches to each part of the investment process can greatly reduce a manager's ability to reap the full rewards of an investment strategy.

A well-structured investment process should also be supported by sound economic logic, diverse information sources, and careful empirical analysis that together produce reliable forecasts and effective implementation. And, of course, a successful investment process should be easy to explain; marketing professionals, consultants, and investors all need to understand a manager's process before they will invest in it.

TRADITIONAL AND QUANTITATIVE APPROACHES TO EQUITY PORTFOLIO MANAGEMENT

At one level, there are as many ways to manage portfolios as there are portfolio managers. After all, developing a unique and innovative investment process is one of the ways managers distinguish themselves from their peers. Nonetheless, at a more general level, there are two basic approaches used by most managers: The traditional, or qualitative, approach and the quantitative approach. Although these two approaches are often sharply contrasted by their proponents, they have been converging over time and actually share many traits. Both apply economic reasoning to identify a small set of key drivers of equity values; both use observable (historical) data to help measure these key drivers; both use expert judgment to develop ways to map these key drivers into the final stock-selection decision; and both evaluate their performance over time. What differs most between traditional and quantitative managers is how they perform these steps.

Traditional managers conduct stock-specific analysis to develop a subjective assessment of each stock's unique attractiveness. Traditional managers talk with senior management, closely study financial statements and other corporate disclosures, conduct detailed, stock-specific competitive analysis, and usually build spreadsheet models of a company's financial statements that provide an explicit link between various forecasts of financial metrics and stock prices. The traditional approach involves detailed analysis of a company and is often well equipped to cope with data errors or structural changes at a company (e.g., restructurings or acquisitions). However, because the traditional approach relies heavily on the judgment of analysts, it is subject to potentially severe subjective biases such as selective perception, hindsight bias, stereotyping, and overconfidence that can reduce forecast quality.[3] Moreover, the traditional approach is more costly to apply, which can make it impracticable for a large investment universe comprising many stocks. The high cost and subjective nature also make it difficult to evaluate the investment process because it is hard to create the history necessary for testing. This testing is important because it helps to distinguish factors that are reflected in stock prices from those that are not. Only factors that are not yet impounded in stock prices can be used to identify profitable trading opportunities. Failure to distinguish between these two types of factors can lead to the familiar "good company, bad stock" problem in which even a great company can be a bad investment if the price paid for the stock is too high.

Quantitative managers use explicit models to map a parsimonious set of measurable metrics into objective forecasts of each stock's return, risk, and cost of trading. The quantitative approach formalizes the relation between the key metrics and forecasts, which makes the approach transparent and largely free of subjective biases. Quantitative analysis can also be highly cost effective. Although the fixed costs of building a robust quantitative model are high, the marginal costs of applying the model, or extending it to a broader investment universe, are low. Consequently, quantitative portfolio managers can choose from a large universe of stocks, including many small and otherwise neglected stocks that have attractive fundamentals. Finally, because the quantitative approach is model-based, it can be tested historically on a wide cross-section of stocks over diverse economic environments. While quantitative analysis can suffer from specification errors and over-fitting, analysts can mitigate these errors by following a well-structured and disciplined research process.

On the negative side, quantitative models can be misleading when there are bad data or significant structural changes at a company (leading to "garbage in, garbage out"). For this reason, most quantitative managers like to spread their bets across many names so that the success of any one position will not make or break the strategy. Traditional managers, conversely, prefer to take fewer, larger bets given their detailed knowledge of the company and the high cost of analysis.

A summary of the major advantages of each approach to equity portfolio management is presented in Exhibit 11.1.[4] Our focus in the rest of this chapter is the process of quantitative equity portfolio management.

---

[3]For a discussion of the systematic errors in judgment and probability assessment that people frequently make, see Daniel Kahneman, Paul Slovic, and Amos Tversky, *Judgment under Uncertainty: Heuristics and Biases* (New York: Cambridge University Press, 1982).
[4]For a comparison of clinical (traditional) and actuarial (quantitative) decision analysis, see Robyn M. Dawes, David Faust, and Paul E. Meehl, "Clinical versus Actuarial Judgment," *Science* 243, no. 4899 (1989): 1668–1674.

EXHIBIT 11.1 Major Advantages of the Traditional and Quantitative Approaches to Equity Portfolio Management

Traditional Approach	
Depth	Although they have views on fewer companies, traditional managers tend to have more in-depth knowledge of the companies they cover. Unlike a computerized model, they should know when data are misleading or unrepresentative.
Regime shifts	Traditional managers may be better equipped to handle regime shifts and recognize situations in which past relations might not be expected to continue.
Key characteristics	Based on their greater in-depth knowledge, traditional managers can better understand the investment themes and underlying metrics that are important for stocks in different industries or countries.
Qualitative factors	Many important factors that may affect an investment decision are not available in any database and are hard to evaluate quantitatively. Examples might include: management and their vision for the company; the value of patents, brands and other intangible assets; product quality; or the impact of new technology.

Quantitative Approach	
Universe	Because a computerized model can quickly evaluate thousands of securities and can update those evaluations daily, it can uncover more opportunities. Further, by spreading their risk across many small bets, quantitative managers can add value with only slightly favorable odds.
Discipline	While individuals often base their decision on only the most salient or distinctive factors, a computerized model will simultaneously evaluate all specified factors before reaching a conclusion.
Verification	Before using any signal to evaluate stocks, quantitative managers will normally validate its historical efficacy and robustness. This provides a framework for weighting the various signals.
Risk management	By its nature, the quantitative approach builds in the notion of statistical risk and can do a better job of controlling unintended risks in the portfolio.
Lower fees	The economies of scale inherent in a quantitative process usually allow quantitative managers to charge lower fees.

FORECASTING STOCK RETURNS, RISKS, AND TRANSACTION COSTS

Developing good forecasts is the first and perhaps most critical step in the investment process. Without good forecasts, the difficult task of forming superior portfolios becomes nearly impossible. In this section we discuss how to use a quantitative approach to generate forecasts of stock returns, risks, and transaction costs. These forecasts are then used in the portfolio construction step described in the next section.

It should be noted that some portfolio managers do not develop explicit forecasts of returns, risks, and transaction costs. Instead, they map a variety of individual stock characteristics directly into portfolio holdings. However, there are limitations with this abbreviated approach. Because the returns and risks corresponding to the various characteristics are not clearly identified, it is difficult to ensure the weights placed on the characteristics are appropriate. Further, measuring risk at the portfolio level is awkward without reliable estimates of the risks of each stock, especially the correlations between stocks. Similarly, controlling turnover is hard when returns and transaction costs are not expressed in consistent units. And, of course, it is difficult to explain a process that comprises a single integrated step.

Forecasting Returns

The process of building a quantitative return-forecasting model can be divided into four closely linked steps: (1) identifying a set of potential return forecasting variables, or signals; (2) testing the effectiveness of each signal, by itself and together with other signals; (3) determining the appropriate weight for each signal in the model; and (4) blending the model's views with market equilibrium to arrive at reasonable forecasts for expected returns.

Identifying a list of potential *signals* might seem like an overwhelming task because the candidate pool can seem almost endless. To narrow the list, it is important to start with fundamental relationships and sound economics. Reports published by Wall Street analysts and books about financial statement analysis may be good sources for ideas. Another potentially valuable resource is academic research in finance and accounting. Academics have the incentive and expertise to identify and carefully analyze new and innovative information sources. Academics have studied a large number of stock price anomalies, and Exhibit 11.2 lists several that have been adopted by many investment managers.[5]

---

[5]For evidence on the performance of several well-known anomalies, see Eugene F. Fama and Kenneth R. French, "Dissecting Anomalies," *Journal of Finance* 63, no. 4 (2008): 1653–1678.

EXHIBIT 11.2 Select Stock Price Anomalies Used in Many Quantitative Equity Models

Growth/Value: Value stocks (high B/P, E/P, CF/P) outperform growth stocks (low B/P, E/P, CF/P).

Post-earnings-announcement drift: Stocks that announce earnings that beat expectations outperform stocks that miss expectations on a subsequent basis.

Short-term price reversal: One-month losers outperform one-month winners.

Intermediate-term price momentum: Six-months to one-year winners outperform losers.

Earnings quality: Stocks with cash earnings outperform stocks with noncash (accrual) earnings.

Stock repurchases: Companies that repurchase shares outperform companies that issue shares.

Analyst earnings estimates and stock recommendations: Changes in analyst stock recommendations and earnings estimates predict subsequent stock returns.

For portfolio managers intent on building a successful investment strategy, it is not enough to simply take the best ideas identified by others and add them to the return-forecasting model. It is also important that these ideas, as expressed by a set of signals, are not yet priced by investors (i.e., are not too popular). Signals that are widely used by other investors will generate lower—and likely less consistent—returns. Further, each potential signal must be thoroughly tested to ensure it works in the context of a manager's strategy across many stocks and during a variety of economic environments. The real challenge is winnowing the list of potential signals to a parsimonious set of reliable forecasting variables. When selecting a set of signals, it is a good idea to include a variety of variables to capture distinct investment themes, such as valuation, momentum, and earnings quality. By diversifying over information sources and variables, there is a good chance that if one signal fails to add value during a quarter or year, another will be there to carry the load.

When evaluating a signal, it is important to make sure the underlying data used to compute the signal are available and largely error free. Checking selected observations by hand and screening for outliers or other influential observations is a useful way to identify data problems. It is also sometimes necessary to transform a signal—for instance, by subtracting the industry mean or taking the natural logarithm—to improve the "shape" of the distribution. To evaluate a signal properly, both univariate and multivariate analysis is important. Univariate analysis provides evidence on the signal's predictive ability when the signal is used alone, whereas multivariate analysis provides evidence on the signal's incremental predictive ability above and beyond other variables considered. For both univariate and multivariate analysis, it is wise to examine the returns to a variety of portfolios formed on the basis of the signal. Sorting stocks into quintiles or deciles is popular, as is regression analysis, where the coefficients represent the return to a portfolio with unit exposure to the signal. These portfolios can be equal-weighted, cap-weighted, or even risk-weighted depending on the model's ultimate purpose. Finally, the return forecasting model should be tested using a realistic simulation that controls the target level of risk, takes account of transaction costs, and imposes appropriate constraints (e.g., the non-negativity constraint for long-only portfolios). In our experience, many promising return-forecasting signals fail to add value in realistic backtests—either because they involve excessive trading; work only for small, illiquid stocks; or contain information that is already captured by other components of the model.

The third step in building a return forecasting model is determining each signal's weight. When computing expected returns, more weight should be put on signals that are more stable; possess greater return potential; deliver more consistent returns; and provide superior diversification benefits. Maintaining exposures to signals that change slowly requires less trading, and hence involves lower transaction costs, than is the case for signals that change rapidly. Other things being equal, a stable signal (such as the ratio of book-to-market equity) should get more weight than a less stable signal (such as one-month price reversal). High, consistent returns are essential to a profitable, low-risk investment strategy; hence, proprietary signals that generate high returns with little risk should get more weight than more common signals that produce lower returns with higher risk. Finally, signals with more diversified payoffs should get more weight because they can hedge overall performance when other signals in the model perform poorly.

The last step in forecasting returns is to make sure the forecasts are reasonable and internally consistent by comparing them with equilibrium views. Return forecasts that ignore equilibrium expectations can create problems in the portfolio construction step. Seemingly reasonable return forecasts can cause an optimizer to maximize errors rather than expected returns, producing extreme, unbalanced portfolios. The problem is caused by return forecasts that are inconsistent with the assumed correlations across stocks. If two stocks (or subportfolios) are highly correlated, then the equilibrium expectation is that their returns should be similar; otherwise, the optimizer will treat the pair of stocks as a (near) arbitrage opportunity by going extremely long the high-return stock and extremely short the low-return stock. However, with hundreds of stocks, it is not always obvious whether certain stocks, or combinations of stocks, are highly correlated and therefore ought to have similar return forecasts. The Black-Litterman model was specifically designed to alleviate this problem. It blends a model's raw return forecasts with *equilibrium expected returns*—which are the returns that would make the benchmark optimal for a given risk model—to produce internally consistent return forecasts that reflect the manager's (or model's) views, yet are consistent with the risk model.[6]

Forecasting Risk

In a portfolio context, the risk of a single stock is a function of the variance of its returns, as well as the covariances between its returns and the returns of other stocks in the portfolio. The variance-covariance matrix of stock returns, or risk model, is used to measure the risk of a portfolio. For equity portfolio management, investors rarely estimate the full variance-covariance matrix directly because the number of individual elements is too large, and for a well-behaved (that is, nonsingular) matrix, the number of observations used to estimate the matrix must significantly exceed the number of stocks in the matrix.[7] For this reason, most equity portfolio managers use a *factor risk model* in which individual variances and covariances are expressed as a function of a small set of stock characteristics—such as industry membership, size, and leverage. This greatly reduces the number of unknown risk parameters that the manager needs to estimate.

When developing an equity factor risk model, it is a good idea to include all of the variables used to forecast returns among the (potentially larger) set of variables used to forecast risks. This way, the risk model "sees" all of the potential risks in an investment strategy, both those managers are willing to accept and those they would like to avoid. Further, a mismatch between the variables in the return and risk models can produce less efficient portfolios in the optimizer. For instance, suppose a return model comprises two signals, each with 50% weight: the book-to-price ratio (B/P) and return on equity (ROE). Suppose the risk model, on the other hand, has only one factor: B/P. When forming a portfolio, the optimizer will manage risk only for the factors in the risk model—B/P but not ROE. This inconsistency between the return and risk models can lead to portfolios with extreme positions and higher-than-expected risk. The portfolio will not reflect the original 50-50 weights on the two signals because the optimizer will dampen the exposure to B/P, but not to ROE. In addition, the risk model's estimate of tracking error will be too low because it will not capture any risk from the portfolio's

---

[6]For a discussion of how to use the Black-Litterman model to incorporate equilibrium views into a return-forecasting model, see Robert Litterman, *Modern Investment Management: An Equilibrium Approach* (Hoboken, N.J.: John Wiley & Sons, 2003).
[7]To see this, suppose there are N stocks. Then the variance-covariance matrix has $N(N + 1)/2$ elements, consisting of N variances and $N(N - 1)/2$ covariances. For an S&P 500 portfolio, for instance, there are $500 \times (500 + 1)/2 = 125{,}250$ unknown parameters to estimate, 500 variances and 124,750 covariances.

exposure to ROE. The most effective way to avoid these two problems is to make sure all of the signals in the return model are included as factors in the risk model (although the converse does not need to be true—that is, there can be risk factors with zero expected returns).

A final issue to consider when developing or selecting a risk model is the frequency of data used in the estimation process. Some popular risk models use monthly returns, whereas many portfolio managers use or have developed risk models that use daily returns. Clearly, when estimating variances and covariances, the more observations, the better. High-frequency data produce more observations and hence more precise and reliable estimates. Further, by giving more weight to recent observations, estimates can be more responsive to changing economic conditions. As a result, risk models that use high-frequency returns should provide more accurate risk estimates.[8]

Forecasting Transaction Costs

Although often overlooked, accurate trade-cost estimates are critical to the equity portfolio management process. After all, what really matters is not a portfolio's gross return, but rather a portfolio's actual return after deducting all relevant costs, including transaction costs. Ignoring transaction costs when forming portfolios can lead to poor performance because implementation costs can reduce, or even eliminate, the advantages achieved through superior stock selection. Conversely, taking account of transaction costs can help produce portfolios with gross excess returns that exceed the costs of trading.

Accurate trading-cost forecasts are also important after portfolio formation, when monitoring the realized costs of trading. A good transaction-cost model can provide a benchmark for what realized costs "should be," and hence whether actual execution costs are reasonable. Detailed trade-cost monitoring can help traders and brokers achieve best execution by driving improvements in trading methods—such as more patient trading, or the selective use of alternative trading mechanisms.

Transaction costs have two components: explicit costs, such as commissions and fees; and implicit costs, or market impact. Commissions and fees tend to be relatively small, and the cost per share does not depend on the number of shares traded. In contrast, market impact costs can be substantial. They reflect the costs of consuming liquidity from the market, costs that increase on a per-share basis with the total number of shares traded.

---

[8]For a detailed discussion of factor risk models, see Peter Zangari, "Equity Risk Factor Models," Chapter 20 in Litterman, *Modern Investment Management: An Equilibrium Approach*.

Market impact costs arise because suppliers of liquidity incur risk. One component of these costs is inventory risk. The liquidity supplier has a risk–return trade-off, and will demand a price concession to compensate for this inventory risk. The larger the trade size and the more illiquid or volatile the stock, the larger are inventory risk and market impact costs. Another consideration is adverse selection risk. Liquidity suppliers are willing to provide a better price to uninformed than informed traders, but since there is no reliable way to distinguish between these two types of traders, the market maker sets an average price, with expected gains from trading with uninformed traders compensating for losses incurred from trading with informed traders. Market impact costs tend to be higher for low-price and small-cap stocks for which adverse selection risk and informational asymmetry tend to be more severe.

Forecasting price impact is difficult. Because researchers only observe prices for completed trades, they cannot determine what a stock's price would have been without these trades. It is therefore impossible to know for sure how much prices moved as a result of the trade. Price impact costs, then, are statistical estimates that are more accurate for larger data samples.

One approach to estimating trade costs is to directly examine the complete record of market prices, tick by tick.[9] These data are noisy due to discrete prices, nonsynchronous reporting of trades and quotes, and input errors. Also, the record does not show orders placed, just those that eventually got executed (which may have been split up from the original, larger order). Research by Lee and Radhakrishna (2000) suggests empirical analysis should be done using aggregated samples of trades rather than individual trades at the tick-by-tick level.[10]

Another approach is for portfolio managers to estimate a proprietary transaction cost model using their own trades and, if available, those of comparable managers. If generating a sufficient sample is feasible, this approach is ideal because the resulting model matches the stock characteristics, investment philosophy, and trading strategy of the individual portfolio manager.[11] Further, models built from actual trading records provide a complementary source of information on market impact costs.

---

[9]See, for example, William J. Breen, Laurie Simon Hodrick, and Robert A. Korajczyk, "Predicting Equity Liquidity," *Management Science* 48, no. 4 (2002): 470–483.

[10]Charles M.C. Lee and Balkrishna Radhakrishna, "Inferring Investor Behavior," *Journal of Financial Markets* 3, no. 2 (2000): 83–111.

[11]For portfolio managers interested in developing a model based on their own trades, see Donald B. Keim and Ananth Madhavan, "The Costs of Institutional Equity Trades: An Overview," *Financial Analysts Journal* 54, no. 4 (1997): 50–69.

CONSTRUCTING PORTFOLIOS

In this section we discuss how to construct portfolios based on the forecasts described in the last section. In particular, we compare rule-based approaches to portfolio optimization. The first step in portfolio construction, however, is to specify the investment goals. While having good forecasts (as described in the previous section) is obviously important, the investor's goals define the portfolio management problem. These goals are usually specified by three major parameters: the benchmark, the risk–return target, and specific restrictions such as the maximum holdings in any single name, industry, or sector.

The benchmark represents the starting point for any active portfolio; it is the client's neutral position—a low-cost alternative to active management in that asset class. For example, investors interested in holding large-cap U.S. stocks might select the S&P 500 or Russell 1000 as their benchmark, while investors interested in holding small-cap stocks might choose the Russell 2000 or the S&P 600. Investors interested in a portfolio of non-U.S. stocks could pick the FTSE 350 (United Kingdom), TOPIX (Japan), or MSCI EAFE (developed world minus North America) indexes. There are a large number of published benchmarks available, or an investor might develop a customized benchmark to represent the neutral position. In all cases, however, the benchmark should be a reasonably low-cost, investable alternative to active management.

Although some investors are content to merely match the returns on their benchmarks, most investors allocate at least some of their assets to active managers. The allocation of risk is done via risk budgeting. In equity portfolio management, active management means overweighting attractive stocks and underweighting unattractive stocks relative to their weights in the benchmark. The difference between a stock's weight in the portfolio and its weight in the benchmark is called its active weight, where a positive active weight corresponds to an overweight position and a negative active weight corresponds to an underweight position. Of course, there is always a chance that these active weighting decisions will cause the portfolio to underperform the benchmark, but one of the basic dictums of modern finance is that to earn higher returns, investors must accept higher risk—which is true of active returns as well as total returns.

A portfolio's *tracking error* measures its risk relative to a benchmark. Tracking error equals the time-series standard deviation of a portfolio's *active return* (which is the difference between the portfolio's return and that of the benchmark). A portfolio's *information ratio* equals its average active return divided by its tracking error. As a measure of return per unit of risk, the information ratio provides a convenient way to compare strategies with different active risk levels.

An *efficient portfolio* is one with the highest expected return for a target level of risk—that is, it has the highest information ratio possible given the risk budget. In the absence of constraints and transaction costs, an efficient portfolio is one in which each stock's marginal contribution to expected return is proportional to its marginal contribution to risk. That is, there are no unintended risks, and all risks are compensated with additional expected returns. How can a portfolio manager construct such an efficient portfolio? Below we compare two approaches: (1) a rule-based system and (2) portfolio optimization.

Building an efficient portfolio is a complex problem. To help simplify this complicated task, many portfolio managers use ad hoc, rule-based methods that partially control exposures to a small number of risk factors. For example, one common approach—called stratified sampling—ranks stocks within buckets formed on the basis of a few key risk factors, such as sector and size. The manager then invests more heavily in the highest-ranked stocks within each bucket, while keeping the portfolio's total weight in each bucket close to that of the benchmark. The resulting portfolio is close to neutral with respect to the identified risk factors (that is, sector and size) while it is overweight attractive stocks and underweight unattractive stocks.

Although stratified sampling may seem sensible, it is not very efficient. Numerous unintended risks can creep into the portfolio, such as an overweight in high-beta stocks, growth stocks, or stocks in certain subsectors. Nor does it allow the manager to explicitly consider trading costs or investment objectives in the portfolio construction problem. Portfolio optimization provides a much better method for balancing expected returns against different sources of risk, trade costs, and investor constraints. An optimizer uses computer algorithms to find the set of weights (or holdings) that maximize the portfolio's expected return, net of trade costs, for a given level of risk. It minimizes uncompensated sources of risk, including sector and style biases. Fortunately, despite the complex math, optimizers require only the various forecasts we've already described and developed in the prior section.

Elsewhere, we demonstrate the benefits of optimization, comparing two portfolios: one constructed using stratified sampling and the other constructed using an optimizer.[12] We designed the optimized portfolio to have the same predicted tracking error as the rule-based portfolio. The results indicate that (1) the optimized portfolio is more efficient in terms of its expected alpha and information ratio for the same level of risk; (2) risk is

---

[12]See Andrew Alford, Robert Jones, and Terence Lim, "Equity Portfolio Management," Chapter 23 in Litterman, *Modern Investment Management: An Equilibrium Approach.*

spread more broadly for the optimized portfolio compared to the rule-based portfolio; (3) more of the risk budget in the optimized portfolio is due to the factors that are expected to generate positive excess returns; and (4) the forecast beta for the optimized portfolio is closer to 1.0, as unintended sources of risk (such as the market timing) are minimized.

Another benefit of optimizers is that they can efficiently account for transaction costs, constraints, selected restrictions, and other account guidelines, making it much easier to create customized client portfolios. Of course, when using an optimizer to construct efficient portfolios, reliable inputs are essential. Data errors that add noise to the return, risk, and transaction cost forecasts can lead to portfolios in which these forecast errors are maximized. Instead of picking stocks with the highest actual expected returns, or the lowest actual risks or transaction costs, the optimizer takes the biggest positions in the stocks with the largest errors, namely, the stocks with the greatest overestimates of expected returns or the greatest underestimates of risks or transaction costs. A robust investment process will screen major data sources for outliers that can severely corrupt one's forecasts. Further, as described in the previous section, return forecasts should be adjusted for equilibrium views using the Black-Litterman model to produce final return forecasts that are more consistent with risk estimates, and with each other. Finally, portfolio managers should impose sensible, but simple, constraints on the optimizer to help guard against the effects of noisy inputs. These constraints could include maximum active weights on individual stocks, industries, or sectors, as well as limitations on the portfolio's active exposure to factors such as size or market beta.

TRADING

Trading is the process of executing the orders derived in the portfolio construction step. To trade a list of stocks efficiently, investors must balance opportunity costs and execution price risk against market impact costs. Trading each stock quickly minimizes lost alpha and price uncertainty due to delay, but impatient trading incurs maximum market impact. However, trading more patiently over a longer period reduces market impact but incurs larger opportunity costs and short-term execution price risk. Striking the right balance is one of the keys to successful trade execution.

The concept of "striking a balance" suggests optimization. Investors can use a trade optimizer to balance the gains from patient trading (e.g., lower market-impact cost) against the risks (e.g., greater deviation between the execution price and the decision price; potentially higher short-term tracking error). Such an optimizer will tend to suggest aggressive trading for names that are liquid and/or have a large effect on portfolio risk, while suggesting patient trading for illiquid names that have less impact on risk. A trade optimizer can also easily handle most real-world trading constraints, such as the need to balance cash in each of many accounts across the trading period (which may last several days).

A trade optimizer can also easily accommodate the time horizon of a manager's views. That is, if a manager is buying a stock primarily for long-term valuation reasons, and the excess return is expected to accrue gradually over time, then the optimizer will likely suggest a patient trading strategy (all else being equal). Conversely, if the manager is buying a stock in expectation of a positive earnings surprise tomorrow, the optimizer is likely to suggest an aggressive trading strategy (again, all else being equal). The trade optimizer can also be programmed to consider short-term return regularities, such as the intraday periodicity and predictability of trading volume and stock prices.[13] Although these types of regularities may be too small to cover trading costs, and should not be used to initiate trades, they can be used to time trades within the day and help minimize execution costs after an investor has independently decided to trade.[14]

To induce traders to follow the desired strategy (the one suggested by the trade optimizer), the portfolio manager needs to give the trader an appropriate benchmark, which provides guidance about how aggressively or patiently to trade. Two widely used benchmarks for aggressive trades are the closing price on the previous day and the opening price on the trade date. Because the values of these two benchmarks are measured prior to any trading, a patient strategy that delays trading heightens execution price risk by increasing the possibility of deviating significantly from the benchmark. Another popular execution benchmark is *the volume-weighted average price* (VWAP) for the stock over the desired trading period, which could be a few minutes or hours for an aggressive trade, or one or more days for a patient trade. However, the VWAP benchmark should only be used for trades that are not too large relative to total volume over the period; otherwise, the trader may be able to influence the benchmark against which he or she is evaluated.

Buy-side traders increasingly make use of algorithmic trading, or computer algorithms that directly access market exchanges, to automatically make certain trading decisions such as the timing, price, quantity, type, and routing of orders. These algorithms may dynamically monitor market conditions across time and trading venues, and reduce market impact by

---

[13]Steven L. Heston, Robert A. Korzjczyk, and Ronnie Sadka, "Intraday patterns in the Cross-section of Stock Returns," *Journal of Finance* 65, no. 4 (2010): 1369–1407.
[14]For a more detailed discussion of trade optimization, see Robert F. Engle and Robert Ferstenberg, "Execution Risk," *Journal of Portfolio Management* 32, no. 2 (2007): 34–44.

breaking large orders into smaller pieces, employing either limit orders or marketable limit orders, or selecting trading venues to submit orders, while closely tracking trading benchmarks. Algorithmic trading provides buy-side traders more anonymity and greater control over their order flow, but tends to work better for more liquid or patient trades.

Principal package trading is another way to lower transaction costs relative to traditional agency methods.[15] Principal trades may be crossed with the principal's existing inventory positions, or allow the portfolio manager to benefit from the longer trading horizon and superior trading ability of certain intermediaries.

EVALUATING RESULTS AND UPDATING THE PROCESS

Once an investment process is up and running, it needs to be constantly reassessed and, if necessary, refined. The first step is to compare actual results to expectations; if realizations differ enough from expectations, process refinements may be necessary. Thus, managers need systems to monitor realized performance, risk, and trading costs and compare them to prior expectations.

A good performance monitoring system should be able to determine not only the degree of over- or underperformance, but also the sources of these excess returns. For example, a good performance attribution system might break excess returns down into those due to market timing (having a different beta than the benchmark), industry tilts, style differences, and stock selection. Such systems are available from a variety of third-party vendors. An even better system would allow the manager to further disaggregate returns to see the effects of each of the proprietary signals used to forecast returns, as well as the effects of constraints and other portfolio requirements. Any system will be more accurate if it can account for daily trading and changes in portfolio exposures. Currently, such systems are not available from outside vendors and need to be developed in-house.

Investors should also compare realized risks to expectations. If realized risk is within a reasonable band around the target, then the manager can assume the risk management techniques are working as intended and no action is required. If realized risk is further from target, the situation may require closer examination, and if realized risk is far from target, some action is usually called for. Investors should monitor realized risk over short intervals such as 20 or 60 days, as well as longer intervals, such as one and

---

[15]Kenneth A. Kavajecz and Donald B. Keim, "Packaging Liquidity: Blind Auctions and Transaction Cost Efficiencies," *Journal of Financial and Quantitative Analysis* 40 (2005): 465–492.

three years. Moreover, investors should monitor the sources of risk to make sure the portfolio is not getting excessive risk from unintended sources, and is getting enough risk from intended sources.[16]

Finally, it is important to monitor trading costs. Are they above or below the costs assumed when making trading decisions? Are they above or below competitors' costs? Are they too high in an absolute sense? If so, managers may need to improve their trade-cost estimates, trading process, or both. There are many services that can report realized trade costs, but most are available with a significant lag, and are inflexible with respect to how they measure and report these costs. With in-house systems, however, managers can compare a variety of trade-cost estimation techniques and get the feedback in a timely enough fashion to act on the results.

The critical question, of course, is what to do with the results of these monitoring systems: When do variations from expectations warrant refinements to the process? This will depend on the size of the variations and their persistence. For example, a manager probably would not throw out a stock-selection signal after one bad month—no matter how bad—but might want to reconsider after several quarters of poor performance, taking into consideration the economic environment and any external factors that might explain the results. It is also important to compare the underperformance to historical simulations. Have similar periods occurred in the past, and if so, were they followed by improvements? In this case, the underperformance is part of the normal risk in that process and no changes may be called for. If not, there may have been a structural change that invalidates the process going forward—for example, if some of the signals have become overly popular, they may no longer be a source of mispricing.

The portfolio manager also needs to consider the reasons for any differences between expectations and realizations. Was underperformance driven, for instance, by faulty signals, binding portfolio constraints, unintended risk, poor trade execution, or random noise? If constraints are to blame, they may be relaxed (but only if doing so would not violate any investment guidelines or incur excessive risk). Alternatively, if the signals are to blame, the manager must decide whether the deviations from expectations are temporary or more enduring. Similarly, any differences between realized and expected risk could be due to poor risk estimates or poor portfolio construction, with the answer determining the response. Excessive trading costs (versus expectations) could reflect poor trading or poor trade-cost estimates,

---

[16]For a discussion of risk monitoring that relies on the concept of the green, yellow, and red zones to compare realized and targeted risk, see Jacob Rosengarten and Peter Zangari, "Risk Monitoring and Performance Measurement," Chapter 17 in Litterman, *Modern Investment Management: An Equilibrium Approach*.

again with different implications for action. Finally, if performance was the result of random effects, no action is necessary.

In summary, ongoing performance, risk, and trade-cost monitoring is an integral part of the equity portfolio management process and should get equal billing with forecasting, portfolio construction, and trading. Monitoring serves as both quality control and a source of new ideas and process improvements. The more sophisticated the monitoring systems, the more useful they are to the process. And although the implications of monitoring involve subtle judgments and careful analysis, better data should lead to better solutions.

KEY POINTS

- Two popular ways to manage equity portfolios are the traditional, or qualitative, approach and the quantitative approach.
- The equity investment process comprises four primary steps: (1) forecasting returns, risks, and transaction costs; (2) constructing portfolios that maximize expected risk-adjusted return net of transaction costs; (3) trading stocks efficiently; and (4) evaluating results and updating the process.
- There are four closely linked steps to building a quantitative equity return-forecasting model: (1) identifying a set of potential return forecasting variables, or signals; (2) testing the effectiveness of each signal, by itself and together with other signals; (3) determining the appropriate weight for each signal in the model; and (4) blending the model's views with market equilibrium to arrive at reasonable forecasts for expected returns.
- Most quantitative equity portfolio managers use a factor risk model in which individual variances and covariances are expressed as a function of a small set of stock characteristics—such as industry membership, size, and leverage.
- Transaction costs consist of explicit costs, such as commissions and fees; and implicit costs, or market impact. The per-share cost of commissions and fees does not depend on the number of shares traded, whereas market impact costs increase on a per-share basis with the total number of shares traded.
- Tracking error measures a portfolio's risk relative to a benchmark. Tracking error equals the time-series standard deviation of a portfolio's active return, the difference between the portfolio's return and that of the benchmark.

- Information ratio is a measure of return per unit of risk, a portfolio's average active return divided by its tracking error.
- Two widely used ways to construct an efficient portfolio are stratified sampling, which is a rule-based system, and portfolio optimization.
- To trade a list of stocks efficiently, investors must balance opportunity costs and execution price risk against market impact costs. Trading each stock quickly minimizes lost alpha and price uncertainty due to delay, but impatient trading incurs maximum market impact. Trading more patiently over a longer period reduces market impact but incurs larger opportunity costs and short-term execution price risk.
- Once an investment process is operational, it should be constantly reassessed and, if necessary, refined. Thus, managers need systems to monitor realized performance, risk, and trading costs and compare them to prior expectations.
- A good performance monitoring system should be able to determine the degree of over- or underperformance as well as the sources of these excess returns, such as market timing, industry tilts, style differences, and stock selection.

QUESTIONS

1. Going forward, the traditional and quantitative approaches to equity portfolio management are likely to converge: Successful investors will make full use of the best available tools. In fact, many portfolio management teams already combine these two approaches. What are some alternative ways of blending the traditional and quantitative approaches, and what are some strengths of each blended approach?
2. Tracking error—the standard deviation of active returns—is a common measure of a portfolio's ex ante risk. What are some limitations of using expected tracking error to measure the ex ante risk of an equity portfolio? When developing an equity factor risk model, why is it a good idea to include all of the return variables (the variables used to calculate stocks' alphas) as factors in the risk model?
3. When developing an equity factor risk model, why is it a good idea to include all of the return variables (the variables used to calculate stocks' alphas) as factors in the risk model?
4. Two widely used methods for constructing equity portfolios are stratified sampling—a type of rule-based approach—and portfolio optimization. What are some of the advantages and disadvantages of each method?

5. Transaction costs comprise two components: explicit costs, such as commissions and fees; and implicit costs, or market impact. What gives rise to market impacts costs? What are typical characteristics of stocks for which their market impact costs tend to be higher?

CHAPTER 12

Long-Short Equity Portfolios

Bruce I. Jacobs, Ph.D.
Principal
Jacobs Levy Equity Management

Kenneth N. Levy, CFA
Principal
Jacobs Levy Equity Management

To create a long-short equity portfolio, the investor buys "winners"—securities that are expected to do well over the investment horizon—and sells short "losers"—securities that are expected to perform poorly. Unlike traditional, long-only equity investing, long-short investing takes full advantage of the investor's insights. Whereas the traditional investor would act on and potentially benefit only from insights about winning securities, the long-short investor can potentially benefit from insights about winners and losers.[1]

As we will see, by combining long and short positions in a single portfolio, the investor increases flexibility in pursuit of return and in control of risk. This increased flexibility reflects the greater freedom afforded the investor to act on negative insights, and also the freedom from traditional index constraints afforded by the ability to reduce risk by offsetting long and short positions. The potential result is improved performance vis-à-vis a traditional long-only portfolio.

---

[1]The requirement that a portfolio hold only long positions is achieved with a portfolio construction constraint prohibiting short selling. Other constraints often present on portfolios include limits on the investment universe and on portfolio active risk. For discussion of the impact of such constraints, see, for example, Bruce I. Jacobs and Kenneth N. Levy, "The Law of One Alpha," *Journal of Portfolio Management* 21, no. 4 (1995): 78–79; and Bruce I. Jacobs and Kenneth N. Levy, "Residual Risk: How Much Is Too Much?" *Journal of Portfolio Management* 22, no. 3 (1996): 10–16.

A long-short portfolio also offers increased flexibility in asset management. For example, the investor can choose to construct a market-neutral long-short portfolio, which eliminates systematic (market) risk while providing the risks and returns of security selection. Alternatively, the investor can combine a market-neutral long-short portfolio with derivatives that perform in line with a desired market benchmark to create a position that offers the security selection performance of the long-short portfolio on top of the chosen asset's performance. That asset may be the market from which the securities were selected or a totally different market. In this way, any skill in security selection can be "transported" to any desired asset class.

This chapter discusses the construction and characteristics of market-neutral long-short portfolios and equitized long-short portfolios and explains the importance of integrated optimization. A market-neutral long-short portfolio offers the active returns and risks of the securities selected for the portfolio, while eliminating the return and risk of the asset class from which the securities were selected. That asset class return and risk can be added back by combining the market-neutral portfolio with an equity market overlay such as stock index futures. The resulting equitized portfolio will offer the active performance of its market-neutral component plus the passive performance of the equity overlay. The active performance of the market-neutral portfolio can be transported to other asset classes by using other types of overlays, including bond index and foreign currency futures or swaps.

Enhanced active, or 120-20 type, portfolios can provide managers and investors with a wider choice of risk-return trade-offs than long-only, market-neutral long-short, or equitized long-short portfolios can provide. Enhanced active portfolios have short positions equal to some percentage of capital (20% in the case of a 120-20 portfolio) and an equal amount of leveraged long positions. Like an equitized long-short portfolio, the enhanced active portfolio retains full sensitivity to underlying market movements and participates fully in the equity market return. Relaxation of the short-selling constraint allows the enhanced active portfolio to achieve security underweights that a long-only portfolio cannot attain, while the ability to invest the proceeds from short sales in additional long positions allows the portfolio to achieve security overweights that an unleveraged long-only portfolio cannot attain.

CONSTRUCTING A MARKET-NEUTRAL PORTFOLIO

In a market-neutral portfolio, the investor holds approximately equal dollar amounts of long and short positions. Of course, careful attention must be paid to the securities' systematic risks: The long positions' price sensitivities

EXHIBIT 12.1 Market-Neutral Deployment of Capital (millions of dollars)

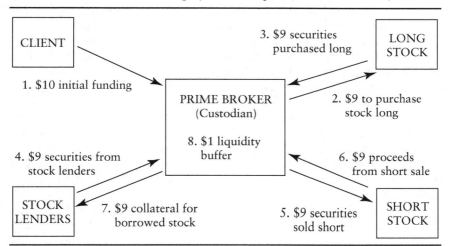

Source: Bruce I. Jacobs and Kenneth N. Levy, "The Long and Short on Long-Short," *Journal of Investing* 6, no. 1 (1997): 73–86.

to broad market movements should virtually offset the short positions' sensitivities, leaving the overall portfolio with negligible systematic risk. This means that the portfolio's value will not rise or fall just because the broad market rises or falls. The portfolio may thus be said to have a beta of zero. The portfolio is not risk-free, however; it retains the risks associated with the selection of the stocks held long and sold short. The value-added provided by insightful security selection, however, should more than compensate for the risk incurred.[2]

Exhibit 12.1 illustrates the operations needed to establish a market-neutral equity strategy, assuming a $10 million initial investment. Keep in mind that these operations are undertaken virtually simultaneously, although they will be discussed in steps.

The Federal Reserve Board requires that short positions be housed in a margin account at a brokerage firm. The first step in setting up a long-short portfolio, then, is to find a "prime broker" to administer the account. This prime broker clears all trades and arranges to borrow the shares to be sold short.

---

[2]See Bruce I. Jacobs and Kenneth N. Levy, "Long/Short Equity Investing," *Journal of Portfolio Management* 20, no. 1 (1993): 52–63 and Bruce I. Jacobs and Kenneth N. Levy, "Investment Analysis: Profiting from a Complex Equity Market," Chapter 2 in *Active Equity Portfolio Management*, ed. Frank J. Fabozzi (Hoboken, N.J.: John Wiley & Sons, 1998).

Exhibit 12.1 shows that, of the initial $10 million investment, $9 million is used to purchase the desired long positions. These are held at the prime broker, where they serve as the collateral necessary, under Federal Reserve Board margin requirements, to establish the desired short positions. The prime broker arranges to borrow the securities to be sold short. Their sale results in cash proceeds, which are delivered to the stock lenders as collateral for the borrowed shares.[3]

Federal Reserve Board Regulation T requires that a margined equity account be at least 50% collateralized to initiate short sales.[4] This means that the investor could buy $10 million of securities and sell short another $10 million, resulting in $20 million in equity positions, long and short. As Exhibit 12.1 shows, however, the investor has bought only $9 million of securities, and sold short an equal amount. The account retains $1 million of the initial investment in cash.

This "liquidity buffer" serves as a pool to meet cash demands on the account. For instance, the account's short positions are marked to market daily. If the prices of the shorted stocks increase, the account must post additional capital with the stock lenders to maintain full collateralization; conversely, if the shorted positions fall in price, the (now overcollateralized) lenders release funds to the long-short account. The liquidity buffer may also be used to reimburse the stock lenders for dividends owed on the shares sold short, although dividends received on stocks held long may be able to meet this cash need. In general, a liquidity buffer equal to 10% of the initial investment is sufficient.

The liquidity buffer will earn interest for the market-neutral account. We assume the interest earned approximates the Treasury bill rate. The $9 million in cash proceeds from the short sales, posted as collateral with the stock lenders, also earns interest. The interest earned is typically allocated among the lenders, the prime broker, and the market-neutral account; the lenders retain a small portion as a lending fee, the prime broker retains a portion to cover expenses and provide some profit, and the long-short account receives the rest. The exact distribution is a matter for negotiation, but we assume the amount rebated to the investor (the "short rebate") approximates the Treasury-bill rate. The investor may incur a larger or a smaller haircut than we have assumed. Retail investors who sell short rarely receive any of the interest on the proceeds.

The overall return to the market-neutral equity portfolio thus has two components—an interest component and an equity component. The

---

[3]In practice, lenders of stock will usually demand that collateral equal something over 100% of the value of the securities lent (usually 102% to 105%).

[4]"Reg T" does not cover U.S. Treasury or municipal bonds or bond funds. Furthermore, Reg T can be circumvented by various means.

performances of the stocks held long and sold short will determine the equity component. As we will see below, this component will be independent of the performance of the equity market from which the stocks have been selected.

Market Neutrality Illustrated

The top half of Exhibit 12.2 illustrates the performance of a market-neutral equity portfolio. It assumes the market rises by 30%, while the long positions rise by 33% and the short positions by 27%. The 33% return increases the value of the $9 million in long positions to $11.97 million, for a $2.97 million gain. The 27% return on the shares sold short increases their value from $9 million to $11.43 million; as the shares are sold short, this translates into a $2.43 million loss for the portfolio.

The net gain from equity positions equals $540,000, or $2.97 million minus $2.43 million. This represents a 6.0% return on the initial equity

EXHIBIT 12.2 Market-Neutral Hypothetical Performance in Bull and Bear Markets (millions of dollars)

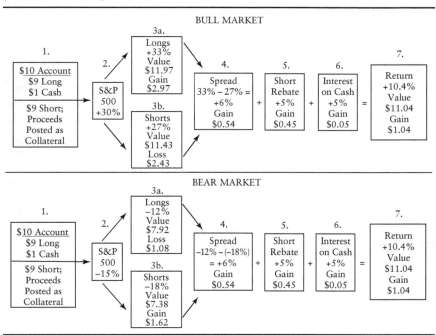

Source: Bruce I. Jacobs and Kenneth N. Levy, "The Long and Short on Long-Short," *Journal of Investing* 6, no. 1 (1997): 73–86.

investment of $9 million, equal to the spread between the returns on the long and short positions (33% minus 27%). As the initial equity investment represented only 90% of the invested capital, however, the equity component's performance translates into a 5.4% return on the initial investment (90% of 6.0%). Of course, if the shorts had outperformed the longs, the return from the equity portion of the portfolio would be negative.

We assume the short rebate (the interest received on the cash proceeds from the short sales) equals 5%. This amounts to $450,000 (5.0% of $9 million). The interest earned on the liquidity buffer adds another $50,000 (5.0% of $1 million). (A lower rate would result, of course, in a lower return.) Thus, at the end of the period, the $10 million initial investment has grown to $11.04 million. The long-short portfolio return of 10.4% comprises a 5% return from interest earnings and a 5.4% return from the equity positions, long and short.

The bottom half of Exhibit 12.2 illustrates the portfolio's performance assuming the market declines by 15%. The long and short positions exhibit the same market-relative performances as above, with the longs falling by 12% and the shorts falling by 18%. In this case, the decline in the prices of the securities held long results in an ending value of $7.92 million, for a loss of $1.08 million. The shares sold short, however, decline in value to $7.38 million, so the portfolio gains $1.62 million from the short positions. The equity positions thus post a gain of $540,000—exactly the same as the net equity result experienced in the up-market case. The interest earnings from the short rebate and the liquidity buffer are the same as when the market rose, so the overall portfolio again grows from $10 million to $11.04 million, for a return of 10.4%. Obviously, if the shorts had fallen less than the longs, or interest rates had declined, the return would be lower.

A market-neutral equity portfolio is designed to return the same amount whether the equity market rises or falls. A properly constructed market-neutral portfolio, if it performs as expected, will incur virtually no systematic, or market, risk; its return will equal its interest earnings plus the net return on (or the spread between) the long and short positions. The equity return spread is purely active, reflecting the investor's stock selection skills; this return spread is not diluted (or augmented) by the underlying market's return.

THE IMPORTANCE OF INTEGRATED OPTIMIZATION

The ability to sell short constitutes a material advantage for a market-neutral investor compared with a long-only investor. Consider, for example, a long-only investor who has an extremely negative view about a typical stock. The investor's ability to benefit from this insight is very limited. The most the investor can do is exclude the stock from the portfolio, in which case the portfolio will have about a 0.01% underweight in the stock, relative to the underlying market (as the median-capitalization stock in the Russell 3000 universe has a weighting of 0.01%). Those who do not consider this to be a material constraint should consider what its effect would be on the investor's ability to overweight a typical stock. It would mean the investor could hold no more than a 0.02% long position in the stock—a 0.01% overweight—no matter how attractive its expected return.

The ability to short, by increasing the investor's leeway to act on his or her insights, has the potential to enhance returns from active security selection. The scope of the improvement, however, depends critically on the way in which the portfolio is constructed. In particular, an integrated optimization that considers both long and short positions simultaneously not only frees the investor from the nonnegativity constraint imposed on long-only portfolios, but also frees the portfolio from the restrictions imposed by securities' benchmark weights. To see this, it is useful to examine in some detail the ways in which market-neutral portfolios can be constructed, and their implications for portfolio performance.

For instance, some investors construct market-neutral portfolios by combining a long-only portfolio, perhaps a preexisting one, with a short-only portfolio. This results in a long-plus-short portfolio. The long side of the portfolio is identical to a long-only portfolio, hence it offers no benefits in terms of incremental return or reduced risk. Furthermore, the short side of the portfolio is statistically equivalent to the long side, hence to the long-only portfolio. In effect,

$$\alpha_L = \alpha_S = \alpha_{LO}$$
$$\omega_L = \omega_S = \omega_{LO}$$

The excess return or alpha, α_L, of the long side of the long-plus-short portfolio will equal the alpha of the short side, α_S, which will equal the alpha of the long-only portfolio, α_{LO}. Furthermore, the residual risk of the long side of the long-plus-short portfolio, ω_L, will equal the residual risk of the short side, ω_S, which will equal the residual risk of the long-only portfolio, ω_{LO}.

These equivalencies reflect the fact that all the portfolios, the long-only portfolio and the long and short components of the long-plus-short portfolio, are constructed relative to a benchmark index. Each portfolio is active in pursuing excess return relative to the underlying benchmark only insofar as it holds securities in weights that depart from their benchmark weights. However, departures from benchmark weights introduce residual risk. Controlling portfolio risk thus involves balancing expected excess (to benchmark) returns against the added risk they introduce. In this balancing act, the investor faces the probability of having to forgo some increment of expected return in order to reduce portfolio residual risk. Portfolio construction is benchmark-constrained.[5]

Consider, for example, an investor who does not have the ability to discriminate between good and bad oil stocks, or who believes that no oil stock will significantly out- or underperform the underlying benchmark in the near future. In long-plus-short, this investor may have to hold some oil stocks in the long portfolio and short some oil stocks in the short portfolio, if only to control each portfolio's residual risk relative to the benchmark.

In long-plus-short, the advantage offered by the flexibility to short is also curtailed by the need to control risk by holding or shorting securities in benchmark-like weights. The ratio of the performance of the long-plus-short portfolio to that of the long-only portfolio can be expressed as follows:

$$\frac{IR_{L+S}}{IR_{LO}} = \sqrt{\frac{2}{1 + \rho_{L+S}}}$$

where IR is the information ratio, or the ratio of excess return to residual risk, α/w, and ρ_{L+S} is the correlation between the alphas of the long and short sides of the long-plus-short portfolio. If this correlation is less than one, the long-plus-short portfolio will enjoy greater diversification and reduced risk relative to a long-only portfolio, for an improvement in IR. However, a long-only portfolio can derive a similar benefit by adding a less than fully correlated asset with comparable risk and return, so this is not a benefit unique to long-short.

Note that the long-only portfolio can also engage in leverage, just like the long-plus-short portfolio. However, a long-only portfolio would have to borrow funds to achieve leverage, and this can have tax consequences for otherwise tax-exempt investors; borrowing shares to sell short does not result in unrelated business taxable income. Furthermore, derivatives such as index futures contracts can be used to make the long-only portfolio market neutral—just like the long-short portfolio. Thus neither market neutrality, nor leverage, nor even shorting alone constitutes an inherent advantage over long-only portfolio construction.[6]

---

[5]Bruce I. Jacobs and Kenneth N. Levy, "More on Long-Short Strategies," *Financial Analysts Journal* 51, no. 2 (1995): 88–90.
[6]See Bruce I. Jacobs and Kenneth N. Levy, "20 Myths About Long-Short," *Financial Analysts Journal* 52, no. 5 (1996): 81–85; and Bruce I. Jacobs and Kenneth N. Levy, "The Long and Short on Long-Short," *Journal of Investing* 6, no. 1 (1997): 73–86.

The Real Benefits of Long-Short

As noted by Jacobs, Levy, and Starer, the real benefits of long-short portfolio construction emerge only when the portfolio is conceived of and constructed as a single, integrated portfolio of long and short positions.[7] In an integrated optimization, selection of the securities to be held long is determined simultaneously with the selection of the securities to be sold short, taking into account the expected returns of the individual securities, the standard deviations of those returns, and the correlations between them, as well as the investor's tolerance for risk. The result is a single portfolio, not one long portfolio and one short portfolio.

With integrated optimization, a long-short portfolio is not constrained by benchmark weights. Once an underlying benchmark has been used to determine the systematic risks of the candidate securities, its role in portfolio construction is effectively over. The offsetting market sensitivities of the aggregate long and aggregate short positions control risk. The investor is not constrained to moving away from or toward benchmark weights. To establish a 1% overweight or a 1% underweight, the investor merely has to allocate 1% of capital long or allocate 1% of capital short.

Suppose, for example, that an investor's strongest insights are about oil stocks, some of which are expected to do especially well and some especially poorly. The investor does not have to restrict the portfolio's holdings of oil stocks to benchmark-like weights in order to control the portfolio's exposure to oil sector risk. The investor can allocate much of the portfolio to oil stocks, held long and sold short. The offsetting long and short positions control the portfolio's exposure to the oil factor.

Conversely, suppose the investor has no insights into oil stock behavior. Unlike the long-only and long-plus-short investors discussed above, the integrated market-neutral investor can totally exclude oil stocks from the portfolio. The exclusion of oil stocks does not increase portfolio risk because the integrated market-neutral portfolio's risk is independent of any security's benchmark weight. At the same time, freed of the need to hold deadweight in the form of securities that offer no abnormal expected returns, the investor can allocate more capital to securities that do offer expected abnormal returns.

Just as one cannot attribute the qualities of water, its wetness say, to its hydrogen or oxygen components separately, one cannot reasonably dissect

---

[7]Bruce I. Jacobs, Kenneth N. Levy, and David Starer, "On the Optimality of Long-Short Strategies," *Financial Analysts Journal* 54, no. 2 (1998): 40–51; and Bruce. I. Jacobs, Kenneth N. Levy, and David Starer, "Long-Short Portfolio Management: An Integrated Approach," *Journal of Portfolio Management* 25, no. 2 (Winter 1999): 23–32.

the performance of an integrated market-neutral portfolio into one element attributable to long positions alone and another attributable to short positions alone. Only jointly do the long and short positions define the portfolio. Rather than being measurable as long and short performances in excess of an underlying benchmark, the performance of an integrated long-short portfolio is measurable as the overall return on the long and short positions—or the spread between the long and short returns—relative to their risk. Compared with the excess return/residual risk of long-only management, this performance should be enhanced by the elimination of benchmark constraints, which allows the market-neutral portfolio increased flexibility to implement investment insights, both long and short.

ADDING BACK A MARKET RETURN

A market-neutral portfolio offers an active return from the specific securities the investor selects to hold long or sell short, plus a return representing an interest rate. The neutral strategy does not reflect either the return or the risk of the underlying equity market. As Exhibit 12.2 illustrated, the value added from stock selection skill, represented by the long-short spread, is independent of the performance of the equity asset class from which the securities were selected.

That value added can be transported to other asset classes through the use of derivatives overlays. An investor can, for example, add back the risk and return of the equity market by purchasing stock index futures equal in amount to the investment in the market-neutral strategy. The resulting "equitized" long-short portfolio captures the performance of the underlying market while allowing the investor to benefit from the enhanced flexibility in stock selection afforded by long-short management.

Exhibit 12.3 illustrates the deployment of capital for equitized long-short portfolio construction. Note that the major difference between Exhibit 12.3 and Exhibit 12.1, other than the addition of the $10 million of stock index futures, is the size of the liquidity buffer. As noted, the liquidity buffer is used, among other things, to meet marks to market on the short positions. With an equitized strategy, an increase in the price of short positions induced by a market rise is generally accompanied by an increase in the price of the futures contract held long; the marks to market on the futures can be used to meet the marks to market on the short positions. The capital freed up from the liquidity buffer is used to margin the futures positions. We assume futures can be purchased on margin of about 5% of the face value of the contracts purchased. Thus, in Exhibit 12.3 as in Exhibit 12.1, $9 million of the initial $10 million investment is assumed available for purchase of securities.

EXHIBIT 12.3 Equitized Deployment of Capital (millions of dollars)

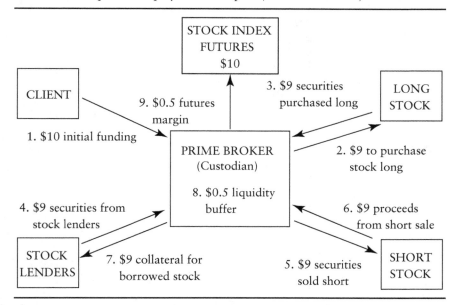

Source: Bruce I. Jacobs and Kenneth N. Levy, "The Long and Short on Long-Short," *Journal of Investing* 6, no. 1 (1997): 73–86.

Exhibit 12.4 illustrates the performance of the equitized long-short portfolio in bull and bear market scenarios, using the same assumptions as Exhibit 12.2. Returns to the long-short portfolio are the same as in Exhibit 12.2. Cash returns are also the same, as the reduced interest from the smaller liquidity buffer is combined with the interest earned on the futures margin.

Total returns on the portfolios in Exhibits 12.2 and 12.4 differ markedly, however. The entire difference is due to the performance of the overall market, which is reflected in the equitized but not the market-neutral portfolio. Unlike the market-neutral portfolio, the equitized portfolio does not behave the same in both bull and bear market scenarios. Its overall return is sensitive to market movements. At the same time, it benefits fully from the return spread of the long-short portfolio, which (insofar as it is positive) serves to augment the increase from an up market and to cushion the decline from a down market.

Return Transportability

In essence, the return on a market-neutral portfolio represents a return to security selection alone, independent of the overall return to the market

EXHIBIT 12.4 Equitized Hypothetical Performance in Bull and Bear Markets (millions of dollars)

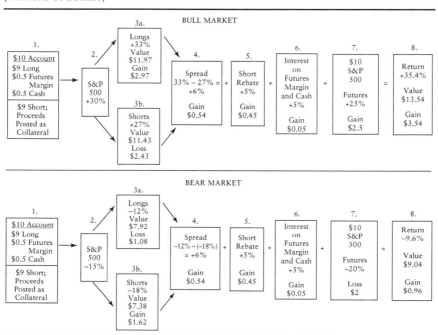

Source: Bruce I. Jacobs and Kenneth N. Levy, "The Long and Short on Long-Short," *Journal of Investing* 6, no. 1 (1997): 73–86.

from which the securities are selected. This return, and all the benefits of long-short construction that it reflects, can be transported to other asset classes through the use of derivatives.[8]

The equitized long-short portfolio transports the return to the equity market class, adding the security selection return (and its associated risk) to the equity market return (and its risk). Other derivatives overlays may be used to establish exposures to fixed income, foreign equity, and so forth.

The "transportability" of the long-short spread has at least two implications for investment management. First, it implies that the identity of a long-short portfolio is flexible. A market-neutral long-short portfolio offers a return (and risk) from security selection on top of a cash return. An equitized

---

[8]See Bruce I. Jacobs and Kenneth N. Levy, "Alpha Transport With Derivatives," *Journal of Portfolio Management* 25, no. 5 (1999): 55–60; and James Rutter, "How to Make Volatility Pay—The Next Step Forward Could Be Portable Alpha," *Global Investor*, June 2003, 8–9.

long-short portfolio offers the security selection return on top of the equity asset class return. Long-short portfolios do not constitute a separate asset class; the existing asset class to which they belong will depend upon the choice of derivatives overlay.

Second, and of perhaps more practical importance, transportability allows the investor to separate security selection skills from asset allocation decisions. This is not an inconsiderable benefit. The task of combining asset allocation with security selection often involves a trade-off. The investor may be able to find active managers who have demonstrated an ability to add value, but the universes exploited by these managers may not encompass the asset class desired by the investor. More often than not, it is the return from security selection that is sacrificed.

Consider the case of an investor who has both large-cap and small-cap equity managers. On the one hand, to the extent that small-cap stocks are less efficiently priced than their large-cap counterparts, the potential of the small-cap manager to add value relative to an underlying small-cap universe may be greater than the potential of the large-cap manager to add value relative to an underlying large-cap universe. The investor may thus want to allocate more to the small-cap than the large-cap manager.

On the other hand, small-cap stocks may be considered too risky in general, or may be expected to underperform larger-cap stocks. In the interest of optimizing overall fund return and risk, the investor may wish to limit the allocation to the small-cap manager and allocate significantly more to the large-cap manager. In that case, however, the investor sacrifices the potential alpha from small-cap security selection in exchange for overall asset class return and risk. The investor's asset allocation decision comes down to a choice between sacrificing security selection return in favor of asset class performance and sacrificing asset class performance in favor of security selection return.

With alpha transport, investors need no longer face such Solomonic decisions. Market-neutral portfolio construction techniques and derivatives can be used to liberate managers, and manager performance, from their underlying asset classes. Investors, or managers, can deploy derivatives to transport the skill of any manager to any asset class. Alpha transport enables the overall fund to add value from both asset and manager allocation.

Enhanced Active 120-20 Portfolio

Two papers by Jacobs, Levy, and Starer explain how to optimize the utility of a portfolio that combines a position in a desired benchmark with long and short positions in benchmark securities.[9] As with the market-neutral

[9]See footnote 6 for references.

equity portfolio, the answer lies in integration: Portfolio construction considers explicitly the risks and returns of the individual securities and the benchmark holding, as well as their correlations.

These papers laid the foundation for enhanced active equity strategies such as 120-20 and 130-30 portfolios. Such portfolios can provide managers and investors with a wider choice of risk-return trade-offs than long-only, market-neutral long-short, or equitized long-short portfolios can provide.

Enhanced active equity portfolios have short positions equal to some percentage of capital (generally 20% or 30%, but possibly 100% or more) and an equal amount of leveraged long positions. A 120-20 portfolio with initial capital of $10 million, for example, sells $2 million of securities short and uses the proceeds from the short sales plus the initial capital to purchase $12 million of securities long.[10] The $2 million in short positions offsets the $2 million in leveraged long positions, leaving a net market exposure of 100%. Like an equitized long-short portfolio, the enhanced active 120-20 portfolio retains full sensitivity to underlying market movements (a beta of one) and participates fully in the equity market return.

If a portfolio manager is able to distinguish between securities that will perform better than the underlying benchmark and those that will perform worse, the 120-20 portfolio will achieve a return higher than the return on the underlying benchmark (at a higher risk level). It can also be expected to outperform a long-only portfolio based on comparable insights because relaxation of the short-selling constraint allows the 120-20 portfolio to achieve security underweights that a long-only portfolio cannot attain, while the ability to invest the proceeds from short sales in additional long positions allows the portfolio to achieve security overweights that an unleveraged long-only portfolio cannot attain. Enhanced active equity strategies thus afford managers greater flexibility in portfolio construction, which allows for fuller exploitation of investment insights.[11]

---

[10]With modern prime brokerage structures ("enhanced prime brokerage"), investors can establish a stock loan account with a broker; rather than being a customer with the broker, the investor serves as a counterparty to the stock loan transaction. This allows the investor to make additional long purchases without borrowing on margin (an important consideration for tax-exempt investors, as borrowing on margin may subject such investors to unrelated business taxable income). Such structures also eliminate the need for a cash buffer, as the shares borrowed to sell short are collateralized by the securities the investor holds long, rather than by short-sale proceeds.
[11]See Bruce I. Jacobs and Kenneth N. Levy, "Enhanced Active Equity Strategies: Relaxing the Long-Only Constraint in the Pursuit of Active Return," *Journal of Portfolio Management* 32, no. 3 (2006): 45–55; and Bruce I. Jacobs and Kenneth N. Levy, "20 Myths About Enhanced Active 120-20 Strategies," *Financial Analysts Journal* 63, no. 4 (2007): 19–26.

Enhanced active equity portfolios are equivalent to equitized market-neutral long-short portfolios in terms of market exposure and security active weights.[12] The equivalency can be observed by "trimming" the equitized portfolio; trimming eliminates any overlap between long and short positions in the same securities.[13] The enhanced active portfolio is, however, more compact and uses less leverage than the equivalent equitized market-neutral portfolio. Furthermore, because the enhanced active equity portfolio uses individual securities rather than derivative overlays to achieve market exposure, it can establish an exposure to any equity benchmark; it is not, like the equitized market-neutral portfolio, dependent on the availability of liquid derivatives. Of course, if the investor wishes to transport the active returns from a market-neutral portfolio to a benchmark that is substantially different from the universe from which the securities were chosen, a market-neutral portfolio in conjunction with an overlay is the preferable course.

SOME CONCERNS ADDRESSED

Long-short construction maximizes the benefit obtained from potentially valuable investment insights by eliminating long-only's constraint on short selling and the need to converge to securities' benchmark weights in order to control portfolio risk. While long-short offers advantages over long-only, however, it also involves complications not encountered in long-only management.

Many of the complications are related to the use of short selling. For example, shares the investor desires to sell short may not be available for borrowing, or shares that have been sold short may be called back by their lenders. Shares sold short are subject to recall by the lender at any time. In most cases, the prime broker will be able to find alternative lenders for the securities subject to recall, but if these are not available, the long-short investor will be subject to "buy-ins" and have to cover the short positions. One also occasionally hears about a "short squeeze," in which speculators buy up lendable stock to force a buy-in at elevated prices. This will be more of a problem for dedicated short sellers who take concentrated positions in

---

[12]See Bruce I. Jacobs and Kenneth N. Levy, "Enhanced Active Equity Portfolios Are Trim Equitized Long-Short Portfolios," *Journal of Portfolio Management* 33, no. 4 (2007): 19–25.

[13]See Bruce I. Jacobs, Kenneth N. Levy, and Harry M. Markowitz, "Portfolio Optimization with Factors, Scenarios, and Realistic Short Positions," *Operations Research* 53, no. 4 (2005): 586–599; and Bruce I. Jacobs, Kenneth N. Levy, and Harry M. Markowitz, "Trimability and Fast Optimization of Long-Short Portfolios," *Financial Analysts Journal* 62, no. 2 (2006): 36–46.

illiquid stocks than for a long-short investor holding small positions diversified across many stocks.

The cost associated with securing and administering lendable stocks averages 25 to 30 basis points. Harder-to-borrow names will require a higher haircut and may even entail negative interest (that is, the short seller pays, rather than receives, interest). This cost is incurred as a haircut on the short rebate the investor receives from the interest earned on the short sale proceeds.

A more serious impediment to long-short strategies may be the discomfort many investors feel with the idea of shorting. While it is true that the risk of a short position is theoretically unlimited because there is no bound on a rise in the price of the shorted security, this source of risk is considerably mitigated in practice. It is unlikely, for example, that the prices of all the securities sold short in a market-neutral portfolio will rise dramatically at the same time, with no offsetting increases in the prices of the securities held long. Also, the trading imperatives of market neutral, which call for keeping dollar amounts of longs and shorts roughly equalized on an ongoing basis, will tend to limit short-side losses because shorts are covered as their prices rise. And if a gap-up in the price of an individual security does not afford the opportunity to cover, the overall portfolio will still be protected provided it is well diversified.

Other perceived impediments to long-short investing are just as illusory. Take, for example, the issue of trading costs. A long-short portfolio that takes full advantage of the allowed leverage will engage in about twice as much trading activity as a comparable unleveraged long-only strategy. The additional trading costs, however, must be weighed against the expanded potential for return. Most investors will be willing to pay the additional trading costs in exchange for the expected incremental return. Nevertheless, leverage is not an inherent part of long-short. Given capital of $10 million, for example, an investor could choose to invest $5 million long and sell $5 million short; trading activity for the resulting long-short portfolio would be roughly equivalent to that for a $10 million long-only portfolio.

The differential between management fees for a long-short versus a long-only portfolio is also largely a reflection of the leverage involved. If one considers the management fee per dollar of securities positions, rather than per dollar of invested capital, there should not be much difference between long-short and long-only. And if one considers the amount of active management provided per fee dollar, long-short may be revealed as substantially less costly than long-only. As we've noted, long-only portfolios contain a sizeable "hidden passive" element; only overweights and underweights relative to the benchmark are truly active. By contrast, virtually the entire long-short portfolio is active.

Because it does not have to converge to securities' benchmark weights in order to control risk, a long-short strategy can take larger positions in securities with higher (and lower) expected returns compared with a long-only portfolio whose ability to take active positions is limited by benchmark weights. It does not necessarily follow, however, that a long-short portfolio is riskier than a long-only portfolio. The long-short portfolio will incur more risk only to the extent that it takes more active positions and/or engages in more leverage. Both the portfolio's "activeness" and its degree of leverage are within the explicit control of the investor. Furthermore, proper portfolio construction should ensure that any incremental risks and costs are compensated by expected incremental returns.

EVALUATING LONG-SHORT

Besides analyzing the operational considerations involved in long-short portfolio construction and management, investors need to evaluate carefully the value-added potential of the security selection approach underpinning it. Any active equity management approach can be adapted to a long-short mode. In the past, investors (including hedge funds) that engaged in short selling tended to focus on in-depth fundamental analyses of specific companies, as they attempted to exploit given situations such as perceived fraud or expected bankruptcy. As short selling began to be incorporated into structured long-short portfolios, however, a more quantitative approach took hold. Today, most long-short managers use a quantitative rather than a traditional judgmental approach.

Traditional judgmental approaches, because of their in-depth nature, are usually limited in the number of stocks they can cover. This in turn limits the range of opportunities that can be exploited by the portfolio. Traditional analyses also generally result in subjective buy, hold, and sell recommendations that are difficult to translate into directions for building portfolios.

By contrast, quantitative approaches can be applied to a large universe of stocks, which tends to increase the number of potential investment opportunities detected. A quantitative process also generally results in numerical estimates of risk and return for the whole range of securities in the universe. Short sale candidates fall out naturally as the lowest-ranking members of the universe. Furthermore, the numerical estimates are eminently suitable inputs for portfolio optimization, allowing for the construction of portfolios that take explicit account of risk in their pursuit of return.

Of course, the performance of a long-short portfolio ultimately depends on the goodness of the insights going into it, whether those insights come from a judgmental or a quantitative approach. We believe that the best insights into security behavior come out of a quantitative approach that grapples with the complexity of the stock market.[14] The market is subject to myriad influences. Mispricing arises from investors' cognitive errors, such as herding or overreaction, and from companies' differing abilities to adapt to changing economic fundamentals. Furthermore, the nature of mispricings changes over time. The market's complexity demands quantitative modeling guided by human insight and ongoing research.

The return to any one stock may demonstrate an exploitable (that is, predictable) response to a number of variables. It is important to examine all these variables simultaneously, so as to isolate the effect of each one. For example, does a consistent abnormal return to small-cap stocks reflect their relatively low P/E levels? A lack of coverage by institutional investors? Tax-related buying and selling? Or some combination of factors? Only by "disentangling" effects can one uncover real profit opportunities.[15]

Good insights also demand breadth of inquiry combined with depth of analysis. Breadth of inquiry maximizes the number of insightful profit opportunities that can be incorporated into a portfolio and provides for greater consistency of return. Depth of analysis, achieved by taking into account the intricacies of stock price behavior, maximizes the "goodness" of such insights, or the potential of each one to add value.[16] Breadth and depth together help to ensure consistent value-added, whether in long-short or long-only portfolio management. Long-short portfolio construction, with the flexibility it affords in pursuing returns and controlling risk, enhances the ability to implement, and profit from, these insights.

KEY POINTS

- Market-neutral long-short portfolios purchase undervalued securities that are expected to increase in price over the investment horizon while selling short an approximately equal dollar amount of overvalued securities that are expected to decline in price.
- Choosing long and short positions with roughly similar average sensitivities to the overall equity market essentially eliminates portfolio exposure to the underlying market (portfolio systematic return and risk).

[14]See James A. White, "How Jacobs and Levy Crunch Stocks for Buying—and Selling," *Wall Street Journal*, March 20, 1991, C1, C9.
[15]See Bruce I. Jacobs and Kenneth N. Levy, "Disentangling Equity Return Regularities: New Insights and Investment Opportunities," *Financial Analysts Journal* 44, no. 3 (1988): 18–44; and Bruce I. Jacobs and Kenneth N. Levy, *Equity Management: Quantitative Analysis for Stock Selection* (New York: McGraw-Hill, 2000).
[16]See Bruce I. Jacobs and Kenneth N. Levy, "Investment Analysis: Profiting from a Complex Market," op. cit.

- Portfolio construction should use an integrated optimization that considers long and short portfolio positions simultaneously; combining a long-only portfolio with a separately optimized short-only portfolio offers no real benefits over a long-only portfolio.
- Integrated optimization frees a long-short portfolio from benchmark constraints and thus improves the portfolio's ability to pursue returns and control risks.
- Integrated optimization is vital not only for market-neutral portfolio construction, but also for equitized long-short portfolios and enhanced active equity strategies such as 120-20 and 130-30 portfolios.
- While a properly constructed market-neutral long-short portfolio does not offer the systematic return and risk of the market from which the securities were selected, that systematic return and risk can be added back by purchasing an equity market overlay such as stock index futures.
- An *equitized* long-short portfolio combines the passive performance of the underlying market with the active performance of a market-neutral portfolio (the returns and risks from the individual securities held long and sold short).
- In place of stock index futures, other passive overlays can be used to provide exposures to other asset classes.
- While long-short portfolios are often depicted as significantly riskier or more costly than long-only portfolios, they are not necessarily either.
- Compared with long-only portfolios based on the same set of insights, long-short portfolios offer investors the opportunity for enhanced portfolio performance and greater flexibility in investment management.

QUESTIONS

1. Name three potential advantages of using short as well as long positions in a portfolio.

2. What is a liquidity buffer, and why might it be necessary?

3. What are the sources of overall return to the market-neutral portfolio?

4. Will a hypothetically ideal market-neutral long-short portfolio earn more if the underlying equity market rises by 15% than if the market falls by 15%?

5. What is integrated optimization and why is it so important?

6. How can a market-neutral long-short portfolio be modified to benefit from the returns available from the overall market?

7. How does an equitized long-short portfolio's return differ from a market-neutral long-short portfolio's return?

8. What's an "enhanced active" 120-20 portfolio?

9. What are some of the issues that may have to be addressed in constructing long-short portfolios?

10. What is the most important determinant of success for a long-short portfolio?

CHAPTER 13

Multifactor Equity Risk Models

Frank J. Fabozzi, Ph.D., CFA, CPA
Professor in the Practice of Finance
Yale School of Management

Raman Vardharaj, CFA
Vice President and Portfolio Manager
OppenheimerFunds

Frank J. Jones, Ph.D.
Professor, Accounting and Finance Department
San Jose State University

Thus far, several chapters have discussed multifactor risk models for equity portfolio management. In Chapter 5, we described the theory of asset pricing in terms of risk factors—the arbitrage pricing theory—and mentioned the different types of multifactor risk models—statistical models, macro models, and fundamental models. The most popular type of model used in practice is the fundamental model. While some asset management firms develop their own model, most use commercially available models. While the development of a fundamental multifactor risk model involves a substantial amount of sophisticated statistical analysis and testing, model development is not the focus of this chapter. Instead, this chapter explains how a multifactor risk model is used in practice to (1) select securities, (2) quantify the risk exposure of a portfolio relative to a benchmark index, (3) construct a portfolio and control risk, and (4) measure performance.

In our illustration, we will use an old version of a model developed by Barra (now MSCI Barra). While that model has been updated, the discussion and illustrations provide the essential points for appreciating the value of using multifactor equity models.

MODEL DESCRIPTION AND ESTIMATION

The basic relationship to be estimated in a multifactor risk model is

$$R_i - R_f = \beta_{i,F1} R_{F1} + \beta_{i,F2} R_{F2} + \ldots + \beta_{i,FH} R_{FH} + e_i$$

where

R_i = rate of return on stock i
R_f = risk-free rate of return
$\beta_{i,Fj}$ = sensitivity of stock i to risk factor j
R_{Fj} = rate of return on risk factor j
e_i = nonfactor (specific) return on security i

The above function is referred to as a *return generating function*.

Fundamental factor models use company and industry attributes and market data as "descriptors." Examples are price/earnings ratios, book/price ratios, estimated earnings growth, and trading activity. The estimation of a fundamental factor model begins with an analysis of historical stock returns and descriptors about a company. In the Barra model, for example, the process of identifying the risk factors begins with monthly returns for 1,900 companies that the descriptors must explain. Descriptors are not the "risk factors" but instead they are the candidates for risk factors. The descriptors are selected in terms of their ability to explain stock returns. That is, all of the descriptors are potential risk factors but only those that appear to be important in explaining stock returns are used in constructing risk factors.

Once the descriptors that are statistically significant in explaining stock returns are identified, they are grouped into "risk indexes" to capture related company attributes. For example, descriptors such as market leverage, book leverage, debt-to-equity ratio, and company's debt rating are combined to obtain a risk index referred to as "leverage." Thus, a risk index is a combination of descriptors that captures a particular attribute of a company.

The Barra fundamental multifactor risk model, the "E3 model" being the latest version, has 13 risk indexes and 55 industry groups. (The descriptors are the same variables that have been consistently found to be important in many well-known academic studies on risk factors.) Exhibit 13.1 lists the 13 risk indexes in the Barra model.[1] Also shown in the exhibit are the descriptors used to construct each risk index. The 55 industry classifications are grouped into 13 sectors. For example, the following three

---

[1]For a more detailed description of each descriptor, see Appendix A in Barra, *Risk Model Handbook United States Equity: Version 3* (Berkeley, CA: Barra, 1998). A listing of the 55 industry groups is provided in Exhibit 13.9.

EXHIBIT 13.1 Barra E3 Model Risk Definitions

Descriptors in Risk Index	Risk Index
Beta times sigma	Volatility
Daily standard deviation	
High-low price	
Log of stock price	
Cumulative range	
Volume beta	
Serial dependence	
Option-implied standard deviation	
Relative strength	Momentum
Historical alpha	
Log of market capitalization	Size
Cube of log of market capitalization	Size Nonlinearity
Share turnover rate (annual)	Trading Activity
Share turnover rate (quarterly)	
Share turnover rate (monthly)	
Share turnover rate (five years)	
Indicator for forward split	
Volume to variance	
Payout ratio over five years	Growth
Variability in capital structure	
Growth rate in total assets	
Earnings growth rate over the last five years	
Analyst-predicted earnings growth	
Recent earnings change	
Analyst-predicted earnings-to-price	Earnings Yield
Trailing annual earnings-to-price	
Historical earnings-to-price	
Book-to-price ratio	Value
Variability in earnings	Earnings Variability
Variability in cash flows	
Extraordinary items in earnings	
Standard deviation of analyst-predicted earnings-to-price	
Market leverage	Leverage
Book leverage	
Debt to total assets	
Senior debt rating	
Exposure to foreign currencies	Currency Sensitivity
Predicted dividend yield	Dividend Yield
Indicator for firms outside US-E3 estimation universe	Non-Estimation Universe Indicator

Adapted from Table 8-1 in Barra, *Risk Model Handbook United States Equity: Version 3* (Berkeley, CA: Barra, 1998), 71–73. Adapted with permission.

industries comprise the energy sector: energy reserves and production, oil refining, and oil services. The consumer noncyclicals sector consists of the following five industries: food and beverages, alcohol, tobacco, home products, and grocery stores. The 13 sectors in the Barra model are basic materials, energy, consumer noncylicals, consumer cyclicals, consumer services, industrials, utility, transport, health care, technology, telecommunications, commercial services, and financial.

Given the risk factors, information about the exposure of every stock to each risk factor ($\beta_{i,Fj}$) is estimated using statistical analysis. For a given time period, the rate of return for each risk factor (R_{Fj}) also can be estimated using statistical analysis. The prediction for the expected return can be obtained from equation (1) for any stock. The nonfactor return (e_i) is found by subtracting the actual return for the period for a stock from the return as predicted by the risk factors.

Moving from individual stocks to portfolios, the predicted return for a portfolio can be computed. The exposure to a given risk factor of a portfolio is simply the weighted average of the exposure of each stock in the portfolio to that risk factor. For example, suppose a portfolio has 42 stocks. Suppose further that stocks 1 through 40 are equally weighted in the portfolio at 2.2%, stock 41 is 5% of the portfolio, and stock 42 is 7% of the portfolio. Then the exposure of the portfolio to risk factor j is

$$0.022\ \beta_{1,Fj} + 0.022\ \beta_{2,Fj} + \ldots + 0.022\ \beta_{40,Fj} + 0.050\ \beta_{41,Fj} + 0.007\ \beta_{42,Fj}$$

The nonfactor error term is measured in the same way as in the case of an individual stock. However, in a well-diversified portfolio, the nonfactor error term will be considerably less for the portfolio than for the individual stocks in the portfolio.

The same analysis can be applied to a stock market index because an index is nothing more than a portfolio of stocks.

RISK DECOMPOSITION

The real usefulness of a linear multifactor model lies in the ease with which the risk of a portfolio with several assets can be estimated. Consider a portfolio with 100 assets. Risk is commonly defined as the variance of the portfolio's returns. So, in this case, we need to find the variance–covariance matrix of the 100 assets. That would require us to estimate 100 variances (one for each of the 100 assets) and 4,950 covariances among the 100 assets. That is, in all we need to estimate 5,050 values, a very difficult undertaking. Suppose, instead, that we use a three-factor model to estimate risk. Then, we need to estimate (1) the three factor loadings for each of the 100 assets (i.e., 300 values), (2) the six values of the factor variance–covariance matrix, and (3) the 100 residual variances (one for each asset). That is, we need to estimate only 406 values in all. This represents a nearly 90% reduction from having to estimate 5,050 values, a huge improvement. Thus, with well-chosen factors, we can substantially reduce the work involved in estimating a portfolio's risk.

Multifactor risk models allow a manager and a client to decompose risk in order to assess the exposure of a portfolio to the risk factors and to assess the *potential* performance of a portfolio relative to a benchmark. This is the portfolio construction and risk control application of the model. Also, the *actual* performance of a portfolio relative to a benchmark can be assessed. This is the performance attribution analysis application of the model.

Barra suggests that there are various ways that a portfolio's total risk can be decomposed when employing a multifactor risk model.[2] Each decomposition approach can be useful to managers depending on the equity portfolio management that they pursue. The four approaches are (1) total risk decomposition, (2) systematic-residual risk decomposition, (3) active risk decomposition, and (4) active systematic-active residual risk decomposition. We describe each below and explain how managers pursuing different strategies discussed in Chapter 8 will find the decomposition helpful in portfolio construction and evaluation.

In all of these approaches to risk decomposition, the total return is first divided into the risk-free return and the total excess return. The *total excess return* is the difference between the *actual* return realized by the portfolio and the risk-free return. The risk associated with the total excess return, called *total excess risk*, is what is further partitioned in the four approaches.

Total Risk Decomposition

There are managers who seek to minimize total risk. For example, a manager pursuing a long-short or market neutral strategy (discussed in Chapter 8), seek to construct a portfolio that minimizes total risk. For such managers, total risk decomposition which breaks down the total excess risk into two components—*common factor risks* (e.g., capitalization and industry exposures) and *specific risk*—is useful. This decomposition is shown in Exhibit 13.2. There is no provision for market risk, only risk attributed to the common factor risks and company-specific influences (i.e., risk unique to a particular company and therefore uncorrelated with the specific risk of other companies). Thus, the market portfolio is not a risk factor considered in this decomposition.

---

[2]See Chapter 4 in Barra, *Risk Model Handbook United States Equity: Version 3*. The discussion to follow in this section follows that in the Barra publication.

EXHIBIT 13.2   Total Risk Decomposition

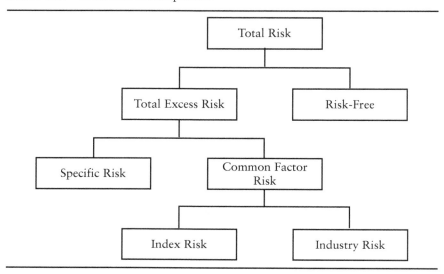

Source: Figure 4.2 in Barra, *Risk Model Handbook United States Equity: Version 3* (Berkeley, CA: Barra, 1998), 34. Reprinted with permission.

Systematic-Residual Risk Decomposition

There are managers who seek to time the market or who intentionally make bets to create a different exposure than that of a market portfolio. Such managers would find it useful to decompose total excess risk into systematic risk and residual risk as shown in Exhibit 13.3. Unlike in the total risk decomposition approach just described, this view brings market risk into the analysis. It is the type of decomposition that was described in Chapter 4, where *systematic risk* is the risk related to a portfolio's beta.

   Residual risk in the systematic-residual risk decomposition is defined in a different way than residual risk is in the total risk decomposition. In the systematic-residual risk decomposition, residual risk is risk that is uncorrelated with the market portfolio. In turn, residual risk is partitioned into specific risk and common factor risk. Notice that the partitioning of risk described here is different from that in the Arbitrage Pricing Theory model described in Chapter 5. In that chapter, all risk factors that could not be diversified away were referred to as "systematic risks." In our discussion here, risk factors that cannot be diversified away are classified as market risk and common factor risk. Systematic risk can be diversified to a negligible level.

EXHIBIT 13.3 Systematic-Residual Risk Decomposition

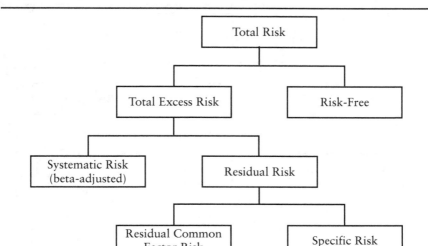

Source: Figure 4.3 in Barra, *Risk Model Handbook United States Equity: Version 3* (Berkeley, CA: Barra, 1998), 34. Reprinted with permission.

Active Risk Decomposition

In previous chapters, the need to assess a portfolio's risk exposure and actual performance relative to a benchmark index is explained. The active risk decomposition approach is useful for that purpose. In this type of decomposition, shown in Exhibit 13.4, the total excess return is divided into *benchmark risk* and *active risk*. Benchmark risk is defined as the risk associated with the benchmark portfolio.

Active risk is the risk that results from the manager's attempt to generate a return that will outperform the benchmark. Another name for active risk is *tracking error*. The active risk is further partitioned into common factor risk and specific risk. This decomposition is useful for managers of index funds and traditionally managed active funds.

Active Systematic-Active Residual Risk Decomposition

There are managers who overlay a market-timing strategy on their stock selection. That is, they not only try to select stocks they believe will outperform but also try to time the purchase of the acquisition. For a manager who pursues such a strategy, it will be important in evaluating performance

EXHIBIT 13.4   Active Risk Decomposition

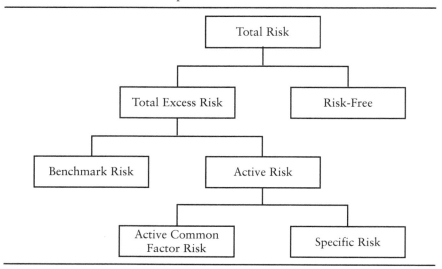

Source: Figure 4.4 in Barra, *Risk Model Handbook United States Equity: Version 3* (Berkeley, CA: Barra, 1998), 34. Reprinted with permission.

to separate market risk from common factor risks. In the active risk decomposition approach just discussed, there is no market risk identified as one of the risk factors.

Since market risk (i.e., systematic risk) is an element of active risk, its inclusion as a source of risk is preferred by managers. When market risk is included, we have the active systematic-active residual risk decomposition approach shown in Exhibit 13.5. Total excess risk is again divided into benchmark risk and active risk. However, active risk is further divided into active systematic risk (i.e., active market risk) and active residual risk. Then active residual risk is divided into common factor risks and specific risk.

Summary of Risk Decomposition

The four approaches to risk decomposition are just different ways of slicing up risk to help a manager in constructing and controlling the risk of a portfolio and for a client to understand how the manager performed. Exhibit 13.6 provides an overview of the four approaches to carving up risk into specific/common factor, systematic/residual, and benchmark/active risks.

EXHIBIT 13.5 Active Systematic-Active Residual Risk Decomposition

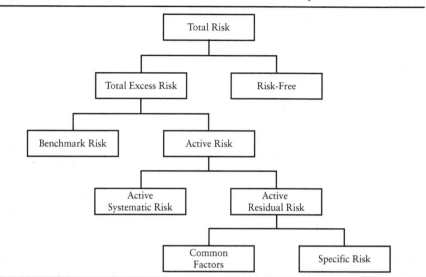

Source: Figure 4.5 in Barra, *Risk Model Handbook United States Equity: Version 3* (Berkeley, CA: Barra, 1998), 37. Reprinted with permission.

EXHIBIT 13.6 Risk Decomposition Overview

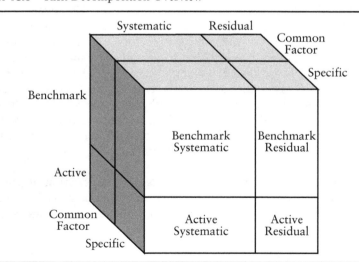

Source: Figure 4.6 in Barra, *Risk Model Handbook United States Equity: Version 3* (Berkeley, Ca.: Barra, 1998), 38. Reprinted with permission.

APPLICATIONS IN PORTFOLIO CONSTRUCTION AND RISK CONTROL

The power of a multifactor risk model is that given the risk factors and the risk factor sensitivities, a portfolio's risk exposure profile can be quantified and controlled. The three examples below show how this can be done so that the a manager can avoid making unintended bets. In the examples, we use the Barra L3 factor model.[3]

A fundamental multifactor risk model can be used to assess whether the current portfolio is consistent with a manager's strengths. Exhibit 13.7 is a list of the top 15 holdings of Portfolio ABC as of December 31, 2008. Exhibit 13.8 is a summary risk decomposition report for the same portfolio. The portfolio had a total market value of $5.4 billion, 868 holdings, and a predicted beta of 1.15.The risk report also shows that the portfolio had an active risk of 6.7%. This is its tracking error with respect to the benchmark, the S&P 500 index. Notice that nearly 93% of the active risk variance (which is 44.8) came from common factor variance (which is 41.6), and only a small proportion came from stock-specific risk variance (also known as *asset selection variance*, which is 3.2). Clearly, the manager of this portfolio had placed fairly large factor bets.

The top portion of Exhibit 13.9 lists the factor risk exposures of Portfolio ABC relative to those of the S&P 500 index, its benchmark. The first column shows the exposures of the portfolio, and the second column shows the exposures of the benchmark. The last column shows the active exposure, which is the difference between the portfolio exposure and the benchmark exposure. The exposures to the risk index factors are measured in units of standard deviation, while the exposures to the industry factors are measured in percentages. The portfolio had a high active exposure to the Volatility risk index factor. That is, the stocks in the portfolio were far more volatile than the stocks in the benchmark. On the other side, the portfolio had a low active exposure to the Size risk index. That is, the stocks in the portfolio were smaller than the benchmark average in terms of market capitalization. The lower portion of Exhibit 13.9 is an abbreviated list of the industry factor exposures.

An important use of such risk reports is the identification of portfolio bets, both explicit and implicit. If, for example, the manager of Portfolio ABC did not intend to place the large bet on the Volatility risk index.

---

[3]The illustrations were created by the authors based on applications suggested in Chapter VI of *United States Equity Model Handbook* (Berkeley, Ca.: Barra, 1996).

EXHIBIT 13.7 Portfolio ABC's Holdings (only the top 15 holdings shown)

Ticker	Security Name	Shares	Price ($)	Weight	Beta	Industry
XOM	Exxon Mobil Corp.	3,080,429	79.83	4.56	0.92	Oil Refining
MSFT	Microsoft Corp.	6,235,154	19.44	2.25	0.95	Computer Software
CVX	Chevron Corp.	1,614,879	73.97	2.21	0.98	Energy Reserves & Production
IBM	International Business Machines Corp.	1,100,900	84.16	1.72	0.83	Computer Software
T	AT&T Inc.	3,226,744	28.50	1.70	0.80	Telephone
HPQ	Hewlett-Packard Co.	2,464,100	36.29	1.66	0.84	Computer Hardware & Business Machines
INTC	Intel Corp.	5,997,300	14.66	1.63	0.87	Semiconductors
COP	ConocoPhillips	1,634,986	51.80	1.57	1.24	Energy Reserves & Production
CSCO	Cisco Systems Inc.	5,186,400	16.30	1.57	0.95	Computer Hardware & Business Machines
JNJ	Johnson & Johnson	1,403,544	59.83	1.56	0.54	Medical Products & Supplies
OXY	Occidental Petroleum Corp.	1,324,426	59.99	1.47	1.26	Energy Reserves & Production
PG	Procter & Gamble Co.	1,249,446	61.82	1.43	0.57	Home Products
GE	General Electric Co.	4,762,984	16.20	1.43	1.41	Heavy Electrical Equipment
PFE	Pfizer Inc.	4,339,092	17.71	1.42	0.61	Drugs
TWX	Time Warner Inc.	1,948,880	30.18	1.09	1.32	Media

337

EXHIBIT 13.8 Portfolio ABC's Summary Risk Decomposition Report

Number of Securities	868
Number of Shares	298,371,041
Average Share Price	$24.91
Weighted Average Share Price	$35.30
Portfolio Ending Market Value	$5,396,530,668
Predicted Beta (vs. Benchmark, S&P 500)	1.15

Barra Risk Decomposition (Variance)

Asset Selection Variance	3.2
Common Factor Variance:	
Risk Indexes	22.5
Industries	11.7
Covariance × 2	7.5
Common Factor Variance	41.6
Active Variance	44.8
Benchmark Variance	749.4
Total Variance	1,016.6

Barra Risk Decomposition (Std. Dev.)

Asset Selection Risk	1.8
Common Factor Risk:	
Risk Indexes	4.7
Industries	3.4
Covariance × 2	
Common Factor Risk	6.5
Active Risk	6.7
Benchmark Risk	27.4
Total Risk	31.9

EXHIBIT 13.9 Analysis of Portfolio ABC's Factor Exposures

Risk Indices (std. dev. units)	Managed[a]	Benchmark[b]	Active[c]
U.S. Volatility	0.321	−0.089	0.410
U.S. Value	0.199	−0.024	0.223
U.S. Earnings Variation	0.149	−0.053	0.202
U.S. Earnings Yield	0.243	0.053	0.191
U.S. Trading Activity	0.161	0.052	0.109
U.S. Leverage	−0.036	−0.110	0.074
U.S. Growth	0.004	−0.069	0.073
U.S. Non-Estimation Universe	0.027	0.000	0.027
U.S. Currency Sensitivity	−0.013	0.007	−0.019
U.S. Momentum	−0.183	−0.043	−0.139
U.S. Yield	−0.115	0.078	−0.194
U.S. Size Non-Linearity	−0.107	0.123	−0.230
U.S. Size	−0.244	0.356	−0.600

Top Three Industries (percentages)	Managed	Benchmark	Active
U.S. Energy Reserves	0.098	0.064	0.033
U.S. Semiconductors	0.052	0.023	0.028
U.S. Mining and Metals	0.036	0.009	0.027

[a] Managed return.
[b] Benchmark return (S&P 500).
[c] Active return = Managed return − Benchmark return.

Risk Control against a Stock Market Index

The objective of equity indexing is to match the performance of some specified stock market index with little tracking error. To do this, the risk profile of the indexed portfolio must match the risk profile of the designated stock market index. Put in other terms, the factor risk exposure of the indexed portfolio must match as closely as possible the exposure of the designated stock market index to the same factors. Any differences in the factor risk exposures result in tracking error. Identification of any differences allows the indexer to rebalance the portfolio to reduce tracking error.

To illustrate this, suppose that an index manager has constructed a portfolio of 50 stocks to match the S&P 500 index. Exhibit 13.10 lists the exposures to the Barra risk indexes of the 50-stock portfolio and the S&P 500 index. The last column in the exhibit shows the difference in exposures. The differences are very small except for the exposures to the Size risk index

EXHIBIT 13.10 Factor Exposures of a 50-Stock Portfolio that Optimally Matches the S&P 500 Index

Risk Indexes (std. dev. units)	Managed[a]	Benchmark[b]	Active[c]
U.S. Volatility	−0.153	−0.089	−0.063
U.S. Momentum	−0.062	−0.043	−0.018
U.S. Size	0.795	0.356	0.440
U.S. Size Non-Linearity	0.164	0.123	0.041
U.S. Trading Activity	−0.001	0.052	−0.053
U.S. Growth	−0.052	−0.069	0.016
U.S. Earnings Yield	0.076	0.053	0.023
U.S. Value	−0.019	−0.024	0.005
U.S. Earnings Variation	−0.122	−0.053	−0.069
U.S. Leverage	−0.176	−0.110	−0.066
U.S. Currency Sensitivity	−0.048	0.007	−0.055
U.S. Yield	0.140	0.078	0.061
U.S. Non-Estimation Universe	0.000	0.000	0.000

[a]Managed return.
[b]Benchmark return (S&P 500).
[c]Active return = Managed return − Benchmark return.

factor. Though not shown in this exhibit, there is a similar list of exposures to the 55 industry factors.

The illustration in Exhibit 13.10 uses price data as of December 31, 2008. It demonstrates how a multifactor risk model can be combined with an optimization model to construct an indexed portfolio when a given number of holdings are sought. Specifically, the portfolio analyzed in the exhibit is the result of an application in which the manager wants a portfolio constructed that matches the S&P 500 index with only 50 stocks and that minimizes tracking error. The optimization model uses the multifactor risk model to construct a 50-stock portfolio with a tracking error versus S&P 500 index of just 2.75%. Since this is the optimal 50-stock portfolio to replicate the S&P 500 index with a minimum tracking error risk, this tells the index manager that if he seeks a lower tracking error, then more stocks must be held. Note, however, that the optimal portfolio changes as time passes and prices move.

Tilting a Portfolio

Now let's look at how an active manager can construct a portfolio to make intentional bets. Suppose that a portfolio manager seeks to construct a portfolio that generates superior returns relative to the S&P 500 by tilting it toward low P/E stocks. At the same time, the manager does not want to increase tracking error significantly. An obvious approach may seem to be to identify all the stocks in the universe that have a lower than average P/E. The problem with this approach is that it introduces unintentional bets with respect to the other risk indexes.

Instead, an optimization method combined with a multifactor risk model can be used to construct the desired portfolio. The necessary inputs to this process are the tilt exposure sought and the benchmark stock market index. Additional constraints can be placed, for example, on the number of stocks to be included in the portfolio. The Barra optimization model can also handle additional specifications such as forecasts of expected returns or alphas on the individual stocks.

In our illustration, the tilt exposure sought is towards low P/E stocks, that is, towards high earnings yield stocks (since earnings yield is the inverse of P/E). The benchmark is the S&P 500. We seek a portfolio that has an average earnings yield that is at least 0.5 standard deviations more than that of the earnings yield of the benchmark. We do not place any limit on the number of stocks to be included in the portfolio. We also do not want the active exposure to any other risk index factor (other than earnings yield) to be more than 0.1 standard deviations in magnitude. This way we avoid placing unintended bets. While we do not report the holdings of the optimal portfolio here, Exhibit 13.11 provides an analysis of that portfolio by comparing the risk exposure of the 50-stock optimal portfolio to that of the S&P 500. Though not shown in this exhibit, there is a similar list of exposures to the 55 industry factors.

KEY POINTS

- There are three types of multifactor equity risk models that are used in practice: statistical, macroeconomic, and fundamental. The most popular is the fundamental model.
- A multifactor equity risk model assumes that stock returns (and hence portfolio returns) can be explained by a linear model with multiple factors, consisting of "risk index" factors such as company size, volatility, momentum, etc and "industry" factors. The portion of the stock return that is not explained by this model is the stock-specific return.
- The risk index factors are measured in standard deviation units, while the industry factors are measured in percentages.
- The real usefulness of a linear multifactor model lies in the ease with which the risk (i.e., the volatility) of a portfolio with several assets can

EXHIBIT 13.11   Factor Exposures of a Portfolio Tilted Towards Earnings Yield

Risk Indexes (std. dev. units)	Managed[a]	Benchmark[b]	Active[c]
U.S. Volatility	−0.050	−0.089	0.039
U.S. Momentum	−0.096	−0.043	−0.052
U.S. Size	0.284	0.356	−0.072
U.S. Size Non-Linearity	0.096	0.123	−0.027
U.S. Trading Activity	0.114	0.052	0.062
U.S. Growth	−0.096	−0.069	−0.027
U.S. Earnings Yield	0.553	0.053	0.500
U.S. Value	0.076	−0.024	0.100
U.S. Earnings Variation	−0.091	−0.053	−0.038
U.S. Leverage	−0.153	−0.110	−0.043
U.S. Currency Sensitivity	0.066	0.007	0.059
U.S. Yield	0.179	0.078	0.100
U.S. Non-Estimation Universe	0.000	0.000	0.000

[a]Managed return.
[b]Benchmark return (S&P 500).
[c]Active return = Managed return − Benchmark return.

be estimated. Instead of estimating the variance-covariance matrix of its assets, it only necessary to estimate the portfolio's factor exposures and the variance-covariance matrix of the factors, a computationally much easier task.

- The variance-covariance matrix of the factors and the factor exposures of stocks are calculated based on a mix of historical and current data, and are updated periodically.
- Total risk of a portfolio can be decomposed in several ways. The partitioning method chosen is based on what is useful given the manager's strategy. The active risk decomposition method is useful for managers of index funds and traditionally managed active funds.
- The level of active risk of a portfolio and the split of the tracking error variance between the common factor portion and the stock-specific portion are useful in assessing if the portfolio is constructed in a way that is consistent with the manager's strengths.
- The list of active factor exposures of a portfolio helps the manager identify its bets, both explicit and implicit. If a manager discovers some unintended bets, then the portfolio can be rebalanced so as to minimize such bets.

- Using a multifactor risk model and an optimization model, a portfolio that has the minimum active risk relative to its benchmark for a given number of assets held can be constructed. This application is useful for passive managers.
- Similarly, a manager can construct a portfolio that tilts towards a specified factor, and has no material active exposure to any other factor. This application is useful for active managers.

QUESTIONS

1. What's "fundamental" about fundamental risk models?
2. A portfolio's risk can be calculated directly based on the variances of the stocks it holds and their correlations to each other. Why then would a portfolio manager choose to calculate portfolio risk indirectly through a factor-based risk model?
3. Can a portfolio manager diversify away to a negligible level both the common factor risk and the specific risk of a portfolio?
4. Is a bottom-up stock-picker portfolio with 50 stocks riskier than a top-down factor-betting portfolio with 500 stocks?
5. Can a portfolio manager use a multifactor risk model to predict if an active portfolio is at greater risk of underperforming its benchmark than outperforming it over the next period? That is, does the "risk model" predict "risk" in the conventional sense?

CHAPTER 14

Fundamentals of Equity Derivatives

Bruce M. Collins, Ph.D.
Professor of Finance
Western Connecticut State University

Frank J. Fabozzi, Ph.D., CFA, CPA
Professor in the Practice of Finance
Yale School of Management

Derivative securities, or simply derivatives, are financial agreements or contracts between two parties that "derive" their value from an underlying asset. The contract specifies the terms of a payout from one party to another. The underlying asset is typically a cash market instrument such as a stock, a bond or a commodity. When the underlying instrument is an equity security, the contract is called an *equity derivative*. The equity security can be a stock, a basket of stocks, an index or a group of indexes.

The purpose of this chapter is to explain these instruments, their investment characteristics, and to provide an overview as to how they are priced. In the next chapter, we look at how equity derivatives can be used in the management of equity portfolios.

THE ROLE OF DERIVATIVES

Equity derivatives have several properties that provide economic benefits that make them excellent candidates for use in equity portfolio management. These properties are linked to the four roles that derivatives serve in portfolio management:

1. *Risk management.* Modifying the risk characteristics of a portfolio.
2. *Returns management.* Enhancing the expected return of a portfolio.

3. *Cost management.* Reducing transaction costs associated with managing a portfolio.
4. *Regulatory management.* Achieving efficiency in the presence of legal, tax, or regulatory obstacles.

We can further reduce the role of derivatives to the single purpose of risk management and incorporate the other three roles into this one role. Thus, it can be argued that equity derivatives are used primarily to manage risk or to buy and sell risk at a favorable price.

Risk management is a dynamic process that allows portfolio managers to identify, measure, and assess the current risk attributes of a portfolio and to measure the potential benefits from taking the risk. Moreover, risk management involves understanding and managing the factors that can have an adverse impact on the targeted rate of return. The objective is to attain a desired return for a given level of corresponding risk on an after-cost basis. This is consistent with the Markowitz efficient frontier and modern portfolio theory discussed in Chapter 3.

The role of equity derivatives in this process is to shift the frontier in favor of the investor by implementing a strategy at a lower cost, lower risk, and higher return or to gain access to an investment that was not available due to some regulatory or other restriction. We can therefore regard the management of equity portfolios as a sophisticated exercise in risk management.

Equity derivatives give investors more degrees of freedom. In the past, the implementation and management of an investment strategy for pension funds, for example, was a function of management style and was carried out in the cash market. Pension funds managed risk by diversifying among management styles. Prior to the advent of the over-the-counter (OTC) derivatives market in the late 1980s and the structured products market in the 1990s, the first risk management tools available to investors were limited to the listed futures and options markets. Although providing a valuable addition to an investor's risk management tool kit, listed derivatives were limited in application due to their standardized features, limited size, and liquidity constraints. The OTC derivatives market gives investors access to longer term products that better match their investment horizon and flexible structures to meet their exact risk–reward requirements. The structured products market allows investors to gain synthetic exposure to risk and return relating to an equity security. The number of unique equity derivative structures is essentially unlimited.

Equity Derivatives Market

There are generally three segments of what we define as the equity derivatives markets. These include the exchange-listed market, the OTC market, and the market for structured products. Often the structured product market is considered an extension of the OTC market.

There are also three general categories of derivatives that are created and traded across three markets: (1) futures and forwards, (2) options, and (3) swaps. The most fundamental derivative securities are futures or forward contracts and options. Swaps and other derivative structures with more complicated payoffs are regarded as hybrid securities, which can be shown to be portfolios of forwards, options, and cash instruments in varying combinations.

The listed market consists of options, warrants, and futures contracts. The principal listed options market consists of exchange-traded options with standardized strike prices, expirations, and payout terms traded on individual stocks, equity indexes, and futures contracts on equity indexes. A FLexible EXchange (FLEX) Option traded on the Chicago Board Options Exchange (CBOE) provides the customization feature of the OTC market, but with the guarantee of the exchange. More recently, the NYSE LIFFE (New York Stock Exchange/London International Financial Futures and Options Exchange) launched a hybrid trading platform that combines the flexibility of the OTC market with the security and benefits associated with exchange-traded derivatives. The listed futures market consists of exchange-traded equity index futures and single stock futures with standardized settlement dates and settlement returns. Other innovations offered by the CBOE include *weeklys*, *quarterlys* and *binaries*. Weeklys are options that are listed for approximately one week to expiration, which provides a cost advantage for investors with derivative needs and short-term horizons. Similarly, quarterlys are options that expire on the last trading day of the calendar quarter. Binaries are options contracts that pay out a pre-determined, fixed amount of money or nothing at all (all or nothing options). This brings the so-called second generation OTC "exotic" options to the listed exchange-traded space.

OTC equity derivatives are not traded on an exchange and have an advantage over listed derivatives because they provide complete flexibility and can be tailored to fit an investment strategy. The OTC equity derivatives market can be divided into four components: OTC forwards, options and warrants, equity-linked debt investments, and equity swaps. Equity forward contracts are not unlike listed futures contracts where the long party agrees to take delivery of a specified number of shares of stock from the counterparty for delivery at some future date for a price agreed upon in the contract. The difference is that forwards are settled at the settlement date while futures are marked-to-the-market. OTC equity options are customized option contracts that can be applied to any equity index, basket of stocks or an individual stock. OTC options are privately negotiated agreements between an investor and an issuing dealer. The structure of the option is completely flexible in terms of strike price, expiration, and payout features. A fundamental difference between listed and OTC derivatives, however, is that listed options and futures contracts are guaranteed by the exchange, while in the OTC market the derivative is the obligation of a nonexchange entity that is the counterparty. Thus, the investor is subject to credit risk or counterparty risk.

Structured products are packaged investment strategies that typically embed equity derivatives technology with other financial instruments.[1] The financial instruments might include a single security, a basket of securities, an index, an interest rate product or a commodity. One common feature of structured products is a principal guarantee. Other features might include tax considerations, returns enhancement or reduced volatility. They are an alternative to direct investment and are often useful for asset allocation purposes.

Other equity derivatives might include exchange traded funds (ETFs), which are index investment products listed and traded on an exchange.

LISTED EQUITY OPTIONS

Equity derivative products are either exchange-traded listed derivatives or OTC derivatives. In this section we will look at listed equity options.[2]

An *option* is a contract in which the option seller grants the option buyer the right to enter into a transaction with the seller to either buy or sell an underlying asset at a specified price on or before a specified date. The specified price is called the *strike price* or *exercise price* and the specified date is called the *expiration date*. The option seller grants this right in exchange for a certain amount of money called the *option premium* or *option price*.

The option seller is also known as the option writer, while the option buyer is the option holder. The asset that is the subject of the option is called the *underlying*. The underlying can be an individual stock, a basket of stocks, a stock index or group of indexes, or another derivative instrument such as a futures contract or an ETF. The option writer can grant the

---

[1]For a more detailed discussion of structured products, see Peter Green and Jeremy Jennings-Mares, "Types of Structured Products," *Equity Derivatives, Documenting and Understanding Equity Derivative Products*, ed. Edmund Parker, (London: Global Business Publishing Ltd., 2009), 85–106.

[2]The CBOE is the largest listed options exchange in the U.S. trading equity, index, ETF, and hybrid options contracts. Eurex is one of the world's leading derivatives exchanges including listed options. It owns the International Securities Exchange (ISE) which is an electronic trading platform for listed options in the United States.

option holder one of two rights. If the right is to purchase the underlying, the option is a *call option*. If the right is to sell the underlying, the option is a *put option*.

An option can also be categorized according to when it may be exercised by the buyer. This is referred to as the *exercise style*. A *European option* can only be exercised at the expiration date of the contract. An *American option* can be exercised any time on or before the expiration date. A *Bermudan option* is in between an American and a European and can only be exercised on certain dates over the life of the option.

The terms of exchange are represented by the contract unit, which is typically 100 shares for an individual stock and a multiple times an index value for a stock index. The terms of exchange are standard for most contracts. The contract terms for a FLEX option can be customized along four dimensions: underlying, strike price, expiration date, and settlement style. These options are discussed further below.

The option holder enters into the contract with an opening transaction. Subsequently, the option holder then has the choice to exercise or to sell the option. The sale of an existing option by the holder is a closing sale.

Listed vs. OTC Equity Options

There are three advantages of listed options relative to OTC options. First, the strike price and expiration dates of the contract are standardized. Second, the direct link between buyer and seller is severed after the order is executed because of the fungible nature of listed options. The Options Clearing Corporation (OCC) serves as the intermediary between buyer and seller. Finally, transaction costs are lower for listed options than their OTC counterparts.

There are many situations in which an institutional investor needs a customized option. Such situations will be identified when we discuss the applications of OTC options in the next chapter. The higher cost of OTC options reflects this customization. However, some OTC exotic option structures may prove to cost less than the closest standardized option because a more specific payout is being bought.

A significant distinction between a listed option and an OTC option is the presence of credit risk or counterparty risk. Only the option buyer is exposed to counterparty risk. Options traded on exchanges and OTC options traded over a network of market makers have different ways of dealing with the problem of credit risk. Organized exchanges reduce counterparty risk by requiring margin, marking to the market daily, imposing size and price limits, and providing an intermediary that takes both sides of a trade. The clearing process provides three levels of protection: (1) the customer's margin, (2) the member firm's guarantee, and (3) the clearing-house. The OTC market has incorporated a variety of terms into the contractual agreement between counterparties to address the issue of credit risk and these are described when we discuss OTC derivatives.

For listed options, there are no margin requirements for the buyer of an option once the option price has been paid in full. Because the option price is the maximum amount that the option buyer can lose, no matter how adverse the price movement of the underlying, margin is not necessary. The option writer has agreed to transfer the risk inherent in a position in the underlying from the option buyer to itself. The writer, on the other, has certain margin requirements.

Basic Features of Listed Options

The basic features of listed options are summarized in Exhibit 14.1. The exhibit is grouped into four categories with each option category presented in terms of its basic features. These include the type of option, underlying, strike price, settlement information, expiration cycle, exercise style, and some trading rules.

Stock options refer to listed options on individual stocks or American Depository Receipts (ADRs). The underlying is 100 shares of the designated stock. All listed stock options in the United States may be exercised any time before the expiration date; that is, they are American style options.

Index options are options where the underlying is a stock index rather than an individual stock. An index call option gives the option buyer the right to buy the underlying stock index, while a put option gives the option buyer the right to sell the underlying stock index. Unlike stock options where a stock can be delivered if the option is exercised by the option holder, it would be extremely complicated to settle an index option by delivering all the stocks that constitute the index. Instead, index options are cash settlement contracts. This means that if the option is exercised by the option holder, the option writer pays cash to the option buyer. There is no delivery of any stocks.

Among the most liquid index options are those on the S&P 100 index (OEX) and the S&P 500 index (SPX). Other indexes that have gained in popularity include options on the Nasdaq 100 Index (NDX) and the Dow Jones Industrial Average Index (DJX). All trade on the CBOE. Index options can be listed as American or European. The S&P 500 index option contract is European, while the OEX is American. Both index option contracts have specific standardized features and contract terms. Moreover, both have short expiration cycles.

EXHIBIT 14.1 Basic Features of Listed Equity Options

Stock Options

Option type	Call or put
Option category	Equity
Underlying security	Individual stock or ADR
Contract value	Equity: 100 shares of common stock or ADRs
Strike price	2½ points when the strike price is between $5 and $25, 10 points when the strike price is over $200. Strikes are adjusted for splits, recapitalizations, etc.
Settlement and delivery	100 shares of stock
Exercise style	American
Expiration cycle	Two near-term months plus two additional months from the January, February, or March quarterly cycles
Transaction Costs	$1–$3 commissions and ⅛ market impact
Position and size limits	Large capitalization stocks have an option position limit of 25,000 contracts (with adjustments for splits, recapitalizations, etc.) on the same side of the market; smaller capitalization stocks have an option position limit of 20,000, 10,500, 7,500 or 4,500 contracts (with adjustments for splits, recapitalizations, etc.) on the same side of the market.

Index Options

Option type	Call or put
Option category	Indexes
Underlying security	Stock index
Contract value	Multiplier × Index price
Strike price	Five points. 10-point intervals in the far-term month.
Settlement and delivery	Cash
Exercise style	American
Expiration cycle	Four near-term months
Transaction costs	$1–$3 commissions and ⅛ market impact
Position and size limits	150,000 contracts on the same side of the market with no more than 100,000 of such contracts in the near-term series

EXHIBIT 14.1   (Continued)
LEAP Options

Option type	Call or put
Option category	LEAP
Underlying security	Individual stock or stock index
Contract value	Equity: 100 shares of common stock or ADRs Index: full or partial value of stock index
Strike price	Equity: same as equity option Index: Based on full or partial value of index. ⅕ value translates into ⅕ strike price
Settlement and delivery	Equity: 100 shares of stock or ADR Index: Cash
Exercise style	American or European
Expiration cycle	May be up to 39 months from the date of initial listing, January expiration only
Transaction costs	$1–$3 commissions and ⅛ market impact
Position and size limits	Same as equity options and index options

FLEX Options

Option type	Call, put, or cap
Option category	Equity: E-FLEX option Index: FLEX option
Underlying security	Individual stock or index
Contract value	Equity: 100 shares of common stock or ADRs Index: multiplier × index value
Strike price	Equity: Calls, same as standard calls Puts, any dollar value or percentage Index: Any index value, percentage, or deviation from index value
Settlement and delivery	Equity: 100 shares of stock Index: Cash
Exercise style	Equity: American or European Index: American, European, or cap
Expiration cycle	Equity: 1 day to 3 years Index: Up to 5 years
Transaction costs	$1–$3 commissions and ⅛ market impact
Position and size limits	Equity: minimum of 250 contracts to create FLEX Index: $10 million minimum to create FLEX No size or position limits

Currently, the CBOE trades approximately 40 index options. Two the latest products that are being prepared for listing as of this writing include the CBOE China Index Options (CYX) and the Morgan Stanley Multinational Company Index (NFT).[3]

Among a wide group of international contracts are options traded on the Dow Jones STOXX 50 and the Dow Jones EURO 50 stock indexes.[4] Other international index options include options traded on the FTSE 100, the CaC-40 and a host of Euro Stoxx indexes.[5] There are over 100 stock index option contracts listed across 26 separate exchanges and 20 countries.

The following mechanics should be noted for index options. The dollar value of the stock index underlying an index option is equal to the current cash index value multiplied by the contract's multiple.[6] That is,

Dollar value of the underlying index = Cash index value × Contract multiple

For example, if the cash index value for the S&P 500 is 1150, then the dollar value of the S&P 500 contract is 1150 × $100 = $115,000.

For a stock option, the price at which the buyer of the option can buy or sell the stock is the strike price. For an index option, the strike index is the index value at which the buyer of the option can buy or sell the underlying stock index. The strike index is converted into a dollar value by multiplying the strike index by the multiple for the contract. For example, if the strike index is 1150, the dollar value is $115,000 (1150 × $100). If an investor purchases a call option on the S&P 500 with a strike index of 1150, and exercises the option when the index value is 1175, then the investor has the right to purchase the index for $115,000 when the market value of the index is $117,500. The buyer of the call option would then receive $2,500 from the option writer.

The next two categories listed in Exhibit 14.1, LEAPS and FLEX options, essentially modify an existing feature of either a stock option, an

---

[3]You can find a complete description of these products at www.cboe.com under products.

[4]The indexes are comprised of 50 industrial, commercial, and financial European blue chip companies.

[5]The EURO STOXX Index is a group of sector indexes and is a broad subset of the STOXX Europe 600 Index. The number of components is variable, and the index encompasses large-, mid-, and small-capitalization companies of 12 Euro zone countries: Austria, Belgium, Finland, France, Germany, Greece, Ireland, Italy, Luxembourg, the Netherlands, Portugal and Spain. There are options and futures contracts available on the indexes.

[6]Non-U.S. index options follow the same valuation specification: Multiplier × Index value. For example, EURO STOXX products are €50 multiplied by the value of the index.

index option, or both. For example, stock option and index option contracts have short expiration cycles. Long-Term Equity Anticipation Securities (LEAPS) are designed to offer options with longer maturities. These contracts are available on individual stocks and some indexes. Stock option LEAPS are comparable to standard stock options except the maturities can range up to 39 months from the origination date. Index options LEAPS differ in size compared with standard index options having a multiplier of 10 rather than 100.

FLEX options allow users to specify the terms of the option contract for either a stock option or an index option. The value of FLEX options is the ability to customize the terms of the contract along four dimensions: underlying, strike price, expiration date, and settlement style. Moreover, the exchange provides a secondary market to offset or alter positions and an independent daily marking of prices. The development of the FLEX option is a response to the growing OTC market. The exchanges seek to make the FLEX option attractive by providing price discovery through a competitive auction market, an active secondary market, daily price valuations, and the virtual elimination of counterparty risk. The FLEX option represents a link between listed options and OTC products.

There are two other categories, ETF options and binary options, that are recent developments in the listed market. The CBOE trades nearly 240 option contracts on ETFs. ETFs are shares of trusts that hold a basket of stocks designed to replicate the performance of a benchmark index. The equity index might be a broad-based index or a narrowly defined sector index. ETFs effectively trade like stocks and options on these products are operationally similar to traditional stock options. Options on ETFs are America style options but are not cash-settled like index options. They are instead physically settled like individual stock options. LEAPS are also offered on some ETF products.

CBOE Binary Options are all or nothing options that allow investors to trade based on market direction.[7] These options are also a link between listed options and OTC products. The contracts pay out a pre-determined fixed amount of $100 or nothing at all. The CBOE lists both calls and puts on the S&P 500 index with a variety of strike prices and expirations. If, at expiration, the price of the underlying index is above the strike, there is a payout of $100 for the buyer in the case of a call option and nothing in the case of a put option. These options trade like ordinary options prior to expiration with the price reflect the market's assessment of the probability that the S&P 500 will exceed or fail to reach a selected strike price. For example,

---

[7]Binary options, also known as digitals, can be structured as "cash or nothing" or "asset of nothing" products. The CBOE S&P 500 binary is a "cash or nothing" structure.

if the strike price for a binary option on the S&P 500 is 1200 then the payout is $100 if the S&P 500 is above 1200 at expiration and 0 otherwise.

Risk and Return Characteristics of Options

Now let's illustrate the risk and return characteristics of the four basic option positions—buying a call option (long a call option), selling a call option (short a call option), buying a put option (long a put option), and selling a put option (short a put option). We will use stock options in our example. The illustrations assume that each option position is held to the expiration date. Also, to simplify the illustrations, we assume that the underlying for each option is for one share of stock rather than 100 shares and we ignore transaction costs.

Buying Call Options

Assume that there is a call option on stock XYZ that expires in one month and has a strike price of $100. The option price is $3. Suppose that the current or spot price of stock XYZ is $100. (The *spot price* is the cash market price.) The profit and loss will depend on the price of stock XYZ at the expiration date. The buyer of a call option benefits if the price rises above the strike price. If the price of stock XYZ is equal to $103, the buyer of a call option breaks even. The maximum loss is the option price, and there is substantial upside potential if the stock price rises above $103. Exhibit 14.2

EXHIBIT 14.2   Profit/Loss Profile at Expiration Call

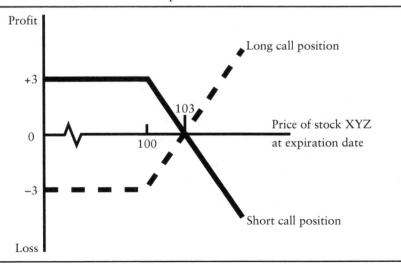

shows using a graph the profit/loss profile for the buyer of this call option at the expiration date.

It is worthwhile to compare the profit and loss profile of the call option buyer with that of an investor taking a long position in one share of stock XYZ. The payoff from the position depends on stock XYZ's price at the expiration date. An investor who takes a long position in stock XYZ realizes a profit of $1 for every $1 increase in stock XYZ's price. As stock XYZ's price falls, however, the investor loses, dollar for dollar. If the price drops by more than $3, the long position in stock XYZ results in a loss of more than $3. The long call position, in contrast, limits the loss to only the option price of $3 but retains the upside potential, which will be $3 less than for the long position in stock XYZ. Which alternative is better, buying the call option or buying the stock? The answer depends on what the investor is attempting to achieve.

Writing Call Options

To illustrate the option seller's, or writer's, position, we use the same call option we used to illustrate buying a call option. The profit/loss profile at expiration of the short call position (that is, the position of the call option writer) is the mirror image of the profit and loss profile of the long call position (the position of the call option buyer). That is, the profit of the short call position for any given price for stock XYZ at the expiration date is the same as the loss of the long call position. Consequently, the maximum profit the short call position can produce is the option price. The maximum loss is not limited because it is the highest price reached by stock XYZ on or before the expiration date, less the option price; this price can be indefinitely high. Exhibit 14.2 shows a graph of the profit/loss profile for the seller of this call option at the expiration date.

Buying Put Options

To illustrate a long put option position, we assume a hypothetical put option on one share of stock XYZ with one month to maturity and a strike price of $100. Assume that the put option is selling for $2 and the spot price of stock XYZ is $100. The profit or loss for this position at the expiration date depends on the market price of stock XYZ. The buyer of a put option benefits if the price falls. Exhibit 14.3 shows a graph of the profit/loss profile for the buyer of this put option at the expiration date. As with all long option positions, the loss is limited to the option price. The profit potential, however, is substantial: The theoretical maximum profit is generated

EXHIBIT 14.3   Profit/Loss Profile at Expiration Put

if stock XYZ's price falls to zero. Contrast this profit potential with that of the buyer of a call option. The theoretical maximum profit for a call buyer cannot be determined beforehand because it depends on the highest price that can be reached by stock XYZ before or at the option expiration date.

To see how an option alters the risk–return profile for an investor, we again compare it with a position in stock XYZ. The long put position is compared with a short position in stock XYZ because such a position would also benefit if the price of the stock falls. While the investor taking a short stock position faces all the downside risk as well as the upside potential, an investor taking the long put position faces limited downside risk (equal to the option price) while still maintaining upside potential reduced by an amount equal to the option price.

Writing Put Options

The profit and loss profile for a short put option is the mirror image of the long put option. The maximum profit to be realized from this position is the option price. The theoretical maximum loss can be substantial should the price of the underlying fall; and if the price were to fall all the way to zero, the loss would be as large as the strike price less the option price the seller received. Exhibit 14.2 shows a graph of the profit/loss profile for the seller of this put option at the expiration date.

The Value of an Option

Now we will look at the basic factors that affect the value of an option and discuss a well-known option pricing model.

Basic Components of the Option Price

The price of an option is a reflection of the option's *intrinsic value* and any additional amount above its intrinsic value. The premium over intrinsic value is often referred to as the *time value.*

Intrinsic Value   The intrinsic value of an option is its economic value if it is exercised immediately. For a call option, the intrinsic value is positive if the spot price (i.e., cash market price) of the underlying is greater than the strike price. For example, if the strike price for a call option is $100 and the spot price of the underlying is $105, the intrinsic value is $5. That is, an option buyer exercising the option and simultaneously selling the underlying would realize $105 from the sale of the underlying, which would be covered by acquiring the underlying from the option writer for $100, thereby netting a $5 gain.

When an option has intrinsic value, it is said to be *in the money* (ITM). When the strike price of a call option exceeds the spot price of the underlying, the call option is said to be *out of the money* (OTM); it has no intrinsic value. An option for which the strike price is equal to the spot price of the underlying is said to be at the money. Both at-the money and out-of-the-money options have an intrinsic value of zero because they are not profitable to exercise.

For a put option, the intrinsic value is equal to the amount by which the spot price of the underlying is below the strike price. For example, if the strike price of a put option is $100 and the spot price of the underlying is $92, the intrinsic value is $8. The buyer of the put option who exercises the put option and simultaneously sells the underlying will net $8 by exercising since the underlying will be sold to the writer for $100 and purchased in the market for $92. The intrinsic value is zero if the strike price is less than or equal to the underlying's spot price.

Time Value   The *time value of an option* is the amount by which the option price exceeds its intrinsic value. The option buyer hopes that at some time prior to expiration, changes in the market price of the underlying will increase the value of the rights conveyed by the option. For this prospect, the option buyer is willing to pay a premium above the intrinsic value. For example, if the price of a call option with a strike price of $100 is $9 when the spot price of the underlying is $105, the time value of this option is $4

($9 minus its intrinsic value of $5). Had the current price of the underlying been $90 instead of $105, then the time value of this option would be the entire $9 because the option has no intrinsic value. Other factors being equal, the time value of an option will increase with the amount of time remaining to expiration since the opportunity for a favorable change in the price of the underlying is greater.

There are two ways in which an option buyer may realize the value of a position taken in an option: the first is to exercise the option, and the second is to sell the option. In the first example above, since the exercise of an option will realize a gain of only $5 and will cause the immediate loss of any time value ($4 in our first example), it is preferable to sell the call. In general, if an option buyer wishes to realize the value of a position, selling will be more economically beneficial than exercising. However, there are circumstances under which it is preferable to exercise prior to the expiration date, depending on whether the total proceeds at the expiration date would be greater by holding the option or by exercising it and reinvesting any cash proceeds received until the expiration date.

Factors that Influence the Option Price

The following six factors influence the option price:

1. Spot price of the underlying.
2. Strike price.
3. Time to expiration of the option.
4. Expected price volatility of the underlying over the life of the option.
5. Short-term risk-free rate over the life of the option.
6. Anticipated cash dividends on the underlying stock or index over the life of the option.

The impact of each of these factors depends on whether (1) the option is a call or a put and (2) the option is an American option or a European option. A summary of the effects of each factor on American put and call option prices is presented in Exhibit 14.4.

Notice how the expected price volatility of the underlying over the life of the option affects the price of both a put and a call option. All other factors being equal, the greater the expected volatility (as measured by the standard deviation or variance) of the price of the underlying, the more an investor would be willing to pay for the option, and the more an option writer would demand for it. This is because the greater the volatility, the greater the probability that the price of the underlying will move in favor of the option buyer at some time before expiration.

EXHIBIT 14.4   Summary of Factors that Effect the Price of an American Option

Factor	Effect of an Increase of Factor on	
	Call Price	Put Price
Spot price of underlying	Increase	Decrease
Strike price	Decrease	Increase
Time to expiration of option	Increase	Increase
Expected price volatility	Increase	Increase
Short-term rate	Increase	Decrease
Anticipated cash dividends	Decrease	Increase

Option Pricing Models

Several models have been developed to determine the theoretical value of an option.[8] The most popular one was developed by Fischer Black and Myron Scholes in 1973 for valuing European call options.[9] Several modifications to their model have followed since then. We discuss this model here to explain how to price an option.

By imposing certain assumptions and using arbitrage arguments, the Black-Scholes option pricing model provides the fair (or theoretical) price of a European call option on a nondividend-paying stock. Basically, the idea behind the arbitrage argument in deriving this and other option pricing models is that if the payoff from owning a call option can be replicated by (1) purchasing the stock underlying the call option and (2) borrowing funds, then the price of the option will be (at most) the cost of creating the replicating strategy.

The formula for the Black-Scholes model is

$$C = SN(d_1) - Xe^{-rt}N(d_2)$$

where

---

[8]The most common are the Black-Scholes-Merton model and the Binomial Pricing models. Other models have been developed to deal with the shortcomings of these two basic models.

[9]Fischer Black and Myron Scholes, "The Pricing of Corporate Liabilities," *Journal of Political Economy* 81 (May–June 1973): 637–659. Today, many practitioners refer to the basic model as the Black-Scholes-Merton model. Robert Merton was awarded the Nobel Prize for economics along with Myron Scholes for their work on options pricing. See R. C. Merton, "Theory of Rational Option Pricing," *Bell Journal of Economics and Management Science*, 4, no. 1 (1973): 141–183.

$$d_1 = \frac{\ln(S/K) + (r + 0.5s^2)t}{s\sqrt{t}}$$

$$d_2 = d_1 - s\sqrt{t}$$

ln = natural logarithm
C   = call option price
S   = price of the underlying
K   = strike price
r   = short-term risk-free rate
e   = 2.718 (natural antilog of 1)
t   = time remaining to the expiration date (measured as a fraction of a year)
s   = standard deviation of the change in stock p
$N(.)$ = the cumulative probability density[10]

Notice that five of the factors that we said earlier in this chapter influence the price of an option are included in the formula. However, the sixth factor, anticipated cash dividends, is not included because the model is for a nondividend-paying stock. In the Black-Scholes model, the direction of the influence of each of these factors is the same as stated earlier. Four of the factors—strike price, price of underlying, time to expiration, and risk-free rate—are easily observed. The standard deviation of the price of the underlying must be estimated. The option price derived from the Black-Scholes model is "fair" in the sense that if any other price existed, it would be possible to earn riskless arbitrage profits by taking an offsetting position in the underlying. That is, if the price of the call option in the market is higher than that derived from the Black-Scholes model, an investor could sell the call option and buy a certain quantity of the underlying. If the reverse is true, that is, the market price of the call option is less than the "fair" price derived from the model, the investor could buy the call option and sell short a certain amount of the underlying. This process of hedging by taking a position in the underlying allows the investor to lock in the riskless arbitrage profit. The number of shares necessary to hedge the position changes as the factors that affect the option price change, so the hedged position must be changed constantly.

To illustrate the Black-Scholes model, assume the following values:

Strike price   = $45
Time remaining to expiration = 183 days

---

[10]The value for $N(.)$ is obtained from a normal distribution function that is tabulated in most statistics textbooks or from spreadsheets that have this built-in function.

Spot stock price   = $47
Expected price volatility   = standard deviation = 25%
Risk-free rate   = 10%

In terms of the values in the formula:

S = 47
K = 45
t = 0.5 (183 days/365, rounded)
s = 0.25
r = 0.10

Substituting these values into the equations above, we get

$$d_1 = \frac{\ln(47/45) + [0.10 + 0.5(0.25)^2]0.5}{0.25\sqrt{0.5}} = 0.6172$$

$$d_2 = 0.6172 - 0.25\sqrt{0.5} = 0.4404$$

From a normal distribution table,

$$N(0.6172) = 0.7315 \text{ and } N(0.4404) = 0.6702$$

Then

$$C = 47(0.7315) - 45(e^{-(0.10)(0.5)})(0.6702) = \$5.69$$

How do we determine the value of put options? There is relationship that shows the relationship among the spot price of the underlying, the call option price, and the put option price. This is called the *put-call parity relationship*. If we can calculate the fair value of a call option, the fair value of a put with the same strike price and expiration on the same stock can be calculated from the put-call parity relationship.

Sensitivity of the Option Price to a Change in Factors

In employing options in investment strategies, a manager would like to know how sensitive the price of an option is to a change in any one of the factors that affect its price. Let's discuss the sensitivity of a call option's price to changes in the price of the underlying, the time to expiration, and expected price volatility. These measures are commonly referred to as the "Greeks" since Greek letters are used to describe them.

The Call Option Price and the Price of the Underlying A manager employing options for risk management wants to know how the option position will change as the price of the underlying changes. Exhibit 14.5 shows the theoretical price of a call option based on the price of the underlying. The horizontal axis is the price of the underlying at any point in time. The vertical axis is the theoretical call option price. The shape of the curve representing the theoretical price of a call option, given the price of the underlying, would be the same regardless of the actual option pricing model used. In particular, the relationship between the price of the underlying and the theoretical call option price is convex.

The line from the origin to the strike price on the horizontal axis in Exhibit 14.5 is the intrinsic value of the call option when the price of the underlying is less than the strike price since the intrinsic value is zero. The 45-degree line extending from the horizontal axis is the intrinsic value of the call option once the price of the underlying exceeds the strike price. The reason is that the intrinsic value of the call option will increase by the same dollar amount as the increase in the price of the underlying. For example, if the strike price is $100 and the price of the underlying increases from $100 to $101, the intrinsic value will increase by $1. If the price of the underlying increases from $101 to $110, the intrinsic value of the option will increase from $1 to $10. Thus, the slope of the line representing the intrinsic value after the strike price is reached is 1.

EXHIBIT 14.5 Theoretical Call Price and Price of Underlying

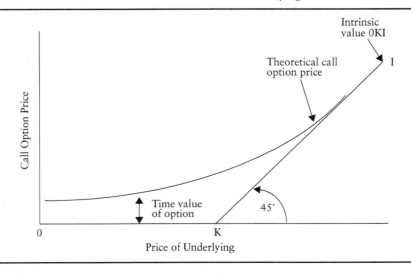

EXHIBIT 14.6   Estimating the Theoretical Option Price

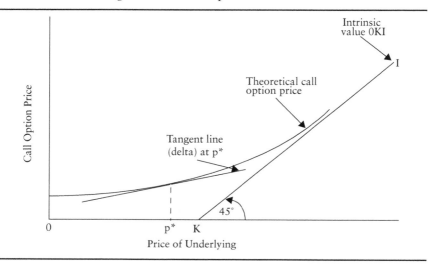

Since the theoretical call option price is shown by the convex curve, the difference between the theoretical call option price and the intrinsic value at any given price for the underlying is the time value of the option. Exhibit 14.6 shows the theoretical call option price, but with a tangent line drawn at the price p*. The tangent line in the exhibit can be used to estimate what the new option price will be (and therefore what the change in the option price will be) if the price of the underlying changes. Because of the convexity of the relationship between the option price and the price of the underlying, the tangent line closely approximates the new option price for a small change in the price of the underlying. For large changes, however, the tangent line does not provide as good an approximation of the new option price. The slope of the tangent line shows how the theoretical call option price will change for small changes in the price of the underlying. The slope of the tangent line is popularly referred to as the *delta* of the option. Specifically,

$$\text{Delta} = \frac{\text{Change in price of call option}}{\text{Change in price of underlying}}$$

For example, a delta of 0.4 means that a $1 change in the price of the underlying will change the price of the call option by approximately $0.40.

Thus, the delta for a call option varies from zero (for call options deep out of the money) to 1 (for call options deep in the money). The delta for a call option at the money is approximately 0.5. The curvature of the convex relationship can also be approximated. This is the rate of change of delta as the price of the underlying changes. The measure is commonly referred to as *gamma* and is defined as follows:

$$\text{Gamma} = \frac{\text{Change in delta}}{\text{Change in price of underlying}}$$

The Call Option Price and Time to Expiration   All other factors constant, the longer the time to expiration, the greater is the option price. Since each day the option moves closer to the expiration date, the time to expiration decreases. The *theta* of an option measures the change in the option price as the time to expiration decreases, or equivalently, it is a measure of time decay. Theta is measured as follows:

$$\text{Theta} = \frac{\text{Change in price of option}}{\text{Decrease in time to expiration}}$$

Assuming that the price of the underlying does not change (which means that the intrinsic value of the option does not change), theta measures how quickly the time value of the option changes as the option moves toward expiration. Buyers of options prefer a low theta so that the option price does not decline quickly as it moves toward the expiration date. An option writer benefits from an option that has a high theta.

The Call Option Price and Expected Price Volatility   All other factors constant, a change in the expected price volatility will change the option price. The *vega* (also called *kappa*) of an option measures the dollar price change in the price of the option for a 1% change in the expected price volatility. That is,

$$\text{Vega} = \frac{\text{Change in option price}}{1\% \text{ change in expected price volatility}}$$

Critique of Black-Scholes Pricing Model

The Black-Scholes pricing model while ground-breaking and innovative is based on a set of assumptions some of which do not hold up in the real world. First of all, the model cannot be used to price American-style options that pay dividends. Second, the underlying assumption that stock returns are normally distributed is inconsistent with the empirical finding of "fat tails" in equity returns. The implication of fat tails is that the Black-Scholes pricing model misprices OTM options. Finally, the model assumes that volatility is constant across the entire price distribution.

Because of these shortcomings, there have been many developments in option pricing models. The most famous perhaps is the binomial option pricing model. The major advantage this model has over the Black-Scholes model is that it can be used to price American-style options. Other modifications have included incorporating stochastic volatility into the model and to consider alternative price distribution that takes into account fat tails.[11]

FUTURES CONTRACTS

A *futures contract* is an agreement between two parties, a buyer and a seller, where the parties agree to transact with respect to the underlying at a predetermined price at a specified date. Both parties are obligated to perform over the life of the contract, and neither party charges a fee. Once the two parties have consummated the trade, the exchange where the futures contract is traded becomes the counterparty to the trade, thereby severing the relationship between the initial parties.

Each futures contract is accompanied by an exact description of the terms of the contract, including a description of the underlying, the contract size, settlement cycles, trading specifications, and position limits. The fact is that in the case of futures contracts, delivery is not the objective of either party because the contracts are used primarily to manage risk or costs.

The nature of the futures contract specifies a buyer and a seller who agree to buy or sell a standard quantity of the underlying at a designated future date. However, when we speak of buyers and sellers, we are simply adopting the language of the futures market, which refers to parties of the contract in terms of the future obligation they are committing themselves to. The buyer of a futures contract agrees to take delivery of the underlying and is said to be *long futures*. Long futures positions benefit when the price of the underlying rises. Since futures can be considered a substitute for a subsequent transaction in the cash market, a long futures position is comparable to holding the underlying without the financial cost of purchasing the underlying or the income that comes from holding the underlying. The seller, on the other hand, is said to be *short futures* and benefits when the price of the underlying declines.

---

[11]Most models used to price options rely on the assumption that asset price behavior can be represented by a geometric Brownian motion. A discussion of the weaknesses of this assumption and presentation of alternative models is found in Chapters 19 and 26 of John C. Hull, *Options, Futures and Other Derivatives*, 7th ed. (Upper Saddle River, N.J.: Pearson Prentice Hall, 2009).

The designated price at which the parties agree to transact is called the *futures price*. The designated date at which the parties must transact is the *settlement date* or *delivery date*. Unlike options, no money changes hands between buyer and seller at the contract's inception. However, the futures broker and the futures exchange require initial margin as a "good faith" deposit. In addition, a minimum amount of funds referred to as *maintenance margin* is required to be maintained in the corresponding futures account. The initial margin and the maintenance margin can be held in the form of short-term credit instruments.

Futures are marked-to-the-market on a daily basis. This means that daily gains or losses in the investor's position are accounted for immediately and reflected in his or her account. The daily cash flow from a futures position is called *variation margin* and essentially means that the futures contract is settled daily. Thus, the buyer of the futures contract pays when the price of the underlying falls and the seller pays when the price of the underlying rises. Variation margin differs from other forms of margin because outflows must be met with cash.

Futures contracts have a settlement cycle and there may be several contracts trading simultaneously. The contract with the closest settlement is call the *nearby futures contract* and is usually the most liquid. The next futures contract is the one that settles just after the near contract. The contract with the furthest away settlement is called the *most distant futures contract*.

Differences between Options and Futures

The fundamental difference between futures and options is that buyer of an option (the long position) has the right but not the obligation to enter into a transaction. The option writer is obligated to transact if the buyer so desires. In contrast, both parties are obligated to perform in the case of a futures contract. In addition, to establish a position, the party who is long futures does not pay the party who is short futures. In contrast, the party long an option must make a payment to the party who is short the option in order to establish the position. The price paid is the option price.

The payout structure also differs between a futures contract and an options contract. The price of an option contract represents the cost of eliminating or modifying the risk–reward relationship of the underlying. In contrast, the payout for a futures contract is a dollar-for-dollar gain or loss for the buyer and seller. The buyer gains at the expense of the seller when the futures price rises, while the buyer suffers a dollar-for dollar loss when the futures price drops.

Thus, futures payout is symmetrical, while the payout for options is skewed. The maximum loss for the option buyer is the option price. The loss to the futures buyer is the full value of the contract. The option buyer has limited downside losses but retains the benefits of an increase in the value in the position of the underlying. The maximum profit that can be realized by the option writer is the option price, which is offset by significant downside exposure. The losses or gains to the buyer and seller of a futures contract are completely symmetrical. Consequently, futures can be used as a hedge against symmetric risk, while options can be used to hedge asymmetric risk.

Features of Futures

The key elements of a futures contract include the futures price, the amount or quantity of the underlying, and the settlement or delivery date.

Stock Index Futures

The underlying for a stock index futures contract is the portfolio of stocks represented by the index.

The value of the underlying portfolio is the value of the index in a specified currency times a number called a *multiplier*. For example, if the current value of the S&P 500 index is 1100, then the seller of a December S&P 500 futures contract is theoretically obligated to deliver in December a portfolio of the 500 stocks that comprise the index. The multiplier for this contract is 250. The portfolio would have to exactly replicate the index with the weights of the stocks equal to their index weights. The current value of one futures contract is $275,000 (= 1100 × 250).

However, because of the problems associated with delivering a portfolio of 500 stocks that exactly replicate the underlying index, stock index futures substitute cash delivery for physical delivery. At final settlement, the futures price equals the spot price and the value of a futures contract is the actual market value of the underlying replicating portfolio that represents the stock index. The contract is marked-to-market based on the settlement price, which is the spot price, and the contract settles. Exhibit 14.7 provides a list of selected stock index futures traded in the United States and Europe.

Single Stock Futures

A *single stock futures* (SSF) contract is an agreement between two parties to buy or sell shares of individual companies (as opposed to a stock index in the case of a stock index futures contract) at some time in the future with the terms agreed upon today. The value of traditional futures contracts is captured by SSFs as well because the agreement requires a low

EXHIBIT 14.7 Selected Equity Futures Contracts Traded in the United States and Europe

Index Futures Contract	Index Description	Exchange	Contract Size
US contracts			
S&P 500	500 cap-weighted stocks	CME	Index × 250 Index × 50 E-mini
S&P MidCap 400	400 cap-weighted stocks	CME	Index × 500 Index × 100 E-mini
Russell 200 Index	2,000 cap-weighted stocks	ICE	Index × 500 Index × 100 mini
S&P Growth Index	165 cap-weighted stocks	CME	Index × 250
S&P Value Index	165 cap-weighted stocks	CME	Index × 250
European contracts			
EURO STOXX 50	50 cap-weighted European stocks	Eurex	Several multiples[a] 5, 10, 25, 50, 100, 200
DAX	30 cap-weighted German stocks	Eurex	Several multiples[a] 5, 10, 25, 50, 100, 200
FTSE 100 Index	100 cap-weighted UK stocks	NYSE Euronext	Index × 10[b]
CAC 40 Index	40-cap-weighted stocks on Euronext Paris	NYSE Euronext	Index × 10[c]

[a]Multiples in euros. Some available in Swiss francs or U.S. dollars.
[b]Multiple in British pounds.
[c]Multiple in euros.

capital commitment upfront in the form of initial margin. Originally there were two key benefits to investors. These included that shorting was not constrained by the uptick rule or complicated by stock loans and a simple long or short strategy in the underlying stock can be created.[12]

SSFs currently trade on numerous exchanges around the world including those in Australia, Denmark, Finland, Hong Kong, Hungary, Portugal, South Africa, Sweden, and, most recently, Canada, the UK, the United States and Iran. As of this writing, there has been modest success for these products. In January 2001, the London International Financial Futures Exchange (LIFFE) introduced SSFs on 30 stocks including seven U.S. companies and the Bourse de Montreal began trading a SSF contract on Nortel Networks.

---

[12]SEC Rule 10a-1(a)(1) (the uptick rule) was removed when Rule 201 Regulation SHO became effective in 2007. In February 2010, the SEC created an alternative rule that triggers a circuit breaker after a stock has fallen 10%. After triggered an uptick rule is in effect.

In May of that year, LIFFE expanded the number by 25 contracts to a total of 65 listed SSF contracts on global stocks.

The importance of the LIFFE development is that it is the first time SSFs have been listed on a major global exchange. The contracts are referred to as Universal Stock Futures (USF) and are standardized futures contracts based on shares of European and U.S. companies. Since the Euronext takeover of LIFFE, it is now part of NYSE Euronext and current trades 143 single stock futures contracts.

Recently, the CBOE, the CME (Chicago Mercantile Exchange) and the CBOT (Chicago Board of Trade) formed a joint venture to establish an electronic trading platform for SSFs called OneChicago, LLC. Trading in SSFs on OneChicago began in November 2002. OneChicago lists futures on 1,548 stocks including some bellwether stocks as IBM, Apple, Google and others.

The standardized features of the contracts for the NYSE Euronext market and the emerging U.S. market at OneChicago include a contract size of 100 shares with quotes in dollars or euros.[13] The minimum tick increment is $0.01 per share or $1 dollar per contract. Settlement calls for the physical delivery of 100 shares (adjusted for corporate events) of stock. The NYSE Euronext contract is also available as cash delivery. There is no daily price limits imposed on the contracts, but OneChicago has position limits of 13,500 net contracts on the 100 shares contracts and 1,350 net contracts on the 1,000 share contracts, which apply only during the last five trading days prior to expiration and are required by CFTC regulation.

PRICING STOCK INDEX FUTURES

Futures contracts are priced based on the spot price and cost of carry considerations. For equity contracts these include the cost of financing a position in the underlying asset, the dividend yield on the underlying stocks, and the time to settlement of the futures contract. The theoretical futures price is derived from the spot price adjusted for the cost of carry. This can be confirmed using risk-free arbitrage arguments.

The logic of the pricing model is that the purchase of a futures contract can be looked at as a temporary substitute for a transaction in the cash market at a later date. Moreover, futures contracts are not assets to be purchased and no money changes hands when the agreement is made. Futures contracts are agreements between two parties that establish the terms of a later transaction. It is these facts that lead us to a pricing relationship

---

[13]OneChicago also offers a 1,000 share contract size and as of this writing the NYSE Euronext Universal stock futures contract for Italy offered 1,000 share size.

between futures contracts and the underlying. The seller of a futures contract is ultimately responsible for delivering the underlying and will demand compensation for incurring the cost of holding it. Thus, the futures price will reflect the cost of financing the underlying. However, the buyer of the futures contract does not hold the underlying and therefore does not receive the dividend. The futures price must be adjusted downward to take this into consideration. The adjustment of the yield for the cost of financing is what is called the *net cost of carry*. The futures price is then based on the net cost of carry, which is the cost of financing adjusted for the yield on the underlying. That is,

Futures price = Spot price + Cost of financing – Dividend yield

The borrowing or financing rate is an interest rate on a money market instrument and the yield in the case of equity futures is the dividend yield on an individual stock or a portfolio of stocks that represent the stock index.

The theoretical futures price derived from this process is a model of the fair value of the futures contract. It is the price that defines a no-arbitrage condition. The no-arbitrage condition is the futures price at which sellers are prepared to sell and buyers are prepared to buy, but no risk-free profit is possible. The theoretical futures price expressed mathematically depends on the treatment of dividends. For individual equities with quarterly dividend payout, the theoretical futures price can be expressed as the spot price adjusted for the present value of expected dividends over the life of the contract and the cost of financing. The expression is given below as

$$F(t,T) = [S(t) - D] \times [1 + R(t,T)]$$

where

$F(t,T)$ = futures price at time t for a contract that settles in the future at time T

$S(t)$ = current spot price

D = present value of dividends expected to be received over the life of the contract

$R(t,T)$ = borrowing rate for a loan with the same time to maturity as the futures settlement date

For example, if the current price of the S&P 500 stock index is 1150, the borrowing rate is 0.4%, the time to settlement is 60 days, and the index is expected to yield 2.14%.[14] An annualized dividend yield of 2.14% corresponds to 4.045 index points when the S&P 500 stock index is 1150 and the contract has 60 days to expiration.

$$1150 \times [0.0214 \times 60/365] = 4.045 \text{ index points}$$

The theoretical futures price can be calculated as follows:

$$D = 4.05/(1 + 0.004)^{60/365} = 4.043$$

$$R = (1 + 0.004)^{(60/365)} - 1 = 0.000656 \text{ or } 0.0656\%$$

$$F(t,60) = [1150 - 4.043] \times 1.000656 = 1146.71$$

If the actual futures price is above or below 1146.71, then risk-free arbitrage is possible. For actual futures prices greater than fair value, the futures contract is overvalued. Arbitrageurs will sell the futures contract, borrow enough funds to purchase the underlying stock index, and hold the position until fair value is restored or until the settlement date of the futures contract.

If, for example, we assume the actual futures price is 1151, then the following positions would lead to risk-free arbitrage:

- Sell the overvalued futures at 1151.
- Borrow an amount equivalent to 1150.
- Purchase a stock portfolio that replicates the index for the equivalent of 1150.

The position can be unwound at the settlement date in 60 days at no risk to the arbitrageur. At the settlement date, the futures settlement price equals the spot price. Assume the spot price is unchanged at 1150. Then,

- Collect 4.045 in dividends.
- Settle the short futures position by delivering the index to the buyer for 1151.
- Repay 1150.755 (1150 × 1.000656) to satisfy the loan (remember the interest rate for the 60 days is 0.0656%).

The net gain is [1151 + 4.045] − 1150.755 = 4.29. That is, the arbitrageur "earned" 4.29 index points or 37 basis points (4.29/1150) without risk

---

[14]The dividend yield and borrowing rate are derived from actual data as of July 2010.

EXHIBIT 14.8 Arbitrage Cash Flows: Short Futures at 1151

Futures Stock Index Settlement Price	Futures Cash Flows	Stock Cash Flows	Interest	Profits
1175	1151 – 1175 = –24	25 + 4.045 = 29.045	0.755	4.29
1165	1151 – 1165 = –14	15 + 4.045 = 19.045	0.755	4.29
1150	1151 – 1150 = 1	0 + 4.045 = 4.045	0.755	4.29
1140	1151 – 1140 = 11	–10 + 4.045 = –5.955	0.755	4.29
1135	1151 – 1135 = 16	–15 + 4.045 = –10.955	0.755	4.29
1125	1151 – 1125 = 26	–25 + 4.045 = –20.955	0.755	4.29

or without making any investment. This activity would continue until the price of the futures converged on fair value.

It does not matter what the settlement price for the index is at the settlement date. This can be clearly shown by treating the futures position and stock position separately. The futures position delivers the difference between the original futures price and the settlement price or 1151 – 1150, which equals 1 index point. The long stock position earned only the dividends and no capital gain. The cost of financing the position in the stock is 0.755 and the net return to the combined short futures and long stock position is 1(futures) + 4.045(stock) less the 0.755 cost of financing, which is a net return of 4.29. Now consider what happens if the spot price is at any other level at the settlement date. Exhibit 14.8 shows the cash flows associated with the arbitrage. We can see from the results that regardless of the movement of the spot price, the arbitrage profit is preserved.

For actual futures prices less than fair value, the futures contract is undervalued. Arbitrageurs will buy the futures contract, short or sell the underlying, lend the proceeds, and hold the position until fair value is restored or until settlement date of the futures contract.

The theoretical futures price can also be expressed mathematically based on a security with a known dividend yield. For equities that pay out a constant dividend over the life of a futures contract, this rendition of the model is appropriate. This may apply to stock index futures contracts where the underlying is an equity index of a large number of stocks. Rather than calculating every dividend, the cumulative dividend payout or the weighted-average dividend produces a constant and known dividend yield. The cost of carry valuation model is modified to reflect the behavior of dividends. This is expressed in the following equation:

$$F(t,T) = S(t) \times [1 + R(t,T) - Y(t,T)]$$

where $Y(t,T)$ is the dividend yield on the underlying over the life of the futures contract and $F(t,T)$, $S(t)$, and $R(t,T)$ are as defined earlier.

For example, if the current price of a stock is 1150, the borrowing rate is 0.4%, the time to settlement is 60 days, and the annualized dividend yield is 2.14%, the theoretical futures price can be calculated as follows:

$$Y = (1 + 0.0214)^{60/365} - 1 = 0.003487 \text{ or } 0.3487\%$$

$$R = (1 + 0.004)^{(60/365)} - 1 = 0.000656 \text{ or } 0.0656\%$$

$$F(t,60) = 1150 \times [1 + 0.000656 - 0.003487] = 1146.75$$

In practice, it is important to remember to use the borrowing rate and dividend yield for the term of the contract and not the annual rates. The arbitrage conditions outlined above still hold in this case. The model is specified differently, but the same outcome is possible. When the actual futures price deviates from the theoretical price suggested by the futures pricing model, arbitrage would be possible and likely. The existence of risk-free arbitrage profits will attract arbitrageurs.

Also in practice, there are several factors that may violate the assumptions of the futures valuation model. Because of these factors, arbitrage must be carried out with some degree of uncertainty and the fair value futures price is not a single price, but actually a range of prices where the upper and lower prices act as boundaries around an arbitrage-free zone. Furthermore, the violation of various assumptions can produce mispricing and risk that reduce arbitrage opportunities.

The futures price ought to gravitate toward fair value when there is a viable and active arbitrage mechanism. Arbitrage activity will only take place beyond the upper and lower limits established by transaction and other costs, uncertain cash flows, and divergent borrowing and lending rates among participants. The variability of the spread between the spot price and futures price, known as the *basis*, is a consequence of mispricing due to changes in the variables that influence the fair value.

The practical aspects of pricing produce a range of prices. This means that the basis can move around without offering a profit motive for arbitrageurs. The perspective of arbitrageurs in the equity futures markets is based on dollar profit but can be viewed in terms of an interest rate. The borrowing or financing rate found in the cost of carry valuation formula assumes borrowing and lending rates are the same. In practice, however, borrowing rates are almost always higher than lending rates. Thus, the model will yield different values depending on the respective borrowing and lending rates facing the user. Every futures price corresponds to an interest rate. We can manipulate the formula and solve for the rate implied by the futures price, which is called the *implied futures rate*. For each market participant there is a theoretical fair value range defined by its respective borrowing and lending rates and transaction costs.

OTC EQUITY DERIVATIVES

An OTC equity derivative can be delivered on a stand-alone basis or as part of a structured product. Structured products involve packaging standard or exotic options, equity swaps, or equity-linked debt into a single product in any combination to meet the risk–return objectives of the investor and may represent an alternative to the cash market even when cash instruments are available.

The four basic components of OTC equity derivatives are equity forwards, OTC options, equity swaps, and equity-linked debt. These components offer an array of product structures that can assist investors in developing and implementing investment strategies that respond to a changing financial world. OTC derivatives can assist the investor with cost minimization, diversification, hedging, asset allocation, and risk management.

Before we provide a product overview, let's look at counterparty risk. For exchange listed derivative products counterparty or credit risk is minimal because of the clearing house associated with the exchange. However, for OTC products there is counterparty risk. For parties taking a position where performance of both parties is required, both parties are exposed to counterparty risk. The OTC market has incorporated a variety of terms into the contractual agreement between counterparties to address the issue of credit risk. These include netting arrangements, position limits, the use of collateral, recouponing, credit triggers, and the establishment of Derivatives Product Companies (DPCs).

Netting arrangements between counterparties are used in master agreements specifying that in the event of default, the bottom line is the net payment owed across all contractual agreements between the two counterparties. *Position limits* may be imposed on a particular counterparty according to the cumulative nature of their positions and creditworthiness. As the OTC market has grown, the creditworthiness of customers has become more diverse. Consequently, dealers are requiring some counterparties to furnish collateral in the form of a liquid shortterm credit instrument. *Recouponing* involves periodically changing the coupon such that the marked-to-market value of the position is zero. For long-term OTC agreements, a *credit trigger provision* allows the dealer to have the position cash settled if the counterparty's credit rating falls below investment grade. Finally, dealers are establishing DPCs as separate business entities to maintain high credit ratings that are crucial in competitively pricing OTC products.

Equity Forwards

Equity forward contracts are OTC products where the underlying equity security can be a single stock, a basket of stocks or based on a stock index.[15] The buyer of the forward is in a long position to take delivery of the underlying at settlement. The seller is responsible for delivery and is short the underlying. The forward price is determined by cost of carry considerations versus the current spot price. The buyer gains if, at settlement, the spot price exceeds the forward price. Equity forwards are a useful mechanism for hedging price risk on either the long or the short side. A long position is stock can be hedged by a short forward contract, while the a short position such as anticipatory purchase can be hedged with a long forward contract.

OTC Options

OTC options can be classified as first generation and second generation options. The latter are called *exotic options*. We describe each type of OTC option below.

First Generation of OTC Options

The basic type of first generation OTC options either extends the standardized structure of an existing listed option or created an option on stocks, stock baskets, or stock indexes without listed options or futures. Thus, OTC options were first used to modify one or more of the features of listed options: the strike price, maturity, size, exercise type (American or European), and delivery mechanism. The terms were tailored to the specific needs of the investor. For example, the strike price can be any level, the maturity date at any time, the contract of any size, the exercise type American or European, the underlying can be a stock, a stock portfolio, or an equity index or a foreign equity index, and the settlement can be physical, in cash or a combination.

An example of how OTC options can differ from listed options is exemplified by an Asian option. Listed options are either European or American in structure relating to the timing of exercise. Asian options are options

---

[15]For a treatment of equity forward contracts see; Julian Barrow and Richard Hart, "Types of OTC Equity Products," in *Equity Derivatives, Documenting and Understanding Equity Derivative Products*, ed. Edmund Parker (London: Global Business Publishing Ltd., 2009), 63–84.

with a payout that is dependent on the average price of the spot price over the life of the option. Due to the averaging process involved, the volatility of the spot price is reduced. Thus, Asian options are cheaper than similar European or American options.

The first generation of OTC options offered flexible solutions to investment situations that listed options did not. For example, hedging strategies using the OTC market allow the investor to achieve customized total risk protection for a specific time horizon. The first generation of OTC options allow investors to fine tune their traditional equity investment strategies through customizing strike prices, and maturities, and choosing any underlying equity security or portfolio of securities. Investors could now improve the management of risk through customized hedging strategies or enhance returns through customized buy writes. In addition, investors could invest in foreign stocks without the need to own them, profit from an industry downturn without the need to short stocks.

Exotics: Second Generation OTC Options

The second generation of OTC equity options includes a set of products that have more complex payoff characteristics than standard American or European call and put options. These second-generation options are sometimes referred to as "exotic" options and are essentially options with specific rules that govern the payoff.[16] Exotic option structures can be created on a stand-alone basis or as part of a broader financing package such as an attachment to a bond issue, which are considered structured products.

Some OTC option structures are path dependent, which means that the value of the option to some extent depends on the price pattern of the underlying asset over the life of the option. In fact, the survival of some options, such as barrier options, depends on this price pattern. Other examples of path dependent options include Asian options, lookback options, and reset options. Another group of OTC option structures has properties similar to step functions. They have fixed singular payoffs when a particular condition is met. Examples of this include digital or binary options and contingent options. A third group of options is classified as multivariate because the payoff is related to more than one underlying asset. Examples of this group include a general category of rainbow options such as spread options and basket options.

Competitive market makers are now prepared to offer investors a broad range of derivative products that satisfy the specific requirements of

---

[16]For a description of exotic options, see Chapter 10 in Bruce M. Collins and Frank J. Fabozzi, *Derivatives and Equity Portfolio Management* (Hoboken, N.J.: John Wiley & Sons, 1999).

investors. The fastest growing portion of this market pertaining to equities involves products with option-like characteristics on major stock indexes or stock portfolios.

Equity Swaps

Equity swaps have the same structure as interest rate swaps in that they are agreements between two counterparties which provide for the periodic exchange of a schedule of cash flows over a specified time period based on some notional amount. For equity swaps at least one of the two payments is linked to the performance of an equity index, a basket of stocks, or a single stock. The unique feature of an equity swap is that the net cash flows are often based on two different markets typically equity, bonds or money markets. In a standard or plain vanilla equity swap, one counterparty agrees to pay the other the total return to an equity index in exchange for receiving either the total return of another asset or a fixed or floating interest rate. All payments are based on a fixed notional amount and payments are made over a fixed time period.

Equity swap structures are very flexible with maturities ranging from a few months to 10 years. The returns of virtually any asset can be swapped for another without incurring the costs associated with a transaction in the cash market. Payment schedules can be denominated in any currency irrespective of the equity asset and payments can be exchanged monthly, quarterly, annually, or at maturity. The equity asset can be any equity index or portfolio of stocks, hedged or unhedged.

Variations of the plain vanilla equity swap include: international equity swaps where the equity return is linked to an international equity index; currency-hedged swaps where the swap is structured to eliminate currency risk; and call swaps where the equity payment is paid only if the equity index appreciates (depreciation will not result in a payment from the counterparty receiving the equity return to the other counterparty because of call protection).

A basic swap structure is illustrated in Exhibit 14.9. In this case, the investor owns a short-term credit instrument that yields LIBOR (London Interbank Offered Rate) plus a spread. The investor then enters into a swap to exchange LIBOR plus the spread for the total return to an equity index. The counterparty pays the total return to the index in exchange for LIBOR plus a spread. Assuming the equity index is the Nikkei 225, a U.S. investor could swap dollar-denominated LIBOR plus a spread for cash flows from the total return to the Nikkei denominated in yen or U.S. dollars. The index could be any foreign or domestic equity index. A

EXHIBIT 14.9   Equity Swaps

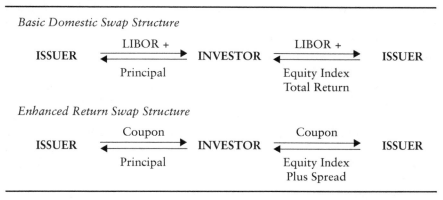

Basic Domestic Swap Structure

Enhanced Return Swap Structure

swap could also be structured to generate superior returns if the financing instrument in the swap yields a higher return than LIBOR.

There are a number of reasons for using equity swaps versus a direct investment in a portfolio of physical shares of equity. These benefits are consistent with the role of derivatives outlined previously. Swaps can serve as an effective mean of cost management by offering lower administrative and execution costs. Swap structures are particularly suitable for returns management because they serve as a substitute for passive index funds or core portfolios with performance benchmarks. There might be regulatory constraints associated with international investments that can be managed with swaps. In addition, swap structures can be devised to effectively manage currency risk.

Equity swaps can be used by fund and portfolio managers for a variety of applications including asset allocation, accessing international markets, enhancing equity returns, hedging equity exposure, and synthetically shorting stocks. A swap structure can create the same economics of a direct investment in an asset. Unlike interest rate swaps where both legs produce positive cash flows, the equity leg can produce a negative cash flow leading to cash outflows on both legs of the swap. An investor who wants to invest $100 million in equities can instead put the money into a short term credit instrument and enter into an equity swap. Every payment date, the investor uses the proceeds from the investment to pay the floating leg and will either invest or divest the equity leg. Thus, this is the equivalent of an equity investment financed with LIBOR.

Another example of an equity swap is a 1-year agreement where the counterparty agrees to pay the investor the total return to the S&P 500 Index in exchange for dollar-denominated LIBOR on a quarterly basis. The investor would pay LIBOR plus a spread × 91/360 × notional amount. This type of equity swap is the economic equivalent of financing a long position in the S&P 500 Index at a spread to LIBOR. The advantages of using the swap are no transaction costs, no sales or dividend withholding tax, and no tracking error or basis risk versus the index.

The basic mechanics of equity swaps are the same regardless of the structure. However, the rules governing the exchange of payments may differ. For example, a U.S. investor wanting to diversify internationally can enter into a swap and, depending on the investment objective, exchange payments on a currency-hedged basis. If the investment objective is to reduce U.S. equity exposure and increase Japanese equity exposure, for example, a swap could be structured to exchange the total returns to the S&P 500 Index for the total returns to the Nikkei 225 Index. If, however, the investment objective is to gain access to the Japanese equity market, a swap can be structured to exchange LIBOR plus a spread for the total returns to the Nikkei 225 Index. This is an example of diversifying internationally and the cash flows can be denominated in either yen or dollars. The advantages of entering into an equity swap to obtain international diversification are that the investor exposure is devoid of tracking error, and the investor incurs no sales tax, custodial fees, withholding fees, or market impact associated with entering and exiting a market. This swap is the economic equivalent of being long the Nikkei 225 financed at a spread to LIBOR at a fixed exchange rate.

STRUCTURED PRODUCTS

It is difficult to precisely define a structured product or separate it from an OTC product. The market is part of the OTC market, but goes beyond the traditional set of OTC products. It includes equity-linked debt investments, but is mostly identified with a "wrapper," which is a legal structure that houses the product by which it is sold to the public. The most common of structures are transferable securities such as a note or a unit in a fund such as an equity certificate. These products are often issued by a *Special Purpose Vehicle* (SPV) that is created specifically to sell the product to the public. The SPV will hold assets that are part of the product and obtain the necessary credit rating to meet the needs of its investors. Structured products are commonly issued to investors by financial institutions. Another differentiating factor for structured products versus OTC products is that some products embed an actively managed portfolio while others have principal protection guarantees. Thus, structured products can be created to enhance returns or manage specific risks. The first structures emerging from the OTC market were equity linked debt products. The wrapper is a note or a bond and the product embeds a derivative structure that can limit downside exposure, cap the upside, offer coupon payments, or include an exotic option like a barrier or Asian option.

KEY POINTS

- The equity security underlying an equity derivative can be a stock, a basket of stocks, an index or a group of indexes.
- Equity derivatives have four basic roles: risk management, returns management, cost management and regulatory management.
- There are three segments of the equity derivatives market: exchange-listed market, OTC market and the market for structured products.
- There are three general categories of derivatives: futures and forwards, options and swaps.
- OTC derivatives provide more flexible terms than listed derivatives and can be customized to meet the specific needs of investors.
- The listed market has sought to incorporate products with OTC characteristics such as FLEX options and binary options.
- The fundamental difference between futures and options is that the buyer of an option has the right but not the obligation to perform whereas the seller of an option is obligated to perform; in contrast, in the case of a futures contract both parties are required to perform
- The payout structure of a futures contract and an options contract differ. The price of an option contract represents the cost of eliminating or modifying the risk–reward relationship of the underlying. The payout for a futures contract is a dollar-for-dollar gain or loss for the buyer and seller. Consequently, a futures payout is symmetrical, while the payout for options is skewed.
- The Black-Scholes model is the basic options pricing model. There are many extensions of this model, but it remains the basic model in practice.
- The factors that affect an option's price are (1) spot price of the underlying, (2) strike price, (3) time to expiration of the option, (4) expected price volatility of the underlying over the life of the option, (5) short-term risk-free rate over the life of the option, and (6) anticipated cash dividends on the underlying stock or index over the life of the option.
- In employing options in investment strategies, a portfolio manager can calculate the sensitivity of the price of an option to a change in any one of the factors that affect its price.
- There are numerous stock index futures contracts that have been developed around the world that can be used to implement an equity investment strategy.

- Single stock futures contracts trade around the world including on the OneChicago exchange in the United States.
- Futures can be priced using a cost of carry valuation model.
- The OTC derivatives market includes equity forwards, options and warrants, equity linked debt and equity swaps.
- Structured products are an extension of the OTC market and can include a "wrapper" to house the product and sell in to the public.

QUESTIONS

1. What are the four roles that equity derivatives serve in equity portfolio management?
2. What are the advantages of listed options versus OTC options?
3. a. What is the dollar value of an S&P 500 index option at expiration if it has a strike price of 1250 and the settlement price is 1265?
   b. How much would the buyer receive?
4. a. What are the factors that affect the price of an American option?
   b. How does each factor impact the price of an American option?
5. What is the delta, theta, and vega of an option?
6. Given the information below, explain how index arbitrage is possible?

Index = 1150
Index futures = 1150
Risk-free rate = 0.5%
Days to expiration = 30
Dividends = 2% annualized

Assume at expiration the index is unchanged.

CHAPTER 15

Using Equity Derivatives in Portfolio Management

Bruce M. Collins, Ph.D.
Professor of Finance
Western Connecticut State University

Frank J. Fabozzi, Ph.D., CFA, CPA
Professor in the Practice of Finance
Yale School of Management

In the previous chapter, we described the basic characteristics of the different types of equity derivatives. We identified four primary roles for derivatives: (1) to modify the risk characteristics of an investment portfolio; (2) to enhance the expected return of a portfolio; (3) to reduce transaction costs associated with managing a portfolio; and (4) to circumvent regulatory obstacles. In this chapter, we discuss several basic applications of these instruments to equity portfolio management that reflect a cross section of these four primary roles across passive, active, and semi-active approaches to equity investment management.[1] In addition, because options will change the risk reward characteristics of an investment portfolio, we also provide an overview of the relationship between expected returns and risk for strategies employing options.

While forward and futures contracts are time dependent linear derivatives with similar payouts and risk characteristics as the underlying, options are nonlinear derivatives that have fundamentally different risk characteristics than the underlying asset. The real value of options in portfolio management regardless of the motivation for their use is that they allow the investor

---

[1] Semi-active might also fall under active strategies. It is semi-active because it involves a core exposure to equities and adding some value without actively pursuing alpha as the case with stock selection.

a means of modifying the risk and return characteristics of their investment portfolio. This makes options valuable vehicles for implementing active or semi-active strategies. The impact of adding options to an existing portfolio or using options as an investment vehicle is to create skewed distributions that reflect different risks than an investment in the underlying asset.[2] For example, the purchase of a call option rather than a stock changes the payout profile of the investment by capping the losses and thus truncates the probability distribution associated with possible outcomes and necessarily changes the expected return and risk of the investment.[3]

EQUITY INVESTMENT MANAGEMENT

Equities represent a significant asset class comprising a major proportion of investors' investment portfolios. The asset allocation for investor spans across equity markets in terms of domestic and international, based on capitalization, style, and investment approach.

There are two basic approaches to equity investment management: passive and active. Common stock portfolio management strategies are discussed in Chapter 9.[4] Passive management involves gaining broad exposure

---

[2]The use of options can create so-called "fat tails" in the returns distribution because volatility changes. Options also create an asymmetric or skewed distribution to reflect their contingent payout pattern. The extent of the skewness depends on the option. In addition, the degree of the volatility affects the peakedness or kurtosis of the distribution as well. High volatility conditions, for example, correspond to distributions with thicker tails and low volatility conditions correspond to distributions with higher peaks. For a discussion of these issues see Nassim Taleb, *Dynamic Hedging* (New York: John Wiley & Sons, 1997).

[3]The probability distribution for an option is not normally distributed as the underlying is assumed to be in Black-Scholes-Merton option pricing model. However, even in the case when returns are not normally distributed, it is still true that the expected returns and variance of the portfolio can be calculated. The normal distribution assumption of Black-Scholes-Merton models allows the mapping to a skewed distribution. The expected returns can be estimated directly from a Taylor expansion, through the use of a factor model (as we do later in the chapter based on CAPM) or through the use of Monte Carlo simulation to generate the probability distribution for the option price.

[4]For an additional discussion of equity portfolio management see Gary Gastineau, Andrew Olma, and Robert Zielinski, "Equity Portfolio Management," Chapter 7 in John Maginn, Donald Tuttle, Dennis McLeavey and Jerald Pinto (eds.), *Managing Investment Portfolios*, (Hoboken, NJ: John Wiley & Sons, 2007). Some have established a third approach called semi-active investing, which traditionally has been considered an active strategy.

to equities as defined by a tracking index such as the S&P 500 stock index.[5] Equity indexing is an approach to equity investing that seeks to replicate the performance of a benchmark. Equity derivatives can be used to as an important investment vehicle for implementing passive strategies. As an alternative to an investment in a replicating portfolio of stocks designed to track the index, investors can use a combination of a long cash investment and stock index futures or an equity swap.[6]

Recall from a previous chapter that active equity investment strategies are designed to outperform a passive equity benchmark. These strategies might use superior stock selection techniques or quantitative techniques to produce superior returns to the benchmark. The specific approach to active management is often categorized according to some concept of style. The most common two styles include growth and value investing. It might also involve a capitalization filter or the use of technical analysis. Once a style has been indentified, a style benchmark is established for measuring performance. Equity derivatives can be used as investment vehicles through a long cash position and a long position in stock index futures based on a style index.[7]

An approach to investment management that falls into an alternative category is long-short investing.[8] The investor can use stock selection to buy undervalued stocks and sell overvalued stocks. Equity derivatives can be used to isolate alpha on the long or short side. For example, a long stock portfolio with positive alpha can be traded against a short stock index futures position that neutralizes systematic risk. Equity swaps can also be used to implement an active or passive strategy.

From Chapter 9, we know that investors developed a strategy known as *enhanced indexing* based on the concept of matching the risk characteristics of a benchmark portfolio with the chance of higher returns. This approach seeks superior risk-adjusted returns versus a benchmark. The other side of this approach is to match expected returns to a benchmark with lower risk.

---

[5]A set of major U.S. and European equity indexes was presented in the previous chapter. Any can be used to implement a passive equity strategy where investors seek to match the performance of the benchmark index.

[6]Other passive investment vehicles might include index mutual funds or exchange-traded funds (ETFs).

[7]An example is the S&P 500 Growth and Value contracts that trade on the Chicago Mercantile Exchange (CME). There are also numerous stock index futures contracts based on capitalization.

[8]Alternative investments are usually regarded as those outside the three major asset classes; stocks, bonds and cash. However, active management strategies that are not long-only and typically implemented by hedge funds also fall into this category. The implementation of an alternative strategy in this context can utilized passive or active investment vehicles or both.

These two approaches are considered *semi-active equity investment strategies*. Once again as with passive and active approaches, the vehicles to implement these strategies can be based on building a stock portfolio or derivatives-based. The derivatives approach can use stock index futures or equity swaps to equitize[9] cash and add value through a nonequity asset. For example, an equity swap can be structured such that the investor receives the total returns to the benchmark and pays LIBOR plus a spread. The investor can achieved added value by investing in a higher return bond.

PORTFOLIO APPLICATIONS OF LISTED OPTIONS

Investors can use the listed options market to address a range of investment problems particularly for active and semi-active managers. We discuss the use of OTC options later. Advantages of listed options relative to OTC options are that they provide accurate and consistent information about pricing and virtually eliminate credit risk. Moreover, because of these characteristics and the standardization of products, listed options often have low transaction costs and moderate to high liquidity. The issue of transaction costs and liquidity can play an important role in the decision to use derivatives as part of the investment process.

Risk Management Strategies

Risk management in the context of equity portfolio management focuses on price risk. Consequently, the strategies discussed here in some way address the risk of a price decline or a loss due to adverse price movement. Options can be used to create asymmetric risk exposures across all or part of the core equity portfolio. This allows the investor to hedge downside risk at a fixed cost with a specific limit to losses should the market turn down. This tactical investment approach can improve risk-adjusted performance versus a benchmark.

The most common strategy for risk management is a *protective put buying strategy*. This strategy is used by investors who currently hold a long position in the underlying security or investors who desire upside exposure and downside protection. The motivation is either to hedge some or all of the total risk. Index put options hedge mostly market risk, while put options on an individual stock hedge the total risk associated with a specific stock. This allows portfolio managers to use protective put strategies for separating tactical and strategic strategies. Consider, for example, a manager who is concerned about nonfinancial events increasing the level of risk in the marketplace. Furthermore, assume the manager is satisfied with the core

---

[9]Equitizing cash involves using derivatives to maintain exposure to equities.

portfolio holdings and the strategic mix. Put options could be employed as a tactical risk reduction strategy designed to preserve capital and still maintain strategic targets for portfolio returns. In recent years, the U.S. equity market has experienced significant volatility. A *protective put buying strategy* implemented in a timely fashion could have produced superior risk-adjusted returns.[10]

Thus, any investor concerned about downside risk is a candidate for a protective put strategy. Nonetheless, protective put strategies may not be suitable for all investors. The value of protective put strategies, however, is that they provide the investor with the ability to invest in volatile stocks with a degree of desired insurance and unlimited profit potential over the life of the strategy.

The protective put involves the purchase of a put option combined with a long stock position. The put option is comparable to an insurance policy written against the long stock position. The option price is the cost of the insurance premium and the amount the option is out-of-the money is the deductible. Just as in the case of insurance, the deductible is inversely related to the insurance premium. The deductible is reduced as the strike price increases, which makes the put option more in-the money or less out-of-the-money. The higher strike price causes the put price to increase and makes the insurance policy more expensive. The put can be paid for through the sale of an out-of-the-money call option creating a *collar strategy*. The upside is limited to the strike price.

Cost Management Strategies

Equity managers are evaluated in terms of performance versus a benchmark. Often costs cause a drag on portfolio performance. Options can be used to manage the cost of maintaining an equity portfolio in a number of ways. Among the strategies is the use of short put and short call positions to serve as a substitute for a limit order in the cash market. Cash-secured put strategies can be used to purchase stocks at the target price, while covered calls or overwrites can be used to sell stocks at the target price. The target price is the one consistent with the portfolio manager's valuation or technical models and the price intended to produce the desired rate of return.

In addition, synthetic strategies may allow the investor to implement a position at a lower cost than a direct investment in the cash market. For example, foreign investors subject to dividend withholding taxes may find a synthetic long stock position using options an attractive alternative to the

---

[10]Since 2000, the equity market has experienced two market corrections in excess of 35%. Protective put strategies or collar strategies could have produced higher risk-adjusted returns.

cash investment. Moreover, there is always an alternative method of creating a position. Synthetic calls, for example, can be created by borrowing, investing in stock, and buying put options. Likewise, a synthetic protective put strategy can be established by buying call options and discount bonds.

Cash-Secured Put

The motivation behind a *cash-secured put strategy* is to reduce market impact costs associated with the purchase of a stock. The strategy can be used by managers to transact in the cash market without bearing the total cost of the perceived risk to the seller. The demand for the stock may bid up the price of the security regardless of the motivation behind the trade. If, for example, the manager believes that the stock is attractive at or below a particular price, a cash-secured put can be established using a strike price consistent with the target price. If the purchase is not motivated by firm-specific information, but is strategic in nature, part of a passive rebalancing, or based on relative valuation models, then using an option mechanism to purchase the stock may make sense.

The strategy is similar to a limit order in the cash market with two notable differences. First, the option approach pays the buyer a premium, while no such premium exists for a limit order. Second, the limit order can be ended at any time, while the option is only extant over the life of the contract.

A cash market transaction may bid up the price of the stock because sellers believe the trade is motivated by new information. The use of short put options is a means to convey the intent of the buyer. The put seller indicates to the market a willingness to accept the downside risk of a further stock price decline. Consequently, this makes it clear to the market that the interested party does not expect an immediate increase in the stock price. This may reduce the immediacy cost of market impact.

Thus, the short put mechanism of purchasing stock may be appropriate for managers with strategic interest in the stock, but no compelling need for immediate execution. The short put premium provides some downside cushion, which further reduces the effective cost of the stock. If the stock rises over the life of the option and the put expires worthless, then an overvalued stock has become more overvalued. If, on the other hand, the manager wants to own the stock immediately, then a put option strategy is not appropriate.

Naked Calls

Similarly, short calls can be used as a mechanism for selling current holdings at a price consistent with the rate of return objective of the manager. The intention is twofold: (1) to reduce market impact costs and (2) to receive a favorable price for selling the stock shares.

Consider a manager who currently holds a number of stocks based on a quantitative valuation model. The model has created a sell price for each holding based on the investment horizon under consideration. The alternative methods for selling a substantial holding are to work it upstairs through a broker/dealer or establish a short call position with a strike price consistent with investment objectives. The disadvantage of a sizable cash market transaction is that the buyer will interpret the sale as information motivated and adjust the price accordingly. This could result in a meaningful decline in price and lower the return contribution of the stock to the overall portfolio.

A naked call can be written with a strike price as a substitute for a limit order. The investor selling the stock is conveying a clearer message to the market regarding intent. The stock is being sold for reasons other than the possession of adverse information regarding the company's future. The seller's intent is clearer for more aggressive OTM strike prices because it requires a rise in price for exercise. The effect of the overwrite position on portfolio performance is positive for neutral to slightly rising markets and negative for declining markets. The trade will undoubtedly incur transaction costs of some kind in either market. However, the prudent use of options is a useful way to be more specific about the motivation behind the trade.

Return Enhancement Strategies

Recall that semi-active management seeks to improve risk-adjusted performance through enhanced returns or less risk. The most popular return enhancement strategies employing listed options are *covered call strategies*. If the investor currently owns the stock and writes a call on that stock, the strategy has been referred to as an "overwrite." If the strategy is implemented all at once (simultaneously buying the stock and selling the call), it is referred to as a "buy write." The essence of the covered call is to trade price appreciation for income. The strategy is appropriate for slightly bullish investors who don't expect much out of the stock and want to produce additional income. These are investors who are willing either to limit upside appreciation for limited downside protection or to manage the costs of selling the underlying stock. The primary motive is to generate additional income from owning the stock.

Although the call premium provides some limited downside protection, this is not an insurance strategy because it has significant downside risk. Consequently, investors should proceed with caution when considering a covered call strategy.

A covered call is less risky than buying the stock because the call premium lowers the break-even recovery price. The strategy behaves like a long stock position when the stock price is below the strike price. On the other hand, the strategy is insensitive to stock prices above the strike price and is therefore capped on the upside. The maximum profit is given by the call premium and the OTM amount of the call option.

Regulatory Issues

The regulation of derivatives markets and equity markets is quite extensive in the United States. The Securities and Exchange Commission (SEC) is the primary regulator of equity markets and option markets. One focus of the SEC is to protect the investor by making certain that brokers identify the suitability of the investor for trading in options. This has mostly been a problem for smaller investors and not for institutional investors. However, numerous institutional investors are still subject to a variety of antiquated restrictions that prohibit such investment management choices as short selling. Options can be used to establish a synthetic short position held in lieu of a short position in the cash market. In addition, options can be useful to foreign investors subject to local tax consequences by avoiding a cash market transaction.

PORTFOLIO APPLICATIONS OF STOCK INDEX FUTURES

Now let's look at how stock index futures can work with passive or active equity investment strategies. Our focus is on how stock index futures can be used to manage all types of equity strategies more efficiently. We begin by examining how futures can help change equity exposure in order to achieve the desired level of exposure at the lowest possible cost. The two strategies examined are hedging strategies (a special case of risk management) and asset allocation strategies.

Stock index futures contracts are often ideal instruments for managing equity exposure in passive or active strategies due to their liquidity, flexibility, and low transaction costs. An equity position of comparable dollar value can be managed in the stock index futures market at a fraction of the cost in the cash market. The futures market is also an alternative means of implementing an investment strategy to the cash market.

The choice of whether to use the cash market or the futures market to alter equity exposure depends on the objectives of the manager and the size of the equity exposure. Despite apparent cost advantages, there are limits to the amount of stock index futures available to large institutional investors such as pension funds due to regulatory, size, and liquidity constraints. Nonetheless, stock index futures can still be an effective and valuable tool for portfolio management.

The motivation behind the choice to change equity exposure is important in deciding between the cash market or the stock index futures market. If the decision is a strategic asset allocation decision then it can be viewed as long term. If, on the other hand, the decision is tactical, it is a short-term situation. Stock index futures allow managers to quickly adjust imbalances in their asset allocation positions effectively without the need to purchase individual stocks. This effectively allows portfolio managers to increase or decrease equity exposure without altering the status of their core portfolio or disturbing their long-term investment objectives.

The appropriate way to analyze the cash and futures alternatives is to compare the costs of the two transactions.

Hedging Market Risk

Since stock index futures were first introduced, the most common application is to hedge market risk. The motivation for hedging market risk might be tactical based on market conditions or strategic as part of an active long-short management strategy or as part of an arbitrage strategy. Active managers with positive alpha derived from long portfolios can neutralize market risk by shorting stock index futures. Arbitragers will buy or sell stock index futures to take advantage of mispricing. Using arbitrage to enhance returns is considered a semi-active approach to equity management. Regardless of the motivation, hedging involves the transfer of risk from one party to another. Stock index futures serve as a valuable hedging instrument for both domestic and global equity portfolio managers. The global proliferation of viable futures contracts has brought the capability from the traditional S&P 500–type funds to a broad range of hedging possibilities. The methodology is identical except that hedging foreign equity positions requires currency hedges as well.

Hedging strategies involve cross-hedging when the hedging instrument is not perfectly correlated with the investor's equity portfolio. This is the case with active portfolios. A perfectly hedged position is one without risk. If the underlying index is the same as the portfolio being hedged, then the hedge is an arbitrage and will generate a certain profit. If the futures contract is fairly priced at the risk-free rate, then the hedge is comparable to a risk-free investment and it will produce the risk-free rate of return. If the portfolio being hedged has some tracking error versus the underlying index, then the rate of return is comparable to a money market instrument with small levels of tracking error.

As a hedging instrument, stock index futures provide investors with a means to manage risk whether holding long or short positions in the equity market. By taking the opposite side of their position, equity managers can insulate the performance of their equity position from market movements. The residual performance is directly related to the level of nonmarket risk in the portfolio. The most sophisticated hedging techniques do not completely eliminate risk because the gains or losses on the futures side do not precisely offset the gains or losses on the cash equity portfolio. Nonetheless, the hedged position is clearly a low-risk strategy particularly when the equity portfolio is highly correlated with the index underlying the stock index futures contract.

For equity portfolios designed to track known indexes with corresponding futures contracts, tracking error is not a huge problem. However, alternative equity portfolios with low correlations might have significant tracking error versus any particular hedging instrument that will subject the hedge to significant risk. This means that stock index futures can only insulate an equity portfolio from some portion of total risk. If the equity portfolio happens to be a broad market index fund, then S&P 500 index futures can pretty much take care of total risk because nonmarket risk was eliminated through diversification. However, when this is not the case and the equity portfolio is subject to significant nonmarket risk, then it exposes the hedging strategy to those same risks.

On the other hand, when the stock index futures contract is based on a broad-market index, it gives managers the ability to hedge systematic risk and take advantage of superior stock selection ability that will produce a positive return even in declining markets. These contracts can be used to isolate the nonmarket component of total risk. This feature benefits active managers who have the ability to pick high-performance stocks, but who do not necessarily like the market. There is no need to stay out of equities. The manager can use stock index futures to remove the market component from the strategy. Over the investment horizon, the returns to the hedged portfolio will include an incremental return to the selected stocks versus the market and any dividends from the stocks.

Hedge Ratios

In order to hedge a position, the amount of the position to be taken in the stock index futures contract must be determined. That is, a risk equivalent position of the cash market portfolio is needed for the stock index futures position in order to hedge the portfolio. The *hedge ratio* indicates the amount of the futures position that must be taken to hedge the cash market portfolio. For example, using the S&P 500 futures contract, a hedge ratio of 1 means that if a manager wants to hedge a \$10 million stock portfolio, a \$10 million S&P 500 futures position must be sold. If the hedge ratio is 0.9, this means that \$9 million of S&P 500 futures contracts must be sold to hedge a \$10 million stock portfolio.

It is tempting to use the portfolio's beta as a hedge ratio because it is an indicator of the sensitivity of the portfolio returns to the stock index returns. It appears, then, to be an ideal sensitivity adjustment. However, applying beta relative to a stock index as a sensitivity adjustment to a stock index futures contract assumes that the index and the futures contract have the same volatility. If futures always sold at their fair value, this would be a reasonable assumption. However, mispricing is an extra element of volatility in a stock index futures contract. Since the stock index futures contract is more volatile than the underlying stock index, using a portfolio beta as a sensitivity measure would result in a portfolio being overhedged.

The most accurate sensitivity adjustment would be the beta of a portfolio relative to the futures contract. It can be shown that the beta of a portfolio relative to a stock index futures contract is equivalent to the product of the portfolio relative to the underlying index and the beta of the index relative to the futures contract.[11] The beta in each case is estimated using regression analysis in which the data are historical returns for the portfolio to be hedged, the stock index, and the stock index futures contract. The regressions estimated are

$$r_P = a_P + B_{PI}r_I + e_P$$

where

r_P = the return on the portfolio to be hedged
r_I = the return on the stock index
B_{PI} = the beta of the portfolio relative to the stock index
a_P = the intercept of the relationship
e_P = the error term

and

$$r_I = a_I + B_{IF}r_F + e_I$$

where

r_F = the return on the stock index futures contract

[11]Edgar Peters, "Hedged Equity Portfolios: Components of Risk and Return," in *Advances in Futures and Options Research*, vol. 1B, ed. by F.J. Fabozzi (Stamford, Conn.: JAI Press, 1987), 75–91.

r_I = the return on the stock index
B_{IF} = the beta of the stock index relative to the stock index futures contract
a_I = the intercept of the relationship
e_I = the error term

Given B_{PI} and B_{IF}, the minimum risk hedge ratio can then be found by:

$$\text{Hedge ratio} = h = B_{PI} \times B_{IF}$$

The hedge ratio h in the above expression is referred to as a *minimum risk hedge ratio* (also called an *optimal hedge ratio*) because the ratio minimizes the variance of returns to the hedged position.

There is a special case where the portfolio beta can be used as the hedge ratio. This is the case if the manager can hedge the portfolio until the settlement date. This is because the return to mispricing is no longer an unknown factor when the portfolio can be held to the futures settlement date.

Given the hedge ratio, the manager must determine the number of stock index futures contracts to sell. The number needed can be calculated using the following three steps after $B\ PI$ and $B\ IF$ are estimated:

Step 1. Determine the "equivalent market index units" of the market by dividing the market value of the portfolio to be hedged by the current value of the futures contract:

$$\text{Equivalent market index units} = \frac{\text{Market value of the portfolio to be hedged}}{\text{Current value of the futures contract}}$$

Step 2. Multiply the equivalent market index units by the hedge ratio to obtain the "beta-adjusted equivalent market index units": Beta-adjusted equivalent market index units":

$$\text{Beta-adjusted equivalent market index units}$$
$$= \text{Hedge ratio} \times \text{Equivalent market index units}$$

or

$$B_{PI} \times B_{IF} \times \text{Equivalent market index units}$$

Step 3. Divide the beta-adjusted equivalent index units by the multiple specified by the stock index futures contract:

$$\text{Number of contracts} = \frac{\text{Beta-adjusted equivalent market index units}}{\text{Multiple of the contract}}$$

Asset Allocation

All investment decisions ultimately are asset allocation decisions. The choice to invest new cash in a domestic index fund instead of a global portfolio or the choice to reduce bond exposure is a clear example. If the decision is a long-term one, then it is a strategic asset allocation decision. Strategic decisions are made with the careful analysis of a client's long-term needs. If, instead, the decision is short-term, it is a tactical asset allocation decision. Tactical asset allocation (TAA) is actually a short-term to intermediate-term timing strategy designed to benefit from identifiable misevaluation in an asset class and seeks to add value to the overall fund performance. TAA could also include a defensive strategy to avoid adverse market movements. The classic example is a shift from equities to bonds or equity to cash in anticipation of a market correction. Asset allocation is not limited to domestic financial assets, but reaches into foreign markets as well. Once the asset allocation decision is made, for the equity investor the implementation of that decision takes place on two levels. First, the asset allocation decision determines the overall exposure to equity as an asset class. Second, the intra-asset allocation determines how the equity exposure is realized—passively or actively. Equity derivatives can play an important role at both levels of the asset allocation process.

The mechanics of implementing asset allocation decisions depend upon the investor's choice of an instrument. Whether managers choose to diversify internationally or not, superior security selection may be blown over by the adverse winds of a bear market. There are several ways that managers can respond to tactical asset allocation models that signal a danger of a market reversal. Tactical asset allocation is comparable to dynamic hedging. The choice to reduce or increase exposure to an asset class effectively hedges one risk in favor of another or none. The instruments to hedge market risk are also available for asset allocation decisions.

Managers have a choice of vehicles and methods to implement an asset allocation strategy. The stock index futures solution is available across a number of countries and asset classes, enabling managers to manage the systematic risk of equity portfolios regardless of the country of origin. The derivatives solution to the asset allocation decision allows managers to separate the security selection decision from the market timing or the asset allocation decision. Later in this chapter we discuss the OTC derivatives alternative to stock index futures.

The choice of whether to use cash or futures to accomplish an allocation-related strategy was discussed earlier. Once again the choice comes down to whether the decision is long term or short term.

Creating an Index Fund

An index fund is a portfolio of securities designed to exactly replicate the returns and risk profile of an established index. Equity indexing is an investment strategy that involves investing funds in a stock portfolio designed to track the performance of an established equity index. Index funds were originally developed as a low-cost passive alternative to active management and as part of a strategic asset allocation plan. As such, plain vanilla index funds were created where the benchmark was the most widely accepted stock market proxy—the S&P 500 Index.

To this day, the most common index fund is designed to track the S&P 500 Index. Recently however, indexing has taken on many different forms and doesn't fit perfectly into the traditional description. The most obvious development has been the use of numerous new benchmarks to represent more narrowly defined stock indexes and foreign stock indexes. However, it wasn't until the last few years that a global proliferation of stock index futures developed to accompany the new equity benchmark investments.

Traditionally, the only approach to establishing an index fund was to purchase a replicating portfolio in the cash market designed to track the S&P 500. With the arrival of equity index derivatives in the early 1980s, synthetic index funds were created. The choices were further expanded in the OTC market with the creation of equity swaps, which we discuss later in the chapter. The return distribution of the S&P 500 Index could be replicated using stock index futures and a money market instrument. The early experience of the S&P 500 Index fund and its synthetic counterpart in the stock index futures market can now be extended to a host of other indexes. Some candidates are indexes with a narrower equity focus and foreign indexes.

As an alternative to holding a cash index fund, a synthetic index fund can be created using stock index futures contracts. The investor purchases stock index futures as a substitute for the cash index and invests the proceeds in a money market instrument. The advantages and disadvantages of using a synthetic index fund versus a cash index fund are the same as those discussed earlier. Based on the assumption of no transaction costs and efficient markets, we know that a synthetic index fund should generate the same returns as a cash index fund. In our next example, however, we relax the assumptions and compare the practical differences between the two applications.

The choice of using the futures market versus the cash market can only be determined by evaluating the trade-offs between costs and risks. The outcome of the synthetic strategy can only match the cash strategy if the following conditions are met:

- The investment amount corresponds to an exact futures amount.
- Interest rates are constant over the investment horizon.
- Expected dividends are realized.
- The futures price is fairly valued when the strategy is initiated.
- All subsequent futures prices are fairly valued.

In practice, these conditions are not exactly met. However, with good estimates of expectations and making the appropriate adjustments to the futures position, under normal market conditions, the risks can be minimized.

The risks of holding a synthetic index fund, for example, must be weighed against the risks of the cash index fund. The two primary sources of risk for using futures are variation margin and price risk. A technique known as "tailing" can be used to minimize the impact of variation margin on returns.[12] Price risk refers to the risk of mispriced futures contracts when the fund is initiated and during times when the position must be rolled into the next settlement cycle. On the other hand, one prominent advantage of a synthetic index fund over a cash index fund is cost. A cash index fund costs 30 to 40 basis points to initiate, while a synthetic index fund costs 2.5 basis points. The cash index fund is also subject to the cost of periodic rebalancings and to cash drag resulting from a delay in investing new cash.

In practice, many index funds hold a replicating portfolio to represent the benchmark and use stock index futures to manage cost and minimize cash drag. The prudent use of futures can provide the means of achieving the investment objective of matching the returns to the benchmark.

Enhanced Index Funds

An index fund is a passive approach to investing where the objective is to exactly or closely match the performance of an agreed upon benchmark. The most common index fund is a plain vanilla S&P 500 index fund. The index fund manager attempts to match the performance of the S&P 500 index on a total return basis. The purpose of an enhanced index fund is to

---

[12]Tailing is a technique designed to minimize the impact of variation margin on returns. The tailing or adjustment factor is applied to the original position such that slightly fewer contracts are bought or sold. The futures position is adjusted by the following formula:

$$\text{Tailing factor} = 1/\text{Term interest rate}$$

The appropriate interest rate is either the term interest rate until expiration of the futures contract, or the term interest rate until the hedge is lifted. Fund managers prefer not to use tailing because it may put a drag on the strategy when the position is moving favorably.

do better than the benchmark index without incurring additional risk. This is considered an active or semi-active strategy.

It is difficult to outperform a benchmark without incurring tracking error risk. Tracking error risk will usually emerge whenever the replicating portfolio is not an exact replica of the benchmark. However, the incremental returns more than compensate for the small increase in risk. Naturally, over time, the enhanced index fund is expected to perform better than the benchmark on a risk-adjusted basis.

There are three basic approaches to enhanced indexing. The first involves changing the composition of the replicating portfolio in order take advantage of valued-added situations. This may include stock selection, sector selection, or a different weighting scheme. The resulting portfolio is usually constructed to minimize tracking error. The replicating portfolio is "tilted" toward superior performance in some way that is expected to provide it with the economic fuel to perform better than the benchmark. The replicating portfolio is put on common ground with the benchmark by trying to match its risk characteristics and not its expected return.

Alternatively, the index fund manager can use a stock replacement program to take advantage of misevaluation in the futures market in order to enhance return. The performance of the index fund is "enhanced" through stock index arbitrage and a stock replacement program. The incremental return is the result of futures pricing inefficiencies rather than estimated misevaluation of equities. The index fund has an additional opportunity for incremental return by reversing the arbitrage at a favorable price as well. In fact, some index funds may enter into a stock replacement program aggressively in order to take advantage of opportunities on the other side of the cash/futures swap.

Consequently, plain vanilla indexing can be viewed as an application of futures in the form of cost management. Enhanced indexing by seeking to capitalize on the mispricing between futures and cash is an example of a return enhancing strategy and falls within the active or semi-active strategy category.

The third way to enhance index funds is to use a structured product vehicle that allows the investor to use leverage or fixed income management to deliver returns above an equity benchmark. For example, an equity swap where the investor manages the fixed income portion to obtain a better return than the swap promises can be added to overall performance of the strategy. Also, warrant structures can utilize leverage as well.

Foreign Market Access

As investment strategies have become international in scope, stock index futures have become an effective means of managing equity exposure and risk exposure in a global portfolio. Once a decision is made to develop and maintain a global investment strategy, the equity manager has to decide how to treat currency risk. The choice to invest internationally subjects the equity portfolio to currency risk and market risk in the country where the investment takes place. The manager is now faced with the task of making prudent investment choices and developing an opinion on currency rates. The risk to the portfolio is that the manager's investment decision was correct, but not realized due to an appreciation in the domestic currency.

The use of stock index futures for implementing a global equity investment strategy can reduce currency risk. The reason is that currency risk is confined to initial margin payments and variation margin. These payments are usually much smaller than the initial value of the equity portfolio. Thus, stock index futures are a viable and important alternative for foreign equity investment compared to investing in the foreign stocks themselves.

The use of stock index futures in a global context shares the same advantages of using stock index futures in a domestic equity investment context. These include high liquidity, rapid execution, low transaction costs, single purchase for broad market exposure, no tracking error, and no custodial costs. A few additional features particularly applicable to foreign investment are that cash settlement avoids the risk of delivery, using stock index futures for country allocation avoids the different settlement periods that may exist between two or more countries, and using futures may avoid withholding taxes. Moreover, in some countries the use of stock index futures allows foreign investors to avoid restrictions on capital movements.

APPLICATIONS OF OTC EQUITY DERIVATIVES

The array of OTC derivative-based equity portfolio management strategies cuts across the two primary categories of investment philosophy—active and passive management. We consider several strategies in this section, which are listed in Exhibit 15.1, together with the purpose of using an OTC derivatives and a product candidate.

Exhibit 15.2 summarizes various OTC equity derivative structures in terms of the role of derivatives for long-term investors and hedgers.[13] A broad spectrum of equity investment activities emanating from the role of derivatives can benefit from these three basic categories of OTC equity derivative structures: options and exotics, equity-linked notes and equity swaps.

---

[13]The investors referred to in Exhibit 15.2 include pension funds, insurance companies, high net work individuals and hedge funds might create an index fund or use active managers to meet their respective investment objectives. All are candidates for using equity derivatives.

EXHIBIT 15.1 The Use of OTC Derivatives for Equity Strategies

Equity Strategy	Purpose	Product Candidate
Return-enhancement strategies	Outperform benchmark	Equity swap
Hedging strategies	Risk management	Exotics, swaps, debt[a]
Spread strategies	Risk management	Equity swaps, exotics
Market access strategies	Reduce costs	Swaps, debt, warrants, exotics
Changing equity exposure	Reduce costs	
Index funds	Outperform benchmark	Swaps, debt, exotics
Standard		Swaps, debt
Enhanced		
Style		
Asset allocation	Risk management	Swaps
Active manager transition	Cost management	Swaps, exotics

[a]Debt refers to equity-linked debt products.

Creation of Structured Product Solutions

One of the most important applications of derivative securities is in the creation of structured product solutions to the financial needs or objectives of an institutional investor.[14] Structured products, which were introduced in the previous chapter, are, like derivative securities, financial products representing contractual agreements between two parties—an issuer (the designer or creator of the structure) and a purchaser (the user or holder of the structure). The structure is designed with a linkage to the performance of an existing security or securities. The linkage could be to an equity index or portfolio, an interest rate, an exchange rate, or a commodity price and based on spreads, correlations, convergences, or divergences. The objective could be to protect principal, enhance returns, defer taxes, gain access to difficult markets, manage costs or manage regulatory risks. The process of creating or establishing a structured product is known as "financial engineering" and involves the creation of a structure that meets the specific needs of the client in terms of the objectives listed above. The value of structured products is that they provide great flexibility in design and application.

Typically, structured products are used to provide some form of principal protection while having the potential for upside returns. Thus, a basic structure consists of a fixed income component and a returns generating

---

[14]For an discussion of structured products see, John C. Braddock, *Derivatives Demystified: Using Structured Financial Products* (New York: John Wiley and Sons, 1997).

EXHIBIT 15.2 OTC Derivative Structures and Investment Management

Derivative Structure	Investor	Role	Application
OTC options and exotics	Long-term Index funds Style funds Active managers Strategic asset allocators	Risk management	Customized protective puts Collar structures Portfolio insurance Currency hedging Asset exposure Probability exposure
		Return management	Index arbitrage Option writing Volatility forecasting Intra-asset allocation Leverage strategies
		Cost management	Option writing Market access Valuation estimation Structured products
		Regulatory management	Foreign market exposure Tax deferral Asset exposure
Equity-linked debt	Long-term Index funds Style funds Active managers Strategic asset allocators	Risk management	Customized structures Collar structures Portfolio insurance Currency hedging Asset exposure
		Return management	Spread premiums
		Cost management	Foreign market cost avoidance Asset allocation
		Regulatory management	Asset exposure Foreign market exposure Capital requirement
Equity swaps	Long-term Index funds Style funds Active managers Strategic asset allocators	Risk management	Diversification Asset allocation Minimize tracking error Currency hedging
		Return management	Tracking portfolio Spread premium
		Cost management	Foreign market cost avoidance Asset allocation
		Regulatory management	Foreign market exposure Tax deferral Asset exposure

component. An alternative basic structure offers a leverage factor that can generate a higher magnitude of returns than a traditional investment or a principal protected structure. Examples of structured products include but are not restricted to warrants, principal protection notes, asset-linked notes, various types of swaps, credit linked products, monetization strategies for restricted or concentrated situations, caps and floor products, and securitized cash flows.

Risk Management Strategies

As we have noted, a common use of derivatives is to hedge financial risk. Stock index futures can only insulate an equity portfolio from some portion of total risk. If the equity portfolio happens to be a broad market index fund, then S&P 500 index futures can pretty much take care of total risk because nonmarket risk was eliminated through diversification. However, when this is not the case and the equity portfolio is subject to significant nonmarket risk, then it exposes the hedging strategy to those same risks.

Stock index futures contracts in which the underlying is a broad market index allow portfolio managers the ability to hedge systematic risk and to take advantage of superior stock selection ability that will produce a positive return even in declining markets. Stock index futures can be used to isolate the nonmarket component of total risk. This feature benefits active managers who have the ability to pick high performance stocks, but who have little market timing skills. There is no need to stay out of equities during volatile markets. The manager can use stock index futures to hedge market risk.

Consequently, over the investment horizon, the returns to the hedged portfolio will include an incremental return to the selected stocks versus the market and any dividends from the stocks. However, the resulting strategy may go beyond the desired risk-return trade-off. OTC derivative structures can be designed to address all these issues and achieve the exact hedged position desired. All costs can be known upfront with no additional risk to investors, with the exception of some credit risk and market failure risk that accompanies all financial transactions.

Despite the benefits of using stock index futures, listed index futures products do not provide a full range of hedging choices for equity investors. OTC equity derivatives go a long way to fill this gap. Investors can choose among equity swaps, equity-linked debt, and a structured option-like product to hedge with greater precision the specific risk they want to shed and to acquire the risk they want to bear. Exhibit 15.3 provides a list of derivative alternatives for hedging equity portfolios.

EXHIBIT 15.3 Hedging with Derivatives

	Hedging Instrument	
Hedging Strategy	Listed	OTC
Reduce Market Risk	Stock index futures	Option, swap, debt
Reduce Total Risk	Multiple SIFs contracts	Option, swap, debt
Change Risk Components	Stock index futures	Option, swap, debt
Reduce Currency Risk	Quanto futures	Option, swap, debt
Reduce Interest Rate Risk	Interest rate derivatives	Option, swap, debt
Reduce Inflation Risk	Interest rate derivatives	Option, swap, debt
	Commodity index derivatives	

With the advent of second-generation "exotic" options, investors can now implement a hedging strategy with the degree of precision they desire. Market risk can be hedged in any country using any derivative structure. Equity swaps can exchange the total return of a portfolio for another less risky asset class. The structure can be designed to hedge currency risk if necessary and desired.

A structured product using exotics can design a payout that is contingent on certain market activity. For example, a barrier put option can be used to obtain a specific degree of protection without paying extra for outcomes that are not relevant. Ladder options can lock in a market decline, while flexible strike options can ratchet up when the market moves opposite to expectations.

Once again, the bottom line is that structured OTC equity derivative products can overcome the risk inherent in cash or futures market hedging strategies. Investors have the means to hedge all or a specific part of total risk.

Asset Allocation

The mechanics of implementing asset allocation decisions depend upon the investor's choice of an investment vehicle. Exhibit 15.4 presents a list of candidates for a global asset shift which changes foreign equity exposure in the overall asset allocation strategy using listed derivatives and OTC derivatives.

The problem is the same one presented in an earlier discussion of equity investment strategies. The choices unfold similarly. The option based solution may suffer from high costs due to a highly volatile portfolio or due to significant liquidity risk. However, exotic option structures provide a means to fine-tune the strategy to reflect very precisely forecasted returns. Basket options, such as index options, are cheaper than a portfolio of options. They also provide a portfolio manager with a means of eliminating tracking error between the underlying for the hedging vehicle and the equity portfolio.

EXHIBIT 15.4   Alternative Investment Vehicles Global Asset Allocation Strategy

Investment Category	Vehicle	Advantages	Disadvantages
Cash market	Stock portfolio	Ownership	Costs and management
Listed derivatives	Stock index futures	Cost	Managing futures
	Stock index options	Listed	Size, standardization
	Flex options	Flexibility, listed	Size, tracking error
Otc options	Baskets	No tracking error	Cost
	Spread	Any market	Cost
	Barriers	Low cost	Volatile markets
	Compound	Low cost	Multiple transactions
Swaps	Equity swap	Quick, efficient	Negative payments
	International swap		Credit risk

Listed options have the additional problem of size limits for standardized contracts. FLEX options resolve some but not all of those limitations. The stock index futures alternative comes with some administrative issues and risks. The equity swap solution incorporates the asset allocation decision into a single transaction, but necessitates a counterparty and has credit risk. In Exhibit 15.5, we present a case where an active manager with $100 million portfolio that is currently allocated 50% equities and 50% bonds and seeks to increase equity exposure to 75%. The equity exposure is currently 100% domestic and the manager wants to diversity into Europe. The swap dealer can structure an equity swap to accomplish this asset allocation objective. The new allocation is $50 million domestic equity, $25 million foreign equity and $25 million bonds.

The derivatives solution to the asset allocation decision allows fund managers or portfolio managers to separate the security selection decision from the market timing or the asset allocation decision. The choice of what mechanism to use to accomplish the investment objective depends on whether the decision is long term or short term and the relative costs.

Return Management Strategies

Return management strategies focus on structuring an investment strategy to increase returns but not risk. Here we include passive index funds and enhanced index funds because they are investment strategies designed to meet the performance criterion of matching or exceeding a benchmark. We could

EXHIBIT 15.5   Asset Allocation Using and Equity Swap Structure

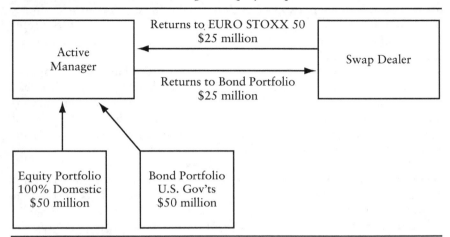

just as easily think of index funds as a means to match the risk characteristics of a benchmark, which is one of the features of this strategy. However, once the risk profile is established, the focus of index funds is performance relative to a benchmark.

The modified index fund strategies might also be called return enhancement strategies. The purpose behind return-enhancement strategies is to increase return without an accompanying increase in risk. This means that an "enhanced" index fund ought to do better than the benchmark index without incurring additional risk. However, it may not be an easy task to outperform a benchmark without incurring tracking error risk. This risk will usually emerge whenever the replicating portfolio does not exactly mimic the composition of the benchmark. Nonetheless, the incremental returns are expected to more than compensate for the small increase in risk and, over time, the enhanced index fund is expected to outperform the benchmark on a risk-adjusted basis.

The goal of indexing is to construct a portfolio to exactly match the performance of the benchmark. When this is accomplished, tracking error is zero. In addition to performance reasons, plan sponsors are attracted to index funds because they provide investment diversification and are a means to control costs. Many plan sponsors have combined active and passive management using index funds as a risk management tool. Index funds can also provide a means for market-timing. Thus we see that index funds can fall into return management, risk management, or cost management categories. This also can fall into a passive or active investment category as well. Part of the reason is that the use of index funds makes performance attribution and cost control more manageable because of the use of an established index as a benchmark. For the plan sponsor, an index fund can represent an entire asset class within the framework of its strategic asset allocation strategy or as part of an intra-asset allocation strategy that mixes active and passive management.

Indexing has taken on many different forms that have broad applications. If we generalize our definition of index funds as a portfolio of stocks designed to match or exceed the returns of a benchmark while maintaining the same risk exposure, then there are many extensions of the original index fund. The many applications of index funds provide a rich landscape for using derivatives to further reduce costs. In fact, the prudent use of equity derivatives can reduce transaction costs to near zero. We regard the reduction of costs as any increase in after-cost return without changing the fundamental composition of the portfolio. This means that the returns are derived from the same sources in the cash market. Thus, it is comparable to getting a better execution in the cash market. Superior execution leads to lower costs, which increases return. The following is a list of index fund applications:

- *Extended funds.* An *extended funds strategy* involves constructing a portfolio linked to an index that "extends" beyond the traditional S&P 500 index and may include a significantly larger group of stocks. The purpose of this strategy is to gain U.S. equity diversification. The universe of over 5,000 stocks across many sectors is more representative of the U.S. equity market and the U.S. economy. In addition, it provides a means of reducing risk versus a more narrow view represented by the S&P 500 index. No real liquid listed derivatives are available to create a synthetic fund. OTC derivative structures such as equity swaps and equity-linked debt instruments can provide an alternative investment vehicle to an exclusive cash approach.

- *Non-S&P 500 index funds.* A non–S&P 500 index funds strategy involves constructing a portfolio linked to a broad-based non–S&P 500 stock index. The strategy underlying these funds is to expand U.S. equity market exposure. Investors who currently have an S&P 500 index fund can combine it with a separate index fund that captures a neglected portion of the market. The end result can effectively be an extended fund with the added advantage of making intra-asset allocation rebalancings when desired. Once we travel outside the plain vanilla index fund, using listed derivatives becomes more difficult. OTC equity derivatives are available for implementing and managing non–S&P 500 index funds.

- *Foreign or international index funds.* A foreign or international index funds strategy seeks to design a portfolio that is linked to a foreign or international stock index. Thus, investors who do not invest beyond the borders of the United States are ignoring about half of world equities. The strategy objective of foreign investments is to gain international diversification. Furthermore, as global financial markets continue to deregulate and integrate, emerging markets in other parts of the world will provide additional opportunities. There are, however, direct investment expenses associated with owning foreign securities that exceed similar domestic investments. These may include larger commissions and spreads, stamp taxes, dividend withholding taxes, custody fees, and research fees. Many of these costs can be better managed through the use of OTC index derivatives.

- *Special-purpose index funds.* A portfolio can be constructed to be linked to the performance of a subindex, such as a market sector, or a portfolio with the same risk profile as a benchmark but with a tilt toward a specific parameter such as yield or price-earnings ratio. This strategy is called a *special-purpose index funds strategy.* Tilted portfolios are designed to enhance the returns to an index fund without assuming additional risk. Sometimes referred to as "enhanced" index funds, this strategy may also involve the use of futures or options to provide incremental return. An enhanced index fund begins with a traditional index fund and then utilizes financing techniques and derivative strategies to enhance return.

Having decided on a passive investment strategy and an appropriate benchmark, the investor's next consideration is how to implement the strategy. A cash market solution needs to address the design and construction of a replicating or tracking portfolio. In the presence of transaction costs, the optimal portfolio may still underperform the benchmark. Thus, in order to overcome the risk of underperformance the investor may have to assume more tracking error risk. The final choice of a replicating portfolio must be made within a cost management framework. The trade-off can be represented by expected tracking error versus expected trading costs. Costs are related to portfolio size and liquidity. Part of the skill of portfolio construction is to find the optimal balance between costs and risk. The marginal trade-off between risk and cost is greater for small sized portfolios.

Earlier we discussed the benefits of using stock index futures to manage an index fund. Synthetic index funds can be created using stock index futures that exactly replicate the returns to the underlying index. Recently, OTC index derivatives have been developed for investors with restrictions on using derivatives. These include equity-linked debt instruments and equity swaps. Equity swaps are important because they are the economic equivalent of financing an equity investment with a fixed-income security, typically a LIBOR-based security. Because there are many stock indexes that are not covered by stock index futures or ETFs, equity index swaps offer a means to invest in these indexes that make them attractive to investors. Equity index swaps provide a low-cost structure that can eliminate tracking risk and provide longer term maturities than stock index futures.

There are some index funds that use futures almost exclusively. It is not practical for large pension funds to rely exclusively on synthetic index funds due to market constraints. Thus, some combination of the cash market and futures market is appropriate. Index funds can be developed as a more dynamic strategy, and can be used as a risk management tool and a platform for better performance. However, stock index futures have their own administrative considerations and are limited in application because they have a linear pay off.

In order to provide a richer body of choices for implementing and managing index funds over the long haul, the use of OTC derivative structures provides the missing link to more complete and effective global risk management solutions to the investment problem. Equity swaps can be used to create the exact desired equity exposure in a single transaction, which makes them convenient, cost effective, and economically sound.

Return Enhancement Strategies

There are three basic approaches to enhanced indexing which apply to other investment strategies as well. These strategies cut across passive and active management, which is why they are often referred to as semi-active strategies. The objective is to increase risk-adjusted returns and this can be accomplished through returns management or risk management. The first approach involves changing the composition of the equity portfolio in order to position the portfolio to take advantage of stocks, stock sectors, some different weighting allotments, or other criteria that the manager believes will cause the portfolio to perform better than a passive benchmark. In the case of index funds, the equity portfolio is the replicating portfolio. Changing the portfolio involves modifying the content of the portfolio and yet maintaining the current level of risk. The resulting portfolio is typically designed to minimize tracking error. For return management strategies, the equity portfolio is designed to match the risk characteristics of a benchmark and not its expected return.

In the second approach, index fund managers can use a stock index futures arbitrage to increase or enhance returns. The strategy is formalized as a stock replacement program, which invests in the less expensive of the cash portfolio or futures. The incremental return is the result of futures pricing inefficiencies rather than estimated mispricing of equities.

OTC equity derivatives can be a useful tool to modify the composition of the portfolio at low cost or to enhance returns. The use of derivatives would enter the picture as part of the implementation process. The investor would first establish the necessary rebalancing to achieve the desired exposure to a new set of stocks on either an individual basis, an industry sector basis, or with the intent to modify a portfolio parameter such as price-earnings ratio. In any case, the result in the cash market is a set of sell orders and a set of buy orders. The investor is shedding some risks in favor of others. The rebalanced portfolio represents the right equity exposure to add incremental return necessary to improve performance with no added risk.

As explained earlier, a structured product can be used to enhance returns by providing a means of accessing other sources of additional returns. Various structures are capable of accomplishing these objectives. For example, investors can invest in a triple-B-rated bond at a spread above Treasuries and enter into an equity swap to receive the total returns to the benchmark index and pay the yield on Treasuries. The spread then enhances the total return to the strategy above the benchmark index. Because of recent market volatility, other types of structures have been developed to improve returns through effective risk management.[15]

Cost Management and Regulatory Management Strategies

We can apply the cost and regulatory management strategies explained earlier using listed options to OTC derivatives as well. The OTC applications extend the benefits further by providing additional flexibility when structuring a strategy. There are also a number of strategies that fall under this category simply because implementing them using derivatives results in lower costs than the cash market alternative. Moreover, in the case of some strategies, implementation in the cash market may have prohibitive regulatory obstacles. An example of both are foreign market access strategies. Derivatives provide investors a means to invest in foreign equities while avoiding some of the costs, tax consequences, and regulatory obstacles simultaneously or separately. This holds true for U.S. investors in equities outside the United States or foreigners investing in U.S. companies.

---

[15]Equity linked note structures that vary the level of principal guarantee and upside participation are available. Also, structures such as provided by "Himalaya products" are linked to the performance of a group of indexes or baskets over an observation period. The best performing index is locked in at that time until the maturity of the product when the investor receives the weighted average performance of the locked in indexes. In seeking protection form market volatility investors hope to improve performance.

Here we review some of the listed option strategies discussed earlier in this chapter, but now using OTC derivatives. We explained the use of short puts as a means of buying stocks using derivatives as a substitute for a limit order in the cash market. This strategy is equally applicable to OTC options, which provide the additional advantage of customization to achieve the specific price and time horizon that meet the investor's needs. Similarly, short calls are a means of selling stocks currently held and targeted for sale. The advantages of the OTC market apply here as well.

In addition to these basic applications, OTC structures can be developed as alternatives to cash market transactions that are tailored to reflect very specific investment opinions or forecasts. These may include any structure that is the economic equivalent of a long or short cash position, but does not require the direct purchase or sale of stock. Other applications which could reduce cost involve an array of exotic structures that are priced lower than standard options. Barrier options can be structured to knock-in under conditions that reflect the price targets of the stock. Spread options allow the manager to generate the performance differential between the current situation and the desired situation without actually buying or selling the stock. Basket options can accomplish the result of buying or selling a basket of stocks simultaneously. Equity swaps can achieve the economic equivalent by an exchange of cash flows. OTC derivatives are equally applicable to cost management or regulatory management.

RISK AND EXPECTED RETURN OF OPTION STRATEGIES

Options are like any other risky asset because they compensate investors for assuming systematic risk. Therefore, if options have higher exposure to systematic risk, investors will require and expect higher returns from holding options. Naturally, call options, which pay off in states of the world where the underlying asset's price rises, will have higher expected returns than the underlying asset. In contrast, put options, which pay off in states of the world where the asset's price declines, will have lower expected returns than the risk-free asset that are often negative.[16] Furthermore, adding options to a stock portfolio or writing options against an existing long position will change the risk-return characteristics of the investment and therefore its expected return.

---

[16]Coval and Shumway find empirical evidence that the returns to option strategies are lower than predicted by the CAPM. They argue that this suggests that other factors besides the market are important for pricing the risk associated with options. (See Joshua D. Coval and Tyler Shumway, "Expected Option Returns," *Journal of Finance* 56, no. 3 (2001): 983–1009.

According to the asset pricing framework of Merton and the Black Scholes model, the instantaneous expected return to an option ought to be the same as the return implied by the CAPM.[17] Hence, it can be shown that an option's instantaneous beta is related to the beta of the underlying stock and the elasticity of the option.[18] Rendleman demonstrates that the expected returns and risks for options should be consistent with the principles of risk and return from the CAPM.[19] He shows the impact on expected returns for various investment strategies that use options. One observation is that call options with high positive betas should have high expected returns and put options with negative betas should have low expected returns. The discussion below follows the presentations by Rendlemen and Coval and Shumway.[20]

Expected Returns from Long Calls and Covered Calls

From the CAPM derived by Merton, the expected value of a call can be derived:

$$E[R_{call}] = R_f + \beta_{call}[E[R_M] - {}_{Rf}]$$

The expected return from buying call options is higher than the underlying stock. However, the difference in returns is less the further the option is in-the-money and converges on the stock's expected return for very high stock prices. The reason for this relationship is that the option's beta exceeds that of the underlying stock and in fact can be much higher. For stocks with positive betas, the beta of the option will be higher because of its exposure to greater systematic risk. The fact that an option is a leveraged position in the underlying would also lead to the higher risk and expected returns conclusion. In a portfolio context, adding an option to a diversified portfolio will heighten the systematic risk in the portfolio. Consequently, investors should require a higher rate of return.

For covered calls, which reduce the risk of holding the stock, the expected return ought to be lower than a long stock position. The important

---

[17]See Robert C. Merton, "An Intertemporal Capital Asset Pricing Model," *Econometrica* 41, no. 5 (1973): 867–887; and Fischer Black and Myron Scholes, "The Pricing of Options and Corporate Liabilities," *Journal of Political Economy* 81, no. 3 (1973): 637–654.
[18]That is, $\beta_{option} = \beta_{stock}(\delta P/\delta S)(S/P)$ where P = price of the option and S = price of the underlying stock.
[19]Richard J. Rendleman, "Option Investing from a Risk-Return Perspective," *Journal of Portfolio Management* 25, special issue (May 1999): 109–121.
[20]Rendleman, "Option Investing from a Risk-Return Perspective"; and Coval and Shumway, "Expected Option Returns." For a graphical treatment of the expected return and risk for option strategies, see Hans E. Stoll and Robert E. Whaley, *Futures and Options: Theory and Applications* (Cincinnati, Ohio: South Western Publishing, 1993).

behavioral aspect of covered call writing from an expected return perspective is that writing calls on a long stock position reduces risk and consequently will lower expected returns. The fact that covered call strategies are viewed as a means to generate income during flat markets does not change the fact that across the spectrum of possible outcomes, risk is lower, as is expected returns.

Expected Returns from Protective

From the CAPM, if a stock has a positive beta, then a put ought to have a negative beta. This can be demonstrated by viewing the put option as a portfolio of a short position and a discount loan. The expected return must necessarily be below the risk-free rate because the equity risk premium is positive. This can be seen in the following expression:

$$E[R_{put}] = R_f + \beta_{put}[E[R_M] - R_f]$$

Investors are willing to hold puts because they view it as purchasing insurance. Hence, a put is bought for the same reasons that motivate consumers to buy automobile or homeowner insurance—to hedge against adverse events. In neither case does the consumer expect to generate earnings because the purchase of an insurance policy is basically the purchase of utility in exchange for the expected loss. Consequently, protective put strategies will lower expected returns compared with a long-only strategy.

For more complicated option-based strategies, the outcomes will also result in a different risk-return profile depending on the payout of the strategy. Straddles, for example, with zero betas ought to return the risk-free rate.

The relationship between expected return and beta for the basic option strategies is illustrated in Exhibit 15.6. From the exhibit, we see that the relationship between strike price and expected return shows that the more in-the-money the option, the closer to the risk-return position of the underlying stock. We also observe that the covered call and the protective put strategy both result in lower risk and expected returns versus the long stock position. The riskless asset and the zero beta straddle ought to be similarly positioned in terms of expected return and beta. On the lower end of the exhibit, we find a similar relationship among put options as call options except with negative betas.[21]

---

[21]See Thomas Schneeweis and Richard Spurgin, "The Benefits of Index Option-Based Strategies for Institutional Portfolios," *Journal of Alternative Investments* 3, no. 4 (2001): 44–52. Schneeweis and Spurgin report that over the period of analysis (1987–1999) passive option-based strategies such as covered calls, protective puts, and collars produced higher risk-adjusted returns than the underlying equity benchmarks.

EXHIBIT 15.6 Expected Return and Beta for Option Strategies

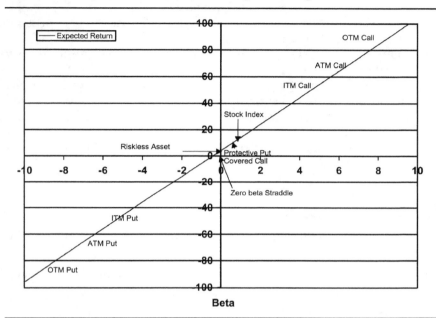

Beta

KEY POINTS

- Equity portfolio management applications fall across the four roles of derivatives (returns management, risk management, cost management, and regulatory management) and the two basic categories of equity investing: passive and active.
- Equity derivatives can be used as investment vehicles by active or passive managers in the context of the four roles of derivatives.
- Portfolio applications exist for listed derivatives and OTC derivatives.
- Protective put buying is the most common risk management strategy using listed options.
- Cash secured puts and naked calls can be used to reduce market impact costs of implementing a strategy.
- Buy writes are the most popular way to use listed options to enhance returns.
- Stock index futures contracts are often ideal instruments for managing equity exposure in passive or active strategies due to their liquidity, flexibility, and low transaction costs.

- Stock index futures can be used to hedge systematic risk, create synthetic index funds or in an enhanced index fund program.
- A hedge ratio is needed to determine the appropriate number of stock index futures in a hedging strategy.
- Equity listed or OTC derivatives can be used to implement an asset allocation program.
- A broad spectrum of equity investment activities emanating from the role of derivatives can benefit from three basic categories of OTC equity derivative structures: options and exotics, equity-linked notes, and equity swaps.
- The instantaneous expected return to an option should be the same as the return implied by the CAPM.

QUESTIONS

1. How can an investor use listed options to protect an equity portfolio from price risk?

2. How can stock index futures be used to create a synthetic index fund?

3. **a.** Explain what an optimal hedge ratio is for portfolio hedging when the index and the futures contracts have the same volatility.
   b. Explain why it is referred to as a minimum hedge ratio.

4. Explain how an investor can use an equity swap structure to reduce domestic equity exposure on a $100 million portfolio from 75% to 70% while increasing bond exposure from 25% to 30%.

5. What are the three basic approaches to enhanced indexing?

Bond Analysis and Portfolio Management

Bonds, Asset-Backed Securities, and Mortgage-Backed Securities

Frank J. Fabozzi, Ph.D., CFA, CPA
Professor in the Practice of Finance
Yale School of Management

In this chapter, the wide range of fixed-income securities is described. They include bonds issued by the U.S. government, federally agency securities, corporations, and municipalities, as well as bonds backed by a pool of loans or receivables: asset-backed securities, residential mortgage-backed securities, and commercial mortgage-backed securities. We begin with the general features of fixed-income securities.

GENERAL FEATURES OF BONDS

We begin our introduction to fixed-income securities or bonds with a description of features common to all of them.

Term to Maturity

The term to maturity of a bond is the number of years over which the issuer has promised to meet the conditions of the obligation. At the maturity date the issuer will pay off any amount the bonds outstanding. The convention is to refer to the "term to maturity" as simply its "maturity" or "term." As we explain later, there may be provisions that allow either the issuer or holder of the debt instrument to alter the term to maturity.

Par Value

The *par value* of a bond is the amount that the issuer agrees to repay the bondholder by the maturity date. This amount is also referred to as the *principal*, *face value*, *redemption value*, or *maturity value*. Bonds can have any par value.

Because bonds can have a different par value, the practice is to quote the price of a bond as a percentage of its par value. A value of 100 means 100% of par value. So, for example, if a bond has a par value of $1,000 and is selling for $900, it would be said to be selling at 90. If a bond with a par value of $5,000 is selling for $5,500, the bond is said to be selling for 110. The reason why a bond sells above or below its par value is explained in Chapter 17.

Coupon Rate

The *coupon rate*, also called the *nominal rate* or the *contract rate*, is the interest rate that the issuer/borrower agrees to pay each year. The dollar amount of the payment, referred to as the *coupon interest payment* or simply *interest payment*, is determined by multiplying the coupon rate by the par value of the bond. For example, the interest payment for a bond with a 7% coupon rate and a par value of $1,000 is $70 (7% times $1,000).

The frequency of interest payments varies by the type of bond. In the United States, the usual practice for bonds is for the issuer to pay the coupon in two semiannual installments. Mortgage-backed securities and asset-backed securities typically pay interest monthly. For bonds issued in some markets outside the United States, coupon payments are made only once per year.

Zero-Coupon Bonds

Not all bonds make periodic coupon interest payments. Bonds that are not contracted to make periodic coupon payments are called *zero-coupon bonds*. The investor realizes interest by buying it substantially below its par value. Interest then is paid at the maturity date, with the interest earned by the investor being the difference between the par value and the price paid for the bond. So, for example, if an investor purchases a zero-coupon bond for 70, the interest realized at the maturity date is 30. This is the difference between the par value (100) and the price paid (70).

There is another type of bond that does not pay interest until the maturity date. This type has contractual coupon payments, but those payments are accrued and distributed along with the maturity value at the maturity date. These instruments are called *accrued coupon instruments* or *accrual securities* or *compound interest securities*.

Floating-Rate Securities

The coupon rate on a bond need not be fixed over the its life. *Floating-rate securities*, sometimes called *floaters* or *variable-rate securities*, have coupon payments that reset periodically according to some reference rate. The typical formula for the coupon rate at the dates when the coupon rate is reset is

$$\text{Reference rate} \pm \text{Quoted margin}$$

The quoted margin is the additional amount that the issuer agrees to pay above the reference rate (if the quoted margin is positive) or the amount less than the reference rate (if the quoted margin is negative). The quoted margin is expressed in terms of *basis points*. A basis point is equal to 0.0001 or 0.01%. Thus, 100 basis points are equal to 1%.

A floating-rate bond may have a restriction on the maximum coupon rate that will be paid at a reset date. The maximum coupon rate is called a *cap*. Because a cap restricts the coupon rate from increasing, a cap is an unattractive feature for the investor. In contrast, there could be a minimum coupon rate specified for a floating-rate security. The minimum coupon rate is called a *floor*. If the coupon reset formula produces a coupon rate that is below the floor, the floor is paid instead. Thus, a floor is an attractive feature for the investor.

Provisions for Paying Off Bonds

The issuer/borrower of a bond agrees to repay the principal by the stated maturity date. The issuer/borrower can agree to repay the entire amount borrowed in one lump sum payment at the maturity date. That is, the issuer/borrower is not required to make any principal repayments prior to the maturity date. Such bonds are said to have a *bullet maturity*.

There are bonds that have a schedule of principal repayments that are made prior to the final maturity of the instrument. Such bonds are said to be *amortizing instruments*.

There are bonds that have a *call provision*. This provision grants the issuer/borrower an option to retire all or part of the issue prior to the stated maturity date. Some issues specify that the issuer must retire a predetermined amount of the issue periodically. Various types of call provisions are discussed below.

Call and Refunding Provisions

A borrower generally wants the right to retire a bond prior to the stated maturity date because it recognizes that at some time in the future the general level of interest rates may fall sufficiently below the coupon rate so that redeeming the issue and replacing it with another bond with a lower coupon rate would be economically beneficial. This right is a disadvantage to the investor since proceeds received must be reinvested at a lower interest rate. As a result, a borrower who wants to include this right as part of a bond must compensate the investor when the issue is sold by offering a higher coupon rate.

The right of the borrower to retire the issue prior to the stated maturity date is referred to as a "call option." If the borrower exercises this right, the issuer is said to "call" the bond. The price that the borrower must pay to retire the issue is referred to as the *call price*. Typically, there is not one call price but a call schedule, which sets forth a call price based on when the borrower exercises the call option.

When a bond is issued, typically the borrower may not call it for a number of years. That is, the issue is said to have a *deferred call*. The date at which the bond may first be called is referred to as the *first call date*. Bonds can be called in whole (the entire issue) or in part (only a portion).

If a bond issue does not have any protection against early call, then it is said to be a *currently callable issue*. But most new bond issues, even if currently callable, usually have some restrictions against certain types of early redemption. The most common restriction is prohibiting the refunding of the bonds for a certain number of years. *Refunding* a bond issue means redeeming bonds with funds obtained through the sale of a new bond issue.

Sinking Fund Provision

An issuer may be required to retire a specified portion of an issue each year. This is referred to as a *sinking fund requirement*. Generally, the issuer may satisfy the sinking fund requirement by either (1) making a cash payment of the face amount of the bonds to be retired to the trustee, who then calls the bonds for redemption using a lottery, or (2) delivering to the trustee bonds purchased in the open market that have a total par value equal to the amount that must be retired.

Options Granted to Bondholders

There are provisions in bonds that gives either the investor and/or the issuer an option to take some action against the other party. The most common type of option embedded is a call feature, which was discussed earlier. This option is granted to the issuer. There are two options that can be granted to the owner of the bond: the right to put the issue and the right to convert the issue.

A bond with a *put provision* grants the investor the right to sell the bond back to the issuer at a specified price on designated dates. The specified price is called the *put price*. The advantage of the put provision to the investor is that if after the issuance date of the bond market interest rates rise above the bond's coupon rate, the investor can force the issuer to redeem the bond at the put price and then reinvest the proceeds at the prevailing higher rate.

A convertible bond is one that grants the investor the right to convert or exchange the bond for a specified number of shares of common stock. Such a feature allows the investor to take advantage of favorable movements in the price of the issuer's common stock. We discuss the features of convertible bonds later in this chapter when we cover corporate bonds.

Medium-Term Notes vs. Bonds

Medium-term notes (MTNs) differ from bonds only in the manner in which they are distributed to investors when they are initially sold. They are offered continuously to investors by an agent of the issuer. Investors can select from several maturity ranges: nine months to one year, more than one year to 18 months, more than 18 months to two years, and so on up to 30 years.

The term *medium-term note* used to describe this bond is misleading. Traditionally, medium term was used to refer to debt issues with a maturity greater than one year but less than 15 years. This is not a characteristic of MTNs since they have been sold with maturities from nine months to 30 years, and even longer. For example, in July 1993, Walt Disney Corporation issued an MTN with a 100-year maturity.

U.S. TREASURY SECURITIES

U.S. Treasury securities are issued by the U.S. Department of the Treasury. These securities are backed by the full faith and credit of the U.S. government. Therefore, they are viewed as default-free securities. Interest income from Treasury securities is subject to federal income taxes but is exempt from state and local income taxes.

Types of Treasury Securities

There are two types of Treasury securities: discount and coupon securities. Treasury coupon securities come in two forms: fixed rate and variable rate securities. Treasury securities are all issued on an auction basis. The auctions are conducted on a competitive bid basis. All U.S. Treasury auctions are single-price auctions. In a single-price auction, all bidders are awarded securities at the highest yield of accepted competitive tenders. For Treasury coupon securities, the most recently auctioned issue is referred to as the *on-the-run issue* or the *current issue*. Securities that are replaced by the on-the-run issue are called *off-the-run issues*.

Treasury Bills

Treasuries are issued at a discount to par value, have no coupon rate, and mature at par value. As discount securities, Treasury bills do not pay coupon interest. Instead, Treasury bills are issued at a discount from their maturity value; the return to the investor is the difference between the maturity value and the purchase price. The current practice of the Treasury is to issue all securities with a maturity of one year or less as discount securities.

Fixed Rate Treasury Notes and Bonds

All securities with initial maturities of two years or more are issued as coupon securities. Coupon securities are issued at approximately par, have a coupon rate, and mature at par value. Treasury coupon securities issued with original maturities of more than one year and no more than 10 years are called *Treasury notes*. Treasury coupon securities with original maturities greater than 10 years are called *Treasury bonds*. Treasury notes and bonds are referred to as *Treasury coupon securities*.

Inflation-Protected Treasury Notes and Bonds

The U.S. Department of the Treasury issues notes and bonds that adjust for inflation. These securities are popularly referred to as *Treasury inflation protection securities* (TIPS) or *Treasury inflation indexed securities* (TIIS). The coupon rate on an issue is set at a fixed rate. That rate is determined via the auction process described later. The coupon rate is called the "real rate" since it is the rate that the investor ultimately earns above the inflation rate. The inflation index that the government has decided to use for the inflation adjustment is the nonseasonally adjusted U.S. City Average All Items Consumer Price Index for All Urban Consumers (CPI-U).

Stripped Treasury Securities

While the U.S. Treasury does not issue zero-coupon notes or bonds, brokerage firms have been able to create such products. The procedure is to purchase Treasury coupon securities and issue receipts representing an ownership interest in each coupon payment on the underlying Treasury securities and a receipt on the underlying Treasury securities' maturity value. This process of separating each coupon payment, as well as the principal, to sell securities backed by them is referred to as "coupon stripping."

To illustrate the process, suppose $500 million of a Treasury bond with a 30-year maturity and a coupon rate of 6% is purchased to create zero-coupon Treasury securities. The cash flow from this Treasury bond is 60 semiannual payments of $15 million each ($500 million times 0.06 divided by 2) and the repayment of principal of $500 million 30 years from now. As there are 61 payments to be made by the Treasury, a receipt representing a single payment claim on each payment is issued, which is effectively a zero-coupon bond. The amount of the maturity value for a receipt on a particular payment, whether coupon or principal, depends on the amount of the payment to be made by the U.S. Treasury on the underlying Treasury bond. In our example, 60 coupon receipts each have a maturity value of $15 million, and one receipt, the principal, has a maturity value of $500 million. The maturity dates for the receipts coincide with the corresponding payment dates for the Treasury securities.

These securities are issued under the U.S. Department of the Treasury's *Separate Trading of Registered Interest and Principal Securities* (STRIPS) program and a referred to in the market as "Treasury strips." They are direct obligations of the U.S. government.

FEDERAL AGENCY SECURITIES

Federal agency securities can be classified by the type of issuer, those issued by federally related institutions and those issued by government sponsored enterprises. *Federally related institutions* (also referred to as *government-owned agencies*) are arms of the federal government and generally do not issue securities directly in the marketplace. The major issuers have been the Tennessee Valley Authority (TVA) and the Private Export Funding Corporation. With the exception of securities of the TVA and the Private Export Funding Corporation, the securities are backed by the full faith and credit of the United States government.

Government sponsored enterprises (GSEs) are privately owned, publicly chartered entities. They were created by Congress to reduce the cost of capital for certain borrowing sectors of the economy deemed to be important enough to warrant assistance. GSE securities are not backed by the full faith and credit of the U.S. government. Consequently, investors purchasing GSEs are exposed to credit risk.

The securities issued by GSEs are one of two types: debentures and mortgage-backed/asset-backed securities. Debentures do not have any specific collateral backing the bond. The ability to repay bondholders depends on the ability of the issuing GSE to generate sufficient cash flows to satisfy the obligation. Several GSEs are frequent issuers of securities and therefore have developed regular programs for securities that they issue.

There are five GSEs that currently issue debentures: Freddie Mac, Fannie Mae, Federal Home Loan Bank System, Federal Farm Credit System, and the Federal Agricultural Mortgage Corporation. The first three are responsible for providing credit to the housing sectors. As of this writing, Fannie Mae and Freddie Mac are under government conservatorship and their future is being debated in Congress. The Federal Agricultural Mortgage Corporation provides the same function for agricultural mortgage loans. The Federal Farm Credit Bank System is responsible for the credit market in the agricultural sector of the economy

CORPORATE BONDS

As the name indicates, corporate bonds are issued by corporations. Corporate bonds are classified by the type of issuer. The four general classifications used by bond information services are: (1) utilities, (2) transportations, (3) industrials, and (4) banks and finance companies.

The promises of a corporate bond issuer and the rights of investors are set forth in great detail in the *bond indenture*. Failure to pay either the principal or interest when due constitutes legal default and court proceedings can be instituted to enforce the contract. Bondholders, as creditors, have a prior legal claim over preferred and common stockholders as to both income and assets of the corporation for the principal and interest due them.

Security for Bonds

The holder of a corporate debt instrument has priority over the equity owners in a bankruptcy proceeding. Moreover, there are creditors who have priority over other creditors.

Either real property or personal property may be pledged to offer security beyond that of the general credit standing of the issuer. With a *mortgage bond*, the issuer has granted the bondholders a lien against the pledged assets. A lien is a legal right to sell mortgaged property to satisfy unpaid obligations to bondholders. In practice, foreclosure and sale of mortgaged property is unusual. If a default occurs, there is usually a financial reorganization of the issuer in which provision is made for settlement of the debt to bondholders. The mortgage lien is important, though, because it gives the mortgage bondholders a strong bargaining position relative to other creditors in determining the terms of a reorganization.

Debenture bonds are not secured by a specific pledge of property, but that does not mean that holders have no claim on property of issuers or on their earnings. Debenture bondholders have the claim of general creditors on all assets of the issuer not pledged specifically to secure other debt. And they even have a claim on pledged assets to the extent that these assets generate proceeds in liquidation that are greater than necessary to satisfy secured creditors. *Subordinated debenture bonds* are issues that rank after secured debt, after debenture bonds, and often after some general creditors in their claim on assets and earnings.

It is important to recognize that while a superior legal status will strengthen a bondholder's chance of recovery in case of default, it will not absolutely prevent bondholders from suffering financial loss when the issuer's ability to generate cash flow adequate to pay its obligations is seriously eroded.

Convertible Bonds

A bond issue may give the bondholder the right to convert the security into a predetermined number of shares of common stock of the issuer. The number of shares of common stock that the bondholder will receive from exercising the call option of a convertible bond is called the *conversion ratio*. The conversion privilege may extend for all or only some portion of the bond's life, and the stated conversion ratio may change over time. It is always adjusted proportionately for stock splits and stock dividends. For example, suppose that a corporation issued a convertible bond with a conversion ratio is 25.32 shares. This means that for each $1,000 of par value of this issue the bondholder exchanges for that firm's common stock, he will receive 25.32 shares.

At the time of issuance of a convertible bond, the issuer effectively grants the bondholder the right to purchase the common stock at a price equal to the par value of the convertible bond divided by the conversion ratio. This price is referred to in the prospectus as the *stated conversion price*. The stated conversion price for the hypothetical convertible bond is $1,000/25.32 or $39.49.

Almost all convertible issues are callable by the issuer. Some convertible bonds are putable. Put options can be classified as "hard" puts and "soft" puts. A hard put is one in which the convertible bond must be redeemed by the issuer only for cash. In the case of a soft put, the issuer has the option to redeem the convertible bond for cash, securities, or a combination of the two.

Corporate Bond Ratings

Professional portfolio managers use various techniques to analyze information on companies and bond issues in order to estimate the ability of the issuer to live up to its future contractual obligations (i.e., to gauge the default risk associated with a bond issue). This activity is known as *credit analysis*.

Some large institutional investors and many investment banking firms have their own credit analysis departments. Few individual investors and institutional bond investors, though, do their own analysis. Instead, they rely primarily on nationally recognized statistical rating organizations that perform credit analysis and issue their conclusions in the form of ratings. The three commercial rating companies are Moody's Investors Service, Standard & Poor's Corporation, and Fitch Ratings.

Rating Symbols

The rating systems use similar symbols, as shown in Exhibit 16.1. In all systems the term "high grade" means low credit risk, or conversely, high probability of future payments. The highest-grade bonds are designated by Moody's by the symbol Aaa, and by the other two rating systems by the symbol AAA. The next highest grade is denoted by the symbol Aa (Moody's) or AA (the other two rating systems); for the third grade all rating systems use A. The next three grades are Baa or BBB, Ba or BB, and B, respectively. There are also C grades.

Bonds rated triple A (AAA or Aaa) are said to be *prime*; double A (AA or Aa) are of *high quality*; single A issues are called *upper medium grade*; and triple B are *medium grade*. Lower-rated bonds are said to have speculative elements or be distinctly speculative.

All rating agencies use rating modifiers to provide a narrower credit quality breakdown within each rating category. S&P and Fitch use a rating modifier of plus and minus. Moody's uses 1, 2, and 3 as its rating modifiers.

Bond issues that are assigned a rating in the top four categories are referred to as *investment-grade bonds*. Issues that carry a rating below the top four categories are referred to as *noninvestment-grade bonds* or *speculative bonds*, or more popularly as *high-yield bonds* or *junk bonds*. Thus, the corporate bond market can be divided into two sectors: the investment-grade and non-investment-grade markets.

Ratings of bonds may change over time. Issuers are upgraded when their likelihood of default (as assessed by the rating company) decreases, and downgraded when their likelihood of default (as assessed by the rating company) increases. The rating companies publish the issues that they are reviewing for possible rating change. To help investors understand how

EXHIBIT 16.1   Summary of Corporate Bond Rating Systems and Symbols

Fitch	Moody's	S&P	Summary Description
Investment Grade—High Creditworthiness			
AAA	Aaa	AAA	Gilt edge, prime, maximum safety
AA+	Aa1	AA+	
AA	Aa2	AA	High-grade, high-credit quality
AA–	Aa3	AA–	
A+	A1	A+	
A	A2	A	Upper-medium grade
A–	A3	A–	
BBB+	Baa1	BBB+	
BBB	Baa2	BBB	Lower-medium grade
BBB–	Baa3	BBB–	
Speculative—Lower Creditworthiness			
BB+	Ba1	BB+	
BB	Ba2	BB	Low grade, speculative
BB–	Ba3	BB–	
B+	B1		
B	B2	B	Highly speculative
B–	B3		
Predominantly Speculative, Substantial Risk, or in Default			
CCC+		CCC+	
CCC	Caa	CCC	Substantial risk, in poor standing
CC	Ca	CC	May be in default, very speculative
C	C	C	Extremely speculative
		CI	Income bonds—no interest being paid
DDD			
DD			Default
D		D	

ratings change over time, the rating agencies publish this information periodically in the form of a table. This table is called a *rating transition matrix*. The table is useful for investors to assess potential downgrades and upgrades. A rating transition matrix is available for different holding periods.

MUNICIPAL SECURITIES

Bonds are issued by state and local governments and by entities that they establish. These securities are popularly referred to as *municipal securities*, despite the fact that they are also issued by states and public agencies and their instruments. Municipal bonds also include bonds issued by the District of Columbia and any possession of the United States—Puerto Rico, the U.S. Virgin Islands, Guam, American Samoa, and the Northern Mariana Islands. An *official statement* describing the issue and the issuer is prepared for new offerings. Municipal securities expose investors to credit risk and are rated by the nationally recognized rating organizations.

There are both tax-exempt and taxable municipal securities. "Tax-exempt" means that interest on a municipal security is exempt from federal income taxation. The tax-exemption of municipal securities applies to interest income, not capital gains. The exemption may or may not extend to taxation at the state and local levels. Each state has its own rules as to how interest on municipal securities is taxed.

Because of the financial difficulties faced by state and local governments and their agencies in recent years, Congress authorized the issuance of a new type of taxable bond under the American Recovery and Investment Act of 2009. These bonds, dubbed *Build America Bonds* (BABs), come in two forms. The first type, called a *direct payment BAB*, is a taxable municipal bond. However, the issuer is subsidized for the higher cost of issuing a taxable bond rather than a tax-exempt bond in the form of a payment from the U.S. Department of the Treasury. The payment is equal to 35% of the interest payments. The second type of BAB is one in which a taxable municipal bond is issued but the bondholders receive a tax credit against their federal income taxes equal to 35% of the interest payment. This form of BAB is called a *tax credit BAB*.

Types of Municipal Securities

There are basically two types of municipal security structures: tax-backed debt and revenue bonds. *Tax-backed bonds* are instruments issued by states, counties, special districts, cities, towns, and school districts that are secured by some form of tax revenue. Tax-backed debt includes general obligation debt, appropriation-backed obligations, bonds supported by public credit enhancement programs, and dedicated tax-backed obligations. We discuss each below. In recent years, states and local governments have issued increasing amounts of bonds where the debt service is to be paid from so-called "dedicated" revenues such as sales taxes, tobacco settlement payments, fees, and penalty payments. Many are structured to mimic the asset-backed securities discussed later.

The second basic type of security structure is found in a revenue bond. *Revenue bonds* are issued for enterprise financings that are secured by the revenues generated by the completed projects themselves, or for general public-purpose financings in which the issuers pledge to the bondholders the tax and revenue resources that were previously part of the general fund. Revenue bonds can be classified by the type of financing. These include utility revenue bonds, transportation revenue bonds, housing revenue bonds, higher education revenue bonds, health care revenue bonds, sports complex and convention center revenue bonds, seaport revenue bonds, and industrial revenue bonds.

Some municipal securities have special security structures. These include insured bonds, bank-backed municipal bonds, and refunded bonds.

Insured bonds, in addition to being secured by the issuer's revenue, are also backed by insurance policies written by commercial insurance companies. Insurance on a municipal bond is an agreement by an insurance company to pay the bondholder any bond principal and/or coupon interest that is due on a stated maturity date but that has not been paid by the bond issuer. Once issued, municipal bond insurance usually extends for the term of the bond issue, and it cannot be canceled by the insurance company. Starting in early 2008, the major bond insurers were either downgraded or faced potential downgrading because of their commitments in the subprime mortgage market, not their involvement in the municipal bond market. As a result, their financial guarantee became a concern and there has been far less issuance of insured municipal bonds.

Although originally issued as either revenue or general obligation bonds, municipals are sometimes refunded. A refunding usually occurs when the original bonds are escrowed or collateralized by direct obligations guaranteed by the U.S. government. By this it is meant that a portfolio of securities guaranteed by the U.S. government is placed in a trust. The portfolio of securities is assembled such that the cash flows from the securities match the obligations that the issuer must pay. Once this portfolio of securities whose cash flows match those of the municipality's obligation is in place, the refunded bonds are no longer secured as either general obligation or revenue bonds. The bonds are now supported by cash flows from the portfolio of securities held in an escrow fund. Such bonds, if escrowed with securities guaranteed by the U.S. government, have little, if any, credit risk. They are the safest municipal bonds available. The escrow fund for a refunded municipal bond can be structured so that the refunded bonds are to be called at the first possible call date or a subsequent call date established in the original bond indenture. Such bonds are known as *prerefunded municipal bonds.* While refunded bonds are usually retired at their first or subsequent call date, some are structured to match the bond to the retirement date. These bonds are known as *escrowed-to-maturity bonds.*

ASSET-BACKED SECURITIES

An *asset-backed security* (ABS) is a security backed by a pool of loans or receivables. A special category of ABSs are securities backed by real estate property, both residential and commercial, and we describe them later in this chapter. The largest types of ABS issued are backed by credit card receivables, auto loans, and student loans.

Although an ABS is not issued by a corporation, this vehicle is used by corporations to raise funds as an alternative to bond issuance. For an issuer that has an opportunity to issuer an ABS or a bond, the decision as to which to issue depends on what the cost is. All other factors constant, an issuer will select the funding source that is less expensive.

The key to structuring an ABS is a third-party entity known as the *special purpose vehicle* (SPV). It is this entity that legally buys the pool of loans or receivables from the company seeking to raise funds and then issues the securities. Unlike a corporate bond where the investors look to the issuer to generate sufficient funds to satisfy the debt obligation, with an ABS investors look to the cash flow from the pool of assets.

Features of ABS

The collateral for an ABS can be classified as either amortizing or non-amortizing assets. *Amortizing assets* are loans in which the borrower's periodic payment consists of scheduled principal and interest payments over the life of the loan. The schedule for the repayment of the principal is called an *amortization schedule. Prepayments* are any excess payment over the scheduled principal payment. Furthermore, prepayments are classified as either voluntary or involuntary. An *involuntary prepayment* occurs when the borrower has defaulted and the asset is repossessed and sold.

In contrast to amortizing assets, *nonamortizing assets* do not have a schedule for the periodic payments that the individual borrower must make. Instead, a nonamortizing asset is one in which the borrower must make a minimum periodic payment. If that payment is less than the interest on the outstanding loan balance, the shortfall is added to the outstanding loan balance. If the periodic payment is greater than the interest on the outstanding loan balance, then the difference is applied to the reduction of the outstanding loan balance. There is no schedule of principal payments (i.e., no amortization schedule) for a nonamortizing asset. Consequently, the concept of a prepayment does not apply.

For an amortizing asset, projection of the cash flows requires projecting prepayments. One factor that may affect prepayments is the prevailing level of interest rates relative to the interest rate on the loan. In projecting prepayments it is critical to determine the extent to which borrowers take advantage of a decline in interest rates below the loan rate in order to refinance the loan. As we see when we discuss valuation modeling in Chapter 18, whether borrowers take advantage of refinancing when interest rates decline determines the valuation methodology. In addition, modeling defaults for the collateral are critical in estimating the cash flows of an ABS. Projecting prepayments for amortizing assets requires an assumption about the default rate and the recovery rate. For a nonamortizing asset, while the concept of a prepayment does not exist, a projection of defaults is still necessary to project how much will be recovered and when.

The maturity of an ABS is not a meaningful parameter. Instead, the "average life" of the security is calculated. This measure is explained later in this chapter.

Credit Enhancements

ABS are credit enhanced. That means that credit support is provided for one or more bondholders in the structure. Typically a double-A or triple-A rating is sought for the most senior bondholder in a deal. The amount of credit enhancement necessary depends on rating agency requirements. There are two general types of credit enhancement structures: external and internal.

External Credit Enhancements

External credit enhancements come in the form of third-party guarantees that provide for first loss protection against losses up to a specified level, for example, 10%. The most common forms of external credit enhancement was at one time insurance from a monoline insurer, but, as with municipal bonds, the financial weakness of these insurers has resulted in less use of this form of credit enhancement.

Internal Credit Enhancements

Internal credit enhancements come in more complicated forms than external credit enhancements. The most common forms of internal credit enhancements are reserve funds, overcollateralization, and senior-subordinated structures.

Reserve Funds   Reserve funds come in two forms: cash reserve funds and excess servicing spread. *Cash reserve funds* are straight deposits of cash generated from issuance proceeds. In this case, part of the underwriting profits from the deal are deposited into a fund.

Excess servicing spread accounts involve the allocation of excess spread or cash into a separate reserve account after paying out the net coupon, servicing fee, and all other expenses on a monthly basis. For example, suppose that the gross weighted average coupon of the collateral is 8%. This means that the collateral is paying about 8%. Payments must be made to bondholders and the servicer and other fees. Suppose that the servicing and other fees are 0.50% and that the net weighted average coupon is 7.25%. The net weighted average coupon is just the rate that is paid to all the bondholders in the structure. Therefore, the amount being paid out is 7.75% (7.25% + 0.50%). Hence, 8% is coming in from the collateral and 7.75% is being paid out, leaving a spread of 0.25% or 25 basis points. This amount is referred to the *excess serving spread* and this amount can be paid into a reserve account. The amount in this excess servicing spread account will gradually increase and can be used to pay for possible future losses.

Overcollateralization   The total par value of the tranches is the liability of the structure. So, if a structure has two tranches with a par value of $300 million, then that is the amount of the liability. The amount of the collateral backing the structure must be at least equal to the amount of the liability. If the amount of the collateral exceeds the amount of the liability of the structure, the deal is said to be *overcollateralized*. The amount of overcollateralization represents a form of internal credit enhancement because it can be used to absorb losses. For example, if the liability of the structure is $300 million and the collateral's value is $320 million, then the structure is overcollateralized by $20 million. Thus, the first $20 million of losses will not result in a loss to any of the tranches.

Senior-Subordinated Structure   In a senior-subordinated structure there is a senior bondholder, also referred to as the "senior tranche," and at least one subordinated bondholder, also called the "subordinated tranche." For example, suppose an ABS deal has $300 million as collateral (i.e., a pool of loans). The structure may look as follows:

Senior tranche	$270 million
Subordinated tranche	$30 million

This means that the first $30 million of losses are absorbed by the subordinated tranche.

The structure can have more than one subordinated tranche. For example, the structure could be as follows:

Senior tranche	$270 million
Subordinated tranche 1	$22 million
Subordinated tranche 2	$8 million

In this structure, the subordinated tranches 1 and 2 are called the *nonsenior tranches*. The senior tranche still has protection up to $30 million as in the previous structure with only one subordinated tranche. In the second structure, the first $8 million of losses is absorbed by the subordinated tranche 2. Hence, this tranche is referred to as the *first-loss tranche*. Subordinated tranche 1 has protection of up to $8 million in losses, the protection provided by the first-loss tranche.

Passthrough vs. Paythrough Structures

A pool of loans or receivables is used as collateral and certificates (securities) are issued with each certificate entitled to a pro rata share of the cash flow from the collateral. So, if a $100 million loan pool is the collateral for an ABS and 10,000 certificates are issued, then the holder of one certificate is entitled to 1/10,000 of the cash flow from the collateral. This type of structure is called a *passthrough structure*.

As explained above, for credit enhancement an ABS deal can be structured as a senior-subordinated structure as follows:

Senior tranche	$280 million	10,000 certificates issued
Subordinated tranche	$20 million	1,000 certificates issued

This structure is called a *passthrough structure* because each certificate holder (senior or subordinate tranche) is entitled to a pro rata share of the cash flow from the collateral. That is, each certificate holder of the senior tranche is entitled to receive 1/10,000 of the cash flow to be paid to the senior tranche from the collateral. Each certificate holder of the subordinated tranche is entitled to receive 1/1,000 of the cash flow to be paid to the subordinated tranche from the collateral.

It common to create a structure such that the senior tranches are carved up into different tranches. This type of ABS structure is referred to as a *paythrough structure*. In this structure, each tranche created will receive the cash flow from the collateral based on a set of rules set forth in the prospectus as to how the priority of the distribution of interest and principal will be distributed to each of the senior tranches. This will be made clear in the next section when we discuss a security called a collateralized mortgage obligation.

RESIDENTIAL MORTGAGE-BACKED SECURITIES

Real estate-backed securities are securities backed by a pool (collection) of mortgage loans. Residential or commercial properties can be used as collateral for such securities. Real estate-backed securities backed by residential mortgage loans include mortgage passthrough securities, stripped mortgage-backed securities, and collateralized mortgage obligations. In this section, we describe residential mortgage-backed securities (RMBS) and in the next section we focus on commercial mortgage-backed securities (CMBS).

Mortgages

The raw material for a mortgage-backed security (MBS) is the mortgage loan. A mortgage loan, or simply mortgage, is a loan secured by the collateral of some specified real estate property, which obliges the borrower to make a predetermined series of payments. The mortgage gives the lender the right if the borrower defaults (i.e., fails to make the contracted payments) to "foreclose" on the loan and seize the property in order to ensure that the debt is paid off. The interest rate on the mortgage loan is called the mortgage rate or contract rate. Here our focus is on residential mortgage loans.

When the lender makes the loan based on the credit of the borrower and on the collateral for the mortgage, the mortgage is said to be a *conventional mortgage*. The lender also may take out mortgage insurance to guarantee the fulfillment of the borrower's obligation. Some borrowers can qualify for mortgage insurance guaranteed by one of three U.S. government agencies: the Federal Housing Administration (FHA), the Veteran's Administration (VA), and the Rural Housing Service (RHS). There are also private mortgage insurers.

There are many types of mortgage designs available in the United States. A mortgage design is a specification of the interest rate, term of the mortgage, and manner in which the borrowed funds are repaid. Here we will discuss the major one: the fixed rate, level payment, fully amortized mortgage. With an understanding of the features of this mortgage, RMBS can be understood.

Fixed Rate, Level Payment, Fully Amortized Mortgage

The basic idea behind the design of the fixed rate, level payment, fully amortized mortgage is that the borrower pays interest and repays principal in equal installments over an agreed-upon period of time, called the maturity or term of the mortgage. The frequency of payment is typically monthly. Each monthly mortgage payment for this mortgage design is due on the first of each month and consists of:

1. Interest of one-twelfth of the annual interest rate times the amount of the outstanding mortgage balance at the beginning of the previous month.
2. A repayment of a portion of the outstanding mortgage balance (principal).

The difference between the monthly mortgage payment and the portion of the payment that represents interest equals the amount that is applied to reduce the outstanding mortgage balance. The monthly mortgage payment is designed so that after the last scheduled monthly payment of the loan is made, the amount of the outstanding mortgage balance is zero (i.e., the mortgage is fully repaid or amortized).

The monthly mortgage payment made by the borrower is not what the investor receives. This is because the mortgage must be serviced. The servicing fee is a portion of the mortgage rate. The interest rate that the investor receives is said to be the *net interest* or *net coupon.*

Homeowners may pay off all or part of their mortgage balance prior to the maturity date. Payments made in excess of the scheduled principal repayments are called *prepayments.* The effect of prepayments is that the amount and timing of the cash flows from a mortgage are not known with certainty. This risk is referred to as *prepayment risk.*

The single most important factor affecting prepayments because of refinancing is the current level of mortgage rates relative to the borrower's contract rate. The more the contract rate exceeds the prevailing mortgage rate, the greater the incentive to refinance the mortgage loan. For refinancing to make economic sense, the interest savings must be greater than the costs associated with refinancing the mortgage. Consequently, in an environment where mortgage rates are declining, the expectations is that refinancing and, therefore, prepayments will increase.

Mortgage Passthrough Securities

Investing in mortgages exposes an investor to default risk and prepayment risk. A more efficient way is to invest in a *mortgage passthrough security.* This is a security created when one or more holders of mortgages form a pool of mortgages and sell shares or participation certificates in the pool. A pool may consist of several thousand or only a few mortgages.

The cash flows of a mortgage passthrough security depend on the cash flows of the underlying mortgages. The cash flows consist of monthly mortgage payments representing interest, the scheduled repayment of principal, and any prepayments for all the mortgages in the pool.

Payments are made to securityholders each month. The coupon rate on a passthrough security, called the *passthrough coupon rate*, is less than the mortgage rate on the underlying pool of mortgage loans by an amount equal to the servicing fee and guarantee fee. Consequently, if there are 10,000 certificates issued, then the holder of one certificate is entitled to 1/10,000 of the cash flow from the pool of mortgages after adjusting for all fees.

Not all of the mortgages that are included in a pool of mortgages that are securitized have the same mortgage rate and the same maturity. Consequently, when describing a passthrough security, a weighted average coupon rate and a weighted average maturity are determined. A *weighted average coupon rate*, or WAC, is found by weighting the mortgage rate of each mortgage loan in the pool by the amount of the mortgage balance outstanding. A *weighted average maturity*, or WAM, is found by weighting the remaining number of months to maturity for each mortgage loan in the pool by the amount of the mortgage balance outstanding.

Agency Passthroughs

Mortgage passthroughs are classified into Government National Mortgage Association (Ginnie Mae) mortgage passthroughs, Federal National Mortgage Association (Fannie Mae) mortgage passthroughs, Federal Home Loan Mortgage Corporation (Freddie Mac) mortgage passthroughs, and private entity mortgage passthroughs.

There are several practices in the market in referring to the mortgage passthroughs issued by these entities. Some market participants simply refer to them as "agency passthroughs." Other market participants refer to the mortgage passthroughs issued by Ginnie Mae as "agency passthroughs" and those issued by the two GSEs as "conventional passthroughs" and then all three are referred to as "agency/conventional passthroughs." Here mortgage passthroughs issued by Ginnie Mae, Fannie Mae, and Freddie Mac will be referred to as agency passthroughs.

For a mortgage to be included in the pool of mortgages that is the collateral for an agency passthrough, the loans must meet the criteria established by the agency. These criteria are referred to as "underwriting standards." A mortgage that meets the underwriting standards is referred to as a "conforming loan" and obviously a loan that fails the underwriting standards is called a "nonconforming loan."

Prepayment Conventions and Cash Flows   In order to value a mortgage pass-through, it is necessary to project its cash flows. The difficulty is that the cash flows are unknown because of prepayments. The only way to project cash flows is to make some assumptions about the prepayment rate over the life of the underlying mortgage pool. The prepayment rate is sometimes referred to as the *speed*. Two conventions have been used as a benchmark for prepayment rates: conditional prepayment rate and Public Securities Association prepayment benchmark.

One convention for projecting prepayments and the cash flows of a passthrough assumes that some fraction of the remaining principal in the pool is prepaid each month for the remaining term of the mortgage. The prepayment rate assumed for a pool, called the *conditional prepayment rate* (CPR), is based on the characteristics of the pool (including its historical prepayment experience) and the current and expected future economic environment.

The CPR is an annual prepayment rate. To estimate monthly prepayments, the CPR must be converted into a monthly prepayment rate, commonly referred to as the *single-monthly mortality rate* (SMM). An SMM of $w\%$ means that approximately $w\%$ of the remaining mortgage balance at the beginning of the month, less the scheduled principal payment, will prepay that month.

The Public Securities Association (PSA) prepayment benchmark is expressed as a monthly series of CPRs. The PSA benchmark assumes that prepayment rates are low for newly originated mortgages and then will speed up as the mortgages become seasoned.

The PSA benchmark assumes the following prepayment rates for 30-year mortgages:

1. A CPR of 0.2% for the first month, increased by 0.2% per year per month for the next 30 months when it reaches 6% per year.
2. A 6% CPR for the remaining years.

Slower or faster speeds are then referred to as some percentage of PSA. For example, 50 PSA means one-half the CPR of the PSA benchmark prepayment rate; 150 PSA means 1.5 times the CPR of the PSA benchmark prepayment rate; 300 PSA means three times the CPR of the benchmark prepayment rate. A prepayment rate of 0 PSA means that no prepayments are assumed.

While we have omitted the details, Exhibit 16.2 shows for selected months the cash flow for a hypothetical mortgage passthrough assuming a WAC of 8.125%, a passthrough rate of 7.5%, and a WAM of 357 months. The cash flow is broken down into three components: (1) interest (based on

EXHIBIT 16.2 Monthly Cash Flow for a $400 million Passthrough with a 7.5% Passthrough Rate, a WAC of 8.125%, and a WAM of 357 Months Assuming 165 PSA

(1)	(2)	(3)	(4)	(5)	(6)	(7)	(8)	(9)
Month	Outstanding Balance	SMM	Mortgage Payment	Net Interest	Scheduled Principal	Prepayment	Total Principal	Cash Flow
1	$400,000,000	0.00111	$2,975,868	$2,500,000	$267,535	$442,389	$709,923	$3,209,923
2	399,290,077	0.00139	2,972,575	2,495,563	269,048	552,847	821,896	3,317,459
3	398,468,181	0.00167	2,968,456	2,490,426	270,495	663,065	933,560	3,423,986
26	350,540,672	0.00835	2,656,123	2,190,879	282,671	2,923,885	3,206,556	5,397,435
27	347,334,116	0.00865	2,633,950	2,170,838	282,209	3,001,955	3,284,164	5,455,002
30	337,568,221	0.00865	2,566,190	2,109,801	280,572	2,917,496	3,198,067	5,307,869
100	170,142,350	0.00865	1,396,958	1,063,390	244,953	1,469,591	1,714,544	2,777,933
101	168,427,806	0.00865	1,384,875	1,052,674	244,478	1,454,765	1,699,243	2,751,916
204	54,021,127	0.00865	565,976	337,632	200,208	465,544	665,752	1,003,384
205	53,355,375	0.00865	561,081	333,471	199,820	459,789	659,609	993,080
357	148,802	0.00865	149,809	930	148,802	0	148,802	149,732

Note: Since the WAM is 357 months, the underlying mortgage pool is seasoned an average of 3 months. Therefore, the CPR for month 27 is 1.65 × 6%.

the passthrough rate), (2) the regularly scheduled principal repayment, and (3) prepayments based on 165 PSA.

The total principal payment reported in Column (8) is the sum of Columns (6) and (7). Finally, the projected monthly cash flow for this passthrough is shown in Column (9). The monthly cash flow is the sum of the interest paid to the passthrough investor [Column (5)] and the total principal payments for the month [Column (8)].

Average Life   The stated maturity of a mortgage passthrough is an inappropriate measure because of principal repayments over time. Instead, market participants calculate an *average life* which is the average time to receipt of principal payments (scheduled principal payments and projected prepayments), weighted by the amount of principal expected. More specifically, the average life is found as follows:

$$\text{Average life} = \frac{\text{Weighted monthly average of principal received}}{12 \times (\text{Total principal to be received})}$$

The average life of a passthrough depends on the PSA prepayment assumption. To see this, the average life is shown below for different prepayment speeds for the mortgage passthrough used to illustrate the cash flows in Exhibit 16.2:

PSA speed	50	100	165	200	300	400	500	600	700
Average life	15.11	11.66	8.76	7.68	5.63	4.44	3.68	3.16	2.78

Contraction Risk and Extension Risk   An investor who owns mortgage passthroughs does not know what the cash flows will be because that depends on prepayments. As noted earlier, this risk is called prepayment risk. However, prepayment risk can be divided into two risks, contraction risk and extension risk. We explain these two risks by means of an example.

Suppose an investor buys a 10% coupon mortgage passthrough at a time when the prevailing mortgage rate is 10%. Suppose further that the expected average life for this mortgage passthrough is nine years based on a prepayment rate of 110 PSA. Let's consider what will happen to prepayments if mortgage rates decline to, say, 6%. The borrower will have an incentive to prepay all or part of the mortgage resulting in a shortening of the average life of the security from what it was expected to be when the security was purchased. For example, the market might expect that the prepayment speed will increase to 200 PSA resulting in a decrease in the average life to six years. The disadvantage to the investor is that the funds received from the prepayments will have to be reinvested at lower interest rates. This risk that the average life of the security will be shortened forcing the investor to reinvest at lower interest rates is referred to as *contraction risk*.

Now let's look at what happens if mortgage rates rise to 14%. Prepayments can be expected to slow down because homeowners will not refinance or partially prepay their mortgages, resulting in an increase in the expected average life. For example, the market might expect the prepayment rate to decrease to 75 PSA that would result in an average life of 12 years. Unfortunately, it is in a rising interest rate environment when investors want prepayments to speed up so that they can reinvest the principal received at the higher market interest rate. This adverse consequence of rising mortgage rates is called *extension risk*.

Therefore, prepayment risk encompasses contraction risk and extension risk. Prepayment risk makes passthrough securities unattractive for certain individuals and financial institutions to hold for purposes of accomplishing their investment objectives. Some individuals and institutional investors are concerned with extension risk and others with contraction risk when they purchase a passthrough security. Is it possible to alter the cash flows of a passthrough to reduce the contraction risk and extension risk for institutional investors? This can be done as we will see when we discuss collateralized mortgage obligations.

Stripped Mortgage-Backed Securities

A mortgage passthrough distributes the cash flow from the underlying pool of mortgages on a pro rata basis to the securityholders. A *stripped mortgage-backed security* (stripped MBS) is created by altering that distribution of principal and interest from a pro rata distribution to an unequal distribution. In the most common type of stripped MBS, all the interest is allocated to one class—the *interest-only class*—and all the principal to the other class—the *principal-only class*.

Principal-Only Securities

A principal-only security, also a called the *PO* or a *principal-only mortgage strip*, is purchased at a substantial discount from par value. The return an investor realizes depends on the speed at which prepayments are made. The faster the prepayments, the higher the investor's return. For example, suppose there is a mortgage pool consisting only of 30-year mortgages, with $400 million in principal, and that investors can purchase POs backed by this mortgage pool for $175 million. The dollar return on this investment will be $225 million. How quickly that dollar return is recovered by PO investors determines the actual return that will be realized. In the extreme case, if all homeowners in the underlying mortgage pool decide to prepay their mortgage loans immediately, PO investors will realize the $225 million immediately. At the other extreme, if all homeowners decide to remain in their homes for 30 years and make no prepayments, the $225 million will be spread out over 30 years, which would result in a lower return for PO investors.

Let's look at how the price of the PO would be expected to change as mortgage rates in the market change. When mortgage rates decline below the contract rate, prepayments are expected to speed up, accelerating payments to the PO holder. Thus, the cash flow of a PO improves (in the sense that principal repayments are received earlier). The cash flow will be discounted at a lower interest rate because the mortgage rate in the market has declined. The result is that the PO price will increase when mortgage rates decline. When mortgage rates rise above the contract rate, prepayments are expected to slow down. The cash flow deteriorates (in the sense that it takes longer to recover principal repayments). Couple this with a higher discount rate, and the price of a PO will fall when mortgage rates rise.

Interest-Only Securities

An interest-only class, also called an *IO* or an *interest-only mortgage strip*, has no par value. In contrast to the PO investor, the IO investor wants prepayments to be slow because the IO investor receives interest only on the amount of the principal outstanding. When prepayments are made, less dollar interest will be received as the outstanding principal declines. In fact, if prepayments are too fast, the IO investor may not recover the amount paid for the IO even if the security is held to maturity.

Let's look at the expected price response of an IO to changes in mortgage rates. If mortgage rates decline below the contract rate, prepayments are expected to accelerate. This would result in a deterioration of the expected cash flow for an IO. While the cash flow will be discounted at a lower rate, the net effect typically is a decline in the price of an IO. If mortgage rates rise above the contract rate, the expected cash flow improves, but the cash flow is discounted at a higher interest rate. The net effect may be either a rise or fall for the IO.

Thus, we see an interesting characteristic of an IO: Its price tends to move in the same direction as the change in mortgage rates (1) when mortgage rates fall below the contract rate and (2) for some range of mortgage rates above the contract rate. Both POs and IOs exhibit substantial price volatility when mortgage rates change. The greater price volatility of the IO and PO compared to the passthrough from which they were created is because the combined price volatility of the IO and PO must be equal to the price volatility of the passthrough.

Agency Collateralized Mortgage Obligations

Some institutional investors are concerned with extension risk and others with contraction risk when they invest in a mortgage passthrough. This problem can be mitigated by redirecting the cash flows of mortgage passthrough securities to different bond classes, called *tranches*, so as to create securities that have different exposure to prepayment risk and, therefore, different risk–return patterns than the passthrough securities from which the tranches were created. As explained in the previous chapter, an asset-backed security can be either a passthrough structure or a paythrough structure. A CMO is an example of a paythrough structure.

When the cash flows of pools of mortgage passthrough securities are redistributed to different bond classes, the resulting securities are called *collateralized mortgage obligations* (CMOs). The creation of a CMO cannot eliminate prepayment risk; it can only distribute the various forms of this risk among different classes of bondholders. The CMO's major financial innovation is that the securities created more closely satisfy the asset/liability needs of institutional investors and thus broaden the appeal of mortgage-backed products to bond investors.

Rather than list the different types of tranches that can be created in a CMO structure, we will show how the tranches can be created. This will provide an excellent illustration of financial engineering. Although there are many different types of CMOs that have been created, we will only look at three of the key innovations in the CMO market: sequential-pay tranches, accrual tranches, and planned amortization-class tranches. Two other important tranches that are not illustrated here are the floating rate tranche and the inverse floating rate tranche.

Sequential-Pay CMOs

A *sequential-pay* CMO is structured so that each class of bond (i.e., tranche) is retired sequentially. To illustrate a sequential-pay CMO, we discuss CMO-1, a hypothetical deal made up to illustrate the basic features of the structure. The collateral for this hypothetical CMO is a hypothetical mortgage passthrough with a total par value of $400 million and the following characteristics: (1) the security's coupon rate is 7.5%, (2) the WAC is 8.125%, and (3) the WAM is 357 months. This is the same mortgage passthrough that we used earlier in this chapter to describe the cash flow of a passthrough based on some PSA assumption.

From this $400 million of collateral, four tranches are created. Their characteristics are summarized in Exhibit 16.3. The total par value of the four tranches is equal to the par value of the collateral (i.e., the mortgage passthrough). In this simple structure, the coupon rate is the same for each tranche and also the same as the coupon rate on the collateral. There is no reason why this must be so, and, in fact, typically the coupon rate varies by tranche.

Now remember that a CMO is created by redistributing the cash flow—interest and principal—to the different tranches based on a set of payment rules. The payment rules at the bottom of Exhibit 16.3 describe how the cash flow from the passthrough (i.e., collateral) is to be distributed to the four tranches. There are separate rules for the payment of the coupon interest and the payment of principal, the principal being the total of the regularly scheduled principal payment and any prepayments.

In CMO-1, each tranche receives periodic coupon interest payments based on the amount of the outstanding balance at the beginning of the month. The disbursement of the principal, however, is made in a special way. A tranche is not entitled to receive principal until the entire principal of the tranche has been paid off. More specifically, tranche A receives all the

EXHIBIT 16.3 CMO-1: A Hypothetical Four-Tranche Sequential-Pay Structure

Tranche	Par Amount	Coupon Rate (%)
A	$194,500,000	7.5
B	36,000,000	7.5
C	96,500,000	7.5
D	73,000,000	7.5
Total	$400,000,000	

Payment rules:

1. *For payment of periodic coupon interest:* Disburse periodic coupon interest to each tranche on the basis of the amount of principal outstanding at the beginning of the period.
2. *For disbursement of principal payments:* Disburse principal payments to tranche A until it is completely paid off. After tranche A is completely paid off, disburse principal payments to tranche B until it is completely paid off. After tranche B is completely paid off, disburse principal payments to tranche C until it is completely paid off. After tranche C is completely paid off, disburse principal payments to tranche D until it is completely paid off.

principal payments until the entire principal amount owed to that tranche, $194,500,000, is paid off; then tranche B begins to receive principal and continues to do so until it is paid the entire $36,000,000. Tranche C then receives principal, and when it is paid off, tranche D starts receiving principal payments.

Although the priority rules for the disbursement of the principal payments are known, the precise amount of the principal in each period is not. This will depend on the cash flow and, therefore, on the principal payments of the collateral, which will depend on the actual prepayment rate of the collateral. An assumed PSA speed allows the cash flow to be projected.

Let's look at what has been accomplished by creating the CMO. First, as shown earlier in this chapter, the average life for the mortgage passthrough is 8.76 years, assuming a prepayment speed of 165 PSA. Exhibit 16.4 shows the average life of the collateral and the four tranches assuming different prepayment speeds. Notice that the four tranches have average lives that are both shorter and longer than the collateral, thereby attracting investors who have a preference for an average life different from that of the collateral.

There is still a major problem: There is considerable variability of the average life for the tranches. We'll see how this can be tackled later on. However, there is some protection provided for each tranche against prepayment risk. This is because prioritizing the distribution of principal (i.e., establishing the payment rules for principal) effectively protects the shorter-term tranche

EXHIBIT 16.4 Average Life for Collateral and Tranches of CMO-1 for Different PSA Assumptions

Prepayment Speed (PSA)	Average Life for				
	Collateral	Tranche A	Tranche B	Tranche C	Tranche D
50	15.11	7.48	15.98	21.02	27.24
100	11.66	4.90	10.86	15.78	24.58
165	8.76	3.48	7.49	11.19	20.27
200	7.68	3.05	6.42	9.60	18.11
300	5.63	2.32	4.64	6.81	13.36
400	4.44	1.94	3.70	5.31	10.34
500	3.68	1.69	3.12	4.38	8.35
600	3.16	1.51	2.74	3.75	6.96
700	2.78	1.38	2.47	3.30	5.95

A in this structure against extension risk. This protection must come from somewhere, so it comes from the three other tranches. Similarly, tranches C and D provide protection against extension risk for tranches A and B. At the same time, tranches C and D benefit because they are provided protection against contraction risk, the protection coming from tranches A and B.

Accrual Bonds

In CMO-1, the payment rules for interest provide for all tranches to be paid interest each month. In many sequential-pay CMO structures, at least one tranche does not receive current interest. Instead, the interest for that tranche would accrue and be added to the principal balance. Such a bond class is commonly referred to as an *accrual tranche*, or a *Z bond* (because the bond is similar to a zero-coupon bond). The interest that would have been paid to the accrual tranche is then used to speed up paying down the principal balance of earlier tranches.

To see this, consider CMO-2, a hypothetical CMO structure with the same collateral as CMO-1 and with four tranches, each with a coupon rate of 7.5%. The structure is shown in Exhibit 16.5. The difference is in the last tranche, Z, which is an accrual tranche.

The inclusion of the accrual tranche results in a shortening of the expected final maturity for tranches A, B, and C. The average lives for tranches A, B, and C are shorter in CMO-2 compared to CMO-1 because of the inclusion of the accrual bond. For example, at 165 PSA, the average lives are as follows:

Structure	Tranche A	Tranche B	Tranche C
CMO-2	2.90	5.86	7.87
CMO-1	3.48	7.49	11.19

The reason for the shortening of the nonaccrual tranches is that the interest that would be paid to the accrual bond is being allocated to the other tranches. Tranche Z in CMO-2 will have a longer average life than tranche D in CMO-1. Thus, shorter-term tranches and a longer-term tranche are created by including an accrual bond. The accrual bond appeals to investors who are concerned with reinvestment risk. Since there are no coupon payments to reinvest, reinvestment risk is eliminated until all the other tranches are paid off.

Planned Amortization–Class Tranches

In a *planned amortization–class* (PAC) CMO structure, if prepayments are within a specified range, the cash flow pattern is known for some of

EXHIBIT 16.5 CMO-2: A Hypothetical Four-Tranche Sequential-Pay Structure with an Accrual Bond Class

Tranche	Par Amount	Coupon Rate (%)
A	$194,500,000	7.5
B	36,000,000	7.5
C	96,500,000	7.5
Z (Accrual)	73,000,000	7.5
Total	$400,000,000	

Payment rules:

1. *For payment of periodic coupon interest:* Disburse periodic coupon interest to tranches A, B, and C on the basis of the amount of principal outstanding at the beginning of the period. For tranche Z, accrue the interest based on the principal plus accrued interest in the previous period. The interest for tranche Z is to be paid to the earlier tranches as a principal pay down.
2. *For disbursement of principal payments:* Disburse principal payments to tranche A until it is completely paid off. After tranche A is completely paid off, disburse principal payments to tranche B until it is completely paid off. After tranche B is completely paid off, disburse principal payments to tranche C until it is completely paid off. After tranche C is completely paid off, disburse principal payments to tranche Z until the original principal balance plus accrued interest is completely paid off.

EXHIBIT 16.6   CMO-3: CMO Structure with One PAC Tranche and One Support Tranche

Tranche	Par Amount	Coupon Rate (%)
P (PAC)	$243,800,000	7.5
S (Support)	156,200,000	7.5
Total	$400,000,000	

Payment rules:

1. *For payment of periodic coupon interest:* Disburse periodic coupon interest to each tranche on the basis of the amount of principal outstanding at the beginning of the period.
2. *For disbursement of principal payments:* Disburse principal payments to tranche P based on its schedule of principal repayments as shown in Exhibit 16.7. Tranche P has priority with respect to current and future principal payments to satisfy the schedule. Any excess principal payments in a month over the amount necessary to satisfy the schedule for tranche P are paid to tranche S. When tranche S is completely paid off, all principal payments are to be made to tranche P regardless of the schedule.

the tranches in the structure, particularly those tranches identified as PAC tranches. The greater predictability of the cash flow for these tranches occurs because there is a principal repayment schedule that must be satisfied. PAC tranches have priority over all other tranches in the CMO structure in receiving principal payments from the underlying collateral. The greater certainty of the cash flow for the PAC tranches comes at the expense of the non-PAC classes, called the *support tranches* or *companion tranches*. It is the support tranches that absorb the prepayment risk.

To illustrate a PAC bond, we will use as collateral the $400 million mortgage passthrough with a coupon rate of 7.5%, a WAC of 8.125%, and a WAM of 357 months. Exhibit 16.6 shows a simple PAC bond structure, CMO-3, that has one PAC bond and one support bond. Suppose a PAC schedule (not shown here) is created by the issuer assuming a PAC collar of 90 PSA to 300 PSA. This characteristic of the collateral allows for the creation of a PAC tranche, assuming that the collateral prepays over its life at a constant speed between 90 PSA and 300 PSA. A schedule of principal repayments that the PAC bondholders are entitled to receive before any other tranche in the CMO is specified. Although there is no assurance that the collateral will prepay between these two speeds, a PAC bond can be structured assuming that it will.

The average life for the PAC tranche and the support tranche in CMO-3 assuming various actual prepayment speeds is shown in Exhibit 16.7. Notice that between 90 PSA and 300 PSA, the average life for the PAC tranche is

EXHIBIT 16.7   Average Life for PAC Tranche and Support Tranche for Different PSA Assumptions

Prepayment Rate (PSA)	PAC Tranche (P)	Support Tranche (S)
0	15.97	27.26
50	9.44	24.00
90	7.26	18.56
100	7.26	18.56
150	7.26	12.57
165	7.26	11.16
200	7.26	8.38
250	7.26	5.37
300	7.26	3.13
350	6.56	2.51
400	5.92	2.17
450	5.38	1.94
500	4.93	1.77
700	3.70	1.37

stable at 7.26 years. However, at slower or faster PSA speeds, the schedule is broken, and the average life changes, lengthening when the prepayment speed is less than 90 PSA and shortening when it is greater than 300 PSA. Even so, there is much greater variability for the average life of the support tranche. The average life for the support tranche is substantial.

Most CMO structures that have a PAC typically have more than one PAC tranche. The tranches are created by carving up a PAC tranche into a series of sequential-pay PAC tranches.

Private-Label Residential MBS

The private-label CMO market encompasses a variety of product and structuring variations. Technically, any deal that is not securitized under an agency or GSE shelf (i.e., Ginnie Mae, Freddie Mac, or Fannie Mae) can be considered private label as the issuing entity has no connection to the U.S. government (either explicit or implicit). Such deals must have some form of credit enhancement in order to create large amounts of investment-grade bonds. The convention in the markets, however, is to limit the private-label sector to the securitization of prime loans. Other products, such as deals backed by subprime loans, are classified as mortgage-related, asset-backed securities, a subset of the ABS category. Subprime loans are loans made to borrowers with impaired credit ratings or where the lender has a weaker priority position in the collateral such as second-lien loans. In some sense, this classification scheme has become fairly arbitrary.

The credit enhancement for a private-label deal typically is obtained by splitting the face value of the loan pool into senior and subordinated bonds. The senior bonds have higher priority with respect to both the receipt of interest and principal and the allocation of realized losses, and are generally created with enough subordination to be rated AAA by the credit rating agencies. In most cases, the subordinate interests are subdivided (or tranched) into a series of bonds that decline sequentially in priority. The subordinate classes normally range from AA in rating to an unrated first-loss piece. These securities are often referenced as the "six-pack," since there are six broad rating grades generally issued by the rating agencies. In the investment-grade category, bonds range from AA to BBB; noninvestment grade ratings decline from BB to the unrated first-loss piece. The structure (or "splits") of a hypothetical deal is shown in Exhibit 16.8, while a schematic detailing how and losses are allocated within the structure is contained in Exhibit 16.9.

FIGURE 16.8   Schematic of Hypothetical Structure with Cash Flow and Loss Allocations

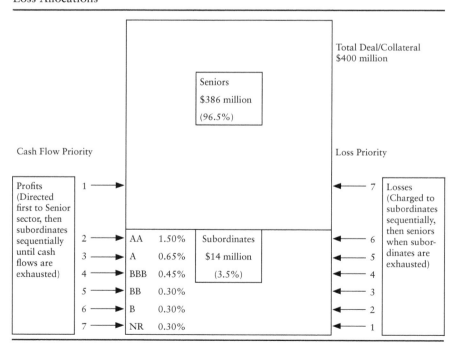

EXHIBIT 16.9 Measuring Subordination by Percentage of Deal Size and Credit Support for a Hypothetical $400 million Deal with 3.5% Initial Subordination

A. Tranche Size as a Percentage of the Total Deal

	Face Value	Percent of Deal
AAA	$386,000,000	96.50%
AA	6,000,000	1.50%
A	2,600,000	0.65%
BBB	1,800,000	0.45%
BB	1,200,000	0.30%
B	1,200,000	0.30%
First loss (nonrated)	1,200,000	0.30%
Total Subordination	14,000,000	3.50%

B. Tranche Size Measured by Percentage of Subordination for Each Rating Level (i.e., credit support)

	Face Value	Credit Support (%)[a]
AAA	$386,000,000	3.50%
AA	6,000,000	2.00%
A	2,600,000	1.35%
BBB	1,800,000	0.90%
BB	1,200,000	0.60%
B	1,200,000	0.30%
First loss (nonrated)	1,200,000	0.00%

[a]Calculated by summing the deal percentages of all tranches junior in priority. As an example, if cumulative losses on the deal were 0.40%, the First Loss and rated B tranches would be fully exhausted, but the tranches rated BB and above would not be affected.

Internal credit enhancement requires two complimentary mechanisms. The cash flows for deals are allocated through the mechanism of a *waterfall*, which dictates the allocation of principal and interest payments to tranches with different degrees of seniority. At the same time, the allocation of realized losses is also governed by a separate prioritization schedule, with the subordinates (subs) typically being impacted in reverse order of priority.

While the original subordination levels are set at the time of issuance (or, more precisely, at the time the attributes of the deal's collateral are finalized), deals with internal credit enhancement are designed such that the amount of credit enhancement grows over time.

Mortgage-Related, Asset-Backed Securities: Subprime MBS

In describing private-label deals, we noted that the emphasis in structures in the mortgage ABS sectors is different from that in structures involving prime first-lien residential loans. Loans that fall into the general category of mortgage ABS are riskier than those in prime deals, either because the loans are granted to borrowers with impaired credit (which greatly increases their expected defaults and losses) or are in an inferior lien position (which creates high-loss severities). As such, these loans are characterized by higher note rates than those in the prime first-lien sector, reflecting risk-based pricing on the part of lenders.

The challenge in structuring mortgage ABS deals is to create cash flow protection and credit enhancement for the senior securities in the most efficient possible way. The optimal form of credit enhancement for deals backed by risky loans with high note rates is the *overcollateralization* (OC) structure. This structure allows the higher note rates associated with these riskier loans to be converted into credit enhancement. In addition to the utilization of excess spread as credit enhancement, deals securitizing these types of risky loans must have higher levels of subordination than in the prime sector. The mechanisms associated with the OC structure are more complex than the traditional shifting interest structures utilized in the prime sector.

For the purposes of our discussion, mortgage ABS deals are collectively referred to as *ABS structures*. As such, these deals should not be confused with ABS deals securitizing assets such as auto loans and credit cards, which have many different features as described earlier in this chapter. Additionally, the term residential deal is also used interchangeably with prime deal in our discussion, utilizing the admittedly oversimplified terminology used in the market.

COMMERCIAL MORTGAGE-BACKED SECURITIES

Commercial mortgage-backed securities (CMBSs) are backed by a pool of commercial mortgage loans on income-producing property—multifamily properties (i.e., apartment buildings), office buildings, industrial properties (including warehouses), shopping centers, hotels, and health care facilities (i.e., senior housing care facilities). The basic building block of the CMBS transaction is a commercial loan that was originated either to finance a commercial purchase or to refinance a prior mortgage obligation.

Commercial mortgage loans are nonrecourse loans. This means that the lender can only look to the income-producing property backing the loan for interest and principal repayment. If there is a default, the lender looks to the proceeds from the sale of the property for repayment and has no recourse to the borrower for any unpaid balance. Basically, this means that the lender must view each property as a stand-alone business and evaluate each property using measures that have been found to be useful in assessing credit risk.

Regardless of the property type, the two measures that have been found to be key indicators of the potential credit performance are the *debt-to-service coverage* (DSC) ratio and the *loan-to-value* (LTV) ratio. The DSC ratio is the ratio of the property's *net operating income* (NOI) divided by the debt service. The NOI is defined as the rental income reduced by cash operating expenses (adjusted for a replacement reserve). A ratio greater than 1 means that the cash flow from the property is sufficient to cover debt servicing. The higher the ratio, the more likely that the borrower will be able to meet debt servicing from the property's cash flow. In computing the LTV, "value" in the ratio is either market value or appraised value. In valuing commercial property, there can be considerable variation in the estimates of the property's market value. The lower the LTV, the greater the protection afforded the lender.

Another characteristic of the underlying loans that is used in gauging the quality of a CMBS deal is the prepayment protection provisions. We review these provisions later. Finally, there are characteristics of the property that affect quality. Specifically, investors and rating agencies look at the concentration of loans by property type and by geographical location.

As with any securitization transaction, the rating agencies will determine the level of credit enhancement to achieve a desired rating level for each tranche in the structure. For example, if certain DSC and LTV ratios are needed, and these ratios cannot be met at the loan level, then subordination is used to achieve these levels.

Call Protection

The degree of call protection available to a CMBS investor is a function of the following two characteristics: (1) call protection available at the loan level and (2) call protection afforded from the actual CMBS structure. At the commercial loan level, call protection can take the following forms: (1) prepayment lockout, (2) defeasance, (3) prepayment penalty points, and (4) yield maintenance charges.

A *prepayment lockout* is a contractual agreement that prohibits any prepayments during a specified period of time, called the *lockout period*. The lockout period at issuance can be from two to five years. After the lockout period, call protection comes in the form of either prepayment penalty points or yield maintenance charges. Prepayment lockout and defeasance are the strongest forms of prepayment protection.

With *defeasance*, rather than prepaying a loan, the borrower provides sufficient funds for the servicer to invest in a portfolio of Treasury securities that replicates the cash flows that would exist in the absence of prepayments. The substitution of the cash flow of a Treasury portfolio for that of the borrower improves the credit quality of the CMBS deal.

Prepayment penalty points are predetermined penalties that must be paid by the borrower if the borrower wishes to refinance. For example, 5-4-3-2-1 is a common prepayment penalty point structure. That is, if the borrower wishes to prepay during the first year, a 5% penalty for a total of $105 rather than $100 (which is the norm in the residential market) must be paid. Likewise, during the second year, a 4% penalty would apply, and so on.

A *yield maintenance charge*, in its simplest terms, is designed to make the lender indifferent as to the timing of prepayments. The yield maintenance charge, also called the *make-whole charge*, makes it uneconomical to refinance solely to get a lower interest rate. Several methods have been used in practice to compute the yield maintenance charge.

The other type of call protection available in CMBS transactions is structural. That is, because the CMBS bond structures are sequential-pay (by rating), the bonds rated AA cannot pay down until the bonds rated AAA are completely retired, and the bonds rated AA must be paid off before the bonds rated A, and so on. However, principal losses due to defaults are impacted from the bottom of the structure upward.

Balloon Maturity Provisions

Many commercial loans backing CMBS transactions are balloon loans that require substantial principal payment at the end of the term of the loan. If the borrower fails to make the balloon payment, the borrower is in default. The lender may extend the loan, and in so doing may modify the original loan terms. During the workout period for the loan, a higher interest rate will be charged, the "default interest rate."

The risk that a borrower will not be able to make the balloon payment because either the borrower cannot arrange for refinancing at the balloon payment date or cannot sell the property to generate sufficient funds to pay off the balloon balance, is called *balloon risk*. Since the term of the loan will be extended by the lender during the workout period, balloon risk is also referred to as *extension risk*.

KEY POINTS

- Bonds have a par value and a coupon rate that can have a fixed or floating interest rate. Bonds can have a bullet maturity or can be amortizing instruments. A bond can be callable by the issuer prior to the maturity date or maybe putable by the bond holder.
- The U.S. Department of Treasury issues both discount and coupon securities. Coupon securities can be either fixed rate or variable rate securities (i.e., inflation-protected securities). U.S. Treasury securities are backed by the full faith and credit of the U.S. government and therefore are viewed as default-free securities.
- Stripped Treasury securities are zero-coupon notes or bonds created by brokerage firms through a process known as coupon stripping under the Treasury's STRIPS program.
- Federal agency securities include securities issued by federally related institutions and government sponsored enterprises. The former are arms of the federal government and generally do not issue securities directly into the marketplace and, with important exceptions, are backed by the full faith and credit of the U.S. government. Government sponsored enterprises are privately owned, publicly chartered entities whose securities are not backed by the full faith and credit of the U.S. government.
- There is a wide range of corporate bonds that can be issued by a corporation that give some creditors priority over other creditors in the case of the bankruptcy of the issuer.
- A convertible bond is a corporate bond where the bond holder has the right to convert the bond into a predetermined number of shares of common stock. Bonds with this feature are typically callable and some are putable.
- The credit risk of a bond is typically gauged by its credit rating as assigned by one or more rating agencies (Moody's Investors Service, Standard & Poor's Corporation, and Fitch Ratings). Investment-grade bonds are issues rated triple B or higher; noninvestment-grade bonds (also called speculative bonds, high-yield bonds, and junk bonds) are bonds rated below triple B. Over time, bonds can be upgraded or downgraded.
- Municipal securities are debt obligations issued by state and local governments, entities that they establish, and by the District of Columbia and any possession of the United States. There are both tax-exempt and taxable municipal securities. For the former interest is exempt from

federal income taxation. Build America Bonds, first issued in 2009, are the largest type of taxable municipal bond.

- The two basic types of security structure in the municipal securities market are tax-backed bonds and revenue bonds. There are also some municipal securities with special security structures: insured, bank-backed municipal bonds, and refunded bonds.

- An asset-backed security is a security backed by a pool of loans or receivables. Unlike a corporate bond where the investors look to the issuer to generate sufficient funds to satisfy the debt obligation, with an ABS investors look to the cash flow from the pool of assets.

- ABS are credit enhanced in order to obtain a credit rating. Credit enhancement means that credit support is provided for one or more bond holders in the structure, with the amount of the credit enhancement necessary determined by the rating agencies.

- There are two general types of credit enhancement structures: external (i.e., credit support from a third party) and internal. Three forms of internal credit enhancement are reserve funds, overcollateralization, and senior-subordinated structures.

- Residential mortgage-backed securities are backed by a pool of residential mortgage loans. The basic form of RMBS is a mortgage passthrough security. Agency mortgage passthroughs are issued by the Government National Mortgage Association (Ginnie Mae), Fannie Mac, and Freddie Mac.

- The cash flow for an RMBS includes interest payments, regularly scheduled principal payments (i.e., amortization), and prepayments. A prepayment is any amount in excess of the regularly scheduled principal payment. Two conventions have been used as a benchmark for prepayment rates: conditional prepayment rate and Public Securities Association prepayment benchmark. The life of an RMBS is measured in terms of its average life.

- An investor in an RMBS is exposed to prepayment risk which can, in turn, be divided into contraction risk and extension risk.

- In the most common type of stripped MBS, all the interest is allocated to one class—the interest-only class—and all the principal to the other class—the principal-only class. Both types of stripped MBS exhibit substantial price volatility when mortgage rates change. The price of an interest-only class tends to move in the same direction as the change in mortgage rates.

- An agency collateralized mortgage obligations is an RMBS created by altering the cash flows from a pool of mortgage passthrough securities to different bond classes (or tranches). By doing so, the prepayment risk associated with the collateral is reallocated to different bond classes so as create securities that more closely satisfy the asset/liability needs of institutional investors.

- There are many different types of CMOs that have been created: sequential-pay tranches, accrual tranches, planned amortization class tranches, floating-rate tranches, and inverse floating-rate tranches.
- Technically, any RMBS that is not an agency or GSE shelf (i.e., Ginnie Mae, Freddie Mac, or Fannie Mae) can be considered private label as the issuing entity has no connection to the U.S. government (either explicit or implicit). Because of the lack of any government backing, such securities must have credit enhancement and this can be in the form of external or internal credit enhancement.
- The private label RMBS market is be divided into two sectors. The first is RMBS backed by prime loans. The other sector is RMBS backed by subprime loans—loans made to borrowers with impaired credit ratings or loans that are second lien (or worse) loans.
- Securities backed by a pool of commercial mortgage loans on income-producing property are called commercial mortgage-backed securities. Income-producing properties include multi-family properties (i.e., apartment buildings), office buildings, industrial properties (including warehouses), shopping centers, hotels, and health care facilities.
- In evaluating the credit risk of all property types, the two measures that have been found to be key indicators of the potential credit performance are the debt-to-service coverage ratio and the loan-to-value ratio.
- Call protection for investors in CMBS is greater than for an RMBS and depends on the call protection available at the loan level and call protection afforded from the actual CMBS structure. At the commercial loan level, call protection can take the form of prepayment lockout, defeasance, prepayment penalty points, and yield maintenance charges.
- Balloon risk for an investor in CMBS is the risk that a borrower in the loan pool will not be able to make the balloon payment at the scheduled date, causing the loan and consequently the CMBS to extend in maturity.

QUESTIONS

1. **a.** What is the advantage of a call provision for an issuer?
   b. What are the disadvantages of a call provision for the bondholder?
2. Explain why you agree or disagree with the following statement: "The debt of government-owned corporations is guaranteed by the full faith and credit of the U.S. government, but that is not the case for the debt of government sponsored enterprises."
3. How do investors gauge the default risk of a bond issue?
4. Why is the maturity of an amortizing bond not a useful measure?
5. Explain why you agree or disagree with the following statements:
   a. "All municipal bonds are exempt from federal income taxes."
   b. "All municipal bonds are exempt from state and local taxes."
6. What is the difference between a municipal tax-backed bond and a municipal revenue bond?
7. **a.** Why is the cash flow of a residential mortgage loan unknown?
   b. In what sense has the investor in a residential mortgage loan granted the borrower (homeowner) a loan similar to a callable bond?
8. Why is an assumed prepayment speed necessary to project the cash flow of a mortgage passthrough security?
9. **a.** What is meant by prepayment risk for a residential mortgage-backed security?
   b. What are contraction risk and extension risk?
   c. "By creating a CMO, an issuer eliminates the prepayment risk associated with the underlying pool of mortgage loans." Do you agree with this statement?
10. **a.** Why is it necessary for a nonagency mortgage-backed security to have credit enhancement?
    b. Who determines the amount of credit enhancement needed?
11. **a.** What is meant by a senior-subordinated structure?
    b. Why is the senior-subordinated structure a form of credit enhancement?
    c. What is the limitation of a third-party guarantee as a form of credit enhancement?
12. What is the difference between a private label and subprime mortgage-backed security? Be sure to mention how they differ in terms of credit enhancement.
13. In a commercial mortgage-backed security, why is balloon risk referred to as extension risk?

CHAPTER 17

Bond Analytics

Basic Valuation, Yield Measures, and Interest Rate Risk Measures

Frank J. Fabozzi, Ph.D., CFA, CPA
Professor in the Practice of Finance
Yale School of Management

In the previous chapter, we discussed the fundamental characteristics of bonds and the wide range of bonds available in the market. In this chapter, we explain the fundamental analytical tools necessary to understand how to analyze bonds and assess their potential performance when interest rates change.

BASIC VALUATION OF OPTION-FREE BONDS

The price of any financial instrument is equal to the present value of the expected cash flows from the financial instrument. Therefore, determining the price requires: (1) an estimate of the expected cash flows and (2) an estimate of the appropriate required yield. The expected cash flows for some financial instruments are simple to compute; for others, the task is more difficult. The *required yield* reflects the yield for financial instruments with comparable risk.

The first step in determining the price of a bond is to estimate its cash flow. The cash flow for a bond that the issuer cannot retire prior to its stated maturity date (that is, an option-free bond) consists of:

1. Periodic coupon interest payments to the maturity date.
2. The par value at maturity.

Our illustrations of bond pricing use three assumptions to simplify the analysis:

1. The coupon payments are made every six months. (For most U.S. bond issues, coupon interest is in fact paid semiannually.)
2. The next coupon payment for the bond is received exactly six months from now.
3. The coupon interest is fixed for the term of the bond.

While our focus in this chapter is on option-free bonds, in Chapter 18 we explain how to value bonds with embedded options.

Consequently, the cash flows for an option-free bond consist of an annuity of a fixed coupon interest payment paid semiannually and the par, or maturity, value. For example, a 20-year bond with a 10% coupon rate and a par, or maturity, value of $1,000 has the following cash flows from coupon interest:

$$\text{Annual coupon interest} = \$1,000 \times 0.10 = \$100$$

$$\text{Semiannual coupon interest} = \$100 / 2 = \$50$$

Therefore, there are 40 semiannual cash flows of $50, and there is a $1,000 cash flow 40 six-month periods from now. Notice the treatment of the par value. It is not treated as if it is received 20 years from now. Instead, it is treated on a basis consistent with the coupon payments, which are semiannual.

The required yield is determined by investigating the yields offered on comparable bonds in the market. In this case, comparable investments would be option-free bonds of the same credit quality and the same maturity. The required yield typically is expressed as an annual interest rate. When the cash flows occur semiannually, the market convention is to use one-half the annual interest rate as the periodic interest rate with which to discount the cash flows.

Given the cash flows of a bond and the required yield, we have all the information needed to price a bond. Because the price of a bond is the present value of the cash flows, it is determined by adding these two present values: (1) the present value of the semiannual coupon payments and (2) the present value of the par, or maturity, value at the maturity date.

In general, the price of a bond can be computed using the following formula:

$$P = \frac{C}{(1+r)^1} + \frac{C}{(1+r)^2} + \frac{C}{(1+r)^3} + \cdots + \frac{C}{(1+r)^n} + \frac{M}{(1+r)^n} \qquad (17.1)$$

where

P = price (in $)

n = number of periods (number of years × 2)

C = semiannual coupon payment (in $)

r = periodic interest rate (required annual yield ÷ 2)

M = maturity value

t = time period when the payment is to be received

To illustrate how to compute the price of a bond, consider a 20-year 10% coupon bond with a par value of $1,000. Let's suppose that the required yield on this bond is 11%. The cash flows for this bond are as follows: (1) 40 semiannual coupon payments of $50 and (2) $1,000 to be received 40 six-month periods from now. The semiannual or periodic interest rate (or periodic required yield) is 5.5% (11% divided by 2).

The present value of the 40 semiannual coupon payments of $50, discounted at 5.5%, is $802.31. The present value of the par, or maturity, value of $1,000 received 40 six-month periods from now, discounted at 5.5%, is $117.46. The price of the bond is then equal to the sum of the two present values: $919.77.

Price–Yield Relationship

A fundamental property of a bond is that its price changes in the opposite direction from the change in the required yield. The reason is that the price of the bond is the present value of the cash flows. As the required yield increases, the present value of the cash flows decreases; hence, the price decreases. The opposite is true when the required yield decreases: The present value of the cash flows increases, and, therefore, the price of the bond increases. This can be seen by examining the price for the 20-year, 10% bond when the required yield is 11%, 10%, and 6.8%. Exhibit 17.1 shows the price of the 20-year, 10% coupon bond for various required yields.

If we graph the price–required yield relationship for any option-free bond, we will find that it has the bowed shape shown in Exhibit 17.2. This shape is referred to as *convex*. The convexity of the price–yield relationship has important implications for the investment properties of a bond, as we explain later in this chapter.

Relationship between Coupon Rate, Required Yield, and Price

As yields in the marketplace change, the only variable that can change to compensate an investor in an existing bond is the price of that bond. When the

EXHIBIT 17.1   Price–Yield Relationship for a 20-Year, 10% Coupon Bond

Yield	Price
0.050	$1,627.57
0.060	1,462.30
0.070	1,320.33
0.080	1,197.93
0.090	1,092.01
0.100	1,000.00
0.110	919.77
0.120	849.54
0.130	787.82
0.140	733.37
0.150	685.14

EXHIBIT 17.2   Shape of the Price–Yield Relationship

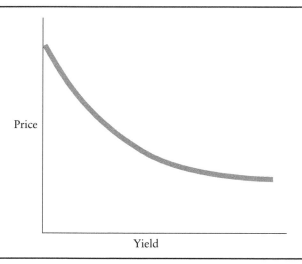

coupon rate is equal to the required yield, the price of the bond will be equal to its par value as we state earlier.

When yields in the marketplace rise above the coupon rate at a given point in time, the price of the bond adjusts so that the investor can realize some additional interest. This is accomplished by the price falling below its par value. The capital appreciation realized by holding the bond to maturity represents a form of interest to the investor to compensate for a coupon rate that is lower than the required yield. When a bond sells below its par value, it is said to be selling at a *discount*. In our earlier calculation of bond price, we saw that when the required yield is greater than the coupon rate, the price of the bond is always lower than the par value ($1,000).

When the required yield in the market is below the coupon rate, the bond must sell above its par value. This is because investors who would have the opportunity to purchase the bond at par would be getting a coupon rate in excess of what the market requires. As a result, investors would bid up the price of the bond because its yield is so attractive. The price would eventually be bid up to a level where the bond offers the required yield in the market. A bond whose price is above its par value is said to be selling at a *premium*.

The relationship between coupon rate, required yield, and price can be summarized as follows:

Coupon rate < Required yield: Price < Par (discount bond)

Coupon rate = Required yield: Price = Par

Coupon rate > Required yield: Price > Par (premium bond)

Relationship between Bond Price and Time If Interest Rates Are Unchanged

If the required yield does not change between the time the bond is purchased and the maturity date, what will happen to the price of the bond? For a bond selling at par value, the coupon rate is equal to the required yield. As the bond moves closer to maturity, the bond will continue to sell at par value. The price of a bond will not remain constant for a bond selling at a premium or a discount, however. A discount bond's price increases as it approaches maturity, assuming the required yield does not change. For a premium bond, the opposite occurs. For both bonds, the price will equal par value at the maturity date.

Reasons for the Change in the Price of a Bond

The price of a bond will change for one or more of the following three reasons:

1. There is a change in the required yield owing to changes in the credit quality of the issuer. That is, the required yield changes because the market now compares the bond yield with yields from a different set of bonds with the same credit risk.

2. There is a change in the price of the bond selling at a premium or a discount without any change in the required yield, simply because the bond is moving toward maturity.
3. There is a change in the required yield owing to a change in the yield on comparable bonds. That is, market interest rates change.

Complications

The framework for pricing a bond discussed in this chapter assumes that: (1) the cash flows are known, (2) one rate is used to discount all cash flows, and (3) one rate is used to discount all cash flows. Let's look at the implications for the pricing of a bond if each assumption is not true.

For option-free bonds, assuming that the issuer does not default, the cash flows are known. For some bonds, however, the cash flows are not known with certainty. This is because an issuer may have an option to call a bond before the stated maturity date. With callable bonds, the cash flows will, in fact, depend on the future level of interest rates relative to the coupon rate. For example, the issuer will typically call a bond when interest rates drop far enough below the coupon rate so that it is economic to retire the bond issue prior to maturity and issue new bonds at a lower coupon rate.[1] Consequently, the cash flows of bonds that may be called prior to maturity are dependent on future interest rates in the marketplace.

Our pricing analysis has assumed that it is appropriate to discount each cash flow using the same discount rate. A bond can be viewed as a package of zero-coupon bonds, in which case a unique discount rate should be used to determine the present value of each cash flow. As will be explained in Chapter 18, this means discounting each cash flow at the spot rate for the period when the cash flow is expected to be received.

Price Quotes

We have assumed in our illustrations that the maturity, or par, value of a bond is $1,000. A bond may have a maturity, or par, value greater or less than $1,000. Consequently, when quoting bond prices, traders quote the price as a percentage of par value. A bond selling at par is quoted as 100, meaning 100% of its par value. A bond selling at a discount will be selling for less than 100; a bond selling at a premium will be selling for more than 100.

The procedure for converting a price quote to a dollar price is as follows:

$$(\text{Price per }\$100\text{ of par value}/100) \times \text{Par value}$$

---

[1]Mortgage-backed securities are another example; the borrower has the right to prepay all or part of the obligation prior to maturity.

For example, if a bond is quoted at 96½ and has a par value of $100,000, then the dollar price is (96.5/100) × $100,000 = $96,500. If a bond is quoted at 103¹⁹⁄₃₂ and has a par value of $1 million, then the dollar price is (103.59375/100) × $1,000,000 = $1,035,937.50.

CONVENTIONAL YIELD MEASURES

Related to the price of a bond is its yield. The price of a bond is calculated from the cash flows and the required yield. The yield of a bond is calculated from the cash flows and the market price plus accrued interest. In this section, we discuss various yield measures and their meaning for evaluating the relative attractiveness of a bond.

There are three bond yield measures commonly quoted by dealers and used by portfolio managers: (1) current yield, (2) yield to maturity, and (3) yield to call. In our illustrations below we assume that the next coupon payment is six months from now and therefore there is no accrued interest.

Current Yield

Current yield relates the annual coupon interest to the market price. The formula for the current yield is

$$\text{Current yield} = \frac{\text{Annual dollar coupon interest}}{\text{Price}}$$

For example, the current yield for a 15-year, 7% coupon bond with a par value of $1,000 selling for $769.40 is 9.10%, as shown:

$$\text{Current yield} = \frac{\$70}{\$769.40} = 0.091\% = 9.1\%$$

The current yield calculation takes into account only the coupon interest and no other source of return that will affect an investor's yield. No consideration is given to the capital gain that the investor will realize when a bond is purchased at a discount and held to maturity; nor is there any recognition of the capital loss that the investor will realize if a bond purchased at a premium is held to maturity. The time value of money is also ignored.

Yield to Maturity

The *yield to maturity* is the interest rate that will make the present value of a bond's remaining cash flows (if held to maturity) equal to the price (plus accrued interest, if any). Mathematically, the yield to maturity, y, for a bond that pays interest semiannually and that has no accrued interest is found by solving the following equation:

$$P = \frac{C}{(1+y)^1} + \frac{C}{(1+y)^2} + \frac{C}{(1+y)^3} + \cdots + \frac{C}{(1+y)^n} + \frac{M}{(1+y)^n} \qquad (17.2)$$

Since the cash flows are every six months, the yield to maturity y found by solving equation (17.2) is a semiannual yield to maturity. This yield can be annualized by either (1) doubling the semiannual yield or (2) compounding the yield. The market convention is to annualize the semiannual yield by simply doubling its value. The yield to maturity computed on the basis of this market convention is called the *bond-equivalent yield*. It is also referred to as a yield on a *bond-equivalent basis*.

The computation of the yield to maturity requires an iterative procedure. To illustrate the computation, consider the bond that we used to compute the current yield. The cash flow for this bond is (1) 30 coupon payments of $35 every six months and (2) $1,000 to be paid 30 six-month periods from now. To get y in equation (17.2), different interest rates must be tried until the present value of the cash flows is equal to the price of $769.42. When a 5% semiannual interest rate is used, the present value of the cash flows is $769.42. Therefore, y is 5%, and is the semiannual yield to maturity. As noted before, the convention in the market is to double the semiannual yield to obtain an annualized yield. Thus, the yield on a bond-equivalent basis for our hypothetical bond is 10%.

The yield-to-maturity calculation takes into account not only the current coupon income but also any capital gain or loss the investor will realize by holding the bond to maturity. In addition, the yield to maturity considers the timing of the cash flows.

The relationship among the coupon rate, current yield, yield to maturity, and bond price is shown in Exhibit 17.3.

EXHIBIT 17.3   Relationship between Coupon Rate, Current Yield, Yield to Maturity, and Bond Price

Bond Selling at	Relationship
Par	Coupon rate = Current yield = Yield to maturity
Discount	Coupon rate < Current yield < Yield to maturity
Premium	Coupon rate > Current yield > Yield to maturity

Yield to Call

As explained in Chapter 16, the issuer may be entitled to call a bond prior to the stated maturity date. When the bond may be called and at what price is specified in the indenture. The price at which the bond may be called is referred to as the *call price*. For some issues, the call price is the same regardless of when the issue is called. For other callable issues, the call price depends on when the issue is called. That is, there is a *call schedule* that specifies a call price for each call date.

For callable issues, the practice has been to calculate a *yield to call* as well as a yield to maturity. The yield to call assumes that the issuer will call the bond at some assumed call date, and the call price is then the call price specified in the call schedule. Typically, investors calculate a *yield to first call* and a *yield to par call*. The yield to first call assumes that the issue will be called on the first call date. The yield to first par call assumes that the issue will be called the first time on the call schedule when the issuer is entitled to call the bond at par value.

The procedure for calculating the yield to any assumed call date is the same as for any yield calculation: Determine the interest rate that will make the present value of the expected cash flows equal to the price plus accrued interest. In the case of yield to first call, the expected cash flows are the coupon payments to the first call date and the call price. For the yield to first par call, the expected cash flows are the coupon payments to the first date at which the issuer may call the bond at par.

To illustrate the computation, consider an 18-year, 11% coupon bond with a maturity value of $1,000 selling for $1,168.97. Suppose that the first call date is 13 years from now and that the call price is $1,055. The cash flows for this bond if it is called in 13 years are (1) 26 coupon payments of $55 every six months and (2) $1,055 due in 26 six-month periods from now. The yield to first call in this example is the one that will make the present value of the cash flows to the first call date equal to the bond's price of $1,168.97. In this case, that periodic interest rate is 4.5%. Therefore, the yield to first call on a bond-equivalent basis is 9%.

Investors typically compute both the yield to call and the yield to maturity for a callable bond selling at a premium. They then select the lower of the two as the yield measure. The lowest yield based on every possible call date and the yield to maturity is referred to as the *yield to worst*.

Potential Sources of a Bond's Dollar Return

An investor who purchases a bond can expect to receive a dollar return from one or more of these sources:

1. The periodic coupon interest payments made by the issuer.
2. Income from reinvestment of the periodic interest payments (the interest-on-interest component).
3. Any capital gain (or capital loss—negative dollar return) when the bond matures, is called, or is sold.

Any measure of a bond's potential yield should take into consideration each of these three potential sources of return. The current yield considers only the coupon interest payments. No consideration is given to any capital gain (or loss) or to interest-on-interest. The yield to maturity takes into account coupon interest and any capital gain (or loss). It also considers the interest-on-interest component; implicit in the yield-to-maturity computation, however, is the assumption that the coupon payments can be reinvested at the computed yield to maturity. The yield to maturity, therefore, is a *promised yield;* that is, it will be realized only if (1) the bond is held to maturity and (2) the coupon interest payments are reinvested at the yield to maturity. If either (1) or (2) fails to occur, the actual yield realized by an investor can be greater than or less than the yield to maturity when the bond is purchased.

The yield to call also takes into account all three potential sources of return. In this case, the assumption is that the coupon payments can be reinvested at the computed yield to call. Therefore, the yield-to-call measure suffers from the same drawback inherent in the implicit assumption of the reinvestment rate for the coupon interest payments. Also, it assumes that the bond will be held until the assumed call date, at which time the bond will be called.

The investor will realize the yield to maturity at the time of purchase only if the bond is held to maturity and the coupon payments can be reinvested at the yield to maturity. The risk that the investor faces is that future reinvestment rates will be less than the yield to maturity at the time the bond is purchased. This risk is called *reinvestment risk.*

Two characteristics of a bond determine the importance of the interest-on-interest component and, therefore, the degree of reinvestment risk: maturity and coupon. For a given yield to maturity and a given coupon rate, the longer the maturity, the more dependent the bond's total dollar return is on the interest-on-interest component in order to realize the yield to maturity at the time of purchase. In other words, the longer the maturity, the greater the reinvestment risk. The implication is that the yield-to-maturity measure for long-term coupon bonds tells little about the potential yield that an investor may realize if the bond is held to maturity. For long-term bonds, the interest-on-interest component may be as high as 80% of the bond's potential total dollar return.

Turning to the coupon rate, for a given maturity and a given yield to maturity, the higher the coupon rate, the more dependent the bond's total dollar return will be on the reinvestment of the coupon payments in order to produce the yield to maturity anticipated at the time of purchase. This means that when maturity and yield to maturity are held constant, premium bonds are more dependent on the interest-on-interest component than are bonds selling at par. Discount bonds are less dependent on the interest-on-interest component than are bonds selling at par. For zero-coupon bonds, none of the bond's total dollar return is dependent on the interest-on-interest component. So a zero-coupon bond has no reinvestment risk if held to maturity. Thus, the yield earned on a zero-coupon bond held to maturity is equal to the promised yield to maturity.

Portfolio Internal Rate of Return

Another measure used to calculate a portfolio yield is the *portfolio internal rate of return*. It is computed by first determining the cash flows for all the bonds in the portfolio, and then finding the interest rate that will make the present value of the cash flows equal to the market value of the portfolio.

To illustrate how to calculate a portfolio's internal rate of return, we will use the three-bond portfolio in Exhibit 17.4. To simplify the illustration, it is assumed that the coupon payment date is the same for each bond. The cash flow for each bond and the portfolio's cash flows are shown in Exhibit 17.5. The portfolio's internal rate of return is the interest rate that will make the present value of the portfolio's cash flows (the last column in Exhibit 17.5) equal to the portfolio's market value of $57,259,000. The interest rate is 4.77%. Doubling this rate to 9.54% gives the portfolio's internal rate of return on a bond-equivalent basis.

The portfolio internal rate of return, while superior to the weighted average portfolio yield, suffers from the same problems as yield measures in general that we discussed earlier: It assumes that the cash flows can be reinvested at the calculated yield. In the case of a portfolio internal rate of return, it assumes that the cash flows can be reinvested at the calculated

EXHIBIT 17.4   Three-Bond Portfolio

Bond	Coupon Rate (%)	Maturity (years)	Par Value ($)	Market Value ($)	Yield to Maturity (%)
B1	7.0	5	10,000,000	9,209,000	9.0
B2	10.5	7	20,000,000	20,000,000	10.5
B3	6.0	3	30,000,000	28,050,000	8.5
Total			60,000,000	57,259,000	

EXHIBIT 17.5 Cash Flow of Three-Bond Portfolio

Period Cash Flow Received	Bond 1	Bond 2	Bond 3	Portfolio
1	$350,000	$1,050,000	$900,000	$2,300,000
2	350,000	1,050,000	900,000	2,300,000
3	350,000	1,050,000	900,000	2,300,000
4	350,000	1,050,000	900,000	2,300,000
5	350,000	1,050,000	900,000	2,300,000
6	350,000	1,050,000	30,900,000	32,300,000
7	350,000	1,050,000	—	1,400,000
8	350,000	1,050,000	—	1,400,000
9	350,000	1,050,000	—	1,400,000
10	10,350,000	1,050,000	—	11,400,000
11	—	1,050,000	—	1,050,000
12	—	1,050,000	—	1,050,000
13	—	1,050,000	—	1,050,000
14	—	21,050,000	—	21,050,000

internal rate of return. Moreover, it assumes that the portfolio is held till the maturity of the longest-maturity bond in the portfolio. For example, if, in our illustration, one of the bonds had a maturity of 30 years, it is assumed that the portfolio is held for 30 years and that all interim cash flows (coupon interest and maturing principal) are reinvested at a rate equal to 9.54%.

TOTAL RETURN

At the time of purchase, an investor is promised a yield, as measured by the yield to maturity, if both of the following conditions are satisfied: (1) The bond is held to maturity, and (2) all coupon interest payments are reinvested at the yield to maturity. We focused on the second assumption, and we showed that the interest-on-interest component for a bond may constitute a substantial portion of the bond's total dollar return. Therefore, reinvesting the coupon interest payments at a rate of interest less than the yield to maturity will produce a lower yield than the yield to maturity.

Rather than assume that the coupon interest payments are reinvested at the yield to maturity, an investor can make an explicit assumption about the reinvestment rate based on expectations. The *total return* is a measure of yield that incorporates an explicit assumption about the reinvestment rate.

The idea underlying total return is simple. The objective is first to compute the total future dollars that will result from investing in a bond assuming a particular reinvestment rate. The total return is then computed as the interest rate that will make the initial investment in the bond grow to the computed total future dollars.

The procedure for computing the total return for a bond held over some investment horizon can be summarized as follows:

Step 1. Compute the total coupon payments plus the interest-on-interest based on the assumed reinvestment rate. The reinvestment rate in this case is one-half the annual interest rate that the investor assumes can be earned on the reinvestment of coupon interest payments.

Step 2. Determine the projected sale price at the end of the planned investment horizon. The projected sale price will depend on the projected required yield at the end of the planned investment horizon. The projected sale price will be equal to the present value of the remaining cash flows of the bond, discounted at the projected required yield.

Step 3. Sum the values computed in steps 1 and 2. The sum is the total future dollars that will be received from the investment given the assumed reinvestment rate and the projected required yield at the end of the investment horizon.

Step 4. Obtain the semiannual total return using the formula:

$$\left(\frac{\text{Total future dollars}}{\text{Purchase price of bond}} \right)^{1/h} - 1 \qquad (17.3)$$

where h is the number of six-month periods in the investment horizon.

Step 5. The semiannual total return found in step 4 must be annualized. There are two alternatives. The first is simply to double the semiannual total return found in step 4. The resulting interest rate is the total return on a bond-equivalent yield basis. The second is to calculate the annual return by compounding the semiannual total return. This is done as follows:

$$(1 + \text{semiannual total return})^2 - 1 \qquad (17.4)$$

A total return calculated using equation (17.4) is called a total return on an *effective rate basis*.

Determination of how to annualize the semiannual total return depends on the situation at hand. The first approach is just a market convention. If an investor is comparing the total return with the return either on other bonds or on a bond index in which yields are calculated on a bond-equivalent basis, then this approach is appropriate. However, if the portfolio objective is to satisfy liabilities that the institution is obligated to pay, and if those liabilities are based on semiannual compounding, then the second approach is appropriate.

To illustrate computation of the total return, suppose that an investor with a three-year investment horizon is considering purchasing a 20-year, 8% coupon bond for $828.40. The yield to maturity for this bond is 10%. The investor expects to be able to reinvest the coupon interest payments at an annual interest rate of 6%, and, at the end of the planned investment horizon, the then-17-year bond will be selling to offer a yield to maturity of 7%. The total return for this bond is found as follows:

Step 1. Compute the total coupon payments plus the interest-on-interest, assuming an annual reinvestment rate of 6%, or 3% every six months. The coupon payments are $40 every six months for three years, or six periods (the planned investment horizon). The total coupon interest plus interest-on-interest is $258.74.

Step 2. Determining the projected sale price at the end of three years, assuming that the required yield to maturity for 17-year bonds is 7%, is accomplished by calculating the present value of 34 coupon payments of $40 plus the present value of the maturity value of $1,000, discounted at 3.5%. The projected sale price is $1,098.51.

Step 3. Adding the amounts in steps 1 and 2 gives total future dollars of $1,357.25.

Step 4. To obtain the semiannual total return, compute the following:

$$\left(\frac{\$1,357.25}{\$828.40} \right)^{1/6} - 1 = 0.0858, \text{ or } 8.58\%$$

Step 5. Doubling 8.58% gives a total return on a bond-equivalent basis of 17.16%. Using equation (17.4), we get the total return on an effective rate basis:

$$(1.0858)^2 - 1 = 17.90\%$$

MEASURING INTEREST RATE RISK

As we explained earlier, a fundamental property of a bond is that its price will change in the opposite direction from the change in the required yield for the bond. This property follows from the fact that the price of a bond is equal to the present value of its expected cash flows. Although all bonds change in price when the required yield changes, they do not change by the same percentage. For example, when the required yield increases by 100 basis points for two bonds, the price of one might fall by 15%, while that of the other might fall by only 1%. To effectively implement bond portfolio strategies, it is necessary to understand why bonds react differently to yield changes. In addition, it is necessary to quantify how a bond's price might react to yield changes. Ideally, a portfolio manager would like a measure that indicates the relationship between changes in required yields and changes in a bond's price. That is, a manager would want to know how a bond's price is expected to change if yields change by, say, 100 basis points.

Here we discuss the characteristics of a bond's price that affect its price volatility. We present two measures that are used to quantify a bond's price volatility. One of these measures, duration, is a measure of the approximate percentage change in a bond's price if yield changes by 100 basis points. Duration, however, provides only an approximation of how the price will change. Duration can be supplemented with another measure that we will discuss, convexity. Together, duration and convexity do an effective job of estimating how a bond's price will change when yields change.

Price Volatility Properties of Option-Free Bonds

The inverse relationship between bond price and yield for an option-free bond is illustrated in Exhibit 17.6 for six hypothetical bonds. The bond prices are shown assuming a par value of $100. When the price–yield relationship for any option-free bond is graphed, it exhibits the convex shape shown in Exhibit 17.2. The price–yield relationship is for a given point in time.

Exhibit 17.7 shows for the six hypothetical bonds in Exhibit 17.5, the percentage change in each bond's price for various changes in the required yield, assuming that the initial yield for all six bonds is 9%. For example, consider the 9%, 25-year bond. If the bond is selling to yield 9%, its price would be 100 (see Exhibit 17.6). If the required yield declines to 8%, the price of that bond would be 110.741 (see Exhibit 17.6). Thus a decline in yield from 9% to 8% would increase the price by 10.74% [(110.741 – 100)/100]. This is the value shown in Exhibit 17.7.

An examination of Exhibit 17.7 reveals several properties concerning the price volatility of an option-free bond.

EXHIBIT 17.6   Price–Yield Relationship for Six Hypothetical Option-Free Bonds

Required Yield	Price at Required Yield Coupon/Maturity in Years					
	9%/5	9%/25	6%/5	6%/25	0%/5	0%/25
6.00%	112.7953	138.5946	100.0000	100.0000	74.4094	22.8107
7.00	108.3166	123.4556	95.8417	88.2722	70.8919	17.9053
8.00	104.0554	110.7410	91.8891	78.5178	67.5564	14.0713
8.50	102.0027	105.1482	89.9864	74.2587	65.9537	12.4795
8.90	100.3966	100.9961	88.4983	71.1105	64.7017	11.3391
8.99	100.0395	100.0988	88.1676	70.4318	64.4236	11.0975
9.00	100.0000	100.0000	88.1309	70.3570	64.3928	11.0170
9.01	99.9604	99.9013	88.0943	70.2824	64.3620	11.0445
9.10	99.6053	99.0199	87.7654	69.6164	64.0855	10.8093
9.50	98.0459	95.2339	86.3214	66.7773	62.8723	9.8242
10.00	96.1391	90.8720	84.5565	63.4881	61.3913	8.7204
11.00	92.4624	83.0685	81.1559	57.6712	58.5431	6.8767
12.00	88.9599	76.3572	77.9197	52.7144	55.8395	5.4288

EXHIBIT 17.7   Instantaneous Percentage Price Change for Six Hypothetical Bonds

Six Hypothetical Bonds, Priced Initially to Yield 9%

9% coupon,	5 years to maturity,	Price = 100.0000
9% coupon,	25 years to maturity,	Price = 100.0000
6% coupon,	5 years to maturity,	Price = 88.1309
6% coupon,	25 years to maturity,	Price = 70.3570
0% coupon,	5 years to maturity,	Price = 64.3928
0% coupon,	25 years to maturity,	Price = 11.0710

Required Yield Changes to	Change in Basis Points	Percentage Price Change, Coupon/Maturity in Years					
		9%/5	9%/25	6%/5	6%/25	0%/5	0%/25
6.00%	−300	12.80	38.59	13.47	42.13	15.56	106.04
7.00	−200	8.32	23.46	8.75	25.46	10.09	61.73
8.00	−100	4.06	10.74	4.26	11.60	4.91	27.10
8.50	−50	2.00	5.15	2.11	5.55	2.42	12.72
8.90	−10	0.40	1.00	0.42	1.07	0.48	2.42
8.99	−1	0.04	0.10	0.04	0.11	0.05	0.24
9.01	1	−0.04	−0.10	−0.04	−0.11	−0.05	−0.24
9.10	10	−0.39	−0.98	−0.41	−1.05	−0.48	−2.36
9.50	50	−1.95	−4.75	−2.05	−5.09	−2.36	−11.26
10.00	100	−3.86	−9.13	−4.06	−9.76	−4.66	−21.23
11.00	200	−7.54	−16.93	−7.91	−18.03	−9.08	−37.89
12.00	300	−11.04	−23.64	−11.59	−25.08	−13.28	−50.96

Property 1. For very small changes in the required yield, the percentage price change for a given bond is roughly the same, whether the required yield increases or decreases.

Property 2. For large changes in the required yield, the percentage price change is not the same for an increase in the required yield as it is for a decrease in the required yield.

Property 3. For a large change in basis points, the percentage price increase is greater than the percentage price decrease. The implication of this property is that if an investor owns a bond, the price appreciation that will be realized if the required yield decreases is greater than the capital loss that will be realized if the required yield rises by the same number of basis points.

An explanation for these three properties of bond price volatility lies in the convex shape of the price–yield relationship. We will investigate this in more detail later.

Factors That Affect a Bond's Price Volatility

Two features of an option-free bond determine its price volatility: coupon and term to maturity. In addition, the yield level at which a bond trades affects its price volatility.

Consider the three 25-year bonds in Exhibit 17.7. For a given change in yield, the zero-coupon bond has the largest price volatility, and the largest coupon bond (the 9% coupon bond) has the smallest price volatility. This is also true for the three five-year bonds. In general, for a given term to maturity and initial yield, the lower the coupon rate, the greater the price volatility of a bond.

Consider next the two 9% coupon bonds in Exhibit 17.7. For a given change in yield, the 25-year bond has the largest price volatility, and the shortest-maturity bond (the five-year bond) has the smallest price volatility. This is also true for the two 6% coupon bonds and the two zero-coupon bonds in Exhibit 17.7. In general, for a given coupon rate and initial yield, the longer the maturity, the greater the price volatility of a bond.

The price volatility of a bond is also affected by the level of interest rates in the economy. Specifically, the higher the level of yields, the lower the price volatility. To illustrate this, let's compare the 9%, 25-year bond trading at two yield levels: 7% and 13%. If the yield increases from 7% to 8%, the bond's price declines by 10.3%; but if the yield increases from 13% to 14%, the bond's price declines by 6.75%.

Measuring Interest Rate Risk Using the Price Value of a Basis Point

To control the interest rate risk of a bond portfolio or a trading position, it is essential to have a measure that quantifies a bond's exposure to changes in interest rates. A portfolio manager can measure the exposure to interest rate changes of a portfolio or trading position by revaluing the bonds held based on various interest rate scenarios. However, the typical way in which interest rate risk is measured is by approximating the impact of a change in interest rates on a bond or a bond portfolio. The two popular measures used are (1) the price value of a basis point and (2) duration and convexity. However, both measures suffer from the problem that they measure only an exposure to a parallel shift in interest rates. That is, it is assumed that the interest rate for all the bonds held will change by the same number of basis of points. There are measures that are used to assess the exposure to changes in the yield curve that we discuss later. Now we focus on the the price value of a basis point.

The *price value of a basis point* (PVBP), also referred to as the *dollar value of an 01* (DV01), measures the change in the price of the bond if the required yield changes by 1 basis point. Note that this measure of price volatility indicates dollar price volatility as opposed to percentage price volatility (price change as a percentage of the initial price). Typically, the price value of a basis point is expressed as the absolute value of the change in price. Owing to property 1 of the price–yield relationship, price volatility is the same for an increase or a decrease of 1 basis point in required yield.

We can illustrate how to calculate the price value of a basis point by using the six bonds in Exhibit 17.6. For each bond, the initial price, the price after increasing the yield by 1 basis point (from 9% to 9.01%), and the price value of a basis point (the difference between the two prices) are shown in Exhibit 17.8.

Measuring Interest Rate Risk Using Duration and Convexity

The most commonly used approach to measure interest rate risk exposure of a portfolio or a trading position is by approximating the impact of a change in interest rates on a bond or a bond portfolio using duration. Duration is a first approximation. To improve upon this approximation, a second measure is estimated and is referred to as convexity. In this section, we explain how duration is estimated for bonds and portfolios. There are different types of duration measures for individual bonds and portfolios. We also explain the limitations of duration. We then discuss how the duration measure can be improved by using a measure called *convexity*.

EXHIBIT 17.8   Price Value of a Basis Point

Bond	Initial Price (9% yield)	Price at 9.01%	Price Value of a Basis Point[a]
5 years, 9% coupon	100.0000	99.9604	0.0396
25 years, 9% coupon	100.0000	99.9013	0.0987
5 years, 6% coupon	88.1309	88.0945	0.0364
25 years, 6% coupon	70.3570	70.2824	0.0746
5 years, zero coupon	64.3928	64.3620	0.0308
25 years, zero coupon	11.0710	11.0445	0.0265

[a]Absolute value per $100 of par value.

Duration

The most obvious way to measure the price sensitivity as a percentage of the security's current price to changes in interest rates is to change rates (i.e., "shock" rates) by a small number of basis points and calculate how a security's value will change as a percentage of the current price. The name popularly used to refer to the approximate percentage price change is duration. The following formula can be used to estimate the duration of a security:

$$\text{Duration} = \frac{V_- - V_+}{2V_0(\Delta y)} \tag{17.5}$$

where

Δy = the change (or shock) in interest rates (in decimal form)
V_0 = the current price of the bond
V_- = the estimated price of the bond if interest rates are decreased by the change in interest rates
V_+ = the estimated price of the bond if interest rates are increased by the change in interest rates

(We use "change in interest rates" and "change in yields" interchangeably.)

It is important to understand that the two values in the numerator of equation (17.5) are the estimated values if interest rates change obtained from a valuation model. Consequently, the duration measure is only as good as the valuation model employed to obtain the estimated values in equation (17.5). The more difficult it is to estimate the value a bond, the less confidence a portfolio manager may have in the estimated duration. We will see that the duration of a portfolio is nothing more than a market-weighted average of the duration of the bonds comprising the portfolio. Hence, a portfolio's duration is sensitive to the estimated duration of the individual bonds.

To illustrate the duration calculation, consider the following option-free bond: a 6% coupon five-year bond trading at par value to yield 6%. The current price is $100. Suppose the yield is changed by 50 basis points. Thus, $\Delta y = 0.005$ and $V_0 = \$100$. This is simple bond to value if interest rates or yield is changed. If the yield is decreased to 5.5%, the price of this bond would be $102.1600. If the yield is increased to 6.5%, the value of this bond would be $97.8944. That is, $V_- = \$102.1600$ and $V_+ = \$97.8944$. Substituting into equation (17.5), we obtain

$$\text{Duration} = \frac{\$102.1600 - \$97.8944}{2(\$100)(0.005)} = 4.27$$

There are various ways in that practitioners have interpreted what the duration of a bond is. We believe the most useful way to think about a bond's duration is as the approximate percentage change in the bond's price for a 100 basis point change in interest rates. Thus a bond with a duration of say 5 will change by approximately 5% for a 100 basis point change in interest rates (i.e., if the yield required for this bond changes by approximately 100 basis points). For a 50 basis point change in interest rates, the bond's price will change by approximately 2.5%; for a 25 basis point change in interest rates, 1.25%, and so on.

Dollar Duration   In estimating the sensitivity of the price of bond to changes in interest rates, we looked at the percentage price change. However, for two bonds with the same duration but trading at different prices, the dollar price change will not be the same. To see this, suppose that we have two bonds, B_1 and B_2, that both have a duration of 5. Suppose further that the current price of B_1 and B_2 are $100 and $90, respectively. A 100 basis point change for both bonds will change the price by approximately 5%. This means a price change of $5 (5% times $100) for B_1 and a price change of $4.5 (5% times $90) for B_2.

The dollar price change of a bond can be measured by multiplying duration by the full dollar price and the number of basis points (in decimal form) and is called the *dollar duration*. That is,

Dollar duration = Duration × Dollar price × Change in rates in decimal

The dollar duration for a 100 basis point change in rates is

$$\text{Dollar duration} = \text{Duration} \times \text{Dollar price} \times 0.01 \qquad (17.6)$$

So, for bonds B_1 and B_2, the dollar duration for a 100 basis point change in rates is

For bond B_1: Dollar duration = $5 \times \$100 \times 0.01 = \$5.0$
For bond B_2: Dollar duration = $5 \times \$90 \times 0.01 = \$4.5$

Knowing the dollar duration allows a portfolio manager to neutralize the risk of bond position. For example, consider a position in bond B_2. If a trader wants to eliminate the interest rate risk exposure of this bond (i.e., hedge the exposure), the trader will look for a position in another financial instrument(s) (for example, an interest rate derivative described in Chapter 22) whose value will change in the opposite direction to bond B_2's price by an amount equal to $4.5. So if the trader has a long position in B_2, the position will decline in value by $4.5 for a 100 basis point increase in interest rates. To hedge this risk exposure, the trader can take a position in another financial instrument whose value increases by $4.5 if interest rates increase by 100 basis points.

Modified Duration and Effective Duration A popular form of duration that is used by practitioners is modified duration. *Modified duration* is the approximate percentage change in a bond's price for a 100 basis point change in interest rates, assuming that the bond's cash flows do not change when interest rates change.[2] What this means is that in calculating the values used in the numerator of the duration formula, the cash flows used to calculate the current price are assumed. Therefore, the change in the bond's value when interest rates change by a small number of basis points is due solely to discounting at the new yield level.

The assumption that the cash flows will not change when interest rates change makes sense for option-free bonds because the payments by the issuer are not altered when interest rates change. This is not the case for callable bond, putable bonds, bonds with accelerated sinking fund options, mortgage-backed securities, and certain types of asset-backed securities (i.e., mortgage related securities). For these securities, a change in interest rates may alter the expected cash flows.

The price–yield relationship for callable bonds and prepayable securites is shown in Exhibit 17.9. As market rates (yields) decline, investors

---

[2]Modified duration is related to another measure commonly cited in the bond market: *Macaulay duration*. The formula for this measure is rarely used in practice so it will not be produced here. Practically speaking, there is very little difference in the computed values for modified duration and Macaulay duration.

EXHIBIT 17.9   Price–Yield Relationship for an Option-Free Bond and a Callable Bond

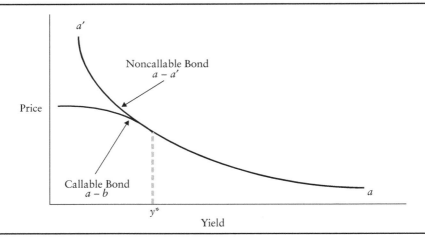

become concerned that these rates will decline further so that the issuer or homeowner will benefit from calling the bond. The precise yield level where investors begin to view the issue likely to be called may not be known, but we do know that there is some level. In Exhibit 17.9, at yield levels below y^*, the price–yield relationship for the callable bond departs from the price–yield relationship for the option-free bond. If, for example, the market yield is such that an option-free bond would be selling for $109, but since it is callable would be called at $104, investors would not pay $109. If they did, and the bond is called, investors would receive $104 (the call price) for a bond they purchased for $109. Notice that for a range of yields below y^*, there is price compression (i.e., there is limited price appreciation as yields decline). The portion of the callable bond price–yield relationship below y^* is said to be *negatively convex*.

Negative convexity means that the price appreciation will be less than the price depreciation for a large change in yield of a given number of basis points. In contrast, a bond that is option-free exhibits positive convexity. This means that the price appreciation will be greater than the price depreciation for a large change in yield.

For bonds with embedded options, there are valuation models that take into account how changes in interest rates will affect cash flows that we will describe in the next section. When the values used in the numerator of equation (17.5) are obtained from a valuation model that takes into account both the discounting at different interest rates and how the cash flows can change, the resulting duration is referred to as *effective duration* or *option-adjusted duration*.

Portfolio Duration   *Portfolio duration* can be obtained by calculating the weighted average of the duration of the bonds in the portfolio. The weight is the proportion of the portfolio that a security comprises. Mathematically, portfolio duration can be calculated as follows:

$$\text{Portfolio duration} = w_1 D_1 + w_2 D_2 + \ldots + w_N D_N \qquad (17.7)$$

where

w_i = market value of bond i/market value of the portfolio
D_i = duration of bond i
N = number of bonds in the portfolio

A portfolio duration of 5, for example, means that for a 100 basis point change in the yield for all 10 bonds, the market value of the portfolio will change by approximately 5%. But keep in mind that the yield on all bonds comprising the portfolio must change by 100 basis points for the duration measure to be most useful. The assumption that all interest rates must change by the same number of basis points is a critical assumption, and its importance cannot be overemphasized. Market practitioners refer to this as the *parallel yield curve shift assumption*.

Contribution to Portfolio Duration   Portfolio managers commonly assess their exposure to an issue in terms of the percentage of that issue in the portfolio. A better measure of exposure of an individual issue to changes in interest rates is in terms of its *contribution to portfolio duration*. This is found by multiplying the percentage that the individual issue is of the portfolio by the duration of the individual issue. That is,

$$\text{Contribution to portfolio duration}$$
$$= \frac{\text{Market value of issue}}{\text{Market value of portfolio}} \times \text{Duration of issue} \qquad (17.8)$$

Notice the contribution to portfolio duration is simply the individual components in portfolio duration formula given by equation (17.7).

While we shown how to compute the contribution to portfolio duration for each bond in a portfolio, the same formula can be used to determine the contribution to portfolio duration for each bond sector represented in a portfolio.

Convexity

The duration measure indicates that regardless of whether interest rates increase or decrease, the approximate percentage price change is the same. However, this does not agree with Property 3 of a bond's price volatility. Specifically, while for small changes in yield the percentage price change will be the same for an increase or decrease in yield, for large changes in yield this is not true. This suggests that duration is only a good approximation of the percentage price change for a small change in yield.

The reason for this is that duration is in fact a first approximation for a small change in yield. The approximation can be improved by using a second approximation. This approximation is referred to as "convexity." The use of this term in the industry is unfortunate since the term convexity is also used to describe the shape or curvature of the price–yield relationship. The convexity measure of a security can be used to approximate the change in price that is not explained by duration.

Convexity Measure   The convexity measure of a bond can be approximated using the following formula:

$$\text{Convexity measure} = \frac{V_+ + V_- - 2V_0}{2V_0 (\Delta y)^2} \tag{17.9}$$

where the notation is the same as used earlier for duration as given by equation (17.5).

For our hypothetical 6%, 25-year bond selling to yield 9%, we know from Exhibit 17.6 that for a 10 basis point change in yield ($\Delta y = 0.001$):

$$V_0 = 70.3570, \; V_- = 71.1105, \text{ and } V_+ = 69.6164$$

Substituting these values into the convexity measure given by equation (17.9):

$$\text{Convexity measure} = \frac{69.6164 + 71.1105 - 2(70.3570)}{2(70.3570)(0.001)^2} = 91.67$$

How to use this convexity measure is discussed shortly. Before doing so, there are three points that should be noted. First, there is no simple interpretation of the convexity measure as there is for duration. Second, it is more common for market participants to refer to the value computed in equation (17.9) as the "convexity of a bond" rather than the "convexity measure of a bond." Finally, the convexity measure reported by dealers and vendors will differ for an option-free bond. The reason is that the value obtained from equation (17.9) will be scaled for the reason explained later.

The procedure for calculating the convexity measure for a portfolio is the same as for calculating a portfolio's duration. That is, the convexity measure for each bond in the portfolio is computed. Then the weighted average of the convexity measure for the bonds in the portfolio is computed to get the portfolio's convexity measure.

Convexity Adjustment to Percentage Price Change   Given the convexity measure, the approximate percentage price change adjustment due to the bond's convexity (i.e., the percentage price change not explained by duration) is

$$\text{Convexity adjustment to percentage price change} \atop = \text{Convexity measure} \times (\Delta y)^2 \times 100 \qquad (17.10)$$

For example, for the 6%, 25-year bond selling to yield 9%, the convexity adjustment to the percentage price change based on duration if the yield increases from 9% to 11% is

$$91.67 \times (0.02)^2 \times 100 = 3.67$$

If the yield decreases from 9% to 7%, the convexity adjustment to the approximate percentage price change based on duration would also be 3.67%.

The approximate percentage price change based on duration and the convexity adjustment is found by adding the two estimates. So, for example, if yields change from 9% to 11%, the estimated percentage price change would be as follows:

Estimated change approximated by duration	=	−21.20%
Convexity adjustment	=	+3.66%
Total estimated percentage price change	=	−17.54%

The actual percentage price change from Exhibit 17.7 is −18.03%. Hence, the approximation has improved.

For a decrease of 200 basis points, from 9% to 7%, the approximate percentage price change would be as follows:

Estimated change approximated by duration	=	+21.20%
Convexity adjustment	=	+3.66%
Total estimated percentage price change	=	+24.86%

The actual percentage price change from Exhibit 17.7 is +25.46%. Once again, we see that duration combined with the convexity adjustment does a good job of estimating the sensitivity of a bond's price change to large changes in yield.

Positive vs. Negative Convexity   Notice that when the convexity measure is positive, we have the situation described earlier that the gain is greater than the loss for a given large change in rates. When a bond (or a bond portfolio) exhibits this behavior, it is said to have *positive convexity*. We can see this in the example above. However, if the convexity measure is negative, we have the situation where the loss will be greater than the gain. For example, suppose that a callable bond has an effective duration of 4 and a convexity measure of –30. This means that the approximate percentage price change for a 200 basis point change is 8%. The convexity adjustment for a 200 basis point change in rates is then

$$-30 \times (0.02)^2 \times 100 = -1.2$$

Therefore, the convexity adjustment is –1.2%, and the approximate percentage price change after adjusting for convexity is the following:

Estimated change approximated by duration = –8.0%
Convexity adjustment   = –1.2%
Total estimated percentage price change   = –9.2%

For a decrease of 200 basis points, the approximate percentage price change would be as follows:

Estimated change approximated by duration = +8.0%
Convexity adjustment   = –1.2%
Total estimated percentage price change   = +6.8%

Notice that the loss is greater than the gain—a property called *negative convexity.*

What does the sign of the convexity mean for a bond portfolio? It means that for a portfolio that has positive convexity, for a large change in interest rates, the absolute value of the change in the portfolio's value will be greater when interest rates decline than when they increase. The opposite is true for a portfolio that has negative convexity.

Scaling the Convexity Measure   The convexity measure as given by equation (17.9) means nothing in isolation. It is the substitution of the computed convexity measure into equation (17.10) that provides the estimated adjustment for convexity. Therefore, it is possible to scale the convexity measure in any way and obtain the same convexity adjustment.

For example, in some books the convexity measure is defined as follows:

$$\text{Convexity measure} = \frac{V_+ + V_- - 2V_0}{V_0 (\Delta y)^2} \qquad (17.11)$$

Equation (17.11) differs from equation (17.9) since it does not include 2 in the denominator. Thus the convexity measure computed using equation (17.11) will be double the convexity measure using equation (17.9). So, for our earlier illustration, since the convexity measure using equation (17.9) is 91.67, the convexity measure using equation (17.11) would be 183.34.

Which is correct, 91.67 or 183.24? Both are. The reason is that the corresponding equation for computing the convexity adjustment would not be given by equation (17.10) if the convexity measure is obtained from equation (17.11). Instead, the corresponding convexity adjustment formula would be equation (17.10) divided by 2.

Some dealers and vendors scale in a different way. Consequently, the convexity measure for our hypothetical bond could be reported as 9.17 or 18.3. It is the modification of equation (17.10) that assures that regardless of how the convexity measure is scaled, it will produce the same approximate percentage change due to convexity.

Standard Convexity and Effective Convexity

The prices used in equation (17.9) to calculate the convexity measure can be obtained by either assuming that when the yield changes the expected cash flows do not change or they do change. In the former case, the resulting convexity is referred to as *standard convexity*. (Actually, in the industry, convexity is not qualified by the adjective "standard.") *Effective convexity*, in contrast, assumes that the cash flows do change when yields change. This is the same distinction made for duration.

As with duration, for bonds with embedded options, there can be quite a difference between the calculated standard convexity and effective convexity. In fact, for all option-free bonds, either convexity measure will have a positive value. For bonds with embedded options, the calculated effective convexity can be negative when the calculated modified convexity is positive.

Measuring Exposure to Yield Curve Changes Key Rate Duration

As explained earlier, duration assumes that when interest rates change, all yields on the yield curve change by the same amount. This is a problem when using duration for a portfolio that will typically have bonds with different maturities. Consequently, it is necessary to be able to measure the exposure of a bond or bond portfolio to shifts in the yield curve. There have been several approaches to measuring yield curve risk. One way is to simply look at the cash flows of the portfolio. The most commonly used measure is *key rate duration*.[3]

The basic principle of key rate duration is to change the yield for a particular maturity of the yield curve and determine the sensitivity of either an individual bond or a portfolio to that change holding all other yields constant. The sensitivity of the change in the bond's value or portfolio's value to a particular change in yield is called *rate duration*. There is a rate duration for every point on the yield curve. Consequently, there is not one rate duration. Rather, there is a set of durations representing each maturity on the yield curve. The total change in value of a bond or a portfolio if all rates change by the same number of basis points is simply the duration of a bond or portfolio.

Practitioners tend to focus on 11 key maturities of the Treasury yield curve. These rate durations are called *key rate durations*. The specific maturities for which a key rate duration is measured are 3 months, 1 year, 2 years, 3 years, 5 years, 7 years, 10 years, 15 years, 20 years, 25 years, and 30 years. Changes in rates between any two key rates are calculated using a linear approximation.

A key rate duration for a particular portfolio maturity should be interpreted as follows: Holding the yield for all other maturities constant, the key rate duration is the approximate percentage change in the value of a portfolio (or bond) for a 100 basis point change in the yield for the maturity whose rate has been changed. Thus, a key rate duration is quantified by changing the yield of the maturity of interest and determining how the value or price changes. In fact, equation (17.5) is used. The prices denoted by V_- and V_+ in the equation are the prices in the case of a bond and the portfolio values in the case of a bond portfolio found by holding all other interest rates constant and changing the yield for the maturity whose key rate duration is sought.

KEY POINTS

- The price of a bond is the present value of the bond's cash flows, the discount rate being equal to the yield offered on comparable bonds. For an option-free bond, the cash flows are the coupon payments and the maturity value.

---

[3]Thomas S.Y. Ho, "Key Rate Durations: Measures of Interest Rate Risks," *Journal of Fixed Income* 2, no. 1 (1992): 29–44.

- The higher (lower) the required yield, the lower (higher) is the price of a bond. Therefore, a bond's price changes in the opposite direction from the change in the required yield.
- When the coupon rate is equal to the required yield, the bond will sell at its par value. When the coupon rate is less (greater) than the required yield, the bond will sell for less (more) than its par value and is said to be selling at a discount (premium).
- The conventional yield measures commonly used by bond market participants are the current yield, yield to maturity, and yield to call.
- The three potential sources of dollar return from investing in a bond—coupon interest, interest-on-interest, and capital gain (or loss); none of the three conventional yield measures deals satisfactorily with all these sources.
- Although the yield to maturity considers all three sources, it is deficient in assuming that all coupon interest can be reinvested at the yield to maturity.
- Reinvestment risk is the risk that the coupon payments will be reinvested at a rate less than the yield to maturity.
- The yield to call assumes that the coupon interest can be reinvested at the yield to call.
- The total return measure is more meaningful than either yield to maturity or yield to call for assessing the relative attractiveness of a bond given the portfolio manager's expectations and planned investment horizon.
- The price–yield relationship for all option-free bonds is convex.
- There are three properties of the price volatility of an option-free bond: (1) For small changes in yield, the percentage price change is symmetric; (2) for large changes in yield, the percentage price change is asymmetric; and (3) for large changes in yield, the price appreciation is greater than the price depreciation for a given change in yield.
- The price volatility of an option-free bond is affected by two characteristics of a bond—maturity and coupon—and the yield level at which a bond trades. For a given maturity and yield, the lower the coupon rate, the greater the price volatility. For a given coupon rate and yield, the lower the coupon rate, the greater the price volatility. For a given coupon rate and maturity, the price volatility is greater the lower the yield.
- There are two measures of bond price volatility: price value of a basis point and duration/convexity.
- The price value of a basis point is the dollar price change of a bond for a one basis point change in interest rates.
- Duration is the approximate percentage change in price for a 100 basis point change in yield. The dollar duration is the approximate dollar price change.

- Modified duration assumes that when interest rates change, the cash flows of a bond will not change. Effective duration assumes that when interest rates change, the cash flows will change and is therefore a better measure of the responsiveness of the price of a bond with an embedded option compared to modified duration.
- While duration is the first approximation as to how the price of a bond or value of a portfolio will change when rates change, a second approximation can be used to improve the estimate of the price change obtained from duration. The second approximation is sometimes called a bond's "convexity." As with duration, a modified convexity and effective convexity measure can be computed.
- Portfolio duration is the weighted average duration of the bonds constituting the portfolio.
- When a portfolio manager attempts to gauge the sensitivity of a bond portfolio to changes in interest rates by computing a portfolio duration, it is assumed that the interest rate for all maturities changes by the same number of basis points.
- The most commonly used approach for estimating the sensitivity of a bond portfolio to unequal changes in interest rates is key rate duration. A rate duration is the approximate change in the value of a portfolio (or bond) to a change in the interest rate of a particular maturity assuming that the interest rate for all other maturities is held constant.
- Practitioners compute a key rate duration, which is simply the rate duration for key maturities.

QUESTIONS

1. Suppose that you are reviewing a price sheet for bonds and see the following prices (per $100 par value) reported. You observe what seem to be several errors. Which bonds seem to be reported incorrectly and explain why?

Bond	Price	Coupon Rate (%)	Required Yield (%)
1	90	6	9
2	96	9	8
3	110	8	6
4	105	0	5
5	107	7	9
6	100	6	6

2. Why may the yield to call for a bond have more than one value?

3. A portfolio manager is considering buying two bonds. Bond A matures in four years and has a coupon rate of 6% payable semiannually. Bond B, of the same credit quality, matures in 10 years and has a coupon rate of 8% payable semiannually. Both bonds are priced at par.
   a. Suppose that the portfolio manager plans to hold the bond that is purchased for four years. Which would be the preferred bond for the portfolio manager to purchase?
   b. Suppose that the portfolio manager plans to hold the bond that is purchased for six years instead of four years. In this case, which would be the preferred bond for the portfolio manager to purchase?

4. Consider a 5% 14-year bond with a maturity value of $100 that is option free and is selling to yield 6%.
   a. What is the bond's price?
   b. What is the price value of a basis point for this bond?
   c. What is the bond's duration using the formula given by equation (17.5) and changing interest rates by 10 basis points?
   d. Is the duration calculated in (c) a modified duration or an effective duration? Explain why?
   e. If market yields change by 100 basis points, what is the approximate percentage change in the bond's price?
   f. If market yields change by 25 basis points, what is the approximate percentage change in the bond's price?
   g. If market yields increase by 50 basis points, what is the approximate dollar price per $100 of par value of this bond?

5. What are the limitations of using duration as a measure of a bond's price sensitivity to interest-rate changes?

6. Consider the following portfolio:

Bond	Market Value	Duration
W	$13 million	2
X	$27 million	7
Y	$60 million	8
Z	$40 million	14

   a. What is the portfolio's duration?
   b. If interest rates for all maturities change by 50 basis points, what is the approximate percentage change in the value of the portfolio?
   c. What is the contribution to portfolio duration for each bond?

7. Consider the following two 10-year corporate bonds that are currently callable:

Bond	Coupon Rate
A	10%
B	5%

Suppose that the current market yield for 10-year corporate bonds is 7%.

a. Which of these two bonds would be expected to exhibit negative convexity?

b. For which of these two bonds would it be more appropriate to use modified duration rather than effective duration.

8. Explain what a 10-year key rate duration of 0.35 means for a portfolio?

CHAPTER 18

Bond Analytics

Spot Rates, Forward Rates, Yield Spreads, and Valuation

Frank J. Fabozzi, Ph.D., CFA, CPA
Professor in the Practice of Finance
Yale School of Management

Steven V. Mann, Ph.D.
Professor of Finance
The Moore School of Business
University of South Carolina

I n Chapter 17, the valuation of option-free bonds was explained. The valuation of more complex bond structures is the subject of this chapter. To understand valuation models, it is necessary to understand several important concepts: spot rates, forward rates, and yield spread measures. So before we explain models for valuing complex bond structures, we will describe these concepts.

ARBITRAGE-FREE BOND VALUATION

The traditional approach to valuation is to discount every cash flow of a bond using the same interest rate. This approach to valuation was described in Chapter 17. The fundamental flaw of this approach is that it views each security as the same package of cash flows. For example, consider a five-year U.S. Treasury note with a 6% coupon rate. The cash flows per $100 of par value would be nine payments of $3 every six months and then payments of $103 for 10 six-month periods. The traditional practice would discount every cash flow using the same discount rate regardless of when the cash flows are delivered in time and the shape of the yield curve. Finance theory tells us that any security should be thought of as a package or portfolio of zero-coupon bonds.

The proper way to view the five-year 6% coupon Treasury note is as a package of zero-coupon instruments whose maturity value is the amount of the cash flow and whose maturity date coincides with the date the cash flow is to be received. Thus, the five-year 6% coupon Treasury issue should be viewed as a package of 10 zero-coupon instruments that mature every six months for the next five years. This approach to valuation does not allow a market participant to realize an arbitrage profit by breaking apart or "stripping" a bond and selling the individual cash flows (i.e., stripped securities) at a higher aggregate value than it would cost to purchase the security in the market. Simply put, arbitrage profits are possible when the sum of the parts is worth more than the whole or vice versa. Because this approach to valuation precludes arbitrage profits, we refer to it as the *arbitrage-free valuation approach*.

By viewing any bond as a package of zero-coupon bonds, a consistent valuation framework can be developed. Viewing a security as a package of zero-coupon bonds means that two bonds with the same maturity and different coupon rates are viewed as different packages of zero-coupon bonds and valued accordingly. Moreover, two cash flows that have identical risk delivered at the same time will be valued using the same discount rate even though they are attached to two different bonds.

To implement the arbitrage-free approach it is necessary to determine the theoretical rate that the U.S. Treasury would have to pay on a zero-coupon Treasury security for each maturity. We say "theoretical" because other than U.S. Treasury bills, the Treasury does not issue zero-coupon bonds. Zero-coupon Treasuries are, however, created by dealer firms. The name given to the zero-coupon Treasury rate is the *Treasury spot rate*. Our next task is to explain how the Treasury spot rate can be calculated.

Theoretical Spot Rates

The theoretical spot rates for Treasury securities represent the appropriate set of interest or discount rates that should be used to value default-free cash flows. A default-free theoretical spot rate can be constructed from the observed Treasury yield curve. The procedure for calculating spot rates can be as simple as extrapolating spot rates from the Treasury yield curve using a bootstrapping method or estimation using econometric modeling. We will not explain either methodology here but instead focus on arbitrage-free valuation given spot rates.[1] Exhibit 18.1 shows the Treasury yields for

---

[1]For an explanation of the methodologies for estimating spot rates, see Frank J. Fabozzi, *Bond Markets, Analysis and Strategies*, 7th ed. (Upper Saddle River, N.J.: Prentice Hall, 2007).

EXHIBIT 18.1   Hypothetical Treasury Par Yield Curve and Corresponding Spot Rate Curve Derived Using a Bootstrapping Methodology

Period	Years	Annual Yield to Maturity (BEY) (%)[a]	Price	Spot Rate (BEY) (%)[a]
1	0.5	3.00	—	3.0000
2	1.0	3.30	—	3.3000
3	1.5	3.50	100.00	3.5053
4	2.0	3.90	100.00	3.9164
5	2.5	4.40	100.00	4.4376
6	3.0	4.70	100.00	4.7520
7	3.5	4.90	100.00	4.9622
8	4.0	5.00	100.00	5.0650
9	4.5	5.10	100.00	5.1701
10	5.0	5.20	100.00	5.2772
11	5.5	5.30	100.00	5.3864
12	6.0	5.40	100.00	5.4976
13	6.5	5.50	100.00	5.6108
14	7.0	5.55	100.00	5.6643
15	7.5	5.60	100.00	5.7193
16	8.0	5.65	100.00	5.7755
17	8.5	5.70	100.00	5.8331
18	9.0	5.80	100.00	5.9584
19	9.5	5.90	100.00	6.0863
20	10.0	6.00	100.00	6.2169

[a]The yield to maturity and the spot rate are annual rates. They are reported as bond-equivalent yields. To obtain the semiannual yield or rate, one half the annual yield or annual rate is used.

different maturities (i.e., if graphed this would be the Treasury yield curve) and the spot rates derived using a bootstrapping methodology.

Valuation Using Treasury Spot Rates

To illustrate how Treasury spot rates are used to compute the arbitrage-free value of a Treasury security, we will use the hypothetical Treasury spot rates shown in the fourth column of Exhibit 18.2 to value an 8%, 10-year Treasury security. The present value of each period's cash flow is shown in the

EXHIBIT 18.2 Determination of the Arbitrage-Free Value of an 8% 10-Year Treasury and Arbitrage Opportunity

Period	Years	Cash Flow ($)	Arbitrage-Free Value		Arbitrage Opportunity		
			Spot Rate (%)	Present Value ($)	Sell for	Buy for	Arbitrage Profit
1	0.5	4	6.05	3.8826	3.8836	3.8632	0.0193
2	1.0	4	6.15	3.7649	3.7649	3.7312	0.0337
3	1.5	4	6.21	3.6494	3.6494	3.6036	0.0458
4	2.0	4	6.26	3.5361	3.5361	3.4804	0.0557
5	2.5	4	6.29	3.4263	3.4263	3.3614	0.6486
6	3.0	4	6.37	3.3141	3.3141	3.2465	0.0676
7	3.5	4	6.38	3.2107	3.3107	3.1355	0.0752
8	4.0	4	6.40	3.1090	3.1090	3.0283	0.0807
9	4.5	4	6.41	3.0113	3.0113	2.9247	0.0866
10	5.0	4	6.48	2.9079	2.9079	2.8247	0.0832
11	5.5	4	6.49	2.8151	2.8151	2.7282	0.0867
12	6.0	4	6.53	2.7203	2.7203	2.6349	0.0854
13	6.5	4	6.63	2.6178	2.6178	2.5448	0.0730
14	7.0	4	6.78	2.5082	2.5082	2.4578	0.0504
15	7.5	4	6.79	2.4242	2.4242	2.3738	0.0504
16	8.0	4	6.81	2.3410	2.3410	2.2926	0.0484
17	8.5	4	6.84	2.2583	2.2583	2.2142	0.0441
18	9.0	4	6.93	2.1666	2.1666	2.1385	0.0281
19	9.5	4	7.05	2.0711	2.0711	2.0654	0.0057
20	10.0	104	7.20	51.2670	51.2670	51.8645	−0.5975
			Total	107.0018	107.0018	106.5141	0.4877

fifth column. The sum of the present values is the arbitrage-free value for the Treasury security. For the 8%, 10-year Treasury it is $107.0018.

Thus far, we have simply asserted that the value of a Treasury security should be based on discounting each cash flow using the corresponding Treasury spot rate. But what if market participants value a security using just the yield for the on-the-run Treasury with a maturity equal to the maturity of the Treasury security being valued? Let's see why the value of a Treasury security should trade close to its arbitrage-free value.

Stripping and Arbitrage-Free Valuation

The key to the arbitrage-free valuation approach is the existence of the Treasury strips market. A dealer has the ability to take apart the cash flows of a Treasury coupon security (i.e., strip the security) and create zero-coupon securities. These zero-coupon securities, which we called *Treasury strips*, can be sold to investors. At what interest rate or yield can these Treasury strips be sold to investors? They can be sold at the Treasury spot rates. If the market price of a Treasury security is less than its value using the arbitrage-free valuation approach, then a dealer can buy the Treasury security, strip it, and sell off the individual Treasury strips so as to generate greater proceeds than the cost of purchasing the Treasury security. The resulting profit is an *arbitrage profit*. Since, as we will see, the value determined by using the Treasury spot rates does not allow for the generation of an arbitrage profit, this is referred to as an "arbitrage-free" approach.

To illustrate this, suppose that the yield for the on-the-run 10-year Treasury issue is 7.08%. Suppose that the 8% coupon 10-year Treasury issue is valued using the traditional approach based on 7.08%. The value based on discounting all the cash flows at 7.08% is $106.5141.

Consider what would happen if the market priced the security at $106.5141. The value based on the Treasury spot rates (Exhibit 18.2) is $107.0018. What can the dealer do? The dealer can buy the 8% 10-year issue for $106.5141, strip it, and sell the Treasury strips at the spot rates shown in Exhibit 18.3. By doing so, the proceeds that will be received by the dealer are $107.0018. This results in an arbitrage profit (ignoring transaction costs) of $0.4877 (= $107.0018 − $106.5141). Dealers recognizing this arbitrage opportunity will bid up the price of the 8% 10-year Treasury issue in order to acquire it and strip it. At what point will the arbitrage profit disappear? When the security is priced at $107.0018, the value that we said is the arbitrage-free value.

To understand in more detail where this arbitrage profit is coming from, look at the last three columns in Exhibit 18.2. The sixth column shows how much each cash flow can be sold for by the dealer if it is stripped. The values in this column are just those in the fifth column. The next-to-last column shows how much the dealer is effectively purchasing the cash flow for if each cash flow is discounted at 7.08%. The sum of the arbitrage profit from each stripped cash flow is the total arbitrage profit and is contained in the last column.

We have just demonstrated how coupon stripping of a Treasury issue will force the market value to be close to the value as determined by the arbitrage-free valuation approach when the market price is less than the arbitrage-free value (i.e., the whole is worth less than the sum of the parts).

What happens when a Treasury issue's market price is greater than the arbitrage-free value? Obviously, a dealer will not want to strip the Treasury issue since the proceeds generated from stripping will be less than the cost of purchasing the issue.

When such situations occur, the dealer can purchase a package of Treasury strips so as to create a synthetic Treasury coupon security that is worth more than the same maturity and same coupon Treasury issue. This process is called reconstitution.

The process of stripping and reconstitution assures that the price of a Treasury issue will not depart materially (depending on transaction costs) from its arbitrage-free value.

Credit Spreads and the Valuation of Non-Treasury Securities

The Treasury spot rates can be used to value any default-free security. For a non-Treasury security, the theoretical value is not as easy to determine. The value of a non-Treasury security is found by discounting the cash flows by the Treasury spot rates plus a yield spread which reflects the additional risks (e.g., default risk, liquidity risks, the risk associated with any embedded options, and so on).

The spot rate used to discount the cash flow of a non-Treasury security can be the Treasury spot rate plus a constant credit spread. For example, suppose the six-month Treasury spot rate is 6.05% and the 10-year Treasury spot rate is 7.20%. Also suppose that a suitable credit spread is 100 basis points. Then a 7.05% spot rate is used to discount a six-month cash flow of a non-Treasury bond and a 8.20% discount rate is used to discount a 10-year cash flow. (Remember that when each semiannual cash flow is discounted, the discount rate used is one-half the spot rate: 3.525% for the six-month spot rate and 4.10% for the 10-year spot rate.)

The drawback of this approach is that there is no reason to expect the credit spread to be the same regardless of when the cash flow is expected to be received. Consequently, the credit spread may vary with a bond's term to maturity. In other words, there is a *term structure of credit spreads*. Generally, credit spreads increase with maturity. This is a typical shape for the term structure of credit spreads. Moreover, the shape of the term structure is not the same for all credit ratings. Typically, the lower the credit rating, the steeper the term structure of credit spreads.

Dealer firms typically estimate the term structure of credit spreads for each credit rating and market sector. Typically, the credit spread increases with maturity. In addition, the shape of the term structure is not the same for all credit ratings. Typically, the lower the credit rating, the steeper the term structure of credit spreads.

EXHIBIT 18.3 Calculation of Arbitrage-Free Value of a Hypothetical 8% 10-Year Non-Treasury Security Using Benchmark Spot Rate Curve

Period	Years	Cash Flow ($)	Treasury Spot Rate (%)	Credit Spread (%)	Benchmark Spot (%)	Present Value ($)
1	0.5	4	6.05	0.30	6.35	3.8769
2	1.0	4	6.15	0.33	6.48	3.7529
3	1.5	4	6.21	0.34	6.55	3.6314
4	2.0	4	6.26	0.37	6.63	3.5108
5	2.5	4	6.29	0.42	6.71	3.3916
6	3.0	4	6.37	0.43	6.80	3.2729
7	3.5	4	6.38	0.44	6.82	3.1632
8	4.0	4	6.40	0.45	6.85	3.0553
9	4.5	4	6.41	0.46	6.87	2.9516
10	5.0	4	6.48	0.52	7.00	2.8357
11	5.5	4	6.49	0.53	7.02	2.7369
12	6.0	4	6.53	0.55	7.08	2.6349
13	6.5	4	6.63	0.58	7.21	2.5241
14	7.0	4	6.78	0.59	7.37	2.4101
15	7.5	4	6.79	0.63	7.42	2.3161
16	8.0	4	6.81	0.64	7.45	2.2281
17	8.5	4	6.84	0.69	7.53	2.1340
18	9.0	4	6.93	0.73	7.66	2.0335
19	9.5	4	7.05	0.77	7.82	1.9301
20	10.0	104	7.20	0.82	8.02	47.3731
					Total	101.7630

When the relevant credit spreads for a given credit rating and market sector are added to the Treasury spot rates, the resulting term structure is used to value the bonds of issuers with that credit rating in that market sector. This term structure is referred to as the *benchmark spot rate curve* or *benchmark zero-coupon rate curve*.

For example, Exhibit 18.3 reproduces the Treasury spot rate curve in Exhibit 18.2. Also shown in the exhibit is a hypothetical term structure of credit spread for a non-Treasury security. The resulting benchmark spot rate curve is in the next-to-the-last column. Like before, it is this spot rate curve that is used to value the securities of issuers that have the same credit rating and are in the same market sector. This is done in Exhibit 18.3 for a hypothetical 8% 10-year issue. The arbitrage-free value is $101.763. Notice that the theoretical value is less than that for an otherwise comparable Treasury security. The arbitrage-free value for an 8% 10-year Treasury is $107.0018 (see Exhibit 18.2).

YIELD SPREAD MEASURES

Traditional yield spread analysis for a non-Treasury security involves calculating the difference between the risky bond's yield and the yield on a comparable maturity benchmark Treasury security. This yield spread measure is referred to as the *nominal spread*.

The nominal spread measure has two drawbacks. For now, the most important is that the nominal spread fails to account for the term structure of spot rates for both bonds. Moreover, as we will see later in this chapter when we discuss the valuation of bonds with embedded options, the nominal spread does not take into consideration the fact that expected interest rate volatility may alter the non-Treasury bond's expected future cash flows. We will focus here only on the first drawback and pose an alternative spread measure that incorporates the spot rate curve. Later we discuss another spread measure, the option-adjusted spread (OAS), for bonds with embedded options.

Zero-Volatility Spread

The *zero-volatility spread*, also referred to as the *Z-spread* or *static spread*, is a measure of the spread that the investor would realize over the entire Treasury spot rate curve if the bond were held to maturity. Unlike the nominal spread, it is not a spread at one point on the yield curve. The Z-spread is the spread that will make the present value of the cash flows from the non-Treasury bond, when discounted at the Treasury rate plus the spread, equal to the non-Treasury bond's market price plus accrued interest. A trial-and-error procedure is used to compute the Z-spread.

To illustrate how this is done, consider the following two five-year bonds:

Issue	Coupon	Price	Yield to Maturity
Treasury	5.055%	100.0000	5.0550%
Non-Treasury	7.000%	101.9576	6.5348%

The nominal spread for the non-Treasury bond is 147.98 basis points. Let's use the information presented in Exhibit 18.4 to determine the

EXHIBIT 18.4   Determination of the Z-Spread for an 7% Five-Year Non-Treasury Issue Selling at $101.9576 to Yield 6.5347%

Period	Years	Cash Flow ($)	Spot Rate (%)	Present Value ($) Assuming a Spread of		
				100 bp	120 bp	150 bp
1	0.5	3.50	4.20	3.4113	3.4080	3.4030
2	1.0	3.50	4.33	3.3207	3.3142	3.3045
3	1.5	3.50	4.39	3.2793	3.2222	3.2081
4	2.0	3.50	4.44	3.1438	3.1315	3.1133
5	2.5	3.50	4.51	3.0553	3.0405	3.0184
6	3.0	3.50	4.54	2.9708	2.9535	2.9278
7	3.5	3.50	4.58	2.8868	2.8672	2.8381
8	4.0	3.50	4.73	2.7921	2.7705	2.7384
9	4.5	3.50	4.90	2.6942	2.6708	2.6360
10	5.0	103.50	5.11	76.6037	75.8643	74.7699
			Total	104.1100	103.2430	101.9580

Z-spread. The third column in the exhibit shows the cash flows for the 7% five-year non-Treasury issue. The fourth column is a hypothetical Treasury spot rate curve that we will employ in this example. Three spread measures are tried: 100, 120, and 150 basis points. As can be seen in the last column of Exhibit 18.4, the present value of the cash flows is equal to the non-Treasury issue's price. Accordingly, 150 basis points is the Z-spread, compared to the nominal spread of 147.98 basis points.

What does the Z-spread represent for this non-Treasury security? Since the Z-spread is relative to the benchmark Treasury spot rate curve, it represents a spread required by the market to compensate for all the risks of holding the non-Treasury bond versus a Treasury security with the same maturity. These risks include the non-Treasury's credit risk, liquidity risk, and the risks associated with any embedded options.

Generally, the divergence is a function of the term structure's shape and the security's characteristics. Among the relevant security characteristics are coupon rate, term to maturity, and type of principal repayment provision—nonamortizing versus amortizing. The steeper the term structure, the greater will be the divergence. For standard coupon-paying bonds with a bullet maturity (i.e., a single payment of principal), the Z-spread and the nominal spread will usually not differ significantly. For monthly-pay amortizing securities the divergence can be substantial in a steep yield curve environment.

A Z-spread can be calculated relative to any benchmark spot rate curve in the same manner. Therefore, when a Z-spread is cited, it must be cited relative to some benchmark spot rate curve. This is essential because it indicates the credit and sector risks that are being considered when the Z-spread is calculated.

FORWARD RATES

We described how a default-free theoretical spot rate curve can be extrapolated from the Treasury yield curve. Additional information useful to market participants can be extrapolated from the default-free theoretical spot rate curve: forward rates. A forward rate is the fundamental unit of yield curve analysis. Forward rates are the building blocks of interest rates just as atoms are the building blocks of solid matter in physics. A forward rate is the discount rate of a single cash flow over a single period. Under certain assumptions, these rates can be viewed as the market's consensus of future interest rates.[2]

Examples of forward rates that can be calculated from the default-free theoretical spot rate curve are the:

- Six-month forward rate six months from now
- Six-month forward rate three years from now
- One-year forward rate one year from now
- Three-year forward rate two years from now
- Five-year forward rates three years from now

We begin by showing how to compute the six-month forward rates. Then we explain how to compute any forward rate between any two periods in the future.

Deriving Six-Month Forward Rates

To illustrate the process of extrapolating six-month forward rates, we use the yield curve and the corresponding spot rate curve from Exhibit 18.1. Suppose an investor has a one-year anticipated investment horizon. In general, an investor has three basic ways to satisfy this maturity preference. First, an investor can purchase a security having a maturity that matches the investment horizon. For example, an investor can buy a one-year zero coupon bond and hold it to maturity. We call this a *buy and hold strategy*.

---

[2]See, Antti Illmanen, "Market's Rate Expectations and Forward Rates," Part 2, *Understanding the Yield Curve* (New York: Salomon Brothers, 1995).

Second, an investor can invest in a series of short-term securities (e.g., buy a six-month zero-coupon bond today, hold it to maturity, and reinvest the proceeds into another six-month zero-coupon bond six months from now.) We call this a *rollover strategy*. Finally, an investor can invest in a security with a maturity greater than the anticipated holding period and sell it at the appropriate time (e.g., buy a two-year zero coupon bond and selling it after one year). If the yield curve is upward-sloping, this strategy is called "riding the yield curve."

For simplicity, let's consider an investor who has a one-year investment horizon and is faced with the following two alternatives. (We return to the riding the yield curve strategy shortly.)

- Buy a one-year Treasury bill (buy-and-hold strategy).
- Buy a six-month Treasury bill, and when it matures in six months, buy another six-month Treasury bill (rollover strategy).

The investor will be indifferent between the two alternatives if they produce the same expected return over the one-year investment horizon. The investor knows the spot rates that are available on the six-month Treasury bill and the one-year Treasury bill. However, the investor does not know what yield will be available on a six-month Treasury bill that will be purchased six months from now (i.e., the second leg of the rollover strategy). That is, the investor does not know the six-month forward rate six months from now. Given the spot rates for the six-month Treasury bill and the one-year Treasury bill, the forward rate on a six-month Treasury bill is the rate that equalizes the expected dollar return between the two alternatives.

To see how that rate can be determined, suppose that an investor purchased a six-month Treasury bill for $\$X$. At the end of six months, the value of this investment would be

$$X(1 + z_1)$$

where z_1 is one-half the bond-equivalent yield (BEY) of the theoretical six-month spot rate. Intuitively, this product tells us how much money the investor will have available to reinvest in the second six-month bill, six months from now.

Let f represent one-half the forward rate (expressed as a BEY) on a six-month Treasury bill available six months from now. If the investor were to rollover her investment by purchasing that bill at that time, then the future dollars available at the end of one year from the $\$X$ investment would be:

$$X(1 + z_1)(1 + f)$$

Note we cannot calculate this expression because we do not know f as of yet.

Now consider the buy-and-hold strategy. Namely, buying the one-year Treasury bill and maturing it. If we let z_2 represent one-half the BEY of the theoretical one-year spot rate, then the future dollars available at the end of one year from the $\$X$ investment would be

$$X(1 + z_2)^2$$

The reason that the squared term appears is that the amount invested is being compounded for two periods at one-half the one-year spot rate due to semiannual compounding.

Now we are prepared to analyze the investor's choices and what this tells us about forward rates. The investor will be indifferent between the two alternatives confronting her if she makes the same dollar investment ($\$X$) and expects to receive the same future dollars from both alternatives at the end of one year. That is, the investor will be indifferent if

$$X(1 + z_1)(1 + f) = X(1 + z_2)^2$$

Dividing both sides by X (the initial investment) leaves the following:

$$(1 + z_1)(1 + f) = (1 + z_2)^2$$

We can interpret the left-side of this expression as the expected holding-period return of the rollover strategy. Likewise, the right-hand side is the expected holding-period return of the buy-and-hold strategy. Given that z_1 and z_2 are known, what does f have to be six months hence for these two strategies to have the same holding-period returns? In simple words, f is the value that makes the right side equal the left side. Note this result is courtesy of the no-arbitrage condition. Solving for f, we get

$$f = \frac{(1 + z_2)^2}{(1 + z_1)} - 1$$

Doubling f gives the BEY for the six-month forward rate six months from now.

We can illustrate the use of this formula with the theoretical spot rates shown in Exhibit 18.1. We know that

Six-month bill spot rate = 0.030, therefore z_1 = 0.0150
One-year bill spot rate = 0.033, therefore z_2 = 0.0165

Substituting into the formula, we have

$$f = \frac{(1.0165)^2}{(1.0150)} - 1 = 0.0180 = 1.8\%$$

Therefore, the six-month forward rate six months from now is 3.6% (1.8% × 2) BEY.

It is quite helpful to think of forward rates as break-even rates. In our example, the yield curve is upward-sloping. As a result, an investor picks up additional yield by investing in the one-year bill rather than the six-month bill. The six-month forward rate tells us how much the six-month spot rate must rise six months from now so that an investor buying the six-month bill and intending to rollover the proceeds into another six-month bill will earn the same one-year holding-period return. Obviously, the six-month spot needs to rise over the next six months to offset the one-year bill's yield advantage. As we have seen, if the six-month spot rate is 3.6% six months from now, an investor will be indifferent between the two strategies. Simply put, forward rates tell us how much the spot curve needs to change over the next period so that all Treasury securities earn the same holding-period return.

The same line of reasoning can be used to obtain the six-month forward rate beginning at any time period in the future. The notation that we use to indicate six-month forward rates is $_1f_m$ where the subscript 1 indicates a one-period (six months in our illustration) rate and the subscript m indicates the period beginning m periods from now. When m is equal to zero, this means the current rate. Thus, the first six-month forward rate is simply the current six-month spot rate. That is, $_1f_0 = z_1$.

The general formula for determining a six-month forward rate is

$$_1f_m = \frac{(1+z_{m+1})^{m+1}}{(1+z_m)^m} - 1$$

This expression tells us if the $m + 1$-period and m-period spot rates are known, the one-period forward rate between periods m and $m + 1$ is computed by dividing $m + 1$-period zero-coupon bond's holding-period return by the m-period zero-coupon bond's holding-period return.

For example, suppose that the six-month forward rate four years (eight six-month periods) from now is sought. In terms of our notation, m is 8 and we seek $_1f_8$. The formula is then

$$_1f_8 = \frac{(1+z_9)^9}{(1+z_8)^8} - 1$$

From Exhibit 18.1, since the four-year spot rate is 5.065% and the 4.5-year spot rate is 5.1701%, z_8 is 2.5325% and z_9 is 2.58505%. Then,

$$_1f_8 = \frac{(1.0258505)^9}{(1.025325)^8} - 1 = 3.0064\%$$

Doubling this rate gives a six-month forward rate four years from now of 6.01%.

The six-month forward rates for the Treasury yield curve and corresponding spot rate curve shown in Exhibit 18.1 are shown below (annualized rates on a bond-equivalent basis):

Notation	Forward Rate	Notation	Forward Rate
$_1f_0$	3.00	$_1f_{10}$	6.48
$_1f_1$	3.60	$_1f_{11}$	6.72
$_1f_2$	3.92	$_1f_{12}$	6.97
$_1f_3$	5.15	$_1f_{13}$	6.36
$_1f_4$	6.54	$_1f_{14}$	6.49
$_1f_5$	6.33	$_1f_{15}$	6.62
$_1f_6$	6.23	$_1f_{16}$	6.76
$_1f_7$	5.79	$_1f_{17}$	8.10
$_1f_8$	6.01	$_1f_{18}$	8.40
$_1f_9$	6.24	$_1f_{19}$	8.72

The set of these forward rates is called the *short-term forward-rate curve*.

Relationship between Spot Rates and Short-Term Forward Rates

Suppose an investor invests $X in a three-year zero-coupon Treasury security. The total proceeds three years (six periods) from now would be

$$X(1 + z_6)^6$$

Alternatively, the investor could buy a six-month Treasury bill and reinvest the proceeds every six months for three years. The future dollars or dollar return will depend on the six-month forward rates. Suppose that the investor can actually reinvest the proceeds maturing every six months at the calculated six-month forward rates shown above. At the end of three years, an investment of $X would generate the following proceeds:

$$X(1 + z_1)(1 + {}_1f_1)(1 + {}_1f_2)(1 + {}_1f_3)(1 + {}_1f_4)(1 + {}_1f_5)$$

Since the two investments must generate the same proceeds at the end of three years, the two previous equations are set equal to one another:

$$X(1 + z_6)^6 = X(1 + z_1)(1 + {}_1f_1)(1 + {}_1f_2)(1 + {}_1f_3)(1 + {}_1f_4)(1 + {}_1f_5)$$

Solving for the 3-year (six-period) spot rate, we have

$$z_6 = [(1 + z_1)(1 + {}_1f_1)(1 + {}_1f_2)(1 + {}_1f_3)(1 + {}_1f_4)(1 + {}_1f_5)]^{1/6} - 1$$

This equation tells us that the three-year spot rate depends on the current six-month spot rate and the five six-month forward rates. Earlier we described a spot rate as the average discount rate of a single cash flow over many periods. We can see now that long-term spot rates are averages of the current single period spot rate and the forward rates. In fact, the right-hand side of this equation is a *geometric* average of the current six-month spot rate and the five six-month forward rates.

In general, the relationship among a *T*-period spot rate, the current six-month spot rate, and the six-month forward rates is as follows:

$$z_T = [(1 + z_1)(1 + {}_1f_1)(1 + {}_1f_2) \cdots (1 + {}_1f_{T-1}]^{1/T} - 1$$

Therefore, discounting at the forward rates will give the same present value as discounting at the spot rates. For example, suppose we have a single default-free cash flow to be delivered three years from today. There are two equivalent ways to discount this cash flow back to time zero. First, discount the cash flow back six periods at one-half the three-year spot rate. Second, discount the cash flow back one period at a time using the appropriate forward rate each period. So, it does not matter whether one discounts cash flows by spot rates or forward rates, the value is the same. The same principle applies with equal force for coupon-paying bonds.

Forward Rates as the Market's Expectation of Future Rates

There are two questions about forward rates that are of interest to portfolio managers. First, are implied forward rates the market's expectation of future spot rates? Second, how well do implied forward rates do at predicting future interest rates? We answer each question in turn.

According to the *pure expectations theory of interest rates*, forward rates exclusively represent expected future spot rates. Thus, the entire yield curve at a given time reflects the market's expectations of the family of future short-term rates. Under this view, an upward-sloping yield curve indicates that the market expects short-term rates to rise throughout the relevant future. Similarly, a flat yield curve reflects an expectation that future short-term rates will be mostly constant, while a downwardsloping yield curve must reflect an expectation that future short-term rates will decline. Of course, there are factors that influence the yield curve other than the market's expectations of future interest rates.

The statement that forward rates reflect the market's consensus of future interest rates is strictly true only if investors do not demand an additional risk premium for holding bonds with longer maturities and if investors' preference for positive convexity (explained in Chapter 17) does not influence the yield curve's shape. Antti Illmanen states in series of articles called *Understanding the Yield Curve*, "Whenever the spot rate curve is upward sloping, the forwards imply rising rates. That is, rising rates are needed to offset long-term bonds' yield advantage. However, it does not necessarily follow that the market expects rising rates."[3] In certain circumstances, risk premiums and the convexity bias can exert considerable influence on yields.

In response to the second question, several empirical studies suggest that forward rates do a poor job in predicting future spot rates.[4] For example, Michele Kreisler and Richard Worley present evidence that suggests there is little or no relationship between the yield curve's slope and subsequent interest rate movements. In other words, increases in rates are as likely to follow positively sloped yield curves as flat or inverted yield curves.[5]

Why then should bond portfolio managers care about implied forward rates? As we have noted, forward rates should be interpreted as break-even levels for future spot rates. By definition, if forward rates are subsequently realized, all government bonds (regardless of maturity) will earn the same one-period return. Given this property, forward rates serve as benchmarks to which we compare our subjective expectations of future interest rates. It is not enough to say "interest rates will rise over the next six months. This is an empty statement—rise relative to what? The "to what" is the implied forward rate. If the yield curve is upward-sloping and one believes spot rates will rise more than suggested by the implied forward rates, then a rollover strategy dominates a buy-and-hold. Conversely, if one believes spot rates will rise by less than the implied forward rates suggest, then the reverse is true.

---

[3]Antti Illmanen, "Market's Rate Expectations and Forward Rate," *Understanding the Yield Curve: Part II* (New York: Salomon Brothers, 1995).
[4]See, for example, John Y. Campbell, Andrew W. Lo and Craig MacKinlay, *The Econometrics of Financial Markets* (Princeton, N.J.: Princeton University Press, 1997).
[5]Michele A. Kreisler and Richard B. Worley, "Value Measures for Managing Interest-Rate Risk," Chapter 3 in *Managing Fixed-Income Portfolios*, ed. Frank J. Fabozzi (New Hope, Pa.: Frank J. Fabozzi Associates, 1997).

OVERVIEW OF THE VALUATION OF BONDS WITH EMBEDDED OPTIONS

To develop an analytical framework for valuing a bond with an embedded option, it is necessary to decompose a bond into its component parts. Consider, for example, the most common bond with an embedded option, a *callable bond*. A callable bond is a bond in which the bondholder has sold the issuer an option (more specifically, a call option) that allows the issuer to repurchase the contractual cash flows of the bond from the time of the bond's first call date until the maturity date.

Consider the following two bonds: (1) a callable bond with an 8% coupon, 20 years to maturity, and callable in five years at 104 and (2) a 10-year 9% coupon bond callable immediately at par. For the first bond, the bondholder owns a five-year option-free bond and has sold a call option granting the issuer the right to call away from the bondholder 15 years of cash flows five years from now for a price of 104. The investor who owns the second bond has a 10-year option-free bond and has sold a call option granting the issuer the right to immediately call the entire 10-year contractual cash flows, or any cash flows remaining at the time the issue is called, for 100.

Effectively, the owner of a callable bond is entering into two separate transactions. First, the investor buys an option-free bond from the issuer for which he pays some price. Then, the investor sells the issuer a call option for which he/she receives the option price. The value of a callable bond is therefore equal to the value of the two component parts. That is,

> Value of a callable bond
> = Value of an option-free bond − Value of a call option

The reason the call option's value is subtracted from the value of the option-free bond is that when the bondholder sells a call option, he/she receives the option price. Actually, the position is more complicated than we just described. The issuer may be entitled to call the bond at the first call date and anytime thereafter, or at the first call date and any subsequent coupon anniversary date. Thus the investor has effectively sold an American-type call option to the issuer, but the call price may vary with the date the call option is exercised. This is because the call schedule for a bond may have a different call price depending on the call date. Moreover, the underlying bond for the call option is the remaining coupon payments that would have been made by the issuer had the bond not been called. For exposition purposes, it is easier to understand the principles associated with the investment characteristics of callable bonds by describing the investor's position as long an option-free bond and short a call option.

The same logic applies to putable bonds. In the case of a putable bond, the bondholder has the right to sell the bond to the issuer at a designated price and time. A putable bond can be broken into two separate transactions. First, the investor buys an option-free bond. Second, the investor buys a put option from the issuer that allows the investor to sell the bond to the issuer. In terms of value,

> Value of a putable bond
> = Value of an option-free bond + Value of a put option

Option-Adjusted Spread and Option Cost

Before presenting the valuation models, we discuss two measures that are derived from a valuation model—option-adjusted spread and option cost.

Option-Adjusted Spread

What an investor seeks to do is to buy a security whose value is greater than its price. A valuation model such as the two described later in this chapter allows an investor to estimate the theoretical value of a security, which at this point would be sufficient to determine the fairness of the price of the security. That is, the investor can say that this bond is 1-point cheap or 2-points cheap, and so on.

A valuation model need not stop here, however. Instead, it can convert the divergence between the security's price observed in the market and the theoretical value derived from the model into a yield spread measure. This step is necessary because many market participants find it more convenient to think in terms of yield spread than price differences.

The *option-adjusted spread* (OAS) was developed as a yield spread measure to convert dollar differences between value and price. Thus, basically, the OAS is used to reconcile value with market price. But what is it a "spread" over? As we shall see when we describe the two valuation methodologies, the OAS is a spread over some benchmark curve. The benchmark curve itself is not a single curve, but a series of curves that allow for changes in interest rates.

The reason that the resulting spread is referred to as "option-adjusted" is because the cash flows of the security whose value we seek are adjusted to reflect any embedded options. In contrast, as explained in the previous chapter, the zero-volatility spread does not consider how the cash flows will change when interest rates change in the future. That is, the zero-volatility spread assumes that interest rate volatility is zero. Consequently, the zero-volatility spread is also referred to as the *static spread.*

While the product of a valuation model is the OAS, the process can be worked in reverse. For a specified OAS, the valuation model can determine the theoretical value of the security that is consistent with that OAS.

Option Cost

The implied cost of the option embedded in any bond can be obtained by calculating the difference between the OAS at the assumed volatility of interest rates and the zero-volatility spread. That is,

$$\text{Option cost} = \text{Zero-volatility spread} - \text{Option-adjusted spread}$$

The reason that the option cost is measured in this way is as follows. In an environment of no interest rate changes, the investor would earn the zero-volatility spread. When future interest rates are uncertain, the spread is different because of the embedded option; the OAS reflects the spread after adjusting for this option. Therefore, the option cost is the difference between the spread that would be earned in a static interest rate environment (the zero-volatility spread) and the spread after adjusting for the option (the OAS).

For callable bonds and mortgage passthrough securities, the option cost is positive. This is because the borrower's ability to alter the cash flow will result in an OAS that is less than the zero-volatility spread. In the case of a putable bond, the OAS is greater than the zero-volatility spread so that the option cost is negative. This occurs because of the investor's ability to alter the cash flow.

In general, when the option cost is positive, this means that the investor has sold or is short an option. This is true for callable bonds and mortgage passthrough securities. A negative value for the option cost means that the investor has purchased or is long an option. A putable bond is an example of a security with a negative option cost. There are certain securities in the mortgage-backed securities market that also have an option cost that is negative.

While the option cost as described above is measured in basis points, it can be translated into a dollar price.

LATTICE MODEL

The first complication in building a model to value bonds with embedded options is that the future cash flows will depend on what happens to interest rates in the future. This means that future interest rates must be considered.

This is incorporated into a valuation model by considering how interest rates can change based on some assumed interest rate volatility. Given the assumed interest rate volatility, an interest rate "tree" representing possible future interest rates consistent with the volatility assumption can be constructed. Since the interest rate tree looks like a lattice, these valuation models are commonly referred to as *lattice models*. It is from the interest rate tree (or lattice) that two important elements in the valuation process are obtained. First, the interest rates on the tree are used to generate the cash flows taking into account the embedded option. Second, the interest rates on the tree are used to compute the present value of the cash flows.

For a given interest rate volatility, there are several interest rate models that have been used in practice to construct an interest rate tree. An *interest rate model* is a probabilistic description of how interest rates can change over the life of the bond. An interest rate model does this by making an assumption about the relationship between the level of short-term interest rates and the interest rate volatility as measured by the standard deviation. A discussion of the various interest rate models that have been suggested in the finance literature and that are used by practitioners in developing valuation models is beyond the scope of this chapter. What is important to understand is that the interest rate models commonly used are based on how short-term interest rates can evolve (i.e., change) over time. Consequently, these interest rate models are referred to as *one-factor models*, where "factor" means only one interest rate is being modeled over time. More complex models consider how more than one interest rate changes over time. For example, an interest rate model can specify how the short-term interest rate and the long-term interest rate can change over time. Such a model is called a *two-factor model*.

Given an interest rate model and an interest rate volatility assumption, it can be assumed that interest rates can realize one of two possible rates in the next period. A valuation model that makes this assumption in creating an interest rate tree is called a *binomial lattice model*, or simply *binomial model*. There are valuation models that assume that interest rates can take on three possible rates in the next period and these models are called *trinomial lattice models*, or simply *trinomial models*. There are even more complex models that assume in creating an interest rate tree that more than three possible rates in the next period can be realized. Regardless of the assumption about how many possible rates can be realized in the next period, the interest rate tree generated must produce a value for the on-the-run Treasury issue that is equal to its observed market price—that is, it must produce an arbitrage-free value. Moreover, the intuition and the methodology for using the interest rate tree (i.e., the backward induction methodology described later) are the same.

Once an interest rate tree is generated that (1) is consistent with both the interest rate volatility assumption and the interest rate model, and (2) generates the observed market price for each on-the-run issue, the next step is to use the interest rate tree to value a bond with an embedded option. The complexity here is that a set of rules must be introduced to determine, for any period, when the embedded option will be exercised. For a callable bond, these rules are called the *call rules*. The rules vary from model builder to model builder.

At this stage, all of this sounds terribly complicated. While the building of a model to value bonds with embedded options is more complex than building a model to value option-free bonds, the basic principles are the same. In the case of valuing an option-free bond, the model that is built is simply a set of spot rates that are used to value cash flows. The spot rates will produce an arbitrage-free value. For a model to value a bond with embedded options, the interest rate tree is used to value future cash flows and the interest rate tree is combined with the call rules to generate the future cash flows. Again, the interest rate tree will produce an arbitrage-free value.

Let's move from theory to practice. Only a few practitioners will develop their own model to value bonds with embedded options. Instead, it is typical for a portfolio manager or analyst to use a model developed by either a dealer firm or a vendor of analytical systems. A fair question is then: Why bother covering a valuation model that is readily available from a third party? The answer is that a valuation model should not be a black box to portfolio managers and analysts. The models in practice share all of the principles described in this chapter, but differ with respect to certain assumptions that can produce quite different results. The reasons for these differences in valuation must be understood. Moreover, third-party models give the user a choice of changing the assumptions. A user who has not "walked through" a valuation model has no appreciation of the significance of these assumptions and therefore of how to assess the impact of these assumptions on the value produced by the model. There is always "modeling risk" when we use the output of a valuation model. This is the risk that the underlying assumptions of a model may be incorrect. Understanding a valuation model permits the user to effectively determine the significance of an assumption.

Below we will use the binomial model to demonstrate all of the issues and assumptions associated with valuing a bond with embedded options. Specifically, it is used to value agency debentures, corporates, and municipal bond structures with embedded options. The reason it is not used to value mortgage-backed securities and certain types of asset-backed securities will be explained when we describe the Monte Carlo simulation valuation model later in this chapter.

EXHIBIT 18.5 On-the-Run Yield Curve and Spot Rates for an Issuer

Maturity (years)	Yield to Maturity (%)	Market Price ($)	Spot Rate (%)
1	3.5	100	3.5000
2	4.2	100	4.2147
3	4.7	100	4.7345
4	5.2	100	5.2707

Binomial Model

To illustrate the binomial valuation methodology, we start with the on-the-run yield curve for the particular issuer whose bonds we want to value. The starting point is the Treasury's on-the-run yield curve. To obtain a particular issuer's on-the-run yield curve, an appropriate credit spread is added to each on-the-run Treasury issue. The credit spread need not be constant for all maturities.

In our illustration, we use the hypothetical on-the-run issues for an issuer shown in Exhibit 18.5. Each bond is trading at par value (100) so the coupon rate is equal to the yield to maturity. We will simplify the illustration by assuming annual-pay bonds. Using a bootstrapping methodology, the spot rates are those shown in the last column of Exhibit 18.5.

Binomial Interest Rate Tree[6]

Once we allow for embedded options, consideration must be given to interest rate volatility. This can be done by introducing a *binomial interest rate tree*. This tree is nothing more than a graphical depiction of the one-period or short rates over time based on some assumption about interest rate volatility. How this tree is constructed is illustrated here.

Exhibit 18.6 provides an example of a binomial interest rate tree. In this tree, each node (bold circle) represents a time period that is equal to one year from the node to its left. Each node is labeled with an N, representing node, and a subscript that indicates the path that the one-year rate took to get to that node. L represents the lower of the two one-year rates and H represents the higher of the two one-year rates. For example, node N_{HH} means to get to that node the following path for one-year rates occurred:

---

[6]The model described in this section was presented in Andrew J. Kalotay, George O. Williams, and Frank J. Fabozzi, "A Model for the Valuation of Bonds and Embedded Options," *Financial Analysts Journal* 49, no. 3 (1993): 35–46.

EXHIBIT 18.6   Four-Year Binomial Interest Rate Tree

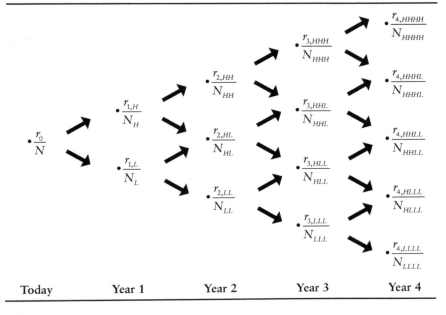

| Today | Year 1 | Year 2 | Year 3 | Year 4 |

The one-year rate realized is the higher of the two rates in the first year and then the higher of the one-year rates in the second year.[7]

Look first at the point denoted by just N in Exhibit 18.6. This is the root of the tree and is nothing more than the current one-year spot rate, or equivalently the current one-year rate, which we denote by r_0. What we have assumed in creating this tree is that the one-year rate can take on two possible rates the next period and the two rates have the same probability of occurring. One rate will be higher than the other. It is assumed that the one-year rate can evolve over time based on a random process called a log-normal random walk with a certain volatility.

We use the following notation to describe the tree in Year 1. Let

σ = assumed volatility of the one-year rate

$r_{1,L}$ = the lower one-year rate one year from now

$r_{1,H}$ = the higher one-year rate one year from now

The relationship between $r_{1,L}$ and $r_{1,H}$ is as follows:

---

[7]Note that N_{HL} is equivalent to N_{LH} in the second year and that in the third year N_{HHL} is equivalent to N_{HLH} and N_{LHH} and that N_{HLL} is equivalent to N_{LLH}. We have simply selected one label for a node rather than clutter up the exhibit.

$$r_{1,H} = r_{1,L}(e^{2\sigma})$$

where e is the base of the natural logarithm 2.71828.

For example, suppose that $r_{1,L}$ is 4.4448% and σ is 10% per year, then

$$r_{1,H} = 4.4448\%(e^{2\times0.10}) = 5.4289\%$$

In Year 2, there are three possible values for the one-year rate, which we will denote as follows:

$r_{2,LL}$ = one-year rate in Year 2 assuming the lower rate in Year 1 and the lower rate in Year 2

$r_{2,HH}$ = one-year rate in Year 2 assuming the higher rate in Year 1 and the higher rate in Year 2

$r_{2,HL}$ = one-year rate in Year 2 assuming the higher rate in Year 1 and the lower rate in Year 2 or equivalently the lower rate in Year 1 and the higher rate in Year 2

The relationship between $r_{2,LL}$ and the other two one-year rates is as follows:

$$r_{2,HH} = r_{2,LL}(e^{4\sigma}) \text{ and } r_{2,HL} = r_{2,LL}(e^{2\sigma})$$

So, for example, if $r_{2,LL}$ is 4.6958%, then assuming once again that σ is 10%, then

$$r_{2,HH} = 4.6958\%(e^{4\times0.10}) = 7.0053\%$$

$$r_{2,HL} = 4.6958\%(e^{4\times0.10}) = 5.7354\%$$

In Year 3, there are four possible values for the one-year rate, which are denoted as follows: $r_{3,HHH}$, $r_{3,HHL}$, $r_{3,HLL}$, and $r_{3,LLL}$, and whose first three rates are related to the last as follows:

$$r_{3,HHH} = (e^{6\sigma})\, r_{3,LLL}$$
$$r_{3,HHL} = (e^{4\sigma})\, r_{3,LLL}$$
$$r_{3,HLL} = (e^{2\sigma})\, r_{3,LLL}$$

Exhibit 18.6 shows the notation for a four-year binomial interest rate tree. We can simplify the notation by letting r_t be the one-year rate t years from now for the lower rate since all the other short rates t years from now depend on that rate.

It can be shown that the standard deviation of the one-year rate is equal to $r_0\sigma$.[8] The standard deviation is a statistical measure of volatility. It is important to see that the process that we assumed generates the binomial interest rate tree (or equivalently the short rates), implies that volatility is measured relative to the current level of rates. For example, if σ is 10% and the one-year rate (r_0) is 4%, then the standard deviation of the one-year rate is 4% × 10% = 0.4% or 40 basis points. However, if the current one-year rate is 12%, the standard deviation of the one-year rate would be 12% × 10% or 120 basis points.

Determining the Value at a Node

To find the value of the bond at a node, we first calculate the bond's value at the two nodes to the right of the node we are interested in. For example, in Exhibit 18.6, suppose we want to determine the bond's value at node N_H. The bond's value at node N_{HH} and N_{HL} must be determined. Hold aside for now how we get these two values because as we will see, the process involves starting from the last year in the tree and working backwards to get the final solution we want, so these two values will be known.

Effectively what we are saying is that if we are at some node, then the value at that node will depend on the future cash flows. In turn, the future cash flows depend on (1) the bond's value one year from now and (2) the coupon payment one year from now. The latter is known. The former depends on whether the one-year rate is the higher or lower rate. The bond's value depending on whether the rate is the higher or lower rate is reported at the two nodes to the right of the node that is the focus of our attention. So, the cash flow at a node will be either (1) the bond's value if the short rate is the higher rate plus the coupon payment, or (2) the bond's value if the short rate is the lower rate plus the coupon payment. For example, suppose that we are interested in the bond's value at N_H. The cash flow will be either the bond's value at N_{HH} plus the coupon payment, or the bond's value at N_{HL} plus the coupon payment.

To get the bond's value at a node we follow the fundamental rule for valuation: The value is the present value of the expected cash flows. The appropriate discount rate to use is the one-year rate at the node. Now there are two present values in this case: the present value if the one-year rate is the higher rate and one if it is the lower rate. Since it is assumed that the probability of both outcomes is equal, an average of the two present values

---

[8]This can be seen by noting that $e^{2\sigma} \approx 1 + 2\sigma$. Then the standard deviation of the one-year rate is

$$\frac{re^{2\sigma} - r}{2} \approx \frac{r + 2\sigma r - r}{2} = \sigma r$$

is computed. The computation is as follows. For any node assuming that the one-year rate is r_* at the node where the valuation is sought and letting:

V_H = the bond's value for the higher one-year rate
V_L = the bond's value for the lower one-year rate
C = coupon payment

then the cash flow at a node is either:

$$V_H + C \text{ for the higher one-year rate}$$

$$V_L + C \text{ for the lower one-year rate}$$

The present value of these two cash flows using the one-year rate at the node, r_*, is

$$\frac{V_H + C}{(1 + r_*)} = \text{present value for the higher one-year rate}$$

$$\frac{V_L + C}{(1 + r_*)} = \text{present value for the lower one-year rate}$$

Then, the value of the bond at the node is found as follows:

$$\text{Value at a node} = \frac{1}{2}\left[\frac{V_H + C}{(1 + r_*)} + \frac{V_L + C}{(1 + r_*)}\right]$$

Constructing the Binomial Interest Rate Tree

The construction of an interest rate tree involves an iterative price in which one begins by creating a one-year interest rate tree to price out the two-year on-the-run issue. The tree will depend on the interest rate volatility assumed. We will not describe the process here.[9]

Assuming a volatility of 10%, Exhibit 18.7 show the one-year tree. Let's see why this is an arbitrage-free tree. If $r_{1,L}$ is 4.4448%, then the corresponding value for the higher one-year rate is 5.4289% (= 4.4448% $e^{2 \times 0.10}$). The bond's value in Year 1 is determined as follows. The bond's value in Year 2 is $104.2. The present value of the bond's value for the higher one-year rate, V_H, is $98.834 (= $104.2/1.054289). The present value of the bond's value for the lower one-year rate, V_L, is $99.766 (= $104.2/1.044448). Adding the

---

[9]The process is explained in Fabozzi, *Bond Markets, Analysis, and Strategies*.

EXHIBIT 18.7 The One-Year Rates for Year 1 Using the Two-Year 4.2% On-the-Run Issue

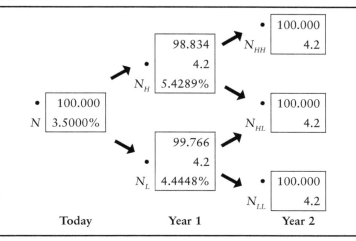

| | Today | Year 1 | Year 2 |

coupon to V_H and V_L, we get $103.034 as the cash flow for the higher rate and $103.966 as the cash flow for the lower rate.

The present value of the two cash flows using the one-year rate at the node to the left, 3.5%, gives:

$$\frac{V_H + C}{1 + r_*} = \frac{\$103.034}{1.035} = \$99.550$$

and

$$\frac{V_L + C}{(1 + r_*)} = \frac{\$103.966}{1.035} = \$100.450$$

The average present value is $100, which is the value at the and is equal to the observed market price of $100.

We can "grow" this tree for one more year by determining r_2. Now we will use the three-year on-the-run issue, the 4.7% coupon bond, to grow the tree. The interest rates on the tree must be such at that they will produce a bond value of $100 (since the three-year on-the-run issue has a market price of $100) and is consistent with (1) a volatility assumption of 10%, (2) a current one-year rate of 3.5%, and (3) the two rates one year from now of 4.4448% (the lower rate) and 5.4289% (the higher rate). Exhibit 18.8 shows the final binomial tree.

EXHIBIT 18.8 Binomial Interest Rate Tree for Valuing Up to a Four-Year Bond for Issuer (10% volatility assumed)

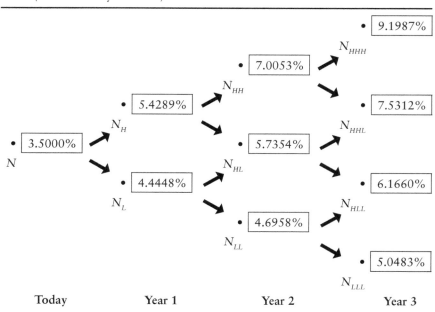

| Today | Year 1 | Year 2 | Year 3 |

Valuing an Option-Free Bond with the Tree

Now consider an option-free bond with four years remaining to maturity and a coupon rate of 6.5%. The value of this bond can be calculated by discounting the cash flow at the spot rates in Exhibit 18.5 as shown in the following calculation:

$$\frac{\$6.5}{(1.035)^1} + \frac{\$6.5}{(1.042147)^2} + \frac{\$6.5}{(1.047345)^{33}} + \frac{\$100 + \$6.5}{(1.052707)^4} = \$104.643$$

An option-free bond that is valued using the binomial interest rate tree should have the same value as discounting by the spot rates.

Thus, Exhibit 18.8 shows the one-year rates or binomial interest rate tree that can then be used to value any bond for this issuer with a maturity up to four years. To illustrate how to use the binomial interest rate tree, consider once again the 6.5% option-free bond with three years remaining to maturity. Also assume that the issuer's on-the-run yield curve is the one in Exhibit 18.6, hence the appropriate binomial interest rate tree is the one in Exhibit 18.8. Exhibit 18.9 shows the various values in the discounting

EXHIBIT 18.9 Valuing an Option-Free Bond with Four Years to Maturity and a Coupon Rate of 6.5% (10% volatility assumed)

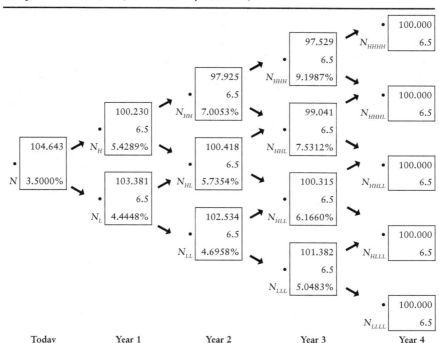

process, and produces a bond value of $104.643. This value is identical to the bond value found when we discounted at the spot rates. This clearly demonstrates that the valuation model is consistent with the standard valuation model for an option-free bond.

Valuing a Callable Bond

Now we demonstrate how the binomial interest rate tree can be applied to value a callable bond. The valuation process proceeds in the same fashion as an option-free bond with one exception: When the call option can be exercised by the issuer, the bond value at a node must be changed to reflect the lesser of its values if it is not called (i.e., the value obtained by applying the recursive valuation formula described previously) and the call price.

For example, consider a 6.5% corporate bond with four years remaining to maturity that is callable in one year at $100. Exhibit 18.10 shows two values at each node of the binomial interest rate tree. The discounting process explained above is used to calculate the first of the two values at each node. The second value is the value based on whether the issue will be called. For simplicity, let's assume that this issuer calls the issue if it exceeds the call price. Then, in Exhibit 18.10 at nodes N_L, N_H, N_{LL}, N_{HL}, N_{LLL}, and N_{HLL} the values from the recursive valuation formula are $101.968, $100.032, $101.723, $100.270, $101.382, and $100.315, respectively. These values exceed the assumed call price ($100) and, therefore, the second value is $100 rather than the calculated value. It is the second value that is used in subsequent calculations. The root of the tree indicates that the value for this callable bond is $102.899.

EXHIBIT 18.10   Valuing a Callable Bond with Four Years to Maturity, a Coupon Rate of 6.5%, and Callable in One Year at 100 (10% volatility assumed)

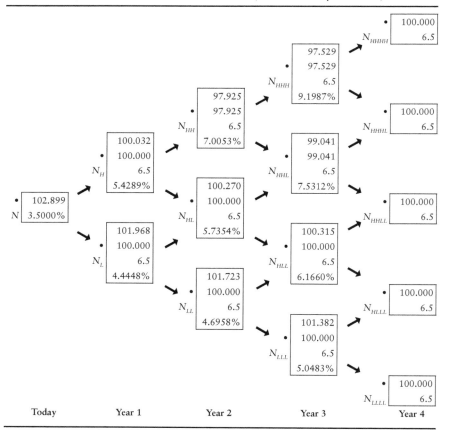

The question we have not addressed in our illustration, which is nonetheless important, is the circumstances under which the issuer will call the bond. A detailed explanation of the call rule is beyond the scope of this chapter. Basically, it involves determining when it would be optimal for the issuer, on an after-tax basis, to call the issue.

Determining the Call Option Value

The value of a callable bond is equal to the value of an option-free bond minus the value of the call option. This means that

> Value of a call option
> = Value of an option-free bond – Value of a callable bond

We have just seen how the value of an option-free bond and the value of a callable bond can be determined. The difference between the two values is therefore the value of the call option.

In our illustration, the value of the option-free bond is $104.643. If the call price is $100 in each year, the value of the callable bond is $102.899. Therefore, the value of the call option is $1.744 (= $104.634 – $102.899).

Extension to Other Embedded Options

The bond valuation framework presented here can be used to analyze other embedded options such as put options, caps and floors on floating rate notes, and the optional accelerated redemption granted to an issuer in fulfilling its sinking fund requirement.

For example, let's consider a putable bond. Suppose that a 6.5% coupon bond with four years remaining to maturity is putable in one year at par ($100). Also assume that the appropriate binomial interest rate tree for this issuer is the one in Exhibit 18.8. It can be demonstrated that the value of this putable bond is $105.327.

Since the value of a putable bond can be expressed as the value of an option-free bond plus the value of a put option on that bond, this means that

> Value of a put option
> = Value of an option-free bond – Value of a putable bond

In our example, since the value of the putable bond is $105.327 and the value of the corresponding option-free bond is $104.643, the value of the put option is –$0.684. The negative sign indicates the issuer has sold the option, or equivalently, the investor has purchased the option.

The framework can also be used to value a bond with multiple or interrelated embedded options. The bond values at each node are altered based on whether one of the options is exercised.

Volatility and the Theoretical Value

In our example, interest rate volatility was assumed to be 10%. The volatility assumption has an important impact on the theoretical value. More specifically, the higher the expected volatility, the higher the value of an option. The same is true for an option embedded in a bond. Correspondingly, this affects the value of the bond with an embedded option. For example, for a callable bond, a higher interest rate volatility assumption means that the value of the call option increases and, since the value of the option-free bond is not affected, the value of the callable bond must be lower. For a putable bond, higher interest rate volatility means that its value will be higher.

To illustrate this, suppose that a 20% volatility is assumed rather than 10%. The value of the hypothetical callable bond is $102.108 if volatility is assumed to be 20% compared to $102.899 if volatility is assumed to be 10%. The hypothetical putable bond at 20% volatility has a value of $106.010 compared to $105.327 at 10% volatility.

In the construction of the binomial interest rate, it was assumed that volatility is the same for each year. The methodology can be extended to incorporate a term structure of volatility.

Option-Adjusted Spread

Suppose the market price of the four-year 6.5% callable bond is $102.218 and the theoretical value assuming 10% volatility is $102.899. This means that this bond is cheap by $0.681 according to the valuation model. The option-adjusted spread is the constant spread that, when added to all the one-year rates on the binomial interest rate tree, will make the arbitrage-free value (i.e., the value produced by the binomial model) equal to the market price.

In our illustration, if the market price is $102.218, the OAS would be the constant spread added to every rate in Exhibit 18.10 that will make the arbitrage-free value equal to $102.218. The solution in this case would be 35 basis points.

As with the value of a bond with an embedded option, the OAS will depend on the volatility assumption. For a given bond price, the higher the interest rate volatility assumed, the lower the OAS for a callable bond. For example, if volatility is 20% rather than 10%, the OAS would be –6 basis points. This illustration clearly demonstrates the importance of the volatility assumption. Assuming volatility of 10%, the OAS is 35 basis points. At

20% volatility, the OAS declines and in this case is negative and therefore the bond is overvalued relative to the model.

How do we interpret the OAS? In general, a nominal spread between two yields reflects differences in the:

1. Credit risk of the two issues.
2. Liquidity risk of the two issues.
3. Option risk of the two issues.

For example, if one of the issues is a non-U.S. Treasury issue with an embedded option and the benchmark interest rates are the rates for the U.S. Treasury on-the-run securities, then the nominal spread is a measure of the difference due to the:

1. Credit risk of the non-Treasury issue.
2. Liquidity risk associated with the non-Treasury issue.
3. Option risk associated with the non-Treasury issue that is not present in Treasury issues.

What the OAS seeks to do is remove from the nominal spread the amount that is due to the option risk. The measure is called an OAS because (1) it is a spread and (2) it adjusts the cash flows for the option when computing the spread to the benchmark interest rates. The second point can be seen from Exhibits 18.9 and 18.10. Notice that at each node the value obtained from the backward induction method is adjusted based on the call option and the call rule. Thus, the resulting spread is "option adjusted."

Consequently, if the Treasury on-the-run issues are used as the benchmark because the call option has been taken into account, the OAS is measuring the compensation for the:

1. Credit risk of the non-Treasury issue.
2. Liquidity risk associated with the non-Treasury issue.

So, for example, an OAS of 160 basis points for a callable BBB industrial issue would mean that based on the valuation model (including the volatility assumption), the OAS is compensation for the credit risk and the lower liquidity of the industrial issue relative to the Treasury benchmark issues. The OAS has removed the compensation for the call feature present in the industrial issue that is not present in the Treasury benchmark interest rates.

However, suppose that the benchmark interest rates are the on-the-run interest rates for the issuer, as in our illustration of how to use the binomial model to value a bond with an embedded option. Then there is no difference in the credit risk between the benchmark interest rates and the non-Treasury issue. That is, the OAS reflects only the difference in the liquidity of an issue relative to the on-the-run issues. The valuation has removed the spread due to the option risk and using the issuer's own benchmark interest rates removes the credit risk.

Suppose instead that the benchmark interest rates used are not of that particular issuer but the on-the-run issues for issuers in the same sector of the bond market and the same credit rating of the issue being analyzed. For example, suppose that the callable bond issue being analyzed is that issued by the XYZ Manufacturing Company, a BBB industrial company. An on-the-run yield curve can be estimated for the XYZ Manufacturing Company. Using that on-the-run yield curve, the OAS reflects the difference in the liquidity risk between the particular callable bond of the XYZ Manufacturing Company analyzed and the on-the-run issues of the XYZ Manufacturing Company. However, if instead the benchmark interest rates used to value the callable bond of the XYZ Manufacturing Company are those of a generic BBB industrial company, the OAS reflects (1) the difference between the liquidity risk of the XYZ Manufacturing Company's callable bond and that of a generic BBB industrial company and (2) differences between event risk/credit risk specific to XYZ Manufacturing Company's issue beyond generic BBB credit risk.

Consequently, we know that an OAS is a spread after adjusting for the embedded option. But we know nothing else until the benchmark interest rates are identified. Without knowing the benchmark used—Treasury on-the-run yield curve, an issuer's on-the-run yield curve, or a generic on-the-run yield curve for issuers in the same sector of the bond market and of the same credit rating—we cannot interpret what the OAS is providing compensation for. Some market participants might view this as unrealistic since most of the time the on-the-run Treasury yield curve is used and therefore the OAS reflects credit risk and liquidity risk. However, vendors of analytical systems and most dealer models allow an investor to specify the benchmark interest rates to be used.

VALUATION OF MBS AND ABS

Now we will demonstrate how to value mortgage-backed and asset-backed securities. We begin by reviewing the conventional framework—static cash flow yield analysis—and its limitations. Then we discuss a more advanced technology, the Monte Carlo model and a by-product of the model, the OAS analysis. The static cash flow yield methodology is the simplest of the two valuation technologies to apply, although it may offer little insight into the relative value of a mortgage-backed or asset-backed security. The option-adjusted spread technology while far superior in valuation is based on assumptions that must be recognized by an investor and the sensitivity of the security's value to changes in those assumptions must be tested.

Static Cash Flow Yield Analysis

As explained in the previous chapter, the yield on any financial instrument is the interest rate that makes the present value of the expected cash flow equal to its market price plus accrued interest. For mortgage-backed and asset-backed securities, the yield calculated is called a *cash flow yield*. The problem in calculating the cash flow yield of a mortgage-backed and asset-backed security is that because of prepayments (voluntary and involuntary) the cash flow is unknown. Consequently, to determine a cash flow yield some assumption about the prepayment rate must be made.

The cash flow for a mortgage-backed and asset-backed security is typically monthly. The convention is to compare the yield on a mortgage-backed security to that of a Treasury coupon security by calculating the MBS's bond-equivalent yield. As explained in the previous chapter, the bond-equivalent yield for a Treasury coupon security is found by doubling the semiannual yield. However, it is incorrect to follow that convention for mortgage-backed and asset-backed securities because the investor has the opportunity to generate greater interest by reinvesting the more frequent cash flows. The market practice/convention is to calculate a yield so as to make it comparable to the yield to maturity on a bond-equivalent yield basis. The formula for annualizing the monthly cash flow yield for a mortgage-backed security is as follows:

$$\text{Bond-equivalent yield} = 2[(1 + i_M)^6 - 1]$$

where i_M is the monthly interest rate that will equate the present value of the projected monthly cash flow to the market price (plus accrued interest) of the security.

As we explained in the previous chapter, all yield measures suffer from problems that limit their use in assessing a security's potential return. The yield to maturity has two major shortcomings as a measure of a bond's potential return. To realize the stated yield to maturity, the investor must: (1) reinvest the coupon payments at a rate equal to the yield to maturity, and (2) hold the bond to the maturity date. The reinvestment of the coupon payments is critical and for long-term bonds can be as much as 80% of the bond's return. The risk of having to reinvest the interest payments at less than the computed yield is called *reinvestment risk*. The risk associated with having to sell the security prior to the maturity date is called *interest rate risk*.

These shortcomings are equally applicable to the cash flow yield measure: (1) the projected cash flows are assumed to be reinvested at the cash flow yield, and (2) the mortgage-backed and asset-backed security is assumed to be held until the final payout based on some prepayment assumption. The importance of reinvestment risk, the risk that the cash flow will have to be reinvested at a rate lower than the cash flow yield, is particularly important for mortgage-backed and asset-backed securities because payments are monthly and both interest and principal (regularly scheduled repayments and prepayments) must be reinvested. Moreover, an additional assumption is that the projected cash flow is actually realized. If the prepayment experience is different from the prepayment rate assumed, the cash flow yield will not be realized.

Given the computed cash flow yield and the average life for a mortgage-backed or asset-backed security based on some prepayment assumption, the next step is to compare the yield to the yield for a comparable Treasury security. "Comparable" is typically defined as a Treasury security with the same maturity as the average life of the security. The difference between the cash flow yield and the yield on a comparable Treasury security is called a *nominal spread*. We described this measure in the previous chapter.

Unfortunately, it is the nominal spread that some investors will use as a measure of relative value. However, this spread masks the fact that a portion of the nominal spread is compensation for accepting prepayment risk. For example, support tranches in agency collateralized mortgage obligations (CMOs) are offered at large nominal spreads. However, the spread embodies the substantial prepayment risk associated with support tranches. An investor who buys solely on the basis of nominal spread—dubbed a "yield hog"—fails to determine whether that nominal spread offers potential compensation given the substantial prepayment risk faced by the holder of a support tranche.

Instead of nominal spread, investors use the OAS measure because it quantifies the potential compensation after adjusting for prepayment risk. Earlier we demonstrated how this measure is computed within the context of the lattice model. Below we will explain how this measure is computed using the model employed for mortgage-backed securities and certain types of asset-backed securities.

Monte Carlo Simulation

In bond valuation modeling, there are two methodologies commonly used to value securities with embedded options—the lattice model and the Monte Carlo model. The lattice model was explained earlier in the chapter. The Monte Carlo simulation model involves simulating a sufficiently large number of potential interest rate paths in order to assess the value of a security along these different paths. This model is the most flexible of the two valuation methodologies for valuing interest rate sensitive instruments where the history of interest rates is important. Mortgage-backed and some asset-backed securities are commonly valued using this model. As explained below, a by-product of a valuation model is the OAS.

Interest Rate History and Path-Dependent Cash Flows

For some fixed income securities and derivative instruments, the periodic cash flows are *path dependent*. This means that the cash flow received in one period is determined not only by the current interest rate level, but also by the path that interest rates took to get to the current level.

In the case of mortgage passthrough securities (or simply, passthroughs), prepayments are path dependent because this month's prepayment rate depends on whether there have been prior opportunities to refinance since the underlying mortgages were originated. Unlike passthroughs, the decision as to whether a corporate issuer will elect to refund an issue when the current rate is below the issue's coupon rate is not dependent on how rates evolved over time to reach the current level.

Pools of passthroughs are used as collateral for the creation of collateralized mortgage obligations (CMOs) as discussed in Chapter 17. Consequently, for CMOs, there are typically two sources of path dependency in a tranche's cash flows. First, the collateral prepayments are path dependent as discussed earlier. Second, the cash flow to be received in the current month by a tranche depends on the outstanding balances of the other tranches in the deal. Thus, we need the history of prepayments to calculate these balances.

Valuing Mortgage-Backed Securities[10]

Conceptually, the valuation of passthroughs using the Monte Carlo method is simple. In practice, however, it is very complex. The simulation involves generating a set of cash flows based on simulated future mortgage refinancing rates, which in turn imply simulated prepayment rates.

Valuation modeling for CMOs is similar to valuation modeling for passthroughs, although the difficulties are amplified because the issuer has reallocated both the prepayment and interest rate risk into smaller pieces and distributed these risks among the tranches. The sensitivity of the

[10]Portions of the material in this section and the one to follow are adapted from Frank J. Fabozzi, Scott F. Richard, and David S. Horowitz, "Valuation of CMOs," Chapter 6 in *Advances in the Valuation and Management of Mortgage-Backed Securities*, ed. Frank J. Fabozzi (Hoboken, N.J.: John Wiley & Sons, 1998).

passthroughs comprising the collateral to these two risks is not transmitted equally to every tranche. Some of the tranches wind up more sensitive to prepayment and interest rate risk than the collateral, while some of them are much less sensitive.

Using Simulation to Generate Interest Rate Paths and Cash Flows   The typical model that Wall Street firms and commercial vendors use to generate random interest rate paths takes as input today's term structure of interest rates and a volatility assumption. The term structure of interest rates is the theoretical spot rate (or zero coupon) curve implied by today's Treasury securities which serve as a benchmark. The volatility assumption determines the dispersion of future interest rates in the simulation. The simulations should be calibrated to the market so that the average simulated price of a zero-coupon Treasury bond equals today's actual price.

Each model has its own model of the evolution of future interest rates and its own volatility assumptions. Typically, there are no important differences in the interest rate models of dealer firms and vendors, although their volatility assumptions can be significantly different.

The random paths of interest rates should be generated from an arbitrage-free model of the future term structure of interest rates. By arbitrage-free it is meant that the model replicates today's term structure of interest rates, an input of the model, and that for all future dates there is no possible arbitrage within the model.

The simulation works by generating many scenarios of future interest rate paths. In each month of the scenario, a monthly interest rate and a mortgage refinancing rate are generated. The monthly interest rates are used to discount the projected cash flows in the scenario. The mortgage refinancing rate is needed to determine the cash flow because it represents the opportunity cost the mortgagor is facing at that time.

If the refinancing rates are high relative to the mortgagor's original coupon rate (i.e., the rate on the mortgagor's loan), the mortgagor will have less incentive to refinance, or even a positive disincentive (i.e., the homeowner will avoid moving in order to avoid refinancing). If the refinancing rate is low relative to the mortgagor's original coupon rate, the mortgagor has an incentive to refinance.

Prepayments are projected by feeding the refinancing rate and loan characteristics, such as age, into a prepayment model. Given the projected prepayments, the cash flow along an interest rate path can be determined.

To make this process more concrete, consider a newly issued mortgage passthrough security with a maturity of 360 months. Exhibit 18.11 shows N simulated interest rate path scenarios. Each scenario consists of a path of 360 simulated one-month future interest rates. Just how many paths should

EXHIBIT 18.11 Simulated Paths of One-Month Future Interest Rates

	Interest Rate Path Number						
Month	1	2	3	...	*n*	...	N
1	$f_1(1)$	$f_1(2)$	$f_1(3)$	...	$f_1(n)$	...	$f_1(N)$
2	$f_2(1)$	$f_2(2)$	$f_2(3)$	...	$f_2(n)$	...	$f_2(N)$
3	$f_3(1)$	$f_3(2)$	$f_3(3)$	...	$f_3(n)$	...	$f_3(N)$
t	$f_t(1)$	$f_t(2)$	$f_t(3)$	...	$f_t(n)$	...	$f_t(N)$
358	$f_{358}(1)$	$f_{358}(2)$	$f_{358}(3)$	...	$f_{358}(n)$	...	$f_{358}(N)$
359	$f_{359}(1)$	$f_{359}(2)$	$f_{359}(3)$	...	$f_{359}(n)$	...	$f_{359}(N)$
360	$f_{360}(1)$	$f_{360}(2)$	$f_{360}(3)$	...	$f_{360}(n)$	...	$f_{360}(N)$

Notation:
$f_t(n)$ = one-month future interest rate for month *t* on path *n*
N = total number of interest rate paths

EXHIBIT 18.12 Simulated Paths of Mortgage Refinancing Rates

	Interest Rate Path Number						
Month	1	2	3	...	*n*	...	N
1	$r_1(1)$	$r_1(2)$	$r_1(3)$	...	$r_1(n)$	...	$r_1(N)$
2	$r_2(1)$	$r_2(2)$	$r_2(3)$	...	$r_2(n)$	...	$r_2(N)$
3	$r_3(1)$	$r_3(2)$	$r_3(3)$	...	$r_3(n)$	...	$r_3(N)$
t	$r_t(1)$	$r_t(2)$	$r_t(3)$	...	$r_t(n)$	...	$r_t(N)$
358	$r_{358}(1)$	$r_{358}(2)$	$r_{358}(3)$	...	$r_{358}(n)$	...	$r_{358}(N)$
359	$r_{359}(1)$	$r_{359}(2)$	$r_{359}(3)$	...	$r_{359}(n)$	...	$r_{359}(N)$
360	$r_{360}(1)$	$r_{360}(2)$	$r_{360}(3)$	...	$r_{360}(n)$	...	$r_{360}(N)$

Notation:
$r_t(n)$ = mortgage refinancing rate for month *t* on path *n*
N = total number of interest rate paths

be generated is explained later. Exhibit 18.12 shows the paths of simulated mortgage refinancing rates corresponding to the scenarios shown in Exhibit 18.11. Assuming these mortgage refinancing rates, the cash flow for each scenario path is shown in Exhibit 18.13.

EXHIBIT 18.13 Simulated Cash Flow on Each of the Interest Rate Paths

	Interest Rate Path Number						
Month	1	2	3	...	n	...	N
1	$C_1(1)$	$C_1(2)$	$C_1(3)$	...	$C_1(n)$	...	$C_1(N)$
2	$C_2(1)$	$C_2(2)$	$C_2(3)$	...	$C_2(n)$	...	$C_2(N)$
3	$C_3(1)$	$C_3(2)$	$C_3(3)$	...	$C_3(n)$	...	$C_3(N)$
t	$C_t(1)$	$C_t(2)$	$C_t(3)$	...	$C_t(n)$	...	$C_t(N)$
358	$C_{358}(1)$	$C_{358}(2)$	$C_{358}(3)$	...	$C_{358}(n)$	...	$C_{358}(N)$
359	$C_{359}(1)$	$C_{359}(2)$	$C_{359}(3)$	...	$C_{359}(n)$	...	$C_{359}(N)$
360	$C_{360}(1)$	$C_{360}(2)$	$C_{360}(3)$	...	$C_{360}(n)$	...	$C_{360}(N)$

Notation:
$C_t(n)$ = cash flow for month t on path n
N = total number of interest rate paths

Calculating the Present Value for a Scenario Interest Rate Path Given the cash flow on an interest rate path, its present value can be calculated. The discount rate for determining the present value is the simulated spot rate for each month on the interest rate path plus an appropriate spread. The spot rate on a path can be determined from the simulated future monthly rates in Exhibit 18.13. The relationship that holds between the simulated spot rate for month T on path n and the simulated future one-month rates is

$$z_T(n) = \{[1 + f_1(n)][1 + f_2(n)]...[2 + f_T(n)]\}^{1/T} - 1$$

where

$z_T(n)$ = simulated spot rate for month T on path n
$f_j(n)$ = simulated future one-month rate for month j on path n

Consequently, the interest rate path for the simulated future one-month rates can be converted to the interest rate path for the simulated monthly spot rates as shown in Exhibit 18.14.

Therefore, the present value of the cash flow for month T on interest rate path n discounted at the simulated spot rate for month T plus some spread is

$$PV[C_T(n)] = \frac{C_T(n)}{[1 + z_T(n) + K]^{1/T}}$$

EXHIBIT 18.14   Simulated Paths of Monthly Spot Rates

Month	Interest Rate Path Number						
	1	2	3	...	n	...	N
1	$z_1(1)$	$z_1(2)$	$z_1(3)$	...	$z_1(n)$	...	$z_1(N)$
2	$z_2(1)$	$z_2(2)$	$z_2(3)$	...	$z_2(n)$	...	$z_2(N)$
3	$z_3(1)$	$z_3(2)$	$z_3(3)$	...	$z_3(n)$	...	$z_3(N)$
t	$z_t(1)$	$z_t(2)$	$z_t(3)$	...	$z_t(n)$	...	$z_t(N)$
358	$z_{358}(1)$	$z_{358}(2)$	$z_{358}(3)$	...	$z_{358}(n)$	...	$z_{358}(N)$
359	$z_{359}(1)$	$z_{359}(2)$	$z_{359}(3)$	...	$z_{359}(n)$	...	$z_{359}(N)$
360	$z_{360}(1)$	$z_{360}(2)$	$z_{360}(3)$	...	$z_{360}(n)$	...	$z_{360}(N)$

Notation:
$z_t(n)$ = spot rate for month t on path n
N = total number of interest rate paths

where

$PV[C_T(n)]$ = present value of cash flow for month T on path n
$C_T(n)$ = cash flow for month T on path n
$z_T(n)$ = spot rate for month T on path n
K = spread

The present value for path n is the sum of the present values of the cash flows for each month on path n. That is,

$$PV[\text{Path}(n)] = PV[C_1(n)] + PV[C_2(n)] + \ldots + PV[C_{360}(n)]$$

where PV[Path(n)] is the present value of interest rate path n.

Determining the Theoretical Value and OAS

The present value of a given interest rate path is the theoretical value of a passthrough if that path was actually realized. The theoretical value of the passthrough can be determined by calculating the average of the theoretical values of all the interest rate paths. That is,

$$\text{Theoretical value} = \frac{PV[\text{Path}(1)] + PV[\text{Path}(2)] + \ldots + PV[\text{Path}(N)]}{N}$$

where N is the number of interest rate paths.

This procedure for valuing a passthrough is also followed for a CMO tranche. The cash flow for each month on each interest rate path is found according to the principal repayment and interest distribution rules of the deal. In order to do this, a model for reverse engineering a CMO deal is needed.

In the Monte Carlo model, the OAS is the spread that, when added to all the spot rates on all interest rate paths, will make the average present value of the paths equal to the observed market price (plus accrued interest). Mathematically, OAS is the value for K (the spread) that will satisfy the following condition:

$$\frac{PV[\text{Path}(1)] + PV[\text{Path}(2)] + \ldots + PV[\text{Path}(N)]}{N} = \text{Market price}$$

where N is the number of interest rate paths. The left-hand side of the above equation looks identical to that of the equation for the theoretical value. The difference is that the objective is to determine what spread, K, will make the model produce a theoretical value equal to the market price.

Special Considerations in Valuing Asset-Backed Securities

The valuation model that should be used for valuing an asset-backed security (ABS) depends on the characteristic of the loans or receivables backing the deal. An ABS can have one of the following three characteristics:

Characteristic 1. The ABS does not have a prepayment option.

Characteristic 2. The ABS has a prepayment option but borrowers do not exhibit a tendency to prepay when refinancing rates fall below the loan rate.

Characteristic 3. The ABS has a prepayment option and borrowers are expected to prepay when refinancing rates fall below the loan rate.

An example of a Characteristic 1–type ABS is a security backed by credit card receivables. An example of a Characteristic 2–type ABS is a security backed by automobile loans. A security backed by closed-end home equity loans where the borrowers are of high quality (i.e., prime borrowers) is an example of a Characteristic 3–type ABS. There are some real-estate backed ABS where the verdict is still out as to the degree to which borrowers take advantage of refinancing opportunities. Specifically, these include securities backed by manufactured housing loans and securities backed by closed-end home equity loans to borrowers classified as low quality borrowers.

There are two possible approaches to valuing an ABS. They are the:

1. Zero-volatility spread (Z-spread) approach.
2. Option-adjusted spread (OAS) approach.

For the Z-spread approach (discussed in the previous chapter), the interest rates used to discount the cash flows are the spot rates plus the zero-volatility spread. The value of an ABS is then the present value of the cash flows based on these discount rates. The Z-spread approach does not consider the prepayment option. Consequently, the Z-spread approach should be used to value Characteristic 1–type ABS. (In terms of the relationship between the Z-spread, OAS, and option cost discussed earlier in this chapter, this means that the value of the option is zero and therefore the Z-spread is equal to the OAS.) Since the Z-spread is equal to the OAS, the Z-spread approach to valuation can be used.

The Z-spread approach can also be used to value Characteristic 2–type ABS because while the borrowers do have a prepayment option, the option is not typically exercised when rates decline below the loan rate. Thus, as with Characteristic 1–type ABS, the Z-spread is equal to the OAS.

The OAS approach—which is considerably more computationally extensive than the Z-spread approach—is used to value securities where there is an embedded option and there is an expectation that the option will be exercised if it makes economic sense for the borrower to do so. Consequently, the OAS approach is used to value Characteristic 3–type ABS. The choice is then whether to use the lattice model or the Monte Carlo simulation model. Since typically the cash flow for an ABS with a prepayment option is interest rate path dependent—as with a mortgage-backed security—the Monte Carlo simulation model is used.

When the Monte Carlo model must be employed for an ABS, then there are some modifications to the model relative to its application for valuing agency mortgage-backed securities. First, instead of the mortgage refinancing rate, the appropriate rate is the borrowing rate for comparable loans of the underlying loan pool. Moreover, an assumption must be made about the relationship between the relevant borrowing rate and the Treasury rate. Second, given the refinancing rates, the collateral's cash flows on each interest rate path can be generated. This requires a prepayment and default/recovery model to project involuntary prepayments.

KEY POINTS

* The traditional approach to bond valuation is to discount every cash flow using the same interest rate. The proper way is to value a bond using an arbitrage-free valuation model which involves viewing any bond as a package of zero-coupon bonds.

- To implement the arbitrage-free approach it is necessary to determine the theoretical rate that the U.S. Treasury would have to pay on a zero-coupon Treasury security for each maturity. The theoretical spot rates for Treasury securities represent the appropriate set of interest rates that should be used to value default-free cash flows.
- The Treasury spot rates can be used to value any default-free security. For a non-Treasury security, the theoretical value is not as easy to determine. The value of a non-Treasury security is found by discounting the cash flows by the Treasury spot rates plus a yield spread which reflects the additional risks.
- Nominal spread is the difference between the yield on a bond and the yield on a comparable maturity benchmark Treasury security. The nominal spread measure has two drawbacks which are overcome by the zero-volatility spread and the option-adjusted spread measures.
- The zero-volatility spread (Z-spread or static spread) is a measure of the spread that the investor would realize over the entire Treasury spot rate curve if the bond were held to maturity. The option-adjusted spread is the spread after adjusting for the value of the embedded option.
- Long-term spot rates are averages of the current single period spot rate and the forward rates.
- To develop an analytical framework for valuing a bond with an embedded option, it is necessary to decompose a bond's value into its component parts.
- The option-adjusted spread is a yield spread measure that converts dollar differences between value and market price.
- The implied cost of the option embedded in any bond can be obtained by calculating the difference between the OAS at the assumed volatility of interest rates and the zero-volatility spread.
- Once an interest rate tree is constructed that (1) is consistent with both the interest rate volatility assumption and the interest rate model and (2) generates the observed market price for each on-the-run issue, the tree can be used to value a bond with an embedded option given a set of rules to determine when the embedded option will be exercised.
- In all valuation models there is modeling risk, which is the risk that the underlying assumptions of a model may be incorrect.
- The lattice model can be used to values callable bond, putable bonds, floating-rate securities with caps and floors, and the optional accelerated redemption feature for a corporate bond with a sinking fund provision.
- The volatility (as measured by the standard deviation) assumption has an important impact on the theoretical value of a bond with an embedded option. More specifically, the higher the expected volatility, the higher the value of the embedded option is.

- The OAS removes from the nominal spread the amount that is due to the option risk. The measure is called an OAS because (1) it is a spread and (2) it adjusts the cash flows for the option when computing the spread to the benchmark interest rates.
- Knowing that the OAS is a spread after adjusting for the embedded option does not mean much unless we know the benchmark interest rates used to calculate the OAS.
- Mortgage-backed securities are valued using the Monte Carlo model.
- For mortgage-backed and asset-backed securities, a cash flow yield is calculated. The problem in calculating the cash flow yield of a mortgage-backed and asset-backed security is that because of prepayments the cash flow is unknown. Consequently, to determine a cash flow yield some assumption about the prepayment rate must be made.
- The nominal spread is the difference between the cash flow yield and the yield on a comparable Treasury security.
- Because mortgage-backed securities are path-dependent bonds, they cannot be valued using the lattice method but instead are valued using the Monte Carlo simulation method.
- Valuation modeling for CMOs is similar to valuation modeling for mortgage passthrough securities, although the difficulties are amplified because the issuer has reallocated both the prepayment and interest rate risk into smaller pieces and distributed these risks among the tranches.
- The valuation model that should be used for valuing an asset-backed security depends on the characteristic of the loans or receivables backing the deal.

QUESTIONS

1. The value of a Treasury security should be based on discounting each cash flow using the corresponding Treasury spot rate. Explain why this is true.

2. **a.** What is the typical relationship between credit spreads and term to maturity?
   b. How does this relationship change as credit ratings decline?

3. Explain what is meant by the nominal spread and the zero volatility spread? How are they computed?

4. Answer the following questions about valuing bonds with embedded options.
   a. Explain how an increase in expected interest rate volatility can decrease the value of a callable bond?

    b. What is the option-adjusted spread (OAS)?

    c. Explain the impact of greater expected interest rate volatility on the option-adjusted spread of a security.

5. Answer the following questions about valuing bonds with embedded options using a binomial interest rate tree:

    a. Why is the procedure for valuing a bond with an embedded option called "backward induction"?

    b. Why is the value produced by a binomial model referred to as an "arbitrage-free" value?

6. Suppose the following information is available from the Treasury spot curve:

    Three-year spot rate = 3.410%

    Four-year spot rate = 3.854%

    Answer the following questions.

    a. What is the implied forward rate on a one-year zero coupon Treasury three years from now quoted on a bond-equivalent basis?

    b. Antti Illmanen states, "Whenever the spot rate curve is upward sloping, the forwards imply rising rates. That is, rising rates are needed to offset long-term bonds' yield advantage. However, it does not mean that the market expects rising rates." Explain this statement.

7. Two portfolio managers are discussing the meaning of option-adjusted spread. Here is what each asserted:

> Manager 1: "The OAS is a measure of the value of the option embedded in the bond. That is, it is the compensation for accepting option risk."

> Manager 2: "The OAS is a measure of the spread relative to the Treasury on-the-run yield curve and reflects compensation for credit risk and liquidity risk."

Comment on each manager's interpretation of OAS.

8. For some MBS and ABS, the cash flows are path-dependent. Explain this statement.

CHAPTER 19

Bond Portfolio Strategies for Outperforming a Benchmark

Bülent Baygün, Ph.D.
Head of Interest Rate Strategy U.S.
BNP Paribas

Robert Tzucker, CFA
Inflation Trading
Credit Suisse

Increasingly, fund managers and, more importantly, chief investment officers are looking to measure the performance of portfolios and portfolio managers in an objective fashion. We believe that the best way to approach the problem is to adopt a "beat the benchmark" approach.

The first question that this approach raises is: "What is an appropriate benchmark?" This chapter addresses this question with a discussion of six widely recognized academic principles of a good index and then looks at a quantitative technique to achieve this goal. A good index should be (1) relevant to the investor, (2) representative of the market, (3) transparent in rules with consistent constituents, (4) investible and replicable, (5) based on high data quality, and (6) independent.

The second question that we address in this chapter follows naturally from the first, which is: "How does one beat a benchmark?" There are countless strategies that can be employed to outperform a benchmark. Outperformance in a bond portfolio is affected through a combination of fixed income asset class preferences, as well as duration and curve positioning choices, relative to the composition of the benchmark.[1] These choices are typically

---

[1]Christopher G. Luck, Thomas M. Richards, Kevin Terhaar, Jeffrey V. Bailey, Wayne A. Kozun, and Lee N. Price, *Benchmarks and Attribution Analysis* (Charlottsville, Va.: AIMR, 2001).

driven by a top-down approach, starting with views on the economy and the projected change in asset valuations. Surely, when considering measures of performance relative to the benchmark, return is but one aspect, the other being the risk taken to achieve the return. Effective portfolio management requires a framework that allows one to quantify risk versus return while balancing one against the other subject to the investment guidelines of the fund.

We also focus on balancing the risk versus return in a portfolio by employing a constrained optimization decision framework. This strategy involves taking views on (1) forward interest rates, (2) economic scenarios, (3) yield curve, (4) asset allocation, (5) duration, (6) risk tolerance, (7) issue selection, and (8) spread relationships.

SELECTING THE BENCHMARK INDEX

Selecting a benchmark by which to measure performance can be as important as the individual investment decisions themselves. The benchmark index is the basis against which all allocation decisions are made, including duration and curve positioning among others. Not only is the index used as a way to evaluate the relative performance of the manager, but it should be considered the best "passive" way to achieve the goals of the fund. If an inappropriate benchmark is selected relative to the goals of the fund, the manager may perform well against the index but fall short of the desired level of return of the fund. We discuss examples of this later in the chapter.

In the current environment there are myriad index providers, each with a different set of qualifying criteria defining the market. Selecting the appropriate index depends upon the needs of the fund. There are some widely recognized academic principles of what constitutes a good index. The major ones are discussed in the following sections. Later in the chapter, we discuss the pros and cons of defining a custom index and methods to accomplish that task while applying the principles described next.

Principle 1: Relevance to the Investor

Any index chosen as a benchmark must be a relevant investment for the investor. One of the most common examples of relevance is the quest to avoid a "natural concentration" between the business risk of the sponsoring entity and the invested portfolio. For example, a defense contractor would seek to benchmark its pension fund to an index with a low concentration of defense-related businesses. For this purpose many investors use custom indexes, excluding specific industries that cause natural concentration, while creating a benchmark. Another example that continues to gain traction is the choosing of an appropriate benchmark for a pension fund. In order to reduce volatility in its funding gap (or limit the possibility of creating a large funding gap), a pension fund manager may wish to use a portfolio of liabilities as a benchmark. The characteristics of the portfolio should closely resemble those of the actual pension fund liabilities. If, for example, the pension fund benchmarks to an index with too short of a duration (pension liabilities typically have very long durations), a move lower in rates could adversely affect its funding gap, even if the fund happens to outperform the index.[2]

Principle 2: Representative of the Market

A good benchmark should provide an accurate picture of the market it claims to represent. For example, if in a market most of the issues of a particular rating or industry sector are below the index size threshold, the performance of the index will be very different from the performance of the market. Hence two indexes, with different minimum thresholds, could exhibit vastly different industry and/or ratings distribution and consequently a vastly different risk–return profile.

Principle 3: Transparent Rules and Consistent Constituents

One of the definitions of a bond index is that it is a rules-based collection of bonds. It is, therefore, imperative that the rules defining the index are transparent and are applied objectively and in a consistent fashion. It is often tempting to bend the rules to accommodate particular market situations such as avoiding undue concentrations of a particular issuer or industry. For example, the downgrade of KPN in September 2001 left it teetering on the edge of the investment-grade threshold. This raised concerns among some high-yield fund managers that KPN would account for over a quarter of the euro high-yield universe were it to make the transition into high yield. These investors sought changes in the index in the form of sector and issuer caps to address this particular situation. If such caps are implemented, they violate the principles that define a good index.

The treatment of unrated paper for investment-grade indexes falls under this category. Many index providers include unrated paper in investment-grade indexes on the premise that if these instruments were to be rated they would end up in the investment grade. The other area where many index providers often vary from each other is the treatment of split-rated bonds, both for the rating tier they represent, as well as to determine whether they form part of the investment-grade universe or not.

---

[2]Frank J. Fabozzi (ed.) *Pension Fund Investment Management*, 2nd ed. (Hoboken, N.J.: John Wiley & Sons, 1997).

Principle 4: Investible and Replicable

An investor should be able to replicate the index and its performance with a small number of instruments as well as with relatively low transaction costs and without moving the market too much. For this reason the index constituents should be a set of bonds that have standard features, are liquid and trade actively in the secondary market. The ability to invest in the index through derivative instruments such as futures and total return swaps is an added attraction of an index.

Indexes with higher threshold levels typically contain fewer illiquid instruments and are thus easy to replicate for obvious reasons, and very often easy to beat as well. The reason for the latter is explained by the presence of a liquidity premium. Everything else being the same, bonds which are more liquid tend to trade at tighter levels than bonds which are less liquid, and the difference is known as the *liquidity premium*. Indexes that have more liquid bonds have lower yields than those with less liquid bonds, and consequently generate lower returns, which in turn implies that they are easier to outperform.

Principle 5: High-Quality Data

It goes without saying that an index is only as good as the data—both prices and static information—that is used to calculate it. Even a well-constituted and well-calculated index is unlikely to represent the moves of the market if it uses distorted prices. Unlike the equity market, where price transparency is high, there have historically been major impediments for getting true market prices for bonds and other over-the-counter (OTC) instruments. Most bond indexes are proprietary indexes that use in-house pricing, and are hence highly susceptible to be distorted by the presence/absence of long/ short positions on the trading book. Often, bonds where the trader has no position are not marked actively and reflect an indicative price and, for that reason, produce erroneous results for return and other calculations. To avoid these pitfalls it is therefore important to ensure that index pricing is from an accurate and reliable source.

Principle 6: Independence

One of the reasons equity indexes are so popular is that the prices used to calculate them are from an independent and a quasi-regulatory source. Independent indexes also make index and bond-level data available from multiple sources. This encourages the development of after-index products including derivatives, as there are multiple dealers active in the market and the resulting competition is good for all participants.

As many market participants observe, the above-mentioned principles are not entirely compatible, and thus create the need to strike the right balance. For example, in the quest to be representative of the market one could sacrifice liquidity of the instruments constituting the index. However, when striking the balance, one has to consider that for an index to be used as a benchmark, the ability to buy the constituent instruments is paramount. Therefore, we argue that Principle 4 is more important than Principle 2.

CREATING A CUSTOM INDEX

It may be that there are no indexes currently constructed that meet the exact needs of the investor. In this case, constructing an index from scratch or combining multiple indexes may very well be worth the time and effort in order to determine the appropriate benchmark. There are several methods that can be employed to create the benchmark index. We will discuss creating a rules-based index as well as using mean-variance frontier analysis to create the appropriate asset class mix within the index.

Rules-Based Indexes

For this exercise, we take a look at an actual index, the rules used to create the index, and how the index can be customized to better suit individual managers. We start by examining the Barclays Capital Global Inflation-Linked Bond Index. This index is a market value—weighted index that tracks the performance of inflation-linked bonds meeting specific credit and issue specific criteria. In the following sections, we look at some of the individual rules governing this index and describe the relevance of each to the above mentioned principles. These rules are reasonably common in creating indexes and can be applied in many situations.[3]

Market Type

In a market index, the debt must be domestic government only, meaning that it must be issued by a government in the currency of that country. This rule pertains to Principles 2, 3, and 4 above in that it is a clear description of the type of debt allowed (Principle 3), representative of the market of inflation-linked debt (Principle 2), and can be invested in easily through cash or total return swaps (Principle 4).

---

[3]David E. Kuenzi, "Strategy Benchmarks," *Journal of Portfolio Management* 29, no. 2 (2003): 46–56.

Inflation Index

The inflation index of each issue must be a commonly used domestic inflation measure. For example, in the United States, not seasonally adjusted CPI would be an acceptable index. This rule eliminates the risk of having a bond that uses a suspect means of indexing, following Principle 3, increasing transparency.

Rating

The rule for this index requires the foreign currency debt rating of the country to be AA–/Aa3 or better to be included in the index (S&P or Moody's, whichever is lower). This would exclude certain sovereign debt such as Greece, which meets the first two index rules, but has a lower rating. The Barclays Global Inflation-Linked Index is designed to have only high-grade sovereign issuance and, therefore, excludes higher-risk sovereigns.

Aggregate Face Value

The aggregate face value of any particular debt issue meeting the other rules must be at least worth $1 billion. In order to create stability and keep bonds from entering and leaving the index frequently, a rule can be imposed that if the bond falls below 90% of that lower limit it will be removed. This prevents bonds from arbitrarily dropping out due to routine currency fluctuations. Rules of this nature are typically devised under Principle 4 to reduce transaction costs and increase the replicability of the index.

Percentage of Index

Issues meeting all the previous criteria will be included in the index based on their market value weight in U.S. dollars at the rebalancing date (typically, the last day of the month). This market value weighting scheme is very popular among indexers for various reasons. First, it is easy to replicate. Second, typically relative market size will also determine relative liquidity. As a result, a smaller market has smaller weights; so, to replicate the index, a manager does not have as much problem sourcing the issues, which keeps costs lower. Although it is a useful rule, it may be problematic with Principle 1, as the construction using market weights may not be an optimal benchmark for an active manager. We explore this issue further in the next section.

Perhaps a manager has a global inflation-linked mandate but is not permitted to invest in issues that have longer than 10 years to maturity. Using the Global Inflation-Linked Index as a benchmark would violate Principle 1 discussed previously due to the irrelevance of the index. It would be unfair to evaluate a manager's performance relative to this benchmark because in the case of a rally, the longer bonds would likely outperform and the portfolio would unfairly be penalized. Likewise, a sell-off would favor the portfolio as longer duration assets underperformed. Instead, a rule can be created to bucket the index into maturities of less than 10 years and maturities of greater than 10 years. Now, the manager can be benchmarked more appropriately and performance more accurately measured. This is a relatively simple example of how rules-based index creation can be used to customize an index, so we will move on to more complicated problems next.

Using Mean–Variance Analysis to Customize an Index

Portfolio theory can play an important role in setting a benchmark for measuring performance. Traditionally, managers use efficient frontiers as a way of determining the most appropriate allocation of assets given either certain return targets or risk limits. Because historical data can only yield one efficient frontier with multiple efficient portfolios, by defining risk limits or targeted returns, the efficient portfolio can be used as a passive benchmark against which to perform tactical asset allocation. Rather than benchmarking against an index that uses arbitrary weighting based on the market value of the constituents, this method allows a manager to make decisions versus a historically efficient allocation, perhaps improving the decision making process. A custom index can also be useful when trying to optimize allocation in concert with the core operations of a business. For example, a bank with a core loan portfolio that would like to use its excess capital to generate returns to supplement their income may need to include that loan portfolio as an asset in the mean/variance analysis construct the most appropriate benchmark.

Setting Up the Problem

In order to create a custom index using mean/variance analysis, certain restrictions will have to be placed on the amount of the index that can consist of a given asset. This prevents, for example, U.S. agency bonds from becoming such a big part of the index that it is impossible to replicate in any size. If so desired, constraints on the size of the assets can also keep at least a nominal allocation to assets that may disappear from the solution if not otherwise constrained. Using minimum inclusion constraints makes sense to a manager that has a mandate to diversify into a certain asset or number of assets to some degree. Once the constraints have been determined, the efficient frontier can be solved using iterative solving software.

EXHIBIT 19.1   Gauging the Size of the Market (as of mid-2005)

Asset Class	Market Value Outstanding ($ billion)	Percentage of Total
U.S. Treasuries (>1 year to maturity)	2,000	66%
TIPS	320	11%
U.S. agency noncallable	690	23%

Source: Barclays Capital, *The Yieldbook.*

Several decisions have to be made before performing the mean variance analysis. First, and arguably most important, the asset classes need to be chosen. In this example, we take the view of a fixed income portfolio manager that is mandated to invest in a combination of noncallable U.S. agency bonds (Fannie Mae, Freddie Mac, Federal Home Loan Bank, etc.), Treasury inflation securities (TIPS), and U.S. Treasuries. Because there are few indexes that describe this universe, creating a custom index may provide the best alternative in this case.

The next step is to determine the constraints that should be imposed on the asset classes to make certain that the index meets the investible and replicable criteria from the previously described rules. The most straightforward way to determine appropriate maximum weights for each asset class is to look at the securities' weight as a proportion of the total weight of all of the asset classes and make a judgment as to a realistic percentage that could be invested based on the size of assets under management. For this exercise, we assume we have $5 billion under management. Comparing this number to the size of each of the classes of assets we are using looks very small. Exhibit 19.1 shows the relative sizes of our investible asset classes. It is immediately clear that our $5 billion under management is dwarfed by the size of securities outstanding, so we are not necessarily constrained by size. However, for the sake of prudence, our index should not consist entirely of one asset, so we will limit the analysis to use no more than 80% of any asset.

Finally, we set up the problem statement so that we can solve for the most efficient index allocation. To accomplish our goal, we perform a constrained optimization by minimizing the variance (risk) of the portfolio for different levels of returns (Markowitz model). The problem we are trying to solve is as follows:

Minimize

$$w^T C w$$

subject to

$$w^T \mu = \mu_p$$
$$w_i \leq 0.8$$
$$\Sigma w_i = 1 \text{ for all } i$$
$$w_i > 0$$

where

w = asset weight vector
C = covariance matrix
μ = expected return vector
μ_p = targeted expected return

The next step is to solve the problem. If a desired return target or a desired risk level is known, the problem can be solved for just one desired return level. If the desired level of return or risk is unknown, the frontier can be created and an efficient mix chosen after evaluating the different portfolio constructions. One thing to remember is that the portfolio return cannot be higher than the highest returning asset as long as no short positions are allowed, which is an assumption we are making, nor can it be lower than the lowest returning asset. To keep things simple and illustrate the point, we have decided to use the minimum risk portfolio as the benchmark. Exhibit 19.2 shows the efficient frontier as well as the market value-weighted index

EXHIBIT 19.2 Efficient Frontier and the Minimum Risk Portfolio

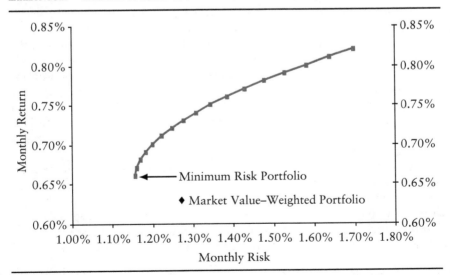

Source: Barclays Capital, *The Yieldbook.*

on a historical risk–return basis. It is obvious that the market value-weighted index is less than efficient, falling far below the frontier. The minimum risk portfolio gives us an advantage on expected return and expected risk.

The minimum risk portfolio consists of 26% Treasuries, 54% agencies, and 20% TIPS. This contrasts starkly from the market value-weighted index which consisted mostly of Treasury debt. One clear advantage of using this new benchmark is that if we choose to have no tactical views and purely match the benchmark, the expected performance of our portfolio is much better than with a market value-weighted index. Another advantage is that the additive value of tactical asset allocation choice can clearly be measured in terms of additional return or reduced risk versus the frontier, which takes into account much more information than a market value-weighted index when constructed. An investor using this technique can develop a custom benchmark for almost any purpose—whether it is to balance risk with the core business or to assist in asset liability management—and generate a meaningful investment hurdle with which to measure performance.[4]

BEATING THE BENCHMARK INDEX

Once the index is selected, the next step is to manage the portfolio around that index while trying to outperform it—or generate "alpha." The starting point in a typical investment strategy is a core view on the economy (GDP growth, inflation expectations, consumer behavior, employment picture, and so on.), which forms the basis of calls on asset prices going forward. For instance, in an environment where employment is rising, inflationary pressures are building, and there is a general surge in asset valuations, the Fed is likely to react by hiking rates, which in turn should give rise to higher rates and a flattening along the entire yield curve. Under these assumptions one could surmise, based on historical relationships, that high-quality asset spreads to Treasuries should widen. Therefore, a portfolio that is structured for this scenario (our "base case") likely would have a short duration bias relative to the index, have curve flattening exposure, and be underweight spread products.

So far the above approach has taken into account only one dimension of investment decisions, namely return. Before executing the strategy, we would want to assess the risks to the portfolio should the markets behave differently than what is depicted in the base case scenario. Typically, that involves stress-testing the portfolio under alternative (risk) scenarios. In other words, one would shock the curve and spreads in different ways and

---

[4]Laurence B. Siegel, *Benchmarks and Investment Management* (Charlottesville, Va.: Research Foundation of AIMR, 2003).

monitor the performance of the portfolio. If performance fell short of the risk guidelines, then one would go back and fix the portfolio in such a way to mitigate the problem—more often than not using ad hoc techniques— and then run the stress test on the revised portfolio. This process would be repeated until desirable risk characteristics are obtained. As an alternative to this iterative process, one could adopt a more formal quantitative framework that aims to optimize some performance criterion, incorporating the base case as well as the risk scenarios at the same time.[5] That is the approach we will describe below, as we have found it to be a very effective way to make informed investment decisions.

Choosing Scenarios for the Optimization

Forward rates should play a central role in the selection of the scenarios. This is a very subtle but important point that may be easily overlooked. Let us explain with some examples: If all the scenarios considered had rates higher than the forwards, the resulting optimal portfolio would undoubtedly have a short duration bias. Similarly, if all the scenarios gave rise to, say, flatter curves than the forwards, then one would end up with flattener positions in the portfolio. That is because in this framework risk assessment is limited to the scenarios under consideration. When all the scenarios are stacked on one side of the forwards it is tantamount to saying "there is no risk of rates being lower (or the curve being steeper) than the forwards." As a result, it would appear as if a portfolio that is short duration (or is fully loaded in flatteners) does not have any potential downside risk—the very characteristic of being optimal. However, it is clear that the portfolios constructed using these lopsided scenarios do not capture the risks in a realistic manner. The same is true when selecting the spread and breakeven scenarios for a portfolio that involves agencies and TIPS.

With this in mind, we consider four scenarios that bracket the current forwards. (All pricing is as of June 21, 2005.) We will not provide a description of the economic backdrop for each one of the scenarios, but suffice it to say that each one depicts significantly different economic conditions giving rise to a broad range of rate and spread changes for the third quarter of 2005 (see Exhibits 19.3, through 19.6). In particular, there are two bearish and two bullish scenarios. In terms of curve movements, two of the scenarios depict a flattening of the curve across all maturities (vis-à-vis the forwards), while one subsumes a steepening, and another one has steepeners in the front-end and flatteners from the five-year on out. Similarly, swap

---

[5]Richard Grinold and Ronald Kahn, *Active Portfolio Management: A Quantitative Approach for Producing Superior Returns and Controlling Risk* (New York: McGraw-Hill, 1999).

EXHIBIT 19.3 Three-Month Treasury Forecasts for Different Scenarios

Yield Levels (%) Current on 6/21/05		Yield Changes (bps)				
		Base Case	Stable Inflation	High Inflation	Growth Slowdown	Forwards
2 yr	3.70	35	10	55	−10	10
5 yr	3.84	36	1	71	−19	7
10 yr	4.06	29	−16	74	−31	4
30 yr	4.34	21	−24	76	−34	2

Source: Barclays Capital

EXHIBIT 19.4 Three-Month Swap Spread Forecasts (bps) for Different Scenarios

	Current	Base Case	Stable Inflation	High Inflation	Growth Slowdown
2 yr	35	34	32	42	30
5 yr	40	42	37	47	34
10 yr	40	42	37	48	34
30 yr	42	43	38	50	34

Source: Barclays Capital

EXHIBIT 19.5 Three-Month Agency–LIBOR Spread Forecasts (bps) for Different Scenarios

	Current	Base Case	Stable Inflation	High Inflation	Growth Slowdown
2 yr	−18	−20	−18	−22	−16
5 yr	−19	−20	−19	−23	−17
10 yr	−7	−9	−4	−12	−3
30 yr	−4	−6	−2	−9	0

Source: Barclays Capital

spreads to Treasuries and Agency–London Interbank Offered Rate (LIBOR) spreads, as well as TIPS breakevens encompass enough variety across the breadth of the scenarios.

Choosing the Optimization Criterion

Now that the scenarios are defined, the next step is to define the criterion for *optimization*. The parameters to optimize over are the market value weights

EXHIBIT 19.6 Three-Month TIPS Breakeven (%) and Inflation Forecasts for Different Scenarios

	Current	Base Case	Stable Inflation	High Inflation	Slow Growth
Jan 07	2.49	2.53	2.35	2.63	2.82
Jan 10	2.43	2.50	2.30	2.61	2.61
Jan 15	2.34	2.43	2.27	2.60	2.42
Jan 25	2.52	2.58	2.43	2.79	2.52
NSA CPI					
June		194.8	194.7	195.0	194.9
July		195.1	194.8	195.4	195.7

of the issues in the universe of eligible securities. Popular choices for the optimization criterion include the following:[6]

- *Maximize expected return.* This approach requires assigning (subjective) probabilities to the various scenarios. This approach has the advantage of being intuitive: most people already have some sense of what scenarios are more likely than others, and like to be able to impose those biases in the way they run their portfolio. Furthermore, it is easy to see the connection between the structure of the portfolio and the probabilities. The disadvantage is that because the criterion is based on average performance across the scenarios, one could not be assured of risks staying below allowable limits in specific scenarios unless there are additional explicit constraints. Another potential downside is that guessing some sensible probabilities adds another layer of subjectivity to what is already a rather subjective process—that is, the choice of a set of scenarios.
- *Maximize return under a specific scenario.* This is a very effective criterion when one has a strong conviction about a certain scenario. The remaining scenarios are treated as risk scenarios, for which underperformance constraints are imposed. The existence of those constraints allows one to balance risks versus return.
- *Maximize the worst case return (maxmin).* This is the most conservative approach that one would employ when (1) the objective is primarily to replicate the benchmark as closely as possible, say for liability matching; or (2) one does not proclaim to have a strong view about the market. Instead of investing based on a specific view, the investor aims

[6]Dimitris Bertsimas and John N. Tsitsiklis, *Introduction to Linear Optimization* (Nashua, N.H.: Athena Scientific, 1997).

for gains across all the scenarios, however modest they may be. This is not the approach that will generate home runs. As long as the scenarios are representative of a broad range of outcomes, the investor should be able to generate modest but consistent returns versus the benchmark.[7]

In our experience, we have found that the maxmin criterion, by its conservative nature, helps limit the volatility of the returns over time. However, the margin of outperformance may be less than desirable for some investors, despite the attractive risk characteristics. Therefore, we leave that criterion aside for now, though we note that it may be an invaluable approach for liability management applications in particular.

There is an interesting relationship between the other two criteria. More specifically, in the absence of any risk constraints under the other scenarios, maximizing return under a specific scenario (e.g., the base case) would be equivalent to assigning a 100% probability to that one scenario and maximizing expected return. Surely, performance could well be dismal under some of the risk scenarios, in particular those that are the "opposite" of the favored scenario. Think of what maximizing return for a bearish scenario would do to performance if a bullish scenario were to materialize. On the other hand, if one were to impose some loss constraints in the risk scenarios, and make those constraints ever more stringent, there would come a point where the optimal portfolio begins to change character and look more like a portfolio driven by the risk scenarios rather than the base-case scenario. At the extreme, where one constrains the portfolio to have a high positive return in the risk scenario, while still maximizing the base case, the result would be the same as if one were maximizing expected return while assigning 100% probability to the risk scenario. In other words, there is a correspondence between the probabilities assigned to various scenarios in the expected return maximization case and the risk constraints in the single-scenario maximization case. As a side note, the two approaches are classified as linear optimization problems, in that both the objective functions and the constraints are linear functions of the optimization parameters (that is, the market value weights).

We prefer the criterion of maximizing return under a specific scenario subject to loss constraints under the risk scenarios. The reason is twofold: we like to be able to impose the loss constraints explicitly (as we want a clear handle on the risks we are taking) and we do not want to create another layer of subjectivity by having to guess probabilities. Yet, we emphasize

[7]Claude Diderich and Wolfgang Marty, "The Min-Max Portfolio Optimization Strategy: An Empirical Study on Balanced Portfolios," in *Lecture Notes in Computer Science*, vol. 1988/2001 (Berlin: Springer, 2001), 201–230.

that what we are doing would be equivalent to maximizing expected return under a specific choice of probabilities.

Defining the Constraints

There are several dimensions in which one could impose constraints on the portfolio. These include duration bands, partial duration bounds, sector allocation constraints, issue weights (both in terms of the percentage of the portfolio, and relative to the float available in the market) and loss constraints as we discussed above.

Duration Bands

Most real-money portfolios cannot deviate significantly from the benchmark duration. The typical band would be 0.25 to 0.5 on either side of the benchmark duration. (Sometimes the band is expressed as a percentage of the benchmark duration.) The duration decision is facilitated by gauging how much the base-case performance improves for an incremental change in duration; that is, if the improvement is marginal beyond a certain duration deviation, then taking additional duration risk is not warranted.

Partial Duration

Typically, unless one imposes some explicit constraints, the optimal portfolio has allocations in all but a few maturity buckets. As a result, the portfolio has an implicit underweight (relative to the benchmark) in those buckets where there is no allocation. If that is not desirable, for fear that relative valuation changes not accounted for in the scenarios may cause tracking error, then one might choose to constrain the partial durations to remain close to those of the benchmark. Of course, curbing potential mismatch comes at a cost: the more constraints one imposes, the less the portfolio can deviate from the benchmark, limiting its upside potential.

Asset Allocation Weights

In a multi-asset portfolio, such as one comprised of Treasuries, agencies, and TIPS, to generate alpha the portfolio manager typically overweights or underweights a specific asset relative to the benchmark. The deviation from the benchmark, especially in spread products, typically has some bounds on it, such as between 90% and 110% of the benchmark allocation, and so on. For example, if agencies were 54% of the benchmark, then the allocation into agencies would have to stay between 48.6% and 59.4% of the portfolio.

Loss Constraints

As we discussed above, the objective is to maximize performance under a base-case scenario, subject to loss constraints under the risk scenarios. The more stringent the constraints, the more the portfolio has to honor them and move away from a structure geared for optimal performance under the base case alone. The choice of the loss constraint depends on how it affects performance under the base case. For instance, if by allowing an incremental loss of 10 basis points (bps) in the risk scenarios, performance in the base case improves by more than 10 bps, then one should relax the loss constraint. However, if the performance improvement is significantly less than the potential incremental risk one takes on, then it is better to use the more restrictive loss constraint.

Issue Weights

In general, one would be better served diversifying the holdings in a portfolio across a large enough set of issues, rather than having concentrated allocations into just a handful of them. Furthermore, when defining the issue size limits in the portfolio, one may need to take into account the total float available in each issue and ensure that no more than a certain percentage of the float is owned by the portfolio. This makes intuitive sense as it will help prevent the portfolio from being subject to technical anomalies in one or two issues. In short, we believe it is advisable to impose a constraint such as "no issue should be more than 10% of the portfolio or 20% of the float."

Putting It All Together: The Optimal Portfolio

We demonstrate the process we have outlined so far with a couple of specific examples. To illustrate the duration decision, separately from the sector allocation decision, we use the Citigroup Treasury Index as the benchmark. As a second example, we turn to sector allocation and choose the minimum risk portfolio defined earlier as the benchmark. To recap, the benchmark consists of 26% Treasuries, 54% agencies, and 20% TIPS in market value terms. In both optimization problems, our objective is to construct a portfolio that is projected to outperform the benchmark in the base case, subject to the following constraints:

- Duration: Within –0.5 to 0.5 years around the benchmark.
- Asset allocation weights: Within ±20% around the benchmark allocation.
- Allowable losses: Up to –30 bps versus the benchmark.

- Issue weights: No one issue to be more than 10% of the portfolio size in market value terms.

The Duration Decision

There is interplay between the duration decision and the maximum losses allowed. The final decision depends on the improvement in performance in the base case. Exhibit 19.7 illustrates the point. Each one of the profiles corresponds to a different level of losses allowed (the loss constraint) and shows the excess return versus the benchmark as a function of the duration deviation. Clearly, when no losses are allowed (the bottom profile), base-case performance improves as duration is shortened—after all, the base case is a bearish move in rates—but up to a certain point. For instance, when duration is matched to the benchmark, the projected excess return is 10 bps, while with a –0.1-year duration deviation the excess return reaches 15 bps. However, in going from –0.1 to –0.2-year, the improvement is a mere 2 bps. Furthermore, there is no incremental improvement for shortening duration past –0.2-year. Therefore, if one favored a very conservative strategy and allowed no losses, shortening duration by 0.1 year would be the way to go.

If the loss constraint is relaxed, there is a marked improvement in performance. For instance in the case where a 10 bp loss is allowed and portfolio duration is matched to the benchmark, excess return is 22 bps. In other words, the return pickup relative to the "no loss" case is 12 bps (22–10

EXHIBIT 19.7 Excess Return as a Function of Duration and Loss Tolerance

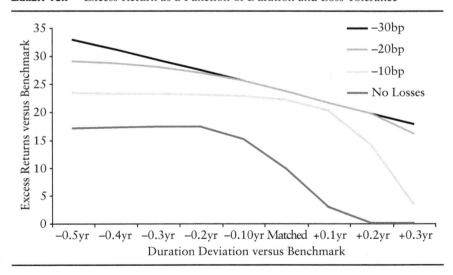

bps), 2 bps higher than the concession given in terms of loss tolerance. It does not seem to make sense to shorten duration in this case, as performance is topped out at 23 bps with any kind of duration mismatch.

Now comes the judgment call. Using the no-loss, matched-duration case as the baseline, we can either (1) boost performance by 12 bps, by taking on the risk of a 10 bps loss but no duration; or (2) add 5 bps of return, by taking on a 0.1-year duration short but no projected losses. We would contend that the latter is a better choice in this case as it does not require making a compromise in terms of loss tolerance (at least within the confines of the scenarios used). However, one could easily argue that targeting a bigger upside potential while relaxing the risk constraints by a small margin is preferable, especially considering that the gains could be attained with no duration mismatch.[8]

The Optimal Portfolio in a Multi-Asset Setting

When constructing the portfolio that comprises Treasuries, agencies and TIPS, we arrive at a clear conclusion following a similar reasoning as in the Treasury-only case: there is no need for duration mismatch, or for allowing losses. The reason is that there are more degrees of freedom in this optimization, as one can enhance performance by choosing to overweight/underweight assets versus one another in addition to, or in lieu of, taking on duration and curve positions.[9]

Because of the asset allocation weight constraints, no one asset can be fully excluded from the portfolio, which makes for good diversification characteristics. Exhibit 19.8 shows the allocation into each one of the assets in the optimization universe. In this case, the portfolio maintains an overweight in TIPS, and an underweight in Treasuries and agencies versus the benchmark, and also has an allocation into cash (10%). The reason for the inclusion of cash is that the portfolio benefits from having a barbelled curve position (that is, overweight in short and long maturity buckets, underweight in intermediate maturities) since the base case involves curve flattening. By taking a position in cash, and coupling that with a bigger position (further out) in the back end of the curve, one can improve exposure to flattening, which is what is happening here. Exhibit 19.9 shows the allocation into different maturity buckets along the curve in each one of the assets,

---

[8]Antti Ilmanen, Rory Byrne, Heinz Gunasekera, and Robert Minikin, "Which Risks Have Been Best Rewarded?" *Journal of Portfolio Management* 30, no. 2 (2004): 53–57; and Antti Ilmanen, "Does Duration Extension Enhance Long-Term Expected Returns?" *Journal of Fixed Income* 6, no. 2 (1996): 23–36.
[9]Mark J. P Anson, "Strategic versus Tactical Asset Allocation," *Journal of Portfolio Management* 30, no. 2 (2004): 8–22.

EXHIBIT 19.8 Percentage of the Market Value Allotted into Each Asset

	Portfolio	Benchmark	Overweight (underweight)
Treasury	11%	26%	−15%
Agency	40%	54%	−14%
TIPS	39%	20%	19%
Cash	10%	0%	10%

EXHIBIT 19.9 Optimal Portfolio Market Value Over/Underweights along the Yield Curve

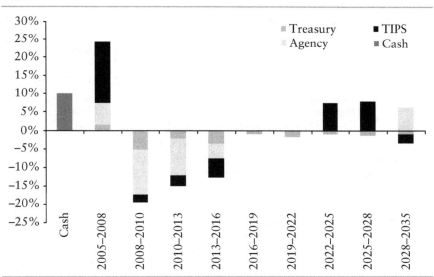

relative to the benchmark composition. It is interesting to note that in the 2022–2028 maturity bucket, the optimal portfolio consists of overweights in TIPS versus Treasuries—roughly, a long TIPS break-even position. In the longest maturity bucket, there is a preference for agencies versus Treasuries and TIPS, which is essentially a long spread position.

KEY POINTS

- The selection of a benchmark index is a process that can carry as much importance as the optimization of the portfolio itself.
- Above all else, the index should be relevant to the investor.

- The goals of the fund should be considered and, if necessary, a customized index should be created to meet the specific needs of the manager.
- When constructing an index using a rules-based method, it is always important to take into account the replicability of the index, the transparency of the rules created and it should be representative of the market.
- Construction of a custom index can be achieved through mean–variance analysis to meet the needs of almost any investor. Using this method allows the manager to measure performance against the most efficient "passive" allocation of assets, which should eventually lead to better, more informed investment decisions.
- Using optimization techniques is a very potent approach to balance risk versus return in a portfolio versus the benchmark.
- Optimization allows one to change risk parameters, monitor the associated change in excess returns, gauge the interplay between duration, curve positioning and asset allocation, all in a well-defined and consistent framework.
- Notwithstanding the fact that the framework is highly quantitative, there are certainly some steps in the analysis that require a judgment call, such as the choice of certain constraints, the decision about what duration/risk tolerance combination to use, etc.
- The choice of the scenarios to be used in the optimization is also critical, in that one should ensure that they cover a wide range of possibilities, bracketing the forwards.
- The projected performance numbers, and more to the point, the risk assessment, is only as good as the quality of the set of scenarios selected.
- Once intuition is gained about how to generate realistic scenarios, and what kind of risk constraints to employ, the discipline of analyzing risks and returns in a unified framework proves invaluable.

QUESTIONS

1. ABCD Asset Management is going to pick a new benchmark for their investment-grade fixed income fund. The investment banking arm of ABCD's parent company, ABCD Capital, publishes an investment-grade bond index which includes Treasuries, agency debt, and mortgages. Name at least two of the principles of a good index that ABCD Asset Management would violate if they chose ABCD Capital's investment-grade bond index as their benchmark and give the reasons why those principles might be violated.

2. a. Discuss the principles as they relate to creating a custom index using the Markowitz model of mean/variance optimization.

b. What do you see as the main issues as they relate to the principles?

3. Specify three different optimization criteria that can be used in scenario-based portfolio construction. Briefly describe the relationship between them, and their respective pros and cons.

4. ABCD asset management has a fund benchmarked against a USD fixed income index, which includes Treasuries, agency debt, TIPS, mortgages and investment-grade corporate bonds. Specify at least four constraints that can be used by ABCD when formulating a scenario-based optimal portfolio versus an index. Also describe briefly how the scenarios should be selected to avoid an implicit bias in positioning.

5. Discuss the interplay between the weighting (or probabilities) in a set of bearish/bullish scenarios, maxmin, and the constraints used in the optimization.

CHAPTER 20

The Art of Fixed Income Portfolio Investing*

Chris P. Dialynas
Managing Director–Portfolio Management
Pacific Investment Management Company

Ellen J. Rachlin
Managing Director–Portfolio Manager
Mariner Investment Group, LLC

The global fixed income portfolio manager's task is to select the optimal combination of fixed income securities and currencies to outperform, on a risk-adjusted basis, a specified fixed income market benchmark index whose characteristics may include global or local, investment grade or high yield, short or long duration, or inclusive of all these characteristics, among many others. Additionally, the global fixed income portfolio manager will strive to post favorable performance versus competitors. But, collectively, the goal of fixed income portfolio management is to provide a meaningful investment result for clients that will complement any multi-asset class portfolio.

Global fixed income portfolio managers must make complex investment choices among the universe of global fixed income products. All global issuers of debt that rely on the public markets for capital, compete for the portfolio manager's investment capital. Issuers that offer securities with the highest risk-adjusted returns will be most attractive to the portfolio manager who selects among these global investment opportunities in such a way that is designed to outperform a benchmark index. Inherent in the invest-

---

*The views and portfolio management techniques expressed in this chapter are those of its authors and do not necessarily reflect the views or investment practices of the authors' employers.

ment decision are choices on duration, country, sector, currency, and product. These choices are built upon forecasts. The portfolio manager allocates capital in accordance with their confidence in their forecast and in context of the current market valuations, market liquidity, and asset volatility. They will choose how much exposure to a variety of risks they are willing to assume such as market, credit, political, liquidity and event. The global fixed income portfolio is a result of their constrained optimization process given these factors.

THE GLOBAL FIXED INCOME PORTFOLIO MANAGER

Because the portfolio manager competes for capital against other portfolio managers over relatively short time periods, investment choices may be far less committed than the loans of supras or other banks. In spite of the fact that the initial term of the commitment (maturity of the bond) is greater than the typical term of a bank loan, the homogeneity of the bond markets, the competition between portfolio managers, and the depth and organization of the bond markets, all contribute to market liquidity. Turnover occurs and prices of the bonds change as the opinions of the portfolio managers effectuate valuation changes.

Within the current global communication revolution, global credit risks are continually assessed from readily available new information. Yet, all of the hazards for the portfolio manager when considering investments in many of the world's developing countries still exist. The portfolio manager must assess the probability within their interest rate forecast that private capital might be suddenly withdrawn from a particular country or company, or that the willingness of the country or company to honor its obligations may change. A sudden withdrawal of funds may have a significant destabilizing effect on the economies and prices of the securities and currencies of emerging capital markets or of other capital markets with comparatively high volatility rates. Conversely, the capital attracted to developing countries from global investment funds, at times, can lead to temporary excesses. These excesses may manifest itself in rapid gross domestic product (GDP) growth, inflation, increasing trade deficits, speculative asset price or financial bubbles, bad loans, and depreciating currencies, among other problems. However, it is the portfolio manager's primary responsibility to determine if a new country path is being established or if excesses are developing. A significant increase in capital to a given market may improve the financial and economic health of that economy, assuming the debt burden is manageable under most economic scenarios.

The global fixed income portfolio manager must assess global economies and their market environments then predict levels of interest rates, slopes of yield curves, and future currency values to determine the performance characteristics, in totality and in context of their investment portfolio. A portfolio manager's task is to predict the optimal combination of fixed income securities and currencies to outperform a particular market index and post favorable performance versus competitors. The portfolio manager selects the optimal combination of securities from the pool of possible choices within the predetermined investment set. That is, a global fixed income manager will choose among sovereigns, supranationals, corporate and mortgage securities, and currencies to determine what type of instrument is the most efficient means of expressing that exposure. With this choice comes the responsibility to assess policy makers' response function and flexibility in order to anticipate, understand, and position for important policy changes.

The professional skills required of global fixed income portfolio managers are complex and challenging. The portfolio manager ultimately utilizes proprietary investment skills to create a portfolio comprised of bonds representative of the set of interest rate, yield curve, currency, country, and credit forecasts in which the portfolio manager believes. The main attributes of a bond portfolio include: (1) duration, (2) cash flow distribution on various yield curves, (3) convexity, (4) credit quality, and (5) nondollar bond and currency exposure. Each selected attribute is the result of multiple and complex evaluation techniques. And the overall risk expected of the portfolio can be derived through a variety of normalization techniques. Alternatively, that is to say, a skilled practitioner should be able to examine a bond portfolio and derive the portfolio's embedded forecasts for: (1) inflation and interest rates, (2) volatility, (3) changes in yield curve shape, (4) intermarket spreads, and (5) intramarket spreads and relative currency values. The portfolio manager must develop a multitude of forecasts to utilize in a variety of ways throughout the investment process. This process will be elaborated on and the practical importance of subtle forecasts demonstrated. Inferences about a particular bond position convey, effectively, the important attributes of a forecast as well as confidence in the forecast. Ultimately, it is the quality of the political-macroeconomic analysis, integrated with the quantification of the asset universe that will yield a rewarding experience.

The creation of an interest rate forecast, which is the overall backdrop for the bond portfolio's construction, in and of itself requires a portfolio manager to call upon knowledge of: (1) economics, (2) politics, (3) history, (4) psychology, and (5) statistics, in addition to other disciplines. A reliable interest rate forecast and an understanding of the differences between that forecast and the implicit forecast of the market are critical to professional bond portfolio management. The portfolio manager must compare the proprietary interest rate forecast to the forward market prices and seek investment opportunities wherever his forecast deviates from market expectations. Therefore, it is insufficient to merely implement an externally developed forecast. The portfolio manager must have in-depth knowledge of the assumptions inherent to the forecast and understand the subsector economic analysis, such as trade account product distribution, monetary targets, noneconomic objectives, cultural norms, tax policies, and the marketplace for which the forecast applies. Indeed, the portfolio manager must create assumptions for what is unknowable and often intuit the intangible influences into actionable portfolio strategies.

It is a miscalculation to assume that a good economic forecast alone allows the portfolio manager to construct a portfolio that performs well. Global economic forecasts are merely an intermediate step in the portfolio manager's effort to devise global interest rate and currency forecasts. Economic forecasts are generally described in terms of real GDP, GDP deflators (inflation rates), unemployment rates, productivity, and current account deficit/reserve changes. The portfolio manager must thoroughly consider all important assumptions and components of their own global interest rate/currency forecast, and assign a measure of confidence to their forecast. Moreover, all possible outcomes, and the probability of those outcomes must be considered to estimate the effect on portfolio valuations should critical assumptions prove incorrect in the context of the investment horizon.

The previous point is illustrated in Exhibit 20.1. The graphics in the exhibit illustrate the volume and the complexity of the information with which portfolio managers are bombarded. Within each graphic is a comment about the importance to a portfolio manager of the microelements of each macrofactor category. The microelements signal secular direction and potential macro/political policy changes.

The portfolio manager must decide whether information is noise, or cyclical or whether it signals the beginning of a long-term trend. To do so, the portfolio manager must look for clues in the numbers and discern seminal changes well before they occur. The task seems utterly impossible. However, as decisions crystallize, the portfolio will take shape, reflecting those decisions while simultaneously assessing the embedded joint portfolio risks.

In simpler terms, although hardly simple, Exhibit 20.2 outlines some of the broad macroeconomic issues in a closed economy. The exhibit illustrates the complexity of the linkages among policy variables, markets, and economic outcomes. Exhibit 20.3 illustrates the complexities of monetary macroeconomic issues while only tangentially providing for an open, global economy. The graphics themselves are substantial and complex, let alone understanding the interrelations delineated. This chapter presents the practical

EXHIBIT 20.1 The Open System: Global Policies and Free Market Prices

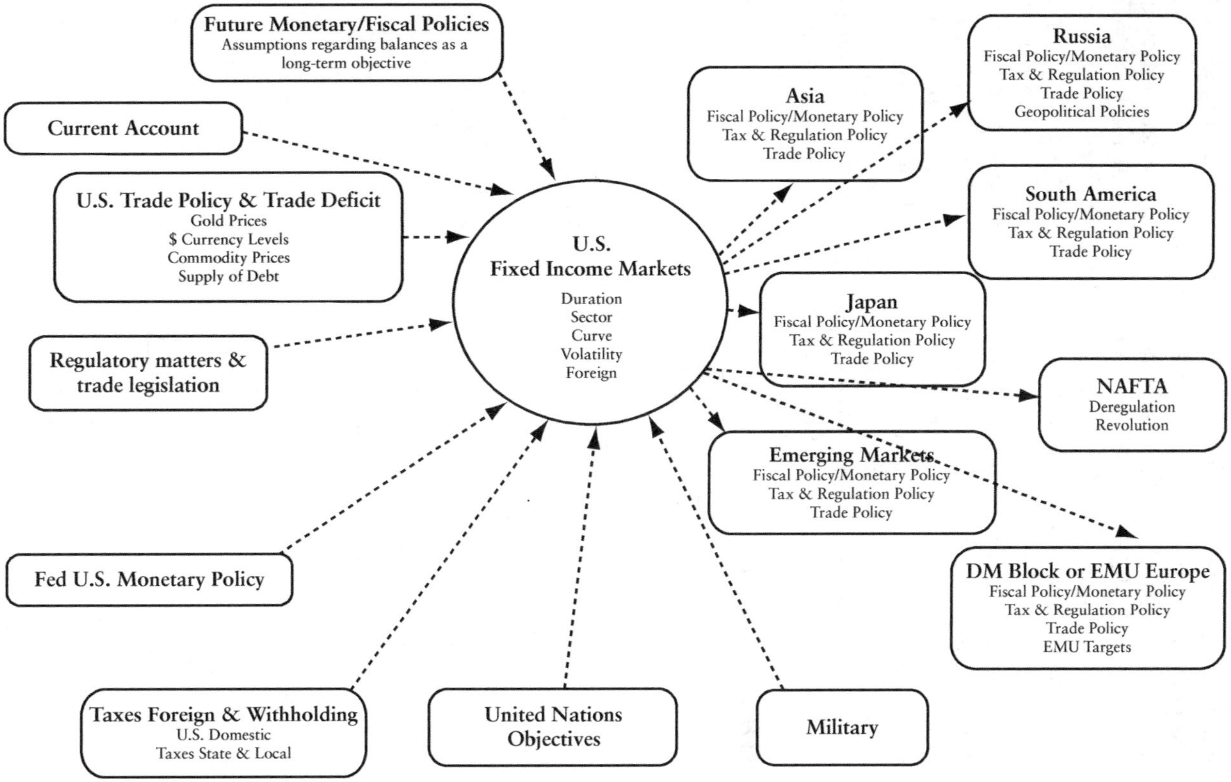

U.S. Fixed Income Markets
Duration
Sector
Curve
Volatility
Foreign

Future Monetary/Fiscal Policies
Assumptions regarding balances as a long-term objective

Current Account

U.S. Trade Policy & Trade Deficit
Gold Prices
$ Currency Levels
Commodity Prices
Supply of Debt

Regulatory matters & trade legislation

Fed U.S. Monetary Policy

Taxes Foreign & Withholding
U.S. Domestic
Taxes State & Local

United Nations Objectives

Military

Russia
Fiscal Policy/Monetary Policy
Tax & Regulation Policy
Trade Policy
Geopolitical Policies

Asia
Fiscal Policy/Monetary Policy
Tax & Regulation Policy
Trade Policy

South America
Fiscal Policy/Monetary Policy
Tax & Regulation Policy
Trade Policy

Japan
Fiscal Policy/Monetary Policy
Tax & Regulation Policy
Trade Policy

Emerging Markets
Fiscal Policy/Monetary Policy
Tax & Regulation Policy
Trade Policy

NAFTA
Deregulation
Revolution

DM Block or EMU Europe
Fiscal Policy/Monetary Policy
Tax & Regulation Policy
Trade Policy
EMU Targets

transition that must be made from global political economist to global fixed income portfolio manager. For clarity's sake, our discussion will be from the perspective of a global fixed income portfolio manager located in the United States. In Exhibit 20.4, observe a simple economic model of an open system with multiple trading partners and the potential impact of subtle economic developments on the management of any fixed income portfolio. Readily observable is the point that decisions regarding foreign bonds and foreign currencies add multiple layers of complexity, particularly in a portfolio management context, where many fixed income products (futures, forwards, swaps, options, etc.) are available for strategy implementation. Moreover, on some level, decisions must be made and constraints developed that relate international exposure to ultimate investment purpose.

There are some practitioners who argue that given the complexity of economic models and volume of macro information, there is a strong case

EXHIBIT 20.2   Closed Economy: Macroeconomic Issues

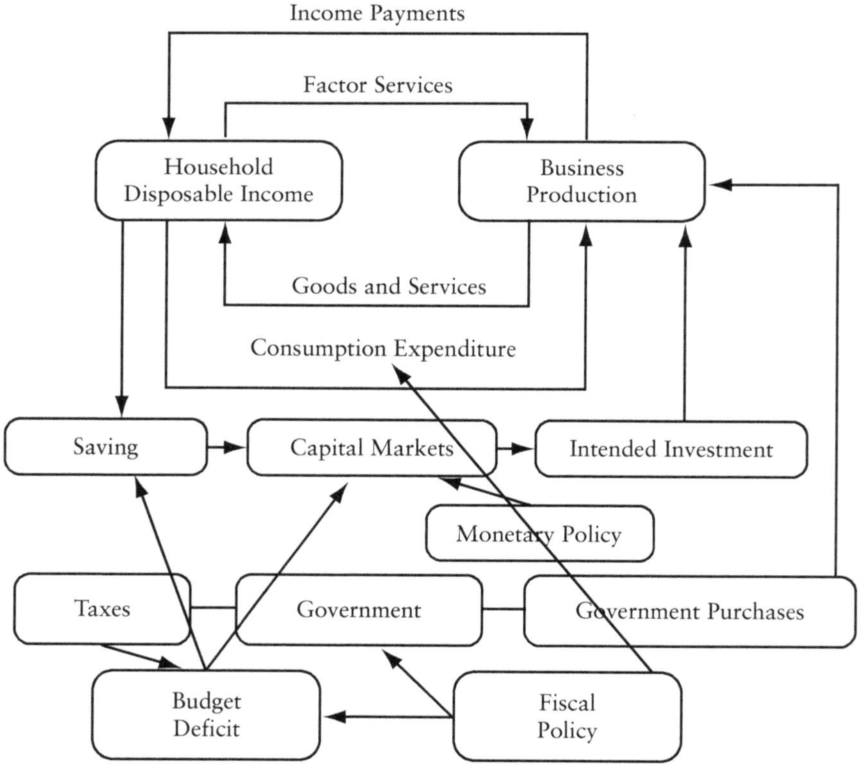

EXHIBIT 20.3 The Fed's "Big Six" Tools

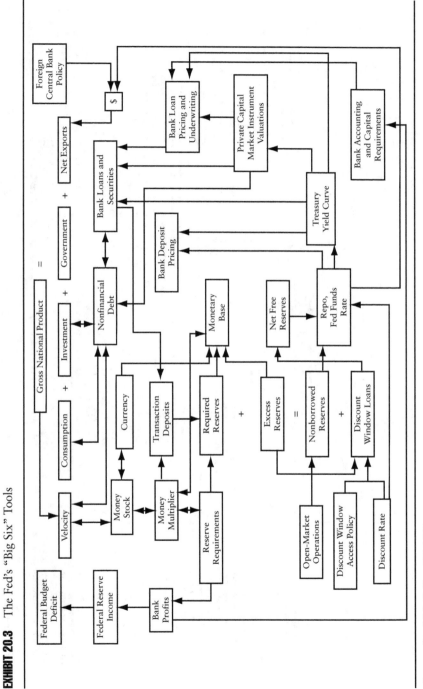

Source: Paul McCulley, PIMCO

EXHIBIT 20.4   Global Bond Markets: Evaluating Impact of Global Monetary and Fiscal Policies

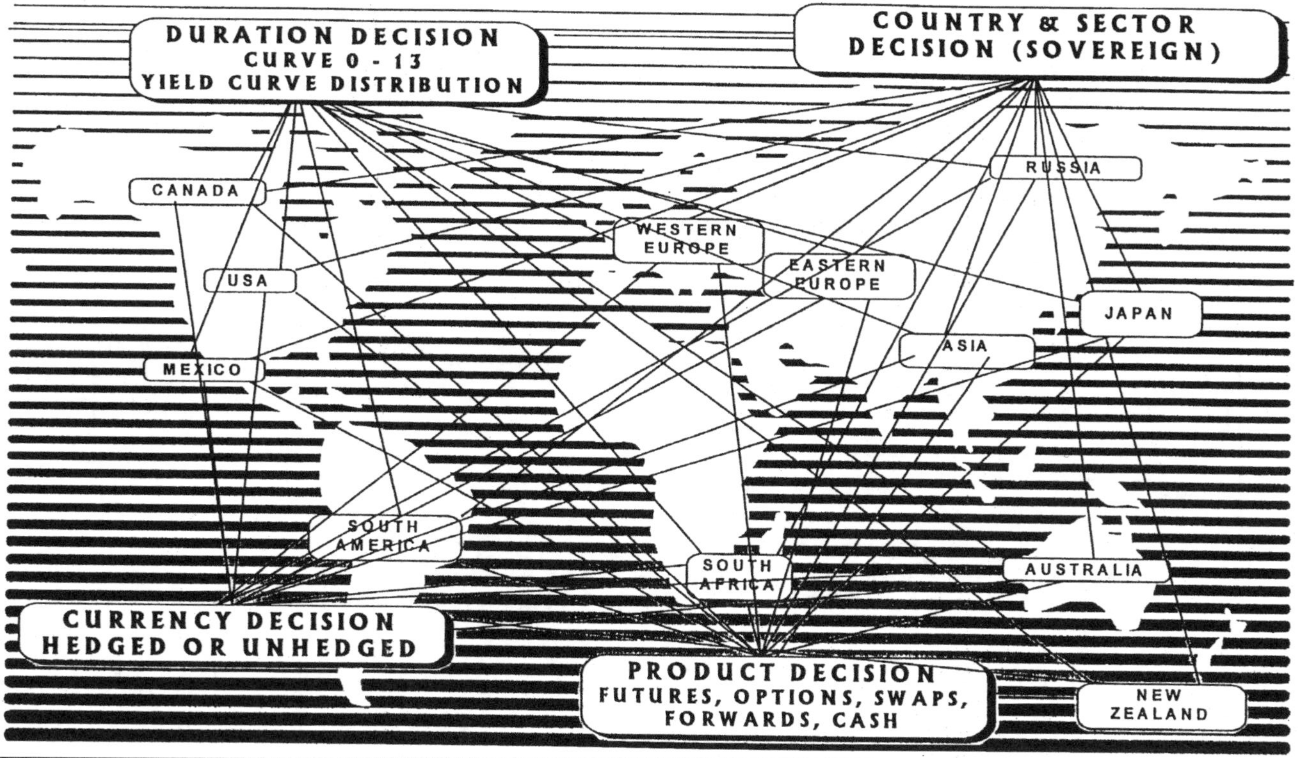

Design: Marie Sacheli

for technical analysis of the bond and currency markets. They argue that all this information is noise because of its sheer volume and potential unreliability and all relevant information can be gleaned from global security and currency prices, and patterns of prices. Technical practitioners believe prices alone are important clues to the future. This practice is prevalent and it is always useful to try to understand other portfolio managers' techniques as their methods may impact the global markets.

THE GLOBAL CHALLENGE

The global fixed income portfolio manager is presented with the challenge of outperforming a widely recognized, well-defined global index benchmark. Generally, the portfolio manager is provided with a clear set of investment guidelines and a large set of investment choices. A reasonable measurement period for all portfolio managers is over a period of time that permits a set of strategies to be implemented and results bear to fruition. This period is usually a business cycle. The challenge is thus defined.

PORTFOLIO PARAMETERS

Ultimately, the portfolio manager must make investment decisions. In practice, this requires the buying and selling of bonds and bond surrogates, and currencies and currency surrogates to create a meaningful portfolio that reflects the desired target parameters. Among the most important parameters are the portfolio's country duration and expected cash flow distribution (yield curve exposure), currency positions, convexity, sector, and credit allocation. These parameters may either be unique or so interrelated that the purity of the choices may become obscured. Nevertheless, the portfolio's definition is within these decision parameters. (In the abstract, however, an efficient and meaningful portfolio can be achieved by merely placing allocations amongst the various market subindexes in combination with a macro-currency allocation scheme.)

For example, the country-specific duration of a portfolio is the most potent source of forecast expression. Large relative positions in currencies are equally important. Extreme duration choices, relative to a market benchmark, represent an expectation for substantially higher or lower interest rates in any given fixed income market as well as a high degree of confidence in the outcome. Implicit within an extreme duration forecast is the expression of expectations for substantial changes in the volatility of interest rates. Similarly, extreme variation in currency composition relative to the benchmark represents an expression about either (1) stable valuations among disparate yield or (2) substantial changes in foreign exchange rates.

Forecast Confidence and Relative Risk

One of the most important assessments that a portfolio manager must make is the degree of confidence in each component of the forecast. Forecast conviction also plays an important role in model usage. Highly confident forecasts may enable the portfolio manager to alter a model or the output of the model to reflect a "biased" distribution of outcomes. In essence, the portfolio manager is affecting the quantitative outcome in a way that is consistent with the qualitative forecast.

Of course, the objective "fair value" determination will be distorted. The various forms of analysis that leads to a forecast were elaborated on previously. A strong conviction, high confidence forecast may result when the secular forecast is consistent with the cyclical forecast and both of those forecasts are consistent with the technical analysis. A weak conviction forecast may result when the conclusions the portfolio manager reaches are subject to a potential major institutional change. The forecast confidence is important because of its influence on the strength of the statement within the portfolio with respect to the portfolio parameters and risk characteristics. Exhibit 20.5 illustrates the generalized statistical implication of forecast confidence. Similarly, for example, institutional arrangements such as those implemented by the International Monetary Fund (IMF) can exert a

EXHIBIT 20.5   Confidence Distributions Low—Low Confidence, Normal—Moderate Confidence Perfect, Truncated—High Confidence

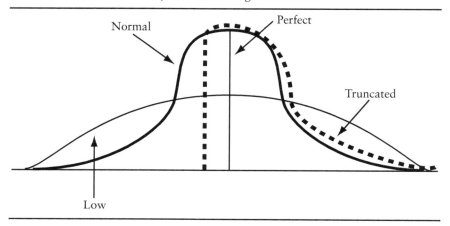

tremendous influence on bond prices. This point will be addressed further in the following section.

A meticulous consideration of confidence levels may also help resolve potential portfolio contradictions. For example, a highly confident bullish country interest rate forecast in conjunction with a low confidence currency forecast would lead the portfolio manager to opt for high country duration and a neutral currency position whenever possible. Of course, in some local currency markets, duration choices are limited to very short maturity bonds and money market instruments.

Below are a few more examples to illustrate the role of forecast confidence in global bond management. However, in the abstract, differences in forecast confidence translates into:

- Low confidence—insure, low risk portfolio.
- Moderate confidence—self-insure.
- High confidence—employ leverage, sell insurance.

Practically speaking, the low confidence forecast would be insured via the strategic purchase of put options or by selling or buying assets in the portfolio to reduce the risk of the portfolio by moving closer to the global index benchmark. Each strategy renders a different set of expected payoffs. The moderate confidence forecast after implied volatility pricing considerations normally results in self-insure strategy with bets consistent with the forecast. The high confidence forecast translates into the execution of extreme leveraged bets consistent with the forecast and the selling of assets with returns derived from a forecast completely contrary. For example, in this latter case, the sale of put options on long bonds would reflect a highly confident forecast for lower yields on long bonds.

Consider a fictitious bond with the following characteristics: 30-year, noncallable Government of Spain bond, putable at par in five years. Let us assess how this bond may be used in two cases: the highly confident forecast and the weakly confident forecast. In both instances, assume that the volatility embedded within the bond's put option is lower than the volatility of conventional put options in the market.

A portfolio manager with a global low-duration, 2.5-year assignment and highly confident that interest rates will fall, will seek ways to increase the portfolio sensitivity to this forecast without dramatically increasing risk. The portfolio manager may decide to use the hypothetical put bond. The bond provides for the upside of a 30-year bond if correct assuming Spain is a high-quality credit risk and the downside of a five-year bond if not correct. In effect, the portfolio manager is long a five-year bond with a call option on a 25-year bond and, therefore, has effectively increased portfolio duration at the expense of yield, which is the alternative strategy.

Assume another portfolio manager with a global market duration assignment holds a low confidence forecast for declining Spanish rates. This portfolio manager decides to sacrifice yield and buys the insurance inherent in the put provision of the bond and is long a 30-year bond with the right to put the last 25 years back to the issuer. The portfolio manager decreases the "expected" cost to the portfolio of being wrong.

A much more powerful example of the importance of understanding forecast confidence to portfolio construction is illustrated in an example which involves the selection of foreign bonds in a political-economic context. Let's assume three portfolio managers hold a very strong conviction that interest rates in Germany will decline. One of the portfolio managers believes in the weakness of the euro, another portfolio manager does not believe in the weakness of the euro, and the third is very uncertain about the prospects for the euro and the U.S. dollar (USD). These beliefs may be expressed:

Portfolio Manager	1	2	3
Bond choice	Spanish	German	Putable Spanish bond (30/5)
Currency choice	USD	Euro	Basket of currencies or call option on Spanish pesetas

REGULATORY CHANGES, DEMOGRAPHIC TRENDS, AND INSTITUTIONAL BIAS

There are many important factors external to the economic system that may critically affect a bond portfolio's performance. To varying extents, these factors are difficult to anticipate. Forces such as demographics, mutual fund growth, and global economic prosperity are trending factors whose dynamics and influence may be discerned. However, sudden, meaningful changes such as tax policy, pension plan allocation rules, guidelines, benefit payout rules, supply of bonds issued, types of bonds issued, central bank policy, and the implementation of credit controls, capital controls, trade treaties, IMF policies, and trade wars, among other issues, are more problematic to contemplate and incorporate.

Other more abrupt aspects of life such as the outbreak of unanticipated wars or the formation of important economic cartels are impossible to predict. All of these factors could induce dramatic changes in the following: (1) direction of interest rates, (2) intermarket yield spreads, (3) shape of the yield curve, (4) volatility of the market and the pricing of expected volatility, (5) exchange rate values, and (6) intracountry yield spread as well as other important financial valuations in addition to an understanding of the investment policies of the reserve-rich central banks and those that are quickly accumulating reserves.

INFORMATION IN THE MARKETS

The global fixed income manager examines the market for information and considers big picture issues of regulations, demographics, and institutional trends before forming an opinion about the more cyclical aspects of current macroeconomic fiscal and monetary policies. There are at least two types of information they will seek:

The first set of information, economic statistics, is readily available in readable format. Some important global economic statistics are contained in Exhibit 20.6. This information is used in a historical business-cycle context to examine the present state of the economy and to derive inferences regarding the future. Pieces of economic statistical data validate or repudiate a particular forecast or portfolio theme.

The second set of important information resides in the marketplace itself. This information is generally available in price form and its meaning or importance must be derived. This market information is in the form of implied forward international government bond rates. These rates may be derived from current international government bond prices. For global fixed income portfolio managers, (1) global yield curves, (2) global money market and repo rates, (3) global public and over-the-counter (OTC) options markets, (4) global futures markets, (5) global forward markets, (6) global credit spread markets, (7) currency markets, and (8) implied breakeven inflation rates, among others, are rich sources of information. Obviously, to the extent models of these decisions are used and they differ or other subjective inputs to the model differ, the inferences will, therefore, differ as well. Practitioners rely often on institutional models provided by external vendors. If institutional models are employed, the portfolio manager must be familiar with the theoretical foundation of the model and cognizant of any biases produced by the model or its inputs.

The importance of inferential market information cannot be overemphasized. This information provides the basis for the performance expectation during a specified period or base case returns for bonds. It, therefore, provides a benchmark from which the portfolio manager's forecast may be expressed. Consider the following scenario, which is exaggerated for illustrative purposes:

Assume a portfolio manager is bearish on U.K. short-term interest rates, expecting a 25 to 75 basis point increase in base rate funds with a very strong

EXHIBIT 20.6 Guide to Bond Portfolio Management

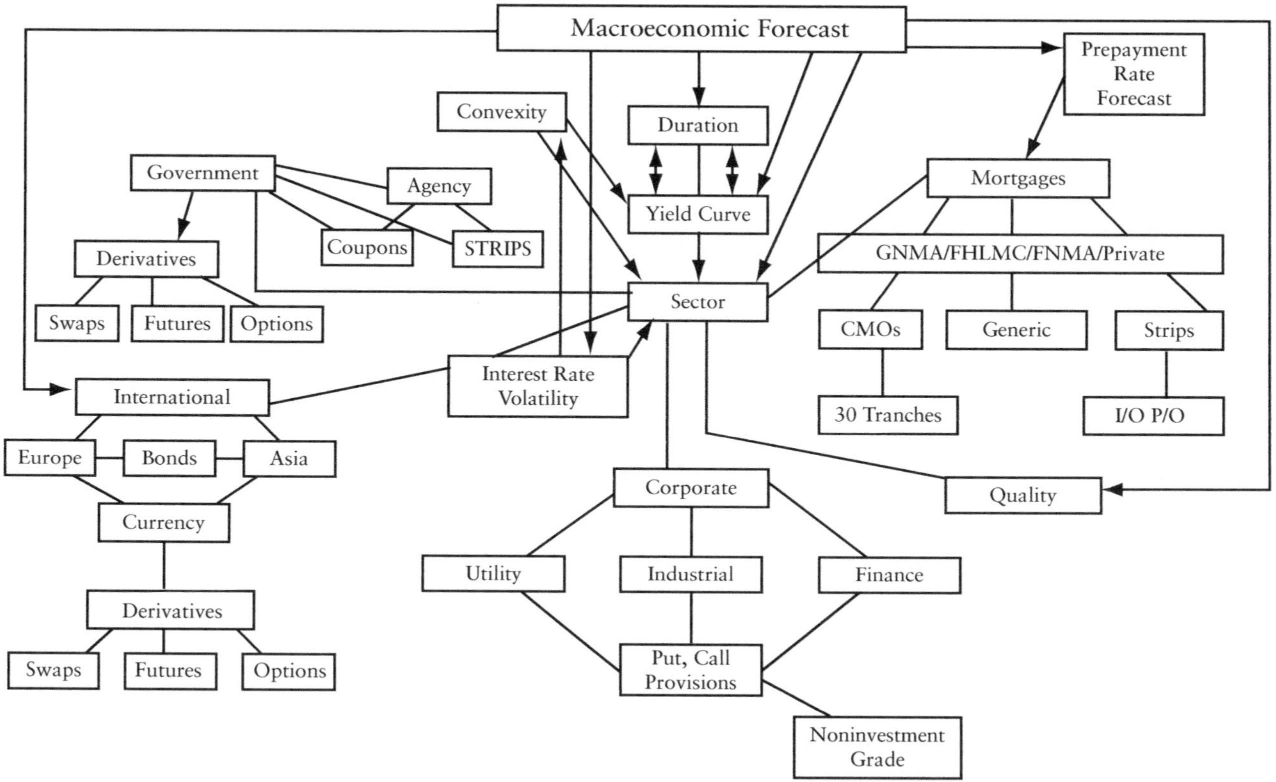

EXHIBIT 20.6 (Continued)

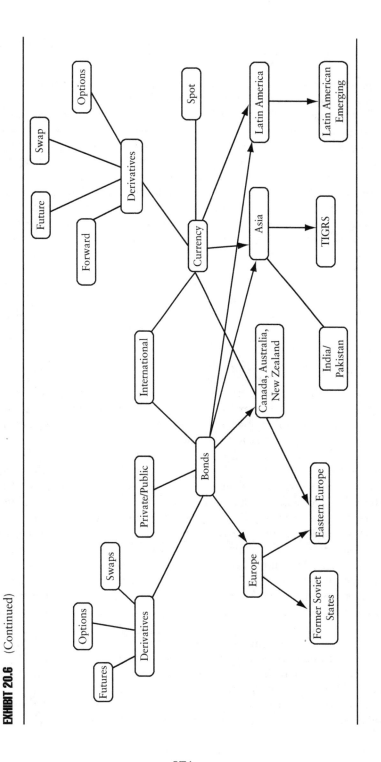

conviction that interest rates will subsequently fall. The portfolio manager has a model reflective of two year gilts. Based upon this forecast, the portfolio manager decides to reduce duration and sell part of the two-year securities position held in the portfolio. Upon further reflection, the portfolio manager decides to consider and analyze market rates. The research reveals the yield curve shape is reflective of a 150 basis point increase in short rates. The futures contracts for Euro sterling have a similar increase priced in for short rates. Paradoxically, although the portfolio manager's expectations for interest rates are bearish, compared to the market's expectations, the manager's expectations are actually bullish. Selling may not be a good idea and in fact, the portfolio manager may consider the possibility of buying.

Discrepancies in inferential information gleaned from different markets regarding the same variable can be very profitable. Sometimes these discrepancies provide a clue to a portfolio manager about a systematic mispricing in a particular market. Unfortunately, most frequently, the discrepant information is a clue that the models are misformulated and that some other variables, such as liquidity differences or carry costs are not being accounted for properly. Other times, the dynamics among the variables are not properly modeled or, perhaps, the dynamics inexplicably change over time. The point, of course, is that while market information is a rich input into evaluating bonds, currencies, and derivatives, the limitations of modeling reinforce the need for the portfolio manager to understand all parts of the process, including model development, and to think carefully about the meaning of the information considered.

The fixed income market has many unique aspects creating both opportunities and challenges. Liquidity can vary from one of the most liquid instruments in the world such as, U.S. Treasury bills, to some of the more illiquid instruments, such as private loans and nonagency mortgages. Some investors can bear this liquidity risk while others will pay large amounts to avoid it. Regulatory differences can also create distortions, such as the usual steepness of the front end of the yield curve created by money market regulations which limit how much maturity and duration risk that money market funds can take. Accounting differences can make banks or other entities more interested in some fixed income securities than others, not for any economic reason, but simply because of accounting treatment of one security versus another.

One of the key facets in constructing the portfolio is to realize that these frictions exist and to try to systematically take advantage of them. The portfolio manager recognizes these elements, as "structural" inefficiencies, and may try to take advantage of them in an effort to add to the risk adjusted returns of portfolios. As an example, one structural peculiarity is the American homeowner's constant need to be able to prepay their home mortgage—which can make agency mortgage backed securities (where an investor sells them this prepayment option) an attractive long-term, risk-adjusted performer. The fixed income market creates many of these opportunities for all of the reasons listed above, and the portfolio manager seeks to take advantage of them as much as possible. As the market evolves and new instruments, regulations, or accounting rules are introduced to the market, these frictions and challenges will likely continue to exist in various forms. Uncertain truths are commonplace in the profession.

DURATION AND YIELD CURVE

The very extreme case of two assets, cash and 30-year U.S. Treasury bonds, provides an example of the clean, unambiguous importance of duration. Over the short term in this portfolio, the vast majority of return performance is determined by the change in long U.S. Treasury rates and the percentage of the portfolio allocated to the long U.S. Treasury. Ambiguities regarding investment intent increase with the number of permissible investment choices. For example, merely adding a zero-coupon bond whose duration is similar to that of the long U.S. Treasury bond complicates the decision process. The zero-coupon bond, although similar in duration to the 30-year U.S. Treasury, has a unique set of performance characteristics. Its dynamic yield curve and volatility changes as well as duration decay will differ over time from the 30-year U.S. Treasury. Although possible, it is unlikely for a crosscurrent of portfolio themes to prevail in this example.

As investment alternatives expand, the crosscurrents of decision making increase at a substantially greater rate. In Exhibit 20.6, the ambiguities of these choices and their impacts are noted by the double arrows indicating feedback effects. The exhibit attempts to include all of the possible investment choices available to the fixed income portfolio manager and to illustrate the volume of decisions that are constantly required to manage an international portfolio.

Forward curves (future yield curves predicted by current interest rates) are rarely, if ever, realized. Monetary policy shifts are enacted, usually, through changes to the policy target rate. These changes indirectly alter the shape of the yield curve and rate volatility levels. The management of yield curve shape changes, capitalizing on disagreements, is a portfolio manager's potent source of superior return. Historically, short-term interest rates have been more volatile than long-term interest rates. An implication of these differentials on historical volatility is that yield curve shapes are unstable. In fact, during the past 20 years there have been numerous large swings in the shape of the yield curve.

Beyond offering a rich arena of yield curve management, shape changes exert significant influences on intermarket and intramarket bond spreads. It is easy to imagine a number of potentially conflicting strategies arising from a given forecast of particular interest rates during a particular period. It is through changes such as those associated with the yield curve coupled with a comprehensive understanding of the various classes of bonds that enable the construction of a portfolio consistent with one's forecasts and convictions. Exhibit 20.6 is a partial representation of sets of bonds and the influences that cause their prices to change and the logical investment strategy per bond type from a given economic and price environment.

VOLATILITY

The portfolio manager must define interest rate volatility, specifying it as a function of both maturity and term. Generally, volatility is a declining function of both maturity and term. Historical data substantiate this proposition. The natural implication of this proposition is that for a given portfolio duration, the portfolio's shorter securities are expected to be more volatile in a yield sense or more risky than its longer bonds. For substantiation of this point, the portfolio manager need only consider the OTC market for options on U.S. Treasury securities to understand the market's pricing of yield curve volatilities.

The assignment or selection of volatility along international yield curves is an important decision for the global fixed income portfolio manager. It not only affects the valuation of imbedded and actual call options but it affects the overall risk adjustments of the portfolio. Risk-adjusted durations, risk-adjusted convexities, and risk-adjusted portfolio yield are partially a function of volatility. Therefore, strategically, the portfolio manager may want to buy volatility on a particular part of a yield curve and sell it at another part to secure the desired risk-adjusted factors.

Volatility itself is an important characteristic that must be accounted for and managed by the portfolio manager in the following contexts:

1. *Option hedging of positions.* As volatility increases, the value of a given option will increase. Therefore, the popular strategy of covered writes, where a portfolio manager shorts an option against an underlying cash position to gain extra income for the portfolio, actually becomes a costly strategy when volatility increases.
2. *Securities with embedded options.* If the bond portfolio manager holds putable bonds, as volatility increases, the value of the embedded option to put the bond to the issuer increases in value as volatility increases. If

the bond portfolio manager is long a callable security, the issuer has the right to call the bond at a particular price. The value of this bond will decrease as volatility increases.

3. *Credit spread trading.* As implied volatility increases, the price of spread products such as emerging market sovereign, international corporate, or international mortgage debt will decrease in value. The market will assign a greater value to the call option and to more liquid securities because bid/ask spreads are volatility dependent.

4. *Trading implied volatility.* A global bond portfolio manager will assess the implied volatility in the markets and may buy or sell different volatilities along the global yield curves depending on their relative assessment of the markets' valuation for these implied volatilities.

Global interest rate volatilities are usually the result of a reversal of long-standing policies. For example, initially, a generous monetary policy in a given country should reduce interest rates in that country and promote growth. But, ultimately, this policy hinders growth as factor price volatility increases. A reversal of monetary policy in a given country with a "tight" mode will raise interest rates and slow economic growth. And sometimes, the monetary policies of one country can have a multicountry interest rate impact. Dramatic changes in fiscal and tax policies also induce volatility in the bond markets. Intrabond/currency market correlations are an important input to the risk-adjustment analysis of global fixed income portfolios.

The volatility exposure characteristic of the global fixed income portfolio is a very important decision. The expectation for a particular volatility factor is an input to the valuation of most bonds in the market. Mortgage securities and corporate bonds generally contain embedded options and are affected substantially by volatility forecasts. Exhibit 20.7 provides a guide for strategy selection based on volatility, yield curve change, and economic forecasts. Details are provided for each sector of the bond markets.

In addition to product-related volatility, which has dominated our discussion so far, let's introduce financial volatility and the macroeconomic effects of prolonged periods of either high or low volatility. Then, let's consider how that may feed back into the portfolio manager's forecasts for interest rates. In general, sustained levels of high volatility will retard economic growth and sustained levels of low volatility will promote economic growth. This truth is the basis for the monetarist's advocacy of low stable money supply growth to achieve sustained, noninflationary economic growth.

If a high degree of volatility is a natural implication of a global interest rate forecast, then the drift component specification and the assumptions for the correlation of volatility along international yield curves are important. (Inferences about volatility are difficult and model dependent.) The

EXHIBIT 20.7 Guide to Strategy Selection Based on Forecasts

Sector/ Forecast	High Volatility	Low Volatility	Lower Rates, Steeper Yield Curve	Lower Rates, Flatter Yield Curve	Higher Rates, Steeper Yield Curve	Higher Rates, Flatter Yield Curve
Corporates						
Growth	Lower-quality noncall-able	Lower-quality callable	Lower-quality non-callable	Lower-quality non-callable putable	Lower-quality callable	Lower-quality putable callable
Recession	Avoid	High quality callable	Avoid	Avoid	Avoid	Avoid
Mortgages						
Growth	Convex PO discount mtgs. PACS	Premium PACS nonagency passthroughs	Current coupon PO long discount CMO	Current coupon PO long Z tranches	Positively convex IO premium passthroughs	Avoid
Recession	Convex IO discount projects PACs	Negatively convex IO passthroughs	Current coupon passthroughs inter-mediate PACs	Long PACs	Positively convex IO premium passthroughs	Positively convex IO premium passthroughs
Governments						
Growth	Barbell	Bullet	Long bullet	Long barbell	Cash	Cash
Recession	Barbell	Bullet	Long bullet	Long barbell	Cash	Cash
Foreign Bonds						
Growth	Industrialized markets low duration (avoid)	Emerging markets low duration				
Recession	Industrialized markets high duration	Industrialized nations high duration				
Foreign Currency						
Growth	Emerging markets	Emerging markets				
Recession	Industrialized markets	Industrialized markets				

576

forecasted volatility expectation can then be compared to the market's pricing—that is, the market's expectation for volatility. The decision to buy or sell volatility in the portfolio is the result of this comparison. Simply stated, if forecasted volatility exceeds (is less than) market volatility, then employ strategies that buy (sell) volatility.

Inflation-Linked Bonds

Most industrialized countries issue inflation protected sovereign bonds. The inflation-protected securities are composed of a nominal coupon, a variable inflation coupon that is determined as a function of future inflation, and a real rate component. The real rate prevailing in the market for any term any time may be greater than or lower than the nominal coupon. In the United States, these securities issued by the U.S. government are referred to as TIPS (U.S. Treasury Inflation Protected Securities) and in Europe these securities are referred to as *linkers*.

Inflation-linked bonds provide investors an opportunity to express forecasts for inflation and real interest rate changes in various countries. Generally speaking, an investor would desire exposure to inflation-linked bonds if inflation is expected to increase relative to inflation expectations or a drop in real interest rates is anticipated. The inflation-linked bonds should perform best if a decline in real rates is coincident with higher inflation. Changes in real interest rates will generally occur asymmetrically along the yield curve and the greatest performance impact will be associated with the longest maturities. While a complete analysis of the choice requires estimates of curve changes on both the inflation-linked and nominal instrument as well as other considerations, a common metric is the expected change in the breakeven inflation rate. This, in its simplest form, is the difference between the inflation-linked bond's real rate and the nominal rate for a bond of the same maturity. When this tool is combined with the idea of country overweight or underweight, the portfolio manager has the opportunity to take a view on relative changes in the breakeven inflation rate of different countries involved.

INTERNATIONAL CORPORATE BONDS

The yield spread of a corporate bond relative to a government bond is negatively correlated to the growth of the economy. Greater economic growth in the global economy generally provides greater profitability to corporations by reducing the probability of default. Yield spreads of corporate bonds over government bonds narrow as default risk diminishes.

Cursory empirical evidence indicates that the inflection points of the yield spreads are related to turning points of bond yields.

A portfolio manager who can confidently identify the transition from recession to growth and vice versa can add substantially to portfolio performance. Not only will he forecast, accurately, the change in the direction of interest rates and aid in currency selection, but he will also add tremendous value with their sector choices. Empirical evidence suggests that low quality corporate bonds satisfy the confident high growth forecast. Holding global government bond rates constant, the most potent relative returns would result from low quality, noncallable, long maturity corporate bonds in improving emerging market countries. Alternatively, corporate bonds should be sold entirely if an economic slowdown or recession is forecast or "buy protection" using credit default swaps to hedge or to profit from widening credit spreads.

Corporate bond spreads reflect the quality of the credit (issuer's credit rating) and the credit quality of the country of domicile. For this reason, corporate bond spreads are likely to be more volatile than government bonds. They may even perform asymmetrically with respect to the direction of volatility changes. Asymmetrical changes in value occur in a typical callable corporate bond for two reasons: the embedded call features and the normal asymmetry associated with quality spread term structures.

Here is an example which better illustrates these issues. Assume we have a corporate bond rated "A" with a 30-year maturity, callable in five years at 105. The prevailing generic quality term spreads for similar structures are as follows: AAA—0.50%, AA—0.65%, A—1.00%, BAA—1.65%, BA—2.75%, and B—4.50%. Exhibit 20.8 illustrates the asymmetry

EXHIBIT 20.8 Credit Spreads, Call Options, and Price Asymmetries
Consider the following hypothetical "A" rated international sovereign bond, denominated in dollars, 7.00%, maturing 9/15/31 priced at 100, callable 9/15/06 at 105

| | Yield Spread | | Price to | Price to | Percent Price Change | |
Rating	(%)	Yield	Call	Maturity	To Call	To Maturity
AAA	0.50	6.50	103.921	106.563	3.92	6.56
AA	0.65	6.65	103.270	104.523	3.27	4.52
A	1.00	7.00	N/A	100.000	0	
Baa	1.65	7.65	N/A	92.396	(7.6)	
Ba	2.75	8.75	N/A	81.531	(18.47)	
B	4.50	10.50	N/A	68.213	(31.79)	

Note: For simplicity, assume a flat term structure at 6.00%, constant credit spreads along the term structure, and a constant term structure volatility.

feature. It shows the possible performance result as the bond spread narrows. Because its duration shrinks, its price does not change significantly relative to the downgrade. If there is a downgrade and the call option goes "out-of-the-money," the price change is quite large. The asymmetry is quite apparent. The portfolio manager must determine how much yield is required to compensate for this risk. The portfolio manager must first assign a particular volatility assumption to each issuer so that the proper yield premium can be determined. The manager may simply choose to assign a probability to both scenarios to assist in the decision process.

INTERNATIONAL INVESTING AND POLITICAL EXTERNALITIES

The actions of government officials and officials of regulatory bodies and agencies can shift market expectations quickly. A perfect macroeconomic forecast and the investments associated with that forecast can be ruined by intervention. As such, the portfolio manager must be concerned with contingent states and a probability assessment of those contingencies.

Fiscal authorities and central banks' intervention have created a form of "government volatility" that may distort risk premiums and artificially drive capital to less-optimal areas. Such actions create yield subsidies crowding out private capital and lead to inefficient capital markets with the risk of unintended consequences

In the emerging markets, for example, an IMF rescue plan can resuscitate a country on the brink of default and instigate a tremendous rally in the bonds. Similarly, in times of conflict, the political decision by a less developed country to allow a developed nation to use its airspace and military bases can provide substantial implicit support to that country's financial assets. The portfolio manager must consider the abstract unexpected.

FOREIGN INVESTMENT SELECTION

The tasks confronting a global fixed income portfolio manager become increasingly complex as global bond markets expand. The development of emerging economies' capital markets have greatly broadened the opportunity set for bond investors. While the U.S. bond market remains the world's largest single market, it accounts for only 35% of the overall global market. A portfolio manager who sticks solely with domestic bonds is missing out on 65% of the world's fixed income opportunities.

The world capital markets present a huge and broadly distributed set of investment considerations and choices. In this analysis, these issues will be simplified at the outset, then a few layers of complexity will be added. Exhibit 20.4 is illustrative of how complex matters can become.

The value inherent to a bond is the enforceability of the bond contract. In a very real way, with substantial historical precedent, investments in bonds of foreign issuers can be void of enforceability powers. Investments in some foreign bonds are, perhaps, more akin to equity-type investments. In this regard, political default risk as opposed to corporate default risk is extremely low but real. This risk should be considered in addition to the volatility risks implied by the options markets for foreign bonds and currencies and should be reflected in the portfolio risk adjustments.

A region/country consideration set for the global fixed income portfolio manager today includes: (1) Canada, (2) Europe, (3) Asia, (4) Australia and New Zealand, (5) Russia and Eastern Europe, (6) Latin America, (7) Middle East, and (8) Africa. Of course, depending on the appetite for global risk, a portfolio manager may wish to consider a more simplified country selection set representative of advanced capital markets, for example, considering only: (1) Canada, (2) Europe, and (3) Japan. In any of the above instances, the analytical focus continues on specific country macroeconomics as in our one country example, both cyclical and secular, but the political analysis would take on greater importance. Additionally, currency valuations are introduced.

Over the long term, cumulative returns from foreign and domestic bonds tend to be similar. Yet the relationship between returns on foreign and U.S. bonds has historically been cyclical.

There are four major components of risk and reward in international bonds: (1) yield, (2) change of interest rates, (3) changes in currency values, and (4) liquidity. The components are a function of market risk, credit risk, and political risk. The last component, liquidity, is particularly significant to the global fixed income portfolio manager when considering emerging-market bonds. Less liquid markets may provide extraordinary yields and performance opportunities but have genuine hazards during periods of rising interest rates or political/economic volatility. By contrast, because the cash, futures, forward, options, and swap markets in the larger international capital markets are fairly well developed, market inferences about volatility expectations and forward break-even rates and prices for both currencies and bonds are more easily discerned. Exhibit 20.9 provides examples of this information. Unfortunately, the same cannot be said for most emerging country markets.

As mentioned above, the global fixed income portfolio manager's analysis of government bonds in foreign countries is similar across all bond markets. However, the portfolio manager must consider the currency risk as a distinct investment decision separated from the decision to invest in the foreign country's bond market. Currency analysis must consider current accounts, trade accounts, capital accounts, monetary policy, fiscal policy,

EXHIBIT 20.9 International Fixed Income Investing

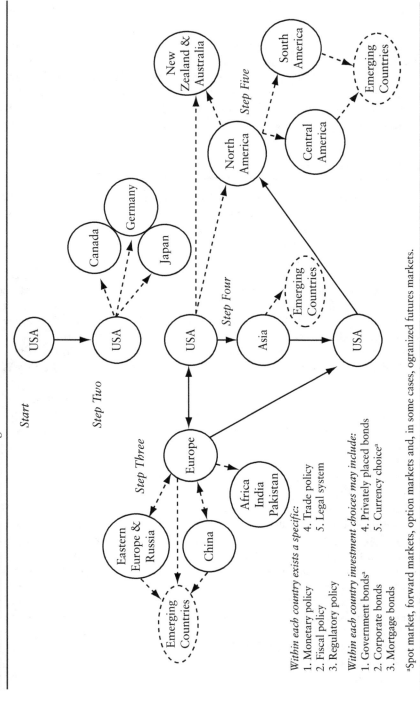

Start

Step Two

Step Three

Step Four

Step Five

Within each country exists a specific:
1. Monetary policy
2. Fiscal policy
3. Regulatory policy
4. Trade policy
5. Legal system

Within each country investment choices may include:
1. Government bonds[a]
2. Corporate bonds
3. Mortgage bonds
4. Privately placed bonds
5. Currency choice[a]

[a]Spot market, forward markets, option markets and, in some cases, ogranized futures markets.

581

as well as regulatory, institutional and tax policies and more. The bond decision ought to be considered as a currency-hedged one, that is, the bond stripped of the currency exposure. By adding currency exposure, the portfolio manager may further increase their chances for higher returns, but they will also take on greater risk or variance of returns via their exposure to a variety of foreign currency price fluctuations.

CURRENCY SELECTION

There are many theories about currency-value determination. The most popular fundamental ones are based on (1) purchasing power parity (PPP), (2) trade balances/capital flows, (3) real interest rate differentials, and (4) growth rates and growth prospects. None of these are very satisfying. Each has proved important but the importance of any one has varied over time. Therefore, technical analysis of the currency markets is quite prevalent.

The portfolio manager must decide upon the relative weights of each of the factors, in conjunction with technical analysis since, most often, the signals will be mixed. For example, PPP may be positive for the currency while the trade balance is negative. The portfolio manager must also consider the influence of cartels, such as European Monetary Union efforts and central bank intervention in the currency markets. A simplified analysis is provided below:

The yen/dollar forward values are derived from the prevailing interest rate term structure differentials between the two markets. For example, 5% difference in one-year rates between the United States and Japan yields an approximate 5% drop in one-year forward currency values. However, forward currency values are affected by other variables as well. So, one can express the conviction that the interest rate term structure differentials are not fully incorporating the influence of those other variables by being long or short the forward currency exchange rates, by golly.

Global bond portfolio performance can be enhanced dramatically when the global fixed income portfolio manager considers as many potential factor changes as possible. When the portfolio manager derives comparative rate forecasts that differ significantly from the current static snapshot of currency rates as evidenced in current forward currency markets, this potential exists. Of course, their conclusions will have an important impact on their global interest rate bets as well. These decisions are inseparable and provide many performance opportunities for the thorough global fixed income portfolio manager. For the leveraged global money manager, currency selection is critical for another reason. The leveraged money manager searches for the cheapest currency from which to borrow funds. The analysis involves comparing various term currencies rates as swapped into one baseline currency, say U.S. dollars, to identify the currency that trades cheapest to LIBOR for the desired term. The leveraged fund manager will borrow in the cheapest currency to finance all their global bond purchases in whatever country he selects.

Potential measures to stem economic crises are another important market phenomena not always captured in currency valuations. A government may impose emergency economic measures such as capital flow restrictions. In response, short-term interest rates soar. Many investors can be effectively trapped with assets whose values plummet. Portfolios overweight in these countries are exposed to this danger and experience greater volatility and reduced return, which completely opposes the presumed positive pattern of return touted with diversification. Episodes can occur in well-developed economies. For example, as the initial attempt at EMU failed in 1992 and countries dropped out such as the United Kingdom, short-term interest rates across Europe soared as each of these countries attempted to protect their currency values. Ultimately, despite state-of-the-art technology and information, only a keen analysis of the political/economic environment would have enabled a global fixed income portfolio manager to escape these episodes.

KEY POINTS

- The global fixed income portfolio manager creates a global bond portfolio, considering all the possible securities within the "benchmark" set of investment possibilities, selecting duration targets and how best to achieve the duration, yield curve positioning and the distribution of cash flows on the yield curve, convexity, credit quality, country selection/hedged international exposure, and nondollar bond or currency exposure. The global portfolio manager strives to post favorable returns versus competitors.
- Global fixed income portfolio managers, whether total or absolute return in discipline, have a significant role to play that benefits not only fixed income investors but emerging and developing countries, as well, by providing more permanent capital to markets that have the potential to yield attractive returns.
- Global fixed income portfolio managers know that market consensus as reflected in current fixed income securities prices on a forward basis can be an incorrect predictor of future rates. A skillful portfolio manager is able to assess all the germane bits of accessible market information and apply knowledgeable market strategies that express disagreement with current global forward prices.

- The basic factors that the global fixed income portfolio manager must consider worldwide include: economic, political, historic, psychological, monetary and fiscal policies, products available, risks associated in buying and selling these products, the impact on other investors on market movements, regulatory issues, and the competitive advantages of other competing portfolio managers.
- Once the global fixed income portfolio manager gathers global information, they can create short- and long-term interest rate and currency forecasts, time frames for performance, as well as alternative strategies should market conditions alter the initial assumptions.
- The global fixed income portfolio manager armed with interest rate and currency forecasts is faced with the eternal trade-off between expected returns or percentage total returns against risk or the variance of the percentage of total returns and liquidity parameters regardless of the set of fixed income investment or benchmark alternatives.

QUESTIONS

1. How can the global bond portfolio manager attempt to determine if capital flows enhance GDP growth or inflation which, in turn, will aid in making investment decisions?

2. Is the current level of interest rates and bond prices a reflection of future economic growth and activity as well a the amount of credit available?

3. What are the main characteristics of a global fixed income portfolio?

4. When should a portfolio manager have the highest conviction in their proprietary forecast?

5. Should the global fixed income portfolio manager focus on less crowded markets in order to more easily access mispriced securities?

CHAPTER 21

Multifactor Fixed Income Risk Models and Their Applications*

Anthony Lazanas, Ph.D.
Managing Director
Barclays Capital

António Baldaque da Silva, Ph.D.
Director
Barclays Capital

Radu Găbudean, Ph.D.
Vice President
Barclays Capital

Arne D. Staal, Ph.D.
Vice President
Barclays Capital

Multifactor models were previously discussed (Chapter 5), and their applications to equity portfolios developed in Chapter 13. Although they share a similar framework, multifactor models in fixed income use different building blocks and provide a different analysis into the risk of a portfolio. In this chapter, we discuss risk modeling construction and applications to fixed income portfolios.

When analyzing their holdings, portfolio managers constantly monitor their exposures, typically net of a benchmark: What is the portfolio duration? How risky is the overweight to credit? How does it relate to the exposure to mortgages? What is the exposure to specific issuers? Even when portfolio holdings and exposures are well known, portfolio managers increasingly

---

*The authors would like to thank Andy Sparks for his valuable comments.

rely on quantitative techniques to translate this information into a common risk language. Risk models can present a coherent view of the portfolio, its exposures, and how they correlate to each other. They can quantify the risk of each exposure and its contribution to the overall risk of the portfolio.

Fixed income securities are exposed to many different types of risk. Multifactor risk models in this area capture these risks by first identifying common sources along different dimensions, the *systematic* risk factors. All risk not captured by systematic factors is considered *idiosyncratic* or security-specific. Typically, fixed income systematic risk factors are divided into two sets: those that influence securities across asset classes (e.g. yield curve risk) and those specific to a particular asset class (e.g. prepayment risk in securitized products).

There are many ways to define systematic risk factors. For instance, they can be defined purely by statistical methods, observed in the markets, or estimated from asset returns. In fixed income, the standard approach is to use pricing models to calculate the analytics that are the natural candidates for risk factor loadings (also called *sensitivities*). In this setting, the risk factors are estimated from cross-sectional asset returns. This is the approach taken in the Barclays Capital Global Risk Model,[1] which is the model used for illustration throughout this chapter.

In this risk model, the forecasted risk of the portfolio is driven by both a systematic and an idiosyncratic (also called *specific, nonsystematic,* and *concentration*) component. The forecasted systematic risk is a function of the mismatch between the portfolio and the benchmark in the exposures to the risk factors, such as yield curve or spreads. The exposures are aggregated from security-level analytics. The systematic risk is also a function of the volatility of the risk factors, as well as the correlations between them. In this setting, the correlation of returns across securities is driven by the correlation of systematic risk factors these securities load on. As the model uses security-level returns and analytics to estimate the factors, we can recover the idiosyncratic return for each security. This is the return net of all systematic factors. The model uses these idiosyncratic returns to estimate rich specifications for the idiosyncratic risk.

---

[1]The Barclays Capital Global Risk Model is available through POINT®, Barclays Capital portfolio management tool. It is a multicurrency cross-asset model that covers many different asset classes across the fixed income and equity markets, including derivatives in these markets. At the heart of the model is a covariance matrix of risk factors. The model has more than 500 factors, many specific to a particular asset class. The asset class models are periodically reviewed. Structure is imposed to increase the robustness of the estimation of such large covariance matrix. The model is estimated from historical data. It is calibrated using extensive security-level historical data and is updated on a monthly basis.

APPROACHES USED TO ANALYZE RISK

In what follows, we turn to the analysis of the risk of a particular portfolio, going through the different approaches typically used. Specifically, consider a portfolio manager that is benchmarked against the Barclays Capital U.S. Aggregate Index. Moreover, suppose she believes interest rates are coming down—so she wants to be long duration—and that she wants some extra yield in her portfolio—meaning investing in bonds with relatively higher spreads. Finally, let us assume that she is mandated to keep the difference between the returns of the portfolio and the benchmark at around 15 basis points, on a monthly basis. Therefore, she has to track a benchmark, but is allowed to deviate from it up to a point in order to express views that hopefully lead to superior returns. A portfolio manager with such a mandate is called an *enhanced indexer*. The amount of deviation allowed is called the *risk budget* (15 basis points in our example) and can be quantified using a risk model. The risk model produces an estimate of the volatility of the difference of the portfolio and benchmark returns, called *tracking error volatility* (TEV).[2] The portfolio manager should keep the TEV at a level equal to or less than her risk budget. For illustration, we construct a portfolio with 50 securities that is consistent with the portfolio manager's views and risk budget and analyze it throughout this chapter.

Market Structure and Exposure Contributions

The first level of analysis that any portfolio manager usually performs is to compare the portfolio holdings in terms of market value with the holdings from the benchmark. For instance, Exhibit 21.1 shows that the composition of the portfolio has several important mismatches when compared with the benchmark. The portfolio is underweighted in Treasuries and government-related securities by 8.4%. This is compensated with an overweight of 12.3% in corporates, especially in the financials sector. Other mismatches include an underweight in mortgage-backed securities (MBS) (–5.8%) and an overweight in commercial mortgage-backed securities (CMBS) (+2.1%).

Interestingly, for an equity manager, this kind of information—for example, applied to the different industries or sectors of the portfolio—would be of paramount importance to the analysis of the risk of her portfolio. For a fixed income portfolio, this is not the case. Although important, this analysis tells us very little about the true active exposures of a fixed income portfolio. What if the Treasuries in the portfolio have significantly longer duration than those in the benchmark—would we be really "short"

---

[2]In this chapter, we refer to TEV, risk, and the standard deviation of the portfolio net returns interchangeably.

EXHIBIT 21.1   Market Weights for Portfolio and Benchmark

Asset Class	Portfolio	Benchmark	Difference
Total	100.0	100.0	0.0
Treasury	30.2	32.1	−1.9
Government-related	5.8	12.3	−6.5
Corporate industrials	9.0	9.7	−0.7
Corporate utilities	2.9	2.1	0.8
Corporate financials	18.6	6.4	12.2
MBS agency	28.4	34.1	−5.8
ABS	0.0	0.3	−0.3
CMBS	5.2	3.1	2.1

in this asset class? What if the spreads from financials in the portfolio are much smaller than those in the benchmark—is the weight mismatch that important?

To answer this kind of questions, we turn into another typical dimension of analysis—the exposure of the portfolio to major sources of risk. An example of such a risk exposure is the duration of the portfolio. Other exposures typically monitored are the spread duration, convexity, spread level, and vega (if the portfolio has many securities with optionality, such as mortgages or callable bonds).

Exhibit 21.2 shows these analytics at the aggregate level for our portfolio, benchmark and the difference between the two. In particular, we can see that the portfolio is long duration (+0.25 years), consistent with the forecast the manager has regarding yield curve moves. In terms of spread duration, the mismatch is somewhat smaller. We can also see that the portfolio has significantly lower negative convexity than the benchmark (−0.15 versus −0.29), probably coming from the smaller weight MBS securities have in the portfolio. The portfolio has also a higher negative vega, but the number is reasonably small for both universes. Finally, the portfolio has significantly higher spreads (100 basis points) than the benchmark. This mismatch is consistent with the manager's goal of having a higher yield in her portfolio, when compared with the benchmark.

The analysis in the Exhibits 21.1 and 21.2 can be combined to deliver a more detailed picture of where the different exposures are coming from. Exhibit 21.3 shows that analysis for the duration of the portfolio. This exhibit shows that the majority of the mismatch in duration contribution (market-weighted duration exposures) comes from the Treasury component of our portfolio (+0.21). Interestingly, even though we are short in Treasuries,

EXHIBIT 21.2 Aggregate Analytics

Analytics	Portfolio	Benchmark	Difference
Duration	4.55	4.30	0.25
Spread duration	4.67	4.56	0.11
Convexity	−0.15	−0.29	0.13
Vega	−0.02	−0.01	−0.01
Spread	157	57	100

EXHIBIT 21.3 Duration Contribution per Asset Class

Duration Contribution	Portfolio	Benchmark	Difference
Total	4.55	4.30	0.25
Treasury	1.92	1.71	0.21
Government-related	0.40	0.49	−0.09
Corporate	1.31	1.19	0.11
Securitized	0.92	0.90	0.02

we are actually long in duration for that asset class. This means that our Treasury portfolio will be negatively impacted, when compared with the benchmark, by an increase in interest rates. Because we are short in Treasuries, this result must mean that our Treasury portfolio is longer in duration than the Treasury component of the benchmark. Conversely, we have a relatively small contribution to excess duration coming from our very large over exposure to corporates. This means that on average the corporate bonds in the portfolio are significantly shorter in duration than those in the benchmark.

Adding Volatility and Correlations into the Analysis

The analysis above gives us some basic understanding of our exposures to different kinds of risk. However, it is still hard to understand how we can compare the level of risk across these different exposures. What is more risky, my long duration exposure of 0.25 years, or my extra spread of 100 basis points? How can I quantify how serious is the vega mismatch on my portfolio? Specifically, the risk of the portfolio is a function of the exposures to the risk factors, but also of how volatile (how "risky") each of the factors is. So to enhance the analysis we bring volatilities into the picture. Exhibit 21.4 shows the outcome of this addition to our example. In particular, it displays the risk of the different exposures of the portfolio

EXHIBIT 21.4   Isolated Risk per Category

Risk Factors Categories	Risk
Curve	8.5
Volatility	1.7
Spread government-related	3.0
Spread corporate	5.1
Spread securitized	3.0

in isolation (that is, if the only active imbalances were those from that particular set of risk factors).

For example, in Exhibit 21.4 one can see that if the only active weight in the portfolio were the mismatch in the yield curve exposures, the risk of the portfolio would be 8.5 basis points per month. By adding volatilities into the analysis, we can now quantify that the mismatch of +0.25 years in duration "costs" the portfolio 8.5 basis points per month of extra volatility, when taken in isolation.[3] Similarly, if the only mismatch were the exposure to corporate spreads, the risk of the portfolio would be 5.1 basis points. Interestingly, we also see that both government-related and securitized sectors have nontrivial risk, despite having smaller imbalances in terms of market weights. By bringing volatilities into the analysis, we can now compare and quantify the impact of each of the imbalances in the portfolio.

For future reference, consider the volatility of the portfolio if all these sources of risk were independent (e.g. correlations were zero). That number would be 10.9 basis points per month.[4] Of course, this scenario is unrealistic, as these sources of risk are not independent. Also, this analysis does not allow us to understand the interplay between the different imbalances. For instance, we know that the isolated risk associated with the curve is 8.5. But this value can be achieved both by being long or short duration. So the isolated number does not allow us to understand the impact of the curve imbalance to the total risk of the portfolio. The net impact certainly depends on the sign of the imbalance. For instance, if the long exposure in curve is diversified away by a long exposure in credit (due, for instance, to negative correlation between rates and credit spreads), a symmetric (short) curve exposure would add to the risk of the long exposure in credit. The risk is clearly smaller in the first case.

---

[3]Later in this chapter, we refer to this risk number as *Isolated TEV*.
[4]We arrive to this number by taking the square root of the sum of squares of all the numbers in the table: $10.9 = (8.5^2 + 1.7^2 + 3.0^2 + 5.1^2 + 3.0^2)^{0.5}$. Moreover, this number would represent the total systematic risk of the portfolio. This definition is developed later in the chapter.

EXHIBIT 21.5   Correlated Risk per Category

Risk Factors Categories	Risk
Total	9.3
Curve	5.9
Volatility	0.1
Spread government-related	0.1
Spread corporate	2.4
Spread securitized	0.7

To alleviate these shortcomings, we bring correlations into the picture. They allow us to understand the net impact of the different exposures to the portfolio's total risk and to detect potential sources of diversification among the imbalances in the portfolio. Exhibit 21.5 reports the contribution of each of the risk factor groups to the total risk, once all correlations are taken into account. The total risk (9.3 bps/month) is smaller than the zero-correlation risk calculated before (10.9 bps/month) due to generally negative correlations between the curve and the spread factors. The exhibit also allows us to isolate the main sources of risk as being curve (5.9 bps/month) and credit spreads (2.4 bps/month), in line with the evidence from the earlier analysis. In particular, the risk of the government-related and securitized spreads is significantly smaller once correlations are taken into account.

The difference in analysis between the isolated and correlated risks reported in Exhibits 21.4 and 21.5 deserves a bit more discussion. For simplicity, assume there are only two sources of risk in the portfolio—yield curve (Y) and spreads (S). The total systematic variance of the portfolio (P) can be illustrated as follows:

$$VAR(P) = VAR(Y + S) = VAR(Y) + VAR(S) + 2COV(Y, S)$$
$$= Y \times Y + S \times S + 2(Y \times S)$$

where we use the product (X) to represent variances and covariances. Another way to represent this summation is using the following matrix:

$$\begin{bmatrix} Y \times Y & Y \times S \\ Y \times S & S \times S \end{bmatrix}$$

The sum of the four elements in the matrix is the variance of the portfolio. The isolated risk (in standard deviation units) reported in Exhibit 21.4 is the square root of the diagonal terms. So the isolated risk due to spreads is represented as

$$Risk_{Spreads}^{Isolated} = \sqrt{S \times S}$$

It would be a function of the exposure to all spread factors, the volatilities of all these factors and the correlations among them.

The correlated risk reported in Exhibit 21.5 is

$$Risk_{Spreads}^{correlated} = [Y \times S + S \times S] / \sqrt{VAR(P)}$$

that is we sum all elements in the row of interest (row 1 for Y, row 2 for S) from the matrix above, and normalize it by the standard deviation of the portfolio. This statistic (1) takes into account correlations and (2) ensures that the correlated risks of all factors add up to the total risk of the portfolio ($Risk_{Curve}^{correlated} + Risk_{Spreads}^{correlated} = \sqrt{VAR(P)} = STD(P)$).[5]

The generic analysis we just performed constitutes the first step into the description of the risk associated with a portfolio. The analysis refers to categories of risk factors (such as "curve" or "spreads"). However, a factor based risk model allows for a significantly deeper analysis of the imbalances the portfolio may have. Each of the risk categories referred to above can be described with a rich set of detailed risk factors. Typically in a fixed income factor model, each asset class has a specific set of risk factors, in addition to the potential set of factors common to all (e.g. curve factors). These asset-specific risk factors are designed to capture the particular sources of risk the asset class is exposed to. In the following section, we go through a risk report built in such a way, emphasizing risk factors that are common or particular to the different asset classes. Along the way, we demonstrate how the report offers insights from both a risk management and a portfolio construction perspective.

A Detailed Risk Report

In this section, we continue the analysis of the portfolio introduced previously, a 50-bond portfolio benchmarked against the Barclays Capital U.S. Aggregate Index. The report package we present was generated using POINT®, Barclays Capital cross-asset portfolio analysis and construction system, and gives a very detailed picture of the risk embedded in the portfolio. The package is divided into four types of reports: summary reports, factor exposure reports, issue/issuer level reports and scenario analysis reports. Some of the information we reviewed earlier can be thought of as summary reports.

---

[5]In this example, we focus only on the systematic component of risk. Later, the normalization is with respect to the total risk of the portfolio, including idiosyncratic risk.

Summary Report

Exhibit 21.6 illustrates a typical risk summary statistics report. It shows that the portfolio has 50 positions, but from only 27 issuers. This number implies limited ability to diversify idiosyncratic risk, as we will see below. The report confirms that the portfolio is long duration (OAD of 4.55 years versus 4.30 years for the benchmark) and has higher yield (yield to worst of 3.71% versus 2.83% for the benchmark) and coupon (4.73% versus 4.46% for the benchmark).

The exhibit also reports that the total volatility of the portfolio (163.3 bps/month) is higher than that of the benchmark (158.1 bps/month). This is not surprising: longer duration, higher spread and less diversification all

EXHIBIT 21.6 Summary Statistics Report

	Portfolio	Benchmark	
A. Parameter			
Positions	50	8191	
Issuers	27	787	
Currencies	1	1	
Market value ($ millions)	200	14,762	
Notional ($ millions)	187	13,750	
B. Analytics	**Portfolio**	**Benchmark**	**Difference**
Coupon	4.73	4.46	0.27
Average life	6.63	6.35	0.27
Yield to worst	3.71	2.83	0.88
Spread	157	57	100
Duration	4.55	4.30	0.25
Vega	−0.02	−0.01	−0.01
Spread duration	4.67	4.56	0.11
Convexity	−0.15	−0.29	0.13
C. Volatility	**Portfolio**	**Benchmark**	**TEV**
Systematic	162.9	158.0	9.3
Idiosyncratic	11.1	5.6	10.1
Total	163.3	158.1	13.7
D. Portfolio Beta			1.03

tend to increase the volatility of a portfolio. Because of its higher volatility, we refer to the portfolio as riskier than the benchmark. Looking into the different components of the portfolio's total volatility, the exhibit reports that the idiosyncratic volatility of the portfolio is significantly smaller than that of the systematic (11.1 bps/month versus 162.9 bps/month, respectively). This is also expected from a portfolio of investment-grade bonds. Given the fact that by construction the systematic and idiosyncratic components of risk are independent, we can calculate the total volatility of the portfolio as

$$TEV_{PTF} = \sqrt{162.9^2 + 11.1^2} = 163.3$$

There are two interesting observations regarding this number: first, the total volatility is smaller than the sum of the volatilities of the two components. This is the diversification benefit that comes from combining independent sources of risk. Second, the total volatility is very close to the systematic one. This may suggest that the idiosyncratic risk is irrelevant. That is an erroneous and dangerous conclusion. In particular, when managing against a benchmark, the focus should be on the net exposures and risk, not on their absolute counterparts. In Exhibit 21.6 the total TEV is reported as 13.7 bps/month. This means that the model forecasts the portfolio return to be typically no more than 14 bps/month higher or lower than the return of the benchmark. This number is in line with the risk budget of our manager. The exhibit also reports idiosyncratic TEV of 10.1 bps/month, which is greater than the systematic TEV (9.3). When measured against the benchmark, our major source of risk is idiosyncratic, contrary to the conclusion one could draw by looking only at the portfolio's volatility. The TEV of our portfolio is also bigger than the difference between the volatilities of the portfolio and benchmark. Again, this is not surprising: the volatility depends on the absolute exposures, while the TEV measures imbalances between these absolute exposures from the portfolio and the benchmark. For the TEV what matters most is the correlation between these absolute exposures. Depending on this correlation, the TEV may be smaller or bigger than the difference in volatilities.

Finally, the report estimates the portfolio to have a beta of 1.03 to the benchmark. This statistic measures the *co-movement* between the portfolio and the benchmark. We can read it as follows: the model forecasts that a movement of 10 bps in the benchmark leads to a movement of 10.3 bps in the portfolio in the same direction. Note that a beta of less than one does not mean that the portfolio is less risky than the benchmark. In the limit, if the portfolio and benchmark are uncorrelated, the portfolio beta is zero but obviously that does not mean that the portfolio has zero risk. Finally, one can compute many different "betas" for the portfolio or subcomponents of

EXHIBIT 21.7   Factor Partition—Risk Analysis

Risk Factor Group	Isolated TEV	Contribution to TEV	Liquidation Effect on TEV	TEV Elasticity (%)
Total	13.7	13.7	−13.7	1.0
Systematic risk	9.3	6.3	−3.6	0.5
Curve	8.5	4.0	−1.5	0.3
Volatility	1.7	0.1	0.0	0.0
Government-related spreads	3.0	0.1	0.2	0.0
Corporate spreads	5.1	1.6	−0.7	0.1
Securitized spreads	3.0	0.5	−0.2	0.1
Idiosyncratic risk	10.1	7.4	−4.4	0.5

it.[6] A simple and widely used one is the "duration beta," given by the ratio of the portfolio duration to that of the benchmark. In our case this ratio is 4.55/4.30 = 1.06. This implies that the portfolio has a return from yield curve movements around 1.06 times larger than that of the benchmark. This beta is larger than the portfolio beta (1.03), meaning that net exposures to other factors (e.g. spreads) "hedge" the portfolio's curve risk.

This first summary report (Exhibit 21.6) allows us to get a glimpse into the risk of the portfolio. However, we want to know in more detail what the source of this risk is. To do that, we turn into the next two summary reports. In the first, risk is partitioned across different groups of risk factors. In the second, the partition is across groups of securities/asset classes.

Exhibit 21.7 shows four different statistics associated with each set of risk factors. The first two were somewhat explored in Exhibit 21.4 and Exhibit 21.5.[7] The exhibit reports in the first column the isolated TEV, that is, the risk associated with that particular set of risk factors only. We see that in an isolated analysis, the systematic and idiosyncratic risks are balanced, at 9.3 and 10.1 respectively. The report also shows the isolated risk associated with the major components of systematic risk. As discussed before, all components of systematic risk have nontrivial isolated risk, but only curve and credit spreads are significant when we look into the contributions to TEV. If we look across factors, the major contributors are idiosyncratic risk, curve and credit spreads. Other systematic exposures are relatively small.

---

[6]For example, see Exhibit 21.13 later in this chapter.
[7]Note that the contribution numbers are different than those from Exhibit 21.5 because there we reported the contribution to systematic—not total—risk.

EXHBIT 21.8   Security Partition—Risk Analysis I

Security	NMW	Contribution to TEV		
Partition Bucket	(%)	Systematic	Idiosyncratic	Total
Total	0.0	6.3	7.4	13.7
Treasuries	−2.0	2.9	0.2	3.1
Government agencies	−5.4	0.5	0.4	0.9
Government nonagencies	−1.0	−1.4	0.1	−1.3
Corporates	12.4	3.4	4.3	7.7
MBS	−5.8	0.9	0.8	1.7
ABS	−0.3	0.0	0.0	0.0
CMBS	2.1	0.0	1.6	1.6

Another look into the correlation comes when we analyze the liquidation effect reported on the table. This number represents the change in TEV when we completely hedge that particular group of risk factors. For instance, if we hedge the curve component of our portfolio, our TEV drops by 1.5 bps/month, from 13.7 to 12.2. One may think that the drop is rather small, given the magnitude of isolated risk the curve represents. However, if we hedge the curve, we also eliminate the beneficial effect the negative correlation between curve and spreads have on the overall risk of the portfolio. Therefore, we have a more limited impact when hedging the curve risk. In fact, for this portfolio we see that hedging any particular set of risk factors has a limited effect in the overall risk.

The TEV elasticity reported in the last column gives another perspective into how the TEV in the portfolio changes when we change the risk loadings. Specifically, it tells us what the percentage change in TEV would be if we changed our exposure to that particular set of factors by 1%. We can see that if we reduce our exposure to corporate spreads by 1%, our TEV would decrease by 0.1%.

We perform a similar analysis in Exhibit 21.8, but applied to a security partition. That is, instead of looking at individual sources of risk (e.g., curve) across all securities, we now aggregate all sources of risk within a security and report analytics for different groups of these securities (e.g., subportfolios). In particular, Exhibit 21.8 reports the results by asset class. We can see that the majority of risk (7.7 bps/month) is coming from the corporate component of the portfolio.[8] Corporates are also the primary contributor to

---

[8]This result does not contradict the findings in Exhibit 21.7, where we see that curve is the major source of risk. Remember that the curve risk can come from our corporate subportfolio.

EXHIBIT 21.9 Security Partition—Risk Analysis II

Security Partition Bucket	Isolated TEV	Liquidation Effect on TEV	TEV Elasticity (%)
Total	13.7	−13.7	1.0
Treasuries	7.4	−1.1	0.2
Government agencies	9.1	2.0	0.1
Government nonagencies	6.7	2.7	−0.1
Corporates	15.2	0.6	0.6
MBS	5.8	−0.5	0.1
ABS	1.1	0.1	0.0
CMBS	5.1	−0.7	0.1

the portfolio's systematic and idiosyncratic components of risk. This is not surprising, given the portfolio's large net market weight (NMW) to this sector. There are two other important sources of risk. The first is the Treasuries subportfolio, with 3.1 bps/month of risk. This risk comes mainly from the mismatch in duration. The second comes from the idiosyncratic risk of the CMBS component of the portfolio. Even though the NMW and systematic risk are not significant for this asset class, the relatively small number of (risky) CMBS positions in the portfolio causes it to have significant idiosyncratic risk (three securities in the portfolio versus 1,735 in the index). Since the portfolio manager is trying to replicate a very large benchmark with only 50 positions, she has to be very confident in the issuers selected. This report highlights the significant name risk the portfolio is exposed to.

Exhibit 21.9 completes the analysis, reporting other important risk statistics about the different asset classes within the portfolio. These statistics mimic the analysis done in terms of risk factor partitions in Exhibit 21.7, so we will not repeat their definitions. We focus on the numbers. In particular, the isolated TEV from the corporate sector is 15.2 bps/month, higher than the total risk of the portfolio. This means that the exposures to the other asset classes, on average, hedge our credit portfolio. The exhibit also reports that the agencies isolated risk is very large. This is due to the large negative net exposure (−5.4%) we have to this asset class. But the risk is fully hedged by the other exposures of the portfolio (e.g. long exposure to credit or long duration on Treasuries), so overall the risk contribution of this asset class is small, as previously discussed. We can even take the analysis a bit further: Exhibit 21.9 shows us through the liquidation effect that if we eliminate the imbalance the portfolio has on agencies, we actually would increase the total risk of the portfolio by 2.0 bps/month. In short, we would be eliminating the hedge this asset class provides to the global portfolio, therefore increasing its risk. The exposures to this asset class were clearly built to counteract other exposures in the portfolio. Finally, Exhibit 21.9 also reports the TEV elasticity of the different components of the portfolio. This number represents the percentage change in TEV if the NMW to that subportfolio changes by 1%, so we need to read the numbers with an opposite sign if the NMW is negative. In particular, if we increase the weight of the agency portfolio in absolute value (making it "more short") by 1%, we would actually increase the TEV by 0.1%. This result shows that the position in agencies provides hedging "on average," but marginally it is already increasing the risk of the portfolio. In other words, the hedging went beyond its optimal value.

This set of summary reports gives us a very clear picture of the major sources of risk and how they relate to each other. In what follows, we focus on the more detailed analysis of the individual systematic sources of risk.

Factor Exposure Reports

At the heart of a multifactor risk model is the definition of the set of systematic factors that drive risk across the portfolio. As described above, there are different types of risk a fixed income portfolio is exposed to. In what follows, we focus on the three major types: curve, credit and prepayment risk. Specifically in what regards the latter two, we use the credit and MBS component of the portfolio, respectively, to illustrate how to measure risks along these dimensions. Moreover, to keep the example simple, we show only a partial view of all relevant factors for these sources of risk. Later in this section we refer briefly to other sources of risk a fixed income portfolio may be exposed to.

Curve Risk   As the previous analysis shows (e.g. Exhibit 21.7), curve is the major source of risk in our portfolio. This kind of risk is embedded in virtually all fixed income securities,[9] therefore mismatches are very penalizing.

When analyzing curve risk, we should use the curve of reference we are interested in. Depending on the portfolio and circumstances, this is typically the government or swap curve.[10] In calm periods, the behavior of the swap curve tends to match that of the government curve. However, during liquidity crises (e.g., the Russian crisis in 1998 or the credit crisis in 2008), they can diverge significantly. To capture these different behaviors adequately, we analyze curve risk using the following decomposition: For government

---

[9]Exceptions are for instance floaters or distressed securities.
[10]Other curves that can be used are, for instance, the municipals (tax free) curve, derivatives-based curves, and the like.

products, the curve risk is assessed using the government curve. For all other products in our portfolio (that usually trade off the swap curve), this risk is measured using both the Treasury curve and swap spreads (i.e., the spreads between the swap and the government curve). Other decompositions are also possible.

The risk associated with each of these curves can be described by the exposure the portfolio has to different points along the curve and a convexity term, and how volatile and correlated the movement in these points of the curve are. For a typical portfolio, a good description of the curve can be achieved by looking at a relatively small number of points along the curve (called key rates), for example 6-month, 2-year, 5-year, 10-year, 20-year, and 30-year. An alternative set of factors used to capture yield curve risk can be defined using statistical analysis of the historical realizations of the various yield curve points. The statistical method used most often is called *principal component analysis* (PCA). This method defines factors that are statistically independent of each other. Typically three or four such factors are sufficient to explain the risk associated with changes of yields across the yield curve. PCA analysis has several shortcomings and must be used with caution. Using a larger set of economic factors, such as the key rate points described above is more intuitive and captures the risk of specialized portfolios better. In our analysis, we follow the key rates approach.

Exhibit 21.10 details the risk in our portfolio associated with the U.S. Treasury curve. It starts by describing all risk factors our portfolio or benchmark load on. As discussed above, we identify the six key rate (KR) points in the curve plus the convexity term as the risk factors associated with U.S. Treasury risk. They are described in the first column of panel A in the exhibit. They measure the risk associated with moves in that particular point in the curve. Exposure to these risk factors is measured by the key rate durations (KRD) for each of the six points. The description of the loading is in the second column of the exhibit, while its value for the portfolio, benchmark and the difference is displayed in the next columns. Key rate durations are also called *partial durations*, as they add up to approximately the duration of the portfolio. Their loadings are constructed by aggregating partial durations across (virtually) all the securities. For instance, for our portfolio, the sum of the key rate durations is 0.14 + 0.86 + 1.30 + 0.77 + 1.02 + 0.47 = 4.56, very close to the total duration of our portfolio.

Looking at the exhibit, we see significant mismatches in the duration profiles between our portfolio and its benchmark, namely at the 10-year and 20-year points on the curve. Specifically, we are short 0.41 years at the 10-year point and long 0.53 years at the 20-year point. How serious is this mismatch? Looking at the factor volatility column, it can be seen that these points on the curve have been very volatile at around 40 bps/month. If we

EXHIBIT 21.10   Treasury Curve Risk

A. Exposures and Factor Volatility

Factor Name	Units	Exposure			Factor Volatility
		Portfolio	Benchmark	Net	
USD 6M key rate	KRD (Yr)	0.14	0.15	−0.01	36.0
USD 2Y key rate	KRD (Yr)	0.86	0.70	0.15	38.0
USD 5Y key rate	KRD (Yr)	1.30	1.25	0.05	44.3
USD 10Y key rate	KRD (Yr)	0.77	1.13	−0.36	44.2
USD 20Y key rate	KRD (Yr)	1.02	0.53	0.49	39.6
USD 30Y key rate	KRD (Yr)	0.47	0.53	−0.06	39.7
USD convexity	OAC	−0.15	−0.29	0.13	8.4

B. Other Risk Statistics

Factor Name	Return Impact of a Typical Move		Marginal Contribution to TEV	TEV Elasticity (%)
	Isolated	Correlated		
USD 6M key rate	0.5	−2.4	6.3	0.0
USD 2Y key rate	−5.8	−4.5	12.2	0.1
USD 5Y key rate	−2.0	−4.5	14.5	0.0
USD 10Y key rate	15.9	−5.0	15.9	−0.4
USD 20Y key rate	−19.5	−5.2	14.9	0.5
USD 30Y key rate	2.5	−5.2	14.8	−0.1
USD convexity	1.1	2.0	1.2	0.0

interpret this volatility as a typical move, the first two columns of panel B show us the potential impact of such a movement in the return of our portfolio, net of benchmark. For instance, a typical move up (+44.2 bps/month) in the 10-year point of the Treasury curve, when considered in isolation, will deliver a positive net return of 15.9 bp.[11] In isolation, the positive impact is expected because we are short that point of the curve. More interesting may be the correlated number on the exhibit. It states the return impact but in a correlated fashion. In the scenario under analysis, a movement in the 10-year point will almost certainly involve a movement of the neighboring

---

[11]This number is obtained by simply multiplying the net exposure by the factor volatility. The sign of the move depends on the interpretation of the factor. In the case of the yield curve movements we know that $R = -KRD \times \Delta KR$. In our example $-(-0.36) \times 44.2 = 15.9$.

points in the curve. So, contrary to the positive isolated effect documented above, the correlated impact of a change up in the 10-year point is actually negative, at −5.0 bps. This result is in line with the overall positive duration exposure the portfolio has: General (correlated) movements up in the curve have negative impact in the portfolio's performance.[12] Finally, and broadly speaking, the ratio of the correlated impact to the factor volatility gives us the model-implied partial empirical duration of the portfolio. For instance, if we focus on the 10-year point, we get 5.0/44.2 = 0.11. This smaller empirical duration is typical in portfolios with spread exposure. The spread exposure tends to empirically hedge some of the curve exposure, given the negative correlation between these two sources of risk. Finally, the exhibit shows the risk associated with convexity. We can see that the benchmark is significantly more negatively convex, so the portfolio is more protected than the benchmark to higher order changes in the yield curve.

There are many other statistics of interest one can analyze regarding the Treasury curve risk of the portfolio. Portfolio managers frequently have questions such as: If I want to reduce the risk of my portfolio by manipulating my Treasury curve exposure, what should I change? What is the most effective move? By how much would my risk actually change? The statistics reported in the columns "Marginal Contribution to TEV" and "TEV Elasticity (%)" of panel B are typically used to answer these questions. Regarding the marginal contributions, the 10-year point has the largest value, showing us that an increase (reduction) of one unit of exposure (in this case one year of duration) to the 10-year point leads to an increase (reduction) of around 16 bps in our TEV.[13] In other words, if we want to reduce risk by manipulating our exposure to the yield curve, the 10-year point seems to present the fastest track. In addition, the exhibit shows that all Treasury risk factors are associated with positive marginal contributions. This means that an increase in the exposure to any of these factors increases the risk (TEV) of the portfolio. This conclusion holds, even for factors for which we have negative exposure (e.g. the 10-year key rate). The reason behind this result is our overall long duration exposure. If we add exposure to it, regardless of the specific point where we add it, we extend our duration even

---

[12]This reversal is clearly related to the fact that the 10-year and the 20-year points in the curve are usually highly correlated. In our case, our short position on the 10-year point is more than compensated by the positive exposure in the 20-year. Netting out, the 20-year effect (long duration) dominates when all changes are taken in a correlated fashion.

[13]The marginal contribution is the derivative of the TEV with respect to the loading of each factor, so its interpretation holds only locally. Therefore, a more realistic reading may be that if we reduce the exposure to the 10-year by 0.1 years, the TEV would be reduced by around 1.6 basis points.

EXHIBIT 21.11   Swap Spread (SS) Risk

Factor Name	Exposure (SS-KRD)			Factor Volatility	Return Impact Correlated	Marginal Contribution to TEV
	Portfolio	Benchmark	Net			
6M SS	0.14	0.13	0.01	39.1	−2.1	5.8
2Y SS	0.52	0.47	0.04	20.4	−2.1	3.0
5Y SS	0.84	0.75	0.09	9.6	−2.0	1.4
10Y SS	0.71	0.68	0.03	14.1	1.7	−1.8
20Y SS	0.34	0.33	0.01	17.0	2.2	−2.7
30Y SS	0.06	0.20	−0.15	20.1	2.4	−3.5

further, increasing the mismatch our portfolio has in terms of duration, and so increasing its risk.[14] This result holds because we take into consideration the correlations between the different points in the Treasury curve. Without correlations, the analysis would be significantly less clear. The exhibit also reports the TEV elasticity of each of the risk factors, a concept introduced earlier. The interpretation is similar to the marginal contribution, but with normalized changes (percentage changes). This normalization makes the numbers more comparable across risk factors of very different nature. It is also useful when considering leveraging the entire portfolio proportionally. In our case, if we increase the exposure to the 10-year key rate point by 10%, from −0.36 to something around −0.40 (effectively reducing our long duration exposure), our TEV would be reduced by 4% (from 13.7 to 13.2 bps/month).

We now turn the analysis to the other component of the curve risk described above: the risk embedded into the portfolio exposure to the swap spread, that is, the spread between the swap and the Treasury curves. All securities that trade against the swap curve (e.g., all typical credit and securitized bonds) are exposed to this risk. Its analysis follows very closely that of the Treasury curve, so we only highlight the major risk characteristics of the portfolio along this dimension. Exhibit 21.11 shows that in general our exposure to the swap spreads is smaller than that of the Treasury curve. Remember that Treasuries do not load on this set of risk factors, so the market-weighted exposures are consequently smaller. Looking at the profile of factor volatilities, one can see that its term structure of volatilities is U-shaped, with the short end extremely volatile and the five-year point having the lowest volatility. When comparing with the Treasury curve volatility profile (see Exhibit 21.10), we can see significant differences, the aftermath

---

[14]This is a rationale very similar to the one used before, where we see all correlated impacts with the same sign.

of a strong liquidity crisis. Regarding net exposures, the exhibit shows that our largest mismatch is at the 30-year point, where we are short by 0.15 years. Interestingly, this is not the most expensive mismatch in terms of risk: when looking at the last column, we see that we would be able to change risk the most by manipulating the short end of our exposure to the swap spread curve, namely the six-month point.

The previous exhibits allow us to understand our exposures to the different types of curve risk and their impact both on the return and risk of our portfolios. They also guide us regarding what changes we can introduce to modify the risk profile of the portfolio. We now turn our attention to sources of risk that are more specific to particular asset classes. In particular, we start with the analysis of credit risk.

Credit Risk Instruments in the portfolio issued by corporations or entities that may default are said to have credit risk. The holders of these securities demand some extra yield—on top of the risk-free yield—to compensate for that risk. The extra yield is usually measured as a spread to a reference curve. For instance, for corporate bonds the reference curve is usually the swap curve. The level of credit spreads determines to a large extent the credit risk exposure associated with the portfolio.[15]

There are several characteristics of credit bonds that are naturally associated with systematic sources of credit spread risk. For instance, depending on the business cycle, particular industries may be going through especially tough times. So industry membership is a natural systematic source of risk. Similarly, bonds with different credit ratings are usually treated as having different levels of credit risk. Credit rating could be another dimension we can use to measure systematic exposure to credit risk. Given these observations, it is common to see factor models for credit risk using industry and rating as the major systematic risk factors. Recent research suggests that risk models that directly use the spreads of the bonds instead of their ratings to assess risk perform better for relatively short/medium horizons of analysis.[16] Under this approach, the loading of a particular bond to a credit risk factor would be the commonly used spread duration, but now multiplied by the bond's spread (the loading is termed DTS = Duration Times Spread = OASD × OAS). By directly using the spread of the bond in the definition of the loading to the credit risk factors, we do not need to assign specific risk factors to

---

[15]Spreads are also compensation for sources of risk other than credit (e.g. liquidity), but for the sake of our argument, we treat them primarily as major indicators of credit risk.

[16]For details, see Arik Ben Dor, Lev Dynkin, Patrick Houweling, Jay Hyman, Erik van Leeuwen, and Olaf Penninga, "A New Measure of Spread Exposure in Credit Portfolios," Barclays Capital publication, February 2010.

capture the rating or any similar quality-like effect. It will be automatically captured by the bond's loading to the credit risk factor, and will adjust as the spread of the bond changes. We use different systematic risk factors only to distinguish among credit risk coming from different industries.[17]

The results of such an approach to the analysis of our portfolio are displayed in Exhibit 21.12 which shows the typical industry risk factors associated with credit risk. The portfolio has net positions in 27 industries, spanning all three major sectors: industrials (IND), Utilities (UTI) and Financials (FIN). We saw before that we have a significant net exposure to financials in terms of market weights (12.2%, see Exhibit 21.1). In terms of risk exposure, Exhibit 21.12 shows that the net DTS attached to the Banking industry is 0.32, clearly the highest across all sectors.[18] However, the marginal contribution to TEV that comes from that industry, although high, is comparable to other industries, namely Brokerage, for which the net exposure is close to zero. This means that these two industries are close substitutes in terms of the current portfolio holdings. Actually, what is very interesting is the fact that the marginal contribution is negative for these industries, even though we are significantly overweighting them. The analysis suggests that if we increase our risk exposure to Banking, our risk would actually decrease. This result is again driven by the strong negative correlation between spreads in financials and the yield curve. Therefore, the exposure in banking is actually helping hedge out our (more risky) long duration position. This kind of analysis is only possible when you account for the correlations across factors. It is of course also dependent on the quality of the correlation estimations the model has.

---

[17]The general principle of a risk model is that the historical returns of assets contain information that can be used to estimate the future volatility of portfolio returns. However, good risk models must have the ability to translate the historical asset returns to the context of the current environment. This translation is made when designing a particular risk model/factor and delivers risk factors that are as invariant as possible. This invariance makes the estimation of the factor distribution much more robust. In the particular case of the DTS, by including the spread in the loading (instead of using only the typical spread duration), we change the nature of the risk factor being estimated. The factor now represents percentage change in spreads, instead of absolute changes in spreads. The former has a significantly more invariant distribution. For more details, see Antonio Silva, "A Note on the New Approach to Credit in the Barclays Capital Global Risk Model," Barclays Capital publication, September 2009.

[18]The DTS units used in the report are based on a OASD stated in years and an OAS in percentage points. Therefore, a bond with an OASD = 5 and an OAS = 200 basis points would have a DTS of 5 × 2 =10. The DTS industry exposures are the weighted sum of the DTS of each of the securities in that industry, the weights being the market weight of each security.

EXHIBIT 21.12   Credit Spread Risk

Factor Name	Exposure (DTS)			Factor Volatility	Return Impact Correlated	Marginal Contribution to TEV
	Portfolio	Benchmark	Net			
IND Chemicals	0.00	0.03	–0.03	15.01	–0.39	0.43
IND Metals	0.00	0.06	–0.06	20.01	–0.16	0.23
IND Paper	0.00	0.01	–0.01	17.04	–0.40	0.49
IND Capital Goods	0.00	0.05	–0.05	14.98	–0.02	0.02
IND Div. Manufacturing	0.00	0.03	–0.03	14.21	–0.62	0.64
IND Auto	0.00	0.01	–0.01	22.18	–0.53	0.85
IND Consumer Cyclical	0.10	0.05	0.06	17.05	–0.26	0.32
IND Retail	0.00	0.05	–0.05	16.95	0.14	–0.17
IND Cons. Non-cyclical	0.00	0.13	–0.13	14.62	–0.22	0.24
IND Health Care	0.00	0.02	–0.02	14.07	0.13	–0.13
IND Pharmaceuticals	0.19	0.06	0.12	15.13	–0.34	0.37
IND Energy	0.12	0.20	–0.07	16.39	–0.29	0.34
IND Technology	0.00	0.06	–0.06	15.52	–0.11	0.12
IND Transportation	0.00	0.05	–0.05	15.09	–0.26	0.29
IND Media Cable	0.24	0.06	0.18	15.83	0.51	–0.58
IND Media Non-cable	0.00	0.04	–0.04	15.94	0.20	–0.23
IND Wirelines	0.09	0.17	–0.08	15.26	0.41	–0.45
IND Wireless	0.00	0.03	–0.03	14.87	1.06	–1.13
UTI Electric	0.28	0.20	0.08	15.79	–0.16	0.18
UTI Gas	0.09	0.10	–0.01	18.51	–0.41	0.55
FIN Banking	0.88	0.56	0.32	18.61	1.19	–1.59
FIN Brokerage	0.00	0.02	–0.02	15.90	1.47	–1.68
FIN Finance Companies	0.08	0.10	–0.02	20.64	0.68	–1.01
FIN Life & Health Insurance	0.12	0.11	0.01	19.96	0.58	–0.84
FIN P&C Insurance	0.00	0.06	–0.06	11.76	0.34	–0.29
FIN Reits	0.14	0.04	0.10	17.68	0.80	–1.02
Non Corporate	0.06	0.23	–0.17	25.27	0.28	–0.50

Although the risk factors used to measure risk are predetermined in a linear factor model, there is extreme flexibility on the way the risk numbers can be aggregated and reported.[19] For example, as explained above, the risk model we use to generate the current risk reports does not use credit ratings as drivers of systematic credit risk. Instead, it relies on the

---

[19]For a detailed methodology on how to performed this customized analysis, please see Antonio Silva, "Risk Attribution with Custom-Defined Risk Factors," Barclays Capital publication, August 2009.

EXHIBIT 21.13   Risk per Rating

Rating	NMW (%)	TEV Contribution	TEV Isolated	TEV Liquidation	TEV Elasticity (%)	Systematic Beta
Total	0.0	13.7	13.7	−13.7	1.0	1.03
AAA	−7.2	10.9	37.4	22.2	0.8	1.12
AA1	−0.3	−0.2	1.0	0.2	0.0	0.00
AA2	0.2	0.3	3.3	0.1	0.0	1.10
AA3	−2.3	−1.3	6.7	2.6	−0.1	0.00
A1	−0.5	0.3	4.2	0.4	0.0	1.51
A2	7.1	3.6	11.2	1.0	0.3	0.77
A3	4.7	1.7	5.8	−0.5	0.1	0.65
BAA1	−0.1	0.3	3.7	0.2	0.0	1.51
BAA2	−3.3	−2.3	11.5	5.9	−0.2	0.00
BAA3	1.7	0.3	7.7	1.7	0.0	0.37

DTS concept. However, once generated, the risk numbers can be reported using any portfolio partition. As an example, Exhibit 21.13 shows the risk breakdown by rating. As reported in this exhibit, the majority of risk is coming from our AAA exposure (10.9 bps/month), the bucket with the biggest mismatch in terms of net weight (−7.2%). This bucket includes Treasury and government-related securities, sectors that are underweighted in the portfolio leading to significant risk. This is even clearer when we look into the isolated TEV numbers. If we had mismatches only on AAAs, the risk of our portfolio would be 37.4 bps/month, instead of the actual 13.7: our other exposures (namely the one to single As) hedge the risk from AAAs. This exhibit also reports the systematic betas associated with each of the rating subportfolios. These betas add up to the portfolio beta, when we use the portfolio weights (not NMW) as weights in the summation. Systematic betas of zero identify buckets for which the portfolio has (close to) no holdings. The exhibit shows that a movement of 10 basis points in the benchmark leads to a 11.2 basis points return in the AAA subcomponent of the portfolio. The beta of 0.37 for the BAA3 component of the portfolio does not signal low volatility for this subportfolio. It indicates mainly low correlation with the benchmark. This is probably due to a larger component of idiosyncratic risk for this set of bonds.

Prepayment Risk   Securitized products are generally exposed to prepayment risk. The most common of the securitized products are the residential MBS

(RMBS or simply MBS), discussed in Chapter 16. These securities represent pools of deals that allow the borrower to prepay their debt before the maturity of the loan/deal, typically when prevailing lending rates are lower. This option means an extra risk to the holder of the security, the risk of holding cash exactly when reinvestment rates are low. Therefore, these securities have two major sources of risk: interest rates (including convexity) and prepayment risk.

Some part of the prepayment risk can be expressed as a function of interest rates via a prepayment model. This risk will be captured as part of interest-rate risk using the key rate durations and the convexity. These securities usually have negative convexity because usually prepayments increase (decrease) with decreasing (increasing) interest rates, thereby reducing price appreciation (increase price depreciation). The remaining part of prepayment risk—that is not captured by the prepayment model—must be modeled with additional systematic risk factors. Typically, the volatility of prepayment speeds (and therefore of risk) on MBS securities depends on three characteristics: program/term of the deal, if the bond is priced at discount or premium (e.g. if the coupon on the bond is bigger than the current mortgage rates) and how seasoned the bond is. This analysis suggests that the systematic risk factors in a risk model should span these three characteristics of the securities.

Exhibit 21.14 shows a potential set of risk factors that capture the three characteristics discussed above. Programs identified as having different prepayment characteristics are the conventional (Fannie Mae) 30-year bonds (the base case used for the analysis), the 15-year conventional (Fannie Mae) bonds, as well as the Ginnie Mae 30- and 15-year bonds. The age of bonds is captured by factors distinguishing between new and aged deals. Finally,

EXHIBIT 21.14 MBS (spread) Prepayment Risk

Factor Name	Exposure (OASD)			Factor Volatility	Return Impact Correlated	Marginal Contribution to TEV
	Portfolio	Benchmark	Net			
MBS New Discount	0.00	0.00	0.00	36.8	−1.2	3.3
MBS New Current	0.00	0.04	−0.04	24.5	−0.3	0.6
MBS New Premium	0.38	0.59	−0.21	29.7	−0.1	0.3
MBS Seasoned Current	0.00	0.00	0.00	25.5	−0.6	1.2
MBS Seasoned Premium	0.65	0.46	0.19	29.8	0.1	−0.2
MBS Ginnie Mae 30Y	0.31	0.21	0.10	6.1	−0.1	0.0
MBS Fannie Mae 15Y	0.00	0.11	−0.11	15.7	0.4	−0.4
MBS Ginnie Mae 15Y	0.00	0.01	−0.01	12.3	0.5	−0.4

each bond is also classified by the price of the security—discount, current or premium. In this example there are no seasoned discounted bonds, given the unprecedented level of mortgage rates as of June 2010. In terms of risk exposures, the exhibit shows that we are currently underweighting 15-year conventional bonds, and overweighting 30-year Ginnie Mae bonds.

Interaction between Sources of Risk   So far we analyzed the major sources of spread risk: credit and prepayment. To do this, we conveniently used two asset classes—credit and agency RMBS, respectively—where one can argue that these sources of risk appear relatively isolated. However, recent developments have made very clear that these sources of risk appear simultaneously in other major asset classes, including non-agency RMBS, home equity loans and CMBS.[20] When designing a risk model for a particular asset class, one should be able to anticipate the nature of the risks the asset class exhibits currently or may encounter in the future. The design and ability to segregate between these two kinds of risk depends also on the richness of the bond indicatives and analytics available to the researcher. For this last point, it is imperative that the researcher understands well the pricing model and assumptions made to generate the analytics typically used as inputs in a risk model. This allows the user to fully understand the output of the model, as well as its applicability and shortcomings.

Other Sources of Risk   There are other sources of systematic risk we did not detail in this section. They may be important sources of risk for particular portfolios. Specific risk models can be designed to address them. We now mention some of them briefly.

Implied Volatility Risk   Many fixed income securities have embedded options (e.g. callable bonds). This means that the expected future volatility (implied volatility[21]) of the interest rate or other discount curves used to price the security plays a role in the value of that option. If expected volatility increases, options generally become more expensive affecting the prices of bonds with embedded options. For example callable bonds will become cheaper with increasing implied volatility since the bond holder is short optionality (the right of the issuer to call the bond). Therefore, the exposure of the portfolio to the implied volatility of the yield curve is also a source of risk that should be accounted for. The sensitivity of securities to changes of implied volatilities is measured by vega, which is calculated using the

---

[20]For a further discussion, see Radu Gabudean, "US Home Equity ABS Risk Model," Barclays Capital publication, October 2009.
[21]The volatility is called implied because it is calculated from the market prices of liquid options with the help of an option-pricing model.

security pricing model. Implied volatility factors can be either calculated by the market prices of liquid fixed income options (caps, floors, and swaptions), or implied by the returns of bonds with embedded options within each asset class.

Liquidity Risk   Many fixed income securities are traded over-the-counter, in decentralized markets. Some trade infrequently, making them illiquid. It is therefore hard to establish their fair price. These bonds are said to be exposed to liquidity risk. The holder of illiquid bonds would have to pay a higher price to liquidate its position, usually meaning selling at a discount. This discount is uncertain and varies across the business cycle. For instance, the discount can be significant in a liquidity crisis, such as the one we experienced in 2008. The uncertainty about this discount means that, everything equal, a more illiquid bond will be riskier. This extra risk can be captured through liquidity risk factors. For instance, in the Treasury markets, one generally refers to the difference in volatility between an on-the-run and an off-the-run Treasury bond as liquidity risk.

Inflation Risk   Inflation-linked securities are priced based on the expectation of future inflation. Uncertainty about this variable adds to the volatility of the bond over and above the volatility from other sources of risk, such as the nominal interest rates. Expected inflation is not an observed variable in the marketplace but can be extracted from the prices on inflation-linked government bonds and inflation swaps. Expected inflation risk factors can be constructed by summarizing this information. The sensitivity of securities to expected inflation is calculated using a specialized pricing model and is usually called *inflation duration*.

Tax-Policy Risk   Many municipal securities are currently tax-exempt. This results in added benefit to their holders. This benefit—incorporated in the price of the security—depends on the level of exemption allowed. Uncertainty around tax policy—tax-policy risk—adds to the risk of these securities. Once again, tax-policy risk factors cannot be observed in the marketplace and must be extracted from the prices of municipal securities. The return of municipal securities in excess of interest rates is driven partially by tax-policy expectations changes. However, it is also driven by changes in the creditworthiness of the municipal issuers as well as other factors. In this case it is difficult to separate tax-policy risk factors from other factors driving municipal bond spreads. Therefore, instead of specific tax-policy factors we usually extract factors representing the overall spread risk of municipal securities. This exercise is performed in a similar way to the credit risk model, where securities are partitioned into groups of "similar" risk by geography, bond-type (general obligation versus revenue), tax-status, and the like.[22]

Issue-Level Reports

The previous analysis focused on the systematic sources of risk. We now turn our attention to the idiosyncratic or security-specific risk embedded in our portfolio. This risk measures the volatility the portfolio has due to news or demand–supply imbalances specific to the individual issues/issuers it holds. Therefore, the idiosyncratic risk is independent across issuers and diversifies away as the number of issues in the portfolio increases: negative news about some issuers is canceled by positive news about others. For relatively small portfolios, the idiosyncratic risk may be a substantial component of the total risk. This can be seen in our example, as our portfolio has only 27 issuers. Exhibit 21.6 shows that the idiosyncratic volatility of our portfolio is 11.1 bps/month, more than twice the idiosyncratic volatility of the benchmark (5.6 bps/month). When looking at the tracking error volatility net of benchmark, Exhibit 21.6 shows that our specific risk is 10.1 bps/month and larger than the systematic component (9.3 bps/month). This means that, typically, a major component of the monthly net return is driven by events affecting only individual issues or issuers. Therefore, monitoring these individual exposures is of paramount importance.

The idiosyncratic risk of each bond is a function of two variables: its net market weight and its idiosyncratic volatility. This last parameter depends on the nature of the bond issuer. For instance, a bond from a distressed firm has much higher idiosyncratic volatility than one from a government-related agency.

Exhibit 21.15 provides a summary of the idiosyncratic risk for the top ten positions by market weight in our portfolio. Not surprisingly, our top seven holdings are Treasuries and MBS securities, in line with the constitution of the index we are using as benchmark. Moreover, these positions have significant market weights, given that our portfolio contains only 50 positions. Even though we see large concentrations, the idiosyncratic TEV for the top holdings is small, as they are not exposed to significant name risk. The last column of the table shows that from this group the largest idiosyncratic risk comes from two corporate bonds (issued by Comcast Cable Communication "CMCSA" and Merrill Lynch "BAC"). This is not surprising, as these are the type of securities with larger event risk. Even within corporates, idiosyncratic risk can be quite diverse. In particular, it usually depends on the industry, duration, and level of distress of the issuer (usually proxied

---

[22]For more discussion, see Arne Staal, "U.S. Municipal Bond Risk Model," Barclays Capital publication, July 2009.

EXHIBIT 21.15 Issue Specific Risk

Identifier	Ticker	Description	Maturity	Spread (bps)	Market Weight (%) Portfolio	Market Weight (%) Net	Idiosyncratic TEV
912828KF	US/T	US Treasury Notes	2/28/2014	4	5.4	5.2	0.4
912828KJ	US/T	US Treasury Notes	3/31/2014	3	5.0	4.8	0.4
912828JW	US/T	US Treasury Notes	12/31/2013	1	4.7	4.5	0.4
912828KN	US/T	US Treasury Notes	4/30/2014	2	3.8	3.6	0.3
FNA04409	FNMA	FNMA Conventional Long T. 30yr	3/1/2039	20	3.2	1.1	0.4
FGB04409	FHLMC	FHLM Gold Guar Single F. 30yr	3/1/2039	25	2.7	1.1	0.4
912810FT	US/T	US Treasury Bonds	2/15/2036	−1	2.3	2.1	0.7
20029PAG	CMCSA	Comcast Cable Communication	5/1/2017	222	2.2	2.2	2.4
59018YSU	BAC	MERRILL LYNCH & CO.	2/3/2014	300	2.1	2.1	2.9
912828KV	US/T	US TREASURY NOTES	5/31/2014	1	2.1	1.9	0.2

by rating, but in our model by the spread of the bond). For instance, the net position for both the CMCSA and BAC bonds is similar (2.2% and 2.1% respectively), but even though the maturity of the BAC bond is significantly shorter, its spread is higher, delivering a higher idiosyncratic risk (2.9 versus 2.4 bps/month). The fact that BAC is a firm from an industry (Financials) that experienced significant volatility in the recent past also contributes to higher idiosyncratic volatility. To manage the idiosyncratic risk in the portfolio one should pay particular attention to mismatches between the portfolio and benchmark for bonds with large spreads or long durations. These would tend to affect disproportionably the idiosyncratic risk of the portfolio.

Although important, the information in Exhibit 21.15 is not enough to fully assess the idiosyncratic risk embedded in the portfolio. For instance, one could buy credit protection to BAC through a credit default swap (CDS). In this case, our exposure to this issuer may not be significant, even though, taken separately, the position reported in this exhibit is relevant. More generally, idiosyncratic risk is independent across issuers, but what happens within a particular issuer? A good risk model should have the ability to account for the fact that the idiosyncratic risk of two securities from the same issuer is correlated, as they are both subject to the same company-specific events. This is especially the case for corporates and emerging market securities. Moreover, it is important to note that the correlation between issues from the same issuer is not constant either. For an issuer in financial distress, all claims to their assets (bonds, equities, convertibles, etc) tend to move together, in absence of specific circumstances. This means that the idiosyncratic correlation between issues from that issuer should be high. Therefore, adding more issues from that issuer to the portfolio does not deliver additional diversification. On the other end, securities from firms that enjoy very strong financial wealth can move quite differently, driven by liquidity or other factors. In this case, one can have some diversification of idiosyncratic risk (although limited) even when adding issues from that same issuer into the portfolio.

To help us understand the net effect of all these points, we need to know the issuers that contribute the most to idiosyncratic risk. When aggregating risk from the issue (as shown in Exhibit 21.15) to the issuer level, the correlations referred to above should be fully taken into account. Exhibit 21.16 shows the results of this exercise, for the ten issuers with the highest idiosyncratic TEV. Our riskiest exposure comes from Johnson & Johnson (JNJ), with 3.7 bps/month of issuer risk. We can also observe that idiosyncratic TEV is not monotonic in the NMW: we have JNJ and President & Fellows of Harvard "HARVRD" with the same NMW, but the former is significantly more risky (3.7 versus 2.0 bps/month). It is possible to have

EXHIBIT 21.16 Issuer Specific Risk

Ticker	Name	Sector	NMW (%)	Idiosyncratic TEV
JNJ	Johnson & Johnson	Pharmaceuticals	2.0	3.7
D	Dominion Resources Inc	Electric	1.8	2.8
CMCSA	Comcast Cable Communication	Media_cable	2.0	2.1
BBT	Bb&T Corporation	Banking	2.0	2.1
HARVRD	Pres&Fellows Of Harvard	Industrial_other	2.0	2.0
AXP	American Express Credit	Banking	1.7	1.8
MS	Morgan Stanley Dean Witter	Banking	1.3	1.7
C	Citigroup Inc	Banking	1.5	1.7
BAC	Merrill Lynch & Co.	Banking	1.6	1.6
RBS	Charter One Bank Fsb	Banking	1.6	1.4

important issuer risk even for names we do not have in our portfolio, if they have significant market weight in the benchmark. Finally, note that because the idiosyncratic risk across issuers is independent, we can easily calculate the cumulative risk of several issuers. For example, the total idiosyncratic risk of the first two issuers is given by

$$TEV_{idio}^{JNJ+D} = \sqrt{3.7^2 + 2.8^2} = 4.6$$

Another important interpretation from this exhibit is that these are our biggest name exposures in our portfolio. In this case, we are overweight in all of them. Therefore, we should not have negative views about any of them. If this is not the case, then we are assuming an unintended name risk. This risk should be promptly taken out of the portfolio, in favor of another issuer with similar characteristics and for which we do not have negative views about. This interactive exercise can easily be performed with a good and flexible optimizer.

Scenario Analysis Report

Scenario analysis is another useful way to gain additional perspective on the portfolio's risk. There are many ways to perform this exercise. For instance, one may want to reprice the whole portfolio under a particular interest rate or spread scenario, and look at the hypothetical return under that scenario. Alternatively, one may look at the holdings of the portfolio and see how

EXHIBIT 21. 17   Historical Systematic Simulated Returns (basis points)

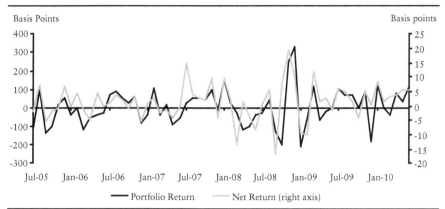

they would have performed under particular stressed historical scenarios (e.g., the 1987 equity crash or the Asian crisis in 1997). One particular problem with this approach is the fact that, given the dynamic nature of the securities, the current portfolio did not exist with the current characteristics along all these historical episodes. A solution may be to try to price the current securities with the market variables at the time. Another solution is to represent the current portfolio as the set of loadings to all systematic risk factors in the factor risk model. We can then multiply these loadings by the historical realizations of the risk factors. The result is a set of historical systematic simulated returns. Exhibit 21.17 presents these returns for our portfolio over the last five years. As expected, the largest volatility came with the crisis of 2008, when the portfolio registered returns between –200 and +300 basis points. The largest underperformance against the benchmark appeared in September 2008, followed by the largest outperformance two months after, both at around 20 basis points.

This analysis has some limitations, especially for the portfolio under consideration, where idiosyncratic exposure is a major source of risk. This kind of risk is always very hard to pin down and obviously less relevant from an historical perspective, as the issuers in our current portfolio may have not witnessed any particular major idiosyncratic event in the past. However, these and other kinds of historical scenario analysis are very important, as they give us some indication of the magnitude of historical returns our portfolio might have encountered. They are usually the starting point for any stress testing. The researcher should always complement these with other nonhistorical scenarios relevant for the particular portfolio under analysis. One way to use the risk model to express such scenarios is discussed in the following section.

APPLICATIONS OF RISK MODELING

In this section, we illustrate several risk model applications typically employed for portfolio management. All applications make use of the fact that the risk model translates into a common, comparable set of numbers the imbalances the portfolio may have across many different dimensions. In some of the applications—risk budgeting and portfolio rebalancing—an optimizer that uses the risk model as an input is the optimal setting to perform the exercise.

Portfolio Construction and Risk Budgeting

Portfolio managers can be divided broadly into indexers (those that measure their returns relative to a benchmark index) and absolute return managers (typically hedge fund managers). In between stand the enhanced indexers we introduced previously in the chapter. All are typically subject to a risk budget that prescribes how much risk they are allowed to take to achieve their objectives: minimize transaction costs and match the index returns for the pure indexers, maximize the net return for the enhanced indexers, or maximize absolute returns for absolute return managers. In any of these cases, the manager has to merge all her views and constraints into a final portfolio. When constructing the portfolio, how can she manage the competing views, while respecting the risk budget? How can the views be combined to minimize the risk? What trade-offs can be made? Many different techniques can be used to structure portfolios in accordance to the manager views. In particular, risk models are widely used to perform this exercise. They perform this task in a simple and objective manner: they can measure how risky each view is and how correlated they are. The manager can then compare the risk with the expected return of each of the views and decide on the optimal allocation across her views.

An example of a portfolio construction exercise using the risk model is the one we performed to construct the portfolio analyzed in the previous section.[23] Exhibit 21.18 shows the exact problem we asked the optimizer to solve. We start the problem by defining an initial portfolio (empty in our case) and a tradable universe—the set of securities we allow the optimizer to buy or sell from. In our case, this is the Barclays Capital U.S. Aggregate index with issues having at least $300 million of amount outstanding (in the Tradable Universe Options pane of the POINT® Optimizer window shown in Exhibit 21.18). The selection of this universe allows us

---

[23]The example is constructed using the POINT® Optimizer. For more details, please refer to Anuj Kumar, "The POINT Optimizer," Barclays Capital publication, June 2010.

EXHIBIT 21.18   Portfolio Construction Optimization Setup in the POINT® Optimizer

Tradable Universe Options

No.	Name	Type	Trade/Buy/Sell	Long/Short
▶ 1	Initial Portfolio	Initial Portfolio	Buy and Sell	Long/Short
2	US Agg 300 Mln (System)	Index	Buy and Sell	Long Only

Objectives

⊙ Minimize   ○ Maximize

No.	Attribute	Measure	Weight	Unit
1	Total TEV	Net vs Bmark	1.00	bps / mo
2	Systematic TEV	Net vs Bmark	0.00	bps / mo
3	Idiosyncratic TEV	Net vs Bmark	0.00	bps / mo

✛ | ✕ | ◀

Common Constraints

Final Portfolio Cash (base currency): ○ Long/Short ○ Long Only ○ Short Only ⊙ No Cash

E...	Description	Measure	Bound	Unit
☑	Budget: Final Portfolio Market Value	Change	100,000,000	USD
☑	Final portfolio maximum gross size	Target		USD
☑	Turnover: Maximum gross size of trades	Target		USD
☑	Maximum number of securities in final portfolio			
☑	Maximum number of trades		50	
☑	Minimum trade size	Target		USD

Constraints on values aggregated by Buckets

No.	Soft	...	Attribute	Universe	Measure	Lower Bound	Upper Bound	Unit
▶ 1	☐		OAD	Final Portfolio	Net vs Bmark	0.25	0.30	yrs
2	☐		OAS	Final Portfolio	Net vs Bmark	100.0	150.0	bps / yr

Constraints on each Issue/Issuer/Ticker

Universe Final Portfolio

No.	Soft	Penalty	Attribute	Universe	For Each	Measure	Lower Bound	Upper Bound	Unit
▶ 1	✛ ☐		Market Value [%]	Final Portfolio	Ticker	Net vs Bmark		2.00000	%

to avoid having small issues in our portfolio, potentially increasing its liquidity. Pertaining to the risk model use (in the Objectives pane of the POINT® Optimizer window), the objective function used in the problem is to minimize Total TEV. This means that we are giving leeway to the risk model to choose a portfolio from the tradeable universe that minimizes the risk relative to the benchmark, in our case the Barclays Capital U.S. Aggregate index. In the Common Constraints pane, additional generic constraints have been imposed: a $100 million final portfolio with a maximum number of 50 securities. In the Constraints on values aggregated by Buckets pane, we force the optimizer to tilt our portfolio to respect the portfolio manager's views: long duration against the benchmark between 0.25 and 0.30 years and spreads between 100 and 150 bps higher than the benchmark. In the Constraints on each Issue/Issuer/Ticker pane, we impose a maximum under-/overweight of 2% per issuer, to ensure proper diversification.[24] The characteristics of the portfolio resulting from this optimization problem were extensively analyzed in the previous section.

Portfolio Rebalancing

Managers are constantly in need to rebalance their portfolios. For instance, as time goes by, the characteristics of the portfolio may drift away from targeted levels. This may be due to the aging of its holdings, market moves, or issuer-specific events such as downgrades or defaults. The periodic re-alignment of a portfolio to its investment guidelines is called portfolio re-balancing. Similar needs arise in many different contexts: when managers receive extra cash to invest, get small changes to their mandates, want to tilt their views, and the like. Similar to portfolio construction, a risk model is very useful in the rebalancing exercise. During rebalancing, the portfolio manager typically seeks to sell bonds currently held and replace them with others having properties more consistent with the overall portfolio goals. Such buy and sell transactions are costly and their cost must be weighted against the benefit from moving the portfolio closer to its initial specifications. A risk model can tell the manager how much risk reduction (or increase) a particular set of transactions can achieve so that she can evaluate the risk adjustment benefits relative to the transaction cost.

As an example, suppose our portfolio manager wants to tone down the heavy overweight she has on banking. She wants to cap that overweight to 5% and wants to do it with no more than 10 trades. Finally, assume she wants no change to the market value of the final portfolio. We can use a setup similar to that of Exhibit 21.18, but adjusting some of the constraints. Exhibit 21.19 shows two of the constraints option panes in the POINT® Optimizer window, changed to allow for the new constraints. Specifically, in the first panel, we allow for 10 trades and, in the second, included an extra constraint for the banking industry.

Exhibit 21.20 shows the trading list suggested by the POINT® Optimizer. Not surprisingly, the biggest sells are of financial companies. To replace them, the optimizer—using the risk model—recommends more holdings of Treasury and corporate bonds. (We need these last to keep the net yield of the portfolio high.) Remember that we concluded that our financial holdings were highly correlated with Treasuries, so the proposed swap is not surprising.

Interestingly, the extra constraint imposed on the optimization problem did not materially change the risk of the portfolio. Results show that the risk actually decreased to around 13 bps/month. This is due to the extra three

---

[24]Another way to ensure diversification would be to include the minimization of the idiosyncratic TEV as a specific goal in the objective function.

EXHIBIT 21.19 Portfolio Rebalancing Optimization Setup in the POINT® Optimizer

Common Constraints

Final Portfolio Cash (base currency):   ⊙ Long/Short   ⊙ Long Only   ⊙ Short Only   ⊙ No Cash

E...	Description	Measure	Bound	Unit
✔	Budget: Final Portfolio Market Value	Change		0 USD
✔	Final portfolio maximum gross size	Target		USD
✔	Turnover: Maximum gross size of trades	Target		USD
✔	Maximum number of securities in final portfolio			
✔	Maximum number of trades			10
✔	Minimum trade size	Target		1,000,000 USD

Constraints on values aggregated by Buckets

No.	Soft	...	Attribute	Universe	Measure	Lower Bound	Upper Bound	Unit
▶ 1	☐		OAD	Final Portfolio	Net vs Bmark	0.25	0.30	yrs
2	☐		OAS	Final Portfolio	Net vs Bmark	100.0	150.0	bps / yr
3	☐		Market Value [%]	Financial Inst. Banki...	Net vs Bmark	0.00000	5.00000	%

EXHIBIT 21. 20 Proposed Trading List

BUYS

Identifier	Description	Position Amount	Market Value
912828KV	US Treasury Notes	967,403	1,000,000
126650BK	CVS Corp-Global	1,696,069	1,518,408
98385XAJ	XTO Energy Inc	2,097,746	2,508,567
FNA05009	FNMA Conventional Long T. 30yr	2,547,359	2,708,258
912828KF	US Treasury Notes	3,786,070	3,882,263
Total			11,617,497

SELLS

Identifier	Description	Position Amount	Market Value
16132NAV	Charter One Bank FSB	–3,229,847	–3,370,981
05531FAF	BB&T Corporation	–2,425,413	–2,499,505
0258M0BZ	American Express Credit	–2,021,013	–2,208,231
3133XN4B	Federal Home Loan Bank	–1,818,417	–2,085,812
740816AB	Pres&Fellows of Harvard	–1,281,616	–1,452,968
Total			–11,617,497

positions added to the portfolio that now has 53 securities. These extra securities allowed the portfolio to reduce both its systematic as well as its idiosyncratic risk.

Scenario Analysis

As described in the previous section, scenario analysis is a very popular tool both for risk management and portfolio construction. In this section, we illustrate another way to construct scenarios, this time using the covariance matrix of the risk model. In this context, users express views on the returns of particular financial variables, indexes, securities, or risk factors, and the scenario analysis tool (using the risk model) calculates their impact on the portfolio's (net) return.

Typically in this kind of scenario analysis, the views one has are only partial views. This means we can have specific views on how particular macrovariables, asset classes, or risk factors will behave; but we hardly have views on all risk factors the portfolio under analysis is exposed to. This is when risk models may be useful. At the heart of the linear factor models described in this chapter is a set of risk factors and the covariance matrix between them. They are being increasingly used in the context of scenario analysis as a way to "complete" specific partial views or scenarios, delivering a full picture of the impact of the scenario in the return of the portfolio. Mechanically, what happens is the following: First, one translates the views into realizations of a subset of risk factors. Then the scenario is completed— using the risk model covariance matrix—to get the realizations of all risk factors. Finally, the portfolio's (net) loadings to all risk factors are used to get its (net) return under that scenario (by multiplying the loadings by the factor realizations under the scenario). This construction implies a set of assumptions that should be carefully understood. For instance, we assume that we can represent or translate our views as risk factor returns. So, if we have a view about the unemployment rate, and this is not a risk factor,[25] we cannot use this procedure to test our scenario. Also, to "complete" the scenario, we generally assume a stationary and normal multivariate distribution between all factors. These assumptions make this analysis less appropriate for looking at extreme events or regime shifts, for instance. But the analysis can be very useful in many circumstances.

As an example, consider using the scenario analysis to compute the model-implied empirical durations (MED) of the portfolio we analyzed in detail previously in this chapter. To do this, we express our views as changes in the curve factors. In our risk model, these are represented by the six key

---

[25]Unemployment rate is not used as a factor in most short- and medium-term risk models.

EXHIBIT 21.21   Scenario Analysis: Analytical and Model-Implied Durations

Universe	Return under Scenario (bp)	Durations MED (scenario)	Analytical
Portfolio	99	3.96	4.55
Benchmark	93	3.72	4.30

EXHIBIT 21. 22   Scenario Analysis: Spread Contraction of 10%

Universe	Restriction on YC movement No Movement	Correlated
Portfolio	31	−3
Benchmark	32	0

rate factors illustrated in Exhibit 21.10. In particular, to calculate the model-implied empirical duration, we are going to assume that all six decrease by 25 bps/month, broadly in line with our managers' views.

Exhibit 21.21 shows that under this scenario, the portfolio returns 99 basis points, against the 93 of the benchmark. As expected given our longer duration, we outperform the benchmark. Due to the other exposures present in the portfolio and benchmark (e.g., spreads) and their average negative correlation with the curve factors, the duration implied by the scenario (MED) for our portfolio is only 3.96 (= 99/25) against the analytical 4.55. The scenario shows a similar decrease in the benchmark's duration.

Another characteristic imposed while constructing the portfolio was a targeted higher spread. As shown in Exhibit 21.2, this resulted in an OAS for the portfolio of 157 bps against the 57 of the benchmark. It would be interesting to evaluate the impact to the portfolio (net) return of a credit spread contraction of 10%. The portfolio is long spread duration (net OASD = 0.11, see Exhibit 21.2), so we may expect our portfolio to overperform in this scenario. To do so, we analyze the results under two spread contraction scenarios: imposing no change in the yield curve (that is, an unchanged yield curve is part of the view) or allowing this change to be "completed" by the correlation matrix. (That is, the change in the yield curve is not part of the scenario. We have no views about it, but we allow it to change in a way historically consistent with our spread view.) Contrary to what one might expect, Exhibit 21.22 shows that the effect in the net return is minimal under both scenarios. The higher spreads deliver no return advantage under this scenario. However, the absolute returns are quite different across the scenarios. When one allows the rates to move in a correlated fashion the net return drops to zero: all positive return from the spread contraction is cancelled by the probable increase in the level of the curve and our long-duration exposure.

These very simple examples illustrate how one can look at reasonable scenarios to study the behavior of the portfolio or the benchmark under different environments. This scenario analysis does increase significantly the intuition the portfolio manager may have regarding the results from the risk model.

KEY POINTS

- Risk models describe the different imbalances of a portfolio using a common language. The imbalances are combined into a consistent and coherent analysis reported by the risk model.
- Risk models provide important insights regarding the different trade-offs existing in the portfolio. They provide guidance regarding how to balance them.
- Risk models in fixed income are unique in two different ways: First, the existence of good pricing models allows us to robustly calculate important analytics regarding the securities. These analytics can be used confidently as inputs into a risk model. Second, returns are not typically used directly to calibrate risk factors. Instead returns are first normalized into more invariant series (e.g. returns normalized by the duration of the bond).
- The fundamental systematic risk of all fixed income securities is interest rate and term structure risk. This is captured by factors representing risk-free rates and swap spreads of various maturities.
- Excess (of interest rates) systematic risk is captured by factors specific to each asset class. The most important components of such risk are credit risk and prepayment risk. Other risk factors that can be important are implied volatility, liquidity, inflation or tax policy.
- Idiosyncratic risk is diversified away in large portfolios and indexes but can become a very significant component of the total risk in small portfolios. The correlation of idiosyncratic risk of securities of the same issuer is nonzero and must be modeled very carefully.
- A good risk model provides detailed information about the exposures of a complex portfolio and can be a valuable tool for portfolio construction and management. It can help managers construct portfolios tracking a particular benchmark, express views subject to a given risk budget, and rebalance a portfolio while avoiding excessive transaction costs. Further, by identifying the exposures where the portfolio has the highest risk sensitivity it can help a portfolio manager reduce (or increase) risk in the most effective way.

QUESTIONS

Answer the questions based on the following information: Consider a portfolio of two equally weighted credit bonds from two different issuers in the same sector. Assume that interest rate risk is modeled by a single variable ΔR, the change of interest rates, and that credit risk in that sector is modeled by another factor $\Delta S/S$, the percentage change of average credit spreads in the sector. Remember this is the DTS factor referred to in the chapter. The loading to this factor is the DTS of the bond. The first bond has interest rate duration $D_1 = 4$yr, spread duration of $SD_1 = 4.5$yr and spread of $S_1 = 400$ bps. The second one has interest rate duration $D_2 = 6$yr, spread duration of $SD_2 = 6.5$yr and spread of $S_2 = 100$ bps. The volatility of the interest rate factor is $\sigma_{\Delta R} = 30$ bps/month, the volatility of the spread factor is $\sigma_{\Delta S/S} = 10\%$/month, and their correlation is $\rho = -30\%$. The idiosyncratic risk of the securities in this sector is proportional to a parameter. Similar to the systematic spread risk, that parameter measures the average percentage change of idiosyncratic spreads in the sector. The volatility of that parameter is $\sigma_{\Delta S/S}^{idio} = 14\%$ / month. The proportionality factor used to calculate idiosyncratic risk is given by the DTS level of the bond.

1. What is the systematic risk of each security?
2. What is the idiosyncratic risk of each security?
3. Which bond is riskier?
4. What is the isolated risk for the portfolio coming from interest rates and sector credit spreads?
5. What are the isolated systematic risk, isolated idiosyncratic risk and the total risk of the portfolio?
6. What are the contributions to total risk of (a) interest rates, (b) sector credit spreads, (c) idiosyncratic risk?
7. What is the correlation between the two bonds' returns?
8. What is the contribution of each bond to total portfolio risk?

CHAPTER 22

Interest Rate Derivatives and Risk Control

Frank J. Fabozzi, Ph.D., CFA, CPA
Professor in the Practice of Finance
Yale School of Management

In Chapters 14 and 15, equity derivatives and their application to equity portfolio management were discussed. There are two general types of fixed income derivatives: interest rate derivatives and credit derivatives. Interest rate derivatives play an important role in managing the interest rate risk of a portfolio or institution and they are the subject of this chapter. In Chapter 23, credit derivatives that can be used to control a portfolio's credit risk exposure are covered.

INTEREST RATE FUTURES AND FORWARD CONTRACTS

A futures contract is an agreement that requires a party to the agreement either to buy or sell something at a designated future date at a predetermined price. The buyer of a futures contract is said to be long the contract. The seller of a futures contract is said to be short the contract. The risk–return feature of futures contracts and the mechanics of trading them are covered in Chapter 14 and will not be repeated here. Instead, we focus on specific contract features, the special considerations in pricing them, and several portfolio applications.

Futures vs. Forward Contracts

A forward contract, just like a futures contract, is an agreement for the future delivery of something at a specified price at the end of a designated period of time. Futures contracts are standardized agreements as to the delivery date (or month) and quality of the deliverable, and are traded on organized exchanges. A forward contract differs in that it is usually nonstandardized (that is, the terms of each contract are negotiated individually between buyer and seller), there is no clearinghouse, and secondary markets are often non-existent or extremely thin. Unlike a futures contract, which is an exchange-traded product, a forward contract is an over-the-counter instrument.

Futures contracts are marked to market at the end of each trading day. Consequently, futures contracts are subject to interim cash flows as additional margin may be required in the case of adverse price movements, or as cash is withdrawn in the case of favorable price movements. A forward contract may or may not be marked to market, depending on the wishes of the two parties. For a forward contract that is not marked to market, there are no interim cash flow effects because no additional margin is required.

Finally, the parties in a forward contract are exposed to credit risk because either party may default on its obligation. This risk is called *counter-party risk*. This risk is minimal in the case of futures contracts because the clearinghouse associated with the exchange guarantees the other side of the transaction. In the case of a forward contract, both parties face counter-party risk. Thus, there exists bilateral counterparty risk.

Other than these differences, most of what we say about futures contracts applies equally to forward contracts.

Exchange-Traded Interest Rate Futures Contracts

Below we describe two commonly used interest rate futures contracts: Treasury bond futures and Eurodollar futures. There are three Treasury note futures contracts—10-year, 5-year, and 2-year—that are also important. However, all three contracts are modeled after the Treasury bond futures contract and are traded on the same exchange.

Treasury Bond Futures

The Treasury bond futures contract is traded on the Chicago Board of Trade (CBOT). The underlying instrument for a Treasury bond futures contract is $100,000 par value of a hypothetical 20-year coupon bond. The coupon rate on the hypothetical bond, called the *notional coupon*, is 6%.

We have been referring to the underlying as a hypothetical Treasury bond. The seller of a Treasury bond futures contract who decides to make delivery rather than liquidate his position by buying the contract prior to the settlement date must deliver some Treasury bond. But what Treasury bond? The CBOT allows the seller to deliver one of several Treasury bonds that the CBOT specifies are acceptable for delivery. The CBOT makes its determination of the Treasury issues that are acceptable for delivery from all outstanding Treasury issues that have at least 15 years to maturity from the first day of the delivery month.

It is important to remember that while the underlying Treasury bond for this contract is a hypothetical issue and therefore cannot itself be delivered into the futures contract, the contract is not a cash settlement contract as is the equity futures contracts described in Chapter 14. The only way to close out a Treasury bond futures contract is to either initiate an offsetting futures position, or to deliver a Treasury issue that is acceptable for delivery.

Conversion Factors The delivery process for the Treasury bond futures contract makes the contract interesting. At the settlement date, the seller of a futures contract (the short) is required to deliver to the buyer (the long) $100,000 par value of a 6% 20-year Treasury bond. Since no such bond exists, the seller must choose from one of the acceptable deliverable Treasury bonds that the CBOT has specified. Suppose the seller is entitled to deliver $100,000 of a 5% 20-year Treasury bond to settle the futures contract. The value of this bond is less than the value of a 6% 20-year bond. If the seller delivers the 5% 20-year bond, this would be unfair to the buyer of the futures contract who contracted to receive $100,000 of a 6% 20-year Treasury bond. Alternatively, suppose the seller delivers $100,000 of a 7% 20-year Treasury bond. The value of a 7% 20-year Treasury bond is greater than that of a 6% 20-year Treasury bond, so this would be a disadvantage to the seller.

How can this problem be resolved? To make delivery equitable to both parties, the CBOT uses conversion factors for adjusting the price of each Treasury issue that can be delivered to satisfy the Treasury bond futures contract. The conversion factor is constant throughout the life of a given futures contract (i.e., a given settlement date) but differs from contract to contract.

Given the conversion factor for an issue and the futures price, the adjusted price is found by multiplying the conversion factor by the futures price. The adjusted price is called the *converted price*.

The price that the buyer must pay the seller when a Treasury bond is delivered is called the *invoice price*. The invoice price is the futures settlement price plus accrued interest. However, as just noted, the seller can deliver one of several acceptable Treasury issues and to make delivery fair to both parties, the invoice price must be adjusted based on the actual Treasury issue delivered. It is the conversion factor that is used to adjust the invoice price. The invoice price is

$$\text{Invoice price} = \text{Contract size} \times \text{Futures settlement price}$$
$$\times \text{Conversion factor} + \text{Accrued interest}$$

Suppose a Treasury bond futures contract settles at 118-16. This means 118.5% of par value or 1.185 times par value. Suppose also that the conversion factor for this issue is 1.2370. Since the contract size is $100,000, the invoice price the buyer pays the seller is

$$\$100,000 \times 1.185 \times 1.2370 + \text{Accrued interest}$$
$$= \$146,584.50 + \text{Accrued interest}$$

Cheapest-to-Deliver Issue   In Chapter 14, the pricing of an equity futures contract is discussed and illustrated using a cash and carry transaction. In that discussion the *implied futures rate* is explained. For the seller of a futures contract (the short), the implied futures rate is an effective lending rate; that is, it is a rate at which funds can be lent or invested. For the buyer of a futures contract (the long), the implied futures rate is an effective borrowing rate. Rather than using the term implied future rate, participants in the interest rate futures area refer to this rate as the *implied repo rate*.

The seller of the futures contract (the short) has the choice of which of the eligible Treasury bonds to deliver to the long to settle the contract. For each eligible Treasury bond issue, the short can calculate an implied repo rate. Remember that the implied repo rate is the rate at which the short is lending funds or, in other words, the rate at which the short is earning on a short-term investment.

This short-term investment comes about by buying a Treasury bond issue and selling the Treasury bond futures contract. The sale of the Treasury bond futures contract locks in a price for the Treasury bond issue purchased at the futures settlement date. Suppose that the futures settlement date is 60 days from now. The short would know the price that will be received in 60 days, which is the converted price specified by the Treasury bond futures contract sold, and the coupon interest earned plus the estimated reinvestment income from reinvesting the coupon interest received over the 60 days. Given the price paid for the Treasury bond issue, a return can be obtained. This is the implied repo rate.

Therefore, in selecting the issue to be delivered, the seller of the futures contract will select from among all the eligible issues the one that will give the highest implied repo rate. The issue that gives the highest implied repo rate is called the *cheapest-to-deliver issue*.

Other Delivery Options   In addition to the choice of which acceptable Treasury issue to deliver—sometimes referred to as the *quality option* or *swap option*—the short has at least two more options granted under CBOT delivery guidelines. The short is permitted to decide when in the delivery month delivery actually will take place. This is called the *timing option*. The other option is the right of the short to give notice of intent to deliver up to 8:00 P.M. Chicago time after the closing of the exchange (3:15 P.M. Chicago time) on the date when the futures settlement price has been fixed. This option is referred to as the *wild card option*. The presence of the quality option, the timing option, and the wild card option—in sum referred to as the *delivery options*—means that the long position can never be sure which Treasury bond will be delivered or when it will be delivered.

Delivery Procedure   For a short who wants to deliver, the delivery procedure involves three days. The first day is the *position day*. On this day, the short notifies the CBOT that it intends to deliver. The short has until 8:00 P.M. central standard time to do so. The second day is the *notice day*. On this day, the short specifies which particular issue will be delivered. The short has until 2:00 P.M. central standard time to make this declaration. (On the last possible notice day in the delivery month, the short has until 3:00 P.M.) The CBOT then selects the long to whom delivery will be made. This is the long position that has been outstanding for the longest period of time. The long is then notified by 4:00 P.M. that delivery will be made. The third day is the *delivery day*. By 10:00 A.M. on this day the short must have in its account the Treasury issue that it specified on the notice day and by 1:00 P.M. must deliver that bond to the long that was assigned by the CBOT to accept delivery. The long pays the short the invoice price upon receipt of the bond.

Pricing of the Treasury Bond Futures Contract   In Chapter 14, it was demonstrated based on a cost of carry model that the theoretical futures price for an equity futures contact is

$$\text{Futures price} = \text{Spot price} + \text{Cost of financing} - \text{Dividend yield}$$

In the case of a fixed income security, the relationship changes to

$$\text{Futures price} = \text{Spot price} + \text{Cost of financing} - \text{Interest earned}$$

The interest earned is the accrued interest on the underlying fixed income instrument.

To derive the theoretical futures price using the arbitrage argument presented for the equity futures contract presented in Chapter 14 (the cost of carry model), we made several assumptions. Below we look at the implications of these assumptions for the pricing of the Treasury bond futures contract.

First, in the cost of carry model, no *interim* cash flows due to variation margin or coupon interest payments (dividend payments in the case of equity futures) were assumed. However, we know that interim cash flows can occur for both of these reasons. Because we assumed no initial margin and variation margin, the price derived is technically the theoretical price for a forward contract that is not marked-to-market. Incorporating interim coupon payments into the pricing model is not difficult. However, the value of the coupon payments at the settlement date will depend on the interest rate at which they can be reinvested. The shorter the maturity of the futures contract and the lower the coupon rate, the less important the reinvestment income is in determining the futures price.

Second, in deriving the theoretical futures price it is assumed that the borrowing and lending rates are equal. Typically, however, the borrowing rate is higher than the lending rate. This was noted in the discussion of equity futures. As a result, there is not one theoretical futures price, but a boundary or range for the futures price where it can be priced such that there is no arbitrage opportunity.

Third, the arbitrage arguments used to derive the theoretical futures price assumes that only one instrument or a package of securities (as in the case of an equity index futures contract) is deliverable. But as just explained, the Treasury bond futures—as well as the Treasury note—are designed to allow the short the choice of delivering one of a number of deliverable issues (the quality or swap option). Because there may be more than one deliverable, market participants track the price of each deliverable bond and determine which issue is the cheapest to deliver. The futures price will then trade in relation to the cheapest-to-deliver issue.

There is the risk that while an issue may be the cheapest to deliver at the time a position in the futures contract is taken, it may not be the cheapest to deliver after that time. A change in the cheapest-to-deliver issue can dramatically alter the futures price. What are the implications of the quality (swap) option on the futures price? Because the swap option is an option granted by the long to the short, the long will want to pay less for the futures contract than indicated above. Therefore, as a result of the quality option, the theoretical futures price must be adjusted as follows:

$$\text{Futures price} = \text{Spot price} + \text{Cost of financing} - \text{Interest earned} \\ - \text{Value of quality option}$$

Market participants have employed theoretical models in attempting to estimate the fair value of the quality option. A discussion of these models is beyond the scope of this chapter.

Finally, in the cost of carry model, a known delivery date is assumed. For Treasury bond and note futures contracts, the short has a timing and wild card option, so the long does not know when the security will be delivered. The effect of the timing and wild card options on the theoretical futures price is the same as with the quality option. These delivery options result in a theoretical futures price that is lower than the one suggested earlier, as shown:

Futures price = Spot price + Cost of financing – Interest earned
– Value of quality option – Value of timing option
– Value of wildcard option

or alternatively,

Futures price = Spot price + Cost of financing – Interest earned
– Delivery options

Market participants attempt to value the delivery options, but a discussion of these models is beyond the scope of this chapter.

Eurodollar Futures Contracts

The Eurodollar futures contracts are traded on both the International Monetary Market of the Chicago Mercantile Exchange and the London International Financial Futures Exchange. The underlying for this contract is the three-month London interbank offered rate (LIBOR).

The contract is for $1 million of face value and is traded on an index price basis. The index price basis in which the contract is quoted is equal to 100 minus the product of the annualized LIBOR futures rate in decimal and 100. For example, a Eurodollar futures price of 94.00 means a three-month LIBOR futures rate of 6% (100 minus 0.06×100).

The Eurodollar futures contract is a cash settlement contract. That is, the parties settle in cash based on LIBOR at the settlement date.

The Eurodollar futures contract allows the buyer of the contract to lock in the rate on three-month LIBOR today for a future three-month period. From the perspective of the seller of a Eurodollar futures contract, the seller is agreeing to lend funds for three months at some future date at the LIBOR futures rate.

The key point here is that the Eurodollar futures contract allows a participant in the financial market to lock in a three-month rate on an investment or a three-month borrowing rate. The three-month period begins in the month that the contract settles.

Controlling Interest Rate Risk with Futures

A key use of interest rate futures is to control a portfolio's interest rate risk. The price of an interest rate futures contract moves in the opposite direction from the change in interest rates: When rates rise, the futures price will fall; when rates fall, the futures price will rise. By buying a futures contract, a portfolio's exposure to a rate increase is increased. That is, the portfolio's duration increases. By selling a futures contract, a portfolio's exposure to a rate increase is decreased. Equivalently, this means that the portfolio's duration is reduced.

A manager with strong expectations about the direction of the future course of interest rates will adjust a portfolio's duration so as to capitalize on those expectations. A manager who wants to position a portfolio in anticipation that rates will rise can sell interest rate futures to reduce duration. A manager who wants to position a portfolio in anticipation of a fall in rates can buy interest rate futures to increase duration.

Before interest rate futures were available, investors who wanted to speculate on interest rates did so with long-term Treasury bonds; they shorted bonds if they expected rates to rise, and they bought them if they expected rates to fall. Using interest rate futures instead of trading long-term Treasuries themselves has three advantages. First, transaction costs for trading futures are lower than trading in the cash market. Second, margin requirements are lower for futures than for Treasury securities; using futures thus permits greater leverage. Finally, it is easier to sell short in the futures market than in the Treasury market. Consequently, while managers can alter the duration of their portfolios with cash market instruments, a quick and inexpensive means for doing so (on either a temporary or permanent basis) is to use futures contracts.

General Principle

The general principle in controlling interest rate risk with futures is to combine the dollar exposure of the current portfolio and that of a futures position so that it is equal to the target dollar exposure. This means that the manager must be able to accurately measure the dollar exposure of both the current portfolio and the futures contract employed to alter the exposure.

As explained in Chapter 17, there are two commonly used measures for approximating the change in the value of a bond or bond portfolio to changes in interest rates: price value of a basis point (PVBP) and duration. PVBP is the dollar price change resulting from a one-basis-point change in yield. Duration is the approximate percentage change in price for a 100 basis point change in rates. There are two measures of duration: modified and effective. As explained in Chapter 17, effective duration is the appropriate measure that should be used for bonds with embedded options. In the foregoing discussion, when we refer to duration, we mean effective duration. Moreover, since the manager is interested in dollar price exposure, it is the effective dollar duration that should be used. For a one basis point change in rates, PVBP is equal to the effective dollar duration for a one basis point change in rates.

As emphasized in Chapter 17, to estimate the effective dollar duration, it is necessary to have a good valuation model. It is the valuation model that is used to determine what the new values for the bonds in the portfolio will be if rates change. The difference between the current values of the bonds in the portfolio and the new values estimated by the valuation model when rates are changed is the dollar price exposure. Consequently, the starting point in controlling interest rate risk is the development of a reliable valuation model and this model is also needed to value the derivative contracts that the manager wants to use to control interest rate exposure.

Suppose that a manager seeks a target duration for the portfolio based on either expectations of interest rates or client-specified exposure. Given the target duration, a target dollar duration for a small basis point change in interest rates can be obtained. For a 50 basis point change in interest rates, for example, the target dollar duration can be found by multiplying the dollar value of the portfolio by the target duration and then dividing by 200. For example, suppose that the manager of a $500 million portfolio wants a target duration of 6. This means that the manager seeks a 3% change in the value of the portfolio for a 50 basis point change in rates (assuming a parallel shift in rates of all maturities). Multiplying the target duration of 6 by $500 million and dividing by 200 gives a target dollar duration of $15 million.

The manager must then determine the dollar duration of the current portfolio. The current dollar duration for a 50 basis point change in interest rates is found by multiplying the current duration by the dollar value of the portfolio and dividing by 200. So, for our $500 million portfolio, suppose that the current duration is 4. The current dollar duration is then $10 million (4 times $500 million divided by 200).

The target dollar duration is then compared to the current dollar duration. The difference between the two dollar durations is the dollar exposure that must be provided by a position in the futures contract. If the target dollar duration exceeds the current dollar duration, a futures position must increase the dollar exposure by the difference. To increase the dollar exposure, an appropriate number of futures contracts must be purchased. If the target dollar duration is less than the current dollar duration, an appropriate number of futures contracts must be sold. That is,

If target dollar duration − Current dollar duration > 0, buy futures
If target dollar duration − Current dollar duration < 0, sell futures

Once a futures position is taken, the portfolio's dollar duration is equal to the current dollar duration without futures plus the dollar duration of the futures position. That is,

$$\text{Portfolio's dollar return} = \text{Current dollar duration without futures} \\ + \text{Dollar duration of futures position}$$

The objective is to control the portfolio's interest rate risk by establishing a futures position such that the portfolio's dollar duration is equal to the target dollar duration. Thus,

$$\text{Portfolio's dollar duration} = \text{Target dollar duration}$$

Or, equivalently,

$$\text{Target dollar duration} = \text{Current dollar duration without futures} \\ + \text{Dollar duration of futures position} \quad (22.1)$$

Over time, the portfolio's dollar duration will move away from the target dollar duration. The manager can alter the futures position to adjust the portfolio's dollar duration to the target dollar duration.

Determining the Number of Contracts

Each futures contract calls for a specified amount of the underlying instrument. When interest rates change, the value of the underlying instrument changes, and therefore the value of the futures contract changes. How much the futures dollar value will change when interest rates change must be estimated. This amount is called the dollar duration per futures contract. For example, suppose the futures price of an interest rate futures contract is 70 and that the underlying instrument has a par value of $100,000. Thus, the futures delivery price is $70,000 (0.70 times $100,000). Suppose that a change in interest rates of 50 basis points results in the futures price changing by about 3 points. Then the dollar duration per futures contract is $2,100 (0.03 times $70,000).

The dollar duration of a futures position is then the number of futures contracts multiplied by the dollar duration per futures contract. That is,

Dollar duration of futures position
= Number of futures contracts × Dollar duration per futures contract (22.2)

How many futures contracts are needed to obtain the target dollar duration? Substituting equation (22.2) into equation (22.1), we get

Number of futures contracts × Dollar duration per futures contract
= Target dollar duration – Current dollar duration without futures   (22.3)

Solving for the number of futures contracts we have

Number of futures contracts

$$= \frac{\text{Target dollar duration} - \text{Current dollar duration without futures}}{\text{Dollar duration per futures contract}} \quad (22.4)$$

Equation (22.4) gives the approximate number of futures contracts that are necessary to adjust the portfolio's dollar duration to the target dollar duration. A positive number means that the futures contract must be purchased; a negative number means that the futures contract must be sold. Notice that if the target dollar duration is greater than the current dollar duration without futures, the numerator is positive and therefore futures contracts are purchased. If the target dollar duration is less than the current dollar duration without futures, the numerator is negative and therefore futures contracts are sold.

Dollar Duration for a Futures Position

Now we turn to how to measure the dollar duration and duration of a bond futures position. Keep in mind what the goal is: It is to measure the sensitivity of a bond futures position to changes in rates.

The general methodology for computing the dollar duration of a futures position for a given change in interest rates is straightforward given a valuation model. The procedure is the same as for computing the dollar duration of any cash market instrument—shock (change) interest rates up and down by the same number of basis points and determine the average dollar price change.

An adjustment is needed for the Treasury bond and note futures contracts. As explained earlier, the pricing of the futures contract depends on the cheapest-to-deliver issue (CTD). The calculation of the dollar duration of a Treasury bond or note futures contract requires determining the effect a change in interest rates will have on the price of the CTD issue, which in turn affects how the futures price will change. The dollar duration of a Treasury bond and note futures contract is determined as follows:

Dollar duration of futures contract

$$= \text{Dollar duration of the CTD issue} \times \frac{\text{Dollar duration of futures contract}}{\text{Dollar duration of CTD issue}}$$

Recall that there is a conversion factor for each issue that is acceptable for delivery for the futures contract. The conversion factor makes delivery equitable to both the buyer and seller of the futures contract. For each deliverable issue, the product of the futures price and the conversion factor is the converted price. Relating this to the equation above, the second ratio is approximately equal to the conversion factor of the cheapest-to-deliver issue. Thus, we can write:

Dollar duration of futures contract

= Dollar duration of the CTD issue × Conversion factor for the CTD issue

Hedging with Interest Rate Futures

Hedging with futures calls for taking a futures position as a temporary substitute for transactions to be made in the cash market at a later date. If cash and futures prices move together, any loss realized by the hedger from one position (whether cash or futures) will be offset by a profit on the other position. Hedging is a special case of controlling interest rate risk. In a hedge, the manager seeks a target duration or target dollar duration of zero.

A *short* (or sell) *hedge* is used to protect against a decline in the cash price of a bond. To execute a short hedge, futures contracts are sold. By establishing a short hedge, the manager has fixed the future cash price and transferred the price risk of ownership to the buyer of the futures contract.

INTEREST RATE SWAPS

In an interest rate swap, two parties agree to exchange periodic interest payments. The dollar amount of the interest payments exchanged is based on some predetermined dollar principal, which is called the *notional principal.* The dollar amount each counterparty pays to the other is the agreed-upon periodic interest rate times the notional principal. The only dollars that are exchanged between the parties are the interest payments, not the notional principal. In the most common type of swap, one party agrees to pay the other party fixed interest payments at designated dates for the life of the contract. This party is referred to as the *fixed rate payer.* The other party, who agrees to make interest rate payments that float with some reference rate, is referred to as the *floating rate payer.*

The reference rates that have been used for the floating rate in an interest rate swap are those on various money market instruments: Treasury bills, the London interbank offered rate, commercial paper, bankers acceptances, certificates of deposit, the federal funds rate, and the prime rate. The most common is the London interbank offered rate. LIBOR is the rate at which prime banks offer to pay on Eurodollar deposits available to other prime banks for a given maturity. Basically, it is viewed as the global cost of bank borrowing. There is not just one rate but a rate for different maturities. For example, there is a one-month LIBOR, three-month LIBOR, six-month LIBOR, etc.

To illustrate an interest rate swap, suppose that for the next five years party X agrees to pay party Y 10% per year, while party Y agrees to pay party X six-month LIBOR (the reference rate). Party X is a fixed rate payer/floating rate receiver, while party Y is a floating rate payer/fixed rate receiver. Assume that the notional principal is $50 million, and that payments are exchanged every six months for the next five years. This means that every six months, party X (the fixed rate payer/floating rate receiver) will pay party Y $2.5 million (10% times $50 million divided by 2). The amount that party Y (the floating rate payer/fixed rate receiver) will pay party X will be six-month LIBOR times $50 million divided by 2. If six-month LIBOR is 7%, party Y will pay party X $1.75 million (7% times $50 million divided by 2). Note that we divide by two because one-half year's interest is being paid.

The convention that has evolved for quoting swaps levels is that a swap dealer sets the floating rate equal to the reference rate and then quotes the fixed rate that will apply. The fixed rate is some spread above the Treasury yield curve with the same term to maturity as the swap.

Interest rate swaps are over-the-counter instruments. This means that they are not traded on an exchange. An institutional investor wishing to enter into a swap transaction can do so through either a securities firm or a commercial bank that transacts in swaps. The risk that the two parties take on when they enter into a swap is that the other party will fail to fulfill its obligations as set forth in the swap agreement. That is, each party faces default risk and therefore there is bilateral counterparty risk.

Risk–Return Characteristics of an Interest Rate Swap

The value of an interest rate swap will fluctuate with market interest rates. To see how, let's consider our hypothetical swap. Suppose that interest rates change immediately after parties X and Y enter into the swap. First, consider what would happen if the market demanded that in any five-year swap the fixed rate payer must pay 11% in order to receive six-month LIBOR. If party X (the fixed rate payer) wants to sell the position to party A, then party A will benefit by having to pay only 10% (the original swap rate agreed upon) rather than 11% (the current swap rate) to receive six-month LIBOR. Party X will want compensation for this benefit. Consequently, the value of party X's position has increased. Thus, if interest rates increase, the fixed rate payer will realize a profit and the floating rate payer will realize a loss.

Next, consider what would happen if interest rates decline to, say, 6%. Now a five-year swap would require a new fixed rate payer to pay 6% rather than 10% to receive six-month LIBOR. If party X wants to sell the position to party B, the latter would demand compensation to take over the position. In other words, if interest rates decline, the fixed rate payer will realize a loss, while the floating rate payer will realize a profit.

Interpreting a Swap Position

There are two ways that a swap position can be interpreted: (1) a package of forward/futures contracts, and (2) a package of cash flows from buying and selling cash market instruments.

Package of Forward Contracts

Contrast the position of the counterparties in an interest rate swap summarized above to the position of the long and short interest rate futures (forward) contract. The long futures position gains if interest rates decline and loses if interest rates rise—this is similar to the risk–return profile for a floating rate payer. The risk–return profile for a fixed rate payer is similar to that of the short futures position: a gain if interest rates increase and a loss if interest rates decrease. By taking a closer look at the interest rate swap we can understand why the risk–return relationships are similar.

Consider party X's position in our previous swap illustration. Party X has agreed to pay 10% and receive six-month LIBOR. More specifically, assuming a $50 million notional principal, X has agreed to buy a commodity called "six-month LIBOR" for $2.5 million. This is effectively a six-month forward contract where X agrees to pay $2.5 million in exchange for delivery of six-month LIBOR. If interest rates increase to 11%, the price of that commodity (six-month LIBOR) is higher, resulting in a gain for the fixed rate payer, who is effectively long a six-month forward contract on six-month LIBOR. The floating rate payer is effectively short a six-month forward contract on six-month LIBOR. There is therefore an implicit forward contract corresponding to each exchange date.

Now we can see why there is a similarity between the risk–return relationship for an interest rate swap and a forward contract. If interest rates increase to, say, 11%, the price of that commodity (six-month LIBOR) increases to $2.75 million (11% times $50 million divided by 2). The long forward position (the fixed rate payer) gains, and the short forward position (the floating rate payer) loses. If interest rates decline to, say, 9%, the price of our commodity decreases to $2.25 million (9% times $50 million divided by 2). The short forward position (the floating rate payer) gains, and the long forward position (the fixed rate payer) loses.

Consequently, interest rate swaps can be viewed as a package of more basic interest rate derivatives, such as forwards. The pricing of an interest rate swap will then depend on the price of a package of forward contracts with the same settlement dates in which the underlying for the forward contract is the same reference rate.

Package of Cash Market Instruments

To understand why a swap can be interpreted as a package of cash market instruments, consider an investor who enters into the transaction below:

- Buy $50 million par of a five-year floating rate bond that pays six-month LIBOR every six months
- Finance the purchase by borrowing $50 million for five years on terms requiring a 10% annual interest rate paid every six months

The cash flows for this transaction are as follows (the subscript for LIBOR indicates the six-month LIBOR as per the terms of the floating rate bond at time t):

Six-Month Period	Cash Flow (in millions of dollars) from:		
	Floating Rate Bond	Borrowing Cost	Net
0	$-$50	$+$50.0	$0
1–9	$+(LIBOR_t/2) \times 50$	-2.5	$+(LIBOR_t/2) \times 50 - 2.5$
10	$+(LIBOR_{10}/2) \times 50 + 50$	-52.5	$+(LIBOR_{10}/2) \times 50 - 2.5$

The second column shows the cash flow from purchasing the five-year floating rate bond. There is a $50 million cash outlay and then 10 cash inflows. The amount of the cash inflows is uncertain because they depend on future LIBOR. The next column shows the cash flow from borrowing $50 million on a fixed rate basis. The last column shows the net cash flow from the entire transaction. As the last column indicates, there is no initial cash flow (no cash inflow or cash outlay). In all 10 six-month periods, the net position results in a cash inflow of LIBOR and a cash outlay of $2.5 million. This net position, however, is identical to the position of a fixed rate payer/floating rate receiver.

It can be seen from the net cash flow that a fixed rate payer has a cash market position that is equivalent to a long position in a floating rate bond and a short position in a fixed rate bond—the short position being the equivalent of borrowing by issuing a fixed rate bond.

What about the position of a floating rate payer? It can be easily demonstrated that the position of a floating rate payer is equivalent to purchasing a fixed rate bond and financing that purchase at a floating rate, where the floating rate is the reference rate for the swap. That is, the position of a floating rate payer is equivalent to a long position in a fixed rate bond and a short position in a floating rate bond.

Swaptions

There are options on interest rate swaps. These derivative contracts are called *swaptions* and grant the option buyer the right to enter into an interest rate swap at a future date. The time until expiration of the swap, the term of the swap, and the swap rate are specified. The swap rate is the strike rate for the option.

A *payer's swaption* entitles the option buyer to enter into an interest rate swap in which the buyer of the option pays a fixed rate and receives a floating rate. Suppose that the strike rate is 6.5%, the term of the swap is three years, and the swaption expires in two years. This means that the buyer of this option some time over the next two years has the right to enter into a three-year interest rate swap where the buyer pays 6.5% (the swap rate which is equal to the strike rate) and receives the reference rate.

In a *receiver's swaption* the buyer of the option has the right to enter into an interest rate swap to pay a floating rate and receive a fixed rate. For example, if the strike rate is 7%, the swap term is five years, and the option expires in one year, the buyer of a receiver's swaption has the right some time over the next year to enter into a five-year interest rate swap in which the buyer receives a swap rate of 7% (i.e., the strike rate) and pays the reference rate.

Controlling Interest Rate Risk with Swaps

Effectively, a position in an interest rate swap is a leveraged position. This agrees with both of the economic interpretations of an interest rate swap explained earlier—it is a leveraged position involving either buying a fixed rate bond and financing on a floating rate basis (i.e., floating rate payer position) or buying a floating rate bond on a fixed rate basis (i.e., fixed rate payer position). So, we would expect that the dollar duration of a swap is a multiple of the bond that effectively underlies the swap.

Using this economic leveraged cash position interpretation of a swap, we can calculate a swap's dollar duration. From the perspective of the floating rate payer, the position can be viewed as follows:

Long a fixed rate bond + Short a floating rate bond

This means that the dollar duration of an interest rate swap from the perspective of a floating rate payer is just the difference between the dollar duration of the two bond positions that comprise the swap. That is,

Dollar duration of a swap for a floating rate payer
= Dollar duration of a fixed rate bond – Dollar duration of a floating rate bond

Most of the interest rate sensitivity of a swap will result from the dollar duration of the fixed rate bond since the dollar duration of the floating rate bond will be small because as interest rates change, the reference rate on a floating rate bond changes. The dollar duration of a floating rate bond is smaller the closer the swap is to its reset date. If the dollar duration of the floating rate bond is close to zero, then

Dollar duration of a swap for a floating rate payer
= Dollar duration of a fixed rate bond

Thus, adding an interest rate swap to a portfolio in which the manager pays a floating rate and receives a fixed rate increases the dollar duration of the portfolio by roughly the dollar duration of the underlying fixed rate bond. This is because it effectively involves buying a fixed rate bond on a leveraged basis.

From the perspective of a fixed rate payer, the dollar duration can be found as follows:

Dollar duration of a swap for a fixed rate payer
= Dollar duration of a floating rate bond – Dollar duration of a fixed rate bond

Again, assuming that the dollar duration of the floater is small, we have

Dollar duration of a swap for a fixed rate payer
= –Dollar duration of a fixed rate bond

Consequently, a manager who adds a swap to a portfolio involving paying fixed and receiving floating decreases the dollar duration of the portfolio by an amount roughly equal to the dollar duration of the fixed rate bond.

The dollar duration of a portfolio that includes a swap is

Dollar duration of assets – Dollar duration of liabilities
+ Dollar duration of a swap position

INTEREST RATE OPTIONS

An option is a contract in which the writer of the option grants the buyer of the option the right, but not the obligation, to purchase from or sell to the writer something at a specified price within a specified period of time (or at a specified date). The risk–return characteristics of an option are explained in Chapter 14, along with the differences between options and futures and the pricing of options.

Exchange-traded interest rate options can be written on a fixed income security or an interest rate futures contract. The former options are called *options on physicals*. *Options on interest rate futures*, called *futures options*, have been far more popular than options on physicals.

Exchange-Traded Futures Options

There are futures options on all the interest rate futures contracts. An option on a futures contract gives the buyer the right to buy from or sell to the writer a designated futures contract at the strike price at any time during the life of the option. If the futures option is a call option, the buyer has the right to purchase one designated futures contract at the strike price. That is, the buyer has the right to acquire a long futures position in the underlying futures contract. If the buyer exercises the call option, the writer acquires a corresponding short position in the futures contract.

A put option on a futures contract grants the buyer the right to sell one designated futures contract to the writer at the strike price. That is, the option buyer has the right to acquire a short position in the designated futures contract. If the put option is exercised, the writer acquires a corresponding long position in the designated futures contract.

As the parties to the futures option will realize a position in a futures contract when the option is exercised, the question is: What will the futures price be? That is, at what futures price will the long be required to pay for the instrument underlying the futures contract, and at what futures price will the short be required to sell the instrument underlying the futures contract?

Upon exercise, the futures price for the futures contract will be set equal to the strike price. The position of the two parties is then immediately marked-to-market in terms of the then-current futures price. Thus, the futures position of the two parties will be at the prevailing futures price. At the same time, the option buyer will receive from the option seller the economic benefit from exercising. In the case of a call futures option, the option writer must pay the difference between the current futures price and the strike price to the buyer of the option. In the case of a put futures option, the option writer must pay the option buyer the difference between the strike price and the current futures price.

For example, suppose an investor buys a call option on some futures contract in which the strike price is 85. Assume also that the futures price is 95 and that the buyer exercises the call option. Upon exercise, the call buyer is given a long position in the futures contract at 85 and the call writer is assigned the corresponding short position in the futures contract at 85. The futures positions of the buyer and the writer are immediately marked-to-market by the exchange. Because the prevailing futures price is 95 and the strike price is 85, the long futures position (the position of the call buyer) realizes a gain of 10, while the short futures position (the position of the call writer) realizes a loss of 10. The call writer pays the exchange 10 and the call buyer receives from the exchange 10. The call buyer, who now has a long futures position at 95, can either liquidate the futures position at 95 or maintain a long futures position. If the former course of action is taken, the call buyer sells a futures contract at the prevailing futures price of 95. There is no gain or loss from liquidating the position. Overall, the call buyer realizes a gain of 10. The call buyer who elects to hold the long futures position will face the same risk and reward of holding such a position, but still realizes a gain of 10 from the exercise of the call option.

Suppose instead that the futures option is a put rather than a call, and the current futures price is 60 rather than 95. Then if the buyer of this put option exercises it, the buyer would have a short position in the futures contract at 85; the option writer would have a long position in the futures contract at 85. The exchange then marks the position to market at the then-current futures price of 60, resulting in a gain to the put buyer of 25 and a loss to the put writer of the same amount. The put buyer who now has a short futures position at 60 can either liquidate the short futures position by buying a futures contract at the prevailing futures price of 60 or maintain the short futures position. In either case the put buyer realizes a gain of 25 from exercising the put option.

Over-the-Counter Options

Over-the-counter options, also called *dealer options*, are purchased by institutional investors who want to hedge the risk associated with a specific security. Typically, the maturity of the option coincides with the time period over which the buyer of the option wants to hedge, so the buyer is not concerned with the option's liquidity.

The parties to any over-the-counter contract are exposed to counterparty risk. In the case of forward contracts where both parties are obligated to perform, both parties face counterparty risk. In contrast, in the case of an option, once the option buyer pays the option price, it has satisfied its obligation. It is only the seller that must perform if the option is exercised. Thus, the option buyer is exposed to counterparty risk—the risk that the option seller will fail to perform.

INTEREST RATE AGREEMENTS (CAPS AND FLOORS)

An *interest rate agreement* is an agreement between two parties whereby one party, for an upfront premium, agrees to compensate the other at specific time periods if the reference rate is different from a predetermined level. When one party agrees to pay the other when the reference rate exceeds a predetermined level, the agreement is referred to as an *interest rate cap* or *ceiling*. The agreement is referred to as an *interest rate floor* when one party agrees to pay the other when the reference rate falls below a predetermined level. The predetermined level is called the *strike rate*.

The terms of an interest rate agreement include:

1. The reference rate.
2. The strike rate that sets the ceiling or floor.
3. The length of the agreement.
4. The frequency of settlement.
5. The notional principal.

For example, suppose that C buys an interest rate cap from D with terms as follows:

1. The reference rate is three-month LIBOR.
2. The strike rate is 6%.
3. The agreement is for four years.
4. Settlement is every three months.
5. The notional principal is $20 million.

Under this agreement, every three months for the next four years, D will pay C whenever three-month LIBOR exceeds 6% at a settlement date. The payment will equal the dollar value of the difference between three-month LIBOR and 6% times the notional principal divided by 4. For example, if three months from now three-month LIBOR on a settlement date is 8%, then D will pay C 2% (8% minus 6%) times $20 million divided by 4, or $100,000. If three-month LIBOR is 6% or less, D does not have to pay anything to C.

In the case of an interest rate floor, assume the same terms as the interest rate cap we just illustrated. In this case, if three-month LIBOR is 8%, C receives nothing from D, but if three-month LIBOR is less than 6%, D compensates C for the difference. For example, if three-month LIBOR is 5%, D will pay C $50,000 (6% minus 5% times $20 million divided by 4).

KEY POINTS

- A forward contract, just like a futures contract, is an agreement for the future delivery of something at a specified price at the end of a designated period of time. In contrast to a futures contracts which are standardized exchange-traded agreements, a forward contract is usually nonstandardized, is an over-the-counter instrument with no clearinghouse (i.e., counterparties are exposed to counterparty risk), and secondary markets are often nonexistent or extremely thin.
- Futures contracts are marked to market at the end of each trading day and therefore subject to interim cash flows as additional margin may be required, whereas a forward contract may or may not be marked to market, depending on the terms negotiated by the two parties.
- The underlying instrument for a Treasury bond futures contract is $100,000 par value of a hypothetical 20-year coupon bond. The nominal coupon rate on the hypothetical bond is 6%. Since there are many acceptable Treasury issues that can be used to satisfy delivery of this contract, conversion factors are used for adjusting the price (the converted price) of each Treasury issue that can be delivered to satisfy the Treasury bond.
- For the Treasury bond futures contract the short will select the issue from among all the eligible issues that can be delivered that offers the highest implied repo rate. The issue that gives the highest implied repo rate is called the cheapest-to-deliver issue.
- The three delivery options available to the short in the Treasury bond futures contract are the swap option, timing option, and wild card option.
- Three-month LIBOR is the underlying instrument for the Eurodollar futures contract, a cash settlement contract. This futures contract allows a participant in the financial market to lock in three-month LIBOR on an investment or a three-month LIBOR funding rate.
- A key use of interest rate futures is to control a portfolio's interest rate risk. The general principle in controlling interest rate risk with futures contracts is to combine the dollar exposure of the current portfolio and that of a futures position so that it is equal to the target dollar exposure.

- In an interest rate swap, the parties agree to exchange periodic interest payments based on a notional principal. In a generic interest rate swap, the fixed rate payer agrees to make fixed interest payments at designated dates for the life of the contract to the counterparty who, in turn, agrees to make floating rate payments based on LIBOR.
- Swaptions are options on swaps that grant the option buyer the right to enter into an interest rate swap at a future date. A payer's swaption entitles the option buyer to enter into a swap paying a fixed rate and receiving a floating rate. A receiver's swaption gives the buyer of the option the right to enter into a swap paying a floating rate and receiving a fixed rate.
- The dollar duration of a swap from the perspective of a floating rate payer is just the difference between the dollar duration of the two bond positions that comprise the swap. Most of the interest rate sensitivity of a swap will result from the dollar duration of the fixed rate bond.
- Adding an interest rate swap to a portfolio in which the manager pays a floating rate and receives a fixed rate increases the dollar duration of the portfolio by roughly the dollar duration of the underlying fixed rate bond. A manager who adds a swap to a portfolio involving paying fixed and receiving floating decreases the dollar duration of the portfolio by an amount roughly equal to the dollar duration of the fixed rate bond.
- Exchange-traded interest rate options can be written on a fixed income security (called physical option) or on an interest rate futures contract (called a futures option).
- An interest rate agreement is an agreement between two parties whereby one party, for an upfront premium, agrees to compensate the other at specific time periods if the reference rate is different from the strike rate. In an interest rate cap, the seller agrees to pay the buyer when the reference rate exceeds the strike rate at a specified date. In an interest rate floor, the seller agrees to pay the buyer when the reference rate falls below the strike rate.

QUESTIONS

1. Explain whether you agree or disagree with the following statement:

   One difference between a futures and forward contract is that futures contracts are marked to market and forward contracts are not.

2. If the target duration for a portfolio is greater than the current portfolio duration, how can the portfolio manager use:

    a. Treasury bond futures contracts to alter the portfolio's duration so as to bring it in line with the target duration?

    b. Interest rate swaps to increase the portfolio's duration so as to bring it in line with the target duration?

3. With respect to Treasury bond futures contract:

    a. What is the role of the conversion factors?

    b. What is the significance of the cheapest-to-deliver issue for a Treasury bond futures contract?

    c. How is the cheapest-to-deliver issue determined?

4. In determining the theoretical price of a Treasury bond futures contracts, explain why it is necessary to modify the standard cost of carry model.

5. When the buyer of a call option on a futures contract exercises, explain the resulting position for the buyer and the writer.

CHAPTER 23

Credit Default Swaps and the Indexes

Stephen J. Antczak, CFA
Head of US Credit Strategy
Societe Generale

Douglas J. Lucas
Managing Director, Global Research
Moody's Investors Service

Frank J. Fabozzi, Ph.D., CFA, CPA
Professor in the Practice of Finance
Yale School of Management

The synthetic markets have grown rapidly in both size and popularity, and now often dominate the volume of trading activity in the corporate credit markets. In this chapter, we provide an overview of single-name credit default swaps (CDS) and the indexes.

Credit derivatives enable the isolation and transfer of credit risk between two parties. They are bilateral financial contracts which allow credit risk to be isolated from the other risks inherent in a financial instrument, such as interest rate risk, and passed from one party to another party. Aside from the ability to isolate credit risk, other reasons for the use of credit derivatives include:

- Asset replication/diversification
- Leverage
- Regulatory capital efficiencies
- Yield enhancement
- Hedging needs
- Liquidity
- Relative value opportunities

The most commonly used credit derivatives employed by bond portfolio managers are single-name credit default swaps and credit default swap indexes. We will discuss these credit derivative products and their applications.

WHAT ARE CREDIT DEFAULT SWAPS?

The typical analogy used for a credit default swap (CDS) is an insurance contract. The purchaser of insurance is buying financial protection against a specified event. For example, a homeowner buys earthquake or flood insurance to "hedge" against a catastrophic event. CDS can be considered a policy used to "hedge" against corporate default.

That said, there are important differences between CDS and insurance contracts. For example, can you imagine a homeowner buying flood protection that pays out in the event of a flood impacting a neighbor's home rather than his or her own? Or how about a homeowner buying protection on a neighbor's house in an amount five, six, or seven times the value of his or her neighbor's home?

It is difficult to envision these things in the context of the insurance market, but these are certainly components of the CDS market. For example, in theory CDS buyers can purchase an unlimited amount of contracts on an underlying reference entity (although if risk managers are doing their jobs, this would not occur). As such, CDS is a way to not only hedge risk, but also a way to take risk—and levered risk at that. Moreover, because homeowners do not necessarily mark-to-market flood insurance that they may have purchased on their (or their neighbor's) house, it cannot be used to protect against other assets being damaged in the event of bad weather (e.g., a boat docked in a nearby lake). But CDS is typically marked-to-market, and as such it can be used for purposes other than to protect against a default by a particular issuer. For example, it can be used to hedge against the mark-to-market risk of an equity option position.

Contract Details and Mechanics

The absolute basic components of a CDS are a credit protection buyer, a credit protection seller, a reference obligor, and reference obligations.

In a CDS, the *credit protection buyer* (or simply protection buyer) purchases credit protection from the *credit protection seller* (or simply protection seller) in a dollar-amount size referred to as the *notional amount* on a *reference obligor*. Potentially, any actual or potential issuer in the debt markets, including corporations, sovereign governments, municipal governments, or supra-nationals, may be a reference obligor. Typically, the

EXHIBIT 23.1 Basic Mechanics of a CDS Contract

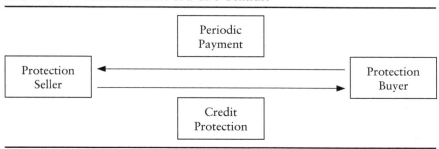

protection buyer pays the protection seller a fee expressed as a number of basis points per annum times the notional amount. These payments are paid by the protection buyer for the life of the swap (which is either maturity or until a credit event occurs). Exhibit 23.1 highlights these flows.

In a typical CDS, the protection buyer pays for the protection premium over several settlement dates rather than upfront, usually quarterly. In the case of quarterly payments, the payment is computed as follows:

Quarterly swap premium payment = Notional amount swap rate (in decimal form)
× Actual number of days in quarter ÷ 360

A reference obligor credit event, should it occur, triggers a payment from the protection seller to the protection buyer. (We define "credit event" later.) With respect to the payment from the protection seller to the protection buyer, the payment depends on whether there is physical or cash settlement. After the payment is made the contract is cancelled.

In *physical settlement,* illustrated in Exhibit 23.2, the protection buyer selects a reference obligation of the reference obligor and delivers it to the protection seller. Usually, any senior unsecured (or any secured) obligation of the reference obligor is a qualified reference obligation. The protection buyer can deliver a par amount of a reference obligation equal to the notional amount of the CDS. The protection seller must then pay the protection buyer par for the reference obligation. The key point here is that after a credit event, reference obligations will most likely trade at a value that is less than par. As such, CDS owners can deliver something worth less than par and receive par for it. After a credit event, as the owner of the reference obligations, the protection seller is free to take whatever steps he or she thinks best to recover the maximum value possible, including working out or selling the assets. If reference obligations have different market values, the protection buyer has what is referred to as the *cheapest-to-deliver*

EXHIBIT 23.2 Following Credit Event: Physical Settlement

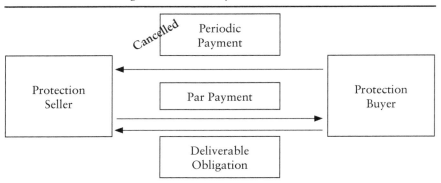

EXHIBIT 23.3 Following Credit Event: Cash Settlement

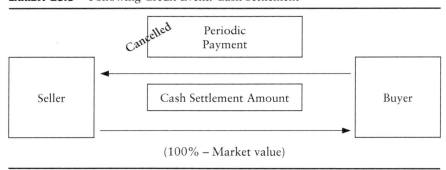

option. This is the choice of finding and delivering the least expensive reference obligation to the protection seller in exchange for par.[1]

In the case of *cash settlement*, the difference between the reference obligation's par value and its market value is paid in cash by the protection seller to the protection buyer. The value of the reference obligation is determined in the market by a specified mark-to-market auction process. This arrangement is illustrated in Exhibit 23.3.

Credit Events

The essential part of a credit default swap is the specific circumstances considered to be *credit events.* The triggering of a credit event is what causes the protection seller to make a protection payment to the protection buyer.

---

[1]This option is similar to the delivery option granted to the short in a Treasury bond and note futures contract.

What constitutes a credit event is defined in the legal documentation for a CDS trade. That documentation, which is the standard contract for a CDS trade developed by the International Swap and Derivatives Association (ISDA), defines six possible credit events that attempt to capture every type of situation that could cause the credit quality of the reference entity to deteriorate:

1. Bankruptcy
2. Failure to pay
3. Obligation default
4. Obligation acceleration
5. Repudiation and moratorium
6. Restructuring

The above definitions are set forth in more detail in the *1999 ISDA Credit Derivatives Definitions* as modified in 2001 by the *Restructuring Supplement to the 1999 ISDA Credit Derivatives Definitions* and then in 2003 by the *2003 ISDA Credit Derivative Definitions*. In the documentation for a specific CDS trade, there is a checkbox whereby the counterparties to the trade specify the credit events that are applicable.[2]

The broader the definition of a credit event, the easier it becomes for a protection payment to be triggered. But the market consensus over the years has been to exclude some credit events and to tighten the definitions for the rest. Parties now generally agree to exclude obligation default and obligation acceleration in nonemerging market corporate CDS. The logic is that these situations do not always rise to the severity intended to trigger a protection payment. And if the situation of the underlying credit is severe, failure to pay will follow shortly anyway.

Similarly, the bankruptcy definition has been tightened. In the 1999 ISDA definitions, the bankruptcy definition contained the phrase "action in furtherance of bankruptcy." In practice, the market discovered this phrase to be vague. If, for example, a debtor under financial stress hires an attorney to help it understand the bankruptcy process, does that mere

---

[2]The growth of the CDS market can partly be attributed to the International Swaps and Derivatives Association's (ISDA) creation of credit derivatives definitions in 1999 (revised in 2003) discussed earlier. ISDA not only eliminated documentation inconsistencies and provided a common negotiating language for all market participants, but also designed a confirmation template that organizes the defined terms into a short, easily understandable, and comparable document. The orderly settlement of the Argentina, Enron, Fannie Mae, Freddie Mac, Lehman Brothers, and WorldCom credit events based on standard ISDA documentation added considerably to the credibility of the documentation and to credit derivative products as well.

consultation qualify as an "action in furtherance of bankruptcy"? This ambiguity was resolved when the phrase was stricken from the bankruptcy definition.

Because repudiation and moratorium are only applicable to sovereign credits, this leaves three remaining credit events common in most corporate underlying CDS: bankruptcy, failure to pay, and restructuring. "Bankruptcy" is the voluntary or involuntary filing of bankruptcy. "Failure to pay" is the failure of the reference obligor to make principal or interest payments on one or more of its obligations. "Restructuring" has been the focus of a great deal of concern and debate.

The Restructuring Debate

Restructuring refers to relaxing the terms of a debtor's loan or bond obligations to take into account the debtor's weakened credit situation. Debt maturities might be extended, coupons lowered, principal reduced, or debt seniority might even be reduced. Restructuring debt is seen as a less disruptive and less costly alternative to the bankruptcy process. While it definitely inflicts a credit loss, the issue in the CDS market is whether, and how, restructuring should be included as a credit event capable of triggering a protection payment.

Restructuring as a credit event is a concern to credit protection sellers. One reason is that it can give the protection buyer an unintended "cheapest-to-deliver" option. When a credit is in bankruptcy, all same-seniority debt trade similarly, regardless of coupon or maturity. This is because the bankruptcy court is apt to treat all debt of the same seniority identically with respect to the distribution of cash or new securities from the bankrupt estate. But this is not the case in a restructuring, where the coupon and maturity of certain obligations issued by the reference entity may remain unaffected by the restructuring. The buyer of protection could find it economically advantageous to search out the cheapest trading debt to purchase and deliver to the protection seller in exchange for par.

Another concern about restructuring is the possible manipulation of the process by bank lenders that have bought credit protection that includes restructuring. The issue is that if a bank controls the restructuring process, and has purchased protection that covers restructuring, the bank has no economic incentive to limit the diminution of the restructured loan. Such a bank could oversee the restructuring of its loan, allow its terms to be slashed, present that loan to the protection seller for a payment of par, and even provide separate new funding to the troubled credit at a higher point in its new capital structure.

On the other side of the issue have been banks, chiefly in Europe, that view restructuring as a legitimate way to work out a problem loan, and thus desire credit protection to cover this eventuality. The regulators of these banks have been reluctant to give capital relief for credit protection that excludes restructuring risk.

Different approaches have been implemented to address the concerns of both protection sellers and protection buyers. There are four standard ISDA definitions dealing with restructuring: "restructuring," "modified restructuring," "modified–modified restructuring," and the elimination of restructuring entirely. Modified restructuring and modified–modified restructuring limit the maturity of deliverable reference obligations in different ways, thus constraining a protection buyer's cheapest-to-deliver option.

How Portfolio Managers Can Use Single-Name CDS

The most obvious way for a portfolio manager to use a single-name CDS is to acquire credit protection for the holding of a credit name in its portfolio. The question is why doesn't the portfolio manager just sell the bonds? There are several reasons. First, the market for corporate bonds may not be very liquid. The portfolio manager may find it beneficial to acquire protection rather than sell the bond when there is poor liquidity. Second, there may be a tax reason for doing so. For example, the portfolio manager may have to hold a corporate bond for two months in order to benefit from a favorable capital gains treatment. A single-name CDS can be used to provide protection against credit risk during that two-month period.

If a portfolio manager wants to purchase the obligation of a corporate entity (i.e., gain long exposure), then the most obvious way to do so is to purchase the bond in the cash market. However, as just noted, because of the illiquidity of the corporate bond market, there may be better execution by transacting in the CDS market. More specifically, the selling of credit protection on a corporate entity provides long credit exposure to that entity. To understand why, consider what happens when a portfolio manager sells credit protection on a reference entity. The portfolio manager receives the swap premium and if there is no credit event, the swap premium is received over the life of the CDS contract. However, this is equivalent to buying the bond of the corporate entity. Instead of receiving coupon interest payments, the portfolio manager receives the swap premium payments. If there is a credit event, then the portfolio manager under the terms of the CDS must make a payment to the credit protection buyer. However, this is equivalent to a loss that would be realized if the bond was purchased. Hence, selling credit protection via a single-name CDS can be economically equivalent to a long position in the reference entity.

Suppose that a portfolio manager wants to short a corporate bond because he believes that the corporation is likely to experience a credit event that will cause a decline in the value of the bond. In the absence of a CDS, the portfolio manager would have to short the bonds in the cash market. However, it is extremely difficult to short corporate bonds. With a liquid single-name CDS, it is easy to effectively short the bond of a corporate entity. Remember that shorting a bond involves making payments to another party and then if the investor is correct and the bond's price declines, the bond can be repurchased at a lower price (i.e., a gain is realized). That is precisely what occurs when a single-name CDS is purchased: the investor makes payments (the swap premium payments) and realizes a gain if a credit event occurs. Hence, buying credit protection via a single-name CDS is equivalent to shorting.

Finally, for a portfolio manager seeking a leveraged position in a corporate bond, this can be achieved by selling credit protection. Selling credit protection is equivalent to a long position in the reference entity. Moreover, as with other derivatives, CDS allows this to be done on a leveraged basis.

CREDIT DEFAULT SWAPS INDEXES

Predefined single-name CDS contracts are also grouped by broad market segments. The three most common are CDS for high-grade corporate bonds (index denoted by CDX.IG), high-yield corporate bonds (index denoted by CDX.HY), and loans (index denoted by LCDX), and help market participants with a number of requirements. The core buyers and sellers of CDX indexes have been index arbitrager players, correlation desks, bank portfolios and proprietary trading desks, and credit hedge funds. Increasingly, greater participation by equity and macro hedge funds has been observed. They are looking for the following from CDX indexes.

- *Barometer of market sentiment.* Credit indexes are averages of a universe of single-name CDS contracts, and provide a snapshot of the market's risk appetite in the same way that the S&P 500 equity index provides a snapshot of equity markets. Note that although there are many similarities between the CDX indexes and equity indexes, some major differences still exist as highlighted in Exhibit 23.4.
- *Hedging tool.* Because of the relatively large trading volume and favorable liquidity provided by both the CDX.HY and LCDX indexes, a number of investors use the products to tactically alter portfolio exposures.
- *Arbitrage and relative value positioning.* One of the more challenging endeavors that many long/short investors face is funding short posi-

EXHIBIT 23.4   Differences between Credit and Equity Indexes

	Credit Indexes	S&P 500
Weighting	Equally weighted	Market cap weighted
Additions/Deletions	Roll to a new series every six months	Changes are made as needed
	Determined by a consortium of dealers	Determined by S&P
Index calculations	Index level driven by demand/supply	Float adjusted market cap/divisor

Data for this table obtained from UBS and Markit Group Limited.

tions; Companies A, B, and C may be high beta and face more fundamental pressures than the average company in the market, but how to pay for shorts and limit mark-to-market risk? Many use the indexes in this regard.

- *Capital structure positioning.* Market participants have increasingly been using the CDX.HY and LCDX indexes in combination with other broad market assets, such as the various equity indexes, oil, and so on, in order to express specific broad market views (e.g., credit crunch will hurt equities more than loans).

The mechanics of a CDS index are slightly different from that of a single-name CDS. A summary of the North American high-grade and high-yield indexes and the European high-grade index is provided in Exhibit 23.5.

For these contracts, there is a swap premium that is paid periodically. If a credit event occurs for a single-name contract, the swap premium payment ceases in the case of a single-name CDS (but paid up to the credit event date) and the contract is terminated. In contrast, for an index, the swap payment continues to be made by the credit protection buyer. However, the amount of the quarterly swap premium payment is reduced. This is because the notional amount is reduced as result of a credit event for the reference obligor.

These broad indexes are available in maturities from one to 10 years, with the greatest liquidity at 5-, 10-, and, 7-year maturities. A new index series is created every six months. At that time, the specific composition of credits in each new series is determined and a new premium level determined for each maturity. Premiums on indexes are exchanged once a quarter on or about the twentieth day of March, June, September, and December. Each name in an index is equally weighted in the indexes. For the North American indexes, only bankruptcy and failure to pay are credit events

EXHIBIT 23.5 Summary of CDX Indexes: North America and Europe

	North America Investment-Grade Index	North America High-Yield Index	Europe Index
Main Index Name	CDX NA IG	CDX NA HY	iTraxx Europe
Main Index Composition	125 corporate names	100 corporate names	125 corporate names
Subindexes	Five industries: consumer, energy, financials, industrials, and technology/media/telecom High volatility	BB rated B rated High beta	Nine industries: autos, consumer, consumer cyclicals, consumer non-cyclicals, energy, senior financials, subordinate financials, industrials, and technology/media/telecom Largest corporates Lower rated (a.k.a. crossover) High volatility

Note: Subindexes are typically relevant for older, off-the-run indexes.
Source: Data for this table obtained from UBS and Markit Group Limited.

even though modified restructuring is commonly a credit event in the North American market. For the European indexes, bankruptcy, failure to pay, and modified–modified restructuring are credit events.

Contrasting the LCDX and CDX Indexes

What differentiates the LCDX from other synthetic corporate debt indexes such as CDX.HY is that it references a collection of loan CDS (i.e., any/all outstanding senior secured bank debt of the reference issuer). Exhibit 23.6 illustrates that LCDX is quite comparable to the CDX.HY index. Both indexes reference the same number of credits (albeit secured loans versus unsecured bonds), offer unfunded exposure, quote on price rather than spread, and follow similar coupon payment mechanics.

Two important differences, however, exist between LCDX and CDX: the recovery assumption and the cancellation of LCDS. First, *recovery* simply reflects the difference in valuations of secured and unsecured debt in the event of bankruptcy. As a first lien instrument, loans typically enjoy a higher recovery rate than unsecured debt in the event of default. Although realized recovery estimates vary (anywhere from 50% to 80%), many assume a 65% recovery for their price/spread calculations, as opposed to 40% for CDX.HY. Second, *cancellation* describes a situation where a firm repays all of its outstanding first lien loans without issuing new first lien

EXHIBIT 23.6 CDX.HY and LCDX Characteristics

	LCDX	CDX.HY
Launch date	5/22/2007	3/27/07 (Series 8)
Constituents	100 equal weight 1st lien LCDS	100 equal weight HY CDS
Roll dates	Semiannual: April 3 and October 3	Semiannual: March 27 and September 26
Coupon	Paid quarterly	Paid quarterly
Coupon payments	Quarterly: Mar–Jun–Sep–Dec 20	Quarterly: Mar–Jun–Sep–Dec 20
Cancellability	Cancellable if all 1st lien secured debt is called; index notional is reduced by 1% following cancellation	NA; Index notional reduced by 1% only if default occurs
Credit event	Bankruptcy or failure to pay debt	Bankruptcy or failure to pay debt
Quotation	Price	Price

Data for this table obtained from Markit Group Limited.

debt, perhaps due to an asset sale, an upgrade to investment-grade status, and so on. In this case, the LCDS is cancelled after 30 days if no debt substitute is found. The original index notional is reduced by 1%.

KEY POINTS

- Credit derivatives enable the isolation and transfer of credit risk between two parties.
- By far, the most popular type of credit derivative is the credit default swap. There are single-name credit default swaps and credit default swap indexes.
- A credit default swap is probably the simplest form of credit risk transference among all credit derivatives. A CDS is used to shift credit exposure to a credit protection seller. The payments are based on the notional amount of the contract.
- The CDS documentation will identify the reference entity (i.e., the issuer of the debt instrument) or the reference obligation. In addition, the documentation will specify what credit events are covered.
- In a CDS, the protection buyer pays a fee, the swap premium, to the protection seller in return for the right to receive a payment conditional upon the occurrence of a credit event. The CDS can call for cash settlement or physical settlement should a credit event occur.
- If reference obligations have different market values, the protection buyer has a cheapest-to-deliver option, which is the option to deliver the least expensive reference obligation to the protection seller in exchange for par.
- Unlike a single-name CDS, the underlying for a credit default swap index is a standardized basket of reference entities. The three most common are CDS for high-grade corporate bonds, high-yield corporate bonds, and loans.
- CDX indexes are used by market participants as a barometer of market sentiment, hedging tool, and arbitrage and relative value positioning.

QUESTIONS

1. How can a single-name credit default swap be used by a portfolio manager who wants to short a reference entity?

2. How can a single-name credit default swap be used by a portfolio manager who is having difficulty acquiring the bonds of a particular corporation in the cash market?

3. How do the mechanics of a single-name credit default swap differ from that of a credit default swap index?

4. How does the LCDX index differ from CDX.HY?

5. How can a portfolio manager use a credit default swap index where the underlying are investment-grade corporate bonds to alter exposure to the corporate bond market?

About the Web Site

This book is accompanied by a web site, www.wiley.com/go/theoryof-investmentmanagement2e.

The web site supplements the materials in the book by offering the solutions to the questions at the end of each chapter.

To receive these free benefits, you will need to follow two simple steps:

1. Enter the following URL in your browser's address bar:

   www.wiley.com/go/theoryofinvestmentmanagement2e.

2. Follow the instructions on the web site to register using your personal e-mail address. You will need a password from this book to complete the registration process. The password is: finance456.

Index

CPSIA information can be obtained
at www.ICGtesting.com
Printed in the USA
BVHW08215722051 9
549069BV00011B/84/P